The Princeton
Companion to
Classical
Japanese Literature

The Princeton Companion to Classical Japanese Literature

BY Earl Miner, Hiroko Odagiri,
AND Robert E. Morrell

Princeton University Press, Princeton, N. J.

Copyright © 1985 by Princeton University Press
Published by Princeton University Press, 41 William Street,
Princeton, New Jersey 08540
In the United Kingdom: Princeton University Press,
Guildford, Surrey

All Rights Reserved
Library of Congress Cataloging in Publication Data will be
found on the last printed page of this book
ISBN 0-691 06599-3

Publication of this book has been aided by grants from
the Whitney Darrow Fund of Princeton University Press
and the Japan Foundation

Clothbound editions of Princeton University Press books
are printed on acid-free paper, and binding materials are
chosen for strength and durability. Paperbacks, although
satisfactory for personal collections, are not usually
suitable for library rebinding

Printed in the United States of America by
Princeton University Press, Princeton, New Jersey

*For
our fellow students of Japanese literature*

NOTICE TO READERS

Few users of this companion will have need to read it all, from preface to index. It is important to read the headnote of any part consulted (for explanation of the contents and the conventions used) before using any section of it.

The location of information can be determined either by running through the table of contents for categories, or by using the index for those authors and titles mentioned in Parts One, Three, and Six.

Cross-References:

> *An asterisk before a name or title indicates that it is entered in Part Three. An asterisk within Part Three signals that the name or title so designated is entered elsewhere in Part Three.

> *italics* Italicized words, other than titles, will be found in Part Four, Literary Terms.

Dates: all are to be taken as A.D. unless otherwise noted. When the ages of authors are mentioned, these approximate the Western system of counting years lived; that is, one year is deducted from the Japanese calculations.

Contents

Preface

Because we mean this *Companion* to be useful, we start with the practical. There is no counterpart to this work, as far as we know, for Japanese or any other literature. It will, therefore, have to be examined carefully to be used to best advantage. The most profitable way to proceed, we believe, is to examine the notice printed opposite the table of contents, then to look at the contents, and then to proceed directly to what is needed; or to use the index, if that covers what is sought, In using any part, it will be useful to consult the opening page or pages of that part. Readers new to Japanese literature, and readers not new but with the necessary leisure, will find that in the history offered in Part One there is information not repeated in other parts. That brief history also provides a conceptual and historical grid for the information in subsequent parts.

That information is provided in considerable variety, consisting of things that we ourselves feel we need to know, to remember, and to have available. In the process, we have used narrative, charts, series, figures, maps, or pictures—in short, whatever seemed most useful and economical of space.

We have defined "classical Japanese literature" conservatively and conventionally. The "classical" formally designates the long period from early times to the Meiji Restoration of 1867–1868. Of course there is very little information about the early times, and the belief that a literature suddenly becomes modern in a certain month is a convenient notion and no more. It is also true that we venture into modern times on occasion, but the arbitrary notion corresponds in historical period or years to what Japanese mean nowadays by "Nihon koten bungaku." In the brief history (Part One), we periodize along lines advised us by Japanese comparativists. We do not, therefore, refer to those larger periods designated "kodai," "chūko," "chūsei," and the rest. It would be convenient to be able to speak of the medieval, but where chūsei begins and where it ends is a matter on which no agreement has been reached.

It is yet more difficult to define "classical *Japanese literature*." The usual Japanese expression for the italicized phrase is "kokubungaku" ("our national literary writings"). The term "bungaku" suggests the study of literature (as in the English phrase, "comparative literature"), more nearly "Literaturwissenschaft" than "Dichtung," "imaginative writing," "belles-lettres," or what we normally include conceptually in "Japanese literature" (although it should not be assumed that the English terms have been immune to change or are always used to designate the same things). One way to show what "classical Japanese literature" means here is to specify what we have not systematically included: writing by Japanese in Chinese; we also do not include Ainu or Ryukyuan literature.

In other words, we define "Japanese literature" as that literature written in Japanese by Japanese, which is to say, as it is conventionally considered in almost all histories of Japanese literature (Nihon bungakushi) and dictionaries of Japanese literature (Nihon bungaku jiten). Our definition of "literature" here relies on similar Japanese decisions. Those decisions are, at least, our points of departure. In fact, we also supply information about writing in Chinese by Japanese, and even about writing by Chinese in Chinese. But those matters are included only if they bear on "Japanese literature." We also range very much farther to provide numerous kinds of historical, religious, and other information not manifestly literary.

It seems that in most cultures, poets emerge by name before other artists do. That was certainly true of Japan—throughout classical literature only *waka* required designation of one's real "name." But on the urging of various people (and against the advice of some others), we have included brief entries in Part Three for artists, musicians, priests, and figures (such as Fujiwara Michinaga and Minamoto Yoshitsune) important to literature in one fashion or another. The table of contents will show some of the range of what is included, and use will reveal it clearly.

Most of the *Companion* consists of lists and series quickly mastered. For that reason, and to allow the index to be brief enough for use, the index includes only what appears in Parts One, Three, and Six.

Although there is no real model for this work, there are Oxford companions for English and American literature. The nondictionary parts of some Japanese old-language dictionaries (kogo jiten) contain information that served as models—and sources. The *Companion* began, however, as a very different book, in which Miner was to write a series of essays on representative Japanese literary kinds. The concept was of a representative critical history. Portions of that early work survive in Part One and in fragments elsewhere, especially in Part Three. Although things had gone far enough in the original direction for Princeton University Press to offer an advance contract, it more and more came to seem that appreciative or theoretical ideas (in that guise) were less needed than a stock of information. Meanwhile, to fill the need for a history, it appeared that Donald Keene would be returning to classical literature in his volumes of literary history, and Konishi Jin'ichi was planning a five-volume history of Japanese literature that would be published in English as well as in Japanese.

While on a Guggenheim fellowship in Japan for four months in 1977–1978, Miner decided to shift to something like what this *Companion* has become. The model for Part One was the much briefer *Nihon Bungakushi* by Konishi Jin'ichi—the book by which Donald Keene long ago discovered him and made him known to many of us in the mid-fifties. It is a model in terms of range and of adjustment between received wisdom and personal preference. The model for Part Three (major authors and works not ascribable to a given author) was harder to find. After looking through various bungaku jiten, Miner decided that the scope of *Shinchō Nihon Bungaku Shōjiten* was right in scale and in kinds of information supplied. We have endeavored to include every *classical* author or work given a single entry in that work, although we have added a large number that are not in it and have often not used material in it. "We" is the proper pronoun, because by that time four of the first five parts had been read by Helen C. McCullough and Hirakawa Sukehiro—and Odagiri had joined Miner in the enterprise. We began to chafe over what was not in our model for that part, and to realize that other parts would be needed. And we felt that for a few great works longer entries were desirable.

Many additions followed. We believed that Japanese theater cannot be explained in terms of entries for works or playwrights alone, and therefore included a part on the major kinds of theater, with one or two that are not major but serve as a sample of many others that have come and gone. We felt the need for information on geography and ranks—and so the *Companion* steadily grew. Sometimes we became dissatisfied with what had been done, even after the *Companion* was accepted for publication. For those matters, we had to start out again. Or it might occur to us, for example, that for a map of the ancient provinces of Japan an additional alphabetical list would help our reader find a province more quickly than the use of simply numbered provinces permits. Then it occurred to us that readers would wish to know which provinces were designated by Sinified -shū names. And so this information was added. Our information was derived from the sources specified in the section on "Principal Immediate Sources."

Odagiri came to Princeton for a summer of great toil, and she has spent a lot of money as well as time in mailing papers to the United States. When it began to seem that our revisions would never end, we learned that Morrell had prepared two substantial, book-length syllabi on literature and Buddhism (and other subjects). He joined the other two of us at what is sometimes called the eleventh hour—but the twelfth was a very long hour, indeed, which ran for months. Morrell's work is found in numerous places, particularly in Parts Three, Four, and Six. And he has made the index.

We have used many, many Japanese and Western works. If we could assume that Japanese scholarship and criticism would end in 1982, or that Princeton University Press would allow us a wholly reset edition every five years, we could include, in Part Three, notice of important Japanese editions and criticism along with Western translations of Japanese works. Fortunately, we cannot make either assumption and so have had to exclude the information because it would become outdated too quickly. Some surrogate information is offered instead. This decision means that we cannot be specific about our debts to major Japanese editions with their commentaries (such as the Iwanami *Nihon Koten Bungaku Taikei* and Shōgakkan *Nihon Koten Bungaku Zenshū*). Some of our literary material comes from the shisōshū, since the line between what is literature and what is "thought" seems to wobble a bit. We have used many reference books, literary histories, general histories, accounts of religion, and specialized studies. We have used the dictionary *Kōjien* for certain kinds of information, along with a number of kogo jiten. We have often had recourse to standard reference books, for which we hope one example may serve: *Haikai Daijiten*, edited by Ijichi Tetsuo et al., (Meiji Shoin, 1957) for renga and haikai.

Some specific decisions have affected what information we included. We endeavored to provide some kind of date for every person entered in Part Three. Many are more heuristic than exact, and a giant "ca." must be thought to apply, particularly to earlier figures and works.

Names and titles present such problems that complete consistency is probably impossible. Major entries of works are under authors in Part Three, unless the work is uncertain or unknown in authorship (and we have been conventional on the subject of authorship). Japanese authors are indexed by surname and then given name or pen name. The index also provides cross-references from English equivalents to the Japanese titles.

We have modernized and simplified names as far as we felt it possible to do so. For pre-Edo names, we have usually dropped the medial "no" except after surnames of one or two syllables: Ki no Tsurayuki and Kamo no Chōmei, but Minamoto Sanetomo and Fujiwara Teika (adding Sadaie, of course). Such usage is in lieu of Kakinomoto no Asomi no Hitomaro (or Fitomaro if a mild version of Old Japanese is used—and lots of unfamiliar sounds and umlauts if a severer rule is applied). Some readers may have other preferences, but they should find our usage comprehensible. For sovereigns and their consorts we have used their usual regnal name without their title, except for a few women for whom a Mon'in is too customary to omit. Similarly, we omit ecclesiastical titles or supply them in parentheses. We have found no way to simplify with any accuracy some of the most cumbersome designations of people, such as certain women of great literary importance: Fujiwara Michitsuna no Haha, Sugawara Takasue no Musume, or Rokujō Saiin Baishi Shinnō no Senji. We have not presumed to supply some obvious but useless information, such as that Sei Shōnagon means Kiyowara Shōnagon, or that Murasaki Shikibu was really a Fujiwara and no doubt known at court, at first at least, as Tō Shikibu.

Since detailed information about our handling of titles is given at the beginning of Part Three, little need be said here. But titles, too, we normalized or chose one of a number of possible versions. We give *Tosa Nikki* and *Genji Monogatari*, as everybody does, rather than the more correct *Tosa no Niki* and *Genji no Monogatari*. Specialists often prefer one term or title to another in more common usage: *Eika Taigai* rather than *Eiga Taigai*, gosan rather than gozan, *Utsuho Monogatari* rather than *Utsubo Monogatari*, and so on. Because it is difficult to distinguish between the pedantic and the clearly correct on the one hand, and between what is familiar and of most use to readers on the other, it is difficult to be consistent. Once a work has been mentioned, abbreviation of the title is feasible. But we have found no way to shorten titles for their entry version or on first mention, even when it means giving *Sakura Hime Zenden Akebono no Sōshi*.

Although it is by no means always simple to determine what is a discrete word in Japanese, our general practice will be clear. It is only necessary to say how we have endeavored to treat titles that end in "shū," "ki," "den," "shō," and so on. It is our general practice to join such Sinified units to the preceding substantive if that is Sinified, and to separate it if the preceding element is either read in Japanese fashion or is a person's name: *Man'yōshū* and *Nansō Satomi Hakkenden*, but *Tsurayuki Shū* and *Kenrei Mon'in Ukyō no Daibu Shū*.

Certain features of our editorial style require special note. Much the most important is that we have decided not to italicize or quote a word in a language other than English unless that word would be so distinguished if English. There is a very important reason for this apart from the cosmetics of the page, itself no mean thing:

in the *Companion* proper, an italicized word—other than a title—is to be found in Part Four, our list of terms.

For example, if a work is said to be a *rekishi monogatari*, the italics (which are used only in the first instance in a section or entry) designate a term defined in Part Four. Another important and related matter:

a title or name with an initial asterisk is entered in Part Three.

It will also be clear that we use a version of the Hepburn system for romanizing Japanese.

We depart from one contemporary usage in respect to titles. It has grown common to adopt librarians' usage for titles—that is, to capitalize only the first word of a title and any subsequent proper noun: *Nansō Satomi hakkenden*, *Uji shūi monogatari*, and so on. We have, however, capitalized all words in titles except particles. In non-library situations few follow librarians' usage for Japanese works when they name Western works. Two of us work in other literatures beside Japanese, and simply do not follow librarians' usage to give, for example, *A midsummer night's dream* or *The decline and fall of the Roman empire*. We have found no rational reason to treat Japanese titles as less worthy of capitals. If one were to argue from the lack of capitals in Japanese then one would have to present Japanese words without breaks between them.

We have tried where possible to give translations of titles, and in particular to use titles supplied by a translator. Now that two excellent translations are called *The Tale of Genji*, we are more or less stuck with "tale" for "monogatari," and we have sought no improvement. Sometimes a work has not been translated, but the meaning of its title is either obvious or can be established. Many titles, however—they multiply heavily in Edo times—are so difficult that only someone who translates or criticizes a work in detail has a right to choose from various possibilities. In those cases we offer no translation.

Although we do not offer information about translations of individual works, there are a number of reference works in English to guide the reader. First, there is a bibliography by Yasuhiro Yoshizaki (as the author is named on the title page) *Studies in Japanese Literature and Language* (Nichigai Associates, 1979).

This is comprehensive chiefly for works in English. Publications by the Japan P.E.N. Club have ranged farther by including translations and studies in other European tongues as well as English, and information on modern as well as classical Japanese literature: see, as a basis, *Japanese Literature in European Languages* (1961). From 1958 to 1971 the club also published a bulletin, *The P.E.N. News*, which reappeared in 1976 as *Japanese Literature Today*. This publication also offers essays on contemporary literary works, accounts of scholarly or critical studies that have made a stir in Japan, and occasional translations of modern poems.

Further information will be found in the annual bibliography of the *Journal of Asian Studies*. That is important for also including books, articles, and translations in fields other than literature. It and other journals devoted to Japanese or Asian matters also offer translations, essays, and reviews (often with invaluable information about major Japanese sources).

There is an especially useful chronology of Japanese literature in *Kokubungaku*, 22 (February 1977). This proceeds in great detail, giving as it were a chapter for each decade in a quasi-narrative form, thereby including information that cannot be presented by the chart used in Part Two and similar schematic devices.

EVERY book is certain to be wrong about some major matters, erroneous in some detail, and somehow inconsistent in presentation. A book as long, as detailed, and as varied as this one is especially susceptible to those faults. We hope that our sins are not as numerous as the sands of Egypt, and that the virtues and utility of the *Companion* will be thought much to outweigh any faults.

The three of us have sought to provide the information we have often sought and have never located in a single place or at all. To the very end we have wished to obtain and present some information we could not find. Sometimes we have disagreed about what to include, how much to say on a given topic, or whether this rather than that was the case. But we have always worked out an accommodation, and the result is that we have done together what none of us could have done alone. It is a conceivable that a reprint may be called for. If so, we would benefit by notice of errors. That notice may be sent to Miner at Princeton, although this preface, like the work itself, should be thought of as having three homes: from west to east, Kamakura, St. Louis, and (as this is written), Washington, D.C.

E. M.

Woodrow Wilson International Center for Scholars
Washington
May 1982

Acknowledgments

For a work of this length with three principals, it is all but impossible to give adequate acknowledgment, and any attempt is not likely to be brief. Toward the end of this *Companion*, we specify our "Principal Immediate Sources." There is considerable common ground between books there and people here.

As mentioned in the preface, an earlier version of parts of what is included here were read by Hirakawa Sukehiro of the University of Tokyo and Helen C. McCullough of the University of California, Berkeley. We are grateful for their corrections and advice. Konishi Jin'ichi has offered advice on numerous details, some small but bothersome, others large. Among the large, he has contributed crucial advice and information about what to include and what to ignore; about the first section of Part One; about Chinese matters; as also about monogatari, and so on. Much of the section on nō in Part Five was essentially rewritten by him, and he very kindly made a special visit from Washington to Princeton to check and correct Parts Three and Four in galley proof. Otherwise, Miner's debts go back so far that adequate acknowledgment is infeasible.

Morrell wishes to express his thanks to his wife, Sachiko Morrell, Librarian at the East Asian Library, Washington University, St. Louis, and to the library for purchase of necessary reference books. Odagiri and Miner wish to express their gratitude to Morrell's colleague, J. T. Rimer, who suggested Morrell's joining in this enterprise.

In addition to our debts to various Japanese publishers with whom she negotiated permissions for the use of figures in Part Ten, Odagiri wishes to thank Professor Nakano Mitsutoshi of Kyushu University, who did so much to arrange permissions for various illustrations. Professor Oka Masahiko of the Kokubungaku Kenkyū Shiryōkan also kindly offered such assistance. She is also grateful to Professors Tsuchida Masao and Ishida Yuriko of Sophia University for raising a number of important issues about an earlier version of the discussion of nō in Part Five. At Odagiri's request, Professor Arashi Yoshindo, now at the Ministry of Education, kindly read through all of Part Nine, making many helpful corrections.

She and Miner also wish to express deep gratitude to Professors Hirakawa

Sukehiro and Satō Seizaburō of the University of Tokyo, for assistance in obtaining a grant for her to do a summer's work on this *Companion* in Princeton.

Miner's record of debts resembles Homer's catalogue of the ships. In addition to individuals mentioned earlier, and to others mentioned later in other connections, there are: Robert H. Brower, with whom he has worked on waka over the years; Ian Hideo Levy on matters concerning the *Man'yōshū*; Richard Bowring, Norma Field, Andrew Pekarik, and Amanda Stinchecum for discussion of works by Murasaki Shikibu; Carol Hochstedler, Richard Kanda, Kenneth Richard, and Thomas C. Rohlich for information about monogatari after the *Genji Monogatari*; Yamashita Hiroaki for lengthy discussion of the *Heike Monogatari* and other gunki monogatari; Barbara Ruch and Susan Matisoff for assistance with popular prototypes of later fiction and drama; Sumie Jones and Alan Woodhull for help on Edo prose narrative; Barbara Thornbury for aid on kabuki; Laurel J. Rodd for assistance on Buddhism; William Malm for designating important musicians; Yoshiaki Shimizu and Christine Kanda for advice about art and artists; and Sumie Jones again for help on Edo thought.

Professor Nakanishi Susumu has assisted in many ways, including those of friendship, on a range of issues from early literature to zuihitsu and collections up to Yokoi Yayū. Professor Haruko Iwasaki helped on arms and armor.

There are others whose help is of long-standing nature. James T. Araki, Howard Hibbett, Donald Keene, E. G. Seidensticker, Makoto Ueda, and Kenneth Yasuda have given invaluable assistance over many years; besides Konishi, William Peterson, Andrew Plaks, and F. W. Mote have given assistance on Chinese matters. With Masao Miyoshi, Miner codirected two National Endowment for the Humanities Institutes, at Princeton in 1979 and at Berkeley in 1981; Miyoshi's presence and liveliness are extraordinary, so that to him and the forty seminar members Miner owes stimulation and much freshly learned.

Miner's typist, Helen Wright, has shown extraordinary patience and dedication in typing some 1,400 pages of manuscript, and it is a pity that the last additional typing and retyping by Miner himself will not assist the printer so well.

Thousands of Chinese and Japanese characters have had to be written into the manuscript. The bulk of this was done by Ojima Reiko, Bob Tadashi Wakabayashi, and Sachiko Morrell, with other work of this kind by the three of us, chiefly Odagiri.

The maps were drawn by Marcia Hart.

There are also various institutions that have offered assistance, whether directly or indirectly related to this book. The Japan Foundation's assistance to Odagiri, and the help of the Library at Washington University, St. Louis, may be mentioned again, along with that of the National Endowment for the Humanities. The Social Science Research Council has made two grants available for brief conferences in Princeton and Washington. These brought fruitful contact with people mentioned thus far, as well as with Eleanor Kerkham and Mark Morris in the former instance, and with Ronald Morse, David Plath, and J. T. Rimer in the latter. The Japan-U. S. Friendship Commission has funded another conference including, besides Professors Jones, Konishi, Nakanishi, and Ueda,

Professors Araki Hiroyuki, Susan Matisoff, Mezaki Tokue, and Noguchi Take-hiko. These intensive, week-long meetings have been unusually informative and productive. The John Simon Guggenheim Foudation gave Miner a fellowship in 1977–1978, during which much of the work for this book was done; the advantage of free time being scarce as it is, this was most beneficial. That fellowship was assisted by Princeton's generous leave policy, and by a fellowship at the Woodrow Wilson Internation Center for Scholars in 1981–1982, where this book was substantially completed. It would be difficult to imagine a more stimulating atmosphere among people from so many, mostly nonliterary, disciplines—with the novel questions that such contact brings, especially in an environment in which the posing of questions seems to be the chief business of the mind.

Versions of Part One, A, "The Development of a Systematic Poetics," were published as "Toward a New Conception of Classical Japanese Poetics" in *Studies on Japanese Culture*, 2 vols. (Tokyo: Japan P. E. N. Club, 1973), 1, 99–113; and as "Nihon no Koten Shigaku" in *Hikaku Bungaku Kenkyū*, no. 36 (1979), pp. 77–97; and elements of the findings appear also in "On the Genesis and Development of Literary Systems," *Critical Inquiry*, 5 (1979), 339–53, 553–68. We are grateful for permission from the Japan P. E. N. Club, the editors of *Hikaku Bungagku Kenkyū*, and the editors of *Critical Inquiry* to use, in adapted form, material that appeared otherwise under their aegis.

Finally, the Department of East Asian Studies at Princeton has given steady support in people's time, in xeroxing facilities, and in office space. Odagiri and Miner wish to express thanks to the department, including its chairman, Marion J. Levy Jr., to Marius B. Jansen, and to the departmental secretariat, Janice Gibson, Ruth Paine, and Hue Su. The staff of the Gest Library and the Marquand Art Library have also assisted generously. The Princeton Research Committee has given financial support to this book over several years, and we are very grateful for that.

These are many people and institutions. But this is a long book, and a difficult one to do, much less to do rightly. What assistance, intellectual and material, can do, assistance has done. In expressing our gratitude, we hope that the book will have a value to others comparable to that of the assistance we have received.

To any we have forgotten, to any we have misused in any way, we extend our apologies as well as our thanks.

The Princeton
Companion to
Classical
Japanese Literature

PART ONE A Brief Literary History

This short history of Japanese Literature offers a simplified conceptual and temporal grid for all that follows. As far as possible, repetition of information presented in Part Three is avoided, except, of course, for mention of authors. It follows that there is information both here and in Part Three necessary to a basic understanding of the work. This part has four sections. The first treats the origin and development of classical Japanese poetics: conceptions of the nature and function of literature. The next three deal with conventionally distinguished periods of Japanese literature, designated according to the logic explained in the preface. These periods involve what may be termed historical fictions, although it does seem that we cannot do without the concept of a period, at least for the sake of convenience in dividing up a discussion of some length. More than that, from our sense of our own present and its individual character, we assume other presents with their own characteristics.

The eight periods distinguished here (or nine, including prehistoric times) are designated by the locations of the seat of government. These matters are discussed in greater detail in the initial part of Section B, which begins the history of literature, as opposed to the history of poetics.

Part Two offers two chronologies, one of the regnal eras by which dates were traditionally calculated, and the other "annals" of Japanese literature. These may be used (with Part Three) to amplify or clarify this first part.

A name or a title preceded by an asterisk has an entry in Part Three, Major Authors and Works. Italicized words (other than titles) are entered in Part Four, Literary Terms.

We recommend a look at the Notice to Readers before the table of contents, and at the preface for a more detailed account of procedures.

A. THE DEVELOPMENT OF A SYSTEMATIC POETICS

The central elements of classical Japanese poetics found fresh expression or alteration with each new major achievement in literature. Yet the essential features endured for centuries. Identifying such fundamental features should assist us in making sense of what is particularly Japanese and also what is particularly historical about Japanese literary history. The identification proves easier if we alienate our subject by positing an alternative—traditional Western poetics and its hazards. That poetics is equally Western and historical, inherently possessing no greater or lesser claim on our understanding of literature than Japanese ideas.

We begin with a postulate: a systematic poetics emerges from the encounter of gifted critical minds with a currently practiced, esteemed genre (by genre is meant lyric, drama, or narrative). Aristotle's esteemed genre was, of course, drama, and he therefore thought in terms that differentiated dramatic art from lyric and narrative. This differentia was, naturally, representation. From representation Aristotle propounded mimesis, not a random or photographic replication of casual happening but an imitation of "universals" of the world and life. This important insight had its limits. It could not adequately account for the Homeric epics or distinguish narrative from lyric, or even dwell on the lyrics of which Greek tragedy were made. But Aristotle's *Poetics* has claimed respect wherever it has been known. Although the treatise itself was lost in ancient times, its ideas were transferred by Alexandrian intermediaries to later classical times and by Arabian mediators to the European Middle Ages.

The important second stage of Western poetics came with the Roman poet, Horace. In his *Art of Poetry* he wrote as a practitioner of lyrics (odes) and satires (including many of his epistles). It is not surprising that confronting these kinds led him, not to presume mimesis, but to a concern with effect on the reader. Affectivism is found throughout Greek ideas about various kinds of knowledge, but it was no more a differentia for literature than it was for rhetoric or philosophy. To Horace, however, the very bases of literature were the delight and the teaching that became traditional in Western conceptions of the ends of literature.

Between them, mimesis and affectivism accounted adequately for the four necessary terms of a literary system: the world, the poet, the poet's expression, and the reader. This system has endured because, and as long as, a prior assumption held. Over the centuries poets and readers assumed that the world is imitable and moving because it is knowable to them. This cognitive presumption permits an essential optimism about literature, even as the universals identified by the followers of Aristotle included hierarchies that tended to social discrimination as much as to moral assurance.

Writers involved in the Romantic fervor of Europe reacted in part against such hierarchies, and they certainly gave greater emphasis to the poet and therefore to expressivist views of literature. As the poet assumed more importance, the world was, as it were, receding from interest, importance, knowability. That recession has continued. For although many critics hold other views, including fresh versions of the mimetic and affective, there have also been many others who doubt the prior postulate that the world is knowable. Others find it increasingly difficult to distinguish poet from reader or expression from world. Many find a sense of liberation from the breakdown of these old cognitive entities. Many others find a fearful loss and an anxiety-ridden self-exposure. There are also some neo-Marxist critics who emphasize a special historicist view, placing the world and poet in an overpowering dialectical scheme founded on a crucially historical view of reality very much at odds with the view of those who would obliterate such distinctions. Somewhat similar changes have come about in modern Japanese views of literature. But classical Japanese poetics offers us a complete alternative to Western poetics in its traditional as well as modern versions.

When Greek poetics emerged, there had been that great Homeric achievement in poetic narrative for which Aristotle did not truly account. When systematic poetics emerged in China and Japan, there was also a major narrative tradition, although it was in prose and actually or purportedly historical. The devisers of Japanese poetics similarly failed to account adequately for prose narrative, although they were certainly aware of it. Japanese were aware, that is, of the *Kojiki and particularly of the *Nihon Shoki (or Nihongi). These are hardly what we think history to be today, but they passed for accounts of what transpired in the Age of the Gods and in early Japan. These prose narratives contain many lyrics, and are at once more literary and less historical, to our modern view, than their Chinese counterparts. Yet in China, in Korea, and especially in Japan, prose narrative was not soon enough encountered by great critical minds as the normative genre for it to provide the basis for a systematic poetics.

That honor went to lyricism. But not to the first lyrics, which are lost in preliterate darkness, nor even to some of the great lyric achievements in early historical times. In Japan, classical poetics would have had a rather different emphasis had there been important critical thinking to encounter the undoubted greatness of the eighth-century collection, the *Man'yōshū. Many of the "long poems," chōka, in that anthology have strong narrative elements, and concern public matters that involve a distinct sense of the relation between human beings and their world. It is not possible to find in later classical Japanese poetry poems comparable to many by *Kakinomoto Hitomaro (fl. ca. 680–700) and *Ōtomo Yakamochi (718–785). In On the Lying in State of Prince Takechi, Hitomaro narrates a battle and assumes a historical continuum. In his poem on The Production of Gold in Michinoku, Yakamochi treats a topic equally absent from later classical poetry. (These poems are Man'yōshū, 2: 199–201; 17: 4094–97—early and late.) Both assume a "public" stance, valuing most highly what all people share rather than that which is idiosyncratic. The sense of what is shared is never wholly lost in classical Japanese literature, but it is defined in terms unlike those of the poems mentioned.

After the Man'yōshū, poets become more subjective. This tendency can be found in not a few of the poems by unknown authors and in many by *Yamabe Akahito (d.? 736) and Yakamochi. The label of subjectivism implies a distinct relation of the poet and the reader to the world, a relation in which the world enters on terms set by the human subject. It is this kind of lyricism, which is of course also known in many other cultures, that is distinctive of most Japanese poetry. It is this lyricism that provides the basis for classical Japanese poetics, as it does not for Western.

Early in the tenth century of this era (ca. 905–920), *Ki no Tsurayuki (868–

945) and others compiled the first of the twenty-one royally commissioned waka collections, the *Kokinshū. Tsurayuki's Japanese preface constitutes the first major piece of vernacular criticism by a Japanese. For centuries, the Kokinshū was a standard, and to say that a given work of another kind was the Kokinshū of that kind bespoke unusual prestige. In rather similar fashion, when later critics wrote about literature, they were much given to echoing phrasing in the first few sentences of Tsurayuki's preface. These sentences reveal an indebtedness—chief among several—to the "Great Preface" to the Chinese Book of Songs (Shikyō, Shih Ching), but the formulation is so very Japanese that many Westerners—and Japanese—have failed to recognize in it the extraordinary importance of its theoretical ideas. We observe Tsurayuki's attempt to differentiate. He begins by speaking emphatically of "the poetry of Japan" (Yamato uta wa . . .).

> The poetry of Japan takes the human heart as seed and flourishes in the countless leaves of words. Because human beings possess interests of so many kinds, it is in poetry that they give expression to the meditations of their hearts in terms of the sights appearing before their eyes and the sounds coming to their ears. Hearing the warbler sing among the blossoms and the frog that lives in the waters—is there any living thing not given to song? It is poetry which, without exertion, moves heaven and earth, stirs the feelings of gods and spirits invisible to the eye, softens the relations between men and women, calms the hearts of fierce warriors.

As later Japanese critics recognized, the crucial terms used by Tsurayuki are *kokoro* and *kotoba*, translated in the first sentence as "heart" and "words." Polarities of this kind appear in many conceptions of literature, and they have counterparts in the "Great Preface." Traditional Western critics speak of art and nature, the world and imitation, and so forth. Critically as well as philosophically, the crucial question involves the relation between the two elements in these polarities. Not many people have troubled to ask about the relation between Tsurayuki's kokoro and kotoba. The answer appears in Tsurayuki's metaphor. In part, the relation is one to be found in nature: we have a seed that produces leaves, leaves that are words (koto no ha: kotoba). The meaning of that "seed" (tane) can be explained by reference to a dictionary and to another literary example. The fifth definition of the word in *Daigenkai* runs, "The basis [motoi] for the generation of matters [koto]. Origin." And as illustration we are given Tsurayuki's first sentence. The literary example comes in a late chapter of the *Genji Monogatari*, "Writing Practice" ("Tenarai"). The nun Imōto says that Ukifune has been brought to her as a replacement for her lost daughter because of her prayers to Kannon. Imōto's priestly brother, Sōzu, has Ukifune's karma in mind as the explanation, and so inquires, "How can a matter be without a seed?" that is, without a cause. ("Tane naki koto wa ikade ka.") Tsurayuki is saying, then, that in Japanese poetry, the human heart is the seed or cause of words.

If what transpires in the human heart is the cause of poetic words, then one central feature of classical Japanese poetics must be termed expressivism. From the human individual's observation, feeling, and thinking comes the motive to express what has been observed, felt, and thought. Tsurayuki's second sentence says as much in nonmetaphorical language. His third sentence extends the principle to creatures other than human. That is to say, we and other living creatures respond to our worlds and, as Tsurayuki insists, the responsive, expressive tendencies inevitably lead to poetry—to the song of human poetry or the songs of the warbler and the frog. Surely this kind of poetic expressivism is particularly appropriate to a theory of literature based on lyricism as the norm. In fact, the Western Romantics came to much the same expressivist conclusions by assuming varieties of lyricism to be the truest poetry. Tsurayuki also wrote of style (*sama*), thereby positing an ideal of technical skill prerequisite to affect (kokoro) and expression (kotoba).

Tsurayuki's concern with the expressive nature of poetry remained his central point in his poetic diary, *Tosa Nikki* (ca. 935). The woman imagined to be keeping the diary ends her journey to the capital from Tosa by writing two poems about the daughter she had lost in the province. Tsurayuki takes great care to let us know quite explicitly how central art is to life, how natural and inevitable is poetic expression. Passing the pine grove on the coast of Uta, where waves have splashed immemorially and cranes have come and gone, the lady observes, "It is impossible merely to look on the splendor of this scenery, and someone composed a poem something like this . . ." (First Month, 9th day). The best statement of all unfortunately involves a famous crux in the diary. (The disputed phrase is the first, "Kō yō no koto mo uta mo," from the Second Month, 9th day.) Here, with the problematic portion italicized, is what Tsurayuki has the woman say:

> *I do not set down these words, nor did I compose the poem,* out of mere love of writing. Surely both in China and Japan art is that which is created when we are unable to suppress our feelings.

Tsurayuki proves consistent, and his view of literature persists. In *Oku no Hosomichi* (*The Narrow Road through the Provinces*), *Matsuo Bashō (1644–1694) expresses himself by pointedly not writing a poem about Matsushima when he visits it. He attends to poems by others, but his silence is, on one view, a kind of Zen Buddhist poem on perhaps the most esteemed beauty spot in Japan. Actually—and this proves how very right Tsurayuki was—Bashō did write some verses, but he was very self-critical and did not think them worthy of Matsushima, of himself, or of inclusion in *Oku no Hosomichi*.

In the *Tosa Nikki*, everybody is a poet. The funniest episode in the diary involves a would-be bard at Ōminato, who brings a gift of food to the ship simply to have an excuse to recite an embarrassingly bad poem. Here the unstated technical assumption comes to light. On another occasion the rough sea captain's orders fall into tanka-cadence (First Month, 6th day, and Second Month, 5th day). Folk songs, boating songs, Chinese poems, poems by Abe no Nakamaro (698–770) and Ariwara Narihira (825–880), and fifty-nine tanka in all make the *Tosa Nikki* abound with poetry of all kinds. The fact that the poems vary so in quality largely shows the different personalities of the persons in the story. The variability also shows Tsurayuki's keen awareness that the irrepressible expressive tendencies we have do not lead to the same quality of poetic expression on every occasion. Natural as poetry is to all people, much as it expresses what is in their hearts, art or technique is required. Something of Tsurayuki's keen sense of artistic requirements (sama) entered into his criticism of even the greatest of his predecessors. In the preface to the *Kokinshū*, his praise of *Ariwara Narihira is tempered by the stricture that his poems "are excessive in heart and deficient in words" (kokoro amarite, kotoba tarazu). Too great an impulse to expression may lead to being cryptic, as with Narihira, or to other verbal inadequacy.

These various remarks and examples show a crucial second element in Tsurayuki's theory. This involves consideration of the heart more than the words of poetry, of the expresser more than what is expressed. The lady diarist said, after all, that "art is that which is created when we are unable to suppress our feelings." It is the response of the human heart that produces expression. In other words, Tsurayuki founds his principle of expressivism upon one of affectivism, just as affectivism entails expressivism. The two are genuinely complementary, and they allow for all four requisite terms of a literary theory: the world to which the poet responds, the responding poet, the poetic expression by the poet, and the reader of that poetic expression, who is then affected in turn. The reader or listener commonly turns poet, having found that the original expression so affected a second heart that a second expression was required. This fact helps account for the social practice of poetic address and reply reflected in the poetic diaries, *monogatari*, and life at the Heian court. This fact also gives special point to the practice of allusion (*honkadori, honzetsu*) and poetic language (*utakotoba, utamakura, makurakotoba*) in Japan as well as in China.

The complementarity of affectivism and expressivism in classical Japanese poetics derives from the fact that they derive from a single critical encounter with lyricism. It was not necessary for centuries to pass and a Japanese Horace to arise for affectivism to be a part of Japanese aesthetics. (On the other hand, a suitable Chinese precedent was usually welcome.) Nor was a new movement like that of the Romantic required to account for the expressivism that was there from the beginning as a counterpart of affectivism. We cannot deny a certain historical awkwardness in the traditional Western poetics, which needed a Horace to complete what an Aristotle had begun. Or rather, there is a peculiar fitness, justice, and wholeness to the Japanese system that did not require addition. It not only accounts for the world, the poet, the expression, and the reader; it also posits as surely as does the mimetic view the knowability of each of those four radical terms. If, for example, the world were unknowable in the strict sense, one could not be positively affected by it, and one would have no ability to express what one knew. By including in a few sentences a range of life from a seed to gods and spirits, Tsurayuki makes clear that all that lives is essentially poetic, and therefore the warbler's song and the poet's words are part of reality. This poetics, which is shared with China and Korea, no doubt has limitations such as any theory founded on any one of the genres will necessarily possess. But Japan was fortunate to have in Tsurayuki a critic with powers to realize as fully as feasible the range of possibility in his theory. Strange as his language may sound for what we think passes as literary criticism, he fathered a theory remarkable at once for completeness and impressiveness.

Classical Japanese literature does not consist solely of lyrics, however. Within about a century of Tsurayuki's formulation there appeared a work usually thought the greatest in all Japanese literature, the *Genji Monogatari* (ca. 1010) This very long work of prose narrative had to be fitted into the critical system if it was to be valued and if the critical system were to continue to make sense. There was, in fact, a lag, with critical estimation rising only in about another century. More to the point, however, the author of this great work knew very well what she was doing, as we can see from the numerous passages on art of one kind or another included with great naturalness by *Murasaki Shikibu. To avoid the best known—that in "Hotaru" ("Fireflies")—let us take that little episode she provides in "Tamakazura." Genji and Murasaki are discussing the distribution of benefactions. His gift to that odd creature, Suetsumuhana of the red nose, brings in return a robe of Chinese style. This robe had seen far better days, as had the language of its accompanying poem, with its "karakoromo" ("robe of far Cathay"), a term long since passed from fashion. Genji is led to reflect both on the persistence of outmoded fashion and the hidebound respect for imagined poetic rules that will seek to arrest natural change in time. He draws the somewhat disquieting inference that what is popular in his own time may seem old-fashioned in another day. In fact, Murasaki Shikibu, like the other best minds of her time, and not only of her time, worried over the question of what should be kept from the past and what should be changed. There are both faults and virtues in clinging to the past—being furumekashi—or in embracing new fashions—being imamekashi. This problem is one of the themes of the work, and is related to numerous other themes, becoming a basis for distinguishing character. As warning examples of either tendency, we have Suetsumuhana at one extreme, and the Lady from Ōmi at something like the opposite. We recall that her author presents her, not as Ōmi no Kimi, but the ridiculous sounding thing, Imahimegimi, the Now Lady.

The importance of this issue was subsequently recognized by two of the poets who did most to raise the esteem of the *Genji Monogatari* to its present position. *Fujiwara Shunzei (1114–1204) and his son *Fujiwara Teika (1162–1241) were led by consideration of these issues to bring new life to Tsurayuki's terms with an awareness of problems not foreseen by Tsurayuki. Their decision led to a slogan, "kotoba furuku, kokoro atarashi." That is, faced with a now established tradition, and yet needing to postulate originality, they advocated the tried and true in realms of language, along with the novel and original in poetic creation. They were themselves somewhat more divided than the slogan implies. But two or three things are quite clear. They were very serious in thinking that poetic diction should be that of the *sandaishū, the first three of the regnal collections. And their stress on the new in poetic conception led to one of the great periods of Japanese poetry.

It does not detract from the importance of Shunzei and Teika to observe that their new conception of poetry would not have been possible without a major achievement of narrative such as the *Genji Monogatari*. Tsurayuki's formulation has many merits, but its lyric base does not allow for conceptions of time and history that are crucial to narrative. Only with the prose narrative of monogatari, and in particular only with a Murasaki Shikibu so given to exploring the nature of narrative literature, can matters of time and history become problematic and therefore important. In his preface to the *Kokinshū*, Tsurayuki had mentioned six poets. His mentioning them led them to be termed the six poetic saints; it did not lead to a historical view of literature such as we find again and again in the *Genji Monogatari*. For that matter, we can see that only after the lyric views of literature had been affected by narrative implications could Teika posit a history, however simple, of Japanese *poetry*. This he did in his preface to *Kindai Shūka* (*Superior Poems of Our Time*). His preface is one of many such critical writings to echo Tsurayuki. But his three-stage history of Japanese poetry required the *Genji Monogatari*, or at least an understanding of time and history such as narrative, alone among the genres, fosters.

The freedom from concern with history and the celebration of the intense moment, of course, distinguish the lyric from narrative and drama, at least in essential emphasis. Immersion in time and history, on the other hand, is necessary to narrative and particularly to prose narrative, with its versions of temporality that lead to extended treatment of at least putative actuality. These are only questions of emphasis. Novels may turn lyrical and songs can seem real. Such matters are also dealt with in the *Genji Monogatari*. In the second chapter, Uma no Kami moves at one moment in his long discussion of women to a comparison involving artisanship and painting. The usual woodworker, he says, fashions his material in ways popular in his time, producing things to be used in that day and then rejected in favor of products in a newer style. On the other hand, some painters aim at astonishing effects, and lose beauty in the process. This contrast also implies a resemblance between two inadequate kinds of art—that of the poor Japanese artisan, and the fundamentally incredible, unreal paintings of some Chinese artists. To that extent, cultural as well as simply temporal elements are involved. Uma no Kami opposes to these poorer examples others that are clearly thought better. Another artisan imparts a genuine beauty to things people actually use. The other, Japanese, painter depicts scenery such as it recognizably is, even including scenes of buildings that suggest familiar human life. Both such superior kinds of art relate to the actual (and both are pointedly Japanese, not Chinese, we observe). The actual world is that known by a Murasaki Shikibu in time, in history, and in experience of her own culture. She seems, perhaps, to approach Aristotle's mimetic inference that art may represent reality and that literary quality arises from what is universal in the actual. But Murasaki Shikibu is wholly Japanese, and her art is first of all conceived in Tsurayuki's terms. When, in "Eawase" ("The Picture Match"), Genji produces the pictorial diary he had painted and written while in exile, everybody present is moved to their depths by what they see. Art remains affective and expressive for Murasaki Shikibu.

The centrality of Tsurayuki's lyric-based poetics remains unchallenged even as it is enlarged and altered. Two rather similar examples testify to this. In the "Hotaru" ("Fireflies") chapter of the *Genji Monogatari*, we discover the young lady Tamakazura comparing her strange life history to that in a version of the *Taketori Monogatari* (a romance completed before the *Tosa Nikki* but extant today only in later versions). Again, in the *Sarashina Nikki* by *Sugawara Takasue's Daughter, the heroine discovers for herself that her life becomes the kind of monogatari that she had been so fond of reading when she was a girl. In both instances, works by other authors are so affective as to be expressive of one's own affected heart. One life history implies another. One life and its times find illumination in another.

These developments testify to the importance of monogatari both to the development of classical Japanese poetics and also to the stability of its central principles. Later works that are all or mostly in prose show much the same tendencies. The literary prose of *Matsuo Bashō is often studied with lyric verse, so it may seem to be an exception. But if we look at *Ihara Saikaku (1643–1693), his contemporary, we shall find no less adherence to the central tenets of Tsurayuki's poetics. The same can be said, for example, of other pairs we might think of: *Oraga Haru* (*This Year of My Life*) by *Kobayashi Issa (1763–1827) and the *Ugetsu Monogatari* (*Tales of Moonlight and Rain*) by *Ueda Akinari (1734–1809). Many have remarked on distinctive features of Japanese prose narrative up to this day, features that they somewhat disconcertedly call lyric. That label is no cause for embarrassment. It is the legacy of Tsurayuki, the property of all classical Japanese literature. But the legacy was used by others to new purposes, and those who esteemed the emergent prose narrative held it with a difference. The old poetics lasted because it could be developed in significant ways to accommodate the valuable insights provided by narrative and, as we must now consider, by drama as well.

*Zeami (Kanze Motokiyo, ?1363–?1443) offers us almost an embarrassing amount of assistance. In addition to his plays, which are in many ways the best criticism of nō, he has left voluminous critical writings. From all these essays three terms may be selected to represent his contribution to classical Japanese poetics. These terms are not easily defined, but let us say that *monomane* is imitation, *yūgen* beauty, and *hana* art. From what we have seen of Aristotle, we might fully expect that a critic of Zeami's powers would concern himself with imitation or representation, since that is the central feature of drama as opposed to lyric and narrative. But the interesting thing about his use of the term "monomane" is that it plays a central, definitive role only in the *Fūshikaden*. It seems that in this early critical work Zeami sought to give expression to the ideas of his father, *Kan'ami (1333–1384). The lack of importance of monomane in Zeami's mature criticism seems to imply that he was moving away from his father's very natural interest in theatrical imitation or representation. It appears that as nō and its actors began to acquire a respectability they had not had earlier, Zeami felt the need to propound a kind of critical theory for his art that would also seem respectable. We might consider as symptoms of the effort to give nō a good name its taking over from standard linked verse, *renga*, the three-part rhythm, *jo-ha-kyū* (preparation, development, fast finale, introduced in Japan from Chinese court music, *gagaku*). But yūgen features more fully in Zeami's aesthetics than in his father's and therefore seems fuller of implication.

Yūgen is a concept that has had books written about it, so that no simple translation or definition can possibly approximate its range of meaning. But this much is clear: the gestalt of meaning, if it may so be called, changes in the course of time, and the critical concept achieved currency as a poetic ideal in the critical pronouncements of Shunzei. In other words, by adapting yūgen to nō criticism, Kan'ami and Zeami were doing nothing other than adapting nō to the basic lyric poetics that had been systematic in Japan since Tsurayuki. Here was a means to give nō the respect that was enjoyed by *waka* and subsequently by monogatari.

In Shunzei's usage, yūgen had elements of darkness, of mystery, and of deprivation, or of an added something that clarifies what it is added to. A beauty compounded of such elements was taken by Shunzei and his admirers to be especially desirable because it was especially profound, especially moving. In his *Mumyōshō*, *Kamo no Chōmei (1153–1216) made clear that even after Shunzei it was not wholly clear what yūgen, a style of mystery and depth, might mean. Or at least he pretends not to know, although since he is the most difficult poet of his time one suspects that when he reports asking *Shun'e about the matter, the reply obtained may be more what Chōmei understood than Shun'e. The reply is especially valuable, however, for the way in which it seems to fit so well with Zeami's concepts of beauty and of theatrical presentation. If that is the case, it is also significant that toward the end he echoes Tsurayuki's preface to the *Kokin-shū* and obviously implies the basic system of affectivism and expressivism. Shun'e is reported to say of yūgen that

> the qualities deemed essential to the style are overtones that do not appear in the words alone and an atmosphere that is not visible in the configuration [*sugata*] of the poem.... On an autumn evening, for example, there is no color in the sky nor any sound, yet although we cannot give any definite reason for it, we are somehow moved to tears.... Or again, it is like the situation of a beautiful woman who, although she has cause for resentment, does not give vent to her feelings in words, but is only faintly discerned—at night, perhaps—to be in a profoundly distressed condition.... Only when the conception is exalted to the highest degree and "the words are too few," will the poem, by expressing one's feeling in this way, have the power of moving Heaven and Earth within the brief confines of a mere thirty-one syllables, and be capable of softening "the hearts of gods and spirits." (*Nihon Kagaku Taikei*, 3, 312–13)

We might almost feel that this is a passage of Zeami's from some context we have forgot, perhaps some essay in which he talks about how to play the role of a woman whose lover is unfaithful without excessive display of feeling. In fact,

Chōmei has waka entirely on his mind and would have been astonished to learn (could be have imagined the later nō) that anyone might think he would write about mere theater in terms of such hallowed canons as those of Tsurayuki. But the resemblance to Zeami's mature criticism shows how very far his critical insights into nō were adapted to the systematic poetics he inherited.

Once this point is fully understood, another requires equal appreciation. Zeami adapted his poetics to the affective-expressive poetics as they had been modified, but he also found a way of doing so that allowed his central insights their due, and a way also that modified the poetic system. This is best understood in terms of his symbol, "hana" or flower, which was earlier translated as "art." This symbol applies to three principal features of Zeami's art. It applies to the skill of the playwright and yet more of the actor, so representing elements at once expressive and relating to his father's idea of monomane. It is not, however, imitation in any ordinary sense, but a most cultivated and subtle power of theatrical expression that Zeami designates. In addition, this symbol designates the effect of the expression on the audience. Skillful expression may induce almost magical effects on its viewers. In this application we discover a version of Tsurayuki's affectivism adapted to the special conditions of drama.

There is one other thing the symbol designates, and this is hardest to elucidate. It is a kind of combination of the first two elements, a hypostasizing of them into a single whole, an abstraction for which "art" seems the only translation. This abstracted sense of aesthetic process and experience seems to be Zeami's special contribution to Japanese aesthetics. We look in vain in earlier criticism for an idea comparable to the Latin *ars* or German *Kunst*. The closest term is one used in a chapter of the *Genji Monogatari*, "Eawase" ("The Picture Match"). This term, *sai* or sae, designates the talent for an art as well as the art, and besides could apply to games as well as to aesthetics, to study of Chinese as well as to practice of Japanese arts (see also the later term, *waza*).

Zeami understood his art and the problems he faced in making that understanding consonant with traditional poetics. But in adapting his concepts to the traditional aesthetics, he succeeded in enlarging the concepts by a degree of abstraction quite uncharacteristic of Japanese criticism up to that point. In the very finest fashion, he exemplifies the talent of making a difficult problem the basis of new thought. In the end, he does not so much solve a problem as make an original contribution. One might say with metaphorical justice that it was he who made a flower bloom among Tsurayuki's countless leaves. But if we recall the affective kokoro or heart and expressive kotoba or words, we can see that Zeami's hana is not really parallel. He sought and found a symbol that was at once apart from kokoro and kotoba and inclusive of them. The basic poetics remains intact but further modified by a degree of abstract thought possible only by virtue of Zeami's dilemma and his originality in resolving it.

Zeami was not the sole master of drama and dramatic criticism, just as nō was not the sole theatrical art practiced with distinction. (The issue of contemporary as against modern reputation is another matter.) We must allow some consideration as well for *jōruri* and *kabuki*. The use of puppets in the one, like the extravaganzas or shifting moods of the other, force on us even more than does nō the issue of representation. What is the relation between artistic expression and the actuality it seeks to express? What is the relation between our aesthetic feelings and actual experience? The answers to these and other questions were provided by the dramatist *Chikamatsu Monzaemon (1653–1724) in what must surely be the briefest of all major critical insights. In *Naniwa Miyage*, Chikamatsu is reported to have said:

> Art is that which lies in the slender margin between truth and falsehood. . . . Participating in the false, it is yet not false. Participating in the true, it is yet not true. . . .
> . . . if one makes a precise copy of a living person, were it Yang Kuei-fei herself, one will be disgusted by it. For this reason, in painting or carving a likeness in wood, there will be some things of close resemblance and others with deviance. After all, deviance is what people like. (*Shingunsho Ruijū*, 6, 325)

It is particularly telling that Chikamatsu's example of art and sculpture is just the kind that Aristotle likes to use, because to the Greeks the art of tragedy is a technē with an almost physical result of imitation. Chikamatsu is led to the same example, as perhaps anyone would be who was used to a theater of puppets or of elaborately got up actors. But who can fail to be struck by his rejection of representation? Put another way, Chikamatsu seems profoundly right in understanding that the basis of art is not representation, although the theater uses representation, as he well knew. He is interested rather in the kind of expression, that which is common to all arts, and the kind of effect, "what people like." As with Zeami's criticism, so in this we find a remarkably skillful adaptation of the basic features of classical Japanese poetics to the special conditions of drama, and vice versa.

Chikamatsu has one further contribution that possesses special value. Because he was such an admirer of the *Genji Monogatari*, I suspect that his concern with truth and falsehood owes not a little to Genji's discussion of monogatari in "Hotaru" ("The Fireflies"). But Chikamatsu arrives at an emphasis different from Genji's sense of literature as teaching what is true by adapted or lesser truth. Instead, the drama he practiced shows him that the matter is essentially a cognitive one. Literature is a kind of knowledge, one that resembles those of the other arts but differs from other kinds of knowledge in terms of those non-falsifiable and therefore nonverifiable elements that art employs. One is hard pressed to say that the pattern on a tea bowl or in modern abstract painting is true. But one is equally hard pressed to say that it is false. Chikamatsu had the genius to extend what all of us can tell from painting and sculpture to an art that uses words as well as the other resources of the theater, and therefore also to extend it to art generally. He goes much beyond a mimetic theory to a cognitive theory such as makes more and more sense as we come to better knowledge of the working of the human brain.

The finest criticism, by Japanese as well as others, is less this kind of explicit theory than what is implicit in the great works of literature. As a dramatist, Chikamatsu encompasses his remarks within a far larger range of proof and of value than these remarks themselves provide. The problem is that we mere readers or theatergoers are normally unable to infer from the works what we can draw out, with some effort, from explicit criticism. It does seem to be true, however, that many readers have experienced some disorientation in moving from Japanese to Western literature or from Western to Japanese. That experience of coming upon unfamiliar and seemingly unmarked ways derives from encounter with a literature embodying a systematic poetics different from one's own literature and its poetics. To a Western reader, the strength of the affective element in Japanese literature is probably the most unusual element, the one hardest to account for, and even the feature that makes the literature seem foreign.

Most peoples like to think that there is something distinctive about their literature, as well as their languages, their histories, or, for that matter, themselves. Such differences are, of course, only comparative. If Western literature seems different from Japanese when those two are the sole basis of comparison, all kinds of literature will look very much alike when they are compared with all kinds of mathematics. Similarly, although Chinese and Japanese literature seem very different when they alone are compared, they look far more alike when Western literature is introduced into the comparison. There are, in fact, a few features of the development of classical Japanese poetics that seem striking in terms of some larger comparisons. In describing them we can indeed find matters that help explain the special character of Japanese literature.

The affective-expressive hypothesis has lasted into modern times, although it is at present only the major postulate among a few other major and many minor ones. As we have seen, that postulate began in the encounter with lyricism as the most valued literary genre, and the poetics that developed was so natural, so secure, that subsequent centuries brought modification but not destruction. By comparison with Western traditional poetics, the lyric base is striking; so is the naturalness with which Japanese poetics accounts for the poet, the world, the expression, and the reader.

The basic poetic system is very much that also of China and Korea, from which Japan has received so much over the centuries. But there are differences. Some are traceable to the differing characters of the languages, some to the experience of an insular rather than a continental nation. Others involve philosophical and religious experience. In all three countries we can find Buddhism, Confucianism, and what for the sake of a neutral category may be termed natural mysticism or magic. In China and Korea, however, Confucianism entered into literature in a far more fundamental sense than it has done in Japan. One might almost say that Japanese literature is fundamentally un-Confucian, as is shown by the number of female writers it has enjoyed in all but the most Confucianism-ridden times. To put it positively, if Confucianism and Taoism have never mattered all that much in Japan, Shinto and Buddhism have. The natural magic of Shinto is related to practices of ritual purity that seem particularly male in emphasis and to practices of shamanism that seem particularly female. The world of Shinto is alive in an unusual degree of compatibility among the natural, the human, and the divine. Perhaps those elements should be said to exist in a continuity, but even that does not convey the kind of positive unity among diverse vital elements that Shinto provides. Buddhism fitted into Japanese life particularly well, whether the early tantric sects like Shingon, which must have suited a land of shamans, or the far later Zen Buddhism, which preferred meditation to action, to words, and to belief as means of enlightenment.

Yet even if we considered all these matters at great length, we would also observe that there are particularly literary explanations for the distinctive features of classical Japanese literature. There appears to be no systematic poetics in the world that has originated by engagement with narrative. Japanese poetics is one of a very large family that originated with lyric presumptions. Besides China and Korea, besides the complex and mixed example of India, besides many rather undeveloped cultures, besides Japanese literature, there is also the family of literatures in the Arabic and related tongues that have founded their poetics on lyricism. It makes little sense to take a vote in such matters, but if one were taken, a lyric-based poetics would gain a majority and a drama-based poetics would be in a distinct minority of one.

Yet Japanese literature and poetics differ from all other lyric-based poetics in two or three striking respects. One of these is the hospitality of its espousers to achievements in other genres. When the Arabs obtained Aristotle's *Poetics*, they hardly knew what to do with it. They had no drama. In the end they made it lyric. But Japan accepted nonliterary genres with great ease by comparison with other countries. Even where, as in China, an impressive prose literature and drama were devised, we observe considerable hostility to admitting them into the status of full, seriously considered arts. One cannot say of Chinese literary history, as one can of Japanese, that the basic poetics was fundamentally adapted as narrative and drama came to be practiced. Practice alone is not enough to alter a poetics in important ways; the practice must also be truly esteemed. In this respect, an account of Chinese poetics would have to deal far more with historical writing, which helps us understand why moral affectivism or didacticism has been of so much greater importance in China than Japan.

A second important matter involves the order of practice of esteemed genres. If the crucial genre is the first one to be esteemed and to be used as a basis for criticism, it is of next importance to observe the sequence in which other esteemed genres appear. The order of appearance of the genres in China resembles that in Japan. But Japan is quite unlike China in the extraordinarily early (absolutely as well as relatively) emergence of great narrative, as also in the quickly acquired esteem of monogatari and nō. It is particularly striking that the order of *esteemed* generic practice differs so strikingly between Japan and the West. In Japan the order is clearly lyric, (prose) narrative, and drama. In the West, the order is drama, and the lyric and satire and (poetic) narrative almost together. But the situation is messier than this. In Japan, critical esteem of kinds after waka often lagged by generations or centuries. The Western Middle Ages lost, until its latest phase, drama as we know it, and prose narrative came into esteem only by the eighteenth century, as one can see from the critical vicissitudes of *Don Quixote.*

Another matter worth commenting on is the remarkably early introduction of subsequently valued new genres in Japan. This is also distinguishes Japan from China in one way and from the West in another. It is remarkable that Japanese aesthetics could accommodate prose narrative so soon after the poetics had been devised out of lyricism. Surely there is no other national literature in which the greatest work appears, as does the *Genji Monogatari,* in little more than a century after the basic poetics had been devised, and in another genre. What might be termed the inherent shock to the poetic system was absorbed with great ease. More than that, it was capitalized on, its insights used to extend the system as it had existed previously. It seems that by being hospitable to literary change, Japanese have managed to gain from the change without losing what they already had. This gain seems beyond price in human terms, and helps explain why classical Japanese literature possesses that variety, personality, and greatness that entitles it to universal esteem. The same is true of the systematic poetics developed over the centuries by Japanese critics.

B. YAMATO, NARA, AND HEIAN LITERATURE (645–1186)

The periods specified here resemble those used in discussing other literatures, and differ largely from accounts of other literatures by use of the Japanese distinction of location of the seat of government to designate literary periods. This does not mean that the dates used correspond exactly to those used by political historians, but only that a correspondence is assumed. The assumption holds that some consonance exists between literary developments and other major happenings in the culture: the political, economic, military, religious, and others. We do not pretend to discuss the issue of whether artistic shifts follow or determine other cultural changes, although we do assume a complex dialectic between the various features of a nation's intellectual life.

Surviving evidence shows that there had been a tradition of oral song and narrative, as no doubt also of proto-theatrical elements. Neither the details nor the chronology of this, our vague Yamato period, can be related with any certainty. Our discussion of Nara literature does, however, involve some glances at earlier times and attention to some materials known about but lost. With the Nara period, we enter literary "historical time." This is hardly to suggest that we know what we wish to know about those early centuries, or for that matter about several later centuries. Because this brief history seeks to deal with what survives and can be known, the length of discussion grows steadily with later periods. Such proportioning is not meant to imply that the Edo period, which is treated in most detail, holds greatest importance in Japanese literature. But with the development of more widely spread education and of printing, there is far more written and much more that survives. Of late Heian and subsequent monogatari, we know about ten times the number of titles than we have works extant. It can only be hoped that the best have survived.

The Nara period is taken, then, to be by definition more or less those years when the capital was situated in or near the Yamato area where Nara itself is found. The Heian period is identified with the literature that developed when the capital was established at Heiankyō, or Kyoto.

Those familiar with Japanese groupings of the periods distinguished will observe that we have more or less followed—without using the accompanying terminology—distinctions between what might be termed three ages of classical Japanese literature. These include the older age (kodai, jōdai), the middle age (chūsei), and the recent age (kinsei). Our divisions may correspond somewhat to these distinctions, but in fact these usual Japanese divisions have not really been used. The reason is simply that Japanese scholars have greater difficulty in agreeing on the terminal times of these "ages" than on the "periods" we distinguish. One well-known scholar has held that the middle age begins in the Nara period, and many others would include later portions (but differing portions) of the Heian period as part of the middle age(s). There are also designations such as the middle-older (chūko) age. In addition the Heian period (sometimes with, sometimes without, the Nara period or post-Heian times) is sometimes referred to as the courtly age (ōchō). In one current literary history, the middle ages (chūsei) are taken to end in 1868. For these reasons, then, we do not use the terminology of ages, although they are well worth mentioning as part of Japanese conceptions of their literary past, and although we have honored them, if that is quite the word, by the groupings of our periods.

In short, our present set of periods includes one—the Yamato—that is more postulated than recoverable; and two that begin with the Nara period (685) and continue with the Heian (793). Between the Yamato and the Nara period, there is in fact some "historical time." But verifiable dates for literature are not easily come by, and for the sake of convenience we have absorbed that earliest part of Japanese literature into the Nara period, the account of which we may now begin.

1. *Yamato and Nara Literature (645–793)*

Although the regnal and era names of early Japan are very evocative to Japanese (see Part Two), very little is known of early rulers, of the origins of the peoples, and of the genesis of the language that made the literature we know. Much of the oldest extant writing survives as oral literature set down by literate scribes or scholars, although ample evidence exists to show that many oral pieces might be thrust into new contexts, as also that oral delivery continued long after the advent of literacy. In fact, literate writers often composed for oral delivery.

The earliest writing valued as Japanese literature is preserved in three main texts, or collections: the *Kojiki, the *Nihon Shoki, and the *Man'yōshū. The first two start off as histories of "the age of the gods" and apparently of certain cultural heroes, especially those of the Yamato people who were edging out such other rivals as those in Izumo on the side of the Japan Sea. The *Records of Ancient Matters* and *The Records of Japan* (Kojiki and Nihon Shoki) are largely prose accounts of the doings of characters with mouth-filling names, interspersed with poems that give the thoughts or words of the characters. The prose is quite straightforward, and there is (in the versions we have) a clear sense of episodic division. Since clarity and analysis are signs of genuine thought, these early records are far less naive than the events depicted may lead one to infer. Moreover, these stories have been interlarded with poems or songs that often seem, to a modern reader, out of sorts with the prose. One explanation holds that, however ill-sorted, the poems were part of the account from the beginning and conveyed the word-spirit or *kotodama*. Another explanation holds that the originals were children's songs, or such work songs as those of rice planting (taueuta), and so on. The affective responses implied by these songs do, however, show that the later affective-expressive poetics was implicit from the beginning of Japanese literature as we know it.

A crucial element in defining literature was, of course, the introduction of a writing system. That event represents the settling of a people into a degree of social and linguistic unity, prosperity, and cultural development that could benefit by relations with Korea and China. Chinese characters had been adopted before the capital was settled in Nara and Yamato generally. Scholars date the emergence of published literature from the reign of Suiko, or about A.D. 595. The borrowed Chinese characters were later used (when not for Chinese itself) in the fashion called *man'yōgana*, one of the most cumbrous systems ever devised. The Chinese characters were used sometimes semantographically for meaning, sometimes for adopted phonetic value, and usually in a mixture. To early Japanese, the benefit of this difficult system was the gift of writing. To modern philologists, the benefit has been the reconstituting of ancient Japanese, with more vowels than the present presumed five, and a wide range of differing pronunciation.

So complex a system could not last, especially since classical Japanese involved inflection of verbs and adjectives, whereas Chinese words have no inflection. In the course of time Chinese characters were used to represent Japanese counterparts of the Chinese semantic values, and some Chinese characters were simplified into two syllabaries, the *hiragana* and *katakana*, or cursive and angular. It also happened that two kinds of words were devised, those based on native Japanese and those, chiefly compounds (similar to English words with Greek roots such as "telephone"), made up of Japanese apprehension of Chinese pronunciation of characters. Such apprehension might come at different times, however, and with differing versions. As a consequence, a given character may have several versions in later Japanese: the Sinified pronunciations (ondoku, *on'yomi*), Japanese pronunciations (kundoku, *kun'yomi*), and in some cases an adapted syllabic pronunciation used for pure Japanese, whether in inflections or simply to avoid Chinese characters. For example, the simple character for "woman" (element 38 女) has, to simplify somewhat, the following versions:

Sinified for compounds, etc.: Jo, jō, nyō, nyo
Japanese: onna, omina, me, musume, (*nouns*)
          meawasu(-seru) (*verb*)
Syllabic: me *as* め (*cursive*)

Modern Japanese literature assumes all three categories. The Sinified versions shade off into sometimes degraded kinds of "Chinese" prose, *kambun*, whereas the purely Japanese was to be the essential, if not the sole version in most of the important literature of the early periods.

This simplification is enough to show that the Japanese writing system is one of the most complex in the world. Japanese children still spend longer learning their system of writing than do their counterparts elsewhere. But this typical compromise by accretion and tolerance has had enormous results. Apart from the possession of literacy, Japanese had access to the study of Chinese as well as to a system all their own. Such a mixed system, or compromise, may be contrasted with that which developed later in Korea. (It seems quite possible that it was Koreans rather than Chinese who devised the model of man'yōgana.) Koreans devised a far more independent and accurately phonetic system for their own pronunciations. This genius allowed them to write the vernacular far more easily than could Japanese. Yet it also permitted the vernacular to be set off from the prestigious Chinese language, leaving two extremes. Korean writers could compose solely in a vernacular or solely in their version of Chinese, whereas Japanese had a multiple, overlapping system as flexible, as capable of great nuance and distinction, as it is complex.

The early prose records represent a number of important motives. The political motive involved establishing the hegemony of one of the peoples making up the early Japanese who managed to impose grounds for its legitimacy. Another aim, very Japanese, very human, was to preserve the past, and particularly to connect the human present with a world of divinities still alive about the writers. The historical writings also testify to a desire to preserve what had happened in earlier reigns, to emulate Chinese writings of attractive kinds, and to legitimize the state—particularly in its royal house.

As has been said, these two Asian literatures—Chinese and Japanese—look very like when contrasted with Western, but side by side look quite different. Both consist of history and lyrics in their early stages, with lyrics the prime example of what is literature. But the early Japanese records are far more animistic and religious than the Chinese, which are for their part more dynastic and Confucian. The protection given by the writing system evolved by the Japanese enabled them to maintain their own culture. It enabled them to select and reject as they pleased. It is quite striking that the three monuments of early Japanese literature have so little of a Buddhist cast to them and so much less of a Confucian coloring.

It is also significant that one of the Chinese-inspired efforts of the Nara period should be the *Fudoki. Instead of being accounts of dynasties viewed cyclically, these are topographical accounts of the seventy-two provinces or kuni that made up ancient Japan (see Part Seven: Geography). Although only some survive (such as *Harima Fudoki*), and probably not many more were completed, the extant ones show the enduring Japanese love of place, of a land populated with divinities of hills and streams and trees as well as with people, and with the distinctions among them not always easily drawn. These accounts of provinces also show an integral sense of time, comparable to the sense of space, going back in unbroken fashion to "the age of the gods."

Although lyrics defined what was literature, there was also prose and, as has been remarked, prose by no means as messy as that of comparable stages in many other literatures. We can be sure that there were also numerous varieties of combination of song and dance (*kabu*, buga) associated with Shinto rites, seasonal festivals, and more or less secular entertainment. This is one way of saying that proto-dramatic elements existed from earliest times, and especially that the sense of performance has always been an important feature of Japanese conceptions of human activity. If feelings demand expression, occasions demand performance.

In other words, the distinctions or implications of Japanese terms often do not wholly coincide with Western counterparts. *Kayō* does include what in English might be termed "folk songs," but the term also designates the songs or poems in the *Kojiki* and *Nihon Shoki*, as well as certain other examples. This fact illustrates one feature of an important principle of literary development in early and later Japan. Japanese tend to assume that their various kinds of sophisticated literature developed from popular origins, with whatever attention to Chinese models along the way. The evidence for this is very rich, in particular for the kinds of drama that emerged in full flower during the Muromachi period and following. The counterpart to this enduring tendency is the subsequent definition of what a given genre or subgenre is in terms of the criteria of what has been developed into sophisticated art and the canons it presumes—as we have seen in the previous section. As a corollary of this second tendency, the Japanese have tended to prize to an unusual degree what was once defined as high art (*ga*). Some kinds of art adapted from continental models have been kept only in Japan, while the models have disappeared in China and Korea. But the same is substantially true of purely Japanese kinds. To consider only the dramatic modes, *nō* and *kyōgen*, it is as if Greece had kept an unbroken tradition of Attic tragedy and the Old Comedy to this day. This tendency is shown as early as the impulse that led to setting down the *Kojiki* and *Nihon Shoki* as well as to the ordering of the various *Fudoki*.

So much said, the glory of this earlier literature is unquestionably the *Man'yōshū*. This "Collection for Ten Thousand Generations" or "of Ten Thousand Leaves" seems likely to prove worthy of its title, so high is its esteem among Japanese. Its 4,516 poems are drawn from a variety of sources, including earlier collections now lost. The poems are of three chief kinds, along with irregular examples from earlier times. The two most important are the "long poem" or *chōka*, which alternates five- and seven-syllable lines to a last couplet of sevens; and the *tanka*, which is an abbreviated chōka in consisting of five lines of five, seven, five, seven, and seven syllables. The tanka are also commonly used to provide one or more *hanka* or envoys to chōka, but they are counted separately from the 265 or so chōka in the traditional numbering of the 4500-odd poems. *Sedōka* are also included. These "head-repeated poems" take their name from a repetition of the last three lines of a tanka, giving five, seven, seven; five, seven, seven. The sedōka never really caught on, and although poets have written chōka into modern times, the tanka was to be the most enduring kind over the centuries. Although the longest chōka in the collection (Book 2, poem 199;

hereafter cited in the style 2: 199) consists of but 149 lines, the *Man'yō* achievement is in no small measure typified by this longer poem. (Japanese and Chinese do not, however, make as much of lines or lineation as do, say, the Greeks, who are apt to define literary kind by prosody.)

Not all the poems in the collection claim attention as world literature by any means, much as many cultivated Japanese respond to their depths over some simple examples that, say, praise the places of the distinctive Yamato countryside. The *Man'yōshū* does, however, include works by a few great poets, the chief of whom is *Kakinomoto Hitomaro.

Hitomaro was a middling courtier in the full sense of both words, not having any great rank or power, and being a court poet to a certain group of the royal house. It is not surprising that the greatest Japanese poets and other writers should be people without genuine power, since that is true the world around. What is worthy of notice is that all people associated with the court, including those of highest rank, should have been expected to write verse, even as the divinities and rulers in the *Kojiki* had been shown expressing themselves in the same way. Hitomaro transcends such expectations and his own service to a given royal clique by a genius that, however inexplicable in the end, includes profound human sympathy directed by kindly ironies, an intelligence that articulates feeling, and a technical virtuosity unequaled for generations.

Some five dozen poems are believed to be certainly by him, and some are attributed to him, or at least are said to be taken from "The Hitomaro Collection" (*Hitomaro Kashū*). On the evidence of the examples chosen, this latter consists chiefly of tanka, and its poems hold considerably less interest than the poems directly assigned to him. Hitomaro is at his greatest with chōka and those tanka envoys that are an inseparable part of the total poetic conception. Those of his poems that hold least interest of a critical kind have great historic import, revealing his efforts to fashion from ritual materials and primitive or at least religious word-spells a genuine literary achievement.

Along with other poets following in his wake, Hitomaro separated out a spectrum of poems from an earlier corpus that is often inseparable from ritual context. His poems are of two principal kinds: those on public subjects and occasions, and those on private. That longest of Man'yō poems referred to earlier is by him: "On the Lying in State of Prince Takechi" (2: 199–201). On behalf of his father, Temmu, Takechi executed the Jinshin War (in 672), thereafter acting as prime minister and being designated as crown prince under his reigning mother, Jitō, for whom Hitomaro was court poet. The poem itself is unique in classical Japanese literature for depicting a battle at length, but it resembles other public poems by this master in that it treats historical events in terms of the motives and acts of the protagonists, and develops the sense of human achievement and loss that colors universal human history.

The private poems he wrote can be exemplified by those on parting from a wife in Iwami, far from Nara, presumably when being recalled for duty elsewhere; and on the death of a wife (marriage customs were so complex that at least two wives must be involved). The second poem on parting (2: 135–37) creates a sense of what it is like to have loved and now to be forced to lose the person who meant so much. The poem is unified by three strands of imagery: that of the sea (moisture often having erotic connotations in Japanese literature), mountains, and trees—all of which might have their divinities. By the second envoy, the poet has been taken by his too rapidly moving horse far from his wife. The second hanka concludes with tree imagery that manages to recall the wife by the seaside:

Akiyama ni	O you yellow leaves,
Otsuru momijiba	That fall upon the autumn slopes—
Shimashiku wa	If only for a moment,
Na chirimagai so	Do not whirl down in such confusion,
Imo ga atari min.	That I may see where my beloved dwells.

This personal grief seems far removed from the Jinshin War and the court of Temmu, Takechi, and Jitō (whose political ambitions were strong and fearless). But public poetry need not deal with martial and political occasions alone. It is essentially a kind that treats of what people share rather than of what distinguishes them as idiosyncratic personalities. In such terms, all Hitomaro's great poems are public, if some less radically so than others.

The crucial quality of the shared can be seen to splendid advantage in a poem less ostensibly either public or private than those mentioned. This has a lengthy specification of the situation that gave rise to it: "On Seeing the Body of a Man Lying among the Stones on the Island of Samine in Sanuki Province" (2: 220–22). The poem recounts the voyage by Hitomaro (and no doubt others, but they go unmentioned) toward Sanuki province in present Shikoku. A typhoon arises, and Hitomaro manages to land on Samine, only barely escaping with his life. There he sees the body of a man, which he addresses half as if the dead person were still alive. They share the uncertain human condition. But the poem begins by praising the divinity and unbroken temporal succession of the history of the landface from which he sets out. The natural forces among which humanity must die are also divine ones giving meaning to life. The chōka and the envoys conclude with attention to the man's wife and the rest of his family. Of course they miss him, not even knowing that he is dead. The wife would be gathering greens for him to eat if she were there, and if this late summer season were not too far advanced for such food. The season past is of course more that of a human lifetime—an irony like Hitomaro's own landing on "The isle so beautiful in name," and so tragic in result.

The second envoy tells of the last human rest in death, of the tragic human condition modified by the divinity of the land, and of the worth of human attachment.

Okitsunami	So you rest your head,
Kiyoru ariso o	Pillowed on the rocky spread-out bedding
Shikitae no	Of this rugged shore,
Makura to makite	While the furious, wind-driven surf
Naseru kimi ka mo.	Pounds ever in from off the sea.

The poem well shows that the more explicitly public poems have private implication, and that the more explicitly private poems are public in what they imply about our lives.

The public quality—in the wider sense—of Hitomaro's poetry is not simply a conviction. It is reflected in his technique as well. His attention to origin, divinity, and praise of the land (or royal line) provides a context in which all may share, because all are embedded in such things. Two technical means assist his ends. Hitomaro uses *makurakotoba* and *jo* to great effect. The former, "pillow-words," and the latter, "prefaces," share the quality of being attributives, of matter prefixed to what follows. It has been common to treat both as decorative features more or less devoid of meaning, parts of a word-hoard like Greek epithets: "wine dark" for "sea," for example. But from the evidence available, Hitomaro devised or refashioned half the makurakotoba he used, and such pillow-words have continued to be invented well into this century. (Later examples do have a hothouse aura, however.) Although they may be little more than decorative in some handlings, for Hitomaro and other responsible poets, the makurakotoba are semiritualistic or traditional and associative elements that enrich the poetic texture by enlarging the realm of experience, and in particular by associating human experience with natural detail, human connection, the rites of social or religious life, and word-magic. They function very differently over the long history of their use, but for Hitomaro, they assist in integrating a public, shared view of human experience.

Such integration is reflected in terms of Hitomaro's ordering, unifying, and articulating by two other techniques: parallelism and complex syntax. Early Japanese songs, presumably from oral originals, often use repetitions and simple parallelisms such as $a-a^1$ or $b-b^1-b^2$. Hitomaro goes farther, interweaving parallelism in such complexities as $a-b-c$, $a^1-b^1-c^1$, $a^2-b^2-c^2$, and other more complex variations. By these means he creates a tension between ordering and the flexible Japanese syntax as well as the fluent nature of the five-seven prosody. This is a primary element in his sustaining of the chōka. But his remarkable syntax also contributes to the complex dynamics of his style. Again and again, as in the Samine poem, he uses ambiguous clause-final verbs. They are ambiguous in being possibly conclusive or "finite" verbs, or else nonconclusive attributive forms modifying a subsequent noun. In such fashion, the chōka of the Samine poem flows as one incomplete syntactic entity to its last word and particle, "tsumara wa." This designates the dead man's wife (it also expresses endearment), with the topic particle that, when used, begins a sentence. The first envoy begins, "Tsuma," so at last going on to complete the unended sentence. For a similar command of extended syntactic complexity, we must await the *Genji Monogatari.*

By common reckoning, Hitomaro is one of the three or four greatest Japanese poets. But there were other Man'yō poets of genuine importance and distinct views of the world. It became traditional to compare *Yamabe Akahito as a poet with Hitomaro—after the tanka became the poetic norm. Akahito dwells on loveliness and purity, with a genius for the unspoiled beauty of the world and people in it. He does so, however, by seeing from afar, and at the cost of excluding by poetic fiat attention to human suffering. His sense of our lives seems not to have taken account of death. Shinto ritual purity of his kind does not consider the realm of defilement that flesh is heir to. The beauty and the limitation are equally marked.

*Yamanoe Okura is often considered today as the second Man'yō poet after Hitomaro. Some scholars today think him a second- or third-generation Korean, an ancestry shared by a considerable portion of notable people at the court. He had close experience of Chinese literature and culture, but for all his supposed background, Japanese remains his language. The background does appear in his Buddhist allusions—a cultural element Hitomaro seems to be unaware of as a poet—and in his treating such social problems as poverty and right conduct. In his "Dialogue" on poverty (5: 892–93), first the poor man speaks of his straitened life, and then the destitute man tells of his even worse lot. The poet ends with a generalizing hanka. Such generalizing, by turns moralistic and sentimental, or both, sometimes mars his poetry. He is at his best when he expresses deep feeling in a broken, crabbed syntax that at once conveys and disciplines his thought. One of the most moving of Man'yō poems is the hanka to his elegy on the death of his son, Furuhi (5: 905). The boy's soul must make its way to the nether realm:

Wakakereba	Since he is so young,
Michiyuki shiraji	He will not know the road to take.
Mai wa sen	I will pay your fee.
Shitae no tsukai	O courier from the realms below,
Oite tōrase.	Bear him there upon your back!

He is also author of Chinese prose pieces and some Chinese verse that appears in the collection. Both of these are equally unprettified, districtly like their author and no one else.

*Ōtomo Yakamochi (d. 785) is considered to be the last compiler of the *Man'yōshū*. In the later books of the collection there are many poems by the numerous Ōtomo family, including most notably himself. He resembles Hitomaro and Okura as a master of chōka, and Akahito as a master of tanka. His chōka are looser, more associative than the work of his best predecessors, and this puts off many readers who reach his poems after reading those of the earlier poets. Only in recent years have a few Japanese critics come to think him worth comparing with Hitomaro, and the grounds for thinking so are valid enough. He does not vie with Hitomaro, Akahito, or Okura in concentration of language, and it is not any single poem that one can cite so much as a large and highly varied canon of achievement. The range in chōka alone is broader than that of his predecessors. If he writes on the discovery of gold in a distant province, the result is something more narrowly or formally public than Hitomaro's poems. He also writes of the shadowed glory of his family (once famous warriors attached to the sovereign), of courtly activities, of deaths, of his life in duty away from the capital—and so on to such very private subjects as dreaming of the loss of a favorite falcon. Yakamochi does not, then, lend himself so easily to quotation or—worse for critics—to categorizing. He must be considered through many poems. And in the consciousness of the past position of his family, he looks back to an earlier glory and independence that the humbler Hitomaro could not have dreamed of. His own life is that of an aristocrat of declined fortunes, and as a result, he brings to the poetry of this early period a subjectivity that is new. Reflection and association, an almost *nō*-like habit of reminiscence marks his writing.

The subjectivity is marked in other ways in his tanka poetry. This is alive with activities having the beauty of Akahito's poems without the deliberate self-denial of what might spoil a ritual purity. If Six-Dynasties Chinese practice had given assistance to parallelism for Hitomaro, it lent Yakamochi techniques of question, confusion over like things, and discrimination of subjectively associated images from nature or from human experience. In such distinction between the human subject as dominant element in poetic experience and the world that provides the experience, Yakamochi not only provides a distinct vision to Man'yō poetry. More than that, he forecasts the direction that poetry was to take pretty much forever after him. If Hitomaro's achievement was a universal one, Yakamochi's was a civilized one. We owe to him the collection of poems by people quite unlike himself, much of what was present when he lived but that might otherwise have been lost. The past is represented in his canon by his numerous fluent chōka. And the future is forecast in his tanka and other poetry by virtue of his attention to what human creatures actively make of the world by their powers of mind. If Hitomaro is the Man'yō poet for all times and peoples, Yakamochi excels as the poet in whom the now established Japanese tradition combines as past, present, and future.

2. *Heian Literature (794–1186)*

The *man'yōgana* writing system of the first great collection and other early writing was one thing that Yakamochi did not modernize. Shortly after his death, that system became more and more difficult, and then impossible, to read until recovered by the pains of scholarly people. In fact, a hiatus occurs in our knowledge of poetic continuity, if not in poetic practice itself. It is often said that a new fashion for matters Chinese intervened, endangering Japanese poetry as a serious art. This is a considerable exaggeration, although it is true that many men were laboring, more or less successfully, over Chinese verse and prose, and that many women were appearing as major authors in the vernacular. Yet within ten years after Yakamochi's death, a new capital had been established, the Heian-kyō. In so short a time does a new spirit manifest itself. And a brief list of major literary events shows, with some formal overlapping in time, the quickly emergent genius of the second early age.

The Heian Age saw unprecedentedly rapid literary development, as it did of other social and cultural features. Although the dates are often only approximate, the fertility as well as the rapidity of literary creation can be tabulated schematically (for further details, see Part Two, C).

887 Poetry matches, *utaawase*, instituted

900 *Taketori Monogatari*, the "parent of all *monogatari*" (the version extant dates from ca. 950)

905 *Kokinshū*, first of the twenty-one *waka* collections royally commissioned

905 Either before or after the *Kokinshū*, the *Ise Monogatari*, greatest of *utamonogatari*

935 *Ki no Tsurayuki's *Tosa Diary*, first poetic memoir, first fictional diary in Japanese, first work of prose narrative extant in original version; a man now writing a memoir in Japanese

974 *Fujiwara Michitsuna no Haha's *Kagerō Nikki*, a poetic memoir bringing the customary, realistic world into literature

990 *Sei Shōnagon's *Makura no Sōshi* (dates not certain), the prime examplar of *zuihitsu* (see Part Six)

1004 *Izumi Shikibu Nikki*, poetic diary or memoir combining romance and realism, scandal and delicacy

1010 *Genji Monogatari*, *tsukurimonogatari*, greatest work of Japanese literature

1085 *Imayō* at their height

Accounts in Japanese or Western languages seldom do justice to the remarkable creativity of this age. Many literary kinds (such as monogatari) and literary institutions (such as utaawase) are generated, canons established, achievements made in literature, as they are also in religious, political, social, and other areas. Not only did the capital grow to perhaps the then most populous city in the world, but decade after decade went by without war.

Certain terms keep recurring in the literature of the period and in that of critics describing it. A few may be mentioned here. There was something of a tug between the old-fashioned (furumekashi) and new-fangled (imamekashi). Most people seemed to wish to be thought up-to-date, as Japanese still do, but those who really had assurance could go one step farther and espouse the old. The standard of *ate* described high quality with overtones of high social status. We are reminded that only nobles of the first five ranks could enter the "cloudland" (kumoi) of the palace. Those who could claim to be the "yoki hito" (good people, those of consequence) were, then, necessarily people of good station, of the right blood, rather than necessarily morally good. The search for the "uruwashi" or beautiful is one that marks the age, and perhaps no word is used so often as "okashi." This may also mean beautiful. It also may mean excelling, elegant (*fūryū*), along with other such positive things. It may also designate the odd, the ridiculous, the laughable—a meaning that one did not wish applied to oneself. To be talked of was bad enough. To be laughed at was to be avoided at all costs. The most famous word to describe the shadows of this world is *aware* or *mono no aware*. This meant (like so many adjectives of the time) that which was heightened in emotion. ("Aware!" conveys a wide range of possible response.) It came to be associated particularly with the long-standing Japanese sense of the evanescent, "hakanashi," which Buddhism did much to accentuate.

The evanescent was related to what was beautiful and valued, whether in nature observed or in human glory. Japanese have always had a strong sense of time and its burdens. This grew with the increasing subjectivity of literature and with the influence of Buddhism on poets and other writers. Shinto taught one to delight in a pure world. Buddhism taught (with the Buddha nature, busshō, of all living things) the insubstantiality of that world. And the most subjective of poets show how well they know that it is the human subject who introduces the problems. The most famous *tanka* conveys something of the paradox. In it (*Kokinshū*, 15: 747) *Ariwara Narihira tells how he visits the house abandoned by his mistress of a year ago. It is spring. The favorite Heian flower, the plum, glows fragrantly in the night under the moonlight.

Tsuki ya aranu	This is not that moon,
Haru ya mukashi no	And it cannot be this is the spring
Haru naranu	Such as the spring I knew;
Waga mi hitotsu wa	I am myself the single thing
Moto no mi ni shite.	Remaining as it ever was.

The point is, of course, that the poet knows how contrary his subjectivity is to the reality of things. The headnote says it is spring and the moon shines beautifully. He feels it cannot be the same, since he lost her. But he *knows* that the natural world is steadfast and that his life has changed.

The poem testifies to the nature of the terms. Mono no aware does not relate simply to a human emotion; it is, rather, the human emotion derived from and yet also presently felt in something understood. Such terms do not merely tell of the affective potential found in the world. They also testify to the need for a person of true feeling (kokoro aru) to express the nature of that experience to someone else equally sensitive. *Ki no Tomonori makes this clear (*Kokinshū*, 1: 38).

Kimi narade	I am at a loss
Tare ni ka misen	To say to whom if not to you
Ume no hana	I might show plum blossoms;
Iro o mo ka o mo	For such beauty and such fragrance
Shiru hito zo shiru.	Only the best judge is a judge at all.

Tomonori has no doubt gone out of his way to find particularly lovely plum blossoms. It is not enough to have them. He must write about them, and what he writes must be sent to the best person, along with some of the flowers and a bit of snow on the bough with them.

In this age, the subject of love emerged as a central concern, and what is particularly to be remarked is the participation of women in creating the ethos of love. At first men set the criteria for poetry. At first they wrote the monogatari that the women read. But even before women took over the genius of Heian literature, there had been female poets such as *Ono no Komachi among the *rokkasen* and *Lady Ise as another passionate female poet. The subject of love answered perfectly to the subjective cast of the literature of the age, and with the *Kokinshū* the tradition was set for royally commissioned anthologies (*chokusenshū;* see Part Six A) to consist of twenty books, the second half of which began with love poetry as the first began with seasonal poems. More than that, love becomes more and more a matter of longing, particularly unfilled yearning— perhaps as the lady waits in vain at dusk for her lover to come. Early in this period, however, the love poems are based much more on actual experience, and the whole range of it is detailed in the *Ise Monogatari*, which consists largely of poems associated with or by Narihira, particularly exchanges of love poems. Short prose contexts fit the poems into little episodes. In episode 141, there is an exchange between the Ise Shrine Priestess and Narihira (also *Kokinshū*, 13: 645). She writes first, by way of exception (the man was supposed to send a next-morning poem).

Kimi ya koshi	My mind is dazzled—
Ware ya yukiken	Did you come to visit me?
Omōezu	Did I go to you?
Yume ka utsutsu ka	Was our night a dream? Reality?
Nete ka samete ka.	Was I sleeping? Or was I awake?

Here we see a great pair of terms emerging in early Heian literature: dream (yume) and reality (utsutsu). The play between them is endless. One may only dream of the reality of love. Yet "dream" may be used to represent love. Dream, in fact, may signify reality, or an illusion that is more convincing than reality. Here is Narihira's reply:

Kakikurasu	Through the blackest shadow
Kokoro no yami ni	Of the darkness of the heart I wander
Madoiniki	In bewilderment—
Yume utsutsu to wa	You who know the world of love, decide:
Yohito sadame yo.	Is my love reality or dream?

This is, of course, much superior to the other poem, but both are typical in concern with the reality of dream and the reverse.

As time went on, some noble houses naturally declined. As more time passed, the nobles began to discover that their society was being encroached upon by the military houses. Even before that had begun, however, it became accepted that the reign of Daigo (897–930) or of Murakami (946–967) represented the golden years. Things usually seem to have been better in the past, but perhaps it was the age of Murakami in which *Murasaki Shikibu situated her radiant hero, Genji. Here was a concept of Japan that did not need to refer to China all the time, since there was now a distinct Japanese cultural ethos that would last. Given the splendors of the court ruled by the Fujiwara regents, the T'ang (or Sung) could be left to shift for itself. This was a court that could define its canons of courtly aesthetics in terms of fūryū and, if that term seemed too Chinese, one could use *miyabi*. Success and grandeur do not themselves make for great literature, however. When greatness occurred, it came from the usual tensions (such as a family once great turning to writing: the best poets of this period are not named Fujiwara); and from some new tensions, as well. These involved a controlling subjectivity whose control was itself understood to be inadequate; Buddhist beliefs held against Shinto; and the abiding sense of human agency in time. These tensions produce the sense of evanescence that is so Japanese, but it also relates to karma (*sukuse*, shukuen). Even the radiant Genji discovers that. And what will not stay proves after all most appealing. This is shown by the old poem:

Sakeba chiru	When they bloom they fall,
Sakaneba koishi	When they do not bloom we yearn
Yamazakura	For mountain cherry flowers ...

This still holds: Japanese cherry blossoms do not stay as long on the bough as they do on the same trees transplanted to North America.

As earlier, at the capital in Nara (and nearby areas), so at Heiankyō—much had been adapted from China: to this day the very layout of the city reflects such a debt. There were little things, such as chrysanthemums (kiku) that began to matter, although Hitomaro had not known them. There were ostensibly large things, such as an examination system and a national or court school (daigaku). But these and other Confucian institutions never really became central in Japan. As we shall see, composition in Chinese did continue to matter, and so did the continental religion. In fact, the Way of the Buddha (butsudō) mattered more in Japan than in China, even as Confucianism had little real impact and as Taoism was more a source for stories than anything else (see Part Six O). Yet it can hardly be said strongly enough that Shinto, the way of the native divinities, continued to supply shamanism (the sovereign being the chief male shaman among so many females), defilements and purifications, rites and superstitions. Such was particularly true away from the court. But the courtiers made them part of their art, as is testified by the initial seasonal books of the ordered collections and by the "Japanese painting" (*yamatoe*) which was the counterpart of Japanese poetry (*yamatouta*). The courtiers also enjoyed leaving the capital for the countryside— to the ancient capital, to Yoshino for cherry blossoms, to the northwest for autumn colors, and to the northeast where so many temples stood in the mountains. Such scenes held divinities of mountain and stream in a world alive with spirit. Buddhism was also not a religion merely of pessimism. It taught Heian courtiers to value living things, to prize efficacious spells, to understand time in terms of aeons as well as seasons, to prize the Buddha's vow to bring enlightenment to all sentient creatures, and to provide expedients (hōben) to those for whom knowledge of the Law is too difficult.

The specific results of these various elements was a vastly expanded literary achievement. The prose of the earliest period is of great value. But the new prose literature tells of what seems immediately human. Now there appeared various writings dealing with what we think of as history. The earlier chronicles are followed by new ones dealing with palpably human times. These include *Shoku Nihongi*, a specified "continuation" of the earlier work. Others are *Nihon Kōki*, dealing with events to 934, and *Shoku Nihon Kōki*, a continuation. Then there were those histories that purport to be "authentic accounts," so testifying at least to a new desire for veracity in history: (*Nihon*) *Montoku Jitsuroku* and *Sandai Jitsuroku*, all written in Chinese (see Part Six B). Lesser matters called for ink, such as the *Kogoshūi*, which attempts a historical justification of the prerogatives of the Imbe family against the Nakatomi and their Fujiwara supporters.

Men continued to write in Chinese, the Latin of Japan—except, of course, that China remained alive, unlike Rome sacked by Visigoths. The *Nihon Ryōiki* deals with numerous matters in its more or less anecdotal fashion, but its discussion of the Buddhist concept of reward according to deeds merges the fictional with the historical so well as to make it difficult to say which is more authoritative—the miracle or what it illustrates. There were also collections of poetry in Chinese (*kanshi*). The best known include the *Bunka Shūreishū* and *Ryōunshū*, both ordered by Saga (r. 809–823), as also the *Keikokushū*, ordered by Junna (r. 823–833). The latter discusses various topics that picture a model reign. There was also a major work on Chinese poetics, the difficult *Bunkyō Hifuron* by the learned, extraordinary *Kūkai, whose brush set down a number of other important works, in perhaps the finest Chinese verse and prose by any Japanese.

Having proved, as it were, their Latinity, men could turn to Japanese letters. In the *Kokinshū*, Ki no Tsurayuki and his fellow compilers chose poems from writers as ancient as Hitomaro to those as recent as themselves. If the *Man'yōshū* was the model for its twenty books (a pattern followed with but few exceptions in later royal collections), the *Kokinshū* was a far more carefully ordered collection. Not only were the two halves led off with six books of seasonal poems and five on love; within these and the other books, the compilers attempted to arrange the poems not by individual author canons but by easy progression. The seasonal poems, for example, go from the beginning of spring to the end of winter, and the love poems go from the man's first interest in a woman just heard of to the end of an affair (albeit with numerous recurrences). Such integration of short poems was to have enormous implication. Along with such other enterprises as the poetry matches (utaawase) and poems connected with pictures on the panels of screens (byōbu no uta), the ordered collections led the way in integrating lyric runs and collections into plotless narrative sequence.

The next two collections ordered by sovereigns of the twenty-one reigns (*nijūichidaishū*) were the *Gosenshū* and *Shūishū*. These later had great prestige (making up, with the *Kokinshū*, the collections of three reigns, *sandaishū*). Their diction supposedly set the standard for waka and renga for some centuries, as also for such other formal poetry as that composed for poetry matches and set sequences (such as *hyakushuuta*). But in fact these two collections show a decline in poetic quality. As might perhaps be expected, the age of ordinary poetry was also an age of scholarship and criticism. In his *Shinsen Zuinō*, *Fujiwara Kintō dealt with the "marrow" of poetics as a conservative critic understood it. In his *Waka Kuhon*, he distinguished nine styles on the basis of the configuration of language (kotoba no sugata) and after-feeling (*yojō*). Kintō had the honor of being ordered sole compiler of the second chokusenshū, the *Shūishū*, already mentioned. In addition, he made a considerable anthology of his own, a counterpart of the one ordered by Kazan (r. 984–986). This was the *Kingyokushū*, which includes Hitomaro, Tsurayuki, together with later poets. He apparently made a collection of his own poems, but any such contribution stood in the shadow of the other collections and of his highly influential collection of Chinese verse and poetry along with Japanese, the *Wakan Rōeishū*, in which his learning is deployed to show that *kagura*, *saibara*, and *kayō* might not only be recited (by *rōei*) but are also to be considered, with waka, part of the main line of Japanese poetry.

The boundaries between poetry and narrative had been breached by the ordered collections, as we have seen. But the genius of narrative, as that is understood in Western literature, was to find expression in prose, commonly with poems. Although the *Ise Monogatari* has been mentioned, something further must be said. The two traditions as to its date put it before or after the *Kokinshū*, which was completed about 920. It seems likely that it is earlier. This greatest of *utamonogatari*—waka stories or tales of poems—commonly uses formulaic beginnings for episodes assumed for generations to deal with Narihira. But in fact such openings typically say only, "Long ago there was a man," not naming Narihira, The combination of prose setting and poetic exchange has no adequate Western counterpart, and although such a combination may seem strange, it has profound significance. Clearly, poetry and prose were not thought to be alien media, and the remarkably earlier emergence of great prose narrative in Japan would not have been possible without such an assumption. It deals, as not a few successors do, with the "world" (yo no naka), that is, with love. If *Ihara Saikaku's versions of those who spend their lives on love have any single ancestor, it must be this collection of well over a hundred brief episodes. With the *Kokinshū*, the *Genji Monogatari*, and the later military romance, the *Heike Monogatari*, this collection of episodes about a man (properly, men) long ago was one of the works studied and restudied, echoed and reechoed as a principal courtly classic (if its hero manages to visit a woman through a broken place in the garden wall, so do countless later lovers). In terms of the sheer quality of its prose narrative, the *Ise Monogatari* is much the least of the three monogatari named, but its principles of the integral nature of successive poems and of poems with prose makes it deserving of such honor.

The monogatari that was characteristic of later developments was more wholly narrative, however, and goes under the other major rubric of *tsukurimonogatari*, although most important exemplars also included poems; since poetry was the basis of social exchange and was expected of every civilized person, that was no accident. The earliest example of this kind is not the most representative. The *Taketori Monogatari* did lead the way, however, by being composed about 900. From such recollections of it as by Tamakazura in the "Hotaru" (Fireflies) chapter of the *Genji Monogatari*, we know that the present version differs from the original. What we have begins with the old bamboo cutter of the title discovering in a joint of bamboo a beautiful three-inch princess. She grows, is wooed, and endures the vicissitudes that a proper heroine usually does in a romance. She disappears at last, ascending to her heavenly home. In a quasi metamorphosis at this ending, the burning of her letters and other relics accounts for the smoke that then rose from Fuji. There can be no doubt but that, as its admirers claim, the work includes a variety of matters. Do we not discover the wretched and the beautiful, the real and the ideal, the earthly and heavenly, the prosaic and poetic? And can we not ask with Tamakazura whether such an account of a heroine's checkered life does not mirror what our own human estate offers? To these questions less enthusiastic readers might ask whether their lives have such remarkable ups with the familiar downs? and whether all those dualities may not be found in most extended narratives, as also whether, in fact, this version of them works to deep human purpose? Those of us who incline toward the latter set of questions will wonder if the work would seem so important if it had appeared two centuries later, even while conceding it both a crucial historical place and admiring its air of a world of innocence and beauty recovered from the mundane. Yes, it is, we may conclude, "the parent and first to appear of monogatari."

Taketori does show a new ability to fashion longer narratives, which means a new art commanding prose style and temporalities. Thereafter the long monogatari (*chōhen* monogatari) is realized as a major literary kind. In the later tenth century, two such longer monogatari appeared (perhaps during the reign of Kazan, 984–986). The *Utsuho Monogatari* begins with things and lore brought back from Persia, and its style does not bear comparison with the best works of Heian literature. But the story does come to grips with real issues of court life, and the unknown author of its twenty parts did know how to integrate a lengthy story. The *Ochikubo Monogatari*, also anonymous, consists of four lengthy parts, and in dealing with the trials of a heroine beset by a malignant stepmother, it is at once given to the stuff of folklore and of real life as it was known to centuries of brides in Japan, well into modern times—even if this one is exaggerated. Happy endings characterize the mukashi monogatari, a fact bespeaking either universal human wish or female readership as imagined by presumably male authors.

The shift from male to female authorship of prose narrative begins in a sense with Tsurayuki's *Tosa Nikki*. Although this was written by the eminent male poet and critic, its famous first sentence says in effect that men have written memoirs and it is now time for a woman to try her hand. This memoir (ca. 935) predates the monogatari just mentioned. It is written as if by a woman who is a principal person in the party of a governor of Tosa returning to the capital (as Tsurayuki had just done in 934–935). As in so many of the memoirs, there is a very high proportion of fact along with poems (about fifty) that include some fiction. There are such realistic details as beginning journeys at night, bartering of food, and fear of pirates. The woman's grief-stricken longing for her lost daughter represents the deepest human experience of the story.

In the late tenth and early eleventh century, women were the major writers. One of the most distinctive—and, as it were, necessary—of them is Fujiwara Michitsuna no Haha, author of the *Kagerō Nikki*, a memoir covering 954 to 974.

She makes it clear that she had read monogatari, and her diary seems almost intended by contrast to bring the realm of imagination into touch with reality. She is concerned with her son, with her errant husband, Kaneie, and above all with the nature of her own existence. In delineating such matters, her memoir is exceptional among the literary diaries for its naming of real years, real places. When she feels bitter about her husband's infidelity, she speaks bitterly. But rather than stay home and sulk, she gets out on visits to religious places far more often than monogatari ever suggest that Heian ladies committed themselves to the out-of-doors. Revision is implied by the excellence of her style and the varying length of treatment, not by time elapsed but by matters that interest her. Revision must also contribute to the sense of veracity the work gives. Not many of us feel altogether comfortable in the presence of a person so self-centered and complaining, but no one has doubted the sense of the reality of her presence. More yet than that, she does not give us *men's* imaginings of what would interest an adolescent girl but adult reality in historical time and real place. It is impossible to conjure a process by which the *Genji Monogatari* could emerge after the *Taketori Monogatari* or even the *Ise Monogatari* without the kinds of understanding exemplified by the *Kagerō Nikki*.

Rather than contributing to the development of something else, *Izumi Shikibu entered this world in the last quarter of the 10th century and became the greatest poet of her time, the way having been prepared by a tradition ready for her talents. Her poems give some vitality to the *Shūishū* and some interest even to the *Goshūishū*. She is the presumed author of the *Izumi Shikibu Nikki*, a memoir suitably thick with poems, dealing with a major portion of the second of her most famous love affairs. At one point she (or the lady of the diary) speaks of her very eyes growing amorous, and not all her sisters at the court of *Jōtō (or Shōtō) Mon'in were amused. Murasaki Shikibu's comment in her *Murasaki Shikibu Nikki* was certainly meant to be harsh, perhaps suggests some jealousy, and may not be far wide of the mark: "licentious" (keshikaranu). Yet few censure Narihira for the same behavior, as if we readily accept the double standard of Heian times.

Izumi Shikibu requires no minced words. She served the same mistress as did Murasaki Shikibu, and there was no better judge of talent. What fascinated men was Izumi Shikibu's sensitivity, wit, and poetry. There is also her personality, in all its uncertainties, a matter of interest to her and to us. She looked out on the world and on people as something *requiring* her response, and practice made her eloquent, whether in reclaiming a drifting lover, mourning her daughter, or sending a priest a poem.

> Kuraki yori　　　　　　Out of this darkness
> Kuraki michi ni zo　　On what a much darker path
> 　Irinu beki　　　　　　　Must I set forth;
> Haruka ni terase　　　Make all clear with your shining,
> Yama no ha no tsuki.　O moon upon the mountain rim.

To an echo of the *Lotus Sūtra* she adds the common figural sense of spiritual illumination in invoking the moon.

In poems such as this there is a discipline of words and thoughts for which the only natural word is intelligence. We have failed to appreciate her poetry as we ought, not just because of textual problems but because of its difficulty. Yet hers is a natural difficulty, without contrivance, part of the meaning. So easy to dismiss or appreciate for shallow reasons, Izumi Shikibu makes with Murasaki Shikibu and the writer we next consider a trio of contemporary great writers such as appears only once again in Japanese literature. That would come in the seventeenth century, with *Matsuo Bashō, *Ihara Saikaku, and *Chikamatsu Monzaemon. We are fortunate not to have to choose between the two triads.

The third member of the Heian trio is *Sei Shōnagon, whose dates are uncertain. She wrote some poems, but she is known as the author of the *Makura no Sōshi*, a prose miscellany in two or five sections, depending on manuscript tradition, and one of the wittiest as well as least classifiable of creations. It fits into—or rather seems to define—that capacious Japanese category of *zuihitsu*, miscellanies, "following the brush," something akin to the essay in its root sense, or to pensées in being a collection of observations on what she saw with her exceptionally clear eyes. If there is little that is transcendent in her masterpiece, it nonetheless tells us a great deal concisely about people and ideas. Those are of her time, but she has a genius for making her people and things at once wholly individual, and yet enduring, valid everywhere human nature is studied. She is a born wit and maker of categories. Her opening section—on dawn being the best time of day for spring, dusk for autumn, and so on—effortlessly distills and defines enduring Japanese tastes.

The greatest writer of the Heian period, and indeed of Japanese literature, is of course another woman, *Murasaki Shikibu. Although her memoir does not really demonstrate her greatness, it does reveal a woman of strong moral judgment and capacity for friendship, as well as the author of at least part of what she terms *Genji no Monogatari*, portions of which, at least, were read aloud at the palace of *Jōtō Mon'in, by Ichijō Tennō, *Fujiwara Michinaga, and *Fujiwara Kintō. She also left behind a personal collection of poems. She does not match Izumi Shikibu as a poet, but the almost eight hundred poems she wrote for her great work are beautifully integrated into its fifty-four parts (to which the poems usually give the titles and often the names of characters).

The *Genji Monogatari* is too complex to be described adequately here (it is like dealing with Dante or James Joyce in a few pages; see the discussion in Part Three). It is now customary to view its fifty-odd parts as making up three sections differing in tone. The first third deals with the rise of her radiant hero, "Hikaru Genji," to a position of effective rule over the land. In this, the author is sometimes said to have taken as her model her contemporary, whom she knew first-hand, Fujiwara Michinaga (966–1027). But the setting a half century or more earlier idealizes Genji as de facto ruler. At all events, matters of government are left implicit, and most readers will be struck by Genji's amours, for which the model may well have been Narihira, although some Japanese scholars have also suggested biographical accounts of *Shōtoku Taishi (574–622) as yet another model. If that more or less legendary prince provides the model, it is one involving the Buddhist countervailing themes developed in the second part of the story. There Genji discovers the transience (*mujō*) of earthly matters as, in all his glory, he finds himself losing the people and command of his world that had mattered most to him. The last portion deals with his successors, his putative son Kaoru and his grandson Prince Niou. Kaoru is genuine and has Genji's sensitivity, but he is thwarted by diffidence, whereas Niou has Genji's authority but is basically dissolute. Apprehension, which is to say misapprehension, governs this last third, which quite properly for Heian literature ends in dream (the last part is "Yume no Ukihashi," "The Floating Bridge of Dreams").

Some doubts have been raised about the authorship or order of various chapters, but the presumed author takes the first part of her name from the heroine of the first two-thirds of the story, Murasaki. Another of the sources for this long work is Po Chü-i's famous narrative poem, *The Song of Endless Grief* (*Ch'ang Hen Ko*), which treats of the tragic love of the Chinese ruler Hsüan Tsung (685–762) for his lower-born concubine Yang Kuei-fei. A brief consideration will show how this poem matters and how it has been transcended. Given the state marriages for great personages such as Genji, it was natural that affairs based on a full committment of passion should usually involve a high-born man with a lesser ranked woman. Genji's mother was such a concubine of a sovereign, and in addition to Murasaki, Genji has other such women, notably Yūgao and the Akashi Lady (both of them born of good rank but fallen on harder times). In the last third of the story, Ukifune—loved both by Kaoru and Niou—provides a reprise. Only one of these women named—Genji's mother—is the concubine of a sovereign, and as to the general situation, that is set forth in a long disquisition on women a man may love in the second chapter ("Hahakigi," "The Dwindle Bush"). The Chinese poem stands as a model, but the higher social role of women in Japan and the power of the author to individualize would have made it possible for the story to be as it is, without the Chinese model, given an author of such genius. Genji is unique among the world's great heroes in knowing how to make an art of life—and subsequently discovering how such an art exquisitely defines his sufferings. In the final third, the equivalent woman, Ukifune, dominates with her own story within the main story of Kaoru, and she achieves a quite special degree of religious peace.

In no other work of Japanese literature do so many characters (far more numerous than those named) come quite so much to life. The whole is resonant with parallels and echoes, rich beyond description with invention and original conception. The style of the prose has extraordinary suppleness and complexity, and what it lacks in the size of its vocabulary it more than makes up for in its syntax and allusiveness. Whereas previous monogatari have happy endings, this does so solely for its first third. The second and third parts demonstrate the author's originality in showing suffering to be the lot of the most sensitive and powerful of human creatures (at the end of the second), and dreadful misunderstanding of what is important to be the fate of lesser characters (at the end of the third).

Peopled with numerous characters, all at once distinct, credible, and interesting, the work sparkles with wit and comedy, but also has nearly constant shadings of sorrow. The author has created a narrator who intervenes when she pleases; and the author slips with ease from relation to action to dialogue or characters' thoughts, switching from one to the next without pause or strain. Long before the traditional novel in the West had yielded to such subjective techniques as "stream of consciousness," the author had learned to command that and a host of other techniques of relation. Among them is a genius for sequentiality in narrative that controls without sacrificing plot, along with a truly extraordinary degree of association, anticipation, and recapitulation by parallels, motifs, and renovation. Perhaps her greatest achievement in respect to world literature is a heroic scale that creates an art of life without lapsing into mere aestheticism. Her greatest achievement within Japanese literature derives from her superlative moral intelligence which, without any didacticism whatever, exerts constant judgment in ways so fine, so assured, that the reader can know them without being able, as critic, to specify the necessary distinctions. For such reasons and many more, a comparatively obscure woman born over a millennium ago wrote not only the greatest work of Japanese literature, but also a prose narrative of a degree of greatness that the world would not see elsewhere for centuries, if indeed it has ever seen it.

Almost a century later men once more began to show their powers as writers. In the wake of Kintō, there appeared other scholars such as *Fujiwara Mototoshi and *Fujiwara Kiyosuke. Each rumbled on in his learned way, producing works that scholars today must pay due respect to. But after them it is a relief to come upon that genuine eccentric, *Minamoto Shunrai (or Toshiyori). He was a gifted poet and compiler of the *Kin'yōshū, the fifth of the twenty-one dynastic collections. (There were not, however, collections for each reign.) When the cloistered Shirakawa (r. 1072–1086, d. 1129) ordered the collection, he had no idea that Shunrai would throw out precedent, produce what is in effect Japan's first collection of contemporary poetry, and give it the somewhat immodest name, Kin'yōshū, Collection of Golden Leaves. Shunrai was told to try again. He did. He was told to try yet again, and this time either he was successful or Shirakawa gave up. This collection is the first of two to be in ten books, and with its 716 poems it is only longer than the next, *Shikashū (ca. 1151–1154, also in ten books, only 411 poems). Although he could turn out as conventional a poem as the next person, Shunrai is properly known as an innovating poet. In his strange ways he was thinking constructively. He genuinely wished to extend the bounds of poetry. He was the first to include tanrenga in one of these ordered collections, and his private collection, Samboku Kikashū, has many excellent pieces. If he is not as great a poet as Izumi Shikibu, he was able in his innovating way to presage the next great period of poetry by using his own eyes to look at the world, respecting what he saw.

Toward the close of the Heian period a number of distinguished works appeared in prose narrative, and along with them some that were not so special but that testify to the flourishing character of narrative. Problems of authorship, kind, and purpose trouble a number of these, but it is quite clear that authors were increasingly aware that they had traditions to guide them.

One of the most important is that storehouse of tales, the *Konjaku Mono-

gatari, Tales of Times Now Past. Stories there are, about 1,200 in thirty-one parts, from which we have lost three parts and stories in some of the others. The collection is the prime exemplar of *setsuwa bungaku,* coming in the wake of the *Nihon Ryōiki* and *Ōe Masafusa's Gōdanshō.* And it led the way for such later collections as *Kohon Setsuwashū, *Kojidan,* and its most worthy successor, *Kokon Chomonjū.* It was apparently put together around the beginning of the twelfth century, but whether there was one compiler or (what seems much more likely) several has yet to be shown. Because so many are stories that were to be used in Buddhist preaching, the compilers are assumed to have been priests. And that seems the more likely because many of the stories have analogues in China, India, and the Near East—parts of the world that Buddhist transmission explains better than anything else. The quality of the stories varies enormously, and some of the fairly numerous secular ones are the most interesting. In range of kind, tone, and subject, these stories fit no one category, but they have had enormous influence on later setsuwa bungaku, including its best successor in later times, the *Uji Shūi Monogatari,* compiled in the early Kamakura period. But secular authors well into the modern period have drawn freely on this repository of prose narrative.

Of these authors of prose narrative at the end of the Heian period, to some of us the greatest is a woman styled as *Sugawara Takasue no Musume (1008– ?). Those who followed her apparently shared this opinion, since they attributed to her works that seem doubtfully hers, a sure sign that a writer is esteemed. The two works that are more or less definitely hers include a diary, the *Sarashina Nikki, which is generally considered to belong to the class of the four best Heian diaries, with the *Tosa Nikki, *Kagerō Nikki,* and *Izumi Shikibu Nikki.* How far it is fictional and how far factual is a question not easily decided. But its single sustained part seems to have been completed about 1060, and it deals with the central figure's life from her thirteenth year forward. It depicts court society on the wane, which lends some credence to the factuality of the account, even if the court was to dominate culture for a long time to come. Its straightforward, attractive style is altogether decorous for the account, and bespeaks an author in command of what she chooses to relate from her special viewpoint as a member of the lower nobility, that of provincial governors (zuryō).

Her masterpiece is, however, the altogether different *Hamamatsu Chūnagon Monogatari,* in five lengthy parts. (As with so many works of the time, there are questions of authorship, but we follow traditional views.) This is thought to have been written about 1053–1058, a mature product of the author's life. Reincarnation and dream figure heavily in this story, creating a magic that is about as far from the author's own life as can be easily imagined: she was from the lower nobility and lacked first-hand experience of the court. The simplest way of describing her story is to say that the hero discovers in a dream that his dead father is now reborn as the third prince of the ruler of the T'ang, that he sets out to see him, and that numerous adventures, including the amatory, are involved, both in China and back in Japan. It is very rare that an author should produce two such different works. This rather obscure author seems to some of us one of the greatest known authors of prose narrative between Murasaki Shikibu and the so-to-speak collective author of the *Heike Monogatari*. In the future she is certain to receive increasing attention.

Common opinion holds the *Sagoromo Monogatari*, whose author is unknown, to be superior to the work just discussed. They share the modern designation of novelistic narratives (shōsetsu monogatari). Often considered second only to the *Genji Monogatari*, the *Sagoromo Monogatari* consists of four long parts perhaps written between 1070 and 1080. The story deals, of course, with Sagoromo, surnamed "the second Genji," and to readers immediately following it was indeed the work second only to that earlier masterpiece. Certainly this story of Sagoromo's amours and rise at court passed on the *Genji* tradition to numerous later stories. The hero greatly resembles his progenitor in success, in a sense surpassing him by ascending—rather implausibly—to the throne. The work is especially appealing in the counterparts of Sagoromo's loves it provides. Their variety and their vicissitudes suggest female authorship (something agreed on by critics, even if the two main contenders for authorship pose problems of proof). With these women—and especially in the wonderful, ill-fated Genji no Miya—female readers must have found it possible to identify themselves, because it is still possible for men as well as women to do so. Heavily laden with Buddhist language, the style also exerts a claim of seriousness on us.

No longer seriously considered to be by Sugawara Takasue no Musume, *Yoru no Nezame* also holds special interest, Because only five of a much larger number of parts survive, it is not easy to describe the story we have as a full, integral one. The heroine, Nezame, and the hero are both highly born, and they share a sorely tried love. The author drew with free hand from Izumi Shikibu's poems and, in conception, *Yoru no Nezame* is almost an amalgam of parts of the *Genji Monogatari*, *Sagoromo Monogatari*, and *Hamamatsu Chūnagon Monogatari*. The extant portions are extraordinarily, deliberately slow-paced. Strange things happen, and the characters have numerous dilemmas. But all is subordinated to a subjectivity yet more dominant over action than are the Uji parts of the *Genji Monogatari*.

The last example given here of lengthier Heian monogatari will be the *Torikaebaya Monogatari*. This anonymous story is the "modern" as opposed to a no longer existing "old" version of the story, and it is a story that may appear to be working out a device. A certain nobleman has a girl child by one, and a boy by another of each of what is mysteriously termed his principal consorts (kita no kata). The title stems from his remark that he wishes they could be exchanged. They are. The girl is brought up as a boy, the boy as a girl. The girl achieves reasonably high office at court; the boy is a lady-in-waiting to a princess. She becomes pregnant, he fathers a child on the princess—and so on, to a perhaps surprisingly dark ending. Once the initial conception is accepted, this story reveals unusual insights into human identity and social role.

There were also shorter stories (tampen monogatari), of which the ten best are to be found in a collection called the *Tsutsumi Chūnagon Monogatari* (ca. 1055). No one knows why such a title should be given to stories that are quite independent of such a character. And it is by no means clear that there is either a single or multiple authorship. This story is racy and that Buddhist, but the materials could have been refashioned by a single author. By comparison with the longer monogatari of the period, however, the distinguishing feature of these stories is wit, humor, and irony. "Ōsaka Koenu Gonchūnagon," for example, offers a parody of Kaoru's unconsummated love with Ōigimi (Waley's Agemaki). Clearly the *Genji Monogatari* has become a central work, but such a spirited parody suggests familiarity less than it does the exhaustion of one important current of Heian literature—or perhaps wicked caricature of someone at court.

In the later Heian period, however, another kind of prose narrative achieved distinction, the *rekishi monogatari*, or historical story. The difference between these and tsukurimonogatari lies not in a simple distinction between fact and fiction but in another simple criterion. The historical accounts set out what happened in named ages and to named and historical (or putatively historical) individuals. It seems quite appropriate that this kind of writing can be traced back to the *Kojiki* and *Nihon Shoki*, because the spirit of recapturing the past through the deeds of the mighty differs little in the two kinds. Of course the divinities and early sovereigns could do wondrous things that would not be credible for mere mortals, but the later standard of historiography is, as will be clear, the stuff of legend and nostalgia, disillusion and hope. These motives no doubt animate historians today, even if they are not confessed, but it is another thing to have modern "scientific" method give sanction, and yet another that the authors of reikishi monogatari should be inclined to include poems.

The dates and authorship of even the principal examples are seldom certain, but the renewed historical emphasis was strong enough to lead to a series of important works that bridge Heian and Kamakura times. In this continuum we are concerned with five distinguished works: 1. *Eiga Monogatari*, 2. *Ōkagami*, 3. *Ima Kagami*, 4. *Mizu Kagami*, 5. *Masukagami*. The last of these is certainly the product of the next period. But it belongs with the previous three titles in Japanese minds as one of the shikyō, or the Four Mirrors of the titles: *The Great Mirror (Ōkagami)*, *The Mirror of the Present (Ima Kagami)*, *The Water Mirror (Mizu Kagami)*, and the later *Larger Mirror (Masukagami)*. (The retrospective title probably recalls the *Four Records* of China: Jese. shiki.)

The *Eiga Monogatari* is not called a mirror, but then the other rekishi monogatari are not called monogatari, either, such being the nomenclature that is traditional. The *Eiga*, which announces flourishing elegance in its title, consists of thirty main parts and ten additional. This lengthy work concerns many people and events, but it celebrates in particular Fujiwara Michinaga (966–1027), under whom the Fujiwara regency and the court reached the apex of its splendor. Another way of putting this is that there is a Michinaga monogatari within the *Eiga Monogatari*, and that the whole is a celebration of the Fujiwara ascendancy, of which he was a conspicuously triumphant example—a man who could once proclaim that the things under heaven were under his sway. The difference between Heian and some later literature comes down to the fact that such a court figure is not seen in downfall here. In fact, although Michinaga's numerous benefactions to temples and shrines introduces religious motifs, the decline and fall is surprisingly slighted, avoided, given the enduring Japanese sense of the transience of earthly glory. If Michinaga is a model for the Radiant Genji, then Murasaki Shikibu saw farther into central Japanese treatment of fame than did the authors of the *Eiga Monogatari*, who did, however, create the great encyclopedia of the details of Heian court life.

Yet the fact is that at the time of writing, the court had well entered into its slow decline. The picture of court glory represents a compensation for the losses being felt. The two centuries or so treated—an even greater span than the seventy or eighty years depicted in the *Genji Monogatari*—help give an historical flavor. The pomp and spaciousness of the account give it a special appeal, and the apparently multiple authorship seems to involve both male and, more probably, female authors. Such varied hands combined to give a certain unity of tone— perhaps rather a testimony to loving concern with details—in their common concern with the Fujiwara house, with the values of the court, with a large number of poems, and above all with a glory that was the more precious for not being entirely realistic for the authors to claim. All this has a certain presence that perhaps the need for historical "mirrors" only reflects at one remove.

After the *Eiga Monogatari* there followed the "four mirrors." The *Ōkagami* (in three, six, or eight parts) is a rekishi monogatari like its predecessor, but it differs in a number of respects. Most obviously, it is a dialogue of sorts. Its central figure, sometimes called the *shite* after the protagonist in nō, is Yotsugi, who is a hardy one aged a hundred and ninety. His principal interlocutor, Shigeki, is a decade younger, although characters of more normal age also appear. Yotsugi's prominence is such that the work is sometimes called the "Yotsugi Monogatari." And in using an old man as a device, it is grouped with three other monogatari— *Taketori Monogatari*, *Utsuho Monogatari*, and *Ochikubo Monogatari*—as an old man's story (okina monogatari). Most readers are more apt to be struck by its nearer resemblance to the *Eiga Monogatari* and *Genji Monogatari* by virtue of its dealing with the glories of the court. It covers a period somewhat similar to that of the former, ca. 850–1026, and in particular it deals with events—the rise of the Fujiwara ascendancy and Michinaga as a conspicuous example. It treats that magnate in a different way, to teach the emptiness of prosperity in terms of the lessons of the Lotus Sutra. This imputed theme brings it closer to the *Genji Monogatari*, as does its style, which resembles the *onnade* or "women's hand." Unlikely as this description may make it seem, the *Ōkagami* is in fact a major source of historical information about the court. As in so much Japanese literature, fiction and fact here join without strain. The anecdotal line of narrative fits perfectly with the fictional frame for historical events, and it is just this poise that establishes the work's *literary* nature.

The *Ima Kagami*, another late Heian rekishi monogatari of uncertain date, follows the *Ōkagami* and is sometimes known as *Zokuōkagami*, a continuation in the sense that its title proclaims it a "mirror of the present." It is written in *kanabun* and, like its two predecessors, has a large number of poems in its three parts. It too deals with the Fujiwara glories, and in particular also with the

Murakami Genji. The speaker is an old woman, Ayame, who relates her story to people who had worshiped at the Hasedera (famous as a Kannon temple especially favored by women), and who was said to be a waiting-lady for Murasaki Shikibu long, long ago. In other words, a deliberate connection is made with the *Genji Monogatari*, with the *Ōkagami* by title and influence, and with the *Eiga Monogatari* in subject matter. Like the later *Mumyōshō* of *Kamo no Chōmei, it has special importance for its richness of comment on art and aesthetics.

The *Mizu Kagami* was put together in the late Heian or early Kamakura period. It differs from its predecessors in having very few poems in its three parts and in having an established authorship. *Nakayama (Fujiwara) Tadachika (1131–1195) wrote a very literary style in kanabun, and once again we have the device of an aged narrator—this time prodigiously old, a sage who has lived since the age of the gods, and who has worshiped (yet again) at the Hasedera. The account covers the fifty-three reigns from the first, so that much is quite unhistorical. In effect, it deals with the fabulous and the historical up to the point where the *Ōkagami* begins. Its method is in some ways the most annalistic if not historical of those prose accounts, since it is given to reign-by-reign details, much like the second and third parts of the *Kojiki* and the last section of the *Nihon Shoki*. The special feature of this "Water Mirror" involves a criticism of the present time at once implicit and explicit in various comments.

The *Masukagami* really belongs to a much later time, that of the Namboku period. It is included here because its title ("Larger Mirror") connects it to the works just considered and for various other literary reasons. After worshiping, this time at a Saga Temple (northwest of Kyoto), the narrator meets a nun over a century old, who relates events of about a century and a half, from the reign of *Gotoba to Godaigo's return from exile in Oki. Once again the style is very literary, and in kanabun. The work is worth association with its predecessors among rekishi monogatari for its concern with court life and because of its use of poetry. It has 200 poems, including a couple of chōka, as does the *Eiga Monogatari*, although that has 627 poems in all. The *Mizu Kagami* provides an exception with but three poems, whereas the *Ōkagami* has 80, and *Ima Kagami* has 145. The lengths vary; so therefore also does the proportion of poems to prose text. Yet three of the four (whatever their dates) share in the Heian sense of poetry as a defining element of prose. The provision of so many poems clearly necessitates a heightened style and presumes an ethos of the court. It seems no accident that the most likely candidate for authorship of the *Masukagami* is *Nijō Yoshimoto (1320–1388), himself a poet and a member of the high court nobility. Yet when all this has been said, this account of the *Masukagami* (and perhaps of the *Mizu Kagami*) has taken them out of their proper period. In a sense, the tradition of rekishi monogatari, so firmly established for treating the court, represents a necessary preparation for the *Heike Monogatari*, the masterpiece of historical tales.

From Murasaki Shikibu to Sugawara Takasue no Musume—and beyond—the finest Heian prose narrative is by women. They would continue to excel as poets and often as prose writers, but it is quite clear that they were fostered as writers in this age as in no other in world history. What the Japanese term the tradition of literature by women (*joryū bungaku*) includes poets as well, so constituting one of the distinctive features of Heian literature and a characteristic distinguishing Japanese from the other literatures of the world. This historical or sociological fact would seem to have something to do with the unusually inventive character of Heian literature. It goes without saying that inventiveness of new literary kinds does not ensure greatness, since in the ages that followed we can find numerous works by men that surpass many by women in this age. Yet the creativity remains a fact, one matched only by the second great burst of inventiveness during and just after the terrible wars that were to rack the nation in the periods to which we soon turn, when men of low or unknown social origins achieved great prominence. Not even in modern times has there been a counterpart of the creativity by Heian women and Muromachi nobodies. And when we add to all this the fact that the greatest work of Japanese literature was produced by a noblewoman of no high rank, when indeed we contemplate the "Genji industry" that so resembles the "Shakespeare industry" in criticism and scholarship, and when we also recall how Tsurayuki had defined the basic features of classical Japanese poetics, it is hard to resist the thought that the inexplicable providence that supplies genius to one age and denies it to another was truly prodigal in its gifts to Heian literature. Human imperfection and limitation clearly abound in early Japan. But the generations that produced the intelligible complexity and normative humanity of Hitomaro's poems and the *Genji Monogatari*, not to mention so much else, established a literature that can be placed beside any other in the world.

C. Kamakura, Nambokuchō, Muromachi, and Azuchi-Momoyama Literature (1186–1603)

Echoing Po Chü-i, *Fujiwara Teika wrote that the strife between the red and the white banners—of the Taira and Minamoto forces in the *Gempei* wars—was no affair of his. He was not alone among poets and ordinary people in trying to work out a safe and productive life among wars and rumors of wars. Many other people were directly concerned with obtaining power, however, and to them and their families—as well as to would-be bystanders like Teika—the times brought intermittent tumult hazarding economic survival, along with crucial matters of life and death. One part of this long period, from about 1467 to 1568 (although other dates are also given) is commonly designated the Sengoku time, referring to the wars in and among the various provinces, and indeed of the nation at large. It applies in a sense to the whole of these four periods, whether we date their inception from the Hōgen War of 1156 or whether we take the distinctive features of the periods as those following the crushing defeat of the Taira at Dannoura in 1185. These convulsions came to their end with the collapse of the Kamakura and Muromachi *bakufu*, with the rise of Toyotomi Hideyoshi (1536–1596), who emerged from humble origins to become effective ruler of Japan in 1585 until, just fifteen years later, the decisive Battle of Sekigahara brought to power Tokugawa Ieyasu (1542–1616). From that decisive resolution of years of struggle the Edo period begins.

If those who sought power by the sword often died by it, the fate of most ordinary people caught up in localities of strife scarcely bears thinking on. Those same little people enjoyed peace, but not much more in Heian times, and the nobility barely managed to survive as a class during the time of wars. Their decline is almost as consistent a motif in Japanese history as the rise of the middle classes in Europe. Even during their protracted but no doubt painful decline, even after their eclipse, the nobility continued to define much of what was important in the literary and other cultural values of the nation.

The finest literature of the periods we now consider not surprisingly took on a dominant tone of seriousness such as was common enough earlier, but that now came essentially to define what life was about. Another way of saying this is that the life of letters became more difficult to master, and that the greatest writers were normally those who managed to live to an advanced age that allowed them to command a mature, complex art. By no means all the writers still cherished were those who stood apart from the struggle for power. *Gotoba was not content to reign or to be a fine poet and patron of artists; but his struggles with the bakufu led to exile in Oki. Taira Tadanori (1144–1184) is said to have risked his life in visiting *Fujiwara Shunzei in the capital so that one of his poems might be included in the *Senzaishū, a commissioned collection that Shunzei was then compiling. One poem was included, anonymously, which was all that Shunzei dared, although Tadanori has found his fame in two episodes of the *Heike Monogatari and in the nō, Tadanori. The ambition to succeed as a literary figure dominated the hearts of the mighty in these periods as it had not before and would not do later. So, at the end of this period, we find *Hosokawa Yūsai, a waka poet, statesman, and warlord writing in terms established by *Ki no Tsurayuki, and in words that seem to speak for the whole period, making clear why literature mattered:

Inishie mo	As throughout the past,
Ima mo kawaranu	So even now it has not changed
Yo no naka ni	In this world of ours:
Kokoro no tane o	The seed engendered in the heart
Nokosu koto no ha.	Lasts after only in poetic words.

Another source of solace was sought, and therefore usually found, in religion. Two major movements distinguish this from the preceding and following period: One was the Christianity that touched many hearts, produced many martyrs, and had a limited effect on literature. The other was the popular Buddhism of Kamakura (the Pure Land sects, Zen, and Nichiren movements). By simplifying the requirements of the religious life solely to calling on the name of Amida (senju nembutsu), Pure Land Buddhism soon became the most widespread and popular form of the ancient faith and, largely unwittingly, fostered a kind of antinomianism. The rigorous meditational and other disciplines of Zen first appealed to warriors and, in time, left a profound mark on arts and letters. Although Zen taught a freedom from scriptures, its Rinzai school produced a vast corpus of writing, as is evident in the so-called literature of the Five Temples, *gosan bungaku*, which was often not literature, which involved numerous differing temples in the Kamakura and Kyoto areas, and which often involved monks so human as to concern themselves more with institutional prosperity than with meditation. Other Zen masters, particularly the stern *Dōgen—who brought back the practice of Sōtō Zen from China in the first half of the thirteenth century—avoided the seduction of easy popularity. Some Japanese think Dōgen the greatest religious philosopher Japan has had. Some say he was less original than given to misunderstanding his Chinese texts. None doubt his single-minded commitment.

The traditional forms of Buddhism—the "Six Nara Sects" as also Heian Tendai and Shingon—did not disappear overnight. The literature of this period continued to reflect the imagery of the *Lotus Sutra* and the esoteric (mikkyō) practices of Shingon, as well as being influenced indirectly by the great institutional structures then centuries old. But traditional Buddhism continued to lose ground to the new movements, and its lingering influence was virtually eliminated with Oda Nobunaga's razing of the great Tendai complex on Mt. Hiei in 1571.

From its early days after *Hōnen established the Pure Land sect in 1175, the movement also had adherents among the powerful. In fact, people of all conditions, from the powerful to prostitutes, were moved by Hōnen's vision of salvation in simple, devout faith.

Pure Land Buddhism shared the same sense, but its means to religious repose differed. Instead of the meditational means of the Zen faiths, instead of the spells of the tantric teachings of early Japanese Buddhism, Jōdo priests preached the comforting doctrine that devout invocation of the Buddha would guarantee birth in the Pure Land. For this reason, it had a profound appeal to common people, who could not afford the luxury of retreat to meditation. But it also had adherents among the powerful, who often found themselves in straits that foreclosed contemplation. According to the *Heike Monogatari*, Tadanori besought a few moments before death to recite the *nembutsu* in elaborate terms.

The third faith was that of Christianity. From 1549, when St. Francis Xavier began to preach in Japan, and for a half century or more, Catholicism attracted many of the humble and the mighty to its vision of salvation and life in the hereafter. *Christian* (or *Kirishitan*) *bungaku* includes no such masterpieces as those inspired by Buddhism, but the thousands of Japanese martyrs for the new faith testified to more than their religion. They showed what all this prolegomenon is meant to emphasize, that the newly evolving literature was imbued with conviction of the precariousness of human life. Such writers turned to the past as well as to the next world to define their present existence, and if such an ill-starred figure as *Minamoto Sanetomo shows that attention to the past and a desire to be a poet guarantee little as to literary quality, he shared with Christians and Buddhists alike many of the same motives in seeking to understand their existence by religion and by literature.

Along with the new faiths, many elements of the old provided continuity with the literary past. But the new writers had their own distinct achievements. The historian could therefore choose to dwell on connections with the past in waka or monogatari and zuihitsu, all of which were practiced with distinction. Or dwell on the new kinds of literature—*renga*, *nō*, and *kyōgen*. Or follow a strict historical line, taking authors as they come. In fact, the ensuing account is quite standard in beginning with the waka of the *Shinkokinshū*—the eighth of the commissioned anthologies and, in sheer quality, probably the greatest of them. This collection dates from about 1201–1216. Since the *Heike Monogatari* is said to have assumed its present twelve-part form about 1350, it commands early attention if historical sequence is to be followed. On the other hand, the later ordered collections of greatest merit—the *Shinchokusenshu*, *Gyokuyōshū*, and *Fūgashū*—have intimate ties with the *Shinkokinshū*. For many such reasons, the ensuing account is somewhat unorthodox and will treat the earlier of our present periods for achievement in waka, monogatari, and zuihitsu, and the later for what it managed with renga and nō. Such tidying-up has many faults, but perhaps may offer some degree of clarity.

1. *Kamakura Literature (1186–1336)*

Writers just before 1200 could, of course, have had no notion that they, unlike their grandparents, were suddenly of the "Kamakura period." But there are stirrings in those years, strivings for fresh things in *monogatari* and *waka*. In the late Heian period, the *Ima Kagami* spends most of its length in comparing the present state of the nobility to its former grandeurs, and it takes no notice of the battles that were becoming a feature of life. It does, however, observe the presence of warriors, who were not worth notice earlier.

Waka revived more fully, however, in the years just before 1200. In 1187, *Fujiwara Shunzei finished his royal collection, the *Senzaishū*, including Taira Tadanori's poem, as we have seen. Much that is old is included, and Shunzei would not have wished it otherwise, being altogether catholic in taste and a person who venerated the poetic language of the past. But he made much of new styles, new understanding. There are poems by the eccentric *Minamoto Shunrai and others by *Minamoto Tsunenobu, who anticipated the increasingly descriptively symbolic ideals of the new age. One of Shunzei's own finest poems appeared in the collection (4: 258):

Yū sareba	As evening falls
Nobe no akikaze	From the fields the autumn wind
Mi ni shimite	Blows chill into the flesh,
Uzura naku nari	And the quails seem to cry out
Fukakusa no sato.	In the deep grass of Fukakusa.

Shunzei's own favorite among his poems, this exemplifies the new poetry he helped bring into being. The desolate scene (Fukakusa had disappeared) well conveys his ideal of *sabi* and especially *yūgen*, of mystery, depth, and beauty in a scene of deprivation. The mystery and depth derive in part from the poem's being an allusive variation, or *honkadori*, on an exchange of poems between Narihira and an anonymous woman (*Ise Monogatari, episode 123; with slight differences, *Kokinshū, 17: 971–72). The romantic aura of two classical works is evoked, and above all the figure of *Narihira. Where is all that now? Yet the allusion adds a depth of now vanished passionate love to an autumn poem on the quintessential autumn time of dusk, as *Sei Shōnagon had postulated.

In the following years, Shunzei attained the unrivaled respect of his poetic contemporaries, even if his court offices were humble. As a fair and catholic critic, he was much in demand during his long lifetime as a judge of other people's poems. At various *utaawase* (poetry matches), he propounded his ideals of sabi and yūgen and put into critical practice his slogan, "traditional language and fresh conceptions" ("kotoba furuku, kokoro atarashi"). The priestly poet *Saigyō sent to Shunzei for judgment on his *jikaawase*, or poetry match with himself, *Mimosusogawa Jika-* (or *Uta-*) *awase*. Saigyō remains one of the three favorite classical poets among Japanese—with *Kakinomoto Hitomaro and *Matsuo Bashō.

The period of Shunzei, Saigyō, Shunzei's greatly gifted son, *Fujiwara Teika, and other splendid poets coincided with the reign and rule as cloistered sovereign (In) of the highly gifted, restless *Gotoba. In addition to commissioning many other kinds of artistic activity, Gotoba sponsored hundred-poem sequences (*hyakushuuta*) and utaawase on an unheard-of scale. He outdid *Fujiwara Yoshitsune's poetry match in 600 rounds by one in 1,500 rounds (these are the **Roppyakuban Utaawase* of 1193 and **Sengohyakuban Utaawase* of 1201). Teika fussed in the Chinese prose of his diary, *Meigetsuki*, that Gotoba would suddenly take into his head some poetic or other notion requiring his courtiers to strain their energies and resources.

The monument to Gotoba's poetic ambitions was the *Shinkokinshū, the eighth anthology, ordered by him, including among the compilers Teika, *Fujiwara Ietaka, and four others. This collection is, with the **Man'yōshū* and *Kokinshū*, the third great collection of court poetry in time and, most Japanese would think, second only to the *Man'yōshū* in greatness. There were, however, sharp disagreements over its compilation. Teika insisted on inclusion of the best poems of their kind. Gotoba was more interested in appropriate poems, and in an ordering that ensured the maximum integration of the collection by editorial techniques of progression and association. Gotoba had the last word, in that when his political machinations earned him exile, he took the collection with him to make it perfect by his lights. Its books or groups of books are indeed beautifully integrated, making what is in effect a sequential, plotless, lyric narrative of its nearly 2,000 poems; a ten-thousand line creation of old and new poems ordered with great skill.

The argument testified to what disagreements always do, the belief that important issues were involved. These poets considered that, in such times of tumult, there were several ways or vocations, *michi*, that could lead to enlightenment. Among them was kadō, the way of poetry. Shunzei brought to bear on poetic composition the meditation, *shikan*, of Tendai Buddhism. That and the serious depth poetry was acquiring imbued the descriptive styles of the age with symbolic import.

One of Saigyō's most famous poems appears as the second of three splendid poems of autumn dusk (sanseki no uta in *Shinkokinshū*, 4: 361–63).

Kokoro naki	While denying his heart,
Mi ni mo aware wa	Even a priest cannot but know
Shirarekeri	The depths of sad beauty:
Shigi tatsu sawa no	From the marsh a longbill
Aki no yūgure.	Flies off in the autumn dusk.

As a priest, he should not feel attracted to the insubstantial things of this world. He does nonetheless. The scene involves, however, a nondescript bird lost in the onset of darkness, leaving a vanishing scene to the observer. Once more, sabi and yūgen, the human condition.

Saigyō wrote many other kinds of poems, including a large number on cherry blossoms, especially at Yoshino, where he seems to have gone frequently for retreat. With him, the Heian favorite, the plum, begins to yield to cherries as the quintessential flower. Among Teika's styles was one of ethereal beauty (*yōembi*), supremely represented by a spring poem (*Shinkokinshū*, 1: 38):

Haru no yo no	The bridge of dreams
Yume no ukihashi	Floating on the brief spring night
Todae shite	Breaks all apart;
Mine ni wakaruru	And from the mountaintop a cloud
Yokogumo no sora.	Takes leave into the open sky.

The subjective first three lines tell us that dawn has broken (the essential hour for spring, according to Sei Shōnagon). The last two lines say that a personified cloud bank takes its leave of a mountain. The whole is otherwise integrated by numerous allusions and nuances, particularly those involving the last chapter of the *Genji Monogatari*, "Yume no Ukihashi" ("The Floating Bridge of Dreams"), in which, besides all that is evoked by the final portion of that masterpiece, a cloud's leaving a mountain is a metaphor for divergence from the religious life (a mountain representing a temple). The last word, sora (sky), also represents the Void (kū, the same character as sora), or the interdependence of all things: the parts may have no persisting self (muga), but their totality is the perfection and freedom of the Absolute itself. That this idea of the Void should underlie the rich imagery of the poets will surprise no reader of the complex poetry of this age.

The other principal poets of the age include Princess Shōkushi (*Shōkushi Naishinnō), Shunzei's Daughter (*Shunzei no Musume), *Fujiwara Ietaka, and *Kamo no Chōmei. When such poets looked away from the wars, they saw with eyes conditioned by the sight of desolation. When they found beauty surpassing the colors of spring flowers and autumn leaves, it was in humble scenes about to vanish into the dark. When the experience of life was most beautiful to them it was the misery of the deserted woman who gained it in an unfinished dream. Loss seems endemic to their understanding. But so does beauty. It is no wonder that the *Shinkokinshū* contains a book of Buddhist poems, *shakkyō*. Such intense depth could only be gained by metaphysical reflection. The poetry lacks the spontaneous response to immediate experience of the best earlier poetry. But by writing fictionally on set topics (*dai*), the poets could take time to reflect on what was meant by a given subject and call to mind the best of the past for refashioning art into their own understanding of precarious, valued life.

That poetry makes much of noun-images. The new developments in mono-gatari make more of verbs and the actions that the poets sought to see through to their essential states. A bit of the new drive in prose narrative will be found in the *Hōbutsushu*, a *setsuwa* collection of stories dominantly religious, although of varying length and date. The new subject was to be war in the *gunki monogatari* (or *gunkimono*). This was exemplified early in the period by the *Hōgen Monogatari*, which dealt with the strife that characterizes so many generations that follow. Its authorship is uncertain, and it deals not with sovereigns but with warriors, as for example Chinzei Hachirō (Minamoto Tametomo, 1139–1170), so often recalled by later writers, including *Kyokutei Bakin in his *Yumiharizuki* and the modern writer Mishima Yukio in one of his plays. Yet the situation of its action reflects historical reality and the continuing relevance of the court: the capital rather than provincial encampments. Such a focus is adjusted by the *Heiji Monogatari*, also ultimately anonymous, whose middle sections are much concerned with the varying locations to which warriors rode off to do battle. Otherwise it shares with the *Hōgen Monogatari* the three-part development so typical of the literature of these times: preparation, action, and result.

The contrast drawn between poetic noun-images and narrative verb-actions is a rude one, but it testifies to the differing appeal between the two kinds of literature. The genius of this new literature was of course slowly formed, and since the finest gunki monogatari have strong Buddhist themes, it must be thought that the quite different *setsuwa bungaku* contributed to their develop-ment or even includes them. A major exemplar of the first kind established on a grand scale by the *Konjaku Monogatari* is the *Uji Shūi Monogatari*, which dates from the early Kamakura period. Although not as highly esteemed today as it was throughout the remainder of classical literature, this collection of about two hundred stories does use a very oral style—one immediate or low, according to taste—that takes notice of the human lot in ways involving humor as well as sobriety. Without such setsuwa and the *rekishi monogatari*, it seems unlikely that the *Heike Monogatari*—the narrative second only to the *Genji Monogatari* in greatness—could have been realized. As a setsuwa collection, the *Uji Shūi Monogatari* may be best thought of in relation to the splendid account of the overthrow of the Taira house in the *Gempei* wars given by the *Heike Mono-gatari*—as a collateral ancestor of a cadet family, one that yet managed to enlarge the milieu of prose narrative to help make possible the capaciousness of its illustrious counterpart.

Like the *Chanson de Roland*, to which it has been interestingly compared, the *Heike Monogatari* has bred many scholarly debates as to its authorship, formation, delivery, texts, sources, and much else. (For this and other reasons, it is slighted here and given an unusually long discussion in Part Three.) The usual twelve-book version known today earns the respect of every reader. It contrasts not only with the waka of the time in style and method, but also with the *Genji Monogatari*. The chapters of the *Genji* are very long. Those of the *Heike* are brief. The syntactic style of the *Genji* offers one of the most complex and elusive verbal media ever created. The style of the *Heike* is in some ways an ideal version of Japanese prose, that rare thing, a wondrous compromise between the finest styles of the Heian narrative and the best styles of the Edo and even modern literature. The *Genji* was meant to be read aloud, with the leisurely pace appropriate to life at court. In its familiar version, the *Heike* was meant to be recited by blind priests to the recitation of *heikyoku*—an exalted oral manner to evoke awe in listeners throughout the land.

Each of the twelve familiar books is divided into episodes—from nine to twenty is the range—and each is well suited in length for recitation. It is easily imagined that people listening to a reciter would ask for the next and the next episode. In practice, however, certain episodes seem to have been sung often and others reserved for special occasions. From all this, not to know the sonorous opening is not to know the work at all. As the praise of its style will have indicated, however, the *Heike* is highly readable as well. Its great theme of the collapse of the Heike is present everywhere, even when—or especially when—the Heike are given sympathy for their virtues or compassion for their sufferings. In fact, the majestic opening bids us see in the fall of the Heike the common end of the great. The deaths of the arrogant Kiyomori or the just Shigemori—and many, many others, even some cowards—remind us of our human condition. Such ends must have spoken yet more directly to those who knew what a sword-swinging age was like. Anyone who has heard a familiar passage recited will know how deeply moving the *Heike* is. The question sometimes raised—can there be any Japanese epic?—is at once pertinent and irrelevant for this work. This, like the *Genji*, is of the stature of the finest Western epics. If the *Heike Monogatari* is in fact not to be thought epic, then that criticism is even more damaging to the concept of epic than to this splendid work.

Poetry after Teika is best understood in terms of his critical writings and social contexts. Teika's *Kindai Shūka* consists of (eighty-three) exemplary poems, as the title suggests, although they are by no means all so recent. One version was sent to Sanetomo, urging him politely to refrain from copying the *Man'yōshū* till he had mastered styles a little closer to home. Sanetomo's *kashū*, the *Kinkaishū*, proved Teika right. This ill-fated shogun's life provides an affecting tale of the times, but the gap between his aspirations and achievements seems greater than many Japanese critics wish to think. He may be mentioned out of duty. Except for his fine late poems, he may be read out of duty. In those last few poems he proved himself fully worthy of his age.

In these years Teika compiled another anthology of poems, the most famous, or familiar, in all Japanese history, the *(Ogura) Hyakunin Isshu*. These hundred poems by as many poets have provided generations of Japanese with a New Year's game and a canon of waka that is almost too familiar to refer to. Unfortunately, his ordering seems to have been lost and we are unable to read the poems in a satisfying sequence of five hundred lines, as we can the 415 lines of *Kindai Shūka*. Just as Horace's *Art of Poetry* produced an *Art of Cookery* and other variations in the eighteenth century, so Teika's imitators provided readers with such amusements as the *Genji Hyakunin Isshu*. Teika's serious purpose was to provide sample poems worthy of attention for their soundness of language and of conception for those who had not yet advanced very far in the way of poetry.

After Teika's death, strife arose over poetic claims, much as in the political realm, and for two of the same reasons: pride and wealth (Teika's estates). In fact, political divisions were also involved. One house claiming inheritance of poetic practice (and estates) consisted of the *Nijō poets, a scholarly but conventional succession of poets. The two other houses, the *Kyōgoku and *Reizei poets, made common cause against their more successful rivals. The Nijō poets may have composed the same poems over and over, but they had a better political sense. As a result, the innovating houses managed to compile only two of the *chokusenshū* after Teika's *Shinchokusenshū* (the sole title among the twenty-one royal collections to boast of its official status as a chokusenshū). The two Kyōgoku-Reizei collections—the *Gyokuyōshū* and *Fūgashū*—are worth the rest and more of those compiled after Teika's collection, and not merely because they are long and integrated in interesting ways, especially in the alternation of the usual close with more distant connections between successive poems.

In this Indian summer for waka, a group of gifted poets brought a fresh view and practice of poetry. The two most powerful are no doubt *Kyōgoku Tamekane and *Yōfuku (or Eifuku) Mon'in. They were not alone. *Reizei Tamehide and two sovereigns, *Fushimi and *Hanazono (long thought compiler of the *Fūgashū*) alone would make the period worthwhile. But with Yōfuku Mon'in, two other women, *Jūsammi Chikako and *Jūnii Tameko, show that women would write poetry as long as the court tradition could be maintained.

This poetry brings a fresh subjectivity to bear with a new objectivity. That is, the love poetry is often so concerned with the states of love that imagery is all but absent, and the seasonal poetry is so concerned with the phenomena of the world that it consists all but entirely of natural imagery. Making the subjective experience of love so very subjective honors, as it were, an objective characteristic of amatory experience, whereas treating the natural world in terms of organized scenes honors our subjective understanding of it. In any event, both kinds of poems share a tendency to some kind of metamorphosis or other development. Here is Yōfuku Mon'in on love (*Gyokuyōshū*, 12: 1707):

Yowarihatsuru	In my grieving heart,
Imawa no kiwa no	Weakened now by your betrayal
Omoi ni wa	To the point of death,
Usa mo aware ni	Even misery takes on pathetic beauty
Naru ni zo arikeru.	And my bitterness is gone.

The speaker and we are astonished by the alteration of her feelings at so critical a moment; and, it may be added, we are faced with great difficulties in this image-free style. Another kind of alteration, and language, will be found in an evening poem by Tamekane: (*Fūgashū*, 8: 794):

Furiharuru	The running hail
Niwa no arare wa	Falls, then stops, and falls again
Katayorite	In patches on the garden;
Iro naru kumo zo	And the beautifully colored clouds
Sora ni kureyuku.	Grow dark in passage through the sky.

Such accurate observation of changes in nature implies the presence of a subjectivity not acknowledged. Saigyō's poem on the longbill is at once more openly subjective, less so in implication, and more symbolic in implication.

During this period there were other poets with new things to say. The rival northern dynasty prepared a collection, the *Shin'yōshū*, that was all too often standard stuff, but that frequently has poems that stand out, as in this love poem by Prince Munenaga, suggesting something of the terrors of the times as a fresh note on the trysting time of dusk (*Shin'yōshū*, 14: 918):

Kono kure mo	Again as twilight falls
Towaren koto wa	How can I count on him to visit?
Yomogiu no	Where rampant grasses grow
Sueba no kaze no	Their tips will agitate with wind
Aki no hageshisa.	In the violence of autumn.

Although he is a better, and more difficult, waka poet, *Kamo no Chōmei will be discussed here as a prose writer, taking us to a new subject but to an earlier period (his dates are 1155–1216). In addition to omitting his poetry, we also pass by the *Hosshinshū*, very likely compiled by him. Two important works remain. The *Mumyōshō* (completed 1209–1210) is a major poetic treatise, if by "treatise" we can designate a composite that is more readily appreciated than described. In the guise of passing on the poetic views of Priest Shun'e, Chōmei offers something of a dialogue. But that is a fiction not rigorously held to. In his time one did not make public the fine points of poetry delivered to you directly, orally. If that is not clear in itself, it becomes so when Chōmei turns learned in discussing *utamakura* (see Part Eight K, Poetic Place Names) and utaawase. Work like that clearly involved research, note-taking and, in short, written delivery. In the end it does not much matter. He presents what he will as he will. As we shall see on other grounds, he was not wholly immersed in his age—and certainly not wholly detached from it. He spent his time in his grass hut (with expeditions to the capital when interest or desire for excitement took him). But the result was a degree of freedom from the poetic debates of his time. One side of the argument in those days was upheld by the conservative Rokujō poets, whose "house" was founded by *Fujiwara Akisue. The other side was led by *Fujiwara Shunzei, founder of the Mikohidari house, which sought to make new even while preserving what was essential from the past. Chōmei's famous, haunting discussion of yūgen (partly quoted in Section A above) shows where his heart really lay, since yūgen was the ideal and slogan of Shunzei.

For every scholarly reader of the *Nameless Treatise* (*Mumyōshō*—not to be confused with the *Mumyōzōshi), there have been thousands of ordinary readers who have enjoyed his *Account of My Hut* (*Hōjōki*). This is said to date from 1212, but like the earlier work it obviously results from a lengthy period of gathering and revising the constituent parts. And it is not without precedent in earlier writings, especially the account kept by *Yoshishige Yasutane. If Chōmei's other familiar work is more or less "untitled," this is one of the three chief exemplars of a kind, *zuihitsu*, that perhaps should be translated "prose miscellanies." But like the other two masterpieces of the kind by Sei Shōnagon earlier and *Kenkō later, it is an art of composite, collective observations. Rather than follow Sei Shōnagon's use of witty, acute categories with examples, Chōmei employs more continuous prose to remark on whatever enters his head about—well, about life.

As we get into the work, we find it easy to assume that his melancholy purpose is to dwell on the vanity of the world (mujō). In famous phrases, mundane life is compared to "the current of a flowing stream" ("yuku kawa no nagare") and on it the bubbles that "here will burst and there re-form" ("katsu kie katsu musubu"). The familiar emblems would not bear the force they do without the remarkably pure, waka-like language he wields. Later, however, we discover that, as in the *Mumyōshō*, Chōmei holds himself at a discreet (not overly far) distance from the world. In another pair of famous phrases, he sets as his ideal "desiring quiet piece" ("shizuka naru o nozomi") and "rejoycing in the absence of wordly grief" ("urei naki o tanoshimi"). This is pure Japanese again, but as with the phrases on the bubbles, it is cast in a parallelism redolent of Chinese. A similarly heightened coloring brightens the dull life of a recluse. There, beside his *Lotus Sūtra* to read and recite, he sets a lute, a zither, and writing materials for poetry. Chōmei not only wrote about his hut. He defined something anew—the life of the poetic recluse—something also implied by the poetry of Saigyō. Chōmei appears to have found an equable answer to the question of what to do with oneself in an age of growing military strife, dispute between the court in Kyoto and the *bakufu* in Kamakura, and an age that was widely thought to be the last age of the Buddhist law (*mappō*). Because they define themselves so much by relation to some group and by daily crowded living, Japanese greatly admire those who seem able to live so purely and serenely alone. The image of Chōmei, the aesthetic recluse, is found not only in Saigyō and his waka, but in Sōgi and his *renga*, and in Matsuo Bashō and his *haikai*. It is the model for the tea ceremony as well, and it found powerful support in the meditative practices of Zen Buddhism. Almost to the end of classical literature, we observe the model in individuals as attractive as *Yokoi Yayū and *Ryōkan.

There were also works that gave new impetus to the literature of memoirs. The *Kenrei Mon'in Chūnagon Nikki* is now lost in the shadow of the *Kenrei Mon'in Ukyō no Daibu Shū (1231). Of the Heike house, Kenrei Mon'in, consort of

Takakura, was one of the few survivors. The triumphant Genji spared her life, but consigned her to live her last days in retreat at Ohara, north of the capital. In addition to the extra, final portion about her in the *Heike Monogatari*, we have *Kenrei Mon'in Ukyō no Daibu's own account of those and former years. It is a melancholy record of her lover lost in battle with the Genji and of scenes of present beauty. By turns a memoir or diary, a monogatari, and a kashū, it tells more of deep emotions recollected than of recollection in tranquillity.

A livelier, more rugged woman, the nun *Abutsu, as she is best known, wrote some fifty years later her *Isayoi (Izayoi) Nikki*, definitely treating a waning world. The diary recounts her trip to Kamakura for litigation over incomes of estates disputed in *Fujiwara Tameie's inheritance from Teika. Much of her account is surprisingly routine for so strong-willed a person. She seems to wish to prove—to an unnecessary degree—that she knows the poetic tradition. Yet hers is one of several works that Matsuo Bashō refers to as a predecessor for his own memoirs of the road (michi no nikki)—what today is termed travel record literature (*kikō bungaku*). Not many people would set off for Kamakura in litigation and write in a form now thought dead, the *chōka* (as well as *tanka*).

A few years later, another diary, *Towazugatari* (completed 1313) was written by another woman, *Gofukakusa In Nijō, or Lady Nijō, in service with the now abdicated Gofukakusa. He seems to have been uncommonly placid about the goings-on of his concubine, if that is what we should call her, and she in turn spends the former part of her diary largely on her relations with high-placed lovers to whom she gives the fancy names of Yuki no Akebono and Ariake no Tsuki. If we accept the most natural interpretation of her title ("I'll Tell You, Even If You Don't Ask"), she is remarkably forthcoming, a latter-day *Izumi Shikibu—less the lover and poet, but more enterprising in other ways. The latter half tells of her taking orders, thus shifting from a predominantly love diary to an intermittent travel account. In the second part there is more pith, more that is fresh, as she visits various places in her freedom as a nun. There is a fine close, but it may be suspected that the excitement of the relatively recent discovery of this work and the account by Lady Ukyō no Daibu will settle down, and that once again greater attention will be given to the works by Chōmei and Kenkō.

The *Tsurezuregusa* by Kenkō is not waka, nikki, or monogatari, but it is a perennial favorite among, and one model of, the zuihitsu kind. As that other outstanding practitioner of the genre, *Sei Shōnagon, might have put it, this is one of the few Works That Are Perfect in Their Kind. It can be said that Kenkō (1283–1351) discovered a couple of centuries before Montaigne that prose was the natural medium for conveying the motions of an inquiring, particularly a self-inquiring, mind. It is, moreover, special to the point of rarity in appealing to young and old alike with a combination of eager tolerance and assuring limitation, beckoning the one and consoling the other. Naturally, many remarks in its 243 sections are long-since famous. "Although he may have many fine traits, a man who has not known the passions of love gives the feeling of a jeweled sake cup without a bottom" (3). "A person's heart is a fool if, in this world, it understands love without being swept by passion" (9). He also says with equal insistence: "Certainly anyone born into this world has many things to pay for" (1). Like Chōmei, and centuries of other Japanese, he found himself moved most by what might seem other than ideally perfect. "Are flowers something to look at only at their peak and the moon only when flawlessly bright?" (37). In the same section, he enunciates another important aesthetic principle, one that unites the *Shinkokinshū*, the *Heike Monogatari*, and subsequent masterpieces as he mingles mujōkan with *mono no aware*: "It is in their changing with passing occasions that makes everything touch one so" (22). No wonder he could feel that the past had such appeal and yet exclaim over life before his eyes: "The very uncertainty of this world is what attracts us so much!" (7). It is not clear whether Kenkō wrote his work before taking first orders (shukke), or whether he or possibly others rewrote what we have later. It would be pleasant to think that we have something like his original version, and that he continued to like it as it is as much as everyone else has since. With this timeless prose, we have a reflection on essentials of earlier literature and an auspice to what endured in the literature that followed.

2. *Nambokuchō, Muromachi, and Azuchi-Momoyama Literature (1336–1603)*

The warfare ushered in with the end of the Heian period intensified after the Kamakura period, adding a greater destruction, and to it confusion. For sixty years (1339–1399), there were two rival lines lines of sovereigns, a claimant in the "south" and in the "north," so giving this period its name, Nambokuchō. In 1467, the violent Ōnin War broke out, for the first time fully centering on the capital. All who could do so fled the fires, depradation, and carnage. A world that had seemed in change but still wholly recognizable was turned topsy-turvy. As a climax to struggle, the unruly factions collected, or were coerced, into groups of mighty opposites in a struggle that at last brought peace under a new military and increasingly "feudal" society. To such anarchy, and the human desire to find order in literature, we owe the striking achievements of *renga* and *nō* as well as distinguished practice in the now passing glory of *waka* and the still sturdy genius of *monogatari*.

Because renga and nō alike developed slowly and from quite different origins, we have the paradox that although in their most distinguished practice nō precedes renga, the canons of renga guided the achievements of nō.

Renga took its origins in waka, particularly in the patterns of progression and association that integrated the ordered collections and sequences such as the *hyakushuuta*. Although poets such as Teika devoted their lives to writing or compiling waka sequences, they also composed renga as a pastime. The results were, of course, less than serious to the poets who applied their souls to poetry as *michi*, or a way to enlightenment. By 1356–1357, *Nijō Yoshimoto (by waka practice rather than birth associated with the *Nijō poets) had compiled the first renga collection, the *Tsukuba Shū*, which thereafter gave renga its name as Tsukuba no michi. The renga master *Sōgi later said that the first of three periods of the art culminating in his own time closed with Yoshimoto. In something like two centuries it had changed from a nonstandard or *mushin* diversion to a poetry worthy of collection and rules by Yoshimoto, himself a cultural arbiter of the time. But since nō and some other writings flowered earlier than did renga, we may consider them before turning to the linked poetry.

From a host of kinds of performance, many comic and all popular, nō developed slowly and then suddenly into what can only be termed its flower (see Part Five, Theaters, for greater detail). Two men, father and son, played crucial roles, although many others and the special conditions of the time made nō what it was. *Kan'ami (1333–1384), as much as anyone, brought into flower *sarugaku no nō*, or nō. Three chief centers of sarugaku flourished in the Yamato-Kyoto area. And in the lifetime of *Zeami (?1364–?1443), nō acquired its essential character, many of its finest plays, as well as recognition from the Ashikaga shogunate. As we have seen (in Section A), it also developed an aesthetic that modified the principles of Japanese aesthetics. In adapting the dominant waka aesthetics, Zeami and others also drew on the *jo-ha-kyū* rhythm instituted for literature by renga. And in seeking to make nō an inclusive, definitive art, the dramatists drew for sources on waka, on the *Ise Monogatari*, the *Genji Monogatari*, the *Heike Monogatari*, and Chinese as well as other native sources of valued literature, not excluding Buddhist conceptions.

The essence of theater is performance, and for that words merely read are inadequate. Yet no matter how often we have heard the initially entered *waki* tell of his journey, our expectations rise afresh. No matter how often we have seen the *shite* in a two-part nō reenter in new mask and robes, the experience catches us again. Always the succession of drum beats or cries from the musicians (*hayashi*) comes in a series that, to the less than trained ear, sounds unexpected and yet just. After today's slow, slow motions, the climactic *mai* will involve the shite in somewhat speeded movements, including stamping of the foot. And, in *Hago-romo*, the raised and bent knee will seem to lift the celestial creature back to her native sky. Like every living theater, nō must be considered precisely as perform-ance (see Part Five).

The central features of this total nō involve a dialectic between text and performance. The words are indeed beautiful, yet their combination of prose and verse spoken by the characters, or the chorus (*jiutai, ji*) weave a pattern largely narrative and lyric. As W. B. Yeats said, nō is reminiscent, and this recollection emphasizes the narrative or lyric cast of the plot. Yet the performance of such a pattern is representational and cannot be understood except on the stage. The canons of all these matters were dealt with in great detail by Zeami, who united in unique combination the genius of playwright, actor, director, and critic. His *Fūshikaden* mingles his father's ideas with his own. His *Kakyō* gives us ideas mostly developed by himself. And the *Sarugaku Dangi* consists of remarks said to be preserved from him. That nō survives today in a form Zeami would have recognized attests in part to his genius and in part to the astonishing Japanese powers of conserving literary achievement. Any surprise we feel over this can only be compounded by the realization that each performance of a play, even by the same actors of the same play in the same week, necessarily varies.

Such variance is a condition of all drama. But dramatic traditions vary in other respects. Greek, Roman, French, and Spanish dramatists rigorously separate their solemn plays from their comic. English drama often mingles the two variously in single plays. On the nō stage in Zeami's time and even now, another mingling was employed. In a standard performance, *kyōgen* were performed as interludes between nō. (Again, see Part Five for details of the theaters, and Part Six, G and H, for titles.) These comedies evoke the laughter that would put at hazard the nobility of nō. (In the current repertory of nō, only one piece—*Sanshō*—involves laughter, and nobody much likes it.) To create a world for which the distinctive human ability to laugh is appropriate, kyōgen involves lower characters in the quotidian problems, and inadequate solutions, of human life. Such is the enduring Japanese, or human, genius of comedy that for the kyōgen representations of quarreling priests, stuffy masters, and rascally servants, audiences in Japan as elsewhere do not require a text before them to appreciate the elaboration of our comic limitations. Comedy and farce offer patterns that recur universally or—what is much the same thing—seem to have an applicability more immediate than the specially endowed characters typical of the more solemn sister art. The most famous servant in kyōgen, *Tarōkaja*, has brothers and sisters throughout the world where comedy is practiced. Kyōgen also introduces wives and even monkeys, but it excludes the topic of romantic love, which it ceded to nō, on its terms, and which was to be taken up later by *jōruri* and *kabuki*. No one who attends to kyōgen, however, will think this a deficiency, except in retrospect (if then).

The peace of a theater must have seemed attractive in an age of wars and rumors of wars. But military experience was too important not to color a good deal of literature. Many such traces mark *Imagawa Ryōshun's diary, *Michiyukiburi* (1371) and even some of the waka in it. This spirit is yet more strongly testified to by the new *gunki monogatari*. The *Soga Monogatari* provides an instance. It may date from ca. 1400 in its twelve-book version, or considerably earlier in its ten-book form. Both deal with the same story of the Soga brothers' revenge. They are based on a historical event that so excited people that the government became alarmed, and people thought that the angry spirits of Gorō and Jūrō required propitiation. Its emphasis makes the *Heike Monogatari* seem courtly by comparison, for the story of this revenge includes no one from the nobility, and its milieu is that of the Genji warriors, the Kantō area.

Not only that, such a revenge story lacks the sweep of the stories of the Gempei wars, with land forces and sea forces opposed, Kyushu and capital, the refined and the rude. It is no wonder that there should appear other versions of these events or works that sought to rival the *Heike Monogatari* by dealing with other subjects. Of the successors to the Heike, one of the best is the *Taiheiki*, which, in spite of the suggestion of its title (that it records the great peace), emerges from the Nambokuchō and its turmoil. It treats the half century between Godaigo and Gomurakami (1318–1368). If it does so without the glories of the *Heike*, it does still manage the feat of telling clearly (at least until its somewhat choppy close) a story about events contemporaneous with the authors. Perhaps they were too close to the events. In any case, two of the people who are known to have participated in the writing have their deaths recorded in the work itself by subsequent authors. That, like its ironic title, provides an emblem of the times.

Yet the *Taiheiki* is neither negligible in itself nor insignificant for the tradition of prose writing. The clarity of its plot has been mentioned. Another matter, one that we might almost pass by, is the fact that its authors were recording what was going on about them as a kind of heroic story. With the rarest exceptions, Western heroic literature deals with the past, involving an implicit contrast with a lesser present. In this respect, the *Taiheiki* and other stories, at once *rekishi monogatari* and gunki monogatari, demonstrate the same impulse to deal with contemporary and continuing matters that we discover in the earlier literature of memoirs in the Heian period.

The *Taiheiki* illustrates the way in which the genres—or at least prose narrative and drama—now influenced each other. As nō had used earlier monogatari for its stories, so the *Taiheiki* drew on plays for some of its dramatic effects. This was the easier to do because the combination of representation and largely narrated plot in *kōwakamai* (see Part Five) was particularly accessible to a narrative with quasi-dramatic encounters. The hospitality of the genres in Japanese literature has many such illustrations. If in the Nara and Heian periods such generosity involves lyric and narrative, in later times it involves narrative and drama in the terms just mentioned.

The early Muromachi period also produced the **Gikeiki* (or *Yoshitsune Ki*). In eight books it tells the story of the most romantic of all Japanese chivalric heroes. By now, so much fiction has been written about Yoshitsune and the other characters in the story that we can no more unravel historical detail from the account than we can reconstruct Burgundy from Wagner's ring cycle. Yet it is worth recalling that Yoshitsune is one of the few Minamoto chieftains to be made much of in the *Heike Monogatari*. As with the *Iliad*, to make much of someone is to spell his doom. The *Gikeiki* does deal with his prowess and triumphs, along with the sinister presence of his brother Yoritomo (who may be as much maligned by these tales as Richard III was by Shakespeare). But Yoshitsune's military strategy, his love affair with Shizuka, his obtaining the loyalty of Benkei, the retreat to Hiraizumi, the fidelity of Izumi Saburō, the perfidy of others, the deaths of those who matter—such things are in fact quite superior to history. There is a combination of character, event, and attitude that quite transcends diurnal reality, and we value the combination not only for its transcendence, important as that is, but for the meaning it bestows on what is otherwise inchoate.

The discovery of artistic and human reality amid confusion and dust was the general enterprise between the Heian and Edo periods. The highest examples of this search, along with the *Heike Monogatari*, are certainly the waka already discussed and the renga that we have postponed discussing: its achievement begins in the former half of the period but reaches its acme only in this latter half.

Along with everyone else who could leave the capital during the Ōnin War, the renga masters packed up their few books and fled. Since they were typically priests, at least in name, they had a freedom of travel and companionship with all other conditions of people. But since so many of them were from low origins, they required financial support to sustain life. This situation led for a time to what is unique in classical Japanese literature, the easy intercourse of the best poets with the nobility, the military, and commoners.

Unlike the waka poets, the renga "priests" or masters were not born to a tradition of learning, but they therefore prized it the more. Again and again we discover them studying with the nobility or learned priests. Again and again we find them writing commentaries on selected classics: the *Ise Monogatari*, waka, the *Genji Monogatari*, and sometimes also, although much more rarely, the *Heike Monogatari*. In fact, some of their commentary opened new ways of understanding: they were more concerned with seeing anew than with upholding some family line on the classics. One fact about renga seems to be exceptional in that matter of desire for learning: in the early fifteenth century, illiterate people also composed renga. This shows that numerous people who before would not have been given attention in any fashion as poets were now emerging. And the emergence testifies to a desire to write poetry.

It might be expected that renga poets would also compose waka, which had much more prestige. In fact, two of the last important waka poets are also known as practitioners of renga. *Shōtetsu was principally a waka poet, important as his linked poetry is, and he deserves special attention for his achievement: in many of his 11,000 poems he managed to bring Reizei ideals into waka, so helping to overcome the stultifying atmosphere fostered by the learned but hidebound Nijō line. He also took the very Japanese step of writing his *Shōtetsu Monogatari*, a "tale of myself." This resembles less the memoirs of earlier times than it does *zuihitsu*, since its concern with poetry more nearly resembles the interests of Chōmei and Kenkō.

The greatest of these interim figures is Bishop *Shinkei, who studied with Shōtetsu. Like *Sugawara Takasue no Musume earlier, Shinkei has a genius not yet adequately honored. The most gifted waka poet following Teika (at least given the personal judgments being expressed here), he is also the most brilliant composer of renga stanzas. No renga poet is as recognizable for style—or for difficulty, which may possibly be the same thing. If he was not the greatest of renga poets, that is because his attachment to waka led him to a concern with the excellence of each individual stanza rather than with the entire, integrated sequence.

The difficulty of his poetry led Shinkei to explain himself in numerous prose writings. For example, in his "Murmurings to Myself," *Sasamegoto* (1463), he writes:

Among the great poets of the past was one who, when asked how we should compose, answered that we should converse with the pampas grass on the withered plain and with the moon fading in the sky at dawn. This gives a heart to locations that cannot speak, makes enlightenment known to places withered by cold.

After such conversations with grass and the moon, difficult and excellent—but also not integratable—poems should perhaps be expected.

Sōgi (1421–1502) was the greatest renga master among many that seemed suddenly to emerge during the fifteenth and early sixteenth centuries. Like many others, he came from humble origins: we do not know where he was born or what kind of family he was from. He became a priest, at least nominally. He wrote waka, which were not up to Shinkei's. When the capital was devastated, he fled to the provinces, where he made friends with commoners, with military chieftains, and with the dispersed nobility. Having studied the classics with a noble friend first in the capital and then in the provinces, he was able to return to the capital and obtain prestige from lectures on the *Ise Monogatari* and *Genji Monogatari*. In explicating these classics and in practicing renga, Sōgi brought a special genius that involved his sense of the modulated whole. The early renga he wrote with Shinkei reflect that master's brilliance in individual stanzas. But such is renga that to write brilliantly throughout is to fail, in whatever a blaze. Sōgi did not fail, but in his triumph he established, or began, the idea of poetry as a profession. This matter aligns *Matsuo Bashō more nearly with Sōgi than with *Saigyō, both of whom he revered.

The standard one-hundred-stanza renga sequence was set down on the outsides—the fronts and the backs—of four folded sheets of paper. To obtain a hundred stanzas on eight sides, the poets wrote eight on the first front and fourth back, but fourteen on each other side:

1st Front	(shoomote)	8 stanzas
Back	(shoura)	14 stanzas
2nd Front	(ni no omote)	14 stanzas
Back	(ni no ura)	14 stanzas
3rd Front	(san no omote)	14 stanzas
Back	(san no ura)	14 stanzas
4th Front	(nagori no omote)	14 stanzas
Back	(nagori no ura)	8 stanzas

The broken lines set off the first front and the fourth back sides of the sheets, because they formally set off the *jo-ha-kyū* divisions that had been passed on to nō from earlier renga. Actually the jo (introduction) commonly spills over for one or more stanzas into the ha (development), and the kyū similarly begins one or more stanzas before the formal end of the ha.

Well before Sōgi, *Nijō Yoshimoto had insisted on varying the impressiveness of stanzas in a renga sequence, even as waka in a *hyakushuuta* were to be varied. Various terms were used to describe gradations at different times, but in general *mon* or design represents the highest and mumon or ji the least impressive. (See Part Four, *renga*.) In decreasing order of impressiveness, then, we have various terms (and more importantly conceptions) that hold for the modulated sequentiality of waka sequences, renga, and *haikai*:

mon (umon)	design
mon-ji (yaya mon)	design-ground (somewhat design)
ji-mon (yaya ji)	ground-design (somewhat ground)
ji (mumon)	ground

Yoshimoto also insisted that connection (kakari) is the soul of renga. In practice, as a close approximation of late integration of waka sequences (particularly by Kyōgoku-Reizei poets), this meant varying the closeness or remoteness of connection between two stanzas (see Part Four, *shinku*). Once again it is possible to postulate four degrees on a decreasing scale of connectedness:

shin(ku)	closely related (stanzas)
shin-so(ku)	close-distantly related (stanzas)
so-shin(ku)	distant-closely related (stanzas)
so(ku)	distantly related (stanzas)

The canons of renga also involved such fairly simple matters as including one flower stanza (simply "hana," not a named flower [na no hana]) per sheet; and one moon stanza ("tsuki," but in the sense of "moon," not "month") per side. The other conventions are so complex as to defy discussion in proportion suitable here. Such details apply, with modification, to haikai as well. For more detailed information, the reader will have to consult specialized works; however, more information will be found in Part Four.

Although the *hyakuin*, one hundred stanzas, was the more or less standard length, fewer were sometimes written (especially in the haikai styles of Matsuo Bashō), and so were multiples, as a thousand stanzas (*senku*) or even ten thousand (*manku*). The number of participating poets also varied. In 1447, twelve poets including Shinkei sat to compose the *Anegakoji Imashinmei Hyakuin*. In 1492, Sōgi composed by himself (over a period of four months) probably the greatest sequence of all, his *Sōgi Dokugin Nanibito Hyakuin*. Normally, a couple of decades of study enabled poets to compose in rapid succession, taking something like three minutes to offer a stanza, have it written down, and checked.

The best known renga is the *Minase Sangin Hyakuin* (1488), composed by Sōgi with *Shōhaku and *Sōchō. Like so many, Shōhaku had taken orders. But he differed from the majority of renga masters in being from the nobility. An especially interesting personality if not the best of the poets, Sōchō resembles most other prominent renga masters at this time in his humble origins. He was the son of a smith, but the swirling times allowed people like him and Sōgi to achieve social prominence—and professional status as poets—by virtue of their talents.

The same three poets composed their best joint effort three years later: *Yunoyama (Yuyama) Sangin Hyakuin*. Shōhaku's opening stanza (*hokku*) sets the season of composition:

Usuyuki ni	Beneath thin snow
ko no ha iro koki	the fallen leaves deepen in tint
yamaji kana	the path upon the hill

(Here, "iro koki" applies, as these expressions often do in renga, doubly: to the coloring of the leaves and the path.) The nature of stanza relation can be seen in two later stanzas. Sōgi wrote the 24th (the first two lines), suggesting that summer will soon yield to autumn. Shōhaku wrote the 25th (the last three lines):

Izumi o kikeba	Listening to a cold summer spring
tada aki no koe	I hear only the voice of autumn
hotaru tobu	and at the house side
sora ni yobukaku	I sit till late at night with fireflies
hashii shite	tracing the sky in flight

A cool sound leads Sōgi to explicit anticipation of autumn. Shōhaku writes another summer stanza (fireflies show as much), transferring to a visual scene. Given the renga-haikai canon that each stanza makes up a semantic unit only with its predecessor (and therefore also only with its successor until the last stanza), we may wonder what Sōchō will do to alter the sense in connecting another stanza (26) to Shōhaku's.

Hotaru tobu	Here at the house side
sora ni yobukaku	I sit till late at night with fireflies
hashii shite	tracing the sky in flight
mono omou tama ya	and left to yearn in vain my soul
nen kata mo naki	finds no way to discover sleep

Sōchō skillfully shifts the topic from summer (for which two successive stanzas sufficed) to a miscellaneous (zō) stanza with love (omou) as a subtopic (see Part Four, dai). He recalls a poem by *Izumi Shikibu, composed "When after being forsaken by a man I made a pilgrimage to Kifune Shrine, and at Mitarashi River [where it was hoped one could be purified of love-yearning] I saw fireflies flying." Sōchō identifies the woman's soul with the fireflies, changing the sex and situation of the speaker—and therefore altering the implications of Shōhaku's from what it meant in connection with Sōgi's. It was thought that one's soul could leave the body to go visiting the person loved. But as the fireflies wander about the sky all night in Shōhaku's stanza, so the yearning woman cannot find the way either to rest or to her lover.

In addition to being a prolific poet, and besides his important commentaries on the classics, Sōgi wrote prose on various poetic and personal subjects. Three representative works are: *Tsukushi Michi no Ki* (1480), *Azuma Mondō* (?1470), and *Oi no Susami* (1479). Also, although it was not published till 1554, his *Shinsen Tsukuba Shū* collects many stanzas from his predecessors and contemporaries. If his legacy remained in such personal writings and collections, as well as in his poetry, it remains true of renga and haikai alike that they flourished only under dominant personalities such as his.

Although Sōgi was the greatest poet of this period, a last prominent renga poet appeared, *Satomura Jōha. Coming so late (1524–1602), he lived right up to the Edo period, a fact not without literary consequence. He too came from humble circumstances, becoming the foremost poet of his time through the usual combination for renga poets: genius, luck, patronage, and long life. So recent is the revival of study of renga that Jōha is not even mentioned in some modern literary histories. But it is now agreed that although his style is sometimes plain, he followed Sōgi in the modulating of sequence by skillful variation of the elements of renga.He is indeed a major poet, but unlike the others, he lived into a new social order, and his founding of a poetic "house" is indicative of the ordering that was so characteristic of the feudal impulses that followed the creative chaos of a warring but literate nation. During Sōgi's lifetime women are mentioned as participating in renga and waka composition at court. By the end of Jōha's life, there are set lines of renga poets, and women are not heard of. In the new age, the government set a policy to "favor men and disfavor women." The policy was successful, and after the anarchy of the second half of this period, all was tidied and set in determined (if often merely formal) order of hierarchies, class, and dominance by a military order that did not favor either those women or nobodies who earlier had been among the principal waka and renga poets.

The age that produced a Zeami and Sōgi was quite unlike any other in classical Japanese literature. It is not so much that we see the decline of women as writers, although that is new in Japanese literature. The crucial thing is rather that the very confused times brought to prominence kinds of literature that wholly depended on *groups* in a given place. This ensemble, group literature (*za* no bungei) includes both the renga and drama (nō and kyōgen alike). If certain charismatic figures could appear—a Zeami or a Sōgi—then a drama or a new kind of poetry would achieve distinction. Perhaps it is not wide of the mark to say that anarchic times required a group effort to achieve greatness. Out of the combination of a few artists sharing a single place for their creativity came renga. So also did nō and kyōgen, realizing and distilling a mixture of constituents of performance into two kinds of dramatic art. In the age that followed, influential personalities were to prove equally important, and for drama the importance of ensemble would remain. But excessive, restrictive order would be the problem, and in that regulated peace nobodies such as Zeami, Sōgi, or women would not find the world of literature as accessible as it had been to people in several generations who seized literature from the threats of war and destruction.

D. THE EDO PERIOD (1603–1868)

Powerful figures began to emerge from the wars. At the beginning of this period, Oda Nobunaga first seemed likely to achieve rule, and then Toyotomi Hideyoshi. Finally, in 1603, the establishment of a new government in Edo by Tokugawa Ieyasu brought peace to an exhausted nation. It also brought totalitarian reaction to anarchy and a desire to put everything and everybody in designated places. It is easier to proclaim laws than have them obeyed, but when an exhausted people welcomes peace, the lawgivers have their chance. The shogunate quickly dispossessed commoners of swords, required provincial magnates alternately to reside in Edo or provide hostages, and in the course of rapid developments left many samurai without a place in society. Edo was for some time an authoritarian seat of power, and it is not surprising that the *kamigata* area near the old capital should have continued to be the nursery of literature, even when the work was not produced by the nobility or warriors but by people of mercantile extraction, members of professional classes, and dispossessed samurai. In the most closely regulated systems, there is disorder enough, but some logic must be sought for any intelligible account. Given the increasingly large numbers of writers, or at least the fuller historical evidence, this account of the age will be subdivided into a Tsurayuki-like set of distinctions as to literary growth: 1. Seed Time: 1603–1672; 2. The Great Flowering: 1673–1724; 3. The Harvest: 1725–1829; 4. Wintry Gleanings: 1830–1867. The reasons for such divisions will become clear, and they follow the spirit of Japanese distinctions, as well.

1. *Seed Time: 1603–1672*

So little of outstanding merit was produced during this period that "the desert" might seem an apter term. Yet in view of the greatness of the ensuing years, we can only assume that the first sixty-five years or so were necessary to sort out and prepare. Since social revolutions concern the possession and exercise of power, they move from a period of anarchy and strife to conservative tidying-up. The new order tidied with the usual authoritarian gusto. In such instances, the question for literature turns on whether the period of imposing order allows for a freedom followed by a repression both dogmatic and antiliterary, or whether the initial ordering will subsequently allow for literature relatively untrammeled by dogma. Fortunately for Japan, the latter was the case. It led to initial uncertainties and then to a renewed great literature.

Japanese literature has no Muses, but its spirit at the Sumiyoshi Shrine ensured that the existing kinds of literature would continue: *waka, renga, nō*, song, and the varieties of prose. Yet in none of them can we discover a genius such as is evident before. In this initial period we search in vain for great plays. And yet from 1610 or 1615 puppets begin to be used in the theater. Moreover, at the beginning of the period Kyoto saw the rise of both male and female players. Of the female the most famous is the troupe, or rather troupes, that went under the name of "Okuni kabuki." The new government's attitude toward women did not help, for although various kinds of female performers were crucial to the development of the drama that followed, the female troupes in Kyoto were effectively quelled by a government that passed edicts in the name of morality. Young male troupes were interdicted on similar grounds, but the times favored adult males.

Poetry also had no great achievements, at least apart from those of the last great renga master, *Satomura Jōha (who has been discussed just previously). In 1614 there appeared a collection of *kouta*, the *Ryūtatsu Kouta Shū*. These "short songs" had been popular since the Muromachi period, and their publication at this time testifies to Japanese desires to prize and keep anything once invented. A nation's song may not constitute its greatest literary glory, but it does testify to enduring poetic energy and to the character of such a force.

If formal poetry had no great achievements either, the future is well represented by *Matsunaga Teitoku (1571–1653). In his early years Teitoku practiced waka and renga. Quite properly, he also concerned himself with poetics, which he studied with some of the important figures at the end of the previous period: with Kujō Tanemichi (1505–1594), one of the last if not greatest of a learned line; with Jōha; with the great political figure and man of the arts, *Hosokawa Yūsai; and with others. Teitoku left behind a collection of *kyōka*. But above all he is remembered for turning to *haikai* (haikai no renga), not yet the distinguished version of this renga offshoot that it was to become. But his *Gosan* (1651) testifies well to the sowing that was necessary before flowering and harvest.

*Kitamura Kigin (1624–1705) began his prolific career a little later. Although a waka and haikai poet of some distinction, he is valued most as the first of a line of distinguished scholars in this age. He wrote on renga and haikai, literary memoirs and *monogatari*. But the monument of his learning is his commentary on the first eight ordered collections of waka, his *Hachidaishū Shō*, which laid a foundation for subsequent study of waka and which, for some of the less often annotated anthologies, remains the first commentary to turn to even now.

Prose writers of other kinds showed fresh life. *Asai Ryōi (d. 1691) had a sense of popular taste that was to become crucial to later writers, as is shown by his *kanazōshi* and similar writings. Among his many works is one dealing with famous scenes along the road from Edo to Kyoto. This *Tōkaidō Meishoki* foretells not only later literary works but also various series of wood block prints. *Suzuki Shōsan (1579–1655) produced a number of works, many tinged by Buddhist elements, that share features of kanazōshi. His *Roankyō*, *Inga Monogatari*, and especially *Ninin Bikuni* maintain some claim on our esteem. His style seldom rose above the ordinary, and his didactic persuasion is not transcended by a higher literary quality. But to have foreshadowed *Ihara Saikaku is something, and among many such somethings, he may be taken to show early signs of spring.

2. *The Great Flowering: 1673–1724*

*Ki no Tsurayuki's saying that all living beings are given to song testifies to the continuity of Japanese literature. His metaphor of seed and plant implied cycles of growth and flower. But the seasons of literature follow no set pattern, and it is simply an accident that after the slow growth of the early years of this period there should follow other apparently natural seasons of development. Tsurayuki's metaphor describes without accounting for the remarkable efflorescence between 1673 and 1724. The time we now consider is not as creative as the Heian period, because so much had been achieved, so many genres created, earlier. But only in the times now being considered has Japan known such a flowering at once of poetry, prose narrative, and drama.

The great triumvirate, one in each genre, consists of course of *Matsuo Bashō (1644–1694), *Ihara Saikaku (1642–1693), and *Chikamatsu Monzaemon (1653–1724), and Chikamatsu's death coincides with the close of the Edo spring. These three not only possessed genius but were the cause of something approaching it in others, so that it is small wonder that they have received more and more attention as Edo literature has come to seem increasingly important. "Has come to seem"—it has not always seemed so. In their own lifetimes, their work held a status much below that of the dusty *waka* of some imitator of imitations of the now stultified Reizei—official waka; and also below the clinked-together *renga* stanzas by samurai with more time than imagination. All three great artists were, by the standards of the time, eminently consignable—and were consigned—to *zoku* status. Their arts were thought inelegant, below the inherited, precedented, and true. On the other hand, no matter the dust of the waka, no matter the clank of the renga, those kinds were by contemporary definition *ga*. They were exemplars of what was canonized by *Ki no Tsurayuki and *Nijō Yoshimoto. To so remarkable an extent did the values of the court hold in a later age. It says a great deal that the not very artistically inclined Edo *bakufu* should still have included renga composition in its annual celebrations (see the account of annual celebrations, *nenjūgyōji*, in Part Seven H). Much the same thing is witnessed by the fact that the followers of Bashō were of lesser social rank and included mostly poets of nonsamurai status. Those who were of the bushi or samurai order were almost uniformly of its lower ranks.

This lag in respect accorded to new kinds of Edo literature far exceeds the time it took for *monogatari* to be appreciated. In the pages that follow, we do not argue that everything written in the Edo period was a product of genius. But Bashō, Saikaku, and Chikamatsu are great writers by modern standards, and it is clear that Bashō himself entered a claim that his art was true art. If he did not speak of it as "ga" in nature, he did in a famous remark rank it with such other "fūga" as the waka of *Saigyō, the renga of *Sōgi, and the tea ceremony of *Sen no Rikyū. Chikamatsu's serious intent is obvious (today) in his plays. The third member has taken longer to attract appreciation, and there may still be some who are unwilling to give up the conception of naughty Saikaku, or of a writer important only for his style. Yet the one serious problem today seems rather that of perspective and catholicity of taste. Bashō has been subjected to bardolatry. And too few people seem able to reach a just appreciation of all three writers. Our general judgment will be clear, and the reasons for it will be given shortly. For others as well as ourselves, the Edo criteria of "ga" and "zoku" simply prove inadequate even while providing guides to historical understanding.

Since poetry seems the place to begin, why not start with a flourish from the master flourisher? Saikaku did nothing by halves when it could be done by multiples. He caught public attention as a *haikai* poet. He had begun in the *Teimon*, the school of *Matsunaga Teitoku. About 1672, however, the popularity of *Nishiyama Sōin's *Danrin* school caught his nervous attention and engaged his allegiance. For a time thereafter he spent energy in producing haikai by prodigious feats of solo composition, as if all other contemporaries were too tardy to work with. It seems safe to say that no one, including Saikaku, has ever read all the verse he wrote. But in 1673 he did publish, as a kind of overture, his *Ikutama Manku*. This prodigious set of ten thousand stanzas makes one think that in a day of guilds the poet had anticipated the industrial revolution and mass production of the Meiji period. But on a single day and night he once produced some 23,500 stanzas—a feat that somehow sounds more impressive when stated as 58,750 lines. This is a far cry from the effort the waka poets of the *Shinkokinshū* had devoted to their poems, and the results were nothing like the haikai of Bashō. But the production (what other word will do?) in one day of so many, many times the total oeuvre of Bashō also tells us something of the energies of the Edo period in its Osaka merchantile guise.

Sōin's Danrin school has suffered in reputation because of Bashō's greatness, but it began sooner, lasted longer, and numbered important poets among its adherents. It also contributed two things to the development of haikai. As against Teitoku's school, the Danrin took from the nonstandard or *mushin* renga of *Sōchō and from renga in general an important criterion. Teitoku's haikai sequences tended to rely on verbal stanzaic connection, *kotobazuke*. Sōin insisted on conceptual connection, *kokorozuke*. This made less of word-play, more of what might be serious poetic procedure. The Danrin school had a second genius of another kind—catholicity—which gained it a sound economic base in appealing to all manner of talents. It ticked along during the great years of Bashō, and survived him. It attracted one of his most gifted followers, *Enomoto Kikaku (1661–1707), who was put off by Bashō's late, simpler stylistic ideal of "lightness" (*karumi*). Kikaku was no haikai producer like Saikaku, and in fact he has a very wide range of excellence, including the somber as well as the exalted. Yet his best work in haikai sequences was done with Bashō. When out of the master's presence, he tended to put individual stanzas on display, glorifying two or three lines at the expense of the longer, integrated sequence.

The *Shōfū* or Shōmon—the school of Bashō—spread over the land but never equaled the Danrin in popularity, although far excelling it in our esteem. Other poets never wrote better than when working with him, and for that reason his styles did not survive his death in terms of like greatness. Haikai of his kind was difficult to write. He revised and considered and revised. It is worth the private effort to try one's hand at his kind of haikai, if only to discover that it occupies a narrow margin such as Chikamatsu postulated for all art. Such effort will show how very difficult it is not to err in the direction either of the affirmative purity of waka or renga, or in the other of jocular lowness of *kyōka* and the later *senryū*. The variants recorded in the standard edition of Bashō's poetry (*Teihon Bashō Taisei*, ed. Ogata Tsutomu, et al. [Sanseidō, 1962]) show that the master found the art no easy feat himself.

Bashō set himself no such high standards in his early work, and it was only something like a decade before his death, about 1684, when he set *sabi* as his ideal, that he found greatness. Many, many discussions of sabi are available. Among them, the two most persuasive account for it in terms of stillness and attenuation. The famous *hokku* on the frog leaping into the old pond proves both contentions (one need only observe Bashō's revisions to see as much). But it also appears that each is brought into being by the addition of contrast. As for stillness, we observe that the essential quiet of that scene depends, for its very existence, on the last line, "mizu no oto," the sound of water as the frog splashes in. As for attenuation, another famous hokku—that on a crow stopping on a withered branch— shows that it depends equally on the addition or poise of the contrary. Again it is in the last line, "aki no kure." As *Sei Shōnagon had postulated, and as centuries of poets had shown, autumn evenings were deemed (with spring dawns) the most movingly poetic of all seasonal phenomena.

Such stillness realized by sound and attenuation of riches testify to the value of the sabi ideal. Yet one does not discover the technique throughout the collection *Minashiguri* (1683), or even fully in *Fuyu no Hi*, the next year. *Fuyu no Hi* does take us to the mature Bashō, however, in its way of departing from convention: it ends in wretchedness rather with than the traditional positive ending for a sequence. He encouraged, it might be said, the essence of Danrin insistence on conceptual connection at the cost of easy conformity. For example, he said that the requirement that an opening stanza end in a *kireji* such as "kana" mattered less than that the opening stanza be seen to be "cut." As he said dauntingly, "If one does not understand such things naturally, it is hard for one to understand them at all."

Bashō had comic and witty gifts, but he took his art seriously because he took life and himself seriously. Some explain this by his interest in Zen Buddhism, for which the direct evidence is rather small, or in earlier Japanese and Chinese poets, for which the proof is ample. Others show copious evidence for his concern with time and death from his account of his reactions when his house in Fukagawa, Edo, was razed and he barely escaped, or from his poetic travel account, *Nozarashi Kikō* (1685). The finest poetic testimony will be found in the four haikai sequences (there are also nearly three hundred hokku) included in *Sarumino* (1691). This was put together by two of his finest haikai colleagues, the modest, gifted *Mukai Kyorai (1651–1704) and the wonderfully versatile *Nozawa Bonchō (d. 1714). All but the last of these sequences are master- pieces of the art, and *Akuoke no deserves to be set beside *Sōgi's solo *Sōgi Dokugin Hyakuin* as a monument of linked poetry. With perhaps the exception of one stanza, it does not reach the beauty of some of Sōgi's, but the tonal range and complexity—not to mention its complicated and beautiful articulation— make this sequence of ninety lines one of the great achievements of Japanese poetry.

Although Saikaku might brandish ten thousand stanzas or more, Bashō's haikai range from the two-stanza *hokkuwaki* to his favorite length of thirty-six stanzas, the *kasen*. (As far as his official collections show, he participated in only one hundred-stanza sequence and did not write solo sequences.) Yet he had other ways of linking stanzas, as is suggested by his likening of a kasen to a journey, and a journey to a kasen in that both begin with one step. That is, he wrote a number of accounts of travel on foot—things his restless spirit led him to. In *Oi no Kobumi* (1687), he coined the phrase, "memoirs (or diaries) of the road" (michi no nikki), which better suits the tradition he saw himself writing in than the usual, fancier, Sinified word, *kikō bungaku*.

The greatest of his travel diaries, *Oku no Hosomichi* (not published till 1703), treats part of his foot travel with a follower, Iwanami Sora (1649–1710; the journey began in 1689). Sora kept a nonliterary diary that shows Bashō sometimes contradicted fact to make art (although most of what he writes is verified), and sometimes invented. The best example comes in the fictional encounter with prostitutes at Ichiburi. The recent explanation for this addition seems true: a desire to give to the journey a renga- or haikai-like sequence by the addition of an episode dealing with the topic of love. This explanation will satisfy only those who are acquainted with the haikai latitude for that topic. The court poets would no more have accepted this than they would have *Yosa Buson's introduction of male homosexual love. Bashō made much of the introduction of love stanzas in the middle section of the *jo-ha-kyū* rhythm that haikai shared with renga and nō, precisely for the agitation that passion brought. The jo of *Oku no Hosomichi* starts with a beautiful, dignified prose poem on time. The lengthy ha or development section includes not only those prostitutes but moments when Bashō shows distinct irritation (for example, over lodging with fleas and with horses pissing nearby, or with overly insistent priests after Sora's health has made it necessary for him to cut out from one part of the journey, leaving the master alone). Bashō's worshiping admirers overlook such responses, and the comic gestures that often accompany others, but they are as integral to his art as the famous accounts of Matsushima, Hiraizumi, and Kisagata, which are also in the development section. The fast finale, or kyū, begins not long after Sora leaves Bashō, and quickly moves through many places and the mention of many people.

The beginning of *Oku no Hosomichi* very nearly says outright that the poet expected to die on that journey. That did not happen, but on a later journey he did fall into his last illness. As he lay dying in Osaka, Bashō had recourse to a word, a concept, that renga and haikai rules demanded be used sparingly: dream (yume). Knowing how closely the old poet identified travel, poetry, and life, we can fully understand the depths of his last famous hokku.

Tabi ni yande   Stricken in travel—
yume wa kareno o   and over withered fields my dreams
kakemeguru   whirl about and about

Bashō's life and his art have exceedingly complex interrelations, but it is not difficult to see from such a stanza as this why Japanese judge him one of their three favorite poets, with *Kakinomoto Hitomaro and *Saigyō. Of the three, the poet stricken in travel is surely the best known and loved. The writer who styled himself the Old Man (okina) in some sequences would have been pleased to know of his subsequent estimation. He would probably also have felt surprise, and might have wished that he had spent yet more time revising his poems.

After Bashō, haikai settled back into ordinary achievement, with the Danrin school continuing on its way. Kyorai decided against taking disciples and went into retirement to think and write about his late master. Bonchō kept writing, and Kikaku who had also already gone his way, continued on it, composing much that is not yet adequately examined. Meanwhile renga and waka also continued to be composed. Little is presently known of the renga of this period. Waka is better known, especially for attempts to bring its language—and therefore its range of experience—closer to that of the times. The kind of study mentioned in respect to *Kitamura Kigin also continued. All in all, however, if we know little about renga, we know something about waka, and it is not such as to rival earlier achievements. *Toda Mosui (1629–1706) published some works of merit, including his critical work, *Higagoto Kurabe* (1697), and collections such as *Tori no Ato* (1702). He wrote: "Since waka uses native Japanese words, there is no reason not to use the language actually employed by people." In practice, he was more conservative, as one of his best poems shows.

Kurekakete	The twilight thickens,
Yamaji no hana ni	And who is it comes on the mountain path
Tare ka kon	To see the blossoms?
Irihi o tsunage	Tie back with the finest thread
Sasagani no ito.	The sun that settles in the west.

This and other poems by Mosui are well composed, but they hardly seem to matter after Bashō.

The drama is another matter. To be feasible as theater, any kind of play must have some degree of popularity and support. Yet to make a lasting aesthetic claim, drama must transcend the commercial and social aspects of theater. Fortunately, the drama of these times did both.

The new drama is often called popular to distinguish it from nō, which of course was still being played. Its popularity is a dual matter, involving both commercial success and the audience primarily appealed to. In terms of the fourfold social division of the time—warriors, peasants, artisans, and merchants (shi-nō-kō-shō)—nō was the possession of the warrior class. The new drama was devised for the artisans and merchants—the townspeople (chōnin), particularly those in the *kamigata* or Kyoto-Osaka area and in Edo. The two new kinds, *jōruri* (*bunraku*) and *kabuki*, are distinguished by the use of manipulated puppets in the former and live male actors in the latter (see Part Five, Theaters, for greater detail). These two kinds of new drama have many roots in ancient dance, mime, and other entertainments. In fact, both drew on a wider range of sources than nō, and draw on nō itself.

We now know that the "Okuni kabuki" of actresses does not have the priority once thought. The belief that they were first has a certain appropriateness in the fact that women had long been shamans and had performed (as miko) in Shinto rites. Moreover, from Kamakura times and following there had been performers such as the *shirabyōshi*. It now seems that "Okuni" is a role or player title such as "Danjūrō." In any event, Okuni kabuki has no priority over that of male actors or, for that matter, over jōruri.

Any dating for these matters depends on one's definitions and sense of a decisive moment. Conservatively put, jōruri emerged at least as early as 1650, although how much earlier is a problem. The usual formal distinction separates the old jōruri (kojōruri) from the new, with the old consisting of plays written before Chikamatsu's *Shusse Kagekiyo* in 1685–1686.

The easiest way to clarify an exceedingly complex development is probably to use Chikamatsu in this fashion as point of reference. The type of performance that he began with was practiced from about 1673 in Osaka at the Okamoto Bun'ya and also in Kyoto at the Kaga no Jō. During these years, jōruri was highly popular, but just about the time that Chikamatsu brought in the "new" variety, kabuki was drawing away the crowds. Toward the end of the Genroku period (1688–1704), when so much flourished in the arts, jōruri once again became more popular. In those days, the author's role was considered the least of four, including also the reciter, the musicians, and the puppet manipulators. Much the same held on the kabuki stage, for although by the Genroku period Chikamatsu was doing better (he was no longer a menial jobman in the theater as well as the author), it has been estimated that in terms of 1975 values, he earned about ¥500,000, whereas the chief actor for whom he was writing, Sakata Tōjūrō (1645–1709), received about ¥15,000,000. Unlike Zeami (or Shakespeare), Chikamatsu did not benefit from being an actor and shareholder. But he persevered, and his situation improved with the years. Two centuries later the kabuki playwright *Kawatake Mokuami had a higher social position, but by then kabuki had become institutionalized.

From about 1677 Chikamatsu was writing jōruri for the Kaga no Jō in Kyoto. The anonymity of plays at the time makes it impossible to be certain which were his. It seems to be assumed (in the face of some later emphases), that his plays tended to the classical and the courtly, as well as the narrative (*monogatari*). If so, that may have been to suit Kyoto tastes. It is clear that his *Yotsugi Soga* (1683) attracted great attention. This version of the Soga brothers' revenge was to have many popular successors, and it itself was so well received that after becoming a hit in Kyoto it was presented in Osaka by that most famous of reciters, *Takemoto Gidayū (1651–1714), at the Takemotoza. As this shows, Chikamatsu had made a name outside Kyoto, and he also wrote a kabuki version "to delight daimyo." Yet jōruri remained his interest into the Genroku period, when for some reason he started writing kabuki.

His move was well timed, since the public seemed to want live actors just then. Because the actor Sakata Tōjūrō had been on good terms with the Kaga no Jō group, the transition was the easier. His first play for Tōjūrō was probably *Yūgiri Shichi Nenki* (1684), and other plays followed. But in 1701 Tōjūrō fell ill, and Chikamatsu went back to jōruri, once more with the tide of public favor. In addition, he began to write for Gidayū, and his financial situation improved markedly.

In moving to Osaka in 1706, he chose one of the three rival municipal centers in Japan. Kyoto and Edo were by no means laggard in theatrical activity, but Osaka was the literary as well as dramatic center of the nation. During this general period of return to jōruri, Chikamatsu wrote some of his greatest plays. One of the major ones was his *Sonezaki Shinjū* (1703). This double love suicide (*shinjū*) was based on a contemporary event that had already been performed as a kabuki, but his new version captured the essentials of jōruri, of shinjū, and of *sewamono*, the plays dealing with contemporary subjects that Osaka drama was to take as its special forte. The Chikamatsu prized by Japanese may be said to be realized with this play on the thwarted love of the hero, Tokubē of an oil merchant's house and Ohatsu from the licensed quarter. Osaka people found at last characters like themselves on the stage, in people made to seem important in their tragic aspirations and in the clash (more or less reconciled) of human passion and ethical values.

Yet Chikamatsu did not rest with one kind of success. The Takemotoza suffered various reverses, including the death of the great Gidayū in 1714. In the same year, urged by a gifted younger contemporary, *Takeda Izumo (1692–1750), Chikamatsu took up an old jōruri play and produced a very different hit, a *jidaimono*, *Kokusen'ya Kassen* (1714). The story of the fabulous career of Coxinga held the stage for three years and made the fortunes of the Takemotoza. Thereafter the dramatist enjoyed the ease of having assistants. He and they had a kind of authors' room in the theater, and with them he wrote a number of plays.

Chikamatsu was known to the public not just as a jōruri and kabuki playwright, but in other guises as well. His verse does not concern us, although it is not altogether negligible, but the published or reading versions of his plays have a real place, even more prominent to his contemporaries than the quarto and folio versions of Shakespeare. In kamigata a kind termed *eiribon* were especially popular (see Part Ten E). These offered a version of the acting text (*daihon*) so revised as normally to have insertion of the characters' names and speech tags along with pictures of major scenes. The version more common in Edo, *eirikyō-genbon*, had the same kind of pictures but involved less addition, having only characters' names above their dialogue.

The distinction between period pieces or jidaimono and contemporary pieces or sewamono is not exact, any more than is the Elizabethan distinction in drama between tragedy and history. There were also some plays that do not fit either category very well, just as there were combinations. Still, the distinction allows us to review Chikamatsu's career and to mirror other plays of the time in it. Among his jidaimono there is *Yotsugi Soga*, his first really popular play. There is *Shusse Kagekiyo*, concerning one of the Taira heroes already treated by Zeami. *Kokusen'ya*, also already mentioned, would once have been called an epic in Hollywood, combining as it were qualities and features of *Ben Hur* and *Gone with the Wind* along with other characteristics from Racine or Restoration English heroic plays.

His sewamono include *Meido no Hikyaku* (1711), which treats a then newsworthy story of a liaison between a woman of the pleasure quarters and one of her customers. There is the *Sonezaki Shinjū*, already mentioned, and *Satsuma Uta* (1704), another *shinjū* play, whose title derives from the poem ("uta") composed by the couple on the way to their death. A somewhat similar play, *Shinjū Nimaizōshi*, refers in its title to the writings left behind to clarify the reasons and details of the suicide. There is also *Shinjū Ten no Amijima* (1720),

Chikamatsu's best-known play today. In it, he provides careful, sympathetic delineation of the lovers, Jihē of the Kamiya and Koharu from the licensed quarters. But the wronged wife, Osan, emerges at once clearly and sympathetically, and her parents are also treated as real people.

A less familar but mature play should suggest something of the continuing interest of Chikamatsu's shinjū plays. Like others of these dramas, *Shinjū Kasane Izutsu* (or *Kasane Izutsu*, 1707) took its story from a couple of events that had occurred three years before, both resulting in suicide. The title relates to the heroine, Ofusa, who is in bond to the licensed house Kasane Izutsu. Her lover, Tokubē, had become enamored of her after having been adopted into a dye-merchant's business, taking his wife's parentage as his own, as was usual in such cases. That fact shows his deep obligation to his wife, Otatsu, and her parents (it is the father who matters in this play). In *Sonezaki Shinjū*, the lovers had been brought to ruin by a villain. In this play, Chikamatsu improves his dramaturgy by having the lovers freely responsible for their end. Hereafter he follows this more natural causation in plays of this kind.

The play has the usual three acts of a sewamono, and altogether twenty-three scenes. As is common, the first and third are much shorter than the second (such is the Japanese taste for what is represented by the jo-ha-kyū pattern). The brief third act begins with a *michiyuki*, one of the simpler ones by Chikamatsu and so easier to translate, as being less complicated than most by word play (*kakekotoba*) and word association (*engo*). This travel piece begins by playing on the title in a literal way, then goes to the lovers' tears. In an ages-old association, the tears are thought to be on the sleeves that wipe their eyes and therefore glisten in the moonlight, which is fading, along with their lives. Although Chikamatsu is considered a prose artist, the passage will give some sense (at least in the original) of his poetic powers, as well. The original is labeled "poetry" (uta), is punctuated for pauses, and is in fives and sevens.

Tsutsu izutsu.	Pipe by well pipe—
izutsu no mizu wa.	the pipe well gives forth water—
nigoranedo.	that once ran clear—
ima wa namida ni	but now with salty tears
kakinigosu	it starts to soil
tsuki mo tamoto ni.	and on their moisted sleeves the moon—
kakikumoru.	also starts to cloud—
ashita no kumo	the morning clouds
yūbe no shimo	and evening dews
Adashigaura no	at the Cove of Evanescence
Utsubobune.	where the hollowed boat—
mi o naki mono to	tells that they will lose themselves
shirinagara ...	although they knew this, too ...

As Ofusa and Tokubē make their last journey, Chikamatsu plays—in time-honored theatrical fashion—on the intersection of theater and world: the lovers voice fear, and perhaps some pride, that they may be made the subject of plays, and they even use the manipulation of puppets as a metaphor. Then, hearing voices (which may be those of pursuers), they recite the familiar first seven words of the Lotus Sutra, saying that those are so few out of the entire 69,384 words. This morning they are in the present world, this evening in the next—and the two will become one. So they set their minds on death.

The educated people in the audience would recognize allusions. The "hollowed boat," or boat carved from a tree trunk and so devoid of physical presence within, as they will shortly be, resonates with overtones of a passage from the *Heike Monogatari. Yet even the illiterate could follow the reciter's spoken words and anguished pauses. We should probably imagine the puppets representing the lovers being brought out in the stage-aisle for jōruri that was the equivalent of the hanamichi for kabuki (see Part Five, Figure 9.) The illusion is the more moving—not just because of the skill of the reciter and puppeteers— but because the characters conceive of themselves as puppets in the causal chain that they have linked.

Such sympathetic and skillfully conveyed insight into characters rent by terrible dilemmas distinguishes Chikamatsu's art of sewamono. His sense of theater is also crucial, and when Ofusa and Tokubē compare themselves to puppets, there is a complex appropriateness in the dramatist's remarking (according to *Hozumi Ikan's Naniwa Miyage) that "the first thing to consider is the puppets." The critic who spoke of the narrow margin between truth and falsehood knew that art required both close approach to reality and an essential distance from it. In Japanese terms, his lovers headed for disaster are not star-crossed by fate but are deeply immersed in their own actions and outcomes. Given the language and thought of the time, they are caught between the ninjō of human passion that meant so much to a mercantile society that was discovering its values, and the giri or ethical duty owed those to whom one is attached: parents, wives, children, relatives, and masters. This was equally real, and it was in clash with equally immediate passion. Details apart, such conflicts provide issues for tragic situations also dealt with by Spanish, French, and English playwrights. It is the resolution by suicide that is less familiar (although the Stoics would have understood it). The lovers caught between giri and ninjō flee to the place of their death, and for such movements Chikamatsu adapts from nō and prose writing the michiyuki, such as we have seen in Shinjū Kasane Izutsu. The complex poetic texture of such passages elevates the act the lovers go to perform, and the Japanese attitude toward suicide also dignifies the deaths.

For centuries, distraught lovers had died by their own actions or hand. Women, especially, took their lives by drowning (cf. Ukifune in the *Genji Monogatari—by no means the first to try). Significantly, many shinjū occur by bodies of water. Two things color the last act. One is the Japanese sense that, whatever the countering ethical claims, whatever the faults of those overcome by passion, taking one's life demontrates a purging, a serenity and purity of motive, entitling such people in extremity to the course they have taken. Chikamatsu also adds strong Buddhist overtones. Moreover, the lives of the urban class under the heavy hand of the military authorities shared not a little with the doom met by so many during the preceding period of civil strife, so that the same invocation of the Buddha's name as one faced death might raise ordinary people—in their eyes, at least—to the level of the dying warriors in the great military tales. In all likelihood, the Buddhist element is Chikamatsu's own way of giving his fragile people a heroism that they recognized and valued, even if it was as rare in their own crises as it had actually been for the warriors, whatever the military tales may say. Since some Greek tragedies end with good fortune and celebration (including the sole extant trilogy, the *Oresteia*), discussion is not much advanced by saying that Jihē and Koharu are too common to be the stuff of true tragedy, or that Buddhism deprives them (and the audience) of the purgation of suffering. Of course, any critic may quibble over the epic stature of the *Heike Monogatari* or the tragic stature of Chikamatsu's shinjū plays. But a better contrast to his art will be found in those Edo kabuki that involve happy endings from forgiving parents, relenting villains, and sudden acquisitions of money to buy the woman out of her bond. Chikamatsu's stories are made of sterner stuff, and his audiences recognized them as dignified versions of their own lives, including degrees of suffering from which they hoped themselves to be free.

Since the present bunraku versions of jōruri represent a rare conservation of a valued theater, complaints are not really justified. But it is a matter of regret that the existing repertoire so steadfastly ignores Chikamatsu in favor of, for example, the no doubt affecting but still less ennobling plays such as *Tsubosaka Reigenki*, in which the blind Sawaichi climactically receives his sight by the intercession of Kannon.

There are certain other residual paradoxes attendant on Chikamatsu's career. He wrote more than 140 plays that are known. Of these, two dozen or so are *kabukikyōgen*. The remaining consist of jōruri. Although about five-sixths of these consist of jidaimono, his finest plays are the sewamono. Its art declined after his death, and the government seems to have felt them dangerous—at least, after an investigation in 1722, shinjū plays were proscribed. (Perhaps that explains the happy endings in Edo kabuki versions.)

It bears emphasizing that Chikamatsu found the locus of suffering in the lives of his contemporaries. This is a very rare thing. In traditional Western drama, comedy deals with the sewamono subjects, and tragedy is distanced in time and usually in place. It is as if Sophocles', Shakespeare's, or Racine's tragedies were set in Athens, London, and Paris in times contemporary with their own. The situation is so exceptional as to require some explanation. If the requirement is clearer than the answer, one likely explanation can be found in the highly narrative character of jōruri. The centrality of the reciter's account provides the "presence," whereas the puppets—remarkable as their handling is—allows for a distance such as time and place or narrative provide in the West. We may recall that after the decline in English drama during the early eighteenth century, Samuel Richardson's masterpiece, his novel *Clarissa Harlowe*, offered English readers a kind of tragedy in narrative that dealt with characters like Chikamatsu's.

Such elements—his sense of theater, his creation of a language that suited and dignified his characters, theaters, and the characters so well—attest to the genius of Chikamatsu. If *Zeami and Bashō wrote in substantially the main line of Japanese literary assumptions, Chikamatsu's achievement was to bring the treatment of a quite different kind of human life into recognizable parity.

Jōruri and kabuki naturally had somewhat different emphases, even in such a kind as jidaimono. Jidaimono leant themselves to depiction of warriors' lives. Such subjects resemble the *gunkimono* or monogatari, and the treatment of daimyo houses was recognized as a distinct kind, *oiemono*. There was also a popular kind in kabuki, the *keiseimono*, plays about beautiful courtesans. These types could be combined, especially by use of a male character dear to kamigata theatergoers, the *yatsushigata*. A yatsushi is usually a daimyo's son beset by problems of his own making—in familiar versions he is reduced by a socially disgraceful love to a wretched condition and appearance. Roles such as this fostered, or were fostered by, the acting style favored in kamigata and developed by Chikamatsu's collaboration with Sakata Tōjūrō. This style was termed *nuregoto*, amorous and pathetic playing, as opposed to the *aragoto* exemplified in Edo—above all by the innovative style of the prominent Edo actor, *Ichikawa Danjūrō (1660–1704), a style of "rough business," more spectacular than sensitive. It is significant that when Danjūrō, consummate actor that he was, played in Kyoto and Osaka, he left behind the aragoto style for which he was so justly famous.

Such professional matters, such practical judgment, are what enable theaters to prosper, whatever literary critics may choose to prefer between one style and another, one issue and another. In the same practical terms, one hit would lead to a sequel or to plays closely modeled on it. When something became popular in jōruri, it was soon translated to the actor's medium of kabuki. As one illustration from many may show, kabuki adapted to its own stage a version of *Sambasō* from jōruri. In the kabuki, *Ayatsuri Sambasō*, or "puppet sambasō," the playing by actors represents that of puppets with exquisite effect. The example is the more pointed because this particular play derives from nō. Yet the main genius of kabuki lay in its basic difference from jōruri: its use of actors. Kabuki is fundamentally more dramatic, or at least less narrative, than jōruri and nō. The aragoto of Danjūrō easily exploited the possibility of movement by a human actor, so that the estrangement and engagement played upon by all literature, but particularly in the theater, naturally dwelt upon the actor in kabuki. Finally, jōruri was limited by the number of characters that could be represented by puppets on its small stage. Kabuki could bring a dozen into play at once without strain, even on the smaller stages of former times (see Part Five). In the place of the purity and dignity that jōruri possesses, kabuki has a wonderful energy, a vitality that can be squandered, rehoarded, and squandered yet again. It can introduce child actors to contrast with adult, and such actions as suicide take on a different quality with live actors. No praise of jōruri or of Chikamatsu—or of Zeami—must be allowed to obscure the genius of kabuki with its live and gifted actors.

Yet it also remains true that in these times dramatic and other literary genius was dominated by the kamigata theaters. In particular, a literary account must consider that the best playwrights were to be found in Kyoto and Osaka. It is appropriate, therefore, to conclude with another kamigata playwright, *Ki no Kaion (1663–1742), not a Chikamatsu, either as to productivity or quality, but the author of some fifty jōruri for the Toyotakeza in Osaka, some of which are worthy of comparison with plays by his elder contemporary.

Born into a family operating a sweets shop in Osaka, Kaion was fortunate in having relatives with literary interests. His father and an uncle were adherents of *Teimon haikai*, and a brother was a *kyōka* poet. Upon inheriting the business, he retired and devoted the rest of his life to literature, including haikai, kyōka, and jōruri. About 1704 he had become an author in the Toyotakeza. There he began his rise as an author, working in competition with Chikamatsu, who wrote for the rival Takemotoza.

Kaion's fifty plays include both jidaimono and sewamono. By comparison with Chikamatsu, he used a style somewhat abstracted and stiff, but he was a real craftsman. One of his most admired plays is a sewamono and shinjū piece, (*Osome Hisamatsu*) *Tamoto no Shirashibori* (1711). As Hisamatsu tells Osome he is dying, she wakes from her reverie, to raise the tension higher: "I thought that I had already died for love in a brief dream." Like Desdemona, she revives with more to say. She invokes the divinities and the Buddha, recalls their pledge to love through the next existences, and worries over their parents' stern refusal to forgive them. Such extension of her words (or thoughts) make her the center of the scene. At last she takes out her sharp, daggerlike scissors, cuts her hair (as if taking vows), and stabs herself. The narrator ends by distancing the action: the story of the lovers goes to every province, he says, with the casks of oil from Hisamatsu's Aburaya; it is the common topic. Such interplay between the plot and the contemporary scene known to the audience is a favorite kind of allusion in many dramatic traditions, and it well represents the concern of the townspeople with their own existence in terms that differed from those of waka, monogatari, and nō. The concern is a genuine one in the Edo period, and we discover various versions of it in the writings of Saikaku, who must now concern us as a master of prose narrative rather than as a mass-producer of haikai.

Bashō spoke to the soul of the age and Chikamatsu to its heart. The more nervous Saikaku, almost an exact contemporary of Bashō, neglected neither but summoned the physical and material vitality of the times in its bravado and fears, its aspirations and failures, its quotidian existence and its hopes that life should hold more than it seems to offer. His daunting energy and his quick, piercing intelligence perfectly suited that unusual, but most human, Genroku combination of sometimes naughty brilliance and down-to-earth practicality that represents no small part of the lives of all of us who are imperfectly human. He and Rabelais are not unlike, and if the French writer was more learned, Saikaku held closer converse with a less pedantic experience of life. He also shows, if showing were necessary, that these times were not solely those of high seriousness. We owe to Saikaku the solace, or safety, that laughter and wit confer on us.

Born into an Osaka chōnin household, Ihara Saikaku wrote haikai from the time he was fifteen. When fame was slow to come by ordinary measures, he engaged in those mammoth sole productions that have been mentioned. One deserves some mention, for although most have been gathering dust since his time, one hundred-stanza sequence (*hyakuin*) is now in print. This is the eighth of sixteen such sequences he composed: a mere four thousand lines that he wrote during one day and night in the third month of 1677. If the title is descriptive enough—*Haikai Ōkukazu* ("A Great Number of Haikai Stanzas")—the sequence is also surprisingly interesting. He observes the obvious haikai rules with due consistency but without mechanical regularity. It is a genuine sequence, although its one failure is telling. His rapid composition led to insufficient variety of degrees of impressiveness and of closeness in stanzaic connection. The result is too great uniformity, too little sense of the sequence as a dynamic unit. Yet there are other qualities that shine through—a narrative emphasis along with a Danrin allusiveness and a characteristic alertness to what was transpiring about him. Such qualities colored his subsequent writing in ways at once evident and subtle.

He was very much one of the principal writers of the time who, without intruding in the manner of a Fielding or Tolstoy, yet gave all he wrote the sign of a single dyer's hand. This is to say that he cultivated his own personality as writer as much as he studied his contemporaries with a quick, penetrating eye. These abilities draw the reader's attention to the story, to the author, and the bond felt with both while reading. Although such qualities seemed to be produced with seemingly effortless mastery, they were accompanied by such heightening that he seemed exotic to his contemporaries, who bestowed on him the nickname of Oranda Saikaku, Saikaku the Hollander. Which is to say in one phrase that he was a consummate if heightened stylist, so up-to-date as almost to be exotic to his contemporaries.

If Saikaku had died at thirty-nine, he would not be much read today. His claim on us derives from his shift of career at that time (like Bashō at a yet later age) to a quite different field. In the next eleven years he brought forth an astonishing number of works, chiefly of the kind known as *ukiyozōshi*. (See Part Four, *sōshi*.) "Ukiyo" has a wide range of associations that grew from the Buddhist sense of this insubstantial world of sorrows. Saikaku's sense implies more particularly what belongs to the present, the varying manifestations of fleeting life in his own times—and what he was to immortalize as *kōshoku*, the human passion of sexual love. In six years, 1682–1687, he produced six works on his chosen purview, which may be set forth with some of the rapidity of his composition: 1. *Kōshoku Ichidai Otoko*, 1682; 2. *Shoen Ōkagami* (or *Kōshoku Nidai Otoko*), 1684; 3. *Wankyū Issei no Monogatari*, 1685; 4. *Kōshoku Gonin Onna*, 1686; 5. *Kōshoku Ichidai Onna*, 1686; 6. *Nanshoku Ōkagami*, 1687. This list is not exhaustive, and probably it will never be known for certain which works attributed to him should be included in his canon. But he and his fellow townspeople knew that the race does not live by love alone, that money must also be had. The list must, then, be extended to two further important works: *Nihon Eitaigura*, 1688; and *Seken .Mune San'yō*, 1692.

The rich style of the kōshoku series might be poised in a set exercise with

Chikamatsu's, since they share such common elements as michiyuki. For if Saikaku's haikai have narrative elements, his prose often turns lyric. The specific cast of his writing would probably have been thought libertine by Chikamatsu, not to mention Zeami, but the elements are not alien to their own art. Saikaku also cultivated features of earlier narrative. His story of a man who devotes his life to love (*Kōshoku Ichidai Otoko*, thought by many his masterpiece) evokes the *Ise Monogatari* and *Genji Monogatari*, those prose works drawn on by writers of waka, nō, renga, and haikai. *Kōshoku Ichidai Onna* draws in similar fashion on old kinds of fiction, particularly on *setsuwa* and diary literature, not to mention poetry by impassioned poets such as *Ono no Komachi. It is particularly telling, although Japanese critics make little of it that, unlike Bashō and Chikamatsu, he draws on Heian prose narrative, ignoring the great military tales. To him and his readers, the struggles of life and death occurred on fields other than those of battle. Men and women in a nearer world were his proper subject.

Saikaku does not totally ignore religion. References to shrines, temples, and ritual observances abound in his writings. Priests are as much a part of his ukiyo as are his lovers, and in fact appear among the laity as lovers, especially in his gallery of male homosexual characters in *Nanshoku Ōkagami*. Yet any given kind of character, apart from the one at the narrative center, is part of the so-to-speak human scenery. When he stressed the conflicts induced by Neoconfucianism between giri and ninjō, he found ample field in exploring the possibilities and hindrances of human love (and making a livelihood). His characters search for a liberty that others might think licentiousness or avaricious. Saikaku knew the audience for which he wrote—and no little of the hearts of those who have read him since, whether such people have given free consent to his stories, have clucked their tongues in disapproval, or have regarded humanity with his own mixture of awe and dry-eyed bemusement.

Yonosuke, the hero of *Ichidai Otoko* (the familiar title), must have given Saikaku's fellow townsmen a certain voyeuristic thrill through the stages of his life devoted to sexual pleasure. Precocious in such matters, like the other men and women devoted to love (or for that matter like the Radiant Genji), Yonosuke must project some kind of male fantasy, and in particular the chōnin's desire to find in sex more power over his world than the authorities in Edo actually allowed. We may ask in terms of fundamental human reality what kind of human power sexual prowess commands by comparison to those who truly govern or truly love? Some critics would think that such a question makes heavy weather of the light-heartedness of a great stylist. But it seems better to some readers to take an author seriously—chic, and wit, and all—following him where his exploration of kōshoku took him. There is no need to suspend common humanity because we pick up a book.

At the end of *Ichidai Otoko*, our now somewhat frazzled playboy has a ship loaded with food, drink, and aphrodisiacs for a rumored Isle of Women. Nothing in the work better suggests the underlying male fantasy. Nothing else shows so tellingly that the townsmen were restricted by the sword-carrying government in Edo from doing much else than make money or love. In the licensed quarters they (not the women there) might find a gilded cage of freedom available nowhere else. The sexual freedom Saikaku allows on such and similar terms gave them imaginary release from bonds they knew to be all too real.

Such an implied darker world becomes more explicit in *Nidai Otoko*. We may let Yonosuke sail off to imagined bliss, but if this later work is made up from leftover materials, as is commonly thought, the residuum has the fantasy stripped away. Women in the licensed quarters, rather than a swashbuckling hero, become the center of attention. To them, immured in their houses, and to the men who visit them, money is a serious issue. Sexual relations imply fetters rather than freedom, a subservience rather than power. This more tragic view of love bordered reality more closely, their lives and death being beneath the notice of the government. In finery or in rags, the women sold into prostitution were basically powerless, and their efforts to achieve individuality are shown to lead to disaster. Buddhist hopes of the kind Chikamatsu saw even in suicide are not considered. Social restraints overpower ordinary female and general human desires.

Saikaku's stories of kōshoku after *Ichidai Otoko* lack the brilliant panache of that work. So much said, it is possible to enter a minority judgment that *Ichidai Onna* and *Gonin Onna* excel in combining such brilliance with the bitter after-taste of *Nidai Otoko*. (This account has at least the virtue of explaining Saikaku's career.) The stories about women deal with the same human passion but remind us of the truer human experience that pleasures are fleeting, that enjoyments are small, and that both have their price, in experience as well as in coin. The later stories catch fire as they deal with lovers in the toils that ruin them, or as the exigencies of age make sexual satisfaction more arduous. After these stories of women, the stories of male homosexuality in *Nanshoku Ōkagami* have a routine character like the catalogue of Don Giovanni's amours sung by Leporello, without the grace of such music.

Both *Nihon Eitaigura* and *Seken Mune San'yō* detail the social, monetary matters of Genroku life so well that they are mines of information to the cultural historian. The former shows how people may make money in a competitive world, the latter how lesser people suffer as debts fall due at year's end. *Nippon Eitaigura* is something of the fiscal equivalent of the sexually possible in *Ichidai Otoko*. *Seken Mune San'yō* offers a counterpart—in its fundamentally anonymous, disparate characters—of the women in bond to the no doubt prosperous owners of the licensed houses.

If we take Saikaku's wit, humor, and daydreams with such seriousness—some might say solemnity—then he seems to have a genuine importance not fully allowable to his contemporaries practicing prose fiction, important as they are. This will be clear from consideration of one of his most gifted fellow authors.

*Ejima Kiseki (1666–1735) was the fourth-generation head of a well known Kyoto shop who tended more to ukiyozōshi than to merchandise. Having served apprenticeship of a kind in jōruri (ca. 1685 ff.), he published a book on actors and then, in 1691, a more important book, *Keisei Irojamisen*. Both were brought out by the important Kyoto publishing house, Hachimonjiya. This work of 1691 treats famous women (keisei) of the licensed quarters in a fashion more reportorial than Saikaku's fictions. *Eisei Kintanki* (1711) continued the handbook vein, treating the customs of lower orders of prostitutes in Shimabara, Shimmachi, Yoshiwara, and so on. It seeks to imitate something of Saikaku's gold and gilt, even as later writers borrowed from it. He subsequently produced a series of books to which he gave a generic title that stuck—*katagimono*. These are accounts of people of a lower social order than himself. Such works include *Seken Musuko Katagi* and *Seken Musume Katagi* (both 1717). The titles inevitably recall Saikaku, but Kiseki deals less with individuals than with a thematic view of their ordinary lives. A few years before (1706), he had brought out *Fūryū Kyokujamisen*, which uses a plot such as might be found in a jōruri or kabuki. From 1711 to 1716, he returned to such writing, gradually declining into narrative adaptation of various plays. He is no Saikaku, but his middle way between reportage and fiction had immense influence on later writers, both in kamigata and Edo.

The flowering attributed to this period involves in part the distinction of the authors mentioned and in part the promise of things to come. It also implies a limitation. When we leave behind the great figures and consider others worthy of mentioning with them, we are left with few writers in any way comparable. It is as though the literary topography is one of mountains and plains, with little between. We may mention with Bashō such poets as *Bonchō, *Kikaku, and *Kyorai, but such another member of the Bashō school as Morikawa Kyoriku (1665–1731) is a lightweight by comparison. In fiction, *Asai Ryōi (d. 1691) does have somewhat greater prominence as a writer of *kanazōshi*, but he is likely to be mentioned most importantly in literary histories for a didactic piece, *Inu Hariko* (1692). If we look beyond to the likes of *Nishizawa Ippū (1665–1731), we find a writer who made his wares of the great, and not so great, leavings of others—a writer able enough but not transcendent.

Something must also be said about the largely intractable, or untranslatable, comic verse of the time. If it is a limitation of Western epics that the humorous is too little appreciated, the same limitation holds for Asian lyricism. *Jōruri* and *kabuki*, like English drama, are rather exceptional in their inclusion of comic elements in serious plays. Much of the world's serious literature avoids the humorous, antiseptically relegating it into genres that may be looked down upon by sober critics. Waka and *ushin renga* disdain the humorous, but with their strong sense of decorum, Japanese have had a lively sense of incongruity. The *Genji Monogatari* has a capaciousness that allows for wit and humor, and this tendency becomes stronger in the Edo period.

The sense of the nonstandard or faintly incongruous can be found in the haikai no uta to be found in the first ordered collection, the *Kokinshū* (ca. 905), and Ki no Tsurayuki, the major compiler of that collection, included comic episodes in his *Tosa Nikki*. Yet it remained for linked poetry to offer a major alternative to the seriousness of waka. Early renga—of the twelfth century—was the grandfather of comic verse in the Edo period. As renga developed into a serious art with the sober assistance of poets like Nijō Yoshimoto, another more playful variant developed in haikai no renga, or haikai. Haikai walks a difficult path, one foot in the earnest and straight path of waka and renga, the other in the lower, dusty byways of quotidian and often wry territory that was to become the world of *senryū*. Such a stanza as this could well appear in a haikai sequence:

Higanoko no	Her scarlet undersash
shigoki de neko no	is what she uses to prevent
koi o seki.	her cat's night of love.

We are to imagine a young woman tying down her female cat, who wishes to join her toms for a night of caterwauling. More than that, the poem enables us to see into the frustrated love life of the woman herself. Quite possibly Matsuo Bashō, certainly *Enomoto Kikaku, could have written such a stanza for a haikai sequence.

It is customary to typify a wide range of Edo comic and satiric verse under the name of senryū. It is more accurate historically to say that there were a number of popular, briefer offshoots of haikai, and that they are sufficiently various as to deserve well the name of miscellaneous or irregular haikai: *zappai*. Bashō would have none of this to him debasing of high art (*fūga*). The *Danrin* and *Teimon* masters saw a financial opportunity in the continuingly popular verse pastimes and so joined other popular judges (*tenja*) in setting topics or stanzas for joined stanzas (*tsukeku*). The most famous of the many judges was *Karai (Hachie-mon) Senryū (1718–90), whose pen name has come to replace *maekuzuke* as a generic name and in fact to name a variety of distinct phenomena. In maeku-zuke, a foundation stanza (*maeku*) could be set by a judge either in the 5-7-5 syllable form or, more commonly, in the 7-7-syllable form. To one of these or to a poetic topic aspirants competed in writing joined stanzas. Although the popu-larity of these pastimes was widespread, they flourished chiefly in Edo, where there were usually about twenty outstanding judges.

Like his predecessors and contemporaries, Senryū held annual competitions for tsukeku on the scale of 10,000, producing mankuawase, which in his case became known as *Senryū Hyō Manku Awase* (*A Ten Thousand-Stanza Competi-tion Judged by Senryū*). It is said that he went through 2,300,000 stanzas, selecting but 3 percent for his annual collection, *Haifū Yanagidaru*. These appeared first in the 1760s but continued long after his death—into the nine-teenth century. During a period of seventy-five years when maekuzuke was popular, a hundred and sixty such collections appeared, almost two a year.

Senryū's predecessor, *Kei Kiitsu (1694–1761) and some others set the hokku-like 5-7-5-syllable stanza as the foundation stanza. The best known of the collections to include maekuzuke of this kind is *Mutamagawa*, compiled by Kiitsu and others (printed 1774). It will be seen that in setting a 7-7 syllable foundation stanza, Senryū and most judges elicited joined stanzas in the 5-7-5 syllable, hokku-like form. And by dropping the foundation stanza in printing stanzas selected from competitions, Senryū reproduced thousands of poems that look like hokku or *haiku*. Witty, pungent verse in that form is what senryū has come to mean, even if historically matters are greatly more complex.

There were many collections, as we have seen. Some had simple, easily translatable titles such as *Sakura no Mi* (*Cherries*, 1767). Some involved literary allusions of an easy kind, as with the collection whose title is the name of the comic, red-nosed lady in the *Genji Monogatari—Suetsumuhana* (1776–1801). Other titles defy translation by their use of typically Edo play on words and characters, as with *Kawazoi Yanagi* (1774–1783) and *Hako Yanagi* (1783; the meaning of *The Boxed Willow* implied by the sound "hako" is contradicted by the use of two different characters substituted for "hako" as "box"). The willow image recurs in this writing because the pen name "Senryū" is a Sinified pronunciation of "Kawayanagi," "River Willow." The most important collection after *Haifū Yanagidaru* was *Haifū Yanagidaru Shūi*. The "gleanings" ("shūi") of the title recalls the third royal collection of waka, the *Shūishū*, and so also to a point does its arrangement. Like two of the royal collections, *Haifū Yanagidaru Shūi* is divided into ten parts. But the compilers set about to establish a non-traditional kind of order for the parts, working on the principle of haikai change (*haikaika*)—that is, the collection is organized chronologically. It is remarkable that this principle, so steadily rejected in the serious poetic collections of Japan, should be honored in this compilation.

It is usually held that senryū degenerated as time wore on, much as sentimentality, the gothic, or the pornographic does in a striving for effect. Later examples often went under the name of *kyōku*, wild or mad stanzas (in counterpart to kyōka, the waka version also popular). As the term "kyōku" implies, the sense of linking remained, much as with the serious hokku that were often anthologized, looking like modern haiku but always having some presumption of potential or actual linking.

Some senryū are mild enough, and simply tell us of our human ways.

Ko o motte	Carrying his child
kinjo no inu no	he memorizes all the names
na o oboe.	of neighborhood dogs.

The father proudly walks about, carrying his first child on fine evenings, and to amuse his young son learns things about their neighborhood that he had never known, in order to impart some paternal lore. Senryū also takes an unblinking look into the seamier side of life.

Tenugui de	With his hand towel
hataite zegen	the whore-buyer dusts off a place
koshi o kake.	and sits down to business.

The only fastidiousness this sordid panderer shows involves using the towel (which commoners often carried) to wipe off a dirty place. Then he turns to the parent or the young woman he is to deal with over terms on buying a young woman into prostitution.

Such examples show the fine observation of human foibles, the kinship with proverbs, and the businesslike assessment of human life that this kind of epigrammatic verse specializes in. But senryū reveals much more. It provides a mine of information about human quirks in a threadbare existence such as most of us fear to know. In this respect, it tells us a great deal about everyday Japanese life (especially in Edo) that we could not learn from other sources. Unfortunately, the other sources are often necessary for us to make sense of senryū, which are harder than other kinds of Japanese verse for the student to understand. Something of the feudal character of life in the Edo period is also implied by senryū: it is as if the mentality of the age required that wit and comedy, at least in verse, be institutionalized, as everything else was. The various anthologies made in Edo testify to such compartmentalizing.

The counterparts in prose of such writing are the *kokkeibon*, of which *Jippensha Ikku is one of the masters. But from Tsurayuki, *Sei Shōnagon, and *Murasaki Shikibu among Heian writers to Ihara Saikaku and modern novelists, we see that many of the greatest writers of prose narrative, like many of the dramatists, encompassed the sphere of comic verse within the larger, more balanced world of total human life.

In only one other area is there real quality. In scholarship we begin to see new vitality and something (if not enough) of that personal note that Sōgi had brought. *Keichū (1640–1701), like *Kigin, is still read for his commentaries, especially on the royal collections, although his now largely superseded work on the *Man'yōshū was in its time probably his most important achievement (*Man'yō Daishōki*, 1690). In addition, he wrote commentaries on numerous other classics, especially poetry, and it is extraordinary that his glosses of even the *Kokinshū* can still be read with profit today. In fact, one often gets Keichū or Kigin without knowing it in the traditional lore handed along by annotators. *Arai Hakuseki (1656–1715) was not so devoted a scholar but was more versatile. His interests ran to public affairs and poetry, as well, and in some ways he is most interesting as an autobiographer. It is perhaps odd that in a tradition as rich in semi-autobiographical writing as that of the Japanese literary and non-literary memoirs there should be relatively little in the way of (public) autobiography as it is usually considered in the West. In fact, Hakuseki is not like Pepys, but his *Oritaku Shiba no Ki* (1716) has genuine interest and a poetic ring that fits it into the Japanese tradition. More than that, this confident or advisor of a shogun could make public matters have genuine literary appeal.

Yet so great is this time at its best that we should not part from it without some sample of its true quality. Here is Bashō, about to begin the journey he wrote about for a major part of the travels in *Oku no Hosomichi*. He set out with time and death on his mind, willing to leave this world to his successors.

The months and days are the wayfarers of the centuries, and as yet another year comes round, it, too, turns traveler. Sailors whose lives float away as they labor on boats, horsemen who encounter old age as they draw the horse around once more by the bit, they also spend their days in travel and make their home in wayfaring. Over the centuries many famous men have met death on the way; and I, too, though I do not know what year it began, have long yielded to the wind like a loosened cloud and, unable to give up my wandering desires, have taken my way along the coast. Last autumn, as I cleaned the old cobwebs from my dilapidated house by the riverside, I found that the year had suddenly drawn to its close. As the sky of the new year filled with the haze of spring, I thought of going beyond the Shirakawa Barrier, and so possessed was I by some peripatetic urge that I thought I had an invitation from the god of travelers himself and so became unable to settle down to anything. I mended my underwear, re-corded my rain hat, and took three bits of moxa cautery. I could not put from my mind how lovely the moon must be at Matsushima. I disposed of my property and moved to Sampū's villa.

Kusa no to mo	My old grass hut
sumikawaru yo zo	changes with the world to new owners
hina no ie.	housing their girls' dolls.

This and the rest of the first eight stanzas of a haikai I left posted on a pillar at Sampū's place.

So off the old poet goes on a foot journey that he identifies with time, life, and death, a characteristic that the travel pieces of his great contemporaries, Chikamatsu and Saikaku, share with him.

3. *The Harvest: 1725–1829*

The century following *Chikamatsu's death is the great age of Edo literature. It is true that no single writer stands out as do the three of the seventeenth century, but there is a very large number of fine authors during the eighteenth century and into the nineteenth. It is curious that almost every important kind of classical literature was originated in kamigata rather than Edo. The only exceptions, if they are exceptions, are some kinds of prose narrative that appear during this time. But the shift from kamigata to Edo in practice is real, and it can best be shown in terms of theater.

Drama flourished in popular esteem after Chikamatsu's death—jōruri in particular, and particularly in Osaka. It is possible to name playwrights involved, and it is possible to name plays. But the growing practice of joint composition makes it difficult to match some of the most famous authors with the most famous plays. The reciter of jōruri had always had a greater importance than the playwright, and about this time reciters introduced bravura effects of great laughter and heart-rent sobs. But technology played an even greater role. The puppets on Chikamatsu's stage were more primitive than the new ones. Faces and hands could now be manipulated—eyes could be closed and rolled. Three operators were now required for each puppet, and of course the result was both that the puppeteers challenged the centrality of the reciter, and the puppets and their show became superior (or any any rate more prominent) than the literary words.

There are four or five playwrights who stand out during this period of greatest popularity for jōruri. One always mentioned is *Takeda Izumo (d. 1747), or Takeda Izumo I, since the name continued to be used. One seldom mentioned is

Matsuda Bunkōdō (fl. ca. 1720–1740), about whom little is known except by theater historians. He was, it seems, the true heir of Chikamatsu in writing plays to be heard as literature, and in avoiding exaggeration when suggestion might do. Takeda Izumo took the opposite approach and became more popular by introducing sudden twists, stage coups, and lavish costumes. Some of his plays (if they really are all by him) have been regarded highly. But he and Bunkōdō were outshone by *Takeda Izumo II (1691–1756).

"Little Izumo" turns out to be large in more than one sense. For one thing, the plays associated with him include a number of the most popular in jōruri and kabuki. For another, "he" consists of himself and collaborators or assistants. The plays include: *Natsumatsuri Naniwa Kagami* (1745), *Sugawara Denju Tenarai Kagami*—called by most people *Terakoya* after the temple-school scene in the fourth act (1746); (*Yoshitsune*) *Sembonzakura* (1747); and (*Kanadehon*) *Chūshingura* (1748), the story of the revenge by the forty-seven masterless samurai. The last three are all-time favorites, equaled in popularity by only a few others. And yet the house of Little Izumo produced these three enduring hits, one a year.

The story behind *Chūshingura* was a historical event that occurred early in the century but that was set—to avoid problems with the censors—in the fourteenth century. Chikamatsu and *Ki no Kaion wrote their versions, along with versions by others. But the *Chūshingura* that really took hold and that provided the basis for subsequent versions is the one by Little Izumo and his associates.

The two Izumos had a wholesome rival in *Namiki Sōsuke (1695–1752). He had gone to Edo for a time, but returned to Osaka, where he wrote some kabuki as well as jōruri. The dates of his versions of *Chūshingura* (1741) and *Sembonzakura* (1747) well show how close was the rivalry. He fell ill while completing another *jidaimono*, surely his masterpiece—*Ichinotani Futaba Gunki* (1751). This is the story familiar to modern kabuki-goers (from one episode) as *Kumagai Jin'ya*. A description will show how sudden, unexpected shifts were introduced into the jōruri of this time, how far the art had changed since Chikamatsu. The familiar versions of the story of Kumagai and Atsumori are found in the *Heike Monogatari* and the nō, *Atsumori*. In earlier versions, Kumagai Naozane is charged to try to find and slay Taira Atsumori, which he does, although touched with sadness and remorse when he discovers the youth of his opponent and the precious flute the lad carried, in a way representing Taira courtliness. The version by Namiki Sōsuke (probably a corporate name also) must have stunned the rapt audience. When Kumagai comes in for a ritual showing of the boy's head, witnesses at the kubi jikken discover with astonishment and horror that Kumagai has substituted his own son as victim, saving Atsumori out of an old debt to the mother. Once the thrilled audience understood that, they were jolted again as the puppet playing Kumagai strips himself of his armor to reveal the priest's robes in which he will spend the rest of his days in order to pray for his son and release himself from evil by rites and austerities.

Osaka jōruri was beset from the mid-eighteenth century by deaths of leading figures, fires, and competition. One important figure distinguished its last days, when most jōruri playwrights were willing to do almost anything to get an audience. This was *Chikamatsu Hanji (1725–1783), a student of the "Little Izumo" and an admirer of Chikamatsu, whose writing name he adopted (the "Hanji" modestly says he is but half a second). He was also the son of Chikamatsu's friend, *Hozumi Ikan, recorder of the dramatist's invaluable remarks on art in *Naniwa Miyage*. Hanji used his inheritance well during the last fifteen years or so of his life. He is known for his skill in *sewamono*, a sure sign of his Osaka and Chikamatsu connections, among them especially *Shimpan Utazaimon* (1780) and *Igagoe Dōchū Sugoroku* (1783). His most famous play is, however, a jidaimono, *Imoseyama Onna Teikin* (1771), which proved to be his great hit and, some think, his masterpiece. It is easy to observe signs of change in Hanji's art, although in him jōruri had a fine dramatist, far finer than its audiences, reciters, and puppeteers deserved. Nevertheless, *Igagoe Dōchū Sugoroku* is adapted from a kabuki. That meant nothing in contemporary terms of authorship, but the significant fact is that a jōruri dramatist now found it necessary to draw on kabuki instead of the reverse. It is also mentioned in accounts of Hanji that the categories of jidaimono and sewamono were beginning to merge. Certainly the tendency became strong in kabuki, thence spilling over into prose narrative, as we shall see with *Tamenaga Shunsui. But even Chikamatsu had experimented with mingling of the two kinds.

Just as Osaka did not immediately cease to produce plays, so had much been going on in Edo. One of the more gifted kabuki dramatists was *Sakurada Jisuke (1734–1806). By 1772, he had written one of his best-received plays, *Gohiiki Kanjinchō*, and shortly thereafter completed two others highly regarded: *Date Kurabe Okuni Kabuki* (1778) and *Keisei Azuma Kagami* (1788).

Theater historians are given, however, to treating *Namiki Gohei (1747–1808) as the pivotal and crucial figure. This is because he seems to represent a cultural shift by moving from Osaka to Edo in 1796. The play that brought him most success was *Godairiki Koi no Fūjime*, written and performed in Osaka (1794), and it is not difficult to see why he took Edo by storm when he took it to the east. He had mastered the tricks of Osaka jōruri and kabuki so that he could either make them combine to strong effect, or make them yield something startling or even contrary to the end for which they had been designed. Some of his special effects caused such uproar in the theaters that the authorities closed the playhouses. His combination of mastery with decadence is inescapable. In *Kanjin Kammon Tekuda no Hajimari* (1789), for example, he plays with the conventions of jidaimono, giving the audience the highly sophisticated satisfaction of contemplating a play whose title alludes to contemporary events *not* treated in the play, a play in which the outcome is disregarded, no character is allowed to make a claim on our respect or affection, and there is a character who makes love with a corpse. This corresponds to certain kinds of late twentieth-century literary art in Japan and the West. But some of us prefer Chikamatsu.

In 1800 the Bunrakuza was established in Osaka. That represented a version of the familiar Japanese institutionalizing of a no longer creative but still respected art. In the Western theatrical metaphor, the curtain had come down on jōruri—even as it was being raised on *bunraku*. The fortunes of the theater were different in Edo, where Namiki Gohei was followed by one of the most authentic but strangest of Japanese dramatists.

*Tsuruya Namboku (1755–1825) had the Edo taste for the startling, finely tuning his macabre plots to the best abilities of the actors. Gore, perversion, and derision of the very conventions he uses characterize his art—or rather partly characterize it. The other part shows a clear mastery of dialogue, action, plot, and indeed of all that can be expected of someone writing plays. He wrote a hundred or more full-length plays, although he started on his own only after the turn of the century. These plays would take a whole day to perform, and although it is true that he wrote with help, it is also true that there is no mistaking his brilliant and lurid art.

One of two plays must be his masterpiece. The one usually so claimed is *Tōkaidō Yotsuya Kaidan* (1825), which may be classed as a sewamono, but in reality should be thought of, as its title shows, as a ghost story, *kaidan*. The various well-turned scenes of the play have continued to thrill houses. Yet throughout the work the scenes are all in a sense variants on, or related to, the central scene, in which the *onnagata* playing the woman Oiwa feigns taking poison and mimes the ghastly contortions of her pain.

A very strong case has been made for the superiority of another play, *Sakurahime Azuma Bunshō* (1817), whose various macabre effects can scarcely be represented in brief. But all the characters, including the Lady Sakura of the title, are shown in steady, spectacular degeneration. The erotics, blood, and various kinds of corruption are played out in the *oiemono* version of jidaimono with a cynical intelligence and a feverish imagination that are remarkable. Whichever of these works we take to be Namboku's masterpiece, with them we come to the end of this harvest time of the Edo period in drama, finishing with a total mastery of outworn conventions and a theater shimmering with gilt before it collapses.

The course of development in poetry runs differently, with far less of the lurid. But again there were some major figures, if not as many as will require consideration for their prose writing. After *Bashō traveled through his dreams to the next world, waka, *kyōka*, and song continued with some of the energy of the drama. But like prose fiction, new poetry of true importance does not appear till the middle of the eighteenth century. In fact, poetry lags. The greatest poet of the time, *Yosa (or Taniguchi) Buson (1716–1783) was devoting himself chiefly to painting from 1755 to 1765. He practiced the style known as *bunjinga*, literati style. As well as such painting, inspired by Chinese example, he wrote a considerable amount of Chinese verse, either in connection with painting or separately. By 1762, however, he had become the chief Yahantei poet. With his remarkable versatility, he had been able to dominate every haikai school with which he chose to associate himself, however briefly. By 1768–1769 he developed a distinct style of his own and had coined the motto, "Return to Bashō!" The Bashō he praised was one with a "dark shudder," which matches with the mature writing of his predecessor, but the collections Buson used as examples were the earlier ones, which do not have such a somber key. If one may guess what this means, Buson knew he was the best poet of his time (he wrote very much the same himself) and that the call to return to Bashō was a cry for excellence, not for a simple renewal of older styles. Since the motto was his, it also implied that he was successor to Bashō. In fact, for the Haikai Revival (as it is called) that he brought about, as for the earlier flowering, it was to be true that the fortunes of greatness were determined by a single charismatic figure who somehow managed to bring forth from others working with him what the others could not produce by themselves.

His haikai career also resembles Bashō's in brevity. Beginning on his own terms at the end of the 1760s, he was spending much of his time painting. By 1771 he was the most famous practitioner of bunjinga. In another dozen years he was dead. After him the Haikai Revival quickly sputtered out. So Buson left behind paintings, Chinese verse, haikai sequences and a number of separate *hokku*, the last being best known and particularly appreciated by innovating modern poets.

Unlike Bashō's, Buson's career was fostered by a rare season of liberalized government. New thought, new actions, fresh experiment were possible. Under such conditions, poetry was sure to develop anew, and the sole question would be of its quality. Buson sought out a clarity of conception, richness of language, and intelligence of execution that manifested itself in wit, striking imagery, and decorous beauty. Neither the age nor his painterly instincts stirred in him the tragic involvement of Bashō. He did, of course, recognize the special genius of haikai as something between what Chikamatsu might have called the narrow margin of waka and renga on the one side and kyōka and senryū on the other. His pronouncements are not as complex as Bashō's, but they often tell us more by implying less. Here is how he described haikai:

Haikai employs low language and esteems that which departs from the low. In departing from the low, it uses the low. The right way of departing from the low is especially difficult.

Nothing could be clearer than that to anyone who has tried writing a sequence of haikai stanzas.

One of the standard critical exercises in Japan is the comparison of Buson to Bashō. The common wisdom holds that the earlier poet is more subjective, more involved in the world he observes, and the later more objective, more remote and more controlling in putting the world under his poetic sway. Numerous echoes by Buson make the comparison with Bashō the more feasible, and nobody seems able to escape making the comparison in some set of terms. Common wisdom also prefers Bashō to Buson although, as with the general preference for the *Shinkokinshū* over the *Kokinshū*, there are distinguished exceptions. What follows must be taken as but one version of many possible.

Buson of course excels Bashō as a painter and as a poet in Chinese. Bashō essentially devoted his life to haikai and *haibun*. The level of Buson's poetry is consistently high, which is quite important, for year after year he wrote more stanzas than did his predecessor. His stanzas may stand by themselves, as a very high proportion of Bashō's do not. When Buson has a bad moment, we still see what he means. When Bashō nods, we find him next to unintelligible. The earlier poet does, however, reach heights and depths of human experience denied Buson. He is also a master at combining hokku with prose in his haibun, as *Oku no Hosomichi* shows so well. Buson does not so excel, although a few words should be spared for one of his neglected works, *Shin Hanatsumi* (1797, although written twenty years before.) Obviously written in emulation of *Kikaku's *Hanatsumi*, this is a rapid composition done as a Buddhist memorial for his dead mother. In its completed version, there are ten units with pictures as well as writing. Mostly composed in a single day, it was interrupted "because of illness," and completed the next day. Buson's accounts of composition tend to be more compositions in their own right than factual records, but in any case we see a new way of combining prose with other art; the style is brilliant, witty, and very difficult. The occasion of the work reminds us that Buson encouraged his wife in haikai, and that one way or another women are again finding it possible to appear publicly as writers, although commonly they are widows who have taken orders, at least nominally.

In the end, Buson's stature as a poet depends on his haikai stanzas. Many outstanding hokku (and other stanzas) might be given here to show his excellence, and among them would be many not familiar from the anthologies. But for haikai proper, we must consider sequences rather than single gems. Near the end of his life, Buson combined with *Takai Kitō (1741–1789) to write two *kasen*, to which they gave the general title *Momosumomo*. For the thirty-six stanzas of each of the two sequences, they allowed themselves eight or nine months, instead of doing a sequence in one day in the usual fashion. Here, if anywhere, we shall find Buson's most mature, most considered poetic art. The first of the two, *Botan Chitte* (*no Maki*), is not so humorous as the second, *Fuyu Kodachi no Maki*, but it is probably even more remarkable than the latter for consistent excellence of the stanzas.

Three stanzas from *Botan Chitte* show something of Buson as haikai poet. (The seventeenth is by Kitō, the two following by Buson.)

17	Kanei aru	For a bell-casting
	hana no mitera ni	at a temple full of cherry flowers
	kami kirite	she cuts her lovely hair
18	haru no yukue no	the destined end of springtime
	nishi ni katabuku	is sunset in the Buddha's west
	Haru no yukue no	The destined end of springtime
	nishi ni katabuku	is sunset in the Buddha's west
19	Noto Dono no	Noritsune's fate
	tsuru oto kasumu	is lost in the hazed-over sound
	tōkata ni	of bow strings far away.

This subsequence is a brilliant example of a run of three spring stanzas (from "hana," "haru," "kasumu") and much else in haikai art. Stanzas seventeen and eighteen share Buddhist elements, and the sacrifice of long hair suggests an ending. Buson's sunset perfectly develops the image of the temple bell. The change in scene is usual and necessary, giving some sense of distance or lightness, but the stanza connection, *tsukeai*, is basically close, heavy.

The opposite is true of the connection between Buson's own two stanzas. The connectedness resides largely in the western reference of eighteen and the death in nineteen of the Taira general at the battle of Dannoura to the west of Edo. ("Destined" and "fate" in the translation are merely implied by the original, and other less similar sounding words might better have been employed if the degree of stanza relation were the sole thing to consider.) So here the connection is as slight as that between seventeen and eighteen is strong. Such alteration in connectedness is the soul of linked poetry, renga as well as haikai, and the example given might be taken as a textbook specimen.

Here are three other stanzas from *Botan Chitte*, with Kitō again leading off and Buson again writing two more in succession.

3	Suwabukite okina ya kado o hiraku ran	Clearing his throat the old gentleman opens the gate with a lofty air
4	muko no erabi ni kitsuru henge	while choosing a son-in-law there has come this apparition
	Muko no erabi ni kitsuru henge	While choosing a son-in-law there has come this apparition
5	toshi furishi chimata no enoki ono irete	as many years go by the town's overgrown nettle-tree submits to the axe

Some degree of connection may be wrested from these stanzas: the opening of the gate in three followed by the coming of an apparition in four, for example. But what connection there is derives solely from juxtaposition (one important technique in *tsukeai*, to be sure). Yet anyone can see that the stanzas are not closely related. In both examples given, Buson makes a very light connection between his own two stanzas, and here he does the same with his first and Kitō's. Given the lengthy period of composition and use of his own stanzas, Buson's decision can only be considered deliberate.

In his haikai marathons, *Ihara Saikaku produced stanzas so rapidly that, although he could sometimes shape them into attractive sequences, there was not enough variety or lightness in their relation. In their two sequences referred to, Buson and Kitō took so long and so emphasized individual stanzas that they went to the opposite extreme, hazarding the integrity of the sequence. It is true that in other sequences composed about this time, and in the usual time of sitting, they show themselves in full command of haikai pace and sequentiality. But there seems something ominous in their setting about so carefully to excel in two show sequences, only to lapse into the same brilliant defect exhibited long before by *Shinkei—writing outstanding stanzas that jeopardized the sequential integrity. When Shinkei performs so, it seems that the art of haikai has not yet been fully realized. When Buson and Kitō do so, it seems the art may be lost. The end of the Haikai Revival after Buson's death offers a form of praise of his importance along with some evidence for the difficulty of the art.

Not that people stopped writing haikai and other kinds of poetry. In the year of Buson's death (1783), there appeared a collection, *Manzai Kyōkashū*, compiled by that Tarō-of-all-trades, *Ōta Nampo (1747–1823). The fact that he could collect so many kyōka, or mad waka, testifies that this art had become more than a simple pastime. No doubt nonsense serves a function like that of sleep in being restorative after the ardors of work or in the midst of sober orthodoxy. Nampo himself seems to have a delightful streak of craziness, writing indifferently in Chinese or Japanese. Here, romanized and with English repetition marks is a Chinese couplet of his. The word involved (in Japanified Chinese) is the character for a bowl such as is used for eating rice.

Wan   ”   ”   ”   wan   ”   ”
   Wan   ”   ”   ”   wan

So this zany proto-dadaism goes on: "From start to finish all one hears is *wan*." This reminds us that "wan wan" is the Japanese for "bow-wow." This from a man who held, like his father, a post of authority in the government and loved Chinese poetry.

Nampo and works associated with him were deservedly popular up and down Japan. Humor testifies to detachment, an ability to regard the world and oneself with some degree of skepticism, and sometimes, at least, to new social urges along with new literary forms. Nampo also worked in prose, producing humorous books of the *kokkeibon* and *hanashibon* kinds. A collection he compiled under one of his many pen names, *Shokusan Hyakushu* (1818) follows the same spirit with kyōka, in fact constituting the single most important collection of "mad waka." Nampo's *Ichiwa Ichigen* contains works from about 1779 to 1820, many by him, and many not. They are of the *zuihitsu* variety. Given his interests, there are some combinations of Chinese and Japanese, humor and earnest, and in general this work, like its collector, was easier to enjoy than it is to classify.

The production of comic waka depends on a continuing tradition of the normal variety to make any current sense. A small number of waka poets may therefore be mentioned, partly for context, partly for the new emphases they bring. *Katō Chikage (1735–1808) was a *kokugakusha* as well as a poet. He was taught not only by his father but by *Kamo no Mabuchi. He had the satisfaction of hearing that his waka poetry was appreciated "even in Kyoto." At this time that awesome news was as much as to say that his poems were skillful but unruffled by unfamiliar words or passions.

*Ozawa Roan (1723–1801) was a better poet, one of the provincial figures who made such a mark in the intellectual world of the times. Although he lived in Kyoto for a time, his life centered in the area of present Nagoya. His roots were in Inuyama, and he settled in Okazaki. He made his name not just in waka, but also in study of Japanese literature and in Chinese studies, where he ranks with such important scholarly figures as *Rai San'yō, *Motoori Norinaga, *Ueda Akinari. For our present purposes, his study of the *Reizei line of poets holds most importance. He advocated "tadagoto no uta," or poems with exact—not over-drawn—words. Here are two of his waka:

Uzumasa no	At Uzumasa
Fukaki hayashi o	The farthest reaches of the woods
Hibikikuru	Begin to tremble
Kaze no to sugoki	As the sound of wind brings terror
Aki no yūgure.	In the fading autumn dusk.
Tsuki hitori	In the heavens
Ame ni kakarite	The only person is the moon,
Aragane no	And rich as nuggets
Tsuchi mo tōre to	The earth is also told, "Now move,"
Teru hikari kana.	By the radiance shimmering down.

Although there is undeniable straining for effect, the result proves to be some of the freshest waka composed in many a decade.

*Murata Harumi (1746–1841) deserves a sentence as a kokugakusha and waka poet, and for his poetic collection, *Kotojiri Shū*. But *Kagawa Kageki (1768–1843) deserves something more. He set out to be the best poet alive and proved more interesting for his theories. At least, being the best waka poet alive was not quite the same as being the best poet. His three central critical principles were "shirabe" or rhythm, "makoto" or forthrightness, and "sei" or actual feeling. He was decidedly free in his ways, steadfastly refusing to give his followers any rule except, "stay with the event and move with the occasion." He comes at the end of this time, and although he scandalized his contemporaries by things that seem pretty tame today, it is fair to say that the poetic revolutions of the Meiji era are anticipated by him.

After Buson (and the still little-studied Kitō deserves another mention), the two best poets are solitary figures. The Sōtō Zen monk *Ryōkan (1758–1831) and *Kobayashi Issa (1763–1827) have other reasons than their isolation to make just estimation difficult. Something of Ryōkan's life is recounted in Part Three, and is fairly clear in its outlines. The problem for study of his Japanese and Chinese poetry lies partly in the fact that his work has been recovered so recently, and partly in its nature. He was a waka poet much indebted to earlier writers—some from the *Man'yōshū*, some from the *Shinkokinshū*, and from the latter particularly *Saigyō and *Fujiwara Teika.

Ryōkan borrows a great deal indeed. But he begs, like a priest, with a difference, an independence. So many Edo waka poets make grand pronounce-ments about using fresh language and saying what they truly feel, then produce commonplace verse. Ryōkan says little about such things, but he does them. The tried—or tired—and true becomes freshly true in his execution. We cannot judge his Chinese poetry apart from the vague impression that, to some degree, it is Japanese poetry written in Chinese characters. But his Japanese work is marked by an independence of mind that is arresting. In some of his poetry, the independence seems to counter the natural stream of waka. But at his best, his poetry brings his life and observations to full realization, making them matter even to those of us coming to him for the first time with the music of the earlier waka poets humming in our ears. It will take some time before Ryōkan is adequately assessed, but even at present it is clear that this solitary figure was as original as he was isolated.

Issa is far better known, but suffers from problems made by himself and by our present ignorance. The difficulties he made involve the self-concern, stridency, and sentimentality of much of his work. But we do discover in his writing what we seldom do in poets of his time, the conviction that poetry matters because it is the best, the necessary, way to deal with most important matters. After making our dutiful way through a good deal of insipid competence among poets his contemporaries, one finds in this feverish creature someone who cared about the divinity of Sumiyoshi (whose tutelary protection of Japanese poetry had little to concern itself with at the time). Issa has a certain shortness of vision, tending to deal with himself, the young, the small. Yet there is still easily available one work of his that stands out, with Ryōkan's, in genuine eminence above other poetry between Buson and modern poets. This is *Oraga Haru* (pub. 1849), a poetic memoir of his life and thoughts in 1819. He was then fifty-six years old, past much of the stridency and defensiveness of earlier years. This work combines hokku with prose in ways that are perhaps less striking than comparable works by Matsuo Bashō and Buson. But there is equal authenticity, whether of a sense of life or of art. The most ardent admirer of Heian poetic memoirs must admit that *Oraga Haru* ranks with the finest of them. But beyond this work, there are problems of ignorance in estimating Issa: he wrote so much that is not currently in print—poetic memoirs, poetic collections, and haikai sequences. So, for reasons different from those attending on Ryōkan, sound estimation of Issa is very difficult at present.

The isolation, the separateness of Ryōkan and Issa seem to suggest that poetry had become a marginal concern in the nineteenth century or, what is much the same thing, that the institutionalized poets who claimed most respect were out of touch with Edo life. This time of harvest is a time of greatness chiefly in prose, a wider but rougher terrain than Ryōkan's hut or Issa's private garden. The genius of Edo literature under a feudal regime led to writing that could appeal to urban readers, preferably in quickly changing fashions. The best writers—apart from a Buson or Issa—knew how to swim with such fast currents, or were men of study and intellect, the scholars who emerged most impressively with learning and new insight. The learned now must be our concern before turning to writers in a bewildering variety of prose fiction.

The gradual and accumulative progress of knowledge holds only indirect importance for writers of poetry and prose fiction. Such building upon earlier knowledge and established or assumed truth is, on the other hand, crucial for scholarship. This time of harvest is therefore appropriately distinguished by a few truly important scholars. Among those already mentioned, two deserve special consideration. Something of a poet, Kamo no Mabuchi (1697–1769) was a formidable, greatly influential scholar. As early as age ten he received direction for study from Kada no Azumamaro (1669–1736), and about sixteen years later was in Kyoto with his master. He was now a poet, and shortly after his teacher's death had formed groups to study the *Hyakunin Isshu* and *Man'yōshū*. He gradually completed a series of studies of the classics that are still studied this long after. Some of these relate to the Shinto affairs hereditary in his house. Among his more recognizably literary studies there are his *Ise Monogatari Koi* (1753), *Kamakura Udaijin Kashū no Jo*, and *Genji Monogatari Shinshaku* (1758).

Mabuchi's most ambitious work centered on the *Man'yōshū*. In 1760 he brought out the first two parts of his *Man'yōkō*. Eight years later the last four parts were done. He concerned himself with topics that have continued to exercise scholars: the compilers, the times the poets lived, poetic styles, poetic changes within the times of the poets, and so on. The motivation for such dedication reflects his family heritage and is explicitly set forth in his *Kaikō* (1765). He depreciates Confucianism and Buddhism as ways of thought not properly Japanese, offering instead the nature of life he discovered in early Japan. His knowledge and Shinto emphasis combined to contribute to a debate over the nature of what is specifically Japanese and therefore over the road proper to the nation.

The eighteenth century achieved glory in Japanese studies by Mabuchi's pupil, Motoori Norinaga (1730–1801), the greatest literary scholar the nation has produced. It would have been a wise seer who could predict as much. He lost his father at ten, and at eighteen was adopted into another family, which he left in three years. He was a failure at the businesses he entered, and when he was sent to Kyoto to study medicine, he squandered on the pleasures of the town much of the money sent by his long-suffering mother. But at last he became seriously interested in kokugaku, and practiced medicine seriously to sustain his studies. He followed a punishing schedule. After a full day of medical practice, he taught his disciples in the evening. Then, after they were gone and the house was quiet, some hours were his own.

He was more prolific of important works than was Mabuchi, and his titles were catchier. One of his first important achievements was *Isonokami Sasame-goto* (1763), a poetic study involving written characters, language, comparison between Chinese and Japanese poetry, and the relation between poetry and ethics. Such novel combinations characterized him and his innovations. In 1779 he brought out *Kotoba no Tama no O*, a linguistic study chiefly based on the poetry of the *hachidaishū*. This was followed by his *Shinkokinshū Mino no Iezuto*, *Dō Orisoe* (1794) and *Kokinshū Tōkagami*, both of which are commentaries on poems in those two anthologies. But his methods differ from those of others. In dealing with the *Shinkokinshū*, he selects scores of poems, elucidating them by others drawn from various earlier commissioned anthologies, and not hesitating to express independent views. His "mirror from afar" for the *Kokinshū* clarified poems by putting them into the language of his contemporaries. Except for the few *chōka* and the Chinese preface, he rendered the whole in the language of his time.

In these same years (ca. 1790) he started one of his most influential works, *Kojikiden* (published complete posthumously in 1822). Devoting the first two parts to preliminaries, he began parts three to seventeen by elucidating the first portions of the text of the **Kojiki*. The rest was then elaborated on in similar detail with help from a student or two. Parts of it take the extraordinary step— alas, by no means common yet today—of providing systematic bibliography and index. Among the stream of studies of the classics there is a zuihitsu, *Tama Katsuma* (begun 1793, published posthumously complete after his death), which resembles the *Arabian Nights* at least in having one thousand and one parts in brief sections that include his observations. Perhaps it is not surprising that he should also deal with that rare Japanese subject, methodology, in *Uiyamabumi* (1798–1799).

His most influential work is his *Genji Monogatari Tama no Ogushi* (1793– 1796). The first and second parts are introductory, and the third gives a chronology of events in the work. That enabled him to go on to postulate bases for assessing each book with corrections of his predecessors. The fourth book corrects **Kitamura Kigin*. The fifth deals with the poems, correcting earlier annotations, offering new. The introductory part provides a view of the whole. Its section, "Shibun Yōryō," is famous for positing *mono no aware* as the thematic and tonal basis of the **Genji Monogatari*. Since Norinaga had developed this concept in *Isonokami Sasamegoto*, in positing it for the masterpiece of Japanese literature he showed that he felt that poetic power was the soul of **Murasaki Shikibu's* work. This poetic basis for mono no aware is not always given attention in comments on his interpretation of the *Genji Monogatari*, nor is the fact that he postulated mono no aware as the soul of other great works of the past, although it is well understood that he opposed this concept to what he thought was a false concept of literature as embodying a loose or coarse morality. By such means, Norinaga emphasized the affective-expressive basis of classical poetics discussed in the first section of this brief history.

His emphasis postulates a Japanese affectivism that need not concern itself with Confucian moral didacticism and yet is not immoral. The concept of mono no aware has historically come to involve two elements: that inherent, for example in autumn twilight, and that felt by a person contemplating autumn twilight. Norinaga's view includes the former, more objective, conception, but emphasizes the more subjective latter conception, since that is the experience that gives literature its directive power in our lives. His own poetry is negligible, but by such industry and such fresh methodology that yielded new insight, Norinaga has influenced the understanding by succeeding generations of many of the greatest works of classical literature. His powers of theoretical conceptualizing and of interpretation remain models—and challenges—for literary study to this day. It seems no accident that his province, Ise, has continued to nurse scholars and critics ever since.

This season of harvest is still so recent that there are important disputes over the poetry and drama written in it. The prose narrative of the time has seemed even more problematical. Some of the problems are terminological and taxonomic—there are names for kinds that flourished briefly and then were adapted into a slightly different kind with a new name. The labels and rapid metamorphoses bespeak a new literary milieu of fashion, and of efforts to push against the limits of what the government would permit. We must allow to writers such as Saikaku and Chikamatsu the creation of a popular literature. But the Edo atmosphere fostered achievement by many popular writers, often of inexpensive little books, or expensive little books, that fetched readers and were soon forgotten. This phenomenon testifies to something closer to a mass culture that was an Edo rather than kamigata phenomenon. The new developments were assisted by printing, whether from wooden blocks or, later, from movable type. But they were also the fruits of a long stable society and an enlarged readership.

Among the world's peoples with lengthy literary traditions, the Japanese are unique in their loving way of preserving the old—as the survival of waka, nō, *kyōgen*, bunraku (jōruri), and even *gagaku* show so well. At the same time, Japanese have always been concerned with being up-to-date, alive to fashion and experiment. Much of the lesser prose literature of Edo exemplifies the passionate desire to be à la mode. And yet some of its literature was didactic, produced for children or for utilitarian purposes. Principal writers combined many of these features, and gradually came to compose works of enormous length, works that seem a world apart from the chapbooks, little stories, and quickly produced tales that make up so much of Edo fiction. No easy means exists to account for this various literature, so that recourse must be taken to some at least of the terms current in Edo.

If what follows seems technical, there is the alternative historical statement such as the one that Tsuga (or Toga) Teishō (1718–1794) originated the *yomihon* ("reading book") with works like (*Kokon Kidan*) *Hanabusa Sōshi* (1749) and *Shigeshige Yawa* (1766). It will be clear that since most of us have difficulty imagining books for purposes other than reading, the technical terminology, however simplified, must be attended to.

Many of the Edo terms for prose fiction refer to physical qualities of the works involved. The most general term is, therefore, *sōshi*, which from long before had designated paper for composition (cf. *Sei Shōnagon's *Makura no Sōshi*). Sheets would be sewed together, normally after folding, to make a thin volume. These could be gathered into larger components, *kan*, which might be assembled into yet larger units, *shū*, sometimes reaching prodigious lengths in sets of shū. *Ezōshi* (or ehon) were only about four pages long and, as their names implied, were illustrated. Like a newspaper, they often dealt with events of the time. And they are also to be found in variants with colored covers such as will be mentioned shortly. Some such sōshi took on special associations. *Otogizōshi*, stories enormously varied in nature, had been written in the Muromachi period, but new works with the same name appeared in the Edo period. *Ukiyozōshi* included, as we have seen, certain kinds of stories circulating in Kamigata from about 1682, with Saikaku's *Ichidai Otoko* as a formal beginning. Chiefly about *chōnin*, they concerned human passion (*ninjō*) and many other subjects; they were popular for about a century. *Kanazōshi* emerged along with or just before ukiyozōshi (ca. 1685) but were simpler to read, as being mostly in *kana* and directed toward a more popular, less educated readership.

Perhaps the simplest way of setting forth the nature of Edo popular literature, more or less under the general rubric of *gesaku*, is to identify the kinds and dates of their appearance or flourishing. It can be seen that some are closely related, but that the terms are not necessarily parallel. The spacings group related kinds.

akahon. Red-covered books. About ten pages. Ca. 1675–1764. Mostly for children: "Shitakiri Suzume," "Momotarō," etc.

kurohon. Black-covered books. Popular ca. 1744–1751. Stage stories, etc.

aohon. Green-covered books. Ten-page units, but as many as ten units might be joined. Ca. 1745–1770. Subjects like those of kurohon.

kibyōshi. Yellow-covered books. Ca. 1770–1805. Dealt with popular matters. Unlike some earlier sōshi, these usually had pictures and even coloring.

kusazōshi. In the broad sense, colored-cover books like the several preceding, and also *gōkan*; in the narrow sense, only gōkan.

gōkan. From ca. 1790 (some say 1805). Popular fiction and romance. Tens of sōshi would be bound into volumes of some size. Often more sophisticated pictures than heretofore.

sharebon. "Smart books." Especially 1764–1788. Chiefly about the licensed quarters, its people, passions, and costumes and those of its visitors.

yomihon. "Reading books." Ca. 1750–1867. Made of five or six kan for sustained reading. Some with plots for didactic ends of a Confucian or Buddhist kind.

kokkeibon. "Humorous books," although of wider purview. Ca. 1801 ff. Well-told stories of events and people familiar to the readers.

ninjōbon. ca. 1818–1867. Books of human feeling. Dealing with Edo licensed quarters, etc., and the customs of the time.

chūbon. Middle-sized books, commonly kokkeibon and ninjōbon.

katagimono. Accounts of people mostly below the author in social class, dealing with their character and lives. Popularized by *Ejima Kiseki's *Seken Musuko Katagi* (1715).

Although this is largely an account of kinds of Edo fiction, the kamigata area yet remained strong. Many books thought typical of "Edo fiction" were in fact published by the Hachimonjiya in Kyoto, and there was steadily increased intercourse between the two areas. It may be possible to bring the various kinds just named to life by associating them with their practitioners, some of whom have appeared earlier.

*Ueda Akinari (1734–1809) transcends such purely historical interest. After Saikaku, he is today the most popular author of prose fiction of the Edo period. Like other really important classical authors, he possessed learning—of the *kokugaku* kind and of Chinese prose fiction. He managed to write both ukiyozōshi and yomihon, although the deprivations and sorrows of his early life would have sunk a lesser man. A certain kind of Westerner would be tempted to Freudianize Akinari. Let us say that he had ample reason while young to exercise his imagination over the range of possible good and evil, over the prominent and the lurid. At twenty-six he found Tama, a young peasant woman from the Kyoto area being brought up by foster parents in Osaka, and knew some measure of happiness. But he found it necessary or desirable to shift his jobs from time to time, and on one occasion lost his possessions in a fire. About the age of forty-five he became financially secure—even though it was in these years that he had to go to Kyoto to quell the rumor that he was dead! He and his wife moved to Kyoto when he was fifty-nine, and he lost her six years later. After twelve more years, after a great deal of writing, his remarkable life ended.

His masterpiece is a collection of stories, *Ugetsu Monogatari* (1768; pub. 1769). In five parts he presents nine stories, each with an air of the fantastic about it. Japanese scholars have unearthed various Chinese origins, and he may be termed a spiritual ancestor of Edgar Allan Poe and the Japanese modern, Akutagawa Ryūnosuke. The fourth story, "Kibitsu no Kama," is one of the most highly esteemed. Its plot somewhat resembles, especially in its opening, a Chikamatsu play or Saikaku story, but the workings are those of Akinari (and Chinese sources): Izawa Shōtarō had been a womanizing kind from his early years. When he betrays his trusting recent bride, Isora, she falls into illness and dies. Her unhappy spirit becomes an avenging ghost, tormenting and at last killing him. Akinari's style has never been in question, but this explanation of his importance seems as unsatisfactory for him as for Saikaku. If a story did not matter to us, we would waste time savoring style. One kind of explanation—that the story is the kind that Akinari's life led him to like—begs the question by putting it at one remove. It seems more likely that, like utopian writing (see the island of women in Saikaku), Akinari's grotesqueries offer double-edged criticism of the present, customary world, which lacks the thrill of the unusual, the threatening, the macabre. Alternatively, Akinari suggests that such things exist but are denied by the complicity of the dull and the wicked. Both these things seem to be involved, but with the other edge of the commonplace seeming much safer than that which would give it spirit in more than one sense.

On such reading, the element of grotesquerie is both a subject and a counter-subject, end and means at once. Much the same holds for parody in his *Kuse Monogatari* (1791) (perhaps also to be read *Kusemono Katari*, a kusemono being a bad, peculiar person). Here his comic tastes find expression in twenty-five short episodes closely modeled on the *Ise Monogatari*. In a style at once close to the original and yet recognizable in his own time, he translates far-off courtly romance into the world of his contemporaries, using parody to transform. The view that Akinari parodies the pretensions of the utamonogatari has considerable truth. But his stylistic fit is remarkably true, and the counter-meaning involves criticism of contemporary life for lacking the beauty, the romance of an earlier world. The weight assigned to such contrasting elements may be variously assessed, but both this work and *Ugetsu Monogatari*, different as they are, provide an integral assessment of the world Akinari knew.

In *Harusame Monogatari* (1808), he collected a number of stories into a yomihon like *Ugetsu*. These seem a distinct letdown after the excitement of the earlier work. All that is involved can scarcely be explained, but many Japanese writers turn to simpler, less perplexed styles in their last phase. Such giants of poetry as *Ki no Tsurayuki, *Fujiwara Teika, and Bashō provide but three examples. Since Akinari takes his characters very seriously in these ten stories without having established their claim on our seriousness, this work seems rather insipid. Its ideals, like those in not a few writings of the time, derive from the native emphases of kokugakusha rather than from Buddhism or Confucianism. Once again we observe that the world Akinari creates offers a criticism of his age, but the exciting counter-theme of the earlier works is lacking, and the tension is less. On the other hand, this collection, like much in the other two works, might have seemed altogether desolating were it not for the evidence of mind at play and the imagined fun.

The importance of Akinari can be conveyed by contrast. *Koikawa Haru-machi (1744–1789) was a gifted illustrator of stories by himself and others. And he had new insights to impart to gesaku. But nobody has ever thought that things mattered as seriously to him, or his readers, as Akinari's writings do. Yet in illustrations and in stories alike, he offers all, and more, that might be expected of a writer with a pen name meaning Love-River Spring-Town.

Two other writers claim much greater attention, even if neither is an Akinari, and even if we consider them out of natural chronology. These are *Santō Kyōden (1761–1816) and *Hiraga Gennai (1728–1797). Kyōden may not measure up to Leonardo da Vinci, but he seems to be one of the rare examples of a happy artist who succeeded in everything he tried. Since some think him the major writer of gesaku, he is worth dwelling upon. His real name was Iwase Sei (apart from other given names as a boy). As Kyōden, he wrote sharebon, kibyōshi, yomihon, and gōkan. As Kitao Masanobu (a name derived from apprenticeship with *Kitao Shigemasa, a distinguished *ukiyoe* artist and illustrator of books), he illustrated stories by himself and others. As Kyōya Denzō (a name adapted from his Kyō-den), he was a successful businessman. By whatever name, he knew the pleasure quarters more inside than out. He was not blessed with *Ihara Saikaku's enormous energy or his genius, but the lesser flights he essayed were performed with the class, the *tsū*, that all aspiring Edokko sought to claim. And he deserves to be read, looked at, and enjoyed when worthier authors and pictorial artists somehow do not fit into our busy days.

Appreciation of gesaku is so relatively new that assured judgments are not easily made. But everybody who has read Kyōden's work thinks that his masterpiece is the comic kibyōshi, *Edo 'Umare Uwaki no Kabayaki* (1785, with later editions; see Part Ten, Figure 91, for an illustration of a cover of the second edition). "Edo 'Umare" means "Born in Edo," but Kyōden uses an archaicism, "mumare" (however then pronounced—probably "umare" or "'nmare") for simple "umare." "Uwaki" means "Lady-Killer," "Playboy with Tsū." "Kabayaki" refers to the Edo fashion of broiling eels. All this refers to the hapless hero, Enjirō, who aspires to being thought a proper uwaki, someone as tsū as can be. (Another illustration in Part Ten, Figure 93, will offer a contrast between the real connoisseurs of the quarters and our feckless hero.)

In Enjirō, Kyōden offers—in the comic guise of a didactic tale—a concoction sharing qualities of a picaresque story and a Bildungsroman, if Western terms are to be used. Kyōden's conception is of a wealthy, pampered, millionaire's son who dimwittedly tries to be thought what he is not. He is distinctive for two things in the pictures: the "En" embroidered on his sleeve and what Kyōden refers to at one point in words as his peony nose, which is represented pictorially by something like three circular forms. In a couple of years the nose became a faddish thing to refer to, and even its creator became blessed by the appellation "Kyōden the Nose." In the story Enjirō is distinguished by two other things: his series of efforts to be thought a true uwaki and his complete failure in each attempt.

Kyōden sought to write something of a sequel in a sharebon, *Tsūgen Sōmagaki* (1787). The title designates "Words of an Amorous Connoisseur" (tsūgen) in the most prestigious house of the Yoshiwara. Enjirō reappears with his two naughty male friends—and without pictures. In its time, it dazzled readers with its astonishing command of details of what was current and necessary to be known about the Yoshiwara and its language, customs, ways. It is barely intelligible today without extensive annotation, although with full commentary it offers copious information about the Yoshiwara, its women, and the men who were thought to be tsū.

Whether because of a desire to try new things, because of the lack of amusement in the bakufu, or for whatever reason, Kyōden's later writings take on an open seriousness that these best-known works do not have. Being sentenced to fifty days of house arrest, manacled, in the spring of 1791 may have been the cause. But we doubt it. Himself as lucky as Enjirō was not, Kyōden grew in fame, prospered in business, and continued to write just this side of censorship.

In going back in time to Gennai, we may pause a moment over a writer of unknown dates but of about this time who took on the ostentatiously humble pen name, Inaka Rōjin Tada no Jijii (Downright Old Uncle Tada from the Country). His *Yūshi Hōgen* (again of uncertain date, although before 1700) somewhat resembles Kyōden's *Edo Umare*. A father and son visit, after some preliminaries, the Yoshiwara. Father seeks to impress son and geisha with his knowledge of the argot of the quarters. He knows it, all right, unlike Enjirō. But, like Enjirō, he fails in his aim, and the more sensitive, delicate son is the person the women invite to stay the night. The father seeks to prove himself tsū. The milder son proves to be by nature an *irogonomi*, at once recalling Chikamatsu's enamored heroes (without their doom) and *Tamenaga Shunsui's later hero (without his prosperity). It is a good story, and it helped further the exploration of brothel life in which sharebon specialized. But it lacks the verve as well as the inventive variety of Kyōden. As it also lacks the imagination of Gennai.

Hiraga Gennai now seems to some of us the most important writer of gesaku—

in its wide sense of Edo popular fiction—if we dismiss Akinari and *Kyokutei Bakin from consideration. Although Kyōden knew his Edo as thoroughly as anyone could, Gennai was a more thoroughgoing intellectual. By the age of twelve, he was studying botany, in which he became proficient. His talents were such that he claimed the attention of Matsudaira Yoritaka, the head of his domain. With such support he launched into studies of Dutch, then the new and learned language for those who wished to find out about the science, the technology, and ways of the West, not to mention gain a better grasp of such things as geography. Although knowledge does not promise literary talent, Gennai had both, and he transformed for a moment the potentialities of kokkeibon. His *Nenashigusa* (1763, 1768) introduced such serious elements as death (by drowning and illness) of the protagonists of its two parts. In retrospect it seems clear that Gennai either would fail in understanding the nature of kokkeibon or make it something different from, something finer than, what others could realize.

The triumphant answer to the question came with his *Fūryū Shidōken Den* (1776). The mordant humor more or less observes the conventions of kokkeibon, but everything else in this narrative transcends the kind. The style is much more complex than that of Kyōden, befitting Gennai's learning. He purports to give the biography of his hero, Shidōken, a well-known storyteller. The work belongs to what in late seventeenth-century and early eighteenth-century England were termed imaginary voyages, and Gennai transforms the kind, much as did Jonathan Swift in *Gulliver's Travels*. Given the nature of his masterwork, and his familiarity with Western matters, it is astonishing that he did not know Swift's most popular work. Gennai narrates Shidōken's visits to numerous countries and places—after being taught by a sage the art of flying. After soaring about various parts of Japan, which are observed with cutting humor, Shidōken sets out on his more distant journey. This takes him across various Asian countries, which are described in detail more imaginative and satiric than real. The resemblances with *Gulliver's Travels* involve countries in which the human shape is distorted—Gennai creats not only giants and midgets but such others as the long-armed and long-legged. Putatively real places from Borneo to—of course— Holland are included. On return, Shidōken visits an Island of Women (again the resemblance with some seventeenth-century English imaginary voyages is uncanny), and he establishes an ideal state. Such a utopia, which is perhaps unique in Japanese literature, serves the same purpose of implicit satire on existing institutions that Western utopias suggest. The work is more miscellaneous, less concentrated than is *Gulliver's Travels*, but its ceaseless inventiveness exceeds that of Swift. An unprejudiced comparison would make for a splendid comparative exercise. Swift's control includes a bitter misanthropy that Gennai did not have. Gennai's loving, detailed sequentiality includes an affirmation in his satire that Swift did not have. He differs from Swift, however, in his obsessive use of sexual matters and extremely elaborated play with language to put received ideas about language into question. When Gennai later turned to jōruri, he wrote well enough and with new somberness. But his literary masterpiece is this prose narrative, which almost puts him into the class of Ueda Akinari and Bakin, since like them he possessed a capacity for fiction that provided an implicit evaluation of his country and times, even while his story remains absorbing reading as fiction. So versatile was he that many of his activities lie outside the scope of this volume. In intelligence, linguistic feat, and range he was a one-man university with full faculties of language, literature, science, and technology.

Toward the end of the 1780s, certain other kibyōshi that dealt bitterly with current happenings were disallowed reprinting. In 1790 the government took the further step of banning sharebon. None of this troubled *Shikitei Samba (1767–1822), another Edokko like Kyōden. He was son of a wood-block engraver and engaged in various trades, marrying in good urban style the daughter of one of the houses he worked for. Somewhat later, having made a bit of a mark as a writer, he set up shop to sell cosmetics and patent medicines, including his own potion, Edo Water. He wrote his fiction as a sideline. Not needing to earn a livelihood by writing, he had leisure to cultivate a vein of ironic comedy in some works and, in general, to evoke in the reader a wry recognition of the nature of ordinary life. He is best known for two kokkeibon: *Ukiyoburo* (1809–1813) and *Ukiyodoko* (1813–1814): the baths and the hairdressers of the "floating world." Only the former was actually completed by Samba, but both have an invention typical of the originator of Edo Water. Relatively few women appear in the second work, which may or may not explain why it tends to deal more with social matters.

It may seem rather obvious (once someone else has thought of it) that a public bath and a hairdresser's shop should provide useful stages on which to bring all kinds of Edo people in moments when they wish to tell of their lives or what interests them, or in order to bring about easily chance encounters that would otherwise require laborious plots. Locality and people—these are very enduring elements in Japanese literature. The episodic or, more positively, the sequential, nature of events must owe not a little to the enduring influence of poems in chokusenshū, setsuwa collections, renga, or (perhaps as good an analogy as any) the anecdotal character of a rekishi monogatari such as *Ōkagami. This is not to suggest sources but to point to something enduringly Japanese (and indeed, universal by way of "framed" stories), in order to stress that the humor with pointed observation of common people belongs to Edo-period literature, even as those stories are about Edokko by an Edokko. Readers at the time living outside Edo found the stories somewhat exotic, as we do.

Samba's fixed location is one way of bringing about numerous situations involving large numbers of characters. Another way, its opposite, is the journey of the picaresque narrative. In Europe, the picaresque seldom shows much concern for its picaro. It would be risky to swear that *Jippensha Ikku (1765–1831) felt abiding concern with his most famous characters, but he could laugh with them as well as at them. Ikku wrote in various kinds of gesaku, in kyōka and senryū as might have been expected. This can be seen from (*Muda Shugyō*) *Kane no Waraji* (1813–1834), which combines accounts of various famous places as a means of characterizing them with such distinct features as their dialects. But such things are lost in the reputation of his masterpiece.

(*Tōkaidōchū*) *Hizakurige* (1802–1822) is one of those works that will be read when many a better ordered, more obviously intelligent, and more dedicated work will be left on the shelf. *Footing It along the Tōkaidō Road* is Ikku's counterpart of Samba's locations. The story is dreadfully uneven, and the scatology becomes a bore with repetition. There are other faults as well. But the two central figures sustain our curiosity and we could wish that the world's mess always held such interest. By getting his rogues out of Edo onto the road, Ikku gained more than a device. He obtained as well a priceless detachment on Edo life and the lower inclinations of us all. Questions whether *Hizakurige* is a masterpiece or a mess do not really apply. Small wonder that the public clamored for more, and that Ikku had to send Yaji and Kita on longer travels than he had first envisaged.

We must now consider the greatest author of prose fiction between Saikaku and Natsume Sōseki in the modern period. Some would rate him lower, some higher, and yet others would think that he is an author whose stock is to be watched as Japanese scholars and critics will surely make more and more of him in the future. The staunchest heart may skip at the thought of *Kyokutei Bakin (1767–1848), since his life and works represent in one sense Akinari writ large. Anyone who has not read these works in their entirety—although it seems unlikely that anyone since the author has read them *all*—must hesitate, or at least acknowledge the limited, personal character of remarks.

Unfortunately, the historian cannot simply relate his life, mentioning the important works in passing. For one thing, the summaries of his works are longer than many earlier works. For another, his life is as full of sudden ups and downs, or downs and plunges, as are his stories. If only to suggest what Bakin struggled with, however, something must be said of his life. At the age of six he greatly impressed his father with a hokku he composed. The father was well employed by the Matsudaira household at that time, but died two years later. At thirteen Bakin took off, leaving a hokku on the door, beginning his Defoe-like struggles. At fifteen he was in Osaka and Kyoto meeting kamigata writers, who strengthened his own determination to write. His mother died when he was eighteen. He refused assistance from his elder brother, and at this time tried his hand at haikai and haibun. At twenty-one he nearly died from an illness. The next year he began his first try at medicine, dropped that, started Confucian studies for a bit, but the following year a meeting with Santō Kyōden set him into prose. While working with Kyōden, he took employment doing this and that, and in 1793 he married into a geta-maker's family. It was the second marriage for his wife, who was three years his senior. Bakin worked hard at making clogs and did well, but the trade was not for him, and he quit. So it goes. His diary describes experiences making charcoal briquets, selling old clothes, and even being reduced to making and selling little things made from the bamboo in his garden. This accounts for the earlier half of his life. The rest was more of the same, except that he managed to write a prodigious amount, began to feel the pains and defects of age, was disappointed in a son; he might loathe the work he was so compulsively attached to, and was reduced to using an amanuensis to complete his longest work. This is *Nansō Satomi Hakkenden*, better known as *Hakkenden*.

He spent thirty-eight years (age forty-seven to seventy-five) on this immense work in ninety-six kan. It features over four hundred people. And it is in the last stages of this work that poor Bakin, losing his sight, had to count the characters off, kanji and kana, one by one, for the printer. For reasons that are more depressing than exhilarating, it is a life calculated to stifle any boast one might be tempted to make of one's own achievements. Few writers have had to endure such privation, few have written so much so complexly, and few have had to wait so long for the fame sought at such a price.

Bakin is usually credited with three major works besides *Hakkenden*. These are *Beibei Kyōdan* (1813), (*Anzetsu*) *Yumiharizuki* (1807–1811), and *Kinseisetsu Bishōnenroku* (1828–1834). *Beibei Kyōdan* is said to be modeled on the **Ochikubo Monogatari* but, instead of treating a romance of the trials of a stepdaughter, it deals with Bakin's frequent concerns: Buddhist causation and conflicts between good and evil. *Kinseisetsu Bishōnenroku*, also a yomihon, is assigned (like so much of Bakin's work) a Chinese original, but its adaptions are also recognized: for example, his characteristic use of a historical character, Mōri Motonari and others involved in the Battle of Itsukushima. The blend of sources, history, and his own story-making is quite typical. But as the title of this work suggests, it also concerns two very attractive youths, romance, and the toils of good and evil in human actions. After brief consideration of *Hakkenden*, *Yumiharizuki* will be our object.

The full title *Nansō Satomi Hakkenden* carries a number of suggestions. For one thing, it implies a range of Chinese sources. Also, there is a postulate of a variety of earlier "Satomi literature," as if there were earlier records of Satomi (*Satomi Ki*), a history of the nine generations of the Satomi (*Satomi Kyūdaiki*), and a war tale of the Satomi (*Satomi Gunki*), and so on. Bakin's borrowings from such earlier works as the **Taiheiki* are a given of scholarship. It is scarcely imaginable that a work of such length should not have had numerous sources, models, and analogues.

The *Hakkenden*, or "story of eight dogs," is really a "hakkenshiden," or "story of eight warriors named dogs." That is, the title derives from its eight samurai with "inu" in their surnames (although some sound more like place names). Each of the eight represents a virtue:

Benevolence	Inuzuka Moritaka
Righteousness	Inukawa Yoshitō
Courtesy	Inuyama Tadatomo
Wisdom	Inukai Nobumichi
Fidelity	Inuta Yasuyori
Loyalty	Inue Masashi
Filial Piety	Inusaka Tanetomo
Service to Elders	Inumura Masanori

These stalwarts and their virtues, the fortunes of the Satomi house, and very much else are dealt with, somewhat in the manner of Spenser, although much less abstractly and with a rapidity we do not associate with *The Faerie Queene*. The story treats a span of about sixty years toward the close of the Muromachi period. As one Japanese critic has put it, echoing others and the experience of all, this work begins and ends with surprising turns; its ups and downs constantly recur; its incidents are riddled with complexities; and it is concerned with the working out of the fates of good and evil characters.

More than the complexity of the story line, Bakin's style is apt to put off less hardy readers. He loves long strings of Chinesey looking characters, complex allusions, arcane references, and extraordinarily rich detail. For all that, by some miracle, the story moves with astonishing speed. Intimidated by the big words but refreshed by the fine imagery, exasperated by the ponderous and excited by ceaselessly fresh invention, the reader in Bakin-land certainly moves over an immense fictional terrain. On reflection, away from the ceaseless agitation of his plots, Bakin's style makes one long for the poise of the *Heike Monogatari*—after all, the *gunkimono* is his model. But instead of ease, Bakin gives quick pushes and unexpected turns; instead of poise, unending, heightened confrontations of good and evil, both qualities being in versions larger than life.

This literary emphasis, and its motives, had appeared in Ueda Akinari. Elements like it will be found in some Heian monogatari, even in the first, the *Taketori Monogatari*. Judging from various comparisons made by Murasaki Shikibu in the *Genji Monogatari*, the spectacular was felt to be a borrowed, Chinese line of fiction. Her opinion receives confirmation in the fact of borrowing by Akinari and Bakin from Chinese plots, however recast those were in terms of military stories of the native past. In style and in its version of life, Bakin's fiction incorporates the agitated, moral, and artificial with the sublime. No wonder he has had to wait for translators.

Since the nature of his work is clear to us, it must have been doubly so to him. So must have been the gap he perceived between life as he knew it in his time and life as he chose to know it in his writing. This discrepancy has its parallel if not its cause in that between his social ambitions and his situation. The heart sinks at the thought of the dogged years of determined, extended creation, of ceaseless invention of an imaginary world for relief from the imperfections of the real by a life of writing he loathed, even as he could not put down his brush. As with Akinari, the life imagined implicitly criticizes the life lived. Yet while a famous comment seems to say just this, it is also depressing that he should say, "The people who know me are those eight virtuous ones." We are used to authors projecting something of themselves into their characters, or even forgetting their characters. But to have to rely upon one's (virtuous) characters for the best knowledge of oneself—that surely is the most damning of quiet comments an author could make on eight decades of Japanese life. One longs for the freer, comic air of Gennai and Kyōden, who look on humanity with more tolerance because they expect less. But with Akinari, Bakin carries the conviction of being a greater writer precisely because he would expect more, would demand morality and genuine heroism from life. When life did not provide such things, art had to make up the deficiency, and he therefore detested the compensating art almost as much as the inadequate life.

Yumiharizuki was published in a mere four years. It was also based on Chinese sources adapted so as to fit with Japanese history and with Japanese military tales, particularly the *Hōgen Monogatari*. There are also certain biographical associations to the idea that apply particularly to *Yumiharizuki*. In addition, there is a simpler pattern than for *Hakkenden*: now there are not eight virtuous or allegorical samurai and corresponding villains, but the single historical figure of Minamoto Tametomo. Perhaps it is this clarification, and some reflection of it in Bakin's style and atmosphere, that gives a sense of freedom that leads to a minority taste (held by one of us) to prefer this work above *Hakkenden*.

Readers do not go to Bakin to relax, although he can be read, as to no small extent he wrote, for escape. The fact is that in some of his paintings and their accompanying writing he could be naughty, engage in visual puns, and show himself capable of a good time. There is some (if not very much) of that Bakin in *Yumiharizuki*. Not that one reads this story for laughs or should expect its author to be fettered by history or probability. When Tametomo is banished to Ōshima, he crosses to the Ryukyus. There the hero pledges love with the crown princess. He quells insurrections and places their only son in line for kingship. The possibility of such actions is one thing, the psychology another, for the male romance with a foreign woman has elements of fantasy we find in *Madame Butterfly* later, and earlier in *Sugawara Takasue no Musume's *Hamamatsu Chūnagon Monogatari*. Something of the nature of the psychology can be understood in the easier reach of characterization, which Bakin effects by various means, especially by dialogue that is highly effective even if it would be strange from other lips. Since characters may surprise us by what they say as well as what they do, there really is a remarkable integrity to Bakin's work. The nature of that integrity puts off many readers, and so does the length of it, making Akinari far more popular. But it seems necessary to consent with what one admiring critic has said of Bakin: the combination of dazzling style with varied architecture of plot makes *Yumiharizuki* and *Hakkenden* outstanding in Japanese narrative. They represent the opposite of the sequential genius of much Japanese literature. Here is scale, moral causality, history re-invented, learning, and ceaseless agitation within an ordered story. Here is *plot*. What keeps this achievement from the greatness of the *Genji Monogatari* and the *Heike Monogatari* is the projection of that world from the desire to possess it, the creation from a felt absence rather than a motivated, assured presence.

It should be clear from even so cursory an account of Bakin's life and times that his writing repaired the deficiencies of his life. The sufferings and sudden vicissitudes in his stories mirror—in enlarged heroic images—his own problems, by offering romance for what was too often grubbing agony. By turning to a heroic past, made exotic by the use of Chinese stories as well as by native history, he compensated for a lack of high tenor in his own life. But the heroic military past examined in an age of peace also criticizes a regime grown soft, a time gone humdrum. The logical causation uniting event to event in the plot makes a sense of life that his own age did not provide, and the sudden turns (yet explained by causation) offer a standard of interest and excitement very much lacking in his time. We can see similar implications in his rich style and in the clear-cut distinction between good and evil. But it also remains true that the reason why he rushes us so from one great event or moral issue to the next is that he really distrusts the possibility of art—no matter how stirring or moral—to compensate as he wishes it to for the grave deficiencies he finds apparent in his world. The only solution to this problem was to write yet more that moved still more quickly and made good confront evil another time. Only his good characters understood him, he said. But that is only half the problem. Worse still, *he* understood the bad.

As with Saikaku, so with Bakin we discover a brilliant prose that offers a species of unintended allegory. Saikaku's world of money and sex does not match Bakin's fancier combination of Chinese romance and Japanese history, but Saikaku faces his subjects head on. And even his later didactic work for samurai has at least something like a real world for his imaginary people. Saikaku's ease in directly engaging his world suggests that he and his world fit each other perfectly, although not on the literal terms. Bakin's difficulties and strong measures imply that he wished to think he saw more deeply into his world than it deserved. The gap between the hollowness of what he saw and the grandiose romance with which he depicts it is one finally bridgeable only by total suspension of disbelief or by entering into his spirit and keeping going, keeping going, on and on and on. If the great Edo harvest is overmellow in his work, the bounty he provides will one day be more widely appreciated. And on that day there will be a sudden fall in the price of gold.

4. *Wintry Gleanings: 1830–1867*

The prodigality of *Bakin looks better and better as we turn to the last season of classical literature. With whatever signs of strain, he is a genuinely imaginative and serious writer. The dates of *Ryūtei Tanehiko (1783–1843) make him a junior contemporary of Bakin's, but his achievement allows us to place him in a lesser category. (As will be evident, the historian must search earnestly for some good writers assignable to this last season.) A versatile writer, Tanehiko specialized in gōkan, but he also wrote kyōka, yomihon, as also later jōruri and kabuki. The work for the theater seems to have assisted this exhibitor of all wares in heightening his art. One of his two most esteemed works, *Nise Murasaki Inaka Genji* (1829) does not promise much in its title (*The Fake Murasaki and Country Genji*). Yet if this has not the depth of Akinari's *Kuse Monogatari*, it does have a storyteller's art. Tanehiko shifts the Genji story to Muromachi times and the Ashikaga shogunate. The young lord Ashikaga Mitsuuji is the Genji character, adding martial prowess to amours. This is said to be one of the most successful adaptations of the Chinese stories so popular at the time, even if its model is very Japanese and its illustrations—fetching pictures by *Utagawa Kunisada—proclaim a Japanese nationality. Because of the Tempō Reform, the story was forebade publication. Some say this proscription led Tanehiko to take his life. Others say that he died of grief. Like the rest of us, he was not made of Bakin's tough fiber.

*Kyoku Sanjin (d. 1836) deserves mention for his most important work,

Kana Majiri Musume Setsuyō (1831–1834). This *ninjōbon* deals with the familiar dilemma of *giri* and passion in a way that brought it to some life.

*Tamenaga Shunsui (1790–1843) wrote more considerable ninjōbon, although since he was a publisher of them, and since his was but one of many hands among others employed, it is not clear whether he wrote some works bearing his name, whether he revised some, or whether he put his name to works really written by others. For all that, he is the one major author of this last phase of classical literature because of a work certainly his own, (*Shunshoku*) *Umegoyomi* (1832–1833). The historian of modern literature would be struck by various anticipations of it found in this story. Coming on it late in this brief history, we are struck more by what it uses from earlier literature. The plot concerns the vicissitudes of Tanjirō, rejected by his well-born father and consigned to adoption by the owner of a Yoshiwara house. There an evil and blocking character (who has a female counterpart later) emerges in the person of the clerk who falsely accuses Tanjirō of helping make away with a family heirloom. This double rejection may account for Tanjirō's mildness, one might say his helplessness. Like male heroes in many jōruri and kabuki *sewamono*, Tanjirō—Tansan—is a lover whose appeal to women seems to derive precisely from his absence of presumed male strength and superiority. The two chief women in his life enter before long. There is the geisha, Yonehachi, who searches for her Tan's hiding place, finds him, and is willing to devote herself, her means, and her bed to him. This creates a series of problems with those who expect her to devote herself to the business of entertaining many rather than one, and an impoverished one at that. The other woman is Ochō, the daughter in the Yoshiwara household into which Tanjirō had been taken. She also loves her Tan, and again, in his gentle, enervated way, he returns the emotion. It is the business of the work to see the frail hero through a number of adventures and get him happily restored at the end in a way that will work out relations with both Yonehachi and Ochō.

The device Shunsui used to effect the reconciliation with Tanjirō's family is one taken from stage *jidaimono*: a trusty servant of the family makes a sudden appearance and manages to use the stolen and lost heirloom to prove innocence and restore the hero. On the stage as well, that jidaimono plot had been combined with the sewamono line, using the gentle *irogonomi* who is so unlike *Ihara Saikaku's Yonosuke. The resolution of the love plot also resembles that of such plays. Tanjirō gets the best of both worlds: Yonehachi as a concubine, Ochō as wife.

It will not seem immediately apparent how such a fabrication exercises a claim on readers, and there are in fact numerous details on which Shunsui could be faulted. These may be suggested by the obvious excess of calling one Yoshiwara establishment Koigakubo or The Cavity of Love. But the fact is that in what matters Shunsui innovates with great risks that he manages to bring off. One moment of risk deals with the physical relations of Tanjirō and Ochō. Sex before marriage was unethical, particularly in the fiction of the age. Shunsui handles the scene with great delicacy, no doubt to elude the censors, but also with the effect of making it seem natural and indeed positive. The other risks are systematic, involving three distinct styles or "layers" of narration, in one of which the narrator-as-author cajoles the reader into seeing the morality of the story or into comradely thought of how difficult it will be to find some means of extracting Tanjirō from his plight of the moment. How such charming confession of authorial difficulty can work with the moral starch is one question, and how both of those work with the greatly circuitous plot is another. But they do—it seems by virtue of a great tact in Shunsui's setting of the relation of his styles or, put another way, of the relation among his narrator, the reader, and the characters. Although his story is therefore much finer than a good yarn in the guise of morality, it does assume that air.

Given such a mixture, it might have been foreseen that the very strength of Shunsui's talent would get him in trouble. The government, being weak on crucial matters, sought to show power in small ones, taking a high line on moral laxity and dangerous thoughts. One writer was driven from Edo. Shunsui was manacled in chains for a time. With much ado, certain illustrated books were banned, along with pictures of actors and courtesans of a kind long since familiar. Only the third Edo kabukiza in Asakusa was left free. If some of the literature seems decadent, it is also clear that a frantic regime was panicking, showing those signs of arbitrary repression that signal the end of an authoritarian government. The writers deserved a better regime, and the government got better writers than it had any right to expect.

Besides Shunsui, there is only one other writer of real value in this close of the Edo period. *Kawatake Mokuami (1816–1893) was extraordinarily prolific, touching prose narrative and other kinds. But he is identified rightly with the kabuki stage, to which he devoted his life, working alongside, as it were, actors and audience alike. What the one could do, and the other wanted, he provided. To some tastes, his plays are intolerably bad. It had been common enough to mingle elements of jidaimono and sewamono on the stage. Mokuami seems to have thrown them in a handful at a time, making sure that the two never had any contact with each other, a jidaimono plot running quite separately from the sewamono story. There is not much that is ennobling to point to. The characters are commonly gangsters. In his handling of the erotic, he manages to outdo even *Tsuruya Namboku. But there are real compensations. Mokuami is able to create credible characters. He has a command of poetic language that his audiences found as memorable as, in *Don Giovanni*, a tune from an earlier opera by Mozart turns out to be. It is in this kind of emphasis on the art itself that makes Mokuami appeal so strongly to a certain kind of contemporary Western taste. Characters are given not simply to remarks such as "all this might be happening in a kabuki," but even to finding ways of advertising their names, or reading from casually discovered paper an announcement of the very play being performed. And so on. All in all, Mokuami is a gifted dramatist who did his best work in the late Edo period.

He is a better poet than Namboku, but he lacks the corrupt or—perhaps rather—the shuddering energy of Namboku. His continuation into modern times is one of the instances of literary continuity, one bit of evidence that the concept of a literary age does not include or exclude all things tidily.

There were numerous other continuities in poetry and prose narrative. Continuity and greatness are not the same thing, however, and early in the modern period the finest major writers of course looked back not simply to a Shunsui but to yet more important writers. Buson became a rallying name, as Bashō had been for him. Akutagawa recalls Akinari, and Mishima Yukio revived the *Hamamatsu Chūnagon Monogatari for his tetralogy. Such filiations suggest what any sensible person would expect, that the great modern writers have adapted classical literature according to their needs, even if Western influences have sometimes seemed overwhelming. In the end, it is not that divinity at Sumiyoshi who determines the lasting integrity of Japanese literature but a unique language shared by an industrious, gifted people who inhabit some not very large islands. The achievement of their classical literature is one of the world's wonders, and if it ends in these wintry gleanings, the new Meiji spring was not far behind.

PART TWO Chronologies

A. PERIODS AND PERIODIZING

As with other literatures, so with Japanese, there is no universally agree-on periodizing, either as to the names of the periods or the times of their duration. For several possibilities, mostly related to political events or nonliterary arts, see Andrew Nathaniel Nelson, *The Modern Reader's Japanese-English Character Dictionary* (Tokyo: Tuttle, 1962), p. 1,017. Our practice is to follow two distinctions now common in Japan. The first relates to the title of our book, involving as it does a distinction between classical literature (koten bungaku 古典文学) and modern literature (gendai bungaku 現代文学). For dividing classical literature, we do not use distinctions as to age (kodai, chūsei, etc.). Reasons are given at the beginning of Part One B; in short, there is no agreement among Japanese as to dates or even as to some names for the ages. Instead, we distinguish periods according to the seat of government, although not exactly in correspondence to political events. In other words, our last literary period is called Edo, after the place where the government was situated, not Tokugawa, as it is sometimes called after the family of the shogunate. We begin the period in 1603, as if everything changed on the last day of the preceding year. Of course we are only representing historical fictions whose truth resides more in general drift and convenience than in any exactitude.

Following common practice, then, we define classical literature as that known to have been written from its beginnings through 1867. In what follows we give lists of the sovereigns (tennō 天皇), including the legendary ones. The twenty-ninth, Kimmei, is taken to begin historical times (from 539), although from archaeological and Chinese evidence more can be known. The Yamato period could be taken to begin in 539, although we take it to begin a century and a half later, in 685, a date from which poetry can be dated with some assurance. In other words, we postulate a legendary period followed by an early historical period from which most literature cannot be dated, and then eight classical periods defined in the terms given, followed by the modern period.

TABLE 2–1. THE PERIODS OF JAPANESE LITERATURE

Legendary	pre–539
Historical	539–645
Yamato 大和	645–711
Nara 奈良	712–793
Heian 平安	794–1186
Kamakura 鎌倉	1186–1336
Nambokuchō 南北朝	1336–1392
Muromachi (Ashikaga) 室町	1392–1573
Azuchi Momoyama 安土桃山	1573–1603
Edo (Tokugawa) 江戸	1603–1868

B. REGNAL AND ERA NAMES OF CLASSICAL JAPAN

Sovereigns before Kimmei (number 29 below) are more legendary than historical. But as Nelson (from whom this section is adapted) observes, legend is also a part of a nation's history. Regnal dates show:

1. the year of accession if known (parentheses indicate the year of "coronation" but are not used when the year of the ceremony was the same as that of succession);
2. the year the reign ended, whether by death or abdication.

Within a given reign, there may be more than one era name. A new one was usually sought to establish an auspicious time. Era names were not systematically developed until Kōtoku (number 36), and there are occasional alternatives to those given here.

Dates are specified by era rather than by reign. Thus Engi 延喜 gannen 元年 and Engi ninen 二年 indicate not just 901 and 902, but also the first and second years of the middle of three eras in the reign of Daigo (number 60). References to a given whole reign are also used, although not for dating a specific year: as Daigo Tennō no on(ōn)toki 醍醐天皇の御時.

It will be apparent that we speak of tennō or sovereigns. There was no notion of an empire, or even its name in the modern sense, during the classical centuries.

Instead of a simple procession of numbered years decreasing (B.C.) or increasing (A.D.), the traditional Japanese dating offered sovereigns—tennō—and, throughout most of classical times, era names for each. Before presenting the historical sequence, we offer two tables for convenience. Table 2-2 relates the sequence of numbered sovereigns to historical periods and their dates. With the period goes an abbreviation of its name. The abbreviation makes it possible next in Table 2–3 to give an alphabetical list of tennō, each with the number assigned in the traditional order, with the dates of reign (real or legendary), and the literary period in which the reign fell.

Using the designations just given, Table 2-3 presents an alphabetical list of sovereigns, legendary with historical, those of the Northern Line along with those counted.

This figure may also serve as an alphabetical index to the chronological table of sovereigns, and so on, in Table 2-4.

TABLE 2–2. OUTLINE OF SOVEREIGNS AND PERIODS

Trad. No.	Abbreviation	Period	Dates
1–28	Leg.	Legendary	pre–539
29–34	Hist.	Historical	539–645
35–43	Yam.	Yamato	645–711
43–50	Nara	Nara	712–793
50–81	Heian	Heian	794–1186
81–96	Kama.	Kamakura	1186–1336
97–100	Namb.	Nambokuchō	1336–1392
——	N.	Northern	1332–1392
101–107	Muro.	Muromachi	1392–1573
107	Az-M.	Azuchi-Momoyama	1573–1603
107–121	Edo	Edo	1603–1868
122–124	Mod.	Modern	1868– ——

TABLE 2–3. ALPHABETICAL LIST OF SOVEREIGNS WITH NUMBER, YEARS OF REIGN, AND PERIOD (Dates in parenthesis are B.C.)

Sovereign	Number	Reign	Period
Ankan	27	531–535	Leg.
Ankō	20	453–456	Leg.
Annei	3	(549–511)	Leg.
Antoku	81	1180–1183	Heian
Bidatsu	30	571–585	Hist.
Buretsu	25	498–506	Leg.
Chōkei	98	1368–1383	Namb.
Chūai	14	191–200	Leg.
Chūkyō	85	1221	Kama.
Daigo	60	897–930	Heian
En'yū	64	969–984	Heian
Fushimi	92	1287–1298	Kama.
Gemmei	43	707–715	Yam.-Nara
Genshō	44	715–724	Nara
Godaigo	96	1318–1339	Kama.-Namb.
Goen'yū	N5	1371–1382	N.
Gofukakusa	89	1246–1259	Kama.
Gofushimi	93	1298–1301	Kama.
Gohanazono	102	1428–1464	Muro.
Gohorikawa	86	1221–1232	Kama.
Goichijō	68	1016–1036	Heian
Gokameyama	99	1383–1392	Namb.
Gokashiwabara	104	1500–1526	Muro.
Gokōgon	N4	1352–1371	N.
Gokomatsu	N6	N1382–1392	N.
Gokomatsu	100	1392–1412	Muro.
Gokōmyō	110	1643–1654	Edo
Gomizunoo	108	1611–1629	Edo
Gomomozono	118	1770–1779	Edo
Gomurakami	97	1339–1368	Namb.

TABLE 2–3. (*continued*)

Sovereign	Number	Reign	Period
Gonara	105	1526–1557	Muro.
Gonijō	94	1301–1308	Kama.
Goreizei	70	1045–1068	Heian
Gosaga	88	1242–1246	Kama.
Gosai	111	1656–1663	Edo
Gosakuramachi	117	1762–1770	Edo
Gosanjō	71	1068–1072	Heian
Goshirakawa	77	1155–1158	Heian
Gosuzaku	69	1036–1045	Heian
Gotoba	82	1183–1198	Heian-Kama.
Gotsuchimikado	103	1465–1500	Muro.
Gouda	91	1274–1287	Kama.
Goyōzei	107	1586–1611	Az. M.-Edo
Hanazono	95	1308–1318	Kama.
Hanzei	18	406–410	Leg.
Heizei	51	806–809	Heian
Higashiyama	113	1687–1709	Edo
Horikawa	73	1086–1107	Heian
Ichijō	66	986–1011	Heian
Ingyō	19	412–453	Leg.
Itoku	4	(510–477)	Leg.
Jimmu	1	(660–585)	Leg.
[Jingū (regent)	14	201–269	Leg.]
Jitō	41	690–697	Yam.
Jomei	34	629–641	Hist.
Junna	53	823–833	Heian
Junnin	47	758–764	Nara
Juntoku	84	1210–1221	Kama.
Kaika	9	(158–98)	Leg.
Kameyama	90	1259–1274	Kama.
Kammu	50	781–806	Nara-Heian
Kazan	65	984–986	Heian
Keikō	12	70–130	Leg.
Keitai	26	506–531	Leg.
Kenzō	23	484–487	Leg.
Kimmei	29	539–571	Hist.
Kōan	6	(392–291)	Leg.
Kōbun	39	671–672	Yam.
Kōgen	8	(214–158)	Leg.
Kōgon	N1	1332–1333	N.
Kōgyoku	35	641–645	Yam.
Kōkaku	119	1779–1817	Edo
Kōken	46	749–758	Nara
Kōkō	58	884–887	Heian
Kōmei	121	1846–1866	Edo
Kōmyō	N2	1333–1348	N.
Kōnin	49	770–781	Nara
Konoe	76	1141–1155	Heian
Kōrei	7	(290–215)	Leg.
Kōshō	5	(475–393)	Leg.
Kōtoku	36	645–654	Yam.

TABLE 2–3. (*continued*)

Sovereign	Number	Reign	Period
Meiji	122	1866–1912	Mod.
Meishō	109	1629–1643	Edo
Mommu	42	697–707	Yama.
Momozono	116	1747–1762	Edo
Montoku	55	850–858	Heian
Murakami	62	946–967	Heian
Nakamikado	114	1709–1735	Edo
Nijō	78	1158–1165	Heian
Nimmyō	54	833–850	Heian
Ninken	24	487–498	Leg.
Ninkō	120	1817–1846	Edo
Nintoku	16	310–399	Leg.
Ōgimachi	106	1557–1586	Muro.
Ōjin	15	269–310	Leg.
Reigen	112	1663–1687	Edo
Reizei	63	967–969	Heian
Richū	17	399–405	Leg.
Rokujō	79	1165–1168	Heian
Saga	52	809–823	Heian
Saimei	37	655–661	Yam.
Sakuramachi	115	1735–1747	Edo
Sanjō	67	1011–1016	Heian
Seimu	13	(130–190)	Leg.
Seinei	22	479–484	Leg.
Seiwa	56	858–876	Heian
Senka	28	535–539	Leg.
Shijō	87	1232–1242	Kama.
Shirakawa	72	1072–1086	Heian
Shōkō	101	1412–1428	Muro.
Shōmu	45	724–749	Nara
Shōtoku	48	764–770	Nara
Shōwa	124	1926– —	Mod.
Suiko	33	592–628	Hist.
Suinin	11	(29)–70	Leg.
Suizei	2	(581–549)	Leg.
Sujin	10	(98–30)	Leg.
Sukō	N3	1348–1351	N.
Sushun	32	587–592	Hist.
Sutoku	75	1123–1141	Heian
Suzaku	61	930–946	Heian
Taishō	123	1912–1926	Mod.
Takakura	80	1168–1180	Heian
Temmu	40	672–686	Yam.
Tenji	38	668–671	Yam.
Toba	74	1107–1123	Heian
Tsuchimikado	83	1198–1210	Kama.
Uda	59	887–897	Heian
Yōmei	31	585–587	Hist.
Yōzei	57	876–884	Heian
Yūryaku	21	456–479	Leg.

The roles of these tennō were to reign, to give legitimacy to government, to give identity to the nation, and to perform rites as shaman-priests, providing a relation of self, people, and traditional divinities.

Sometimes a tennō also ruled, but if so the rule was likely to be through close associates or after abdication, using a later sovereign as figurehead. More often, while the tennō reigned and did the duties proper to office, some other group exercised power through various offices. These matters are represented in Part Nine, Ranks and Offices.

For the activities of a given year at court and elsewhere, see Part Seven, Times, Directions, and Related Symbolism.

The names by which tennō are known are regnal rather than personal. So it is only outside Japan that the 124th sovereign, Shōwa (Tennō) would be referred to as Hirohito.

The traditional and still used system of dating involves years within a sovereign's regnal name, beginning with the first as year one of that era. Thus, since Shōwa ascended in 1926 by modern Western reckoning, Shōwa 5 is 1930, Shōwa 25 is 1950, and so on—not 1931, 1951, etc., because the first year of ascension must be counted as year one.

As in any royal system, the heir designate is assumed to ascend as sovereign immediately on the death (or abdication) of the predecessor. This means that at the end of the reign of one sovereign and at the beginning of the reign of the next, a given year by Western reckoning may have two regnal era designations. Thus 1926 was Taishō 15 until Shōwa ascended, after which it was Shōwa 1.

The modern examples are simpler than the premodern ones. Since earlier sovereigns are known by their regnal names, and since *dates* are calculated within names of regnal *eras*, if (as was very common), the regnal era name was changed, a given sovereign's period of reign became broken into more than one era for purposes of dating. To take a fairly simple example, there was the short reign of Kōkō (number 58 in the traditional numbering). He ascended in 884, which was therefore Kōkō 1 or Kōkō gannen (original year 光孝元年) as well as, before his ascension, Yōzei 9 (陽成). The next year, however, Kōkō changed his regnal era name to Ninna (仁和). In other words, much of 885 is not known as Kōkō 2, but Ninna 1, 886 is Ninna 2, 887 is Ninna 3. And since he died that year, 887 is thereafter also Uda 1 (宇多). There were various reasons for choosing a new regnal era name. Most commonly a new one designated some new purpose or a desire to part from natural or other calamities. In any event, reigns like those of Ichijō (number 66), Horikawa (number 73), and Godaigo (number 96) created multiple regnal eras that must be used for traditional dating, or for deriving modern Western dating from the traditional dates.

There is a further complication for the years 1332–1392. References made by traditional dates—in literary as well as historical discussions—may sometimes refer to the Northern line for dating, even though the Southern is usually used. We therefore enter those Northern sovereigns after the appropriate run of Southern and, as suggested, also the three sovereigns of modern times as a matter of convenience.

Female tennō are indicated by a † before their names.
Regnal dates show:

1. the year of accession if known (parentheses indicate the year of "coronation" but are not used when the year of the ceremony was the same as that of succession)
2. the year the reign ended, whether by death or abdication.

For early tennō, information in square brackets derives from modern historical and archaeological findings.

TABLE 2–4. SOVEREIGNS, REGNAL ERAS, AND DATES (WITH FIRST YEAR OF ERAS)

Legendary (Pre–539)

1.	神武	Jimmu, (660)–585 B.C.
2.	綏靖	Suizei, 581–549
3.	安寧	Annei, 549–511
4.	懿徳	Itoku, 510–477
5.	孝昭	Kōshō, 475–393
6.	孝安	Kōan, 392–291
7.	孝霊	Kōrei, 290–215
8.	孝元	Kōgen, 214–158
9.	開化	Kaika, 158–98
10.	崇神	Sujin, 98 (97)–30 [died ca. A.D. 258]
11.	垂仁	Suinin, (29 B.C.)–A.D. 70
12.	景行	Keikō, 70 (71)–130 [accession ca. 300]
13.	成務	Seimu, 130 (131)–190
14.	仲哀	Chūai, 191 (192)–200
	神功皇后	†Jingū Kōgō (regent), 201–269
15.	応神	Ōjin, 269 (270)–310
16.	仁徳	Nintoku, 310 (313)–399 [accession ca. 395; died ca. 427]
17.	履中	Richū, 399 (400)–405
18.	反正	Hanzei, (406)–410
19.	允恭	Ingyō, (412)–453
20.	安康	Ankō, 453–456
21.	雄略	Yūryaku, 456–479 [sends embassy to China in 478]
22.	清寧	Seinei, 479 (480)–484
23.	顕宗	Kenzō, 484 (485)–487 (or Kensō)
24.	仁賢	Ninken, 487 (488)–498
25.	武烈	Buretsu, 498–506
26.	継体	Keitai, 506 (507)–531
27.	安閑	Ankan, 531–535
28.	宣化	Senka, 535–539

Historical (539–645)

29.	欽明	Kimmei, 539–571
30.	敏達	Bidatsu, 571 (572)–585

TABLE 2–4. (*continued*)

<hr>

Historical (539–645)

31.	用明	Yōmei, 585–587
32.	崇峻	Sushun, 587–592
33.	推古	†Suiko, 592–628
34.	舒明	Jomei, (629)–641
35.	皇極	†Kōgyoku, 641 (642)–645 (same woman as Saimei, 37)

Yamato (645–711)

36.	孝徳	Kōtoku, 645–654	
		大化 Taika	645
		白雉 Hakuchi	650
37.	斉明	†Saimei, (655)–661 (same woman as Kōgyoku, 35; Saimei is usual dictionary name)	
38.	天智	Tenji, (668)–671	
39.	弘文	Kōbun, 671–672	
		白鳳 Hakuhō	672
40.	天武	Temmu, (672)–686	
		朱鳥 Shuchō	686
41.	持統	†Jitō, (690)–697	
42.	文武	Mommu, 697–707	
		大宝 Daihō	701
		慶雲 Kyōun (or Keiun)	704
43.	元明	†Gemmei, 707–715	
		和銅 Wadō	708

Nara (712–793)

44.	元正	†Genshō, 715–724	
		霊亀 Reiki	715
		養老 Yōrō	717
45.	聖武	Shōmu, 724–749	
		神亀 Jinki	724
		天平 Tempyō	729
46.	孝謙	†Kōken, 749–758 (same woman as Shōtoku, 48)	
		天平感宝 Tempyōkampō	749
		天平勝宝 Tempyōshōhō	749
		天平宝字 Tempyōhōji	757
47.	淳仁	Junnin, 758–764	
48.	称徳	†Shōtoku, 764–770 (same woman as Kōken, 46; Shōtoku is usual dictionary entry name)	
		天平神護 Tempyōjingo	765
		神護景雲 Jingokeiun	767
49.	光仁	Kōnin, 770–781	
		宝亀 Hōki	770

Heian (794–1186)

50.	桓武	Kammu, 781–806	
		天応 Ten'ō	781
		延暦 Enryaku	782

TABLE 2–4. (*continued*)

Heian (794–1186)	

51. 平城	Heizei, 806–809	
	大同 Daidō	806
52. 嵯峨	Saga, 809–823	
	弘仁 Kōnin	810
53. 淳和	Junna, 823–833	
	天長 Tenchō	824
54. 仁明	Nimmyō, 833–850	
	承和 Jōwa	834
	嘉祥 Kajō	848
55. 文徳	Montoku, 850–858	
	仁寿 Ninju	851
	斉衡 Saikō	854
	天安 Tenan (or Tennan)	857
56. 清和	Seiwa, 858–876	
	貞観 Jōgan	859
57. 陽成	Yōzei, 876 (877)–884	
	元慶 Gangyō	877
58. 光孝	Kōkō, 884–887	
	仁和 Ninna	885
59. 宇多	Uda, 887–897	
	寛平 Kampyō	889
60. 醍醐	Daigo, 897–930	
	昌泰 Shōtai	898
	延喜 Engi	901
	延長 Enchō	923
61. 朱雀	Suzaku, 930–946	
	承平 Jōhei	931
	天慶 Tengyō	938
62. 村上	Murakami, 946–967	
	天暦 Tenryaku	947
	天徳 Tentoku	957
	応和 Ōwa	961
	康保 Kōhō	964
63. 冷泉	Reizei, 967–969	
	安和 Anna	968
64. 円融	En'yū, 969–984	
	天禄 Tenroku	970
	天延 Ten'en	973
	貞元 Jōgen	976
	天元 Tengen	978
	永観 Eikan	983
65. 花山	Kazan, 984–986	
	寛和 Kanna	985
66. 一条	Ichijō, 986–1011	
	永延 Eien	987
	永柞 Eiso	989
	正暦 Shōryaku	990

Tᴀʙʟᴇ 2–4. (*continued*)

		Heian (794–1186)	
	長徳	Chōtoku	995
	長保	Chōhō	999
	寛弘	Kankō	1004
67.	三条	Sanjō, 1011–1016	
	長和	Chōwa	1012
68.	後一条	Goichijō, 1016–1036	
	寛仁	Kannin	1017
	治安	Jian	1021
	万寿	Manju	1024
	長元	Chōgen	1028
69.	後朱雀	Gosuzaku, 1036–1045	
	長暦	Chōryaku	1037
	長久	Chōkyū	1040
	寛徳	Kantoku	1044
70.	後冷泉	Goreizei, 1045–1068	
	永承	'Eijō	1046
	天喜	Tengi	1053
	康平	Kōhei	1058
	治暦	Jiryaku	1065
71.	後三条	Gosanjō, 1068–1072	
	延久	Enkyū	1069
72.	白河	Shirakawa, 1072–1086	
	承保	Jōhō	1074
	承暦	Jōryaku	1077
	永保	Eihō	1081
	応徳	Ōtoku	1084
73.	堀河	Horikawa, 1086–1107	
	寛治	Kanji	1087
	嘉保	Kahō	1094
	永長	Eichō	1096
	承徳	Jōtoku	1097
	康和	Kōwa	1099
	長治	Chōji	1104
	嘉承	Kajō	1106
74.	鳥羽	Toba, 1107–1123	
	天仁	Tennin	1108
	天永	Ten'ei	1110
	永久	Eikyū	1113
	元永	Gen'ei	1118
	保安	Hōan	1120
75.	崇徳	Sutoku, 1123–1141	
	天治	Tenji	1124
	大治	Daiji	1126
	天承	Tenjō	1131
	長承	Chōjō	1132
	保延	Hōen	1135
76.	近衛	Konoe, 1141–1155	

TABLE 2–4. (*continued*)

		Heian (794–1186)	
		永治 Eiji	1141
		康治 Kōji	1142
		天養 Ten'yō	1144
		久安 Kyūan	1145
		仁平 Nimpyō	1151
		久寿 Kyūju	1154
77.	後白河	Goshirakawa, 1155–1158	
		保元 Hōgen	1156
78.	二条	Nijō, 1158–1165	
		平治 Heiji	1159
		永暦 Eiryaku	1160
		応保 Ōhō	1161
		長寛 Chōkan	1163
79.	六条	Rokujō, 1165–1168	
		永万 Eiman	1165
		仁安 Nin'an	1166
80.	高倉	Takakura, 1168–1180	
		嘉応 Kaō	1169
		承安 Jōan	1171
		安元 Angen	1175
		治承 Jishō	1177
81.	安徳	Antoku, 1180–1183	
		養和 Yōwa	1181
		寿永 Juei	1182
		Kamakura (1186–1336)	
82.	後鳥羽	Gotoba, 1183 (1184)–1198	
		元暦 Genryaku	1184
		文治 Bunji	1185
		建久 Kenkyū	1190
83.	土御門	Tsuchimikado, 1198–1210	
		正治 Shōji	1199
		建仁 Kennin	1201
		元久 Genkyū	1204
		建永 Ken'ei	1206
		承元 Jōgen	1207
84.	順徳	Juntoku, 1210–1221	
		建暦 Kenryaku	1211
		建保 Kempō	1213
		承久 Jōkyū	1219
85.	仲恭	Chūkyō, 1221	
86.	後堀河	Gohorikawa, 1221–1232	
		貞応 Jōō	1222
		元仁 Gennin	1224
		嘉禄 Karoku	1225
		安貞 Antei	1227
		寛喜 Kangi	1229

TABLE 2–4. (*continued*)

		Kamakura (1186–1336)	
87.	四条	Shijō, 1232–1242	
		貞永 Jōei	1232
		天福 Tempuku	1233
		文暦 Bunryaku	1234
		嘉禎 Katei	1235
		暦仁 Ryakunin	1238
		延応 En'ō	1239
		仁治 Ninji	1240
88.	後嵯峨	Gosaga, 1242–1246	
		寛元 Kangen	1243
89.	後深草	Gofukakusa, 1246–1259	
		宝治 Hōji	1247
		建長 Kenchō	1249
		康元 Kōgen	1256
		正嘉 Shōka	1257
90.	亀山	Kameyama, 1259–1274	
		正元 Shōgen	1259
		文応 Bun'ō	1260
		弘長 Kōchō	1261
		文永 Bun'ei	1264
91.	後宇多	Gouda, 1274–1287	
		建治 Kenji	1275
		弘安 Kōan	1278
92.	伏見	Fushimi, 1287 (1288)–1298	
		正応 Shōō	1288
		永仁 Einin	1293
93.	後伏見	Gofushimi, 1298–1301	
		正安 Shōan	1299
94.	後二条	Gonijō, 1301–1308	
		乾元 Kengen	1302
		嘉元 Kagen	1303
		徳治 Tokuji	1306
95.	花園	Hanazono, 1308–1318	
		延慶 Engyō	1308
		応長 Ōchō	1311
		正和 Shōwa	1312
		文保 Bumpō	1317
96.	後醍醐	Godaigo, 1318–1339	
		元応 Gen'ō	1319
		元亨 Genkyō	1321
		正中 Shōchū	1324
		嘉暦 Karyaku	1326
		元徳 Gentoku	1329
		元弘 Genkō	1331
		建武 Kemmu	1334
		延元 Engen	1336

Table 2–4. (*continued*)

<table>
<tr><td colspan="4" align="center">Nambokuchō (1336–1392)</td></tr>
<tr><td>97.</td><td>後村上</td><td>Gomurakami, 1339 (coronation?)–1368</td><td></td></tr>
<tr><td></td><td></td><td>興国 Kōkoku</td><td>1340</td></tr>
<tr><td></td><td></td><td>正平 Shōhei</td><td>1346</td></tr>
<tr><td>98.</td><td>長慶</td><td>Chōkei, 1368 (coronation?)–1383</td><td></td></tr>
<tr><td></td><td></td><td>建徳 Kentoku</td><td>1370</td></tr>
<tr><td></td><td></td><td>文中 Bunchū</td><td>1372</td></tr>
<tr><td></td><td></td><td>天授 Tenju</td><td>1375</td></tr>
<tr><td></td><td></td><td>弘和 Kōwa</td><td>1381</td></tr>
<tr><td>99.</td><td>後亀山</td><td>Gokameyama, 1383–1392</td><td></td></tr>
<tr><td></td><td></td><td>元中 Genchū</td><td>1384</td></tr>
<tr><td></td><td></td><td>明徳 Meitoku</td><td>1390</td></tr>
</table>

<table>
<tr><td colspan="4" align="center">*The Brief Northern Dynasty*</td></tr>
<tr><td>1.</td><td>光厳</td><td>Kōgon, 1332–1333</td><td></td></tr>
<tr><td></td><td></td><td>正慶 Shōkei</td><td>1332</td></tr>
<tr><td>2.</td><td>光明</td><td>Kōmyō, 1333 (1337)–1348</td><td></td></tr>
<tr><td></td><td></td><td>暦応 Ryakuō</td><td>1338</td></tr>
<tr><td></td><td></td><td>康永 Kōei</td><td>1342</td></tr>
<tr><td></td><td></td><td>貞和 Jōwa</td><td>1345</td></tr>
<tr><td>3.</td><td>崇光</td><td>Sukō, 1348 (1349)–1351</td><td></td></tr>
<tr><td></td><td></td><td>観応 Kan'ō</td><td>1350</td></tr>
<tr><td>4.</td><td>後光厳</td><td>Gokōgon, 1352 (1353)–1371</td><td></td></tr>
<tr><td></td><td></td><td>文和 Bunna</td><td>1352</td></tr>
<tr><td></td><td></td><td>延文 Embun</td><td>1356</td></tr>
<tr><td></td><td></td><td>康安 Kōan</td><td>1361</td></tr>
<tr><td></td><td></td><td>貞治 Jōji</td><td>1362</td></tr>
<tr><td></td><td></td><td>応安 Ōan</td><td>1368</td></tr>
<tr><td>5.</td><td>後円融</td><td>Goen'yū, 1371 (1374)–1382</td><td></td></tr>
<tr><td></td><td></td><td>永和 Eiwa</td><td>1375</td></tr>
<tr><td></td><td></td><td>康暦 Kōryaku</td><td>1379</td></tr>
<tr><td></td><td></td><td>永徳 Eitoku</td><td>1381</td></tr>
<tr><td>6.</td><td>後小松</td><td>Gokomatsu, 1382–1392
(becoming 100th in main line)</td><td></td></tr>
<tr><td></td><td></td><td>至徳 Shitoku</td><td>1384</td></tr>
<tr><td></td><td></td><td>嘉慶 Kakei (or Kakyo)</td><td>1387</td></tr>
<tr><td></td><td></td><td>康応 Kōō</td><td>1389</td></tr>
<tr><td></td><td></td><td>明徳 Meitoku</td><td>1390</td></tr>
</table>

<table>
<tr><td colspan="4" align="center">Muromachi (1392–1573)</td></tr>
<tr><td>100.</td><td>後小松</td><td>Gokomatsu, 1392–1412</td><td></td></tr>
<tr><td></td><td></td><td>応永 Ōei</td><td>1394</td></tr>
<tr><td>101.</td><td>称光</td><td>Shōkō, 1412 (1414)–1428</td><td></td></tr>
<tr><td></td><td></td><td>正長 Shōchō</td><td>1428</td></tr>
</table>

TABLE 2–4. (*continued*)

Muromachi (1392–1573)

102.	後花園	Gohanazono, 1428 (1429)–1464	
		永享 Eikyō	1429
		嘉吉 Kakitsu	1441
		文安 Bun'an (or Bunnan)	1444
		宝徳 Hōtoku	1449
		享徳 Kyōtoku	1452
		康正 Kōshō	1455
		長禄 Chōroku	1457
		寛正 Kanshō	1460
103.	後土御門	Gotsuchimikado, (1465)–1500	
		文正 Bunshō	1466
		応仁 Ōnin	1467
		文明 Bummei	1469
		長享 Chōkyō	1487
		延徳 Entoku	1489
		明応 Meiō	1492
104.	後柏原	Gokashiwabara, 1500 (1521)–1526	
		文亀 Bunki	1501
		永正 Eishō	1504
		大永 Daiei	1521
105.	後奈良	Gonara, 1526 (1536)–1557	
		享禄 Kyōroku	1528
		天文 Tembun (or Temmon)	1532
		弘治 Kōji	1555
106.	正親町	Ōgimachi, 1557 (1560)–1586	
		永禄 Eiroku	1558
		元亀 Genki	1570
		天正 Tenshō	1573

Azuchi-Momoyama (1573–1603)

107.	後陽成	Goyōzei, 1586–1611	
		文禄 Bunroku	1592
		慶長 Keichō	1596

Edo (1603–1688)

108.	後水尾	Gomizunoo, 1611–1629	
		元和 Genna	1615
		寛永 Kan'ei	1624
109.	明正	Meishō, 1629 (1630)–1643	
110.	後光明	Gokōmyō, 1643–1654	
		正保 Shōhō	1644
		慶安 Keian	1648
		承応 Jōō	1652
		明暦 Meireki	1655
111.	後西	Gosai, (1656)–1663	
		万治 Manji	1658
		寛文 Kambun	1661

TABLE 2–4. (*continued*)

<hr>

Azuchi-Momoyama (1573–1603)

112.	霊元	Reigen, 1663–1687	
		延宝 Empō	1673
		天和 Tenna	1681
		貞享 Jōkyō	1684
113.	東山	Higashiyama, 1687–1709	
		元禄 Genroku	1688
		宝永 Hōei	1704
114.	中御門	Nakamikado, 1709 (1710)–1735	
		正徳 Shōtoku	1711
		享保 Kyōhō	1716
115.	桜町	Sakuramachi, 1735–1747	
		天文 Gembun	1736
		寛保 Kampō	1741
		延享 Enkyō	1744
116.	桃園	Momozono, 1747–1762	
		寛延 Kan'en	1748
		宝暦 Hōreki	1751
117.	後桜町	Gosakuramachi, (1763)–1770	
		明和 Meiwa	1764
118.	後桃園	Gomomozono, 1770 (1771)–1779	
		安永 An'ei	1772
119.	光格	Kōkaku, 1779 (1780)–1817	
		天明 Temmei	1781
		寛政 Kansei	1789
		享和 Kyōwa	1801
		文化 Bunka	1804
120.	仁孝	Ninkō, 1817–1846	
		文政 Bunsei	1818
		天保 Tempō (or Tembō)	1830
		弘化 Kōka	1844
121.	孝明	Kōmei, 1846 (1847)–1866	
		嘉永 Kaei	1848
		安政 Ansei	1854
		万延 Man'en	1860
		文久 Bunkyū	1861
		元治 Genji	1864
		慶応 Keiō	1865

<hr>

Modern (1868——)

122.	明治	Meiji, 1866 (1868)–1912	
		明治 Meiji	1868
123.	大正	Taishō, 1912 (1915)–1926	
		大正 Taishō	1912
124.	昭和	Present Sovereign, 1926 (1928)– —	
		昭和 Shōwa	1926

<hr>

C. ANNALS OF WORKS AND EVENTS

Symbols and abbreviations

ca.	about this time
done	by this time
hereafter	after this time
in part	written in part by this date
comp.	the person(s) named compiled or edited the work named
( )	a *date* in parentheses after a title indicates the date of completion or publication; a *title* in parentheses is an alternative in part or whole
*	indicates a person or title found in Part Three, Major Authors and Works
italics	italicized words other than titles will be found in Part Four, Literary Terms

About These Annals

The dates given are definite as far as possible as to completion, publication, mention of a major part, or starting. The older the work, in general the less is certain. Most of the dates have been taken from *Nihon Bungaku Shōjiten*, edited by Itō Sei, et al. (Shinchōsha, 1976), and *Kōjien*, 2nd ed. (Iwanami, 1969). Other sources would sometimes give different dates, readings of titles and names, and so on. Even when not so indicated, dates may therefore be approximate or disputed.

A special issue of *Kokubungaku*, vol. 22 (February 1977) devotes an article to the literature of each decade, 670–1870.

The excellent *Nihonshi Jiten*, edited by Takayanagi and Takeuchi, 2nd ed. (Kadokawa, 1964), gives more detailed political and historical information; it also includes literary figures and works.

TABLE 2–5. WORKS AND EVENTS

Date	Works, Kinds	Events
	Yamato Period (645–711)	
607		Hōryūji built
622		*Shōtoku Taishi d.
645		Taika Reform
671		Tamai (field dance) performed at palace
672		Jinshin War
698 ca.		*Bugaku* and *sangaku* from China
701		A court school (daigaku) founded on Confucian lines; Taihō Code
710		Capital moved to Heijōkyō

Tᴀʙʟᴇ 2–5. (*continued*)

Date	Works, Kinds	Events
	Nara Period (712–793)	
712	Ō no Yasumaro finishes *Kojiki* revisions	
713	*Fudoki* ordered	
715	*Harima Fudoki* in existence	
718	*Hitachi Fudoki* in existence	
720	*Nihon Shoki (Nihongi)* comp. by Prince Toneri, Ō no Yasumaro	
732	*Izumo Fudoki* in existence	
750 ca.		Li Po and Tu Fu fl.
751	*Kaifūsō	
753 ca.	*Bussokusekika	
759 ca.	Later poems of the *Man'yōshū	
770		Kagura performed sometime in this decade
772	*Fujiwara Hamanari, *Kakyō Hyōshiki*	
	Heian Period (794–1186)	
794		Capital moved to Heiankyō
797	*Shoku Nihongi*; *Kūkai, *Sangō Shiki*	
806		Po Chü-i, *Song of Everlasting Sorrow*
814	Ono no Minemori et al. comp. *Ryōunshū*	
815	Fujiwara Fuyutsugu et al. comp. *Bunka Shūreishū*	
819	*Kūkai, *Bunkyō Hifuron*	
822		*Saichō d.
823	*Nihon Ryōiki (Reiiki)*	
827	Yoshimine Yasuyo comp. *Keikokushū*	
846		Po Chü-i d.
858		Fujiwara Yoshifusa introduces sesshō government
880		Fujiwara Mototsune first kampaku
885 ca.	*Zaiminbukyōke Utaawase* (first poetry match)	
893	*Shinsen Man'yōshū* done; *Kampyō no Kisai (or Kisaki) no Miya no Utaawase*	
894		Embassies to China stopped
897–930		Reign of Daigo (without sesshō or kampaku)
901–933	Two traditions say *Taketori Monogatari* done before/after this time	
905–920	*Kokinshū*. Two traditions say *Ise Monogatari* done before/after *Kokinshū*	

TABLE 2–5. (*continued*)

Date	Works, Kinds	Events
908 ca.		*Rōei* popularized
913 ca.	**Kagura* and **azumaasobiuta written*	
927		*Engi Shiki*
930–934	*Ki no Tsurayuki, Shinsenshū	
935	*Ki no Tsurayuki, Tosa Nikki	
937	*Minamoto Shitagō, Wamyō Ruijūshō	
938		Nembutsuodori introduced
940	*Shōmonki	
945	*Mibu no Tadamine, *Wakatai Jūsshu*; sometime hereafter, *Tsurayuki Shū*	
946–967		Reign of Murakami
951	*Yamato Monogatari* done (some say 956); *Ise Shū*	
958 ca.	*Gosenshū done	
960	*Tentoku Dairi Utaawase*	
967 ca.	*Heichū Monogatari	
974 ca.	*Fujiwara Michitsuna no Haha, *Kagerō Nikki*	
982 ca.	*Utsuho (Utsubo) Monogatari	
987 ca.	*Kokin Rokujō	
996 ca.	*Sei Shōnagon, *Makura no Sōshi*; other traditions say later	
1008 ca.	*Izumi Shikibu Nikki	
1011 ca.	*Murasaki Shikibu, **Genji Monogatari*; *Fujiwara Kintō, *Wakan Rōeishū*	
1023		*Dengaku* performed at palace
1030 ca.	*Eiga Monogatari	
1041	*Fujiwara Kintō, *Waka Kuhon* and *Shinsen Zuinō* done	
1043–51		Years of war
1053 ca.	*Sugawara Takasue no Musume, *Hamamatsu Chūnagon Monogatari*	
1055	*Rokujō Saiin Monogatari Utaawase*	
1058	*Fujiwara Akihira, *Shinsarugakuki*	
1060 ca.	*Sugawara Takasue no Musume, *Sarashina Nikki*	
1076 ca.	*Sagoromo Monogatari	
1083–86		Years of war
1086	*Goshūishū	Shirakawa begins insei system
1095	*Ōe Masafusa, *Kairaishiki* (on puppeteers), *Rakuyō Dengakuki*	
1107	*Ōe Masafusa, *Gōdanshō*; ca. **Konjaku Monogatari (Shū)*	
1111	*Ōe Masafusa, *Gōshidai*	
1119 ca.	*Ōkagami	
1123	*Fujiwara Mototoshi, *Shinsen Rōeishū* done	

TABLE 2–5. (*continued*)

Date	Works, Kinds	Events
1126	*Kin' yōshū*, 2nd compilation	
1134	*Uchigiki Shū* done	
1140	*Honchō Zokumonzui* hereafter	
1144	*Fujiwara Kiyosuke, Ōgishō* done	
1151	*Shikashū*	
1156		Hōgen War breaks out
1159		Heiji War breaks out
1165	*Fujiwara Kiyosuke comp. Shokushikashū*; *Kenshō, Konsenshū*	
1167		Taira Kiyomori is Dajō Daijin
1170 ca.	*Imakagami*	
1175		Female *dengaku* appears
1178	*Fujiwara Shunzei, Chōshū Eisō* in part	
1185		Minamoto defeat Taira at Dannoura
	Near the end of the Heian Period: *Tsutsumi Chūnagon Monogatari*; *Yoru no Nezame*; Genji Monogatari Emaki; *Kohon Setsuwashū*; *Torikaeba ya Monogatari*	

Kamakura Period (1186–1336)

Date	Works, Kinds	Events
	Near the beginning of the Kamakura Period: *Hōgen Monogatari*; *Ujishūi Monogatari*; and some say *Heiji Monogatari*; also *Sumiyoshi Monogatari* present form (original early Heian)	
1187	*Fujiwara Shunzei comp. *Senzaishū*; *Saigyō, Mimosusogawa Utaawase	
1190	*Saigyō, Sankashū*	
1192		*Minamoto Yoritomo assumes shogunate, establishes *bakufu* at Kamakura
1193	*Roppyakuban Utaawase*	
1195	*Mizukagami* done	
1197	*Fujiwara Shunzei, Korai Fūteishō*	
1200		Nara *sarugaku* players act before Tsuchimikado
1202	*Kamo no Chōmei, Mumyōshō*; Sengohyakuban Utaawase done	
1205	*Shinkokinshū* presented rev. 1216	
1209	*Fujiwara Teika, Kindai Shūka*, 1st version	
1212	*Kamo no Chōmei, *Hōjōki*	Hōnen d.
1218 ca.	*Heike Monogatari*	

TABLE 2–5. (*continued*)

Date	Works, Kinds	Events
1219	*Fujiwara Teika, *Maigetsushō*; *Ken-shun Mon'in Chūnagon Nikki* in part; ca. *Minamoto Sanetomo, *Kinkaishū*; *Jien, *Gukanshō*	
1223 ca.	*Kaidōki*	
1232 ca.	*Kenrei Mon'in Ukyō no Daibu Shū*	Sarugaku popular in Kyoto
1234	*Fujiwara Teika comp. *Shinchoku-senshū*	
1235 ca.	*Fujiwara Teika comp. *Ogura Hya-kunin Isshu*	
1239		Bakufu bans sale of human beings
1241	*Izumi Shikibu, *Izumi Shikibu Shū* done?	
1242	*Tōkan Kikō*; ca.; *Juntoku comp. *Yakumo Mishō*	
1251	*Fujiwara Tameie comp. *Shokugo-senshū*	
1252		Princes' bakufu established at Kamakura
1252 ca.	*Gofukakusa In Ben no Naishi, *Ben no Naishi Nikki*	
1259	*Nichiren, *Risshō Ankokuron*; ca. *Gempei Jōsuiki* (*Seisuiki*)	
1265	*Shokukokinshū*	
1269	*Senkaku, *Man'yōshū Chūshaku*	
1271 ca.	*Fūgashū*	
1274 ca.	*Fujiwara Tameie, *Eiga Ittei*	
1278 ca.	*Shokushūishū*	
1280	*Abutsu Ni, *Isayoi* (*Izayoi*) *Nikki*; *Asukai Gayū, *Haru no Miyamaji*	
1287 ca.	*Kyōgoku Tamekane, *Tamekane Kyō Wakashō*	
1292 ca.	*Fushimi In no Nakatsukasa Naishi, *Nakatsukasa Naishi Nikki*	
1303	*Nijō Tameyo comp. *Shingosenshū*	
1306 ca.	*Gufukakusa In Nijō, *Towazugatari*	
1308 ca.		Heikyoku becomes popular
1310	*Kyōgoku Tamekane, *Engyō Ryōkyō Sochinjō*	
1310–15 ca.		Dengaku popular
1316		Hōjō Takatoki learns dengaku performance
1320	*Shokusenzaishū*	
1320–25 ca.		Small coins made for commoners; pawn shops appear
1326	*Shokugoshūishū*	
1330	*Kenkō, *Tsurezuregusa* begun	
1331		Genkō War

Table 2–5. (*continued*)

Date	Works, Kinds	Events
1331–92		Northern Dynasty
1336		Ashikaga Takauji, shogun, establishes *bakufu* in Muromachi

Nambokuchō Period (1336–1392)

Date	Works, Kinds	Events
1339	*Kitabatake Chikafusa, *Jinnō Shōtōki*	
1346	*Fūgashū* in preparation	
1349		*Dengaku* being performed at Shijō Kawaramachi, Kyoto
1353	*Nijō Yoshimoto, *Ojima no Kuchi-zusami*	
1357	*Nijō Yoshimoto, *Tsukubashū*	
1358	*Yoshino Shūi*	
1359	*Shinsenzaishū*	
1361	*Shintōshū*	
1366	*Nenjū Gyōji Utaawase*	
1371	*Imagawa Ryōshun, *Michiyukiburi*	
1372	*Nijō Yoshimoto, *Renga Shinshiki* and *Tsukuba Mondō*; *Taiheiki*	
1374 ca.	*Masukagami*	
1375	*Nanchō Gohyakuban Utaawase*	Ashikaga Yoshimitsu sees *nō* at Kumano, takes *Zeami under his patronage
1381	*Munenaga Shinnō comp. *Shin'yōshū*	
1384	*Bontō, *Sodeshita Shū*	
1385	*Nijō Yoshimoto, *Ishiyama Hyakuin*	
1387	*Nijō Yoshimoto, *Kinrai Fūteishō*	

Muromachi Period (1392–1573)

Date	Works, Kinds	Events
1399	*Soga Monogatari* (begun late Kamakura) completed early Muromachi	Ōei War
1400	*Zeami, *Fūshikaden*	
1418	*Shōtetsu, *Nagusamegusa*	
1420	*Zeami, *Shikadō*	
1423	*Zeami, *Sandō*	
1424	*Zeami, *Kakyō*	
1430	*Zeami, *Sarugaku Dangi*	
1432		Female *sarugaku* begins
1439	*Shinzokukokinshū*	
1441		*Kōwakamai* is remarked on
1448	*Shōtetsu, *Shōtetsu Monogatari*	
1455	*Komparu Zenchiku, *Rokurin Ichiro no Ki*	
1460 ca.		*Renga* vogue under way
1463	*Shinkei, *Sasamegoto*	

TABLE 2–5. (*continued*)

Date	Works, Kinds	Events
1466 ca.		*Kōwakamai* begins in Kyoto area
1467	*Komparu Zenchiku, *Shidō Yōshō*	Ōnin War (to 1477)
1468	*Sōgi, *Azuma Mondō*	
1469		Painter *Sesshū returns from China
1472	*Ichijō Kanera (Kaneyoshi), *Kachō Yojō*	
1479	*Sōgi, *Oi no Susami*	
1480	*Sōgi, *Tsukushi Michi no Ki*	ca. Tea ceremony in vogue
1488	*Sōgi, *Shōhaku, *Sōchō, *Minase Sangin Hyakuin*	
1491	*Sōgi, *Shōhaku, *Sōchō, *Yunoyama (Yuyama) Sangin Hyakuin*	
1495	*Sōgi, *Sōgi Dokugin Nanibito Hyakuin*	
1518	*Kanginshū*	
1525	*Arakida Moritake, *Yononaka Hyaku-shu*	
1540	*Arakida Moritake, *Dokugin Senku*	
1543		Portuguese ships arrive
1549		St. Francis Xavier preaches
1554	*Yamazaki Sōkan comp. (*Shinsen*) *Inu Tsukubashū*	
1560		*Shamisen* adapted to Japanese use
1563	*Satomura Jōha, *Shōmyōin Tsuizen Dokugin Senku*	
1577		Puppeteers officially recognized

Azuchi Momoyama Period (1573–1603)

Date	Works, Kinds	Events
1585	*Satomura Jōha, *Renga Shihōshō*, *Bōfu Tsuizen Dokugin*	Toyotomi Hideyoshi is ruler
1587	*Hosokawa Yūsai, *Kyūshūdō no Ki*	Christianity proscribed
1593 ca.	*Isoho* [Aesop] *Monogatari* etc. appear from Christian sources	Wooden movable type comes into use; Portuguese Roman letters in use
1595 ca.		Puppeteers, reciters combine in Kyoto, producing *kojōruri*
1597 ca.	"Okuni" acts *kabuki* in Kyoto	
1598		Hideyoshi d.
1600		Battle of Sekigahara

Edo Period (1603–1868)

Date	Works, Kinds	Events
1603		Tokugawa Ieyasu shogun
1614	*Ryūtatsu Koutashū* published (popular since ca. 1600)	

Table 2–5. (*continued*)

Date	Works, Kinds	Events
1614 ca.		Puppet *jōruri* appears on stage in several places
1615		Seven *kabuki* theaters permitted in Kyoto; Toyotomi line exterminated in Osaka
1619 ca.		Japanese Christians martyred
1623	*Anrakuan Sakuden, *Seisuishō*	
1629		Public acting, dancing by women proscribed
1637		Tokugawa Ieyasu establishes *bakufu* in Edo; Shimabara War
1639		Christianity strictly forbidden to all daimyo; Japan closed
1645 ca.		*Kanazōshi* popular
1648	*Kitamura Kigin begins publishing works on *haikai*, etc.	
1651	*Matsunaga Teitoku, *Gosan*	
1652		Boy *kabuki* theater proscribed; six *kabuki* theaters permitted in Osaka
1657		Great Fire of Edo
1660	*Asai Ryōi, *Tōkaidō Meishoki*	ca. *Jōruri* popular in Edo
1663	*Suzuki Shōsan, *Ninin Bikuni*	
1666	*Asai Ryōi, *Otogi Bōko*	
1673	*Ihara Saikaku, *Ikutama Manku*	
1675	*Nishiyama Sōin, *Danrin Toppyakuin*	ca. *Danrin haikai* well established
1680		Study of Dutch begins
1682	*Ihara Saikaku, *Kōshoku Ichidai Otoko*	*Ukiyozōshi* appear
1683	*Matsuo Bashō, *Minashiguri*; *Chikamatsu Monzaemon, *Yotsugi Soga*	
1684		Osaka Takemoto Gidayu Za founded
1685	*Matsuo Bashō, *Nozarashi Kikō*; *Chikamatsu Monzaemon, *Shusse Kagekiyo*	
1689		*Matsuo Bashō begins trip treated in *Oku no Hosomichi*
1691	*Mukai Kyorai, *Nozawa Bonchō comp. *Sarumino* (*haikai* by Bashō and his school)	
1692	*Ihara Saikaku, *Seken Mune San'yō*	
1697	*Toda Mosui, *Higagoto Shirabe*	

TABLE 2–5. (*continued*)

Date	Works, Kinds	Events
1699	*Chikamatsu Monzaemon, *Keisei Hotoke no Hara*	
1701	*Ejima Kiseki, *Keisei Irojamisen*	
1702	*Mukai Kyorai, *Kyorai Shō* (to 1704)	
1703	*Chikamatsu Monzaemon, *Sonezaki Shinjū*	Osaka Toyotakeza founded
1704		Danjūrō I d.
1706	*Chikamatsu Monzaemon, *Shinjū Nimaiezōshi*	
1707	*Chikamatsu Monzaemon, *Shinjū Kasane Izutsu*	
1711	*Ejima Kiseki, *Keisei Kintanki*	
1715	*Chikamatsu Monzaemon, *Kokusen'ya Kassen*	
1720	*Chikamatsu Monzaemon, *Shinjū Ten no Amijima*	Western books proscribed
1720		Publication of love suicide stories prohibited
1734	*Takeda Izumo, *Ashiya Dōman Ōuchi Kagami*	Three men now required to manipulate puppets
1748	*Takeda Izumo II, *Kanadehon Chūshingura*	
1751	*Namiki Sōsuke, *Ichinotani Futaba Gunki*	
1755 ca.		Distinct Edo language formed
1758		Revolving *kabuki* stage invented
1763	*Motoori Norinaga, *Isonokami Sasamegoto*	
1765	*Kamo no Mabuchi, *Kokuikō*	
1768	*Ueda Akinari, *Ugetsu Monogatari*; *Hiraga Gennai, *Nenashigusa*	
1770	*Inaka Rōjin Tada no Jijii *Yūshi Hōgen*	
1773	*Sakurada Jisuke, *Gohiiki Kanjinchō*	
1774 ca.		*Kibyōshi* appear
1778	*Namiki Gohei, *Kimmon Gosan no Kiri*; *Sakurada Jisuke, *Date Kurabe Gkuni Kabuki*	
1779	*Koikawa Harumachi, *Mudaiki*	
1780	*Chikamatsu Hanji, *Shimpan Utazaimon*	ca. *Kyōka, senryū* popular
1783	*Ōta Nampo, *Manzai Kyōkashū*; *Chikamatsu Hanji, *Igagoe Dōchū Sugoroku*	
1784	*Takai Kitō comp. *Yosa Buson, *Buson Shū*	
1785	*Santō Kyōden, *Edo Umare Uwaki no Kabayaki*	

TABLE 2–5. (*continued*)

Date	Works, Kinds	Events
1787	*Santō Kyōden, *Tsūgen Sōmagaki*	Price riots in Edo and Osaka
1789 ca.		*Kibyōshi* bitterly treating current events-banned
1790	*Motoori Norinaga, *Kojikiden* and *Kotoba no Tama no O*	*Sharebon* banned; Neoconfucianism proclaimed sole orthodoxy
1791	*Ueda Akinari, *Kuse Monogatari*	Punishment decreed for publishing *sharebon*
1797	*Yosa Buson, *Shin Hanatsumi*; *Motoori Norinaga, *Kokinshū Tōkagami*	Edo *rakugo* banned
1798	*Shikitei Samba, *Tatsumi Fugen*	
1799	*Motoori Norinaga, *Genji Monogatari Tama no Ogushi*	
1800		Bunrakuza begins
1802	*Jippensha Ikku, *(Tōkai) (dōchū) Hizakurige* (to 1822); *Katō Chikage, *Ukeragahana*	
1804	From this time, *Ryōkan active as a poet	*Ezōshi* banned; those associated with *Ehon Taiheiki* and *Bakemono Taiheiki* punished
1805	*Santō Kyōden, *Sakurahime Zenden Akebonozōshi*	
1807	*Kyokutei Bakin, *Chinsetsu Yumiharizuki* (1810)	
1808	*Ueda Akinari, *Harusame Monogatari* and *Tandai Shōshinroku*; *Tsuruya Namboku, *Toki mo Kikiyō Shusse no Ukejō*	
1809	*Shikitei Samba, *Ukiyoburo* (to 1813)	
1811	*Ozawa Roan, *Rokujō Eisō*	
1813	*Murata Harumi, *Kotojirishū*; *Kyokutei Bakin, *Beibei Kyōdan*; *Shikitei Samba, *Ukiyodoko* in progress	
1814	*Kyokutei Bakin, *(Nansō Satomi) Hakkenden*	
1815	*Ryūtei Tanehiko, *Shohenjitate*	
1819	*Kobayashi Issa, *Oraga Haru*; *Jippensha Ikku, *Seidan no Mine no Hatsuhana*	
1820	*Ōta Nampo, *Ichiwa Ichigen*	
1825	*Tsuruya Namboku, *Tōkaidō Yotsuya Kaidan*	Bakufu orders all foreign ships be driven away
1826 ca.	*Rai San'yō begins *Nihon Gaishi*	
1828	*Kyokutei Bakin, *Kinsei Setsu Bishōnenroku*	

TABLE 2–5. (*continued*)

Date	Works, Kinds	Events
1829	*Ryūtei Tanehiko, *Nise Murasaki Inaka Genji* (1842)	
1830	*Kagawa Kageki, *Keien Isshi*	ca. *Ninjō* literature popular
1831	*Kyoku Sanjin, *Kanamajiri Musume Setsuyō*	
1832	*Tamenaga Shunsui, (*Shunshoku*) *Umegoyomi* (1833)	
1842		Tamenaga Shunsui manacled; pictures of actors and courtesans banned; general government repression of writers
1853		Perry's black ships arrive

PART THREE Major Authors and Works

Many readers may have occasion to come first to this part. If so, their investigations will be assisted by attention to the notice opposite the table of contents and by examination of that table. The essential information to remember is that an asterisk before a name or title designates an author or work found in this part; and that an italicized word, other than a title, designates a term given in Part Four (such a term is italicized only on its first appearance in a given entry). In other words, no Japanese word or phrase is otherwise given quotation marks or italicized unless its English counterpart would be.

There are here many more than three hundred entries by "name" and well over one hundred by title. Since the "names" are often appellations that vary from century to century in kind, our policy has been to simplify and normalize to the extent consistent with clarity.

Given problems of authorship, it is often difficult to decide whether to enter a given work by its title or in an author entry. We have followed our models (see the Sources, pp. 515ff.). In practice that means that works are entered here by title when they are anonymous, multiple in authorship or compilation, or debatable as to authorship. Where authorship is reasonably certain or otherwise uncomplicated, a work is given under an author entry. That means that many hundreds of works are included in author entries.

A reader uncertain of authorship can begin with the Index, using the title of the work. Wherever possible, here and in the Index, we have offered translations of titles—with two exceptions. One is when they are obvious in context (such as "Ise's personal collection, *Ise Shū*.") The other involves those titles that cannot be rendered in English until the choice is justified by an accompanying translation. This is radically true of many Edo titles. They sometimes involve plays on words and sounds: for example, Tsuruya Namboku's *Nazo no Obi Chotto Tokube*. Or they may involve Chinese characters at variance from their pronunciation, such as Tsuga Teishō's *Hitsujigusa* 莠句冊.

Following our models, we have not thought certain kinds of simplification possible. Even when cumbersome, some appellations have been given in full, such as "Kenrei Mon'in Ukyō no Daibu." In typical instances we enter individuals under the equivalents of surnames: for example, "Matsuo Bashō." But we also include cross-references, as from "Bashō." Where a writer is widely known by more than one surname, we follow our models for choice of entry and supply cross-references. For example, our entry is "Yosa Buson," with cross-references from both "Taniguchi Buson" and "Buson"; and we stay with "Yosa," although it now seems that the proper pronunciation is "Yoza."

We have been able to simplify in certain other ways. When a person is known by several styles or pen names as an artist, the entry uses the most familiar: "Santō Kyōden" rather than "Kitao Masanobu": and "Matsuo Bashō" rather than "Matsuo Tōsei."

In addition, titles such as "Tennō," "In," "Hōshi," and "Sōzu" are omitted for sovereigns and religious figures.

Wherever feasible without loss of clarity, we have simplified names. The medial "no" normally in use until Edo times is almost uniformly dropped, except for persons with surnames of one or two syllables. So a Heian writer such as "Ariwara Narihira" is understood to be "Ariwara no Narihira." Accompanying designations of court office (kabane) in early times or designations of appointments (such as "Satsuma no Kami") are omitted. Thus we give "Kakinomoto Hitomaro" and "Taira Tadanori" rather than "Kakinomoto no Asomi (no) Hitomaro," and so on.

Where Sinified as well as Japanese readings for names exist, the more familiar in actual usage today is given: "Fujiwara Teika" rather than "Fujiwara Sadaie", and "Fujiwara Ietaka" rather than "Fujiwara Karyū." The alternatives are normally supplied.

Names and titles sometimes have elements not normally used, or have some alternative. When the normally unused or alternative part initiates an entry, the alphabetizing is based on the first commonly used element: "(Fujiwara) Jūnii Tameko" is in the "J" series rather than in the "F," for example. Otherwise, elements commonly not used are sometimes dropped but usually put into parentheses: "*Kokin(waka)shū*." When the matter is too complex for such means, lengthier or repetitive means are used: "*Yoru no Nezame* (or *Yowa no Nezame*, or *Nezame*)."

Characters are supplied for names and titles for at least the entry. But they are omitted when manifest. For example, in the entry for "Izumi Shikibu," the characters for the name are given, but they are not given for the "*Izumi Shikibu Nikki*." In all truth, the characters will not be manifest to someone who knows no Japanese, but their presence would not assist such persons, either.

The designation "parts" is used in lieu of "scrolls," "books," "fascicles," "chapters," and so on to represent a wide range of terms— 巻 (maki, kan), 帖 (jō), and so forth.

The authors and others identified by name entries are chiefly people who wrote literary works in Japanese. But, to increase the utility of this section, attention has also been given—usually in briefer form—to writers in Chinese, and to religious figures, philosophers, scholars, historians, and artists in kinds other than literary.

The attempt has been to scale the length of an entry to the degree of literary importance. Of course insufficient knowledge of earlier writers often makes that aim impossible to realize.

Other information germane to these authors and works is in Part One.

ABE NO NAKAMARO 阿倍仲麻呂. Ca. 700–770. Nara-period scholar, *waka* poet. Little is known of him except that he went to China to study in 717, remaining there for one reason or another until his death. He lives as a poet for one famous poem (*Kokinshū*, 9:406) in which the sight of the moon in China reminds him of its rise over the Hill of Mikasa in Nara.

ABUTSU 阿仏. D. 1283. Mid-Kamakura *waka* poet and diarist. Although her background and canon are not wholly clear, she had remarkable strength of character and was a versatile writer. She became a wife of *Fujiwara Tameie, whose sons later divided over political, poetic, and fiscal disputes, her concern being for her sons, chiefly *Reizei Tamesuke. On his behalf she made a journey to the *bakufu* in Kamakura to seek favorable adjudication. The account of her journey in 1280 is set forth in the *Isayoi* (or *Izayoi*) *Nikki* 十六夜日記 (*The Diary of the Waning Moon*), in which she includes many poems, including *chōka*. Shortly after Tameie took orders, she did also, administering affairs so energetically that she became known as "the female master." She acquired considerable knowledge of the *Genji Monogatari* and is known as a poet for some 330 poems. Among her many other works, her *Niwa no Oshie* 庭の訓 (*Domestic Instructions*) treats her daughter's service at court in terms of a handbook for other ladies-in-waiting. Her *Yoru no Tsuru* 夜の鶴 (*The Crane's Night Lessons*) (1278–1283) collects the poetic teachings of Tameie. And her *Utatane* うたたね (*That Brief Sleep*), written late, is a kind of diary or autobiography treating such matters as an old love affair in days before Tameie. Everything she did and wrote leaves the imprint of an ambitious, powerful personality.

AGUI SCHOOL. See *Shintōshū*.

AKAHITO. See YAMABE AKAHITO.

AKAZOME EMON 赤染衛門. Fl. 976–1041. Mid-Heian *waka* poet. After serving for a time in the palace of *Fujiwara Michinaga, she later served *Jōtō Mon'in. Late in life, over eighty, she took orders. She was one of the group of brilliant women assembled at court in her time—along with *Murasaki Shikibu, *Sei Shōnagon, and *Izumi Shikibu. She participated in numerous *utaawase*, was named one of the Thirty-Six Older Poetic Sages (chūko sanjūrokkasen) and, strange as it seems, was once thought at least equal to *Izumi Shikibu. Her poems appear in royal and other collections from the

Shūishū on. In addition to her personal collection, *Akazome Emon Shū*, she is associated with the *Eiga Monogatari*, not infrequently being considered its author, author in part, or compiler.

AKINARI. See UEDA AKINARI.

AKISUE. See FUJIAWARA AKISUE.

AKUOKE NO NO MAKI 灰汁桶のの巻 (*At the Tub of Ashes*), also called *Kirigirisu* きりぎりす (*As Crickets Chirp*). Early Edo 36-stanza *haikai* sequence composed in autumn, 1690. The poets are *Nozawa Bonchō (*hokku*), *Matsuo Bashō (*waki*), *Okada Yasui (*daisan*, *ageku*), and *Mukai Kyorai. Bashō urged his fellow poets to squeeze the marrow from their bones in writing this sequence. The result is neither quite regular nor irregular; but for individual stanzas, the stanzaic connection (*tsukeai*), and for nearly every other feature it is a model, and perhaps the acme, of Bashō-style haikai. It was included in *Sarumino* (see Part Six).

ANDŌ HIROSHIGE 安藤広重. 1797–1858. Late Edo ukiyo-e print artist. A highly productive artist with many subjects, he is best known for his series on famous places; his fifty-three prints on stations of the road from Edo to Kyoto (*Tōkaidō Gojūsantsugi*, *The Fifty-Three Stations of the Tōkaidō*) is probably the most famous of all ukiyo-e series. Although he often captures striking scenes, their elements compose into a single whole without compositional tension, as with *Katsushika Hokusai.

ANEGAKŌJI IMASHIMMEI HYAKUIN 姉小路 今神明百韻 (*One Hundred Stanzas at Imashimmei Shrine*). A mid-Muromachi hundred-stanza renga sequence composed at the Anegakōji Shrine, probably in 1447. Thirteen poets participated, of whom the best known are *Sōzei (who wrote the winter *hokku* and the *ageku*), *Chikamasa (who wrote the *waki*), *Shinkei, and *Senjun. There is also one *Kō. The sequence suffers at points from unevenness, as is natural with so many poets. But it quite impressively shows gifted poets at work.

ANRAKUAN SAKUDEN 安楽庵策伝. 1554–1642. Early Edo priest, tea master, writer. His chief literary work, *Seisuishō* 醒睡笑 (*Sobering Laughter*, 1623), is a humorous composition in eight parts that had great influence on *hanashibon* and *rakugo*, the latter of which he is credited with inventing.

AOKI MOKUBEI 青木木米. 1767–1833. Late Edo potter. After turning deaf, he was also known as

Rōbei 轟米. Most distinguished for the graceful lines of his pottery, he also showed talent in painting.

ARAI HAKUSEKI 新井白石 1657–1725. Mid-Edo scholar, poet in Chinese, historian, autobiographer, and political figure. Although he began working in his father's shop, he had talents that were recognized by a series of rising appointment that culminated in his becoming the most trusted adviser of the future and then appointed shogun, Tokugawa Ienobu. Some—perhaps including himself— thought he made Ienobu's policy. There was a stubborn integrity to him. His love of Chinese poetry gave strength to what he wrote in Japanese prose. His historical study gave perspective to his political views. Once he put his thoughts in order, he acted with great determination. On three occasions he became masterless (a rōnin), only to recover; and his advice to Ienobu was given with unusual strength and candor. When he could not get on with later shoguns, he expressed himself in writing.

Although not all his works are lengthy, they are numerous and, in their totality, are exceptional in the degree to which they look outward upon the world and inward upon himself. Among his extrospective works, one is Sairan Igen 采覽異言 (1713). This uses material known in Japan from the work of the Jesuit Matteo Ricci and deals with geography as well as some matters treating with many parts of the Western world. About this time Hakuseki met another Jesuit, Giovanni Battista Sidotti, who had somehow gotten to Japan, despite bakufu interdictions. Hakuseki and Sidotti seem to have got on well, with the Japanese admiring the courage of the Italian visitor. The philosophical and religious outlooks of the two men differed greatly, but Hakuseki took the opportunity to learn about geography and astronomy. From this experience and other sources, Hakuseki wrote his Seiyō Kibun 西洋紀聞 (Hearing about the West, 1715), which he added to an edition of Sairan Igen.

From Heian times, Japan had had many autobiographical accounts in nikki and haibun form, among others. But Hakuseki wrote what is generally regarded and esteemed as the first Japanese autobiography in the prose terms known in the West. This draws heavily on materials he had written earlier in order to fashion an account of his public self or person. He began with what he had heard of his grandparents and had observed of his parents, dealing also in no small measure with matters related to his experience in public affairs. The result is a work, Oritaku Shiba no Ki 折たく柴の記 (Told Round a Brushwood Fire, ca. 1716–1717), the sole prose biography in classical Japanese literature worthy of being set beside Rousseau's Confessions.

If this seems to describe Hakuseki as in some way non-Japanese, the description is wrong. Like all other major Edo figures with public interests, he was concerned with what mattered in his time and nation, and he was interested in the usual native and Chinese matters. His Tōga 東雅 (1719, in twenty parts) is a kind of encyclopedic dictionary. With his great linguistic skills, he made an unsual distinction between the spoken and written varieties of Japanese, using Chinese models of linguistic or lexicographic writings and interpretation of the Chinese Shih Ching (J. Shikyō; Classic of Songs) to elucidate language.

The historical elements in Oritaku Shiba no Ki are but one kind of earnest of Hakuseki's importance as a historian. His historical writings proper include Koshitsū 古史通 (A Survey of Ancient Historical Writings, 1716) and Dokushi Yoron 読史余論 (A Reading of History, 1712).

Hakuseki is also one of the important Japanese poets in Chinese. His Hakuseki Shisō 白石詩草 (Hakuseki's Poetic Drafts) attracted attention in Korea and China. If his prose alone is considered, there is justice to the claim that he is the greatest Edo writer of bakufu and samurai life, as *Ihara Saikaku is of the lives of chōnin. He belongs among the select circle of Edo intellectuals that includes *Kamo no Mabuchi, *Ogyū Sorai, *Hiraga Gennai, and *Motoori Norinaga.

ARAKIDA MORITAKE 荒木田守武. 1473–1549. Late Muromachi renga and haikai poet. He held an important post at the Ise Shrines, but he is best known for having set haikai on its distinctive way by efforts shared with *Yamazaki Sōkan. He studied renga with *Sōgi, *Sōchō, and others. Although not a negligible renga poet, he helped make haikai no renga an art distinct from mushin renga. This was done mostly by example, in such sequences as his Dokugin Hyakuin 独吟百韻 (Solo Hyakuin) of 1531 and such others as his Yongin Hyakuin 四吟百韻 (Hyakuin by Four Poets, date unknown). The Yo no Naka Hyakushu 世中百首 (One Hundred Poems on Worldly Affairs, 1525) especially was taken as exemplary.

His greatest work is, however, a senku haikai sequence first called Haikai no Renga Dokugin Senku 誹諧之連歌独吟千句 (A Thousand-Stanza Solo Haikai Sequence), better known today as Moritake (Dokugin) Senku 守武(独吟)千句 (Moritake's Thousand-Stanza [Solo] Sequence). There are some doubts as to whether it was written in five days, as he once claimed, but there is no question about its contribution to the development of haikai. It seems to have been written in recollection of Sōgi's Mishima Senku. The first three stanzas of one hyakuin give a fair sample of his style: "Less in the flower/than present in the nose/the spring fragrance;/In the light of the hazy moon/the wild boar grows old;/On the spring night/is not the dream entirely that of a cow?" ("Hana yori mo/hana ni arikeru/nioi kana;/Tsuki wa oboro ni/fuku-ru inoshishi;/Haru no yo no/yume ya sanagara/ushi naran.") The language is waka or renga-like in its Japanese purity. But the play on "hana" ("flower" and "nose"), like the introduction of an aging wild beast, or more especially the introduction of a cow into the evocative context of a dream on a spring night show both the *haikaika*, or haikai change, and the love of words in Moritake's style.

His vein of haikai humor is perhaps best represented by another kind of writing, the more miscellaneous *Moritake Zuihitsu* 守武随筆 (*Moritake's Essays*), which reached a popular audience.

ARIIE. See FUJIWARA ARIIE.

ARIWARA NARIHIRA 在原業平. 825–880. Early Heian *waka* poet. For so famous a poet, little is known of him, and legend has eclipsed fact. His friendship with the ill-starred Prince Koretaka became a pattern of friendship, and the use of some of his poems with those by others in the **Ise Monogatari* set a model for dashing courtly lovers. If in one episode he uses a broken place in a wall to effect a rendezvous, so, following that example, do numerous other lovers, including Niou in the "Ukifune" part of the **Genji Monogatari*. The canon of poems certainly by him is small, but it includes the most famous of *tanka* (**Kokinshū*, 15: 747) on the moon and spring that seem to change while he alone remains as he was in past. The fame of the poem was so great that those using it for allusion (*honkadori*) were expected to regard the words as sacrosanct (*nushi aru kotoba*) and allude to it only conceptually. **Ki no Tsurayuki's half-grudging, half-admiring comment in the preface to the *Kokinshū* that Narihira's mind (or heart) was too great and his words too few well captures the intense intellectuality of his style. He is one of the *rokkasen* and *sanjūrokkasen*.

ARIWARA YUKIHIRA 在原行平. ?818–?893. Early Heian *waka* poet, courtier. As a poet he stands in the shadow of his younger brother, **Ariwara Narihira. But he was considerably involved in court affairs, becoming a middle counsellor (*chūnagon*) and head of the bureau of civil affairs after holding other appointments. Although not as famous as **Sugawara Michizane, he shared Michizane's fate as a prey to Fujiwara hegemony and as an exiled poet. Numerous works deal with, parallel, or allude to his exile in Suma. Among them are the "Suma" chapter of **Murasaki Shikibu's *Genji Monogatari*; the *nō*, *Matsukaze*, is another conspicuous example. *Renga*, *jōruri*, and *haikai* also recall him and his poems. In those poems and in his legend, he lives on as one of the unfortunate heroes periodically remembered when another person suffers similar exile or suffering.

ASAI RYŌI 浅井了意. D. 1691. Early Edo *kanazōshi* writer, once head of a Kyoto temple. He is known as the finest writer of kanazōshi. His works

include two guides to famous places: *Kyō Suzume* 京雀 (*The Sparrows of Kyoto*, 1665) and *Tōkaidō Meishoki* 東海道名所記 (*Famous Sights Along the Tōkaidō*, ca. 1660). He also wrote ghost stories: *Otogi Bōko* 御伽婢子 (*The Protective Doll*, 1660) and *Inu Hariko* 狗張子 (*The Toy Dog*, 1692); as also didactic writings such as *Kanninki* 堪忍記 (*The Chronicle of Forbearance*, 1655) and reportage as in *Kanameishi* かなめ石 (*The Cornerstone*, ca. 1662). In a style imitative of **Ihara Saikaku's *Ichidai Otoko*, he fashioned his *Ukiyo Monogatari* 浮世物語 (*Tale of the Floating World*, by 1662). These and other works were snapped up by an eager readership, so it is natural that he should have exercised extensive influence on other popular writers.

ASAYAMA BONTŌ. See BONTŌ.

ASUKAI GAYŪ (MASAARI) 飛鳥井雅有. 1241–1301. Mid-Kamakura political figure, poet. Although a nobleman who rose to high rank, he called Kamakura his home and occupied a place of repute in the *bakufu* there. As a poet, he is represented by eighty-six poems—in the insipid vein of the **Nijō poets—in the **Zokukokinshū* and later collections, and by his personal collection, *Rinjo Wakashū* 隣女和歌集 (*The Woman Next Door*). He also gained a reputation for his knowledge of the classics, particularly of the **Kokinshū* and **Genji Monogatari*. He has a reputation for a certain decadence in his earlier writings, and today he is best known for his records of five journeys, none of the accounts very long but all by a man of taste and concerning various parts of the country. In what is perhaps their order of composition, these include: *Mumyō no Ki* 無名の記 (*The Untitled Account*, ca. 1269), *Mogami no Kawaji* 最上の河路 (*The Mogami River Route*, ca. 1269), *Saga no Kayoi* 嵯峨のかよひ (*Trips to Saga*, 1269), *Miyakoji no Wakare* 都路のわかれ (*Parting on the Kyoto Road*, 1277), and *Haru no Miyamaji* 春の深山路 (*Spring Paths in Remote Mountains*, 1280). These are remarkable in using the *kana* style associated with earlier works by court ladies, and it seems generally agreed that in the last and lengthiest his style and subject best succeed, to the point of becoming a story with himself at the center. His other work is less profound, but all his travel writings give sensible accounts by a man of some position who was esteemed by his contemporaries for his literary knowledge.

ATSUTANE. See HIRATA ATSUTANE.

AYATARI. See TAKEBE AYATARI.

AZUMA KAGAMI 吾妻鏡 or 東鑑, etc, (*Mirror of the East*). A Kamakura history in fifty-two parts (of which the forty-fifth is missing), dealing with the struggle leading to the formation of the Kamakura *bakufu* and beyond, 1180–1266. The title shows that the author was aware of writing about an area not the capital, and in fact this is said to be the first historical account of a military house, that of *Minamoto Yoritomo. Commentators remark on its diarylike style and presume that the unknown author was a bakufu official. Its greatest use is for study of Kamakura political and military history. See *Jōkyūki.

AZUMAMARO. See KADA NO AZUMAMARO.

BAISHŌRON 梅松論. Namboku *rekishi monogatari* in two parts, completed about 1349. This has strong elements of a *gunki monogatari* such as the *Taiheiki*, whose omissions it seems to be designed to repair. It uses the guise of a rekishi monogatari such as the *Ōkagami*, however: a temple setting and a sage delivering information about the past.

At a temple in Kitano a large group gathers. A very high ecclesiastical official appears before them to relate the glories of the Ashikaga shogunate to 1336 and the merits of the Hosokawa in assisting the growth of the splendors of the Ashikaga. For a record of this kind, and one clearly by a military figure sympathetic to Ashikaga Takauji, this is thought to be an unusually reliable account. The author is not known. But *Imagawa Ryōshun wrote in his *Nan Taiheiki* about Hosokawa Kazuuji 細川 和氏 (1290–1342) as author of *Musōki* 夢想記 (*An Account of a Dream*), which may be this work. Kazuuji fits the specifications well.

BAKIN. See KYOKUTEI BAKIN.

BAKUSUI. See HORI BAKUSUI.

BAN NOBUTOMO 伴信友. 1773–1846. Late Edo *kokugakusha*. Dedicated as he was to the methods of *Motoori Norinaga, he nonetheless opposed his contemporary, *Hirata Atsutane, who had similar ideals. He specialized in study that would correct past historical error, something particularly true of his efforts to revise the accounts in the *Rikkokushi* in *Kana no Motosue* 仮字本末 (printed 1850), or assemble miscellaneous investigations, as in *Hikobae* 比古婆衣 (printed in 20 vols., 1847–1907). The dates show that these works really belong to the modern period, although many of his three hundred volumes were published earlier. Others of his works usually mentioned as of most importance are *Jimmeichō Kōshō* 神名帳考証 (1807) and *Nagara no Yamakaze* 長等の山風 (*The Mountain Wind at Nagara*), the second of which seems slight today and is certainly brief. The attention given it formerly must have derived from its affecting story of *Tenji, his Ōmi court, and his enemies.

BANSAI. See KATŌ BANSAI.

BANZAN. See KUMAZAW BANZAN.

BASHŌ. See MATSUO BASHŌ.

BOKUYŌ. See NAKARAI BOKUYŌ.

BONCHŌ. See NOZAWA BONCHŌ.

BONTŌ(AN) 梵燈(庵). 1349–1427. Namboku-Muromachi *renga* and *waka* poet, surname Asayama. He was in the employ of the Ashikaga shogunate, entrusted with important missions. It is not known when he took orders and received the name by which he is known. He did travel a good deal, lived for a time in a hermitage at Matsushima, and returned to the capital in 1407 or 1408. After the death of *Nijō Yoshimoto, he became the leading authority on renga. He studied waka with *Reizei Tamehide, getting poems into two royal collections. His renga studies were conducted under Yoshimoto and Shūa. He participated in numerous important renga sequences, including *Ishiyama Hyakuin* 石山百韻 (*A Hundred Stanzas at Ishiyama*). His works include *Chōtanshō* 長短抄 (*On the Long and the Short*, 1390); and the somewhat more systematic *Bontōan Shu Hentōsho* 梵灯庵主返答書 (*Replies by Master Bontōan*, 1417). His selection of renga stanzas, *Bontō Rengaawase Jūgoban* 梵灯連歌合十五番 (*A Renga Match in Fifteen Rounds*, 1415), was read and marked by Gokomatsu of the northern line of sovereigns (r. 1382–1412).

Bontō was not simply a poet of importance, but also a teacher with great impact on another long-lived generation of renga masters. *Sōzei's *Shoshin Kyūeishū*, for example, is said to transmit Bontō's teaching.

BUNCHŌ. See TANI BUNCHŌ.

BUNKA SHŪREISHŪ 文華秀麗集 (*Glories and Graces*). Early Heian *kanshi* collection (*chokusenshū*) second such collection in Japan (after the *Ryōunshū*). Ordered by Saga (r. 809–823), compiled by Fujiwara Fuyutsugu and others by 818, the collection includes 148 poems by twenty-six poets, chief among them Saga, with 34 poems. Seven-character lines dominate over five-character lines; Six Dynasties' witty techniques give a further flavor to the work; and the introduction of a slight Buddhist element also provides novelty.

BUNNA SENKU 文和千句 (*A Thousand Stanzas in the Bunna Era*). A Muromachi thousand-stanza *renga* sequence composed in the forth and fifth months of 1355 at the palace of *Nijō Yoshimoto. In the first of the ten *hyakuin* (all that exists in a modern edition), eleven poets participated, the greatest being *Gusai (also Kyūzai, etc.), Shūa, and Yoshimoto. This hyakuin shows renga developed as a mature art. The sequence is quite regular—for example in its number of flower and moon stanzas, although there are somewhat more spring stanzas than usual and fewer on love. For so many poets, the connection and flow is excellent.

BUSON. See YOSA BUSON.

CHIKAMASA. See CHIUN.

CHIKAMATSU HANJI 近松半二. 1725–1783. Mid-Edo *jōruri* author. Born in Osaka, his career was mostly spent there. By living in the licensed quarters for a time and writing at the Osaka Takemotoza he seems to have acquired the varied experience needed. Out of some fifty pieces, twenty or more belong to these dozen years he served as apprentice or as a writer subordinate to other playwrights. Among his later *jidaimono*, two of the best known are *Honchō Nijūshikō* 本朝二十四孝 (*Japan's Twenty-four Filial Ones*, 1767), dealing with the Sengoku period, and *Imoseyama Onna Teikin* 妹背山婦女庭訓 (*The Imoseyama Female Analects*, 1771), dealing with the tribulations of Fujiwara Kamatari (614–669), an unusually early subject for the stage. Two of his most admired *sewamono* are *Shimpan Utazaimon* 新版歌祭文 (*Newly Printed Poetic Prayers*, 1780) and *Igagoe Dōchū Sugoroku* 伊賀越道中双六 (*Backgammon on the Crossing to Iga*, 1783). It frequently happened that *kabuki* drew on *jōruri* for plays and effects. Chikamatsu Hanji found ways of getting kabuki elements into jōruri, with the result that his influence has remained even in the present *bunraku*.

CHIKAFUSA. See KITABATAKE CHIKAFUSA.

CHIKAGE. See KATŌ CHIKAGE.

CHIKAMATSU MONZAEMON 近松門左衛門. 1653–1724. Early Edo *jōruri* and *kabuki* dramatist. Such is Chikamatsu's importance to drama that the jōruri plays written before him are assigned to the class of old jōruri. Yet he arrived at his art almost by accident. His family came from a distinguished samurai house, and things might have continued the same had not his father, for some reason, become masterless, and one branch of the family—including Chikamatsu—visited Kyoto. Then, as earlier, it was the center of literary culture, and apparently Chikamatsu began to write jōruri, even while still leading a more typical samurai life. Fact and legend are not easily sorted out, but there is a story that he may have contributed to a play when he was but fourteen.

In 1683 he gained attention with the great success of *Yotsugi Soga* 世継曽我 (*The Soga Successors*), followed by *Shusse Kagekiyo* 出世景清 (*Kagekiyo Victorious*, 1685). By the time he wrote one of his greatest kabuki, *Keisei Hotoke no Hara* 傾城仏の原 (*The Courtesan at Hotoke no Hara*, 1699), he was sufficiently in command of his art and audience to merge features of the *oiemono* kind of *jidaimono* and *sewamono*, in treating the fortunes of his hero, Sakata Tōjūrō, a move that was to affect not only later kabuki but also the prose fiction of *gesaku* writers such as *Tamenaga Shunsui.

Chikamatsu is best known for his jōruri plays, mostly written for the Takemotoza in Osaka, although early on he worked in Kyoto and had plays performed in Edo at various times. Among his eleven sewamono, the three most famous are *Sonezaki Shinjū* 曽根崎心中 (*The Love Suicides at Sonezaki*, 1703), *Meido no Hikyaku* 冥途の飛脚 (*The Courier for Hell*, 1711), and *Shinjū Ten no Amijima* 心中天網島 *The Love Suicides at Amijima*, 1720). All three involve a son of a mercantile house in a love affair with a woman from the licensed quarters. The first and third end with the lovers' suicide (*shinjū*). The protagonist of *Meido no Hikyaku* commits a number of wicked acts until he is at last captured by authorities. The men of the shinjū plays are by comparison gentle, weak, and doomed, whereas this villain bound for hell distinguishes himself by sheer force of personality, somewhat like Yonosuke in the *Kōshoku Ichidai Otoko* by *Ihara Saikaku.

Kokusen'ya, or Coxinga, the hero of *Kokusen'ya Kassen* 国性爺合戦 (*The Battles of Coxinga*, 1715) is not so much forceful as many times larger than life. In this jidaimono jōruri, the puppets wonderfully act out the fantastic heroism situated now in Ming China, now in Japan (the birthplaces of Coxinga's two parents).

The imagination required to create these and other plays of so widely ranging variety of tone and character makes Chikamatsu a fit member of the great triumvirate of seventeenth-century writers, including *Matsuo Bashō and Saikaku. Bashō is many times over the favorite of the three, and indeed the favorite poet of Japanese. Saikaku is probably preferred to Chikamatsu because it is easier to savor to the full Saikaku's narration in a way one cannot the texts for plays written for theaters that have since been modified. Unfortunately, Chikamatsu's jōruri are seldom performed by the Bunrakuza, so that we grope toward a just estimate. He lacks some of Bashō's ability to discover himself—beckoning others to discover themselves—in the world to hand. He also lacks some of Saikaku's restless energy. But he shows with greater seeming truth, and certainly more forcefully, the constraints on individual townspeople's lives in the repressive Edo climate. He also reveals how, with fantasy and religion, his audience came to terms with the social chains they wore.

Just as jōruri and kabuki lack the prestige of *nō*, Chikamatsu has not the high reputation of *Zeami. But if the remarks quoted from him by *Hozumi Ikan at the opening of *Naniwa Miyage* are characteristic of his thoughts about literature, the absence of a body of criticism by him is the most grievously missed might-have-been in all Japanese criticism. His influence can be found far beyond the theaters of the century and the next, and when closely considered, his plays tell us more about his times than do even the works of Bashō and Saikaku.

CHIKAZANE. See Koma no Chikazane

CHIKUDEN. See Tanomura Chikuden.

(NINAGAWA) CHIUN (or CHIKAMASA) (蜷川) 智蘊 (or 親当.) D. 1448. Muromachi military figure and *renga* poet. He served the shogun Ashikaga Yoshinori in military affairs. His study of various Japanese and Chinese cultural matters was under the tutelage of the learned, eccentric *Ikkyū, and he studied renga under *Bontō. By the 1430s he emerged as a poet, taking part in a ten-thousand-stanza renga sequence at Kitano. He became acquainted with the renga masters *Shinkei, *Senjun, and *Gyōjo, with whom he participated in the well-esteemed *Anegakōji Imashimmei Hyakuin. He left behind a collection, *Chikamasa Kushū* 親当句集 (*Chikamasa's Stanzas*). Like *Sōi, he is a representative of the military men who were turning to renga in those days of social turmoil. At its best, his style has elegance and sometimes an aura of mysterious beauty somewhat like *Fujiwara Teika's *yōen* style.

CHIYO 千代. 1703–1775. *Haikai* poet. Born in Kaga, she is sometimes called "Kaga no Chiyojo." She is said to have married at about seventeen, to have delivered one son, to have lost him and her husband, and to have returned to her native house. This is not certain. About fifty she did take orders and is sometimes known as the Nun Chiyo (Chiyo Ni). She had composed haikai in her girlhood, and even in adulthood she has a vein of sentimentality that is never wholly out of fashion in the world, and often in fashion, especially for popular audiences. In 1763 she had published. *Chiyo Ni Kushū* 千代尼 句集(*Nun Chiyo's Stanzas*).

CHŌSHŌSHI. See Kinoshita Chōshōshi.

CHŌMEI. See Kamo no Chōmei.

CHORA. See Miura Chora.

DENGYŌ DAISHI. See Saichō.

DŌGEN 道元 1200–1253. Also called Kigen Dōgen 希玄道元. Early Kamakura religious thinker, founder of Sōtō Zen Buddhism in Japan. Dōgen began his religious training on Tendai's Mt. Hiei, but in 1223 he went to China to study with the Ts'ao-tung (Sōtō) master Ju-ching (J., Nyojō, 1163–1228). On his return to Japan in 1227, Dōgen wrote his *Fukan Zazengi* 普観坐禅儀 (*General Advice on the Principles of Zazen*) in which he advocated "zazen only" ("shikan taza"), a method which, unlike Chih-i's shikan meditation, rejected accommodation with other religious practices, including the "kōan-introspection" ("kanna") zen of the Rinzai schools.

His major theoretical work, composed beween 1231 and 1253, is the ninety-five-chapter *Shōbogenzō* 正法眼蔵 (*The Eye Treasury of the Right Dharma*). *Shōbōgenzō Zuimonki* 正法眼蔵随聞記 (*Gleanings from Master Dōgen's Sayings*) is a popular introduction to Dōgen's life and thought compiled by his disciple Ejō, ca. 1235–1238. In 1246, in Echizen province, Dōgen established Eiheiji temple, which became the headquarters of the Sōtō sect.

Although Dōgen left behind a number of poems, including some sixty *tanka* collected in the *Sanshō Dōei* 傘松道詠 (*Dōgen's Poetry Collection*, 1420), his effect on literature derives chiefly from his religious influence, extending to such writers as the *nō* playwright and theorist, *Zeami.

DOHŌ. See Hattori Dohō.

DŌHO. See Igarashi Dōho.

DŌMYAKU SENSEI 銅脈先生. 1752–1801. Late Edo writer of *kyōshi* and other comic literature. Like his slightly older friend, *Ōta Nampo, Dōmyaku enlivened the reading of the latter half of the eighteenth century. Born in Kyoto, he served the court nobility and studied Chinese. His maiden effort, *Taihei Gafu* 太平楽府 (*The Nonsense Song Bureau*, 1769), won a popularity encouraging him to write a number of books. In addition to comic Chinese verse, he wrote *kyōbun* or comic Japanese prose, as in his *Katakana Seisuiki* 片仮名世酔記 (1772), as well as comic Chinese prose, *kokkeibon*, and *sharebon*.

EIFUKU MON'IN. See Yōfuku Mon'in.

EIFUKU MON'IN NAISHI. See Yōfuku Mon'in Naishi.

EIGA MONOGATARI 栄花(栄華)物語(*The Tale of Flowering Splendor*). Late Heian *rekishi monogatari* (ca. 1092). Its forty parts are considered to consist of thirty main and ten additional units by different hands. Other opinions as to authorship hold that the last three chapters are by yet a third hand, or that each of the forty was by a different author. Whatever the authorship, there is a degree of unity from the subject of the glory (eiga) of the court depicted and from the attention to the main character, *Fujiwara Michinaga, under whom the Fujiwara regency and the court reached its cultural and political pinnacle.

Most opinions hold to female authorship, or at least to participation by women in gathering materials. A tradition going as far back as the Kamakura period and accepted in some fashion by many holds the work to be by *Akazome Emon, an attribution some think derives from her service at the most cultured royal household of the time, that of *Jōtō Mon'in, where *Murasaki Shikibu and *Izumi Shikibu were the chief literary figures. It seems likely that Akazome Emon had some part in the work: as author of one of the several works presumed as sources, as a compiler of such sources, as a kind of editor—or as more than one of these.

Another attribution credits the first twenty-seven books (in which poems are the most numerous) to another woman, Idewa no Ben, daughter of Taira Suenobu—hence her full appellation, Dewa no Kami, Taira Suenobu no Musume Idewa no Ben. On this view, the other thirteen books are by some unknown court lady.

Whatever the authorship, the writing of it was completed sometime after the second month of 1092, and the work inaugurated *rekishi monogatari*, historical tales, including such important successors as *Ōkagami*, *Masukagami*, and *Heike Monogatari*. The splendors mentioned by the title are those of the two centuries and of the fifteen reigns from Uda (r. 887–897) to part of the reign of Horikawa (r. 1086–1107). The first thirty parts cover 140 years of those two centuries, and the last ten the remainder. The literary value of the story is somewhat heightened by its being freed from annalistic organization, and by the fact that the long account is integrated by theme, plot, and characters. It might be termed a court *monogatari*, a Fujiwara monogatari, or indeed for much of it "The Michinaga Monogatari." The story of rise to grandeur is told the more effectively by the inclusion of darker shadowing—spirit possessions (mononoke), illnesses, and death. By comparison with the first thirty chapters, the remaining ten—dealing with what followed Michinaga—are less closely coherent. In this last quarter, Michinaga's son Yorimichi (and other descendants) do serve as protagonists, but attention is less closely focused. The main subject becomes court life, especially as viewed by women's eyes.

It may be that the last ten parts were designed as a parallel with the closing portion of the *Genji Monogatari*, whose last ten chapters are traditionally regarded as a unit (Uji jūjō). If so, the tone differs. One of the remarkable features of the *Eiga Monogatari* is the absence of the strong sense of evanescence (*mujō*), of the illusory nature of worldly glory. Since the *Genji Monogatari* was written by a contemporary of Michinaga, and included so strong a sense of evanescence, the absence of such a tone in a work written toward the end of the court's dominance of power reveals an unusual expression of nostalgia by celebrating former glories in a way maintaining their presence even after they were gone. Yet, especially in the chapters with Michinaga as hero, the idea of splendor is held with conviction. Above all, it is an encyclopedic work, rich in details of dress, customs, and so on.

EISAI (or **YŌSAI**) 栄西. 1141–1215. Founder of Rinzai Zen in the early Kamakura period. He began his priestly career in the Tendai sect, and throughout his life maintained a syncretic attitude toward Zen and other modes of religious practice. On his second trip to China in 1189 Eisai received the Rinzai (Linchi) seal of transmission. However, his teacher belonged to the line of Huang-lung (1002–1069) rather than to the influential Yang-ch'i (992–1049) line transmitted through *Enni, *Musō, *Ikkyū, and *Hakuin. Upon his return to Japan in 1191, Eisai began to propagate the "Daruma School" (Daruma-shū), so-called from the name of the semilegendary founder of Chinese Ch'an, Bodhidharma (d. 528?). He was appointed abbot of the Jufukuji in Kamakura in 1200; and the construction of his headquarters in Kyoto, the Kenninji, was begun in 1202. His major apology is the *Kōzen Gokokuron* 興禅護国論 (*Propagation of Zen as a Defense of the Nation*, 1198). Although Eisai did *not* introduce tea to Japan, he did return from China with tea seeds and promoted the use of the beverage in his *Kissa Yōjōki* 喫茶養生記 (*Drink Tea and Prolong Life*, 1214).

EITOKU. See KANŌ EITOKU.

EJIMA KISEKI 江島其磧. 1666–1735. Early Edo writer of *ukiyozōshi*. Although he was the fourth proprietor of a famous Kyoto rice-cake shop, he lacked a head for the enterprise and gave up the business to become a writer. He got under way in the middle of the Genroku era by writing two or three *jōruri*. From them it was a natural move to his *Yakusha Kuchijamisen* 役者口三味線 (*The Versatile Actor*, 1699), with its comments on actors. From that it was in turn not difficult to move to women in the pleasure quarters. So he did in *Keisei Irojamisen* 傾城色三味線 (*The Courtesan's Amorous Shamisen*, 1701), causing something of a sensation by the novel practice of giving real names. His skill in arranging materials and, of course, his new idea helped make him popular, even if one looks in vain for the depth or vitality of *Ihara Saikaku.

Kiseki then tried his hand at a less gilded topic in *Keisei Kintanki* 傾城禁短気 (*Courtesans Forbidden to Lose Temper*, 1711), which depicts the training and other features of the lives of lower-ranking women in the licensed quarters.

His next innovation has brought him special notice: *katagimono*. This kind of writing dealt with boys or girls, teachers, tea masters—nobody terribly impressive. The trick was to catch the stereotype, to fix the outlines much as a cartoonist makes people recognizable by distortion. He devoted one such book to young men and another to young women: *Seken Musuko Katagi* 世間子息気質 (*Characters of Worldly Young Men*, 1715) and *Seken Musume Katagi* 世間娘気質 (*Characters of Worldly Young Women*, 1717). It may be noted how one work by him catches in the title an element or two from a previous title.

Kiseki's works were popular, and later writers learned from them. *Jippensha Ikku, *Shikitei Samba, and *Ryūtei Tanehiko are among those. Yet in spite of all this, in spite of being a mainstay as author for the Hachimonjiya publishing house in Kyoto, Kiseki ended his life in poverty. It seems that his inventiveness failed him. He turned to adapting works by others, no doubt ending as a cautionary tale for Kyoto sons of mercantile houses to stay clear of literature.

EKISAI. See KARIYA EKISAI.

ENNI BEN'EN 円爾弁円. 1202–1280. Early Kamakura Rinzai Zen priest. After education at various temples in Japan, he went to Sung China in 1235. On his return in 1241 he taught in many places, especially at the *gosan* temples in Kyoto and Kamakura. He started the Shōichi school of gosan Zen Buddhism and founded Tōfukuji.

ENNIN 円仁 (or **JIKAKU DAISHI** 慈覚大師). 793–864. A disciple of *Saichō and the third abbot of the Enryakuji, Ennin is noted for having introduced esotericism into Tendai. This tradition, known as taimitsu, is based on the teachings of the *Dainichikyō,* the *Kongōchōgyō,* and the *Soshitchikyō.* (Part Six O). Ennin is best known for the account of his visit to China from 838 to 847, the *Nittō Guhō Junrei Gyōki* 入唐求法巡礼行記 (*The Record of a Pilgrimage to China in Search of the Law*). His trip coincided with the great persecution of Buddhism in China in 845; and the details of his life there give us an invaluable insight into T'ang society.

ENOMOTO (TAKARAI) KIKAKU 榎本（宝井）其角. 1661–1707. Early Edo *haikai* poet, one of the ten worthies among followers of *Matsuo Bashō. The first of Bashō's followers, he was also the most gifted, eccentric, and most independent-minded. "At my hut," wrote Bashō, "there stand a peach and a cherry tree. Among my followers are Kikaku and [*Hattori] Ransetsu." Given Bashō's pen name at the time, Tōsei 桃青 (Peach Green), this puts Kikaku above the rest.

Born in Edo, a precocious poet, he became associated with Bashō at twelve and never acquired the full deference that others felt for the master. Quick, prolific, witty, strange, and often spectacular, he had a streak of wild imagination in him. In a duo *kasen* such as *Shi Akindo,* Bashō has to work hard to keep up with him—or at least to maintain coherence. *Mukai Kyorai well compared Kikaku to *Fujiwara Teika for the brilliance of his writing. In other terms, Kikaku represents the Edo haikai temper, as *Nozawa Bonchō does that of *kamigata.* One or the other deserves the title of the second poet of the age after Bashō.

He was closest to the master from about 1682 to 1689. In 1683, he edited *Minashiguri,* and in 1689 he wrote the preface to *Sarumino,* two of the best collections of the school (see Part Six F). He also edited a collection, *Kareobana* 枯尾花 (*Withered Pampas Plumes*), honoring Bashō's memory in the year of his death (1694). This is a handsome gesture, since he had disagreed with Bashō vigorously over the *karumi* or simpler style Bashō propounded near the end of his life. By all odds the most brilliant poet of the time, he somewhat resembles in artistic temper *Ihara Saikaku, and his haikai shares with Saikaku's certain *Danrin* features, especially a fondness for allusion. The streak of wildness in his personality relates partly to his Edo character, and it was expressed among other ways in his heavy drinking, for which Bashō chided him in vain. He and Bonchō have a marvelous sense of humor, with Kikaku the more witty of the two. But he has not the humanity of Bonchō—nor, of course, of Bashō.

ENSHŪ. See KOBORI ENSHŪ.

ESOPO NO FABULAS. See *Isoho Monogatari.*

ETENRAKU 越天楽. The most famous piece of Chinese court music (*gagaku*) in Japan. It was brought to mid-Heian Japan from China, where it has since been lost. The dance that it originally accompanied has been not been preserved in Japan. It has been set in three of the gagaku modes and in one, the hyō(jō), the melodic elements of the piece became highly appreciated. Later, words were added to make it a highly popular *imayō* or present-day song that led to a special type known as eten-raku imayō. It is one of numerous instances in Japan of art moving from higher to lower social spheres (the reverse is also common).

FUBOKU(WAKA)SHŌ 夫木（和歌）抄 (*The Japanese Collection*). Late Kamakura privately selected *waka* collection in thirty-six parts. The compiler was Fujiwara (Katsumada) Nagakiyo 藤原（勝間田）長清, a poetic follower of *Reizei Tamesuke. It seems to have been completed about 1310, perhaps with later changes. As befits a Reizei collection, it is far more freely conceived than would have been a counterpart by *Nijō poets. The thirty-six parts (not twenty or ten), *imayō* as well as waka, and many unusual poems make the work quite special. Since the poems in such a collection were thought to be exemplary (*shūka*), the choices are the more remarkable, making even the *Gyokuyōshū* seem fairly standard. The characters for the first word of the title take portions of 扶桑, that is, a word for Japan, Fusō. (Chinese had used the characters to designate the area to their east where the sun rose and later as another name for Japan.)

FUDOKI 風土記. Topographies. In 713, on a Chinese analogy, Gemmei Tennō ordered the provinces to compile topographies dealing with geographical and other natural features, customs, and interesting stories from the provinces. Only five have survived: from the provinces of Izumo 出雲, Harima, 播磨, Hitachi 常陸, Hizen 肥前, and Bungo 豊後. Of these, only the *Izumo (no Kuni no) Fudoki* has survived complete. Fragments of the others exist in quotations in notes to such works as the *Nihon Shoki* and *Man'yōshū*. Gemmei's motive was in part the glory of her royal house, but the surveys would also have features akin to a census that would assist her rule of the country. Some of the earliest prose narratives are to be found in surviving portions of the *Fudoki*, often written in ornate Chinese.

FŪGA(WAKA)SHŪ 風雅(和歌)集 (*Collection [of Japanese Poetry] of Elegance*). Nambokuchō royal *waka* collection (*chokusenshū*); seventeenth of twenty-one. Compiled 1343–1349 by Kōgon (r. 1332–1333, of the northern line) with the active participation of *Hanazono (r. 1308–1318). Hanazono's care had a precedent in Gotoba's concern over the *Shinkokinshū*, but this is the sole official anthology compiled by a sovereign rather than by a subject. That Hanazono furnished the Japanese and Chinese prefaces is equally exceptional. Based on the *Kokinshū* model, this has twenty books; its 2,211 poems make it the third largest of the *nijūichidaishū* (see *Gyokuyōshū* and *Shinsenzaishū*). The title lays claim to a true art, signaling the efforts of the *Kyōgoku poets and *Reizei poets to honor their innovative work as an entity opposed to that of the conservative *Nijō poets, a number of whose poems are, however, included. This is the last really important official anthology, and resembles the *Gyokuyōshū* in the method of integration and the identity of its poets, although some new ones of the two innovative schools have been added. See Part Six A.

FUJIMOTO KIZAN 藤本箕山. 1626–1704. Kizan is known for his *Shikidō Ōkagami* 色道大鏡 (*The Great Mirror of the Art of Love*), a *kanazōshi*. As this work shows, the "mirror book" (see *kagamimono*) became, in time, more elaborate and directed more frequently or directly to townspeople (*chōnin*), sometimes treating amorous subjects, including male homosexuality. Kizan's work was one of the sources drawn on by *Ihara Saikaku for his *Kōshoku Ichidai Otoko*, after which books of this kind were known as *ukiyozōshi*.

FUJIWARA AKIHIRA (MEIGŌ) 藤原明衡. 989–1066. Mid-Heian scholar and writer of Chinese poetry. His time of most active literary work was from 1037 to 1040, although his fame rests chiefly on collections made or printed later. Chief among these is *Honchō Monzui* 本朝文粋 (*Choice Pieces by Japanese Poets*, 1058–1064), which includes compositions in Chinese dating from about 810 to 1015. His collection differs from the *Ryōunshū and *Bunka Shūreishū in being privately done, in not being a *chokusenshū*. He also departed in conception, both by making a collection for reading rather than recitation and, in later versions, by including prose as well as verse. The changing conception naturally produced variance among manuscript versions. The expanded collection includes, whatever the divisions, some seventy writers, chiefly those from the two learned houses, the Sugawara and Ōe.

His other collections include *Honchō Shūku* 本朝秀句 (*Exemplary Lines by Japanese Poets*, ca. 1066) and Japan's first collection of exemplary letters, *Meigō Ōrai* 明衡往来 (*Meigō's Correspondence*, 1066). These compilations seemed to have satisfied the hunger for learned anthologies felt at the time. Yet other collections made by him appeared in the century following his death. His was the hardworking, productive, and not very happy life known to scholars in other times and countries, and today his Chinese style is considered quite unsatisfactory.

FUJIWARA AKISUE 藤原顕季. 1055–1123. Late Heian *waka* poet, scholar. He had a good if not spectacular court career, involving governorships of several provinces and promotions to good rank. The residence he established at the crossing of Rokujō and Karasuma in Kyoto led to an appellation, Rokujō Suri no Daibu 六条修理大夫, so that his personal collection is called *Rokujō Suri no Daibu Shū*. The location and his prolific descendants gave rise to the name of "Rokujō" to represent conservative and scholarly poetry (see Fujiwara Akisuke, Kiyosuke, Motosuke and Ariie; also Kenshō). In time, this group became opposed to the more innovative Mikohidari branch of the Fujiwara poets: see Fujiwara Shunzei. Akisue took part in many poetic activities, including *utaawase* and *hyakushuuta*. In 1109 he sponsored the *Akisue Kyō no Ie no Utaawase* 顕季卿家歌合 (*The Poetry Match at Lord Akisue's*). His deep scholarly interests can be characterized by his role in encouraging study of the *Man'yōshū*, something in which he took such part that he more than anyone else promoted *Kakinomoto Hitomaro to the status of a protective divinity of Japanese poetry. His own poetry is technically faultless, as proper as it is learned and familiar. It appeared in numerous official collections beginning with the *Goshūishū* as well as many unofficial collections (*shisenshū*), and well represents the *Fujiwara style*.

FUJIWARA ARIIE 藤原有家. 1155–1216. Early Kamakura *waka* poet. He is one of the representative poets in, and one of the compilers of, the *Shinkokinshū*. Perhaps because of the small number of his poems extant, he is not accorded highest marks by critics today. But at his best, his few poems show affinity to styles of *Fujiwara Teika. Some of his poems combine syntactic fragments of well-defined noun images with word association (*engo*) or allusive variation (*honkadori*) to integrate his works. In such poems the fragmentation conveys both intensity and a symbolism that heightens the descriptive techniques of the age to a higher level by means of generalization that conveys the essence of an experience. He has but one poem included in the **Senzaishū* and nineteen in the *Shinkokinshū*. If he had a personal collection, it is lost.

FUJIWARA HAMANARI 藤原浜成. 724–790. Nara poet, critic, court official. Although not much is known of him or his poetry, he is venerated for his producing the first critical work on Japanese poetry. Adapting Chinese criticism, he distinguished in his *Kakyō Hyōshiki* 歌経標式 (or *Hamanari Shiki*, completed ca. 772) three poetic styles and seven kinds of poetic faults (*uta no yamai*, kahei). This is not yet major criticism, but his attention to poetic faults would long be a feature of judgments in *utaawase*.

FUJIWARA IETAKA (KARYŪ) 藤原家隆. 1158–1237. Early Kamakura *waka* poet. He showed his talent at a youthful age. And he belongs to the network of **Shinkokinshū* poets by marriage to a daughter of **Jakuren as well as by involvement in the compilation of that collection. He participated in numerous poetry matches (*utaawase*) and wrote a number of poetic sequences. He left behind a personal collection known both as *Minishū* 壬二集 and *Gyokuginshū* 玉吟集 (*Collection of Jeweled Songs*). All accounts treat him as an attractive, loyal person. He persisted in fidelity to **Gotoba, even after Gotoba had been exiled.

His poetic styles include most of those traditional and common in his age, including among the latter the descriptive symbolism that marks much of its best poetry in one fashion or another. Although a few poems are touched by **Fujiwara Teika's *yōembi* or style of ethereal beauty, even fewer have the depth of *yūgen* propounded by **Fujiwara Shunzei. Instead, he seems to have inclined to a clearer, purer style, more beauty of *kotoba* than depth of *kokoro*. This was recognized in a passage by **Shōtetsu that mixed praise and hesitation: "Ietaka employed decorous language (*kotoba*) and composed in a lofty, graceful style. For such reasons, **Fujiwara Teika appreciated the poetry, including forty-three poems in the **Shinkokinshū. . . . Teika did have some worry about the lack of splendor (hanayakasa) in Ietaka's style and wondered if its qualities could be transmitted to his descendants" (*Shōtetsu Monogatari*). It is also true, however, that **Sen no Rikyū took one of Ietaka's poems to represent ideals of the tea ceremony, even though he admired Teika far more.

FUJIWARA KINTŌ 藤原公任. 966–1041. Mid-Heian *waka* poet and critic. Although his political ambitions were thwarted, he rose to high court rank and to esteem as a critic. By nineteen he was participating in poetry matches at court, and his prestige led in due course to appointment as a judge at such *utaawase*, and he was also appointed as the first person to compile an official collection alone. This was to be the **Shūishū* (ca. 968–1008), which seems to have circulated in draft as *Shūishō* 拾遺抄 until Kazan (r. 984–986), who had commissioned it, revised it at last to his liking. Most of the poets exemplified date from about a century before, and the poems included are smooth, undisturbing, and style-worn.

The dates of his other works are not clear, but most are believed to fall between 1004 and 1012. He is best known for his poetic treatise, *Shinsen Zuinō* 新撰髄脳 (*The Essentials of Poetry, Newly Compiled*), which argues for refined thought and clever conception. As its title indicates, his *Waka Kuhon* 和歌九品 identifies and illustrates nine styles of waka. His *Kingyokushū* 金玉集 (*Gold and Jewels*) offers a selection of poems he thought exemplary. Because Japanese criticism so often has functioned since by example or formularies of this kind, this is perhaps Kintō's most important innovation. His collection of Japanese and Chinese verse, *Wakan Rōeishū* (ca. 1013) was greatly influential. His personal collection, *Kintō Kyō Shū* 公任卿集 (*Lord Kintō's Collection*), is of unknown date. Everyone grants Kintō's historical importance, but few still read his poems.

FUJIWARA KIYOSUKE 藤原清輔. 1104–1177. Late Heian *waka* poet, critic, second son of **Fujiwara Akisuke. A very learned poet and student of poetry, Kiyosuke was also a mediocre poet who got embroiled in some of the testier controversies of his time. His *Fukurozōshi* 袋草紙 (*Book of Folded Pages*) details his early debate with his father over compilation of the **Shikashū* (ca. 1151–1154). It is a work filled with interesting anecdotes about people as well as statements and accounts important to the history of Japanese poetry, including *renga*. His *Ōgishō* 奥儀抄 (*Poetic Profundities*, 1124–1144) is characteristic of him in its loving preservation of the poetic lore of the past. **Kamo no Chōmei said, "There is no one worth putting beside him for knowledge of poetry." But for those who value the practice of poetry, Kiyosuke's more liberal rival, **Fujiwara Shunzei, holds far greater interest.

FUJIWARA MASATSUNE 藤原雅経. 1170–1221. Early Kamakura *waka* poet, founder of the Asukai 飛鳥井 house of poets and calligraphers. He studied poetry with both **Fujiwara Shunzei and **Fujiwara Teika. With the latter, he was one of the compilers of the **Shinkokinshū. As this implies, he was at the center of many poetic events, participating in a number of poetry matches and waka sequences, and holding a reputation among his contemporaries that has not survived the centuries. He has a personal collection, *Asukai Shū* 明日香井集.

FUJIWARA MEIGŌ. See FUJIWARA AKIHIRA.

FUJIWARA MICHINAGA 藤原道長. 966–1027. Mid-Heian court minister. By political acumen and good fortune, he managed to marry a daughter to one sovereign, have her give birth to two other tennō, and by these and related means obtain effective control of the state. Under him, his immediate branch of the Fujiwara house aggrandized both the instruments and the art of power. He wrote poems, as every Heian court member did, but he is remembered in literature for the glimpses we gain of him in *Murasaki Shikibu's diary, perhaps as a model for the hero of her *Genji Monogatari*, and for the depiction of him amid his splendors in the *Eiga Monogatari* and *Ōkagami*.

FUJIWARA MICHITOSHI 藤原通俊. 1047–1099. Late Heian *waka* poet, courtier. Born in a house distinguished for learning more than for high rank or power, Michitoshi composed poetry early in life. He also had the good fortune to excite the trust of Shirakawa (r. 1072–1086) and Horikawa (1086–1107), just as they were instituting the *insei* system, whereby a sovereign abdicated to free himself from ceremony and devote himself to exercise of real power. Michitoshi was kept very busy, but he advanced in rank and power beyond what his family had known. He did manage to appear from time to time at *utaawase* and other poetic gatherings.

In 1075 Shirakawa commissioned Michitoshi to compile a new collection. The order caused some scandal, since Michitoshi was only thirty-seven and had nothing like the poetic reputation of *Minamoto Tsunenobu. What was to become the *Goshūishū* moved ahead very slowly. In 1084 Michitoshi at last took time away from his court affairs, and two years later presented the collection with his own Japanese preface. Tsunenobu harshly criticized the selections in his *Nan Goshūi*, to which Michitoshi replied in his *Goshūi Mondō* 後拾遺問答 (*Reply on the Goshūishū*, 1094). Michitoshi was far from being the critic, and farther yet from being the poet, that Tsunenobu was. A careful, conservative taste governs the collection, giving it a rather insipid uniformity, except that in many selections he showed that he understood the importance of the descriptive poetry that had emerged in his generation.

FUJIWARA MICHITSUNA NO HAHA 藤原道綱母. Mid-Heian diarist. A wife of a major court figure, Fujiwara Kaneie, she married in 954 and, as her "name" shows, she was Mother of Fujiwara Michitsuna. Little information is available other than what she reveals in her *Kagerō Nikki* 蜻蛉日記 (*The Gossamer Years*), one of the four major Heian diary classics. It covers the period 954 to 974, and

she justly describes its three parts in psychological terms as "a diary concerning myself only." What she tells is very much presented from her own view, even when it concerns others. In the first part, for example, we learn of her responses to: Kaneie's failure to behave toward her by the proper mores of the time; her father's unhappy departure for the provinces; the birth of her son, Michitsuna; Kaneie's taking up with a woman below their class; the deaths of her mother and the reigning Murakami; an illness of Kaneie; and so on. She had a reputation as a poet, but it is the factuality—or at least the self-absorbed, grudging, and yet careful notice of others—that sets her diary apart from other classics of its kind. There is never any doubt of her feelings, even if they are so often given to complaint. It is difficult to decide whether she is the most realistic of the major diarists, or simply the most tortured by ordinary human realities. But she probably presents the facts of a woman's life in her time with more accuracy, or less embellishment, than other authors of like gifts; and it comes as a shock to recall that *Murasaki Shikibu's *Genji Monogatari* makes of these same years something of a golden era. The diary seems to have far more of the fact of human existence as it was known, even if less of the truth of human aspirations. Later literature by women seems far more palatable but, by comparison, more fashioned from the hopes than the realities of life.

FUJIWARA MOTOTOSHI 藤原基俊. ?–1142 or 1143. Late Heian *waka* poet and critic. Although he came from a highly placed family, he advanced but little in rank and position. Many stories exist of his severity as judge in *utaawase*, and some of the most amusing concern his rigor or foolishness in trying to criticize, at such poetry matches, his rival, *Minamoto Shunrai, who was odd enough, but in another way. He once fumed over Shunrai's writing a poem about a heron (tazu) dwelling in the clouds. Shunrai waited his while and pointed out that he had written of a dragon (tatsu—the words would have been written the same in the *kanabun* of the time), echoing a Chinese tale. When judging rounds of poems by Shunrai and himself, he awarded himself most of the wins, so violating decorums of behavior.

He seems to have terrorized many people at poetry matches with his irascibility and learning. If there was no real poetry in his reactionary criticism, his poetry is at least reactionary in the same way. He did manage to get over one hundred poems into official collections, beginning with the *Kin'yōshū* (compiled by none other than Shunrai, who had his problems, too). His private collection is called simply *Mototoshi Shū*. He also compiled a private waka collection, the *Shin Sanjūrokunin Kasen* 新三十六人歌仙 (*The New Thirty-Six Poetic Sages*, appeared 1260) as well as *Shinsen Rōeishū* 新撰朗詠集 (*A New Collection of Poetic Recitations*, 1106–1123). Perhaps the nicest thing to be said about him is that, very late in Mototoshi's life, *Fujiwara Shunzei allowed himself to be taught by this learned, hidebound scholar for a time.

FUJIWARA SADAIE. See FUJIWARA TEIKA.

FUJIWARA SEIKA 藤原惺窩. 1561–1619. Early Edo scholar of Chinese studies. He represents in striking fashion both his family past and his sense of his present. A twelfth-generation descendant of *Fujiwara Teika in the line of *Reizei poets, he practiced *waka* and Japanese prose with facility. But he is known for other innovations. By seven he was studying in one temple, and at seventeen was working at Shōkokuji. He began to switch from Buddhist to Confucian study, soon acquiring a name for himself in this new subject. About thirty he switched to official *Shushigaku*. Apparently thinking he would consolidate his mastery in this new field by going to Ming China, he set out in 1597, only to be sent back to shore when his boat capsized. His students included leading intellectuals of the next phase of the Edo period, and if any single person may be said to have been the early popularizer of Neoconfucianism in Japan, the credit must be his.

FUJIWARA SHUNZEI (TOSHINARI) 藤原俊成. 1114–1204. Late Heian, early Kamakura *waka* poet and critic. Son of Toshitada (himself a poet), Shunzei began writing at an early age. By ca. 1131–1132 he was participating in poetry matches and thereafter wrote poetic sequences (especially *hyaku-shuuta*). His taste or personality led him to admire many styles, a reason why he was so successful in obtaining respect for his own innovations. His early ideal was the poet *Minamoto Shunrai, but he also made a point of studying poetics (about 1158) with that formidable archconservative, *Fujiwara Mototoshi. When he participated in the *Horikawa Hyakushu* enterprise, he showed that he could write in old as well as innovative styles, so mattering to poets of all tastes. By this time he had become a sympathetic judge for other poets, including *Saigyō, who looked to him for judgment and encouragement.

For some reason, Shunzei had only one poem included in the *Shikashū*. Somewhat similarly, his official court post was the lowly one of building overseer for the dowager consort. Although he later rose in the official court ranks, he never achieved much more by way of court position.

His worldly fortunes improved from the middle years of the century, although he contracted a serious illness in 1176. His equitable nature and catholic tastes made him a highly respected participant and judge at poetry matches. He departed from precedent to say what was good about the poems matched in a given round, awarding the victory to the better, rather than excluding on the basis of real or imagined faults, as Mototoshi had. He also used his judgments as a means of inculcating his own poetic ideals, which thereby came more and more to prevail. Such judgments at *utaawase* remain to this day a major source for understanding poetic developments in his age.

Above all, he propounded *yūgen*, which in turn he related to *sabi*. He modified the darkness and deprivation the terms partly imply by various means —a sense of beauty, allusions to older poems and narratives, intense Buddhist contemplation, and Shinto conceptions of a pure world. The typical style for expressing such elements was one of descriptive symbolism, not using exact metaphors, symbols, or allegory, but a poem's general configuration (*sugata*), traditional diction (*kotoba*), and fresh conception (*kokoro*) to convey the depth and resonance of yūgen. Of course this achievement was not solely his own, as Shunzei recognized in the praise he bestowed on such predecessors as *Minamoto Tsunenobu and *Minamoto Shunrai. Yet there is a sense in which Shunzei fathered not only *Fujiwara Teika but also one of the two greatest ages of Japanese poetry, "the age of the *Shinkokinshū*."

In 1187 he received the honor of a commission to compile the seventh official anthology, the *Senzaishū*. The collection represents a full range of poets and styles, including the conservative—Shunzei effected change the more easily precisely because he was not a radical. His collection is the first to make much of *Saigyō, and introduces a number of gifted younger poets in his circle, including his son Teika. Such poets, the yūgen style, the victory of descriptive symbolism seem to us the things to matter about the *Senzaishū*. At the time of its completion, however, tongues wagged over the inclusion of more poems by Shunrai than Mototoshi. To the end of his life he was quietly influencing poetic developments by being involved in the preparation or judgment of sequences and poetry matches, doing groundwork for the *Shinkokinshū*, and above all encouraging younger writers of talent.

In part his criticism must be ferreted from numerous pronouncements at utaawase, but there are also more general matters of importance and works to point to. His writings include a study of poetry in the *Man'yōshū*, and it is with Shunzei that a major revaluation of earlier works takes place. He was the first to make evident the greatness of *Murasaki Shikibu's *Genji Monogatari*. He combed the personal collections of earlier poets in search of poems that anticipated the styles in which he was interested, so revealing new dimensions to poets who had seemed wholly cut and dried. One theory, not widely held, claims him as the author of the diary of *Izumi Shikibu. That seems unlikely, but the *Senzaishū* is the first official collection to include poems from that diary. Many features of his criticism culminate in his two-part *Korai Fūteishō* 古来風体抄 (*Poetic Styles Past and Present*, 1197). This conspectus of former and present styles is a typically catholic collection. By long search, Shunzei found exemplary poems to illustrate various kinds of styles he identified. The examples are often so numerous as to seem miscellaneous rather than illustrative of a given, single style. But by review and inventory, Shunzei sets forth a kind of enduring canon of poetry to his time. The canon could be read, and it could be imitated by aspiring poets. There is also in Shunzei's conception more than the rudiments of a historical consciousness of Japanese poetry.

One of the finest poets of the next generation, *Shokushi Naishinnō, used her rank to compliment Shunzei. Her request for a collection of his own poems led to the Chōshū Eisō 長秋詠藻 (Shunzei's Collection for Her Former Majesty, 1178; "Chōshū" was an appellation of the wife of the former sovereign, whom Shunzei at least nominally served). Other poems by Shunzei seem to have been added by later editors, and he had two other collections made, as well. At his best a great poet, Shunzei fostered greatness in others. Trusted by his contemporaries and a promoter of fine poetry of whatever kind or school, his is one of the most attractive personalities in Japanese literature and criticism.

FUJIWARA SHUNZEI (TOSHINARI) NO MUSUME 藤原俊成女. Ca. ?1175–?1250. Early Kamakura waka poet. In reality Shunzei's granddaughter, she seems to have been adopted by reason of her outstanding poetic talents. About 750 of her poems survive, including those in Shunzei Kyō no Musume no Shū 俊成卿女集 (The Collection of Lord Shunzei's Daughter) and the 116 that appear in royal collections beginning with the *Shinkokinshū. She is one of the finest poets of her age, especially in her command of that style of ethereal beauty (yōembi) that was the early mature ideal of *Fujiwara Teika, Shunzei's son. It is natural to compare her with the other most gifted female poet of the age, *Shokushi Naishinnō, whom she does not quite match. But she shows great ease with seasonal and love topics—features of which she often merges—and like Princess Shokushi, she maintained brilliantly the tradition of the passionate woman poet. There is a tradition that she was author of the *Mumyōzōshi, an important treatise on monogatari, but the evidence does not suffice for proof. In 1202 she served at the palace of *Gotoba, and about the age of forty took orders, thereafter being known by the religious names of Saga no Zenni or Koshibe no Zenni.

FUJIWARA TAKANOBU 藤原隆信. 1142–1205. Late Heian, early Kamakura court official, painter, waka poet. He did not hold high rank and, toward the end of his life, took orders. It is an exaggeration to say he brought into being realistic Japanese portraiture, but it is difficult to find many predecessors of the two famous portraits attributed to him—those of Minamoto Yoritomo and Taira Shigemori in Jingoji. He has a poetic collection, Fujiwara Tokanobu Ason Shū.

FUJIWARA TAMEIE 藤原為家. 1198–1275. Kamakura waka poet. Third in the line of Mikohidari poets of the Fujiwara house, heir to his grandfather, *Fujiwara Shunzei, and first of the *Nijō poets. While young, Tameie caused Teika no end of fret for his indifference to poetry and addiction to kickball (kemari). But about the age of twenty he suddenly turned to poetry and by 1222 he could produce one thousand poems in five days. He participated as poet or judge in a large number of poetic activities, including utaawase and hyakushu. In 1248 he was commissioned by Gosaga to compile the *Shokugosenshū. By this time, he had managed to get caught in a crossfire between rival poetic factions, being notably deficient in his grandfather's catholic tastes and diplomatic ways as much as in his father's brilliance. His disappointments included not being permitted to compile alone the *Shokukokinshū, on which he had been working for some time. Well on in years he took as wife *Abutsu, a forceful personality who was genitress of the *Reizei Poets. In his Eiga Ittei 詠歌一体 (The Style of Composition, 1274?) he set as ideal gentle diction and a purity expressed in poetic configuration (sugata). The ideal well describes his own poetry which, fresh as it may have seemed to some at the time, will hardly strike a reader today as daring. Such were the reputation he inherited and his own talent, however, that well over three hundred of his poems were included in official collections beginning with the *Shinchokusenshū compiled by his father. He annotated the *Kokinshū, *Gosenshū, and *Genji Monogatari. In recent years some have thought him compiler of the *Fūyōshū, but the attribution is not widely accepted.

FUJIWARA TEIKA (SADAIE) 藤原定家. 1162–1241. Early Kamakura waka poet, critic. He is impossible to sentimentalize, as are *Saigyō and *Matsuo Bashō, but with them and *Kakinomoto Hitomaro, he is regarded as one of Japan's four greatest poets. His long life obscures the fact of his almost constant illness from his teens, as his reputation also hides the series of adversities he sometimes brought on himself, as when he got into a fight with Minamoto Masayuki at the royal palace. He seems to have inherited little of the congeniality of his father, *Fujiwara Shunzei, but to have acquired even greater poetic ability. His poetic styles underwent a complex series of changes over the years. So did his criticism, prose writing, and editing. What follows first treats the poet and man, and then the rest of his achievement.

In 1186, he became allied to the Kujō house, coming into contact with *Fujiwara Yoshitsune and *Jien. In the same year he participated in the Futamigaura Hyakushu 二見浦百首 (The Futamigaura One Hundred Poem Sequence) fostered by Saigyō. He had already produced such famous poems as his one of the "three autumn twilights" later included in the *Shinkokinshū. When he altered his style about 1187 to a verbally and conceptually more complex kind, he was censured by many contemporaries, although some of these poems are now regarded as among his finest. He stubbornly persisted in what he felt certain to be right, seeking to establish his way in a series of waka sequences. In the autumn of 1193, Yoshitsune held a famous poetry match in six hundred rounds, the *Roppyakuban Utaawase, in which Teika participated in a full range of fresh styles that set him apart from the conservative Rokujō school. During the last decade of the century, he wrote more brilliantly than any of his contemporaries. His future seemed bright. But with the fall of the Kujō house in 1196, and his fortune associated with it, his remaining days seemed to involve poverty and very little hope.

For a person of such strong will, Teika sometimes showed what can only be called opportunism. He seems to have decided that his fortune lay with impressing the now retired Gotoba, with whom he was not on the best of terms. In 1200 he produced a waka sequence of great beauty, Shōji Ninen In Shodo Onhyakushu 正治二年院初度御百首 (A Hundred Poem Sequence of the Shōji Era). So impressive was the achievement that there began a relationship with the retired and ambitious sovereign that did far more for Japanese poetry than for the equanimity of either man. Things began well, and Teika was appointed to the Bureau of Poetry in 1201. The association continued with his contribution to Gotoba's spectacular Poetry Contest in 1500 Rounds (*Sengohyakuban Utaawase), in which Teika participated as a judge as well as a poet. In 1202, with five other poets, he received from Gotoba a commission to compile the eighth official collection, what was to become the *Shinkokinshū. Teika and his royal master disagreed about the principles of selection. Gotoba wished to include lesser poems among better, both to set off great by middling poems and to make for a smoother, fuller integration by techniques of association and progression. Since this was to be the genius of renga, which begins in a somewhat serious way at this time, and later of haikai, Gotoba's preferences clearly had the future in claim. Teika held to a standard of enduring excellence, wishing to admit only outstanding poems, and giving sequential integration second priority. Gotoba complained that Teika would reject poems by himself that were well suited to collection and, worse still, poems even by his father: so impossible did he seem in his standards. Shunzei died in 1204, thereby holding up celebrations for the completion of the collection—which Gotoba later revised in exile in a shorter version suiting his own preferences.

During these years Teika actually advanced in rank much beyond that of his father. And in 1216 he gave himself the satisfaction of making a collection of his poems, Shūi Gusō 拾遺愚草 (Meager Gleanings). But relations between Gotoba and him worsened, leading to censure and punishment in 1220. The poetic strife suddenly altered when the Kamakura regime banished Gotoba to Oki for his fomenting of the Jōkyū War (1221) in an attempt to reassert the power of the royal cause against the military overlords. Now the connection of the Kujō house with the Saionji family—the nobles closest to the Kamakura government—led to a recovery for it and, in its wake, Teika.

His last two decades, spent in old age and increasing infirmity, were nonetheless years of unaccustomed prosperity. Such good fortune in worldly terms may explain why he now wrote less poetry, although a minority view holds that his taste had turned to renga. From 1235, problems with his legs more or less restricted him to his house, making him unable to participate in poetry contests at court. Perhaps to occupy himself, perhaps to give his nervous intelligence an outlet, he made much of a kind of scriptorium he had in his house. Numerous classical works were copied out under his study and close scrutiny, some in his own hand, entirely or in part.

About this time, his poetry changed again. When Gohorikawa (r. 1221–1232) commissioned Teika to compile an official collection—the *Shinchokusenshū—he practiced a simpler style than he had used previously. Yet this style of "integral conception" (ushin) had in common the intensity (or much of it), the beauty, and the clarity common to his poetry throughout his career. In 1233 he took orders, and eight years later he died.

Some of Teika's other writings were designed to instruct aspiring poets. In 1209 he sent one version of his Kindai Shūka 近代秀歌 (Superior Poems of Our Time) to *Minamoto Sanetomo. In the preface, he argues that poetry had reached its first height in the Kampyō era (ca. 890); that after flourishing for a time, it entered into marked decline; and that it began to revive again in recent times, thanks to poets like *Minamoto Tsunenobu and *Minamoto Shunrai. However rudimentary, this is the first explicit poetic history in Japan, building to be sure on his father's Korai Fūteishō and other works, but having a design and specificity, a historical plan that is new. His and his father's review of earlier literature—and especially the temporalities necessary to such narratives as *Murasaki Shikibu's Genji Monogatari—assisted in the formation of a new idea of the literature of the past and indeed of literature itself. After dealing with such other matters as the handling of allusion, Teika sets forth eighty-three exemplary poems (shūka) for Sanetomo to take as models.

His Maigetsu Shō 毎月抄 (Monthly Notes, 1219) has more detailed criticism, arguing the merits of his late ushin stylistic ideal and distinguishing ten styles exemplifying it. The ten are illustrated by "superior poems" in Teika Jittei 定家十体 (Teika's Ten Styles,

1202–1213). *Eika (Eiga) Taigai* 詠歌大概 (*General Rules of Poetic Composition*, 1216) resembles *Kindai Shūka* closely and shares seventy-two poems with it. His *Nishidaishū* 二四代集 (*The Collection of Eight Eras*, 1234–1235) was perhaps intended to be called *Hachidaishō* 八代抄 (*A Treatise on the Collections of Eight Eras*). Whatever the case, it is his longest exemplary collection, with about eighteen hundred poems, much more like his father's *Korai Fūteishō* than his other exemplary compilations. Sometime between 1229 and 1236, Teika compiled a shorter version, *Hyakunin Shūka* 百人秀歌 (*Outstanding Poems by a Hundred Poets*), which actually includes 101 poets rather than the 100 mentioned in the title. Perhaps Teika was later requested to add one of his own, and kept the title from his sense of proper form. Most now think again that he also compiled the most famous of all such short, exemplary collections, (*Ogura*) *Hyakunin Isshu* (小倉)百人一首 ([*The Ogura Collection of*] *Single Poems by a Hundred Poets*), although his descendants may have revised it. Its present order is held to differ from the original, perhaps because the poems were removed as slips or cards pasted on a screen. Ingenious attempts to reorder in Teika's original manner have not carried conviction. Several other poetic treatises are extant.

Beginning in his teens (1180) and for fifty-six years (to 1235), Teika kept a Chinese diary, *Meigetsuki* 明月記 (*The Record of the Clear Moon*), a great resource for historians but written in a handwriting that became difficult to read as disease afflicted his hands. (In 1980 the Reizei family made public the manuscripts of this and other works. A degree of revision and revaluation was made possible.) Earlier he had had the reputation of being able to copy without error, an ability that no doubt accounts for the standards he exercised in having classical texts copied out. The "Teika texts" (Teikabon) are among the most highly prized for the *Kokinshū*, *Ise Monogatari*, and *Genji Monogatari*.

Two collections of his comments appeared from other hands: *Teika Monogatari* 定家物語 (*The Story of Teika*) and *Teika Kyō Sōgo* 定家卿相語 (*Talks with Lord Teika*). These testify to his importance in the eyes of his contemporaries and successors, as does also the attribution of spurious works to him, and the *nō*, *Teika*, a lengthy piece on his supposed amour with *Shokushi Naishinnō. He is said to have written a number of *monogatari* while young. The best candidate as a genuine work is probably the *Matsura no Miya Monogatari* 松浦宮物語 (*The Tale of the Matsura Palace*). This *giko monogatari* somewhat resembles the *Hamamatsu Chūnagon Monogatari* by *Sugawara Takasue no Musume in its play with credibilities.

Teika left behind oral teaching and many manuscripts for his children. Among the chief of these is that personal selection of his poems, *Shūi Gusō*

拾遺愚草 (1216–1233). Building on his father's efforts, he had indeed begun a poetic house. His grandchildren and their mothers quarreled over property, politics, and poetry. They separated into three lines that came to be known by the names of Nijō (led by Tameuji), Reizei (led by Tamesuke), and Kyōgoku (led by Tamenori). The Nijō won most of the economic and political struggles but were insipid poets. The Reizei was then the weakest, but it obtained a number of crucial manuscripts (handing over their own forgeries to the Nijō), and showed the greatest staying power as a school of *waka*, even into modern times. The Kyōgoku made a party with the Reizei and produced even better poets in those generations. Together they managed to keep poetry alive, as is shown in the last two important official collections, the *Gyokuyōshū* and *Fūgashū*. All branches of the family venerated in their ways their intense, brilliant ancestor. In being commissioned to compile the *Shinchokusenshū*, he became the first person to have the honor of compiler twice. The poet who had tolerated nothing but excellence now devised that simpler style. This foreshadows the last phase of the career of *Matsuo Bashō, and we ought to recall that Teika also wrote *renga*. There is no other Japanese poet of such intensity and such a range of lyric achievement.

FUJIWARA TOSHINARI. See Fᴜᴊɪᴡᴀʀᴀ Sʜᴜɴᴢᴇɪ.

FUJIWARA (KUJŌ) YOSHITSUNE 藤原(九条) 良経. 1169–1206. Early Kamakura *waka* poet, courtier. From a family of the upper nobility, he held various important court offices. He was gifted in calligraphy, Chinese poetry, and painting, but his literary fame rests on his *waka*. His best poetry is descriptive, with energy of language and thought, symbolism, and beauty. A poem of his opens the *Shinkokinshū*, which includes seventy-eight others by him—more than any other poet except for *Saigyō and *Jien. His personal collection is called *Akishino Gesseishū* 秋篠月清集 (*Yoshitsune's Clear Moon at Akishino*). His sudden death at thirty-seven deprived the age of one of its great poets just as he was reaching his prime.

FUKUZAWA YUKICHI 福沢諭吉. 1834–1901. Late Edo-early modern thinker, publicist, educator, critic, founder of Keiō University. Although essentially a modern figure, he is included here because his concern with education and his background in Dutch studies illustrates the way in which late Edo concerns were transmitted to modern times.

FUMIKUNI. See Nᴀᴋᴀᴍᴜʀᴀ Fᴜᴍɪᴋᴜɴɪ.

FUN'YA YASUHIDE 文屋康秀. Fl. ca. 858–888. Early Heian *waka* poet, one of the *rokkasen*, or six poetic sages. The designation hardly prepares one for the fact that he has but five poems in the *Kokinshū.

FURUTA ORIBE 古田織部. 1543–1615. Azuchi-Momoyama tea master, founder of the Oribe tea ceremonial, and predecessor of *Sen no Rikyū.

FUSHIMI 伏見. 1265–1317. The ninety-second sovereign in traditional numbering (r. 1288–1298). From his youth he studied Japanese classics—the *Kokinshū, *Genji Monogatari, *Man'yōshū, and so on. He is known to have written over two thousand poems and was well represented in the *Gyokuyōshū and *Fūgashū. Although not as great a poet as his consort, *Yōfuku Mon'in, he was certainly a gifted one and, like her, was strongly influenced by the innovative poetic ideals of *Kyogoku Tamekane, whom he commissioned to compile what became the longest *chokusenshū*, the *Gyokuyōshū.

FUSHIMI IN NO NAKATSUKASA NAISHI 伏見院中務内侍. Dates unknown. Late Kamakura diarist, poet. Although she has two poems in the *Gyokuyōshū, she is best known for her diary, *Nakatsukasa Naishi Nikki* 中務内侍日記. Covering the author's years of service at court from 1280 to 1292, it poises an attachment to this life against a sense of evanescence, revealing an attractive if not forceful personality.

FŪYŌ(WAKA)SHŪ 風葉(和歌)集 (*The Collection of Wind-Blown Leaves*). Mid-Kamakura *waka* collection in eighteen existing parts of twenty original, and with a preface on the *Kokinshū model. Ordered in 1271 by Ōmiya In Saionji Kitsushi (Gosaga's consort), it was probably compiled fairly soon thereafter by her ladies-in-waiting, although some credit *Fujiwara Tameie with selection.

The striking feature of the collection involves its taking all its poems from *monogatari*, about 200 of which are drawn on to supply its 1410 poems. The *Genji Monogatari provided almost a sixth of the poems (180), the *Utsuho Monogatari almost a tenth (110), and the *Sagoromo Monogatari a twentieth (56). Since only 10 percent of the 200 monogatari are now extant, the collection provides an invaluable window on a lost literature. It also demonstrates the esteem with which monogatari had come to be held after *Fujiwara Shunzei and his son *Fujiwara Teika, and it gives valuable evidence of the poetic taste of the time. Finally, it may be said to provide a mirror image of the *uta monogatari*.

FŪZOKU MONZEN 風俗文選 (*Popular Literary Selections*). A *haibun* collection of ten parts that appeared in 1705 under the title, *Honchō Monzen* 本朝文選 (*Japanese Literary Selections*), later altered to the more familiar version. Both titles allude, in their second word, to a major sixth-century Chinese collection of various writings, *Wen Hsüan*

(*Monzen*), although the resemblances are not as great as the shared titles would suggest (*Honchō Monzen* means *The Japanese Monzen*).

The Japanese collection is the first to offer a selection of haibun by various writers—by *Matsuo Bashō and other writers of his school. The twenty-nine authors represented include, besides Bashō, *Enomoto Kikaku, *Mukai Kyorai, and other major figures of the school. The 116 selections are of varying length and are categorized by terms that commonly reflect Chinese practice (for example, fu 賦, the Chinese meaning of which is sometimes rendered "rhyme-prose," sometimes "rhapsody," an ornate and rhetorical kind of writing).

Bashō is most fully represented and, as might be expected, among his works included are a number of accounts of travel (*kikō* is one of the categories) and such other works well known to Bashō scholars as *Genjūan no Ki* (*ki* being yet another category). With such major authors of haibun being selected for their best-known works, it was natural that the collection would have considerable influence. The best-loved of subsequent examples of haibun collections is no doubt *Yokoi Yayū's *Uzuragoromo*.

It cannot be said that, in classical times, haikai, much less haibun, achieved status as an elegant or standard (*ga*) art in prevailing judgment. But this collection is a major one by modern standards, and it affirms both the seriousness and pride of artistry of the Bashō school.

GEIAMI 芸阿弥. 1431–1485. Late Muromachi painter, second of the "Three Ami's" (see Nōami). Patronized by the Ashikaga *bakufu*, Geiami excelled at ink wash paintings, in which he incorporated Chinese elements. He also showed talent for *renga* and other arts.

GEMPEI JŌSUIKI (or *SEISUIKI*) 源平盛衰記 (*An Account of the Gempei Wars*). Late Kamakura or early Namboku *gunki monogatari* in forty-eight parts. Although various people have been proposed as single authors, it seems to have been produced by a succession of priests. This story of the *Gempei wars offers an alternative to the greater version in the *Heike Monogatari, containing a number of incidents not found in that story. In particular, *Minamoto Yoritomo emerges as a more important figure, altering the focus from one centered on Kyoto to one centered on the eastern provinces. In general plot, however, the two works are much the same, since this also begins with the highly effective "Gion Shōja" opening, recounts the events of the strife, and ends with the "Kanjō no Maki" on Kenrei Mon'in's last years in Ohara.

The story seems not to have undergone as much revision, and its audience is less well implied. Some say that it may be meant as a more popular version of the story shared with the *Heike Monogatari*, but that is scarcely possible in any sense other than vulgarizing. Other guesses, perhaps more likely, hold that it was meant for solitary reading, for recitation, or for preaching with gestures and intonations. It is more accurate than the *Heike Monogatari* in certain respects, some of its accounts being verifiable from various diaries of the time. It is also less of a piece than the *Heike Monogatari*, in that it is easier to sort out *setsuwa* characteristics, *michiyuki*, and Chinese borrowings. It is known to have influenced the *Taiheiki* in style. Some incidents not shared with the *Heike Monogatari* reappear in *nō*, *kōwakamai*, *otogizōshi*, *jōruri*, and *gesaku* writing. If its rival did not exist, this might well be considered the masterpiece of heroic literature.

GENJI MONOGATARI. See Murasaki Shikibu.

GENNAI. See Hiraga Gennai.

GENSHIN 源信. 942–1017. Mid-Heian religious figure. His ecclesiastical activities and virtuous life at Yokawa in the Mount Hiei area made him widely known, among lay as well as clerical people. Genshin and Kakuun (953–1007), the two leading disciples of the powerful abbot Ryōgen (912–985), established complementary movements within Tendai: the Eshin and the Danna schools, each transmitting doctrines into which *Saichō was said to have been initiated while in China. Genshin's Eshin school emphasized the doctrine of Original Enlightenment (*hongaku*), stressing "the descent from Buddhahood to mortality"; by contrast, the Danna school emphasized "the process of ascending from mortality up to Buddhahood." Both schools of Tendai scholasticism, orally transmitted for the most part, taught "meditation on Amida Buddha through one's own introspection of mind" (Ui)—thus forming a bridge to the Pure Land movements of the Kamakura period. Genshin's major work, the *Ōjōyōshū* 往生要集 (*Essentials of Deliverance*) is said to have appealed especially to members of the nobility forced out of power by the central Fujiwara magnates. His writing led to *ōjōden* and was a major influence on the leaders of the developing Pure Land movements, including *Hōnen and *Shinran. About a dozen of his *tanka* are scattered throughout the royal collections. Genshin is the model for Yokawa no Sōzu in the closing parts of the *Genji Monogatari*. He is unique in being featured for piety and learning in the greatest examples of *tsukuri monogatari*, *rekishi monogatari*, *gunki monogatari*, *setsuwa*, and in *nō*.

GIKEIKI 義経記 (*The Story of Yoshitsune*). Muromachi *gunki monogatari* in eight parts. Sometimes the title is read *Yoshitsune Ki*. The author, more likely the authors, of various stages are not known, but the style seems to indicate that a well-educated person made the final version. According to one theory, the work grew from stories told in north-eastern Japan of the *setsuwa* kind—brief, illustrative—concerning Yoshitsune. (Yoshitsune met his end at Hiraizumi, not far distant from Sendai.) These were then gradually put together to make this work and such another as the *Hōgan Monogatari* ("Hōgan" being another designation by title for Yoshitsune). The explanation seems quite plausible.

The *Gikeiki* can be regarded as something of a continuation of the *Heike Monogatari*, taking one of its many characters and adding others to lead to a decisive end. It begins, however, at a point before the end of the earlier work, with Ushiwaka, youngest son of Minamoto Yoshitomo, seeking to escape the net of Taira forces. Yoshitsune makes his appearance in the second part, and bit by bit we meet the other familiar characters of the story—the warrior-monk, Benkei; the lovely and loyal Shizuka; and Satō Tadanobu. It ends in 1188 with the death in battle of Benkei at the Koromo River at Hiraizumi, and the suicides of Yoshitsune and his family when betrayed to forces of his merciless brother, Yoritomo.

By this and other works, Yoshitsune was made into the most chivalric figure in Japanese history, there being versions of different episodes in all main kinds of Japanese drama and in fiction. The process of heroicizing and romanticizing history has now made it impossible to get a clear historical view of Yoshitsune or Yoritomo. The hero became an ideal that at once mollified and concealed the cruelty of military life.

GOFUKAKUSA IN BEN NO NAISHI 後深草院弁内侍. Dates unknown. Kamakura *waka* poet, diarist. She served Gofukakusa (r. 1246–1259) from his accession to 1252, recording in her diary what went on at court, and in her poems writing the kind of thing expected from a woman of her class and position. But her work has no special interest except to the student of those years.

GOFUKAKUSA IN NIJŌ 後深草院二条. B. 1258. Late Kamakura *waka* poet, diarist. She served Gofukakusa (r. 1246–1259) and later *Yōfuku Mon'in, who was a highly gifted poet and consort of Fushimi (r. 1288–1298). Her diary is unusual in the title she gave it—not *nikki*, *monogatari*, or (*ka*)*shū*—but *Towazugatari* とはずがたり (*The Unrequested Tale* or *Lady Nijō's Confessions*). That suggests a life sufficiently complex (and therefore worth knowing about) as to defy requests to explain it. But she does, with a keen sense of which details to include to establish a sense of her world or to interest the reader.

The account runs over a number of years to about 1313, always interesting and in general quite convincing, since its tone differs with her age and situation. At an early age she was settled in the palace as a concubine of Gofukakusa. He seems not to have greatly minded her relations with other men, as long as they were fairly discreet. To her chief lovers she gave names that may have been meant to be cryptic or that may have referred to poems they wrote. There are Yuki no Akebono (Sunrise on the Snow, referring to the distinguished nobleman, Saionji Sanekane) and Ariake no Tsuki (Melting Moon at Dawn, the younger brother of Gofukakusa).

These affairs and her court service occupy the first three of the five parts of her work. The last two parts show her a nun, and they give a particularly interesting account of her travels. She was welcomed at the Kamakura *bakufu*, not to mention places far less cultivated, for what a woman so close to the center of cultural things, and so accomplished, could explain. There is a suitably interesting and elegiac close. Thoroughly pleasurable and convincing, it is one of the most readable of court diaries, with a style suiting its purposes, even if it does not rise to the heights of some others.

GOFUSHIMI 後伏見. 1288–1336. Ninety-third sovereign in traditional count (r. 1298–1301), *waka* poet. He was one of the strongest supporters of the liberal Kyōgoku and Reizei waka styles. His poems first appeared in the *Shingosenshū*, but he is better represented in the *Fūgashū* and the *Gyokuyōshū*.

GOHEI. See NAMIKI GOHEI.

GONSUI. See IKENISHI GONSUI.

GOSAN(BUNGAKU) 五山 (文学); also GOZAN. The (literature of the) five temples in Kyoto and five in Kamakura. The five are sets of that number in Kyoto and in Kamakura from the Kamakura to the early Edo period. From time to time the temples included might change, and there were not always ten. Among the most important were Nanzenji and Shōkokuji in Kyoto; and Kenchōji and Engakuji in Kamakura. Although at first their new ideas were imported from China, their rivalry with old sects for support and their symbolic discourse excited resistance ranging from the ecclesiastical to the poetic (see *darumauta*), the lore of the gosan monks made increasing headway. Being so highly literate, the monks appealed first to the court and to educated warriors.

Although from Nara times Japan was never without some lively legacy from China, the gosan groups imported a host of new ideas with a degree of close mastery of them and rigor of standards that had not been known for some time. In addition to their religious teachings, meditational practices, and ecclesiastical organization, gosan teaching brought Confucianism new emphases, Sung aesthetics, and stricter observance of Chinese poetic canons. Besides their practice of Chinese letters, the gosan monks engaged in *waka*, *wakan renku*, and *renga*. Among its outstanding writers and striking personalities, this Rinzai intellectual movement included *Ikkyū, *Kokan, *Musō, Sesson Yūbai (1290–

1346), Chūgan Engetsu (1300–1375), Gidō Shūshin (1325–1388), and Zekkai (Chūshin; 1336–1405).

GOSEN(WAKA)SHŪ 後撰 (和歌) 集 (*Later Collection [of Japanese] Poetry*). Mid-Heian (951ff.) royal *waka* collection (*chokusenshū*): second of twenty-one. Ordered by Murakami (r. 946–967), it was compiled by the so-called Five Men of the Pear Jar Room: Ōnakatomi Yoshinobu, Kiyowara Motosuke, *Minamoto Shitagō, Ki no Tokibumi, and Sakanoe Mochiki. The five were learned men, but as the title chosen suggests, the 1,426 poems are "later gleanings" after the *Kokinshū*, whose model is followed in the twenty books and other features of arrangement. There is no preface. A chief feature of interest appears in the often lengthy headnotes, many of which seem to have been provided by the compilers to provide settings that would make the poems appropriate, if fictional responses, to experience. See Part Six A.

GOSHŪI(WAKA)SHŪ 後拾遺 (和歌) 集 (*Later Collection of Gleanings [of Japanese Poetry]*). Late Heian royal *waka* collection (*chokusenshū*); fourth of the *nijūichidaishū*. Ordered by Shirakawa (r. 1072–1086) in 1078 and completed in 1086. The compiler, *Fujiwara Michitoshi, also supplied a Japanese preface. Modeled on the *Kokinshū*, it has twenty books, 1,200 poems. Michitoshi's conservative tastes are very much in evidence, but his collection is fresh in its representation of the women poets who had dominated poetry for several decades, and of new descriptive styles. See Part Six A.

GOTOBA 後鳥羽 or Gotoba In 後鳥羽院. 1180–1239. Early Kamakura *waka* poet, sovereign (r. 1183–1198). After abdicating to exercise more power in retirement (hence his usual name, Gotoba In) he became immersed in politics. But he remained an active patron of many arts, and he ordered the *Shinkokinshū*, taking a major interest in its compiling and being one of its major poets. The compilers of the collection, particularly *Fujiwara Teika, had a number of disagreements about poems to include or exclude. (See the entry for Teika.)

His ideas about Teika, and of course much more about poetry, were set down in *Gotoba no In Gokuden* 後鳥羽院御口伝 (*The Secret Teachings of Gotoba In*), a major source for understanding the poetic issues and ideas of the time. There is also a personal collection, *Gotoba In Gyoshū* 後鳥羽院御集 (*The Collection of Gotoba In*). In addition to poems by him in official collections, he has eighteen renga stanzas in *Nijō Yoshimoto's *Tsukuba Shū*. His waka follows in general the stylistic ideals of *Fujiwara Shunzei, and the descriptive styles practiced by the best poets of the time. The later years of his life were not happy. He was banished to Oki after his ill-conceived attempt to overthrow the *bakufu* failed in the Jōkyū War of 1221. There he prepared a version of the *Shinkokinshū* at once shorter and mȯre to his liking. Exile must have been very trying for his restless spirit, for which poetry and other arts seemed his one sphere of repose. See *Jokyūki*.

GUSAI (or KYŪZAI, KYŪSEI, KASEI) 救済. 1284–1378. He was long-lived like most other important *renga* masters, and like theirs his ancestry is uncertain, although his dates are clearer than those of many. His career coincided with the first flowering of renga, of which he is one of the truly great masters. In spite of his later close association with *Nijō Yoshimoto, who adhered to the conservative *Nijō poets in *waka*, Gusai studied waka with *Reizei Tamesuke. Around 1315 he made appearance as an important renga poet, but after about 1319 nothing is known of him for some two decades. These were years when Godaigo (r. 1318–1339) was unsuccessfully seeking to wrest power from the Kamakura shogunate—more properly, from its Hōjō regents. Perhaps, like renga masters a century and a quarter later, Gusai found it advisable to leave the capital for travel.

By 1339 he had reappeared, to participate in a well-known renga sequence and thereafter became the first renga poet of his time. By 1341 he had become close to Yoshimoto, at whose house he took part in a very important 1,000-stanza renga composition, the *Bunna Senku* of 1355. His great achievement as a poet, and what surely made him appeal to Yoshimoto, was the fresh, genuinely poetic nature of his style. In particular, as renga was just gaining consideration as a serious art, he showed that it could rise well above pastime, above the comic, undignified, *mushin* kind it had been. He also managed the yet more difficult feat of making renga not simply serious but different in its seriousness from waka. Sometimes the difference lies in expression (*kotoba*), sometimes in conception (*kokoro*). Yoshimoto recognized the achievement when he compiled the first renga collection (*Tsukuba Shū*). Gusai's 126 stanzas outnumber those of any other poet. It does not really matter that he seems to have assisted Yoshimoto in the collection.

The two of them seem to have divided the public renga world of the time into the poetry of Gusai and the criticism of Yoshimoto. Yet just as Yoshimoto was a skillful renga poet (and by his high social position lent authority to the new art), so Gusai's insights helped shape the critical treatises of his highly placed friend. In particular, Yoshimoto's *Renga Shinshiki* (1372) shows the influence of the poet then nearly ninety. If Yoshimoto gave renga respectability, Gusai's art showed that it was deserved.

GYŌFŪ. See SEIHAKUDŌ GYŌFŪ.

GYŌJO 行助. 1405–1469. Muromachi *renga* poet. After taking orders, he studied renga with *Sōzei and, in 1444, they, *Chiun, and others participated in a well-esteemed hundred-stanza renga. Later he

participated notably in a number of thousand-stanza sequences. *Sōgi praised him for depth of conception in stanzaic connection and included him as one of seven poets in the *Chikurinshō*. He died young for an important renga poet and, some say, by his own hand.

GYOKUDŌ. See URAGAMI GYOKUDŌ.

GYOKUYŌ(WAKA)SHŪ 玉葉(和歌)集 (*Collection of Jeweled Leaves [of Japanese Poetry]*). Late Kamakura royal *waka* collection (*chokusenshū*); fourteenth of twenty-one. After considerable maneuvering by would-be compilers, *Fushimi (r. 1287–1298) ordered compilation by *Kyōgoku Tamekane in 1312, who finished the next year. Tamekane must have been busy for some time earlier, since the 2,796 (or 2,801, depending on the version) poems make this the longest of the official anthologies: perhaps he feared that there would be no second chance for the Kyōgoku-Reizei poets to be represented in another collection. But see *Fūgashū*. On the model of the *Kokinshū*, this has twenty parts. This and the *Fūgashū* take the perfected method of integrating a collection realized by the *Shinkokinshū a step further, using *renga*-style variations in closer and more distant connection. The finest poets besides Tamekane are *Yōfuku Mon'in, *Hanazono, *Fushimi, *Jūsammi Minamoto Chikako (Shinshi), *Jusammi Tameko, and others of the Kyōgoku-Reizei schools. There is no preface. See Part Six A.

HAKUIN 白隠. 1685–1768. Mid-Edo Rinzai Zen reformer, painter, calligrapher, and poet. Hakuin was so successful in teaching by *kōan* that virtually all modern Rinzai masters trace their lineage to him. He began his religious career at the Shōinji, a small rural temple in his native village of Hara in Suruga southwest of Hakone. On going to the temple Myōshinji in Kyoto, he acquired fame as a great master. He was also a devoted traveler and avoided attention, seeking instead to reach out to common people. His work holds considerable variety, including, of course, religious writing. His *Yabukōji* 藪柑子 (*Evergreen Shrub*, 1753) includes a discussion of the famous *kōan* that Hakuin had originated himself, the sound of a single hand clapping (sekishu no onjō). *Yasen Kanwa* 夜船閑話 (*A Chat on a Boat in the Evening*, 1757) and the short, *imayō*-style "Zazen Wasan" 坐禅和讃 ("Song in Praise of Meditation") are among his most popular writings. He has also left a *kashū*, the *Moshiogusa* 藻塩草 (*Brinish Seaweed*, 1759).

HAKUSHI MONJŪ 白氏文集 (*The Po Collection*). A collection of writings by the T'ang poet, Po Chü-i (Japanese Haku Kyoi 白居易 or Haku Rakuten 白楽天, 772–846). This collection seems to have begun with fifty parts, selections by the poet, and was later extended to seventy or more. By virtue of the familiarity among Japanese poets with this collection, Po Chü-i became the favorite poet of Heian times—some say because his poetry was reputed to be easy. He was the Chinese poet to whom allusions, and from whom recollections, were most frequent in Heian Japan. His verses were often used for *kudai waka*, and he epitomized Chinese poetry. So far was that the case that a *nō*, *Haku Rakuten*, depicted the divinity of Sumiyoshi, who represented Japan and its poetry, driving away an invasion by the Chinese poet and his nation's prestigious poetry. He maintained a high reputation even when other Chinese poets came to be favorites—Tu Fu, for example. The major Chinese influence on *Murasaki Shikibu's Genji Monogatari* is his narrative poem on the disastrous love of the ruler Hsüan Tsung for the great beauty Yang Kuei-fei, *Ch'ang Hen Ko* 長恨歌 (Japanese *Chōgonka*; *The Enduring Remorse*), and he is the Chinese poet not only on that great author's mind but also on those of her male contemporaries. This collection helped make such influence possible.

HAMADA CHINSEKI 浜田珍碩. D. ?1737. Early Edo *haikai* poet. Said to have been a physician, he lived in Zeze near Lake Biwa. About 1689 he joined the school of *Matsuo Bashō. He is represented in *Sarumino* and compiled *Hisago* and *Fukagawa* among other principal Bashō-style collections (see Part Six). He also is known as Shadō 酒堂.

HAMAMATSU CHŪNAGON MONOGATARI. See SUGAWARA TAKASUE NO MUSUME.

HAMAOMI. See SHIMIZU HAMAOMI.

HANA SANJIN 鼻山人. 1790–1858. Late Edo writer of *gesaku*. Among his various kinds of gesaku, for *sharebon* and *ninjōbon* he usually used this Hana (Nose) pen name. The reason is tedious to explain, but will be clear from the entry on his teacher, *Santō Kyōden. For *yomihon*, *kokkeibon*, and *gōkan*, he usually used the name Tōri Sanjin 東里山人. But he used numerous other styles as well. Although a member of the bakufu police force, after gaining experience elsewhere, he worked under Santō Kyōden. His first known work was the gōkan, *Shareta Shingata* 儷た新形. His most important sharebon is taken to be *Sato Kagami* 花街鑑 (1822); his best ninjōbon *Fūzoku Suiko Den* 風俗粋好伝 (1825) and *Kuruwa Zōdan* 廓雑談 (1826). During the middle 1820s, Sanjin hit his stride, giving some last touches to and making of ninjōbon —with *Tamenaga Shunsui—a settled, accepted kind of fiction. About 1830, he unwisely resigned his position with the police. He must have thought all lay clear for prosperous days as a writer. But he was somewhat given to nostalgia for a past he had not known and seems to have lost touch with his age and his audience. His last years were spent in reduced, demeaning circumstances. Very much a gesaku

writer, his credit will continue to fluctuate with the esteem given such popular writing.

HANAWA HOKINOICHI 塙保己一. 1746–1821. Late Edo scholar of earlier Japanese works. Born into a Musashi farming family, he was in Edo studying by the age of twelve. *Kamo no Mabuchi was his most famous teacher. His labors were prodigious, and it comes as a shock that he and his students, rather than some Meiji corporate enterprise, compiled *Gunsho Ruijū* 群書類従 (*Classified Collections of Japanese Classics*—530 parts (1779–1819). This compendium of over 1,200 writings of various kinds is still a major scholarly source. It was supplemented by *Zoku Gunsho Ruijū* (72 parts) by his son Tadatomo (1807–1862).

HANAZONO 花園. 1297–1348. Ninety-fifth sovereign in the traditional count (r. 1308–1318), Kamakura *waka* poet. Although he possessed great proficiency in calligraphy and painting as well as devoted understanding of Zen Buddhism, he is best known artistically as a waka poet in the innovative Kyōgoku and Reizei styles. He was especially close to *Kyōgoku Tamekane, the main poetic mover and critic of the age. Tamekane, his archrival the conservative *Fujiwara (Nijō) Tameyo, and many other poets are mentioned in his detailed diary, which covers the years 1310–1322. It was long believed that he compiled the last truly important official waka collection, the *Fūgashū. Recent evidence shows, however, that the compiler was Kōgon (r. 1332–1333). Hanazono did supervise compilation as well as supply both the Japanese and Chinese prefaces to the collection. Historians and critics have found useful his strangely named diary, *Hanazono In Tennō Shinki* 花園院天皇宸記 (*Diary of the Cloistered Reigning Hanazono*). A gifted, attractive person.

HARIMA (NO KUNI NO) FUDOKI. See *Fudoki*.

HARITSU. See OGAWA HARITSU.

HARUMACHI. See KOIKAWA HARUMACHI.

HARUMI. See MURATA HARUMI.

HARUNOBU. See SUZUKI HARUNOBU.

HASEGAWA TŌHAKU 長谷川等伯. 1539–1610. Momoyama painter, founder of the Hasegawa school. He seems to have begun with Buddhist painting, but on moving to Kyoto and studying the Kanō style, he turned to secular work, developing his own freer style in opposition to the Kanō school, much like *Kaihō Yūshō. In addition to the usual subjects for ink-wash painting, he showed talent for portraits and depictions of birds and flowers.

HATTORI TOHŌ (or **DOHŌ**) 服部土芳. 1657– 1730. Early Edo *haikai* poet. Born in Iga Ueno (Mie) thirteen years after *Matsuo Bashō, of a family of high-ranking retainers of the local samurai lord, Tōdō, he knew Bashō from about the age of ten, met him again in 1685, and followed his haikai style from 1688. Dohō's hermitage, called Minomushian, had contemporary fame, and not simply because he entertained Bashō there. He first appeared as a poet in *Sarumino* (see Part Six). His *Sanzōshi* 三冊子 (*Three Books*, ca. 1702) is one of the principal sources of our knowledge about Bashō. Each is familiarly designated by the color of its original cover—white, red, or black. He also edited a collection of Bashō's stanzas and included his own poetry written between 1688 and 1729 in his *Minomushian Shū* 蓑虫庵集 (*Collection of the Bagworm Hermitage*).

HATTORI NANKAKU 服部南郭. 1683–1759. Mid-Edo Chinese scholar, poet. Reared by his father as a *waka* poet, he lost him in 1695 and moved the next year to Edo. There he entered into service with the lord of Mino, Yanagisawa Yoshiyasu. He studied Confucianism in that household, and in 1716 he left service there to found an academy that flourished with samurai patronage. His works include an anecdotal history of Japan written in Chinese, *Daitō Seigo* 大東世語 (*An Account of the Great Eastern World*, 1750) and two collections of Chinese compositions: *Nankaku Sensei Bunshū* (or *Monjū*) 南郭先生文集 (*Professor Nankaku's Literary Collection*, 1758), and *Tōshisen Kokujikai* 唐詩選国字解 (*A Japanese Glossary of Selected Poems in Chinese*, 1792). His Chinese poetry, which he claimed followed the pure, ancient manner of Tu Fu, was highly popular and read for years after his death, although scarcely a line of it has since gone uncriticized for faults.

HATTORI RANSETSU 服部嵐雪. 1654–1707. Early Edo *haikai* poet. Born in Edo of a samurai family, he served several daimyo. After *Enomoto Kikaku and *Matsukura Ranran, he was among the first disciples of *Matsuo Bashō. Like Ranran, he was one of twenty followers whose solo *kasen* were published in 1680. He participated in various sequences and collections of the Bashō school, including *Minashiguri* and *Sarumino* (see Part Six) as well as in a *ryōgin* or duo kasen with Bashō in 1689. When he published his own collection, *Wakana Shū* 若菜集 (*The Collection of Young Shoots*), he dedicated it to the memory of Bashō. He has some of the playful eccentricity often found in adherents of Zen Buddhism, but perhaps the source was his familiarity with Kikaku; in any event he is one of the traditional four worthies in the Bashō school.

HAYASHI RAZAN 林羅山. 1583–1657. Early Edo scholar of Chinese, poet. Although not one of the great thinkers, as a popularizer of the orthodox Neoconfucianism (*shushigaku*) he was very influential. His life also shows that the social code was

flexible enought to allow for his rise. Born to a Kyoto townspeople's family, he studied a variety of subjects under priests. He might have become one himself, but declined in his teens. He began his study of Neoconfucianism at seventeen. Before long his arguments as to its importance came to the attention of the first Tokugawa shogun, Ieyasu, who appointed him to head the governmental school to propound the philosophy as official doctrine. In doing so he founded the Hayashi school. Such are his productive talents that his Chinese poems alone require 175 parts for printing, and his *Razan Bunshū* 羅山文集 (*A Collection of Razan's Works*, 1662), 75. Annals and historical writings must also be added, such as *Honchō Tsugan* 本朝通鑑 (*A General History of Our State*, comp. 1644–1670). Among those collections, special collections, and further collections, there is also a concern with native literature, as befits a person once connected with *Matsunaga Teitoku. These include *Genji Monogatari Shonengetsu Kō* 源氏物語諸年月考 (*A Study of Various Chronologies in the Genji Monogatari*) and similar studies of the *nijūichidaishū*.

HEICHŪ MONOGATARI 平中物語 (*The Tale of Heichū* [or *Sadabun*]. Mid-Heian *uta monogatari*, also called *Heichū Nikki* and, after the more or less central figure, *Sadabun Nikki*. Composed by an unknown author drawing on the poems of Taira Sadabun (also Sadabumi; d. ca. 923), it is sometimes supposed to have been written near Sadabun's death, although most opinions set a later date.

The thirty-eight episodes contain 150 poems (including a *chōka* and *tanrenga*). Although patterned on the *Ise Monogatari* and *Yamato Monogatari*, this curiously combines in its order seasonal classifications based on *waka* categories with more extended narrative units than those in the *Ise Monogatari*. In spite of the dominance of the waka classifications, a given episode does not therefore make as much of a single poem—or in spite of the narrative prominence, the waka classifications are stronger than in earlier uta monogatari. The substance of the episodes is consistently amatory.

HEIJI MONOGATARI 平治物語 (*The Tale of the Heiji War*). Kamakura *gunki monogatari* in three parts. Also called *Heiji Ki*. Because of its resemblance to the *Hōgen Monogatari*, written about events just prior to those dealt with here, a common writer has sometimes been assumed. But authorship is unknown. The *Heiji Monogatari* shows that the Taira have now gained power under Taira Kiyomori, but ends with those seeds of the Minamoto rivalry that were to lead to the *Gempei wars and the story told in the *Heike Monogatari*. Although that work excels this and the *Hōgen Monogatari*, these two made that achievement possible by demonstration of methods to individualize many characters, relate incidents, and develop the *wakan konkōbun* style of Japanese. They also were recited by *biwa hōshi* and helped give Japan a heroic literature.

Among the many characters of this story, three stand out. Fujiwara Nobuyori (1133–1159) is the active agent. He plots overthrow of the Taira hegemony and loses. After various dodges, he is captured and executed. Taira Kiyomori (1118–1181) is of course virtual dictator of the court and government. To readers of the *Heike Monogatari*, Kiyomori seems of more human proportions here; it is fascinating to see him in assured control while we think of what lies ahead. The same is true in another sense for Minamoto Yoritomo. He appears toward the end, defeated but spared, an exile vowing to revive this family. He leaves his designated place of exile to revive the Genji cause. He is more on stage than in the *Heike Monogatari*, more sympathetic than in the **Gikeiki*.

Like the *Hōgen* and *Heike Monogatari*, this is oriented toward the court and the capital, drawing on the nobility as well as warriors, poems as well as prose. It shares not only these with the *Hōgen Monogatari* but also the three parts, the ordering of events in them and the style. These works use the first part to deal with events leading up to the central outburst; and second to deal with battles; and the third to show the aftermath. The *Heiji Monogatari* innovates by introducing incidental characters who enrich the main story line.

There are ten or more kinds of text in existence. Many are distinguished by being texts for recitation. Others are notable for illustration. The early illustrated texts are of great value by virtue of their proximity in time to the events recounted, giving an unusually clear visual version of Kamakura details. The first part of the story provides incidents for the three famous pictures in the *Heiji Monogatari Emaki* ... 絵巻: "The Burning of Sanjō Palace," "Shinzei," and "The Royal Progress to Rokuhara."

HEIKE MONOGATARI 平家物語 (*The Tale of the Heike*). Kamakura *gunki monogatari*. The story of the struggles between the Taira (Heike) and Minamoto (Genji) houses is told in many versions and has a cultural familiarity for Japanese like the Bible or Arthurian legend. Its subject is the downfall of the Heike, along with events leading up to that, or following from it. In style, meaningfulness, organization, and emphasis it is the second greatest of Japanese narratives after the **Genji Monogatari*.

The action covers about sixty years, ca. 1131–1191, and occurs over wide areas of central and western Japan. Unlike some other versions of the same events, it pays less attention to what transpires in the northern and eastern areas.

In one sense, it is almost impossible to say what is meant by "*Heike Monogatari*." Three kinds of texts in many versions existed: 1. versions for historical records; 2. versions for priests to read or use in itinerant preaching; and 3. versions for the *biwa hōshi* to recite. Some critics think that an early three-part version existed, and that a six-part version followed. One surviving example of the story, the **Gempei Jōsuiki*, is, however, in forty-eight parts. Early versions of types 1 and 2 are usually in *kambun*, whereas versions of 3 are in the more natural written Japanese of the time, *wakan konkōbun*.

Some version of the events dealt with seems to have been put together within about three decades after 1191. In the late Kamakura period, performance lines divided into two—the Ichikata 一方 and Yasaka 八坂. The Ichikata line is best known for its Kakuichi version, named after the biwa hōshi or reciter, Kakuichi 覚一. For most purposes, this version is what is usually meant when the work is named. It is said that one Nyoichi 如一 founded the Ichikata school (so named by its writing of ichi or "ones" as one of the text marks) and that Kakuichi effectively reworked the *Heike Monogatari*. But it is impossible to say what we owe to him for the design and style of the work. Certainly many earlier writers and reciters made contributions, and earlier versions must have helped create incidents and canons of telling. Another important element was the desire of at least a part of the country to look upon the fate of the proud Taira house as a romantic and tragic series of events, as appealing as they are sad.

The Kakuichi version consists of twelve books and a sequel, the "Kanjō no Maki," dealing with the widowed Kenrei Mon'in's last days in a temple in Ohara, north of Kyoto. The preceding twelve books of the Kakuichi version are numbered rather than titled. On the other hand, each episode (*sōwa*) within the twelve has a title. And the episodes are further divisible in terms of units for recitation. The coincidence of various formulas (saru hodo ni) being one of the strong ones in marking a division) with marginal markings like ku and kudoki—口, 口説—seem to suggest strong divisions, new material. Many of the details of the smaller-scale organization of the parts are disputed, but the very nature of the issues debated seems clearer than the structure of the whole. There is simply no agreed-on opinion as to whether the work exists in two major parts, or three or more. Recent study has tended to agree that there are probably six unequal divisions, but those who agree on that do not agree on what the divisions are.

Of course the important works in a literature naturally draw attention, and varied attention arouses various opinions. Yet the lack of agreement as to the structure of the work is the more worth remarking, since there is such general agreement on the tonal and spiritual unity of it. Perhaps compositeness is a better word than unity. At times the style offers forthright narrative relation. But the resounding Sinified opening is in another key of verse-prose, in which a basic 7-5-syllable pattern is varied for emphasis:

Gion shōja no / Kane no koe   7/5
Shogyō mujō no / Hibiki ari   7/5
Shara sōju no / Hana no iro   7/5
Jōsha hissui no / Kotowari o arawasu   7/9
Ogoreru hito mo / Hisashikarazu   7/6
Tada haru no yo no / Yume no gotoshi   7/6
Takeki mono mo / Tsui ni wa horobinu   6/8
Hitoe ni kaze no / Mae no chiri ni onaji.   7/9

The impermanence spoken of is that *mujō* that sounds through Japanese literature, and the teak trees are those that shed their flowers as Shakamuni died—entered Nirvana. So that a translation adhering to the line succession as far as possible might run:

At the Jetavana Temple / The bell gives voice
To the impermanence of all / As it reverberates.
That the pairs of teak trees, / In the hue of their flowers,
Show the downfall of the splendid / Is a matter of reason.
The magnificent ones as well / Will not continue long,
Only like a night in spring / When dreams are brief.
The most stalwart ones as well / Are overthrown in the end,
As one before the tempest / They are blown away like dust.

It is clear that those magnificent ones doomed to fail are the Taira, the Heike of the title. It is equally clear that the glory from which they fall is as real as the fact of falling.

Comparison of the *Heike Monogatari* with other accounts of the *Gempei* wars shows that it comes from a group that understands the faults of the Taira lords but differs from those who have the eastern view that is so directly sympathetic with Minamoto Yoritomo, whose role in the *Heike Monogatari* is surprisingly small. On the Minamoto side the two most impressive figures are Yoshitsune, whose fabled death at the instigation of his brother, Yoritomo, lies ahead, and Kiso Yoshinaka, the violent, proud, and valiant man whose efforts for the Minamoto cause do not save him from the wrath of Yoritomo. As numerous signs show, then, this is a story about the doom of those who are glorious. It is also, perhaps, even more concerned with the glory of the doomed. Recent criticism has shown clearly that the attitude or viewpoint assumed is that of the people of Kyoto. They know the proud Taira, who had been ordering them around. But the Taira are people who have accepted court values and Kyoto ways. The Minamoto seem by comparison to be rigid men of iron (with exceptions like Yoshitsune, whose time in Kyoto has been a redeeming feature).

The Taira side includes a very large cast. It includes, of course, Kiyomori, who had taken his house to the pinnacle of its fame, winning control, as the Fujiwara had done earlier, over the sovereign and major court offices. His macabre death provides one of the set pieces in the book—one of a series of endings (saigo) to lives that increases with frequency near the end, each person illustrating the character achieved in life by the art of dying practiced. Kiyomori's eldest son, Shigemori, provides a foil for the haughty father. One of the bravest, he is also the best of the Heike, and his death is a sign that the Heike have lost moral authority.

The work is a *gunki monogatari* if any is at all. But its features are softened and colored more warmly by features of stories familiar to the court in Kyoto. One symptom is the importance of women. Kenrei Mon'in has learned suffering long before that sequel. Yoshinaka's end features an Amazonian heroine, his lover, Tomoe. The efforts of Yokobue to find her lover (10, "Yokobue") are rich in many kinds of sorrow. The story features characters of many kinds, usually as appealing as they are imperfect, and yet in their suffering larger than life. The story oscillates between Heike and Genji, high and low, crowds and lonely scenes, men and women, adults and children. There is no question of the greatness of the story—next only to *Murasaki Shikibu's Genji Monogatari. Whether this story of heroism is an epic is a question whose counterpart is whether or not there is in other literatures a *monogatari* of this kind.

One of the glories of the *Heike Monogatari* is its style, which is as rich as oral delivery could allow, and as vigorous as the efforts of many tellers could effect. By some miracle, it combines the Sinified and the Japanese, the *onnade* of Heian monogatari with *otokode* befitting war. Where the style of the *Genji Monogatari* seems to us today perplexingly complex, this style is clear. Where the *Genji Monogatari* suggests a slowing and inward turn to narrative, this shows a world in turmoil. The courtly world of the earlier work tends more to nighttime, indoor scenes, and to deeply affecting encounters with a few—usually two—characters at a time. The world of the *Heike Monogatari* is by contrast one of daylight, of the outdoors, of issues and trends that catch up the individual along with crowds here and battles there. The work is far from the last literary benefit that the Kyoto outlook would bestow on the rest of the nation, but it is one of the greatest and certainly the greatest of its kind.

HENJŌ 遍昭. 816–?890. Early Heian *waka* poet, Tendai cleric, disciple of *Ennin. He is one of the six poetic sages—*rokkasen*—for having been mentioned with five other poets in *Ki no Tsurayuki's Japanese preface to the *Kokinshū*, and is included as well as one of the thirty-six poetic worthies (*sanjūrokkasen*). Although he has a playful poetic exchange with *Ono no Komachi, and his fame is beyond question, not much is known of him. (The *Yamato Monogatari* writes of a love affair with

Komachi, but that is taken to be fabricated.) He appears to have taken orders in grief over the death of Nimmyō (r. 833–850). He has a brief personal collection, *Henjō Shū*. Only thirty-five of his poems appear in official collections beginning with the *Kokinshū*, and it is hard not to think that he was overrated by Tsurayuki and others.

HIEDA NO ARE 稗田阿礼. Fl. ?670–?690. Nara lady (toneri) at the court of Temmu Tennō. Little is known of her, except that she was so famous for her powers of memory that, at Temmu's command, she memorized a number of oral and written materials that she then recited to Ō no Yasumaro for compilation, leading to the **Kojiki.*

HINO NO TAKEMUKI 日野竹向き. Fl. ca. 1330–1350. Nambokuchō diarist. Daughter of Hino no Sukena (her formal given name was Meishi 名子), she married Saionji Kimmune. Her husband was deeply involved in the chaotic political events of the time and, during the Kemmu Restoration, was executed in 1335 on the charge of planning assassination of Godaigo. Takemuki seems to have spent much of the rest of her life in the effort to restore the fortunes of her husband's family and to rear her son, Sanetoshi. It is thought that by 1349 she had completed her diary, *Takemuki ga Ki,* 竹向きが記 (*The Diary of Takemuki*), which records, or recalls, the previous fifteen or twenty years. Her poetry does not equal that of **Kenrei Mon'in Ukyō no Daibu, but her prose is superior, and her account has a good deal more action. She has some claim to being the last important female writer in a long line. It would be many generations before society fostered another woman like her as a prose writer.

HIRAGA GENNAI 平賀源内. 1728–1779. Mid-Edo writer of *kokkeibon* and *jōruri*, scholar of Dutch, botanist—a "renaissance man." A remarkably versatile person, he began study of plants at twelve and by eighteen had so impressed his feudal superior, Matsudaira Yoriyasu, that he was taken into service.

Although the concern here is with his literary interests, he was a social commentator, tutor or secretary to *bakufu* officials, a philologist, dictionary compiler, teacher in his own school, and commentator on history, law, music, martial science, and politics. That range of interest would be remarkable in any country at any time, but they were especially timely in late eighteenth-century Japan. His Dutch studies and curiosity enabled him to produce the first asbestos and first electric generator in Japan, as also to be a pioneer in Western-style oil painting.

At twenty-four he began Dutch studies at Nagasaki, becoming acquainted with recent Western learning, particularly in his favorite subject, botany. Growing tired of service, he resigned his

samurai status in 1751. Three years later he left Osaka for Edo, where he threw himself into a burst of activity, establishing (in 1757) Japan's first produce association, studying Confucianism and also *kokugaku*, the latter under **Kamo no Mabuchi. In 1763 his two most important works began to appear: *Nenashigusa* 根無草 (*Rootless Grass*) and *Fūryū Shidōken Den* 風流志道軒伝 (*The Dashing Life of Shidōken*). Drawing on the earlier *Sayoarashi* (1689), Gennai treated in *Nenashigusa* (1763, 1768) human dissipations and depravities, but in terms of credible individuals of his own time. The first part deals with a person who dies from drowning, the second with death by illness—both based on contemporary individuals. His biting style was very popular.

His masterpiece, *Fūryū Shidōken Den*, purports to be a biography of Fukai Shidōken. It tells how a sage teaches the hero to fly. So he does, visiting the various regions of Japan, and then going abroad, to countries imaginary and real—although the distinction is largely formal. The countries include a land of giants and a land of midgets, a land of long-armed and a land of long-legged people, as well as Borneo and Holland. At one point he institutes an ideal state. His last stop is at the Island of Women (Nyogogashima, whither the aged Yonosuke of **Ihara Saikaku's *Kōshoku Ichidai Otoko* sets forth at last with cronies, before returning to Japan. The conspectus provided by the travels offers an implicit characterization (including some satire on Japan and a government that forebade leaving the country). Interestingly enough, it is independent of Swift's *Gulliver's Travels.*

In these works he seeks to correct widely held errors, or self-serving social pretense, by complex parodic reasoning. All we encounter (he holds) has a front side (omote) of appearance or sham and a hidden back side (ura) of truth. Since the truthful backside is hidden, it is a lie; and the appearances of the front are necessary to ascertain truth. There is no good in appeal to authority: in the preface to *Nenashigusa* he speaks of "the Buddha's fraudulence, Lao-tze's and Chuang-tze's balderdash, and Lady Murasaki's zillion lies." There is also an unsettling dynamism: truth may become a lie, and a lie truth. Yet throughout these verbal gestures, a "lie" really means "fiction," and "truth" is similarly compromised.

Gennai's paradoxes are designed to expose the falsity of usual presumptions. He uses other means as well. There are three kinds of lists: of synonyms, of matters inventoried, and of reasons to argue by. This is Rabelaisian to a degree, but he may include among synonyms something that seems antithetical: the point being shock, uncertainty, and reason to consider its back side. His famous Hiraga buri (Hiraga style) has other specifiable characteristics. He combines all the languages to which he had access (including a smattering of Sanskrit). His

Japanese itself is multiple, uncertain. Different levels, dialects, argot, and jargon enter. Often he reads Chinese as if it were Japanese. That is, a sentence may have an explicit (front) meaning in terms of the Chinese characters used. But the accompanying *kana* (supposedly there to assist pronunciation) give a very different (back) meaning. *Nenashigusa* deals with these matters and these ways largely in sexual terms, and *Fūryū Shidōken Den* in social. In both (as in other works) a reader will find a lot of sheer fun in the intellectual play. But there is earnest in Gennai's jest: he sometimes comes close to suggesting that front and back, lie and truth, are toys of language and behavior. His practical interests and evident satiric concerns are, in this matter, the most reassuring elements of his work.

These stories naturally had a great impact on other writers and developments in Japanese prose fiction. By 1770, however, Gennai had turned to jōruri, bringing out his first play, *Shinrei Yaguchi no Watashi* 神霊矢口渡, thereby enlivening the Edo puppet theatre with his enormous vitality. He wrote other works, including the posthumously edited *Fūrai Rikubushū* 風来六部集 (1780), and he also found time to introduce Western principles of art to his contemporaries. He is one of the greatest figures of his time, literary and otherwise, possessing an energy for which *Ihara Saikaku seems the only precedent among Edo writers. That vitality led to a wildness of life. He wounded a man in a trivial incident such as he might have written up in exciting terms, and he died while imprisoned for the act.

HIRAGA MOTOYOSHI 平賀元義. 1800–1865. Late Edo *waka* poet. After study of various other subjects, he turned to literary and antiquarian matters. His waka style emulated features of the *Man'yōshū*, and his preferences influenced leading modern poets such as Masaoka Shiki.

HIRATA ATSUTANE 平田篤胤. 1776–1843. Late Edo *kokugaku* scholar. By the age of seven he was into Neoconfucian studies, and by nineteen had studied medical and martial matters as well. He studied under the son of *Motoori Norinaga, Haruniwa, while his own talents gained steady recognition. His move to Kyoto in 1809 put him into touch with Shinto scholars. His *Tamano Mihashira* 霊能真柱 (1812) shows signs of independence from the Norinaga school. He was one of those who argued for the existence of *jindai moji*, a Japanese written language supposedly predating the introduction of Chinese characters. His fanciful argument was set forth in *Shinji Hifumi Den* 神字日文傳 (*Japanese Writing in the Divine Script*, 1819). Although his study was not really directed against the Edo shogunate, in 1841 the government forbade publications of his works. By then, however, his followers had spread his ideas throughout Japan, widely influencing late Edo attitudes, even if his

thought has had nothing like the lasting importance of Motoori Norinaga's.

HIROKATA. See YASHIRO HIROKATA.

HIROSE TANSŌ 広瀬淡窓. 1782–1856. *Kanshi* poet, student and teacher of Chinese learning. His poems were published in 1837, his collected works in many volumes later. It is particularly striking that he opened a school at which he taught, in time, over 4,000 boys from all parts of the country, anticipating the Meiji urge to education and showing that much that is thought to be characteristic of Meiji Japan had begun earlier.

HIROSHIGE. See ANDŌ HIROSHIGE.

HISHIKAWA MORONOBU 菱川師宣. D. ca. 1695. Early Edo ukiyoe artist. Moving to Edo from the provinces, he spent more than thirty years as a painter and artist of woodblock prints. Although the prints were largely for books printed from blocks, he stimulated further artistic developments.

HITACHI (NO KUNI NO) FUDOKI. See *Fudoki*.

HITOMARO. See KAKINOMOTO HITOMARO.

HŌBUTSUSHŪ 宝物集 (*A Collection of Treasures*). Early Kamakura *setsuwa* collection. One to seven parts in various versions. Some other works attribute the compilation to Taira Yasuyori 平康頼 (dates unknown but active ca. 1190–1200). The treasures of the title are the things that people esteem, things climaxed—or transcended—by the Law of the Buddha. The doctrine of the various stories is very much that of Tendai Buddhism, especially as formulated by *Genshin. The *wakan konkō* prose style exercised influence on various *monogatari*, including even the *Heike Monogatari*.

HŌGEN MONOGATARI 保元物語 (*The Tale of The Hōgen War*). Kamakura *gunki monogatari* in three parts. Resembling the slightly later *Heiji Monogatari* so much in subject, style, and ordering, it has sometimes been thought to be written by the same person. But, authorship is unknown. Both works were quickly taken up for oral delivery by *biwa hōshi*. The many surviving manuscripts have left a complex textual problem.

The title derives from the Hōgen War (1156), a strife with many principal characters, none of whom dominates the work. On the death in 1156 of his predecessor (the retired Toba), the retired Sutoku (r. 1123–1141) decided to enlist allies in order to exercise control of royal authority and power. To that end he engaged the forces of Fujiwara Yorinaga, Minamoto Tameyoshi, and Minamoto Tametomo. On the other side, the reigning sovereign, Goshirakawa (r. 1155–1158) obtained forces led by Lay

Priest Shinzei, Taira Kiyomori, and Minamoto Yoshitomo. Battle is engaged in the second part, coming to a stirring climax when Chinzei Hachirō Tametomo issues forth, seven feet tall, releasing deadly arrows. They do not avail, Sutoku's forces are vanquished, and Sutoku is forced to take orders. One passionate effort follows the next, each adding a tragedy. In the third section, Tameyoshi's wife commits suicide, Sutoku is exiled to Sanuki (in Shikoku), and the military action ends, leaving ample seeds for further trouble, as the *Heiji Monogatari* and *Heike Monogatari* were to show.

The opposition of royal powers divides houses, so there is not the sense of clear and titanic division that came with the *Gempei* wars. If the scale is not so large or the issues so clearly drawn as some later, there is ample tragedy in the ruin of so many people by the heedless and basically petty struggles within the royal house. Characters are well individualized, although it will be noticed that the personality of Kiyomori is less awesome than in the monogatari to come. This and the *Heiji Monogatari* make an excellent pair, both in their mastery of narrative and in their development of the *wakan konkōbun* style of Japanese. In both respects, they laid the ground for the *Heike Monogatari*.

HŌITSU. See SAKAI HŌITSU.

HOKUSAI. See KATSUSHIKA HOKUSAI.

HŌNEN 法然. 1133–1212. Early Kamakura religious figure, founder of the Jōdo (Pure Land) sect. Hōnen advocated the Sole-practice Calling upon the Name of the Buddha (senju *nembutsu* 専修 念仏) in 1175, the date frequently cited for the founding of the Jōdo sect. In 1198, at the request of his influential patron, Kujō Kanezane (1148–1207), Hōnen wrote his major work, the *Senjaku* (or *Senchaku*) [*Hongan Nembutsu*] *Shū* 選択〔本願念仏〕集, *Collection of Passages* [*on the Original Vow and the Nembutsu*]. Hōnen's message was eagerly received by courtiers and warriors, farmers and prostitutes. People of all classes found in his teaching a clarity and hope amid the chaos of the day. Hōnen himself had need of the hope he taught, since at seventy-four he was banished to Shikoku for four years. He died a year later, having written during a long last illness the *Ichimai Kishōmon* 一枚起請文, *The One-Page Testament*. The Pure Land movement by Hōnen was a major influence on Japanese religion, society, and literature for centuries to come. See also *Shinran.

HONNAMI (or **HON'AMI**) **KŌETSU** 本阿弥 光悦. 1558–1637. Early Edo artist, born in Kyoto. He acquired proficiency in so many arts that he is difficult to place. Skilled in swordsmanship, he was also thought one of the three great calligraphers of his time. In addition, he was a master of tea and skilled at raised gold lacquer. But if one achievement had to be singled out, it would probably be his pottery in the Kyoto rakuyaki style.

HORI BAKUSUI 堀麦水. 1718–1783. Mid-Edo *haikai* poet. Born in Kaga, he studied haikai in the school of *Kagami Shikō (a Mino poet), one of the ten Bashō worthies. He then switched to a less well-known teacher from Ise, with whom he did well enough for a time until his style became attenuated by a precious classicism. When he later read the *shōfū* collection, *Minashiguri* (see Part Six), he was bowled over. In his eagerness to lend his services to the serious reformation of haikai, he showed the humorless zeal of a convert, and he degenerated as a poet.

HŌSEIDŌ KISANJI 朋誠堂喜三二. 1735–1813. Late Edo writer of *sharebon* and *kibyōshi*. One of the few important *gesaku* writers from samurai origin, he began writing *haikai* while still young, and seems to have produced his first sharebon about 1773. Thereafter many writings followed. Some have the complex or contrived titles of so much Edo literature for stage and reading, such as *Koto Shamisen* 滑都酒美選 (1783). Other titles include *Kagekiyo Hyakunin Isshu* 景清百人一首 *(1782)* and *Nagaiki Mitaiki* 長生見度記 (1783). He became a leading writer, but in 1788 his *Bumbu Nidō Mangokudōshi* 文武二道万石通 offended the government, and he was forbidden to publish any more prose fiction. As a result, he turned in his last years to *kyōka*, something for which his samurai education and haikai writing had well fitted him.

HOSOKAWA YŪSAI 細川幽斎. 1534–1610. Political figure, warrior, *waka* poet, critic. His family was of the three principal military lords of local domains (shugo daimyo) to furnish advisers (kanrei) to the Ashikaga shoguns, two of whom Yūsai served. He was born as the shogunate was tottering and the nation was torn by civil wars; he lived into the age of Toyotomi Hideyoshi and even Tokugawa Ieyasu. His artistic tastes included tea ceremony and calligraphy, but the art of the *Kokinshū, or the tradition of waka, was as important to him as life itself, and it was felt that full learning rested only with him. Although when divorced from his life, his poetry is less interesting, he might have felt the reverse. Besides his personal collection, *Shūmyōshū* 衆妙集 (*Yūsai's Collection of General Principles*, 1671), he wrote a travel account, *Kyūshū Michi no Ki* 九州道 の記 (*An Account of Travel to Kyūshū*, 1587), and left behind a commentary, *Hyakunin Isshu Shō* 百人一 首抄 (*A Treatise on the Hyakunin Isshu*; see *Fujiwara Teika*).

HOZUMI IKAN 穂積以貫. 1692–1769. Early Edo Confucianist. After being educated, he settled down in Osaka and set up school. For literary purposes the most important of his works is *Naniwa Miyage*

難波みやげ (*A Present from Naniwa*), in which he records ideas about drama and art delivered by *Chikamatsu Monzaemon.

HYAKUNIN ISSHU. See *karuta*, FUJIWARA TEIKA.

ICHIJŌ KANERA (or KANEYOSHI) 一条兼良. 1402–1481. Mid-Muromachi *waka*, *renga* poet, critic. Like his father, he held the highest court titles (when they had more status than power). During the disastrous Ōnin War, he turned to scholarship, writing extensively on the *Genji Monogatari, *Ise Monogatari*, and *Kokinshū*, as well as passing on his learning to such important writers as the renga poet *Sōgi. His renga treatises also exerted considerable influence. In the combination of rank, learning, and character, he was the foremost nobleman of his day.

ICHIKAWA DANJŪRŌ 市川団十郎. 1660–1704. Early Edo *kabuki* actor. By all accounts one of the most creative and greatest of earlier actors, he established the Ichikawa house and provided kabuki with one of the most famous of actors' names (a succession of later actors bore it). He made famous the Edo *aragoto* style of acting (see Part Five).

ICHINAKA WA NO MAKI 市中はの巻 (*Throughout The Town*); also called *Natsu no Tsuki* 夏の月 (*The Summer Moon*). An early Edo thirty-six-stanza *haikai* sequence (*kasen*) composed in the summer of 1690 by *Nozawa Bonchō (*hokku*), *Matsuo Bashō (*waki*), and *Mukai Kyorai (*daisan, ageku*). The sequence was later included in *Sarumino* (see Part Six). Within the limits of controlled beauty, this is one of the more irregular sequences composed by Bashō and his followers. It is full of humor, surprise, and details of quotidian life. It is a model of freedom within haikai canons.

ICHŪ. See OKANISHI ICHŪ.

IETAKA. See FUJIWARA IETAKA.

IGARASHI DŌHO 五十嵐道甫. Dates unknown. Azuchi-Momoyama artist of raised gold lacquer. His splendid techniques well suited contemporary taste for costly decoration. For about two decades following 1624, he worked for the Maeda daimate in Kanazawa, where he established the Kaga school of his art.

IHARA SAIKAKU 井原西鶴. 1642–1693. Early Edo writer of *haikai, ukiyozōshi*, and other kinds. Although prose narrative of the Edo period took on greatness with his writings, he began as a haikai poet, and his distinction in such poetry left lasting effect on the organization of some, and the style of many, of his best known writings. An Osaka *chōnin* through and through, he began writing haikai in the *Teimon* style, switching to the *Danrin* for his best poetry. He performed spectacular feats of solo haikai composition at one sitting, *ōkukazu* or *yakazu*. After managing 1,000 stanzas so in 1666, then 1,600 in 1667, and then 10,000 in his *Ikutama Manku* 生玉万句 (1673), he went on to the feat of 16,000 in one day and night. This was his *Saikaku Haikai Ōkukazu* 西鶴俳諧大句数 (*Saikaku's Mass-Produced Haikai*, 1677), in which a group of wearied scribes barely managed to copy down the stanzas (or first lines of stanzas) he dictated. By some miracle, he follows the important rules of haikai, is highly allusive in the Danrin style, and composed groups of *hyakuin* that are still well worth reading.

His haikai style is often said to have a *monogatari* or narrative element, which means that the stanzaic connection, or *tsukeai*, tends to look back as much as look ahead to the next stanza. But this characterization is also a retrospective judgment based on the ukiyozōshi he subsequently wrote. Of these, *Kōshoku Ichidai Otoko* 好色一代男 (*One Man Who Devoted His Life to Love*, 1682) established *kōshoku* literature with instant success. It deals in two long parts (each divided into shorter episodes) with the amatory experiences of Yonosuke. Each of the parts is modeled on the pattern of a haikai hyakuin. Both have the haikai *jo-ha-kyū*. Each of the brief episodes can be classified as miscellaneous (*zō*) or, more often, seasonal as to topic in the *renga* and haikai fashion (however adapted to Saikaku's narrative purposes). The affirmative end expected of a haikai sequence finds expression in Yonosuke's coming into a large inheritance at the end of the first part and in his bravado as a tottering old man at the end of the second, when he sails off to an Island of Women with a few cronies and a stock of provisions including aphrodisiacs and other such wares. His later kōshoku writings are less indebted to haikai, and they are generally of more somber tone. The alteration begins with *Kōshoku Nidai Otoko* 好色二代男 (*Two Men Who Devoted Their Lives to Love*, 1684), and finds full expression in the bleak *Kōshoku Gonin Onna* 好色五人女 (*Five Women Who Devoted Their Lives to Love*, 1686), the latter of which has a rather perfunctory happy ending to the story of the fifth woman, in the manner of a haikai sequence. Something of the élan of Yonosuke is partially recovered in *Kōshoku Ichidai Onna* 好色一代女 (*One Woman Who Devoted Her Life to Love*, 1686) and in *Nanshoku Ōkagami* 男色大鑑 (*The Mirror of Love Between Men*, 1687).

Ever restless, ever changing, Saikaku turned to more didactic or prudential writing toward the end of his life. In 1687 he published his *Budō Denraiki* 武道伝来記 (*An Account of Traditional Samurai Behavior*) and the next year his *Buke Giri Monogatari* 武家義理物語 (*Tales of Samurai Duty*), two works explaining and inculcating samurai mores. These and some others of his late writings have remained the preserve of specialists. But two other works addressed to his fellow chōnin are among the well-studied works of his copious production. These are the optimistic *Nihon Eitaigura* 日本永代蔵 (*The Everlasting Japanese Storehouse*, 1688), in which various examples and precepts tell one how to make a fortune; and the bleak *Seken Mune San'yō* 世間胸算用 (*Heartfelt Worldly Calculations*, 1692), which details by numerous examples the sad shifts of the poor in dealing with the necessity to pay, or evade, debts falling due at the end of the year.

As such variety shows, Saikaku had an enormous fund of invention. If he seemed to repeat himself in a given kind, it was always with some radical difference. Besides restlessness and inventiveness, he possessed great vitality, an energy marking his work from his haikai forward. None of his many imitators ever matched his coruscating, flexible style. With such a lively capacity, conventionally associated by sociologists with chōnin prominence in the cultural life of the time, went a genius for establishing new ways of understanding and conceptions that could be either romantic or bleakly realistic. Such brilliance, with the undercurrent of pessimistic assessment of chōnin life, makes him a worthy member of the triumvirate of genius at the time with *Matsuo Bashō (almost an exact contemporary) and *Chikamatsu Monzaemon (the somewhat younger member of the group). Although he was once taken for a mere stylist, his works show with brilliant insight the swaggering hopes and the nagging fears of townspeople under a repressive government. And as long as human nature remains what it has always been, his focus on money and sex will represent pressing features of life to readers far removed from Osaka mercantile society.

IIO SŌGI. See Sōgi.

IKENISHI GONSUI, 池西言水. 1650–1722. Early Edo *haikai* poet. Beginning under the tutelage of *Matsue Shigeyori, he was one of those who, like *Matsuo Bashō, saw the need to make haikai a more seriously considered art. He never became as prominent as his insight deserved, but he is still well regarded for the appeal of his stanzas and has a collection of sequences and *hokku*, *Azuma Nikki* 東日記 (*Collection from the East*, pr. 1681).

IKE NO TAIGA 池大雅. 1723–1776. Mid-Edo painter of the *nanga* style. Combining a conceptual simplicity with splendor of execution, his painting has its own unusual appeal. He was also outstanding as a calligrapher.

IKKU. See Jippensha Ikku.

IKKYŪ (SŌJUN) 一休 (宗純). 1394–1481. Mid-Muromachi poet in Chinese, ecclesiastical figure. A Rinzai Zen Buddhist priest of a degree of eccentricity unusual even among them, he nonetheless became forty-seventh head of Daitokuji. He asso-

ciated with a wide variety of people, from sovereigns to *Sōchō, *Zeami, *Komparu Zenchiku, and various women, in spite of his celibate vows. In addition to his Chinese poetry, he left a number of personal accounts. He exercised wide personal and religious influence on contemporary and later writers.

IKUTA KENGYŌ 生田検校. 1656–1715. Mid-Edo koto composer, performer, and founder of the Ikuta school. He studied under Kitajima Kengyō before establishing his own school in Kyoto. "Kengyō" was a style given various blind musicians and others. See also *Yamada Kengyō and *Yatsuhashi Kengyō.

IMAGAWA RYŌSHUN 今川了俊. B. 1326. Early Muromachi *waka* and *renga* poet, diarist, political figure. Born into a daimyo family that stimulated him to study waka, he worked chiefly with the liberal *Reizei poets and *Kyōgoku poets. He also studied *renga* with *Gusai and others. His waka sometimes showed traces of his military inheritance, and his renga a restraint encouraged by the precepts of *Nijō Yoshimoto. From about 1367 he became identified with the cause of the northern court, a devotion leading to various assignments, including prolonged residence in Kyushu. His *Michiyukiburi* 道ゆきぶり (*Traveling*) tells of a trip there in 1371 and after.

His writings on waka include *Nigonshō* 二言抄 (*A Treatise of Two Words* ca. 1403) and *Ryōshun Kagakusho* 了俊歌学書 (*Ryōshun's Poetics*, 1410). Besides his personal collection, *Gonjinshū* 言塵集 (*Ryōshun's Collection of Verbal Dust*, 1406), he has numerous other writings including a diary, *Ryōshun Nikki* (1412). Much of his voluminous critical writing is surprisingly tepid, offering less of Reizei poetics than we could hope for. There is one exception, his denunciation of the *Taiheiki* in his *Nan Taiheiki* 難太平記 (*Faulting the Taiheiki*, 1402). Otherwise, his waka, renga, and diaries hold more interest.

IMA KAGAMI 今鏡 (*The Mirror of the Present*). Late Heian *rekishi monogatari* in ten parts. Authorship is variously ascribed. That of Fujiwara Tametsune 藤原為経 is the least dubious, if not wholly certain. The work is believed to have been completed ca. 1180, and it covers all or part of thirteen reigns, 146 years from 1025 to 1170. In other words, it begins where the *Ōkagami left off. The influence of the earlier work is evident in the narration, as well.

After a pilgrimage to Hasedera (much favored by women), the narrator goes on to Kasuga Plain near Nara, where he meets a very old woman related to Yotsugi (the chief speaker in *Ōkagami). The aged creature, Ayame, had served *Murasaki Shikibu. Since this is little more than a framing device, there is not the sprightly conversation found in *Ōkagami.

After a preface, the first three parts deal with sovereigns, the next five with such clans as the Fujiwara and Murakami Genji, and the last two with things heard about. Its historical conception can be traced to the *Eiga Monogatari*, but it describes a lesser world for the nobility. Many court triumphs are set forth, but a sense of downward slide emerges in the increased strength of evanescence and illusory quality of grandeur already present in the *Ōkagami*.

In lieu of dynastic or court achievements, the author (who must have been acquainted with such things) emphasizes literature, discussing *chokusen-shū*, poetry matches, *hyakushuuta*, and even *renga*. At one point, the author refers to the work as a *tsukuri monogatari*, so relating it to such a masterpiece as the *Genji Monogatari*. It is not of that order, but it is appropriately enough written in *kanabun*, is possessed of 145 poems, and is very useful for knowledge of poetry in its time.

INAKA RŌJIN TADA NO JIJII 田舎老人多田爺. Dates unknown. Late Edo *sharebon* author. The unknown person who took this portentously humble name (something like Downright Old Uncle Tada from the Country) left Osaka for Edo and there wrote one work of importance, *Yūshi Hōgen* 遊子方言 (*The Courtesans' Dialect*, 1770), dealing with the licensed quarters in so effectively realistic a way as to have influence on later writers of sharebon and other short fiction.

INAWASHIRO KENSAI 猪苗代兼載. 1452–1510. Mid-Muromachi *renga* poet. Having been attracted to the art by *Shinkei while the latter was in the east fleeing the Ōnin War, he went to the capital before turning twenty, as things settled down. There he associated with other principal renga poets, including *Sōgi, whom he assisted in compiling the *Shinsen Tsukuba Shū*. He wrote about his travels and, like other renga poets, lectured on such classics as *Murasaki Shikibu's *Genji Monogatari*. Among his other works there are a treatise, *Wakakusayama* 若草山 (*The Hill of Wakakusa*, 1497) and a poetic collection, *Sono no Chiri* 園の塵 (*The Dust of the Garden*, ca. 1508).

IPPŪ. See NISHIZAWA IPPŪ.

I-RO-HA UTA. See Part Four.

ISE 伊勢. Dates unknown: ?877–?940. Early Heian *waka* poet. Although certain other works have been attributed to her, she is known properly from poems in the *Kokinshū*, from later collections, and from her personal collection, the *Ise Shū*. A writer of passionate and witty poetry, she resembles *Ono no Komachi, although without such great intensity or such a host of legends surrounding her. In fact, she is known almost wholly from her rather small canon of appealing poems. She is one of the thirty-six poetic sages (*sanjūrokkasen*) and, appropriately enough, makes up with Komachi the twin jewels of poetry.

ISE MONOGATARI 伊勢物語 (*Tales of Ise*). Early Heian *uta monogatari*. This is taken to be the prime exemplar of uta monogatari, with the *Yamato Monogatari* and *Heichū Monogatari* less esteemed. In the usual text, there are 125 incidents (involving 209 poems) of varying but brief length. At the center is a figure presumed to be modeled on *Ariwara Narihira, many of whose poems are used. Alternative titles also use another version of his name, *Zaigo Chūjō Nikki* 在五中将日記 (*The Narihira Diary*) and *Zaigo ga Monogatari* 在五が物語 (*The Tale of Narihira*).

The brief episodes commonly begin, "Formerly there was a certain man" ("Mukashi otoko arikeri"), such a situation or brief action leading to one or more poems. The sense of the past and of that man contribute to the aura of Narihira, although only thirty-five poems can be identified as his. Some others involve known replies to his poems, or poems to which he replied. Yet others are taken from the *Man'yōshū*, the *sandaishū* (see also Part Six), and various personal collections by other poets.

The date of composition is not clear, but the usual assumption—that it was sometime after the compilation of the *Kokinshū*—seems secure. Otherwise it would be difficult to account for the presence of poems by *Ki no Tsurayuki or the closeness of occasional prose contexts to headnotes in that collection. Yet the total effect differs by virtue of the consistent importance of the prose contexts: this is, after all, a *monogatari*, if of *waka* episodes.

Although the *Ise Monogatari* is more unified in a Western sense than is the *Yamato Monogatari*, that fact does not account for the enormous prestige of the work or for the hold it exerts on those who read it closely. It has the variety and pace that is the genius of Japanese literature. The courtly lover, a Narihira figure, does dominate, even if by no means all the stories fit that mold (five are distinctly uncourtly). And there is that general aura in most of the brief episodes, where the very lack of names gives a dreamlike version of romance.

More than that, the work is poised between a poetic collection and a *tsukurimonogatari*, participating in the virtues of both. Its collective character shows the interest in fluctuating human experience that is a feature of the love books of the royal collections. The compositeness (with enough that is different to give the desired asymmetry), the causal use of motivation, the ellipses of explanation, and the exploration of the reaches of human passion far beyond what cursory reading offers—none of these were wasted on *Murasaki Shikibu. It is impossible to designate another Japanese work that rivals this one for delicacy and for realization of the balance between prose and verse, potential and actualization.

There is a sense in which Murasaki Shikibu writes large the *Ise Monogatari* in her *Genji Monogatari*, and not simply because her Genji has long been thought to be modeled on that Narihira figure, the man of the past. The *Ise Monogatari* was recognized with the *Genji Monogatari* by the *renga* masters as one of the two classics of monogatari literature central to their art. In fact, the renga masters like *Sōgi achieved social status not by their poetry but by their lectures on these two works. One of *Zeami's greatest *nō*, *Izutsu*, uses the seventeenth episode (dan) of the work, along with other echoes from it, to characterize the love of Ki no Aritsune's Daughter and Narihira. The *kokugakusha* made the work a devoted object of study. And there were even parodies, including the *Nise Monogatari*, sometimes (but wrongly, it is now thought) attributed to *Karasuma Mitsuhiro, and the *Kuse Monogatari* by *Ueda Akinari.

The legacy of the work is broader still, in some respects—not as a cause or influence so much as a major early exemplar of much that is most characteristic in Japanese literature. In many Edo stories of love in books or plays there are descendants of the Narihira figure, the *irogonomi* character. One of the greatest re-creations is the Yonosuke of *Ihara Saikaku's *Kōshoku Ichidai Otoko*. More importantly in some ways, the work's varied, sequential, and collective or composite genius corresponds not simply to love books in the *chokusenshū*, and not simply to *waka*, renga, and *haikai* sequences, but to the sense that literature may be organized in looser terms than pedants may think.

It is, finally, a work extraordinarily rich in half-hidden detail. The attentive folklorist, psychologist, and historian reap rewards akin to those of the poet and novelist as readers. Neither these subtle details nor the magical aura of the work is likely to be captured by translation, but the student of Japanese literature will find the *Ise Monogatari* one of the most surprisingly rich, as also richly surprising, works of all classical literature.

ISE NO TAYŪ (ŌSUKE) 伊勢大輔. Fl. ca. 1000–1025? Mid-Heian *waka* poet. Known almost solely for her participation in poetry matches and for her personal collection, *Ise no Tayū Shū* 伊勢大輔集, she is one of the principal poets of her time, although not as great or as interesting as *Izumi Shikibu.

ISSA. See KOBAYASHI ISSA.

ISOHO MONOGATARI 伊曽保(イソホ)物語 (*Aesop's Fables*). Selections were published as part of the *kirishitan bungaku* of Catholic missionaries during the late Muromachi and early Edo periods. Although the name given for this entry is the usual modern one, the exact titles varied. A printing of 1593—*Esopo no Fabulas*—was the first book published in Japan from movable type. More literary versions of an *Isoho Monogatari* were published between ca. 1615 and 1640.

ITŌ JINSAI 伊藤仁斎. 1627–1705. Early Edo Confucian scholar. His father a Kyoto townsman and his mother a woman from a house known for *renga*, he turned to the more abstract subject of Confucianism. His school of *kogaku* became one of the three principal ones toward the end of the seventeenth century. His scholarly bent was expressed in commentaries on Confucian classics, as being represented in his *Rongo Kogi* 論語古義 (*Old Interpretations of the Analects*, pr. 1712), *Mōshi Kogi* 孟子古義 (*Old Interpretations of Mencius*, pr. 1720), and so on.

IZUMI SHIKIBU 和泉式部. ?976–?. Mid-Heian *waka* poet, diarist. Apart from the fact that she was the greatest poet of her time and served at the remarkable court of *Jōtō Mon'in with *Akazome Emon and *Murasaki Shikibu (who could not abide her), what is "known" of her derives chiefly by inference drawn from, or supposition occasioned by, her writing. She seems to have had a large number of lovers, and was thus something of a female equivalent of *Ariwara Narihira. The two most illustrious of her partners were Prince Tametaka, with whom her affair ended with his death in 1002, and his half-brother Atsumichi, with whom she entered into a liaison the next year. Much of the course of the latter affair is the basis for the *Izumi Shikibu Nikki* (date and even authorship uncertain, although usually thought to be by her), one of the four principal Heian diaries. From her marriage with Tachibana Michisada, for a time governor of Izumi, she derives part of her name. By him she had a daughter, Koshikibu, herself a good poet. When the daughter died giving birth to a child, Izumi Shikibu mourned her in a poem. Her personal collection, the *Izumi Shikibu Shū*, exists in five distinct versions, varying from 647 to 902 poems.

Her diary depicts a woman of extraordinary sensibility—it is that, expressed in prose compositions, gestures, and of course poems that brings back her prince (Atsumichi, though fictionalized), again and again, even when he has heard the most appalling rumors about her. The lady is said to feel, at one point, that her very eyes felt amorous, and that may have added to her appeal, harshly as she was sometimes judged by the double standard of her time. After long resisting the prince's offer to take residence in his palace, she decides to "yield to fate" ("sukuse ni makasete") and go. Just then one of their worst misunderstandings occurs, and so the story takes a further twist. At last the prince does take her to his palace, where she is made so much of that the prince's consort is offended by the humiliation and retires to her mother's house. This triumphant ending for the lady is told in a different style and without poems. One plausible explanation for this holds that the *poetic* version of love conventionally ends unhappily, and that in order to achieve a happy ending like that in a *monogatari*, the change was required.

Atsumichi fell in love with her in 1003 and died in 1007 at age 26, probably younger than she. It is very unclear what she did during her later years. One tradition holds that she took religious orders. There is nothing implausible about that, but it may derive from misdating a poem by her in the *Shūishū* (20:1342), which is in fact the greatest religious *waka* of the age. If we consider the poetry rather than the very shadowy life, there are problems enough with the different collections. But some things are clear. Her poetry makes a considerable canon, treats various topics with full command, is often packed to the point of difficulty in reading, and constitutes the great poetic achievement of the time.

IZUMO. See TAKEDA IZUMO.

IZUMO FUDOKI. See *Fudoki.*

JAKUREN 寂蓮. ?1139–1202. Early Kamakura *waka* poet, priest. He was a nephew of *Fujiwara Shunzei, who adopted him as a son. He served briefly at the court of Goshirakawa (r. 1155–1158). About 1172 he took orders. Starting about six years before he had begun to appear as a prominent poet at *utaawase* and other poetic gatherings. During this period, he was on close terms with the conservative Rokujō house of poets, especially with *Fujiwara Kiyosuke and *Akisuke, and most active in support of the newly risen Taira house. Perhaps it was then that he and *Taira Tadanori became acquainted, as it was also perhaps he who introduced Tadanori to Shunzei. After a time his study with Shunzei naturally led him to align himself with the much more original Mikohidari house (of which Shunzei was the acknowledged leader) and his step-brother, *Fujiwara Teika, the greatest among several peers.

Jakuren made numerous trips, such as then seemed natural to a priest, especially one who was also a poet. He went to Mount Kōya, Izumo, Kamakura, and other places, although he never ventured as far away or for so long as *Saigyō. The attractions of the capital included its temples and its poetry meetings. He took part in one of the most famous of poetry matches, the *Roppyakuban Utaawase* (1193). His new poetic allegiance brought him into conflict with a third pillar of the Rokujō house, *Kenshō.

An account of 1172–1173 described his poetic style as one with nobility, likening it to the suffering of a beautiful woman. It does have a beauty, and a sense of darkness such as Shunzei's ideals of *sabi* and *yūgen* entailed. Most of his poetry lacks, however, the force of the poetry of Teika, Saigyō, and *Shokushi Naishinnō. Shunzei included seven of his poems in the *Senzaishū,* and he is well represented

in the *Shinkokinshū,* with thirty-five poems. He had been appointed one of the compilers of that collection but died before selection was completed. His personal collection, *Jakuren Hōshi Shū,* is sufficiently fine to offer a mirror not only of his talents but of the achievements of the age.

JIEN 慈円. 1155–1225. Early Kamakura *waka* poet, ecclesiastical figure, historian. A son of a noble family of very high rank, he was studious and earnest from his youth. By thirty-seven, partly by reason of his family connections, partly for his attainments, he was head priest of Tendai Buddhism and later became archbishop (daisōjō). His literary interests led him to join the innovating poets surrounding the venerable *Fujiwara Shunzei. Through him he met Shunzei's son, *Fujiwara Teika, the aged *Saigyō, and others. His nephew, *Fujiwara Yoshitsune, also exercised influence on him. He composed a substantial number of poems. His personal collection, the *Shūgyokushū* 拾玉集 (*The Collection of Gathered Jewels,* 1236 and later versions) is an ample collection, and after Saigyō he has the most poems in the *Shinkokinshū* (92).

*Gotoba thought him equal to any poet alive. That judgment has not stood the test of time. But he was a fine, representative poet, and at times he rises high. He also had better political sense than Gotoba, declining to get into tricky relations with the Kamakura *bakufu.* In his concern with developments in his time, he twice felt that he had divine revelations in dreams. So he came to write about the principles of true government (which necessitated rule under the regency of his own Fujiwara house) from ancient to present times in his *Gukanshō* 愚管抄 (*The Future and the Past,* 1219–1220; six parts). This runs from the legendary first sovereign, Jimmu, to the author's own age. The work, which is well written in *kanabun,* is prized for its detail about Jien's time. His name lives on for it, for his religious service, and for some few excellent poems.

JIKAKU DAISHI. See ENNIN.

JIKKUN* (or *JIKKIN) SHŌ 十訓抄 (*A Treatise of Ten Rules*). Mid-Kamakura *setsuwa* collection (ca. 1252). As the title indicates, this is designed as a compilation of ten moral principles, although various Edo-period printings run from two to twelve parts. According to one manuscript, the compiler was the lay priest, Rokuhara Nirōzaemon 六波羅二﨟左衛門. Nothing is known of him, although information has been discovered concerning someone bearing such a name who served about that time at Rokuhara in eastern Kyoto.

The collection includes about 280 stories under ten heads (or divisions) distinguished by a particular something not to be done or, more often, to be done. Such things as the didactic intent, a Confucian element, and a contemporary concern with military features have been distinguished. Yet no small number of the stories depict the ethos of the Japanese court. Contrary to the expressed didactic intent, and to the character of some earlier setsuwa collections, this one often seems to have a perfunctory or lame moral, with greatest interest taken in representing the colloquial, the humorous, and the exciting. What is least didactic in main emphasis usually has the greatest literary value. The compiler's claim in the preface that the stories are chosen for being true is as may be. But it is a well known fact that one of his stories (6:35) served as the source for Akutagawa Ryūnosuke's fantasy, *Jigokuhen* (Hell-Screen). Such a mixture of the didactic, real, and fantastic may imply that the stories were meant to be read rather than recited or used as moral examples by priests (see Part Six).

JINSAI. See ITŌ JINSAI.

JIPPENSHA IKKU 十返舎一九. 1765–1831. Late Edo *gesaku* writer. Even among prolific Edo prose writers, Ikku is something of a prodigy. Although he lived principally in Edo, he spent some time in Osaka, where he left the samurai service that had taken him there and became a townsman. Between about 1795 and 1801, he produced nearly twenty *kibyōshi* a year, and thereafter wrote *sharebon*, *kokkeibon*, and numerous other kinds. To take longer works, he left behind 360 *gōkan*. There is also some verse—*kyōka* and *senryū*. There are also pictures, and nobody knows what all else.

He had a knack for anticipating what readers wanted before they knew it themselves. He is not simply a popular writer, or he would not have been praised by *Kyokutei Bakin as the finest writer of *gesaku* and the first to live by his writing. Yet it must be said that even his best work is uneven in quality, repetitive, and, in fact, weak in ordering. Perhaps that is why his greatest work had, in a sense, its own organization, the road from Edo to Kyoto. This is *Tōkaidōchū Hizakurige* 東海道中膝栗毛 (*Footing It along the Tōkaidō*)—also *Dōchū Hizakurige*, *Hizakurige*. The first part was an instant success in 1802. During the next twenty years he kept adding to it. In the most familiar first part, his two rascals, Yajirōbē and Kitahachi (or, as everybody knows them, Yaji and Kita) make their way along the Tōkaidō, station by station, adventure by adventure. They have very little money, Edo cleverness, not much real intelligence, and an often winning earthiness that tires before it offends.

Knowing that he had a winner, Ikku not only added on—and on; he also tried to change the tune in another book by showing two yokels on the road here and there, looking into famous places and recording local dialects. This was (*Muda Shugyō*) *Kane no Waraji* (方言修業) 金草鞋 (1813–1834). It has its interests, but its pair of travelers are Yaji and

Kita's poor country cousins. Only genuine addicts of Edo literature have read all of both these works (especialy as added to) or have ventured farther. Ikku is not to be taken whole, but as such yarns as the Goemomburo or Kyoto episodes in *Hizakurige* show, he really must be taken in part.

JISUKE. See SAKURADA JISUKE.

JIUN 慈雲. 1718–1804. Mid-Edo Shingon reformer, Sanskrit scholar, calligrapher, and poet. For three years beginning in 1736, after he had already taken Buddhist orders, Jiun studied the tenets of early Confucianism under Itō Tōgai, and later practiced Zen. In 1744 he took up residence at the Chōeiji temple near Osaka, where he formulated a system of regulations for the religious life based on the precepts of primitive Buddhism (shōbō ritsu). His concern for the ideals of early Buddhism led him to examine original Sanskrit sources and resulted in a monumental study of approximately a thousand parts, the *Bongaku Shinryō* 梵学津梁 (*A Bridge to Indian Studies*, ca. 1766). He composed popular writings classed as *kana hōgo* and other successful works such as *Hito to Naru Michi* 人となる道 (*The Way to Become a Person*). His prolific literary output also includes a substantial collection of poetry assembled by his disciples, the *Jiun Sonja Wakashū* 慈雲尊者和歌集 (*The Venerable Jiun's Waka*).

JŌCHŌ 定朝. D. 1057. Mid-Heian sculptor. He had a great reputation in his time and in following generations, but only one work has survived the wars and fires that have razed so much Buddhist art. Fortunately, what survived is the famous image of the Amida Buddha at the temple Byōdōin in Uji.

JŌHA. See SATOMURA JŌHA.

JŌJIN AJARI NO HAHA 成尋阿闍梨母. B. ca. 985, d. after 1073. Early Heian diarist, *waka* poet; the Mother of Master Jōjin. Her diary was discovered in court archives in 1930 and published in 1935. It covers the years 1067–1073. She starts by saying that she has attained her 80th year and has an unexampled tale to tell. The tale concerns her son Jōjin who, in 1072, went to Sung China. He died there. The diary really concerns a mother's love for her son, a love she yearns to communicate to him on his return.

JŌKYŪKI 承久記 (*An Account of the Jōkyū War*). A late Kamakura or early Nambuko *gunki monogatari* in two parts, dealing with a war that was *Gotoba's misguided attempt to enlist the support of warriors and others not in sympathy with the Kamakura *bakufu* to restore royal power. The attempted restoration failed, Gotoba was banished to Oki, and two other sovereigns under his thumb were also exiled. This work is of interest in presenting a Kyoto view of the attempt, as a supplement to closing portions of the *Azuma Kagami* and as a work written in comprehensible Japanese. Its historical value exceeds its literary worth, however.

JOSETSU 如拙. Dates unknown. Fourteenth or early fifteenth-century painter, priest. He worked particularly in ink wash, and his career was spent in the Kyoto *Gosan temples. A portrait of Ashikaga Yoshimitsu remains as an example of his secular work.

JŌTŌ (or SHŌTŌ) MON'IN 上東門院. 988–1074. Mid-Heian royal consort, patron. She was daughter of *Fujiwara Michinaga, who achieved his power by marrying her to Ichijō as principal consort and by her bearing two future tennō, Goichijō and Gosuzaku. Her given name was Shōshi or Akiko 彰子; she took the name by which she is known in 1026. Her court was brilliant as the focus of Michinaga's efforts to display power. It was the finest literary salon of the time, with *Murasaki Shikibu, *Izumi Shikibu, and other women of great talent serving her. In Murasaki Shikibu's *Diary* we learn, among other things, that the writer coached her mistress in Chinese.

(FUJIWARA) JUNII TAMEKO (藤原)従二位為子. Ca. 1251–ca. 1316). Late Kamakura *waka* poet. She was elder sister of the central poetic figure of the day, *Kyōgoku Tamekane. She served at the court of the other most gifted woman, *Yōfuku Mon'in, absorbing some of her mistress's poetic intensity, and modeling her styles on those of her brother and mistress. She wrote hundred-poem sequences and participated in poetry matches involving the *Kyōgoku poets and *Reizei poets. She is represented in several collections, chiefly the *Gyokuyōshū* and *Fūgashū*, in the latter of which she has thirty-nine poems.

JUNTOKU 順徳. 1197–1242. Early Kamakura *waka* poet, sovereign (r. 1210–1221). Son of *Gotoba, he followed his father's poetic interests from an early age, composing well by the time he was fourteen. From 1215 he appeared in important poetry matches and had compiled notable *hyakushuuta*. A personal collection (now bearing his name as Juntoku In) completed in 1220–1221 was submitted to his father and *Fujiwara Teika for their judgments. He was embroiled in his father's efforts against the Kamakura *bakufu*, and was exiled to Sado as a result. From there he sent a hyakushuuta to his father and Teika for judgment. His poems appear in numerous collections. Offering a compromise among the conflicting poetic ideals of the age, his work is such as neither to offend us today nor to transcend his age.

He wrote two treatises uncertain as to their circumstances: *Kimpishō* 禁秘抄 (*The Top-secret Treatise*) and *Yakumo Mishō* 八雲御抄 (*His Majesty's Yakumo Treatise*). The former deals with matters of royalty and court custom. The latter is very valuable for what it shows of the poetic opinions and practice of the age. Its six parts have labels that do not always seem to describe their contents, but each part claims attention. Part One, Virtues, deals with six poetic virtues but more extensively with kinds of poems, styles, poetic faults, and so on. Part Two, Methods, discusses *utaawase*, authors, and so on. Part Three, Details, concerns times, places, persons, commodities, etc. Part Four, Language, deals with that topic in numerous guises. Part Five, Famous Places, distinguishes such *utamakura* by class (such as hills, mountains, names). Part Six, Preparation, offers his own poetics. This is a poet's encyclopedia, showing genuine learning. Originality was not required by such a treatise, nor was it supplied.

JUSAMMI MINAMOTO CHIKAKO (SHINSHI) 従三位源親子. Fl. ca. 1300. Late Kamakura *waka* poet. She wrote in the styles of *Kyōgoku Tamekane and participated in the poetic events of the *Kyōgoku poets and *Reizei poets. Her poetry began to appear in the *Shingosenshū*, but she is better represented in the *Gyokuyōshū* and *Fūgashū*, in the latter of which she has fifteen poems. Her personal collection is called *Gondainagon Naishinosuke Shū* 権大納言典侍集.

KADA NO AZUMAMARO 荷田春満. 1669–1736. Mid-Edo *kokugaku* scholar. He came from a family heading a shrine in Fushimi. After service to a prince, he went to Edo, where he was employed by the shogunate to verify and arrange historical records. In time he returned home to study and teach, specializing in matters of early Japan. His works on the *Kojiki, *Nihon Shoki, and *Man'yōshū do not in themselves bear comparison with the work of many later kokugaku scholars. But by opposing the early Japanese works that he favored to tenets of official Neoconfucianism, and in a few other respects, he anticipated central features of a major line of Edo thought, and exercised influence on *Kamo no Mabuchi in particular.

KAGAMI SHIKŌ 各務支考. 1665–1731. Early Edo *haikai* poet, one of the ten worthies of the Bashō school. Born in Mino (Gifu), he joined the Bashō school in 1690, when the master was staying in Ōmi (Shiga). He specialized in ideas about poetry, and in *Kuzu no Matsubara* 葛の松原 (*The Pine Grove with Kudzu*, 1692), he explained Bashō's principles in the light of earlier practice. He accompanied the Old Master on his last journey, and co-edited *Zoku Sarumino* (1698; see Part Six). After Bashō's death, he edited a memorial, *Oi Nikki* 笈日記 (*The Diary of the Book Satchel*, preface dated 1695), and continued to turn out serious accounts of Bashō's poetic principles.

Having won himself a reputation in this line, he began to invent ideas for the dead poet. These he transported around the country, whether as talks or as supposedly authentic writings. Sometimes he explained matters truthfully, and sometimes he held a pious memorial service for Bashō. But neither truth nor piety shackled him. In 1711 he made a last testament, pretended to have died, and went into hiding with a follower or two, going under names such as White Insanity (Hakukyō) or Mad Watanabe (Watanabe no Kyō—Watanabe being his mother's family name).

Other members of the Shōmon were not much amused, and the laity was bewildered. By the next century, *Yosa Buson classified Shikō with the most ineffectual poets of Bashō's school, as "Peasant-style Bashō." Yet the confusion helped spread the popularity, and *some* of the things Shikō wrote or said were true. He also launched the practice of writing Chinese poems in Japanese syllables (*kanashi*), something that really need not be examined very far to get the idea of this gifted lunatic.

KAGA NO CHIYO. See Chiyo.

KAGAWA KAGEKI 香川景樹. 1768–1843. Late Edo *waka* poet and critic. In his youth Kageki conceived the ambition to be the best poet in the world. He did not make it, but he tried. After going to Kyoto to study with *Ozawa Roan, he set out on his own, propounding rhythmic beauty (shirabe) as the goal. Poetry was not, he said, a matter of rationality, but of natural rhythm, which was in turn based on forthrightness (makoto). Some of his large number of poems were collected by himself in *Keien Isshi* 桂園一枝 (*A Shoot from the Judas-Tree Garden*, pub. 1830). Many of his pronouncements were attacked by contemporaries, but it is rare to find a poet who criticizes his own poetry, as he does. That, and a split in opinion about his poetry right up to Meiji times, make this an unusual collection. His critical studies include works on *waka*, particularly the *Kokinshū*, and *Ki no Tsurayuki's *Tosa Nikki*.

KAGEKI. See Kagawa Kageki.

KAIBARA EKIKEN 貝原益軒. 1630–1714. Early Edo Neoconfucianist. He was born into a lesser samurai family serving the Fukuoka domain of the Kuroda house in Kyushu, his home base most of his life. He must have set some kind of record as a traveling Neoconfucianist, with five trips to study at nearby Nagasaki, twelve to Edo, and twenty-four to Kyoto. His Neoconfucianism was of the increasingly orthodox *shushigaku* kind. Although afflicted with various illnesses, Ekiken was a prodigious worker and a voluminous writer. He had historical interests as well, including an account of the

Kuroda house and the ingeniously titled *Chikuzen Zoku Fudoki* 筑前続風土紀 (*The Topography of Chikuzen, Continued*, 1703). After the age of seventy, he wrote ten didactic works. A part of one of them, *Onna Daigaku* 女大学 (*The Greater Learning for Women*) is so belittling of women that it seems to have had some answer in a work of the same title by *Kyoku Sanjin. He is best remembered for the breadth of his interests, including not only Neoconfucianism but botany and history, natural history and philology.

KAIDŌKI 海道記 (*A Record of Travel on the Coast Road*). Early Kamakura travel account. In spite of earlier attributions, the authorship of this is unknown, apart from its having been written (it seems to be assumed) by the same man who wrote the *Tōkan Kikō* two decades later. This, the superior, relates events after the author took orders, spending a reclusive life in Kyoto. He then decides on a walking trip to Kamakura, starting early in the fourth month of 1223. After eighteen days on the road, he spends another ten or so visiting famous places in the area. By the fifth month, he begins to worry about his octogenarian mother left in the capital, to which he returns and finishes off his narrative. Reflection on his trip enables him to strengthen his religious resolve. The account ends with an essayistic cast more like certain examples of *zuihitsu* than most travel accounts. The style, in an attractive version of *wakan konkōbun*, makes comparison the easier.

KAIFŪSŌ 懐風藻 (*Yearnings for the Ancient Chinese Style*). Late Nara, one-book collection of poetry in Chinese. In fact, although neither in Japanese nor royally commissioned, this is the first poetic collection published in Japan, and the first work of belles lettres. The compiler's identity is uncertain, although various names have been mentioned. The preface allows for dating about 751. It also says that 120 selections from sixty-four writers are included; extant versions are slightly curtailed. The collection includes, at the end, some poems written later, judging (it is said) by their style.

The poets are largely sovereigns, other members of the high nobility, and priests (see *Nagaya no Ōkimi). This suggests that continental learning has not yet been widely disseminated. On the other hand, there is enough Buddhism, Confucianism, and Taoism here to suggest that these ways of thought have grown familiar to the court circle.

The topics of the poems are fairly standard from the continental models, and even when describing scenery, the poets use Chinese tags and morals. The collection seems to have had little influence on later writing, including Japanese poetry in Chinese. But topics it made respectable—such as the Seventh Night story (tanabata) and grievances (*jukkai*)—were to have a long life. The style is said to be that of the early T'ang (which is tantamount to saying late Six Dynasties), which shows the time lag for Japan at this time. Some critics are impressed by certain poems, but their examples seem pale beside poems in the *Man'yōshū* or T'ang poetry (see Part Six).

KAIHO SEIRYŌ 海保青陵. 1755–1817. Mid-Edo economist. Born in Edo, he was of the house of the Miyazu domain in Tango. His service took him on many travels. Late in life, he settled in Kyoto, where he opened a private school. He was concerned with the economic needs of the populace much in advance of his time, and before the development of the "dismal science."

KAIHŌ YŪSHŌ 海北友松. 1533–1615. Azuchi-Momoyama painter, founder of the Kaihō School. From Ōmi, he studied painting with *Kanō Motonobu, and later favored Sung and Mongol dynasties painting. After serving the court of Goyōzei (r. 1586–1611) for a time, he was patronized by Toyotomi Hideyoshi, for whom he did genre paintings with groups of people, ink-wash paintings, screen paintings, and so on. He was less committed to a school style than the Kanōs, and he had some talent as a writer.

KAION. See KI NO KAION.

KAKEI. See YAMAMOTO KAKEI.

KAKIEMON 柿右衛門. Dates unknown. Early Edo potter of Arita (and a name sustained through generations of artists). Techniques newly introduced from Korea allowed for high temperatures that produced a new whiteness and strength to the base, making thinner walls possible, along with a field for brilliant reds and other colors. The ware was so long continued and so well copied that "Kakiemon" by now designates a style rather than an individual.

KAKINOMOTO HITOMARO 柿本人麻呂. Yamato *waka* poet. Dates unknown; d. 708–715 at about fifty? Little is known, apart from what can be inferred from his poems and their occasions, about this court poet who survives in a relatively small canon. Yet those poems are all that need be known to consider him one of the four greatest Japanese poets, along with *Fujiwara Teika, *Sōgi, and *Matsuo Bashō. And when reading those poems one gains a sense of purity, majesty, unity, and goodness without simplification that make him—to all who prize these qualities—Japan's most appealing poet. With *Yamabe Akahito, *Yamanoe Okura, and *Ōtomo Yakamochi, he is one of the four principal poets of the *Man'yōshū, a collection that greatly benefits from having his poems near the beginning and Yakamochi's toward the end.

The collection contains nineteen *chōka* by Hitomaro, and about seventy-five *tanka*, many of them

used as envoys (*hanka*) to the chōka. There are also some 380 poems (depending on how one counts) derived from the *Hitomaro Kashū*, but it is not at all clear whether this or that example can be thought his. Some or many may be by Hitomaro, and indeed not all are inferior. Some are palpably not his, by reason of folk or other origin. One group of critics think the collection was based on youthful poems (but how many early Japanese collections are of that kind?). Others think, probably rightly, that poems by him are included with poems by others. It is to be expected that the Homers of a nation's poetry should have spurious poems attributed to them. Because none of the approximately nineteen chōka and seventy-five tanka said to be by him are also said to be from the *Hitomaro Collection*, any assured estimation must simply ignore the collection; there are sufficient riches in the more or less certainly canonical poems.

These can be divided into two main groups, the first consisting of those written by him as court poet for three sovereigns: Temmu (r. 673–686), Jitō (690–697), and Mommu (697–707); and those written on occasions in his own life that do not involve the rulers. The distinction helps us distinguish between such poems as that on the ruined capital at Ōmi (1: 29–31) or on the death of Prince Takechi as poems on affairs of state, on the one hand, and poems on parting from his wife (2: 131–33; 135–37) or on the death of his wife (2: 207–209; 210–12), on the other. But the distinctions must be qualified. For one thing, his court service was chiefly devoted to extolling the personal, special cause of Jitō, one of the most strong-minded of Japan's female sovereigns (indeed, "female" may be left out of the comparison). It is not at all clear that assassination was not among her means of seeking to gain power for her cause. Wife of Temmu, mother of Prince Takechi, she was at the center of numerous intrigues. She groomed her son to succeed her, although he died before he could do so. Takechi had led the forces of Temmu and Jitō in the Jinshin War (672), and on his death Hitomaro wrote a poem (2: 199–201) that is the longest in the *Man'yōshū*, consisting of a chōka of 149 lines and two envoys, 159 lines in all. His personal poems also contain elements resembling those in his official poems, in that the individual, personal occasion is set in a context that enables others to share the experience. On these grounds, his poetry is all more or less public in nature, emphasizing the unified, shared nature of the events of human life.

Great poetry need not arise from the pleasantest of circumstances, whether personal or public, and Hitomaro's very evidently transcends the seemingly sordid dynastic conflicts or the personal troubles that give rise to his art. Perhaps the finest example of such transcendence, and no doubt the poem with which to begin study of Hitomaro, is that "On Seeing the Body of a Man Lying among the Stones on the Island of Samine in Sanuki Province" (2: 220–22). It relates how the poet (and however many others—they are never explicitly mentioned) left by boat from Naka and, on the Inland Sea, were beset by a typhoon. The storm drove the boat ashore on Samine, just in time to keep it from a worse fate. On the shore lies a man's body. Out of these circumstances, Hitomaro made a poem that begins by invoking the divinity of the land in which he and his fellows live. After this overture, the disastrous voyage is described. Then there is the encounter with the dead man (such contact might have caused ritual pollution, and some read the poem as a lustration, as an exorcism of the wrath of the spirit of the dead man, or as some other kind of appeasement). Among the elements making the poem so moving are the poet's wonder over a divine world in which people nonetheless suffer the shipwreck of death, the identification of the living poet with the dead man, the assumption that the dead man had a normal human sphere including wife and family, a kindly irony that both treats the dead man as if alive and capable of being addressed and also makes it very clear that a tragedy has occurred.

Similar elements are found in other poems, whether personal or public. We inhabit an awesome, good world. There are very normal and yet outstanding people in it. The good world and fine people share in the tragedies from which no one is exempt. Yet the world is pure, all is normal, and all is precious as well. The poet hesitates to speak, and yet must speak. Anything he can think of heightens awe while reminding us of human limits. The poet draws on all his resources for beauty of conception and expression, enlarges constantly into a context of tragic moments. Nothing is too complex for poetry (including the machinations of Jitō), and nothing is too simple for notice (his child by his dead wife will not be pacified by the distraught ineptitude of a father who cannot supply it with milk).

In this poetic world several features stand out. One is the total unity of world and people, time and nature, public and private motivations. In a sense, the unity is achieved by omission. It is a Shinto world from which Buddhism—which later Japanese had no difficulty in making their own— is conspicuously absent. Such unified understanding of the world gains expression in a remarkably diverse and yet single style. The tanka envoys are not simply added but are means of completing what the chōka develops. Again and again, a whole chōka— or some very long portion of it—flows on and on as a single syntactic unit. The forty-five lines of the chōka in the poem on the dead man at Samine constitute an incomplete sentence, ending with its topic, "tsumara wa," something like "and as for your wife who is so dear to you." The first envoy begins, "Tsuma no," so picking up the topic of that immensely long and complex, yet incomplete, sentence preceding it, bringing it to a close in its five lines. The next envoy returns to the dead man pillowed on the stones while the still storm-driven waves crash on the alien coast.

Some of the means by which Hitomaro creates such magnificent, majestic effects are evident. Others are debated. The syntax is one kind of obvious means. So are his makurakotoba, those pillow-words that can be used decoratively or, as in his hands, meaningfully. Unlike the epic similes of Western epics, which they resemble in some ways, his makurakotoba do not function to introduce the world of the familiar and homely into the heroic world. They are used instead to elevate by associating the individual or personal world with the exalted and divine; or they function to unify the complex, diverse elements of a poem. It is difficult to speak of a period for which we have so little evidence, but given the evidence available, Hitomaro either revised or coined half the makurakotoba he used.

Most Japanese critics agree that Hitomaro, who left Buddhism out of his poetry, nonetheless benefited from other aspects of the new learning introduced from the continent. In any ordinary or a priori sense, that agreement is impossible to refute. But it is also next to impossible to prove. Where else, one wonders, could this poet have found models for such lengthy and so harmoniously integrated poems? Where else hints for such a complex verse texture? But no Chinese or Korean poems can be suggested as individual models. The absence of the new religion speaks for itself. Perhaps the closest we can come to evidence of Hitomaro's knowledge of Chinese poetry will be found in the highly complex parallelism that he employs. How, we may ask, could this conspicuous feature of so much poetry in Chinese been used so complexly without his knowing Chinese poetry in some fashion? And yet his parallelism differs from Chinese, and if he owed a debt, its total assimilation makes the concept of indebtedness require another kind of explanation that is far to seek. Of all Chinese kinds available at the time, the fu most resembles what Hitomaro achieved—a work lengthy by Asian standards of poetry, rich in texture of imagery and metaphor, and often given to praise. Yet such continental "rhyme-prose" is alien to Hitomaro's syntactic medium, one of the most distinctive features of his writing.

Much the same problem is involved with any attempt to posit Japanese models. In the oral poetry preserved in the *Kojiki and *Nihon Shoki there are a few longish poems, and there are prose narratives punctuated with poems. Purely poetic models using these elements may once have existed in works now lost, or may not, but certainly Hitomaro's poetry has a narrative cast to its lyricism. Yet the fact of the matter is that the comparison is one founded on desperation, since his poems have a wholeness that requires no prose context, and it is also genuine literate poetry attributable to a single historical poet. His overtures, which deal again and again with the divine origins of the royal house, or with the divinity and goodness of the natural world, are sometimes compared with the *norito* of Shinto liturgy. There is no question but that the poet knew Shinto rites. But there is a question of dating— whether in fact his poems do not precede extant examples of *norito*.

The search for explanations of what we value is as important as natural. But the problem with Hitomaro resembles that with *Murasaki Shikibu and other great writers who seem to appear without the preparation that we perhaps too readily assume exists to account for the greatness that suddenly flowers in a literature. In the end, we can only say lamely that Hitomaro is a poet lost in the obscurity of early Japanese literature, and that no one who has read his poetry has ever had cause to question that he is a poet recognizably great and distinct. From this middling courtier we have poems of rich, unaffected, and yet complex humanity, with the vision of a world at once unitary in what we may choose to call its ontological or metaphysical assumptions, and rich with an irony that affirms to this day the nature of our common humanity.

KAMESUKE. See Nagawa Kamesuke.

KAMIJIMA ONITSURA. See Uejima Onitsura.

KAMO NO CHŌMEI 鴨長明. 1155–1216. Early Kamakura *waka* poet, critic, compiler, prose stylist. "Chōmei" is sometimes read "Nagaakira." He was embarked on a good career at court in his teens, when he was serving Takamatsu Nyoin, a consort of Nijō (r. 1158–1165). After losing his father at seventeen or eighteen and Takamatsu Nyoin when he was twenty-one, he gave up active life at court and devoted himself to the arts. Besides his poetry, he acquired considerable proficiency with the lute (biwa). Such pursuits did not require that he cut himself off from the world entirely and, in fact, he managed to keep on good terms both with members of the freshly-founded *bakufu* in Kamakura and with their royal opponent, *Gotoba. At thirty-one and thirty-two traveled to Ise, a trip recorded in his *Ise Ki* 伊勢記 (*An Account of an Ise Journey*, 1186; only extracts extant). Money occasionally became a problem that was usually solved by some royal benefaction or by some work at the Kamo Shrine, where his family held hereditary office. His opposition to the head of the shrine led him to a fuller retirement. He first exiled himself north of the capital in Ohara. He declined a royal request that he return by a poem. Later he took orders, having been enlightened (he said) about his brief existence. But to the end his life was as much aesthetic as religious, a true *tonseisha*.

A few years later he moved to Yamashiro, where his main preoccupation was writing his *Mumyōshō*

無名抄 (*The Nameless Treatise*, 1209–1210). In this, not so much a poetic treatise as a *zuihitsu*-poetics, he goes over a number of topics and personalities in ways that seem ever fresh. There is gossip about poetry parties, poets of the past and poets of the present, poetic principles and the conventional topics of verse (*utamakura*). His discussion of *yūgen* is but one of the many passages that have proved indispensable to our understanding of poetry at the time. Chōmei's views are the more interesting for two features of his writing. For one thing, he presents himself as a person not belonging to either of the divided critical factions of the time, not wholly with the liberal or new ideals of *Fujiwara Shunzei and the Mikohidari Fujiwara nor with the conservative Rokujō house. It is also interesting that he puts his thoughts into the mouth of his teacher, *Shun'e. This gives a voice of authority, to be sure. It also reminds us somewhat of the method of the *Ōkagami.

In 1211 he went to Kamakura to teach poetry to the young shogun, *Minamoto Sanetomo. Since they could not agree about it, he returned to his hut. Around 1214–1215 he compiled a *setsuwa* collection, *Hosshinshū* 発心集 (*A Collection of Religious Awakenings*; his authorship has been questioned, but his role seems most probable). It is typical of Chōmei that he should write the collection in Japanese. Early versions seem to have been in three, six, or eight parts. Surviving versions run from the manuscript version of 64 stories in five parts to the printed versions of 102 stories in eight parts. Chōmei has a preface and postscript. As the title indicates, the collection is concerned with religious awakening, as also with reclusive life and with death. These are staples of Buddhist piety, and Chōmei draws on other authors for interesting stories. But to an unusual degree, he relies on his own experience— what he saw, heard, thought. There are many passages recalling the *zuihitsu* style of his *Hōjōki* 方丈記 (*An Account of My Hut*; ca. 1212), and also touches of diarylike elements as well as associative connections that would have been natural to a *waka* poet of his time. This work is discussed at some length in Part One. See also *hosshintan*.

In all three of his major prose works—*Mumyōshō*, *Hōjōki*, and *Hosshinshū*—Chōmei shows to perfection the art of making what interests him interest others (see the discussion in Part One). The *Hōjōki* is justly thought to be his masterpiece, but its ability to bring a topic to life will be found in the other two works as well. The one thing too often forgotten about him is his greatness as a poet. Unlike his prose, his poetry is difficult, resembling *Izumi Shikibu before him or *Kyōgoku Tamekane after him. But their difficulties usually appear in love poems. His seasonal poems are also very complex, so that the closest comparison is probably to *Shinkei. Both poets have yet to be duly appreciated.

KAMO NO MABUCHI 賀茂真淵. 1697–1769. Mid-Edo *kokugaku* scholar, *waka* poet. He was descended from a family of shrine officials. At ten, he began literary studies. At nineteen he started on Chinese, but his inheritance in Shinto and his interests did not favor that line. He next went to Kyoto, and then to Edo, taking part in a poetry match on the way. When he lost his teacher, he decided to begin his own school.

From that began one of the most influential approaches to Japanese studies. He started with groups studying the *Hyakunin Isshu* (see *Fujiwara Teika) and the *Man'yōshū*. His teaching led to a series of studies of major (and some minor) classics: an early one of the *Man'yōshū* is followed by others on the *Ise Monogatari*, *Kamakura Udaijin Kashū*, *Genji Monogatari*, and *kagura*. These studies appeared between 1752 and 1766. Two studies in particular deserve attention. His *Man'yō Kō* 万葉考 (*Study of the Man'yōshū*, 1760–68) is a massive study (six parts by Mabuchi, then another six, and then eight by his followers) dealing with seemingly everything from the title of the collection to the styles of its poetry. His best-known work is his *Kokui Kō* 国意考 (*A Study of Our National Temper*, 1765), in which he uses poetry to oppose such imported teachings as Buddhism and Confucianism, and advocates instead ideals based on native religion and literature. His school outlasted him, and he is one of the greatest of Edo kokugaku scholars. His poetic talents are not so major. He began writing under the influence of *Shinkokinshū* poets. Later he wrote so little that it is hard to say what his emphasis may be, but most critics think they detect elements of the *Man'yōshū* in it. That is of a piece with his efforts to revive what is most anciently Japanese.

KAN'AMI 観阿弥 (or **KANZE KIYOTSUGU** 観世清次). 1333–1384. Namboku *nō* leader, actor, author. He left the family of nō actors into which he had been born to set up his company in Ise, moving thereafter to Yamato. His great achievement was to make nō into a coherent, consistent art by synthesizing or standardizing diverse elements then existing in *sarugaku*, *dengaku*, *utamai*, and so on. He was willing to draw on contemporary music of certain kinds and also popular versions of *katarimono* to harmonize with dramatic elements. But it was the acting that mattered most to him. His even greater son, *Zeami, passes on his father's ideas most clearly in *Fūshikaden*, where the concept of representation (*monomane*) is crucial.

When in 1375 Ashikaga Yoshimitsu began to patronize Zeami, Kan'ami withdrew. Toward the end he moved to Suruga (Shizuoka) to stage religious nō, and died six months later. Various of his plays are still acted.

KANAMURA. See Kasa no Kanamura.

KAN CHAZAN (or **SAZAN**) 菅茶山. 1748–1827. Late Edo *kanshi* poet, Confucianist. From Bingo (modern Hiroshima) he went to Kyoto to study Neoconfucianism and kanshi. Over the years his skill in Sung-style poetry is said to have effected a complete change in the style of Chinese poetry written in *kamigata*. Some are of the opinion that during the Edo period there was no better Japanese poet in Chinese than he. On his return to Bingo, he opened his own school, and *Rai San'yō studied under him. His many works include *Kōyō Sekiyō Sonshashi* 黄葉夕陽村舎詩 (*Village Poems of the Red Setting Sun on Yellow Leaves*) and *Fude no Susabi* 筆のすさび (*Writing for Play*).

KANERA. See Ichijō Kanera.

KANEYOSHI. See Ichijō Kanera.

KANGINSHŪ 閑吟集 (*Songs for Leisure Hours*). Mid-Muromachi *kayō* collection. According to some, the compiler was the *renga* poet *Sōchō, who would have liked these songs, and might have written the carefree lines of the Japanese preface, which delightfully celebrates reclusive life. But there is no adequate proof. The Chinese preface is dated 1518 and is said to offer a critical study of *kouta*.

The collection is ordered on the pattern of a *chokusenshū*: the order of the four seasons, love, and miscellaneous topics. The 311 songs are also classified. There are 229 kouta 小歌 (miscellaneous songs), 50 yamato-bushi 大和節 (Yamato rhythms), 7 ginshiku 吟詩句 (poetic songs), 3 hōka no uta 放下歌 (songs for hōka), 8 hayauta 早歌 (light songs), 10 dengaku 田楽 (field songs), 2 Ōmibushi 近江節 (Ōmi rhythms), and 2 kyōgen kouta 狂言小歌 (*kyōgen* songs). The prosody chiefly uses some combination of the traditional fives and sevens, usually with an initial seven, but some are more irregular and colloquial. About two-thirds of the songs have love elements, whatever their formal category.

The collection greatly influenced a number of later anthologies and exercised influence on women's *kabuki* and songs set to the shamisen.

KANŌ EITOKU 狩野永徳. 1543–1590. Azuchi-Momoyama painter, fifth generation of the school. He is credited with magnificent paintings for the Azuchi castle of Oda Nobunaga and the Osaka castle of Toyotomi Hideyoshi, but the fall of both rulers led to the loss of much of that painting. What survives shows that he well suited the tastes of the time for splendor.

KANŌ MASANOBU 狩野正信. 1434–1530. Late Muromachi painter, founder of the Kanō school. He studied ink wash painting under *Shūbun, and in a timely way possessed the requisite talents when the later Ashikaga shoguns developed a taste for painting.

KANŌ MOTONOBU 狩野元信. 1476–1559. Late Muromachi painter, son of Masanobu. Motonobu introduced a great change in the styles he inherited from his father, so setting the Kanō school on the artistic road it largely followed thereafter.

KANŌ NAONOBU 狩野尚信. 1607–1650. Early Edo painter. He worked for the Tokugawa shogunate both in Kyoto and Edo. Besides murals for Nijō castle, he did a good deal of the ink wash painting for which the Kanō school was well known.

KANŌ TAN'YŪ 狩野探幽. 1602–1674. Early Edo painter. He was a kind of court painter for the Tokugawa shogunate, which favored his spacious pictures. Many remain in Nijō palace, Kyoto, and in Nagoya castle.

KANZE KIYOTSUGU. See KAN'AMI.

KANZE MOTOKIYO. See ZEAMI.

KARAGOROMO KISSHŪ 唐衣橘洲. 1743–1802. Mid-Edo *kyōka* poet. Little is known about him. He is credited with having made kyōka popular by beginning a group to sponsor it. The group included *Ōta Nampo, about whom more is known. But it seems to be agreed that Kisshū's *Kyōka Wakaba Shū* 狂歌若葉集 (*Fresh Leaves of Mad Poems*, 1783) rivals Nampo's collection published the same year, and that one or the other was the foremost kyōka poet of Edo times. He left behind a personal collection, *Suichikushū* 酔竹集 (1802), which deserves knowing.

KARAI SENRYŪ 柄井川柳. 1718–1790. Mid-Edo *haikai* poet, originator of *senryū*. From Asakusa in Edo, he emerged as a poetic authority as *maekuzuke* was acquiring great popularity. In his variety of that kind, a judge (*tenja*) like himself would set a foundation stanza (*maeku*) in 7-7 syllables to which aspirants would add their stanzas (*tsukeku*) for judgment. These added stanzas would be in 5-7-5 syllables. He was not only one of the most popular of about twenty prominent Edo judges at the time but also a man of entrprise. Judges before him had been assembling about 10,000 stanzas in intermittent competitions. Beginning in 1757, Senryū began his annual competitions, *Senryū Hyō Manku Awase* 川柳評万句合, which proved so popular that they continued in his name to 1797, after his lifetime. It is said that he selected about 80,000, or 3 percent, from over 2,300,000 stanzas submitted. These were set forth in *Haifū Yanagidaru* 誹風柳多留, collections that continued to 1833, well after his death. The title is a reminder of the close relation of senryū to haikai, or more properly that it is a kind of *zappai*, irregular haikai. And although various kinds were in existence, the importance of Senryū is plain in that his pen name should have come to designate one kind, even after it had ceased to be the kind he practiced.

KARASUMA MITSUHIRO 烏丸光広. 1579–1630. Early Edo *waka* poet. He studied *Kokin denjū* and waka under *Hosokawa Yūsai. In 1609 he ran afoul of authorities, but was pardoned two years later and eventually rose to decent rank. When only twenty-one, he was ordered by Goyōzei (r. 1586–1611) to visit Yūsai on the battlefield to copy down knowledge of waka, lest the principles of poetry be forever lost. He was author of various works and has a ten-book personal poetic collection, *Kōyō Wakashū* 黄葉和歌集 (*Collection of Yellow Leaves*, pub. 1669). Although his poetry is mostly in the line of the insipid *Nijō poets, it is periodically enlivened by a sensibility nurtured on Zen Buddhism. Perhaps the conservative emphasis of his poetics as well as poetry was natural when the nation was convulsed with war. It is a pity that he is no longer credited with certain *kanazōshi: Mesamashigusa* 目覚し草 (*The Plants that Wake You Up*), *Chikusai* 竹斎, and *Nise Monogatari* 仁勢物語, a parody of the *Ise Monogatari*.

KARIYA EKISAI 狩谷棭斎. 1775–1835. Late Edo *kokugaku* scholar. His work was influenced by such more important scholars as *Murata Harumi and *Yashiro Hirokata. With one exception it resembles that of most such scholars in his time: he shows an interest in Chinese antiquity unusual in a scholar of the native past, and therefore he deserves some credit as a comparatist.

KASA NO IRATSUME 笠女郎. Dates unknown. A Nara *waka* poet, she is known today for a handful of *tanka* sent to *Ōtomo Yakamochi. Although far from the greatest poet of the *Man'yōshū, she seems to be one of the first to write in the style of the passionate woman poet, which has lasted over the centuries, and has featured such gifted writers as *Ono no Komachi, *Ise, *Izumi Shikibu, *Shokushi Naishinnō and, in modern times, Yosano Akiko.

KASA NO KANAMURA 笠金村. Dates unknown. Nara *waka* poet, important poet in the *Man'yōshū. A personal collection, *Kasa no Asomi no Kanamura Shū* 笠朝臣金村集, existed about 730, but is not extant. The *Man'yōshū* includes thirty-four of his *chōka* and fourteen *tanka*. He is esteemed for his personal note. To a surprising degree for a court poet, he avoids (in the poems we have) engagement with public events. Although a fine poet, he falls well behind the four greatest poets represented in the collection (*Kakinomoto Hitomaro, *Yamabe Akahito, *Yamanoe Okura, and *Ōtomo Yakamochi).

KATŌ BANSAI 加藤磐斎. 1621–1674. Early Edo *haikai* poet, critic. Born in Kyoto, from an early age he studied haikai, *waka*, and poetics with *Matsunaga Teitoku. He composed haikai sequences with *Kitamura Kigin, *Yasuhara Teishitsu, and other notables. Later he turned to criticism of earlier works by *Kenkō and *Sei Shōnagon. He also left some waka.

KATŌ CHIKAGE 加藤千蔭. 1735–1808. Late Edo scholar of *kokugaku*, *waka* poet. He studied first with his father and then with *Kamo no Mabuchi. After Mabuchi's death, he became the leader of kokugaku studies in Edo. His status as a waka poet was, as they say, known even in Kyoto; it is certainly well attested to in *Ukeragahana* うけらが花 (*Chikage's Poetic Flowers*, 1802). By no means a negligible poet, he belongs to the rank after *Ozawa Roan. He has many other accomplishments; he was a painter as well as a poet. But he was above all a scholar who produced valuable commentaries on the *Man'yōshū, *Genji Monogatari, and *Ise Monogatari, and he produced manuscript copies of the *Genji Monogatari*, *Utsuho Monogatari, and other works in his much esteemed hand.

KATŌ KYŌTAI 加藤暁台. 1732–1792. Mid-Edo *haikai* poet. Born in Nagoya, he served for a time in the Tokugawa home household, but in 1759 he went to Edo. From about the age of twenty he had been studying haikai under a couple of masters whose names are no longer familiar. Writing under various pen names, he settled on the style of Kyōtai with his *Ateishū* 蛙啼集 (*Frog Croakings*, 1763). He was in Kyoto about 1774. From his contact there with *Yosa Buson at the height of the Haikai Revival, he produced his best poetry. In 1783 he brought out a work honoring *Matsuo Bashō as founder of the true style of haikai: *Fūra Nembutsu* 風羅念仏. In that year Buson died and, nine years later, so did Kyōtai, in Kyoto.

KATORI NAHIKO 楫取魚彦. 1723–1782. Late Edo *kokugaku* scholar, *waka* poet. His more literary studies follow in the school of *Kamo no Mabuchi. Perhaps because of his study of early Japanese grammar, he attempted in his waka—of which few remain—to recapture the atmosphere of the *Man'yōshū.

KATSUSHIKA HOKUSAI 葛飾北斎. 1760–1849. Late Edo artist of *ukiyoe* prints, founder of the Hokusai school. After the usual apprenticeship, his unusual gifts and interest in Western art led to a style in which he depicted a wide range of subjects— actors, beautiful women, animals, birds, butterflies, and above all landscapes in which a total striking effect possesses highly particularized and sometimes startling detail.

KAWATAKE MOKUAMI 河竹黙阿弥. 1816– 1893. Late Edo, modern *kabuki* dramatist. He rep-

resents the most distinguished dramatic transition from Edo to Meiji times. He was enormously prolific, showing his talents at an early age and working ceaselessly thereafter. It is not clear whether the twenty-eight volumes of his collected works testify to a remaining zest in Edo Japan or to the accumulating energy of the modern period. But his career shows the division between classical and modern literature is less just than we often think.

KAYA SHIRAO 加舎白雄. 1738–1791. Mid-Edo *haikai* poet. Born possibly in Shinano—or more likely in Edo—where in 1780 he set up his Shunjū hermitage. His poetry is well regarded, although some find his puritanical attitude dislikable. In any case it is his own, unlike his highly derivative criticism.

KAZAN 花山 (or **KAZAN IN**). 968–1008. R. 984– 986. Mid-Heian *waka* poet. A fine poet, if not the greatest of royal poets in Japan. About 115 or 120 of his poems survive to show his seriousness in many examples that tend to the darker tones of suffering and *jukkai* that he knew all too well in his lifetime.

KAZAN. See WATANABE KAZAN.

KAZAN IN NAGACHIKA 花山院長親. D. 1429. Nambokuchō-Early Muromachi poet, prose writer, courtier. He had close associations with the southern court. The *Shin'yōshū* includes twenty-five of his poems, and he was often in the circle about *Munenaga Shinnō. To express his loyalty to Chōkei (r. 1368–1383), he wrote his highly esteemed *Kōun Senshu* 耕雲千首 (*A Thousand Poems by Kōun*), "Kōun" being one of his pen names. Later he took orders, went to Kyoto, and after a time settled at the Nanzenji.

About 1394 he took up writing again with his *Ryōseiki* 両聖記 on spirits visiting China. His *Kōun Kuden* 耕雲口伝 (*Kōun's Instructions*, 1408) and *Kōun Kikō* 耕雲紀行 (*Kōun's Travel*, 1419) are not outstanding works, but they show how Zen Buddhism and Sung thought had entered literature. In 1414 he judged a poetry match in seven hundred rounds (only the preface is left), and later left behind criticism of earlier classics, of which his *Genji Kokagami* 源氏小鏡 (*A Little Account of The Genji Monogatari*, 1423–1428) is a notable example.

KEICHŪ 契沖. 1640–1701. Early Edo student of classics. At an early age he took orders as a Shingon monk and later lived a reclusive life at various temples. His religious name was Kūshin. To him Japan owes the foundation of disciplined study of its literary classics. He brought to bear an exceptionally severe mind and determined method, leading to studies of the *Kokinshū, Hyakunin Isshu (see *Fujiwara Teika), and many, many other collections, diaries, and *monogatari*. His work is remarkable for its painstaking efforts to achieve accuracy. He was a very difficult master to work with, placing on his students the same rigorous demands he laid on himself. Such has been, however, the continuing importance of his work that it received the hard-won praise of *Motoori Norinaga. He was still being published well into the Meiji era, and his method of reading the *Man'yōshū is still taught. His best-known study today is Man'yō Daishōki 万葉代匠記, but he remains a philological scholar to respect in his other work, as well.

KEIKAI. See Nihon Ryōiki.

KEI KIITSU 慶紀逸. 1695–1762. Haikai poet and judge (tenja). Kiitsu stands in the shadow of his successor, *Karai Senryū. But like his successor, he was held in high reputation as a judge of stanzas submitted in maekuzuke fashion. He varied from usual practice in setting as a foundation stanza one in 5-7-5 syllables—like a hokku in haikai, for adding stanzas (tsukeku) in 7-7 syllables. Many examples of these irregular haikai compositions (zappai) were published by him and others in the collection Mutamagawa 武玉川 (1750; printed 1774).

KEIKOKUSHŪ 経国集 (Collection of National Polity). Early Heian kanshi collection in twenty parts. Ordered by Junna (r. 923–933), it was compiled by Yoshimine Yasuyo, Shigeno Sadanushi, and others in 827. According to its preface, the twenty parts included 178 poets and 998 poems, but existing versions are truncated. The poets include Junna and his predecessor, Saga (r. 809–823), Nara and Heian court officials, priests such as *Kūkai, and women such as Uchiko Naishinnō. Clearly this represented a spread of continental learning, and this third collection of Chinese poetry (see Part Six) shows many more poets writing with assurance, even if such niceties of Chinese poetry such as rhyme-tones may have eluded them.

KENGYŌ. See Ikuta Kengyō; Yamada Kengyō; Yatsuhashi Kengyō.

KENJUN 賢順. 1547–1636. Muromachi to early Edo musician, composer, waka poet. While yet a boy, he lost his father to death in battle. Thereafter he entered a temple and at an early age became a priest. He studied koto music for gagaku and also the seven-stringed Chinese zither. Although most famous as the founder of Tsukushi koto playing, he also gained a reputation for imayō and attracted a wide following.

KENKŌ 兼好 (or **YOSHIDA KANEYOSHI** 吉田兼好). ca. 1283–ca. 1352. Nambokuchō poet and essayist. Very few authors have given the world a nonfictional prose work that continues to be read and loved, even by secondary-school students, cen-turies after their death. *Sei Shōnagon and *Kamo no Chōmei are among such authors, but they are usually read in abstract, whereas Kenkō's Tsurezuregusa つれづれ草(徒然草) (Essays in Idleness, 1330–1331) is read whole. His work is one of the prime exemplars of that Japanese kind of prose, zuihitsu, a term implying not so much essays as miscellaneous reflections, observations. Such was his reputation from his own time and following that many other works have been attributed to him, none with any certainty. In fact, he became something of a legend, reduced to a single man only in modern times.

He was born into a well-connected family with hereditary Shinto connections (one brother was, however, a Tendai priest). He is often mentioned by his contemporaries and such followers or later admirers as Shōtetsu, in part because of service to Gonijō (r. 1301–1308), in part for his connections with the Ashikaga bakufu, in part for his reputation as a poet, and in no small part for the romantic gossip surrounding him. At some point (by 1320) he had become a priest. He studied poetry in the flagging style of the *Nijō poets, and today his former reputation as a poet seems overblown. According to the *Taiheiki and other works, he was asked by one Kō no Moronao to write a love letter to a certain man's wife. She refused to respond, and Moronao grew angry with the hapless Kenkō. His contemporaries thought him a worldly-wise cleric, and he was. Yet for his masterpiece, the reverse is true: it is by a Buddhist author with unusual tolerance for the world and human weakness. Many more profound authors appeal less to fallible readers (see Part One, pp. 54–55 on Tsurezuregusa).

KENREI MON'IN UKYŌ NO DAIBU 建礼門院右京大夫. B. ca. 1157. Early Kamakura waka poet, diarist. She served twice at the court of *Gotoba, but from about 1195 she entered service with Kenrei Mon'in (consort of Takakura, r. 1168–1180), and it is from that service that she derives part of her name. During this period there occurred the love affair that dominated her life and later her memory, when her lover—Taira Sukemori—was killed at the Battle of Dannoura (1185). That catastrophic turn for the Heike cause involved Kenrei Mon'in's being sent to a temple in Ohara. Our author went with her mistress, but after a few years moved away. It seems that it was a good deal later that she put together her Kenrei Mon'in Ukyō no Daibu Shū. As with so many of these works, this is part kashū (there are three hundred poems), part chronological nikki and part monogatari, or at least uta monogatari (the prose often provides context and build-up for the poems). Such realizing of a balance among kinds, along with the elegiac or plaintive tone and the highly skillful ordering of her work, claim admiration. She was enough of a poet to have twenty-two poems included in various official collections, beginning with the *Shinchokusenshū. Some have thought her author of a sequel to the *Genji Monogatari, Yamaji no Tsuyu* 山路の露 (*Dew on the Mountain Path*).

KENSAI. See INAWASHIRO KENSAI.

KENSHŌ 顕昭. Ca. 1128–ca. 1210. Late Heian *waka* poet, critic. In his time, there were two major, competing groups of poets. His was the Rokujō, set against the Mikohidari group (also a Fujiwara family) led by *Fujiwara Shunzei. On his side was another learned critic, *Fujiwara Kiyosuke. Both brothers produced a number of treatises on poetry, both were stuffed with learning, and both were highly conservative. His learning issued in commentaries on works as early as the *Man'yōshū and as contemporary as current poetry contests. He compiled a number of collections of his own work and of that by others. His own poems are represented in many collections, and he participated in the most prestigious poetry matches of the time, the *Roppyakuban Utaawase* and *Sengohyakuban Utaawase*. He wrote a work protesting Shunzei's judgments at the former, and got into a yet more famous dispute with *Jakuren. He and his brother were unquestionably among the learned poets of their time, but their opponents also had learning, as well as a poetic genius denied the brothers.

KENSHUN MON'IN CHŪNAGON 建春門院中納言. B. 1157. Early Kamakura diarist. Her interest derives as much from her connections as from her diary, *Kenshun Mon'in Chūnagon Nikki*, or *Tamakiharu*. Daughter of *Fujiwara Shunzei and sister of *Fujiwara Teika, she derives her name from service to the daughter of Goshirakawa (r. 1155–1158). She lived amid the upheavals of court connected with the *Gempei* wars. In 1183 she entered service with *Shōkushi Naishinnō, a princess more broadminded than the diarist, who was very staid. For all her propriety, although she took orders at forty-nine, that did not prevent her from staying at court. She died somewhere between the ages of sixty-two and sixty-nine. The first half of her diary concerns her service with Kenshun Mon'in, and the second, dealing with later matters, was completed by Teika. Highly particularized as it is, it has useful historical information and detailed description of court life at the time. But its literary worth is less conspicuous than that of many earlier diaries by court ladies.

KENZAN. See OGATA KENZAN.

KIBI NO MAKIBI 吉備真備. 693–775. Nara scholar, courtier. He studied in China from 717 to 735, acting as a kind of cultural ambassador for Kōken (r. 749–758). She directed him to bring back fruits of T'ang learning, which he did, including various Chinese works, especially on Confucianism and government. After his return, he held various important court appointments.

KIGIN. See KITAMURA KIGIN.

KIKAKU. See ENOMOTO KIKAKU.

KINEYA 杵屋. An Edo line of *nagauta* 長唄 composers, shamisen performers. The house used certain traditional names for its chief musicians, much as actors did. Since musicians using one style were often promoted to bear a senior style, the history of individuals bearing the Kineya name and the various styles is quite complex. The senior style was Kangorō 勘五郎 which, according to tradition, began in the early seventeenth century, but probably emerged later. The third musician to bear the name lived 1829–1877, and the fifth 1875–1917. The first Kangorō was also considered the first Rokuzaemon 六左衛門. This line was augmented by extra or courtesy titles, including musicians often equaling those who bore the style in regular succession. The junior line of Kisaburō 喜三郎 first appears in 1702 and has continued into modern times, although a number who bore the style later became known as one generation or another of Kangorō. Confusing as this is, nagauta had a profound influence on *jōruri*, *kabuki*, and other literary kinds, so that the prominence of the Kineya school cannot be overlooked.

KINKAFU 琴歌譜 (*Songs for the Zither*). A Heian book of music, in one part, of unknown authorship and date. One copy is dated 981, and references to the work show its popularity during the Heian period. The books gives the music for nineteen songs for the wagon (an earlier version of the koto) and, in *man'yōgana*, twenty-two song texts. They are *ōnuta*, contributing to maintenance of courtly traditions, ceremonies, and pleasures.

KI NO KAION 紀海音. 1663–1742. Early Edo writer of *jōruri*, *haikai*, and *kyōka*. His father had a taste for *Teimon* haikai and his eldest brother for *kyōka*. His interests first followed his father's, but he later turned to *Danrin* haikai. In early middle age he gave deep thought to entering the priesthood, but he gave up the idea, and at the relatively advanced age of forty-three he took up writing jōruri for the Toyotakeza in Osaka, where he entered into competition with *Chikamatsu Monzaemon. In the eighteen years after 1706, he wrote some fifty plays. Among his *sewamono* are: *Osome Hisamatsu Tamoto no Shirashibori* お染・久松袖の白絞り(1711, one of his *shinjū* plays), *Yaoya Oshichi* 八百屋お七 (*Oshichi of the Greengrocer's*, ca. 1711–1715), and *Keisei Sandogasa* 傾城三度笠 (1713). His *jidaimono* include: *Kamakura Sandaiki* 鎌倉三代記 (1718) and *Keisei Mugen no Kane* 傾城無間鐘 (1723).

Kaion initiates no great departures, and is instead someone who makes better what had been. Literary students will have heard of Chikamatsu long before him, but the truth is that he exercised greater influence on later drama than did Chikamatsu. As he contemplated his successes later in life, he reverted to the joys of composing haikai and took up kyōka as a pleasure.

KINOSHITA CHŌSHŌSHI 木下長嘯子. 1569–1649. Early Edo *waka* poet. After being involved in the wars that concluded with the foundation of the Edo *bakufu* (he was nephew-in-law of Toyotomi Hideyoshi), he lost his land holdings and took orders to begin a second life as a poet. His admirers included *Hosokawa Yūsai, *Fujiwara Seika, *Hayashi Razan, and *Matsunaga Teitoku. He had a sense of the poetic tastes evolving, so that his *Kyohaku Shū* 挙白集 (*Chōshōshi's Collection*, 1649) exercised some influence even on *Matsuo Bashō. But in general he stands on the other side of the transition from waka and *renga* to haikai.

KI NO TOMONORI 紀友則. Fl. ca. ?850–?904. Early Heian *waka* poet, one of the *sanjūrokkasen*. He had a hand in compiling the first official collection, the *Kokinshū*, but because that includes a poem by his kinsman; *Ki no Tsurayuki, mourning his death, he must have died between about 900 and 905. Little is known about him except that he had a middling post at court and that he is author of poems in the *Kokinshū* and sixty-four more in later collections. Although his reputation has never been of the highest, in a handful of seasonal and love poems he much excels a large group of later poets who get more space in the usual literary histories. There is a personal collection, *Tomonori Shū*, which confirms what little we know about his poetry and him from other sources.

KI NO TSURAYUKI 紀貫之. Ca. 872–945. Early Heian *waka* poet, critic, diarist. He was greatly admired for his learning, for his waka, for his Chinese poetry, for the expression he gave to the styles of art and life in his time, and for his aesthetic definition of what seemed to be inchoate seems to take on attractive form. His role in the compilation of the *Kokinshū* is a conspicuous example. He also altered existing art. For example, although most of the poetry he inherited was written from actual situations, his many compositions to go with pictures on folding screens introduced an element of fictionality that was to have enormous impact on waka.

His role in the design of the *Kokinshū* can no longer be distinguished with any assurance from the roles of the other compilers. Since two of the people involved were kinsmen, however, and since he has more poems in the collection than any other poet, it seems safe to say that he was the leading spirit. The design of the collection seems to be accepted as something inevitable, but the lack of such design in the *Man'yōshū* or the Chinese collections to which he is supposedly indebted tells us that the compi-lation of the *Kokinshū* is probably the most creative act in all Japanese poetry. Not only are subsequent waka collections (official and personal) modeled on it, but so also, in various ways, are *utaawase, hyaku-shuuta, renga, haikai*, and even modern *haiku*. The importance of his Japanese preface to the collection is dealt with in Part One.

Tsurayuki's criticism stresses the naturalness of affective and expressive acts. But in his more formal poetry he reveals a compelling devotion to craft. His poetry appears not only in the *Kokinshū* and later official collections but also in two versions of his personal collection, *Tsurayuki Shū* 貫之集. Both were made by later, unknown hands. One compiler included about nine hundred poems, the other about seven hundred—including a large number of poems to go with screen paintings.

His *Tosa Nikki* 土佐日記 (*The Tosa Diary*, ca. 935) is not only one of the principal Heian literary diaries but also the first; in fact, it is the oldest piece of Japanese prose literature extant in its original form. He presents it as if recorded by a woman accompanying the party of a governor leaving Tosa to return to the capital (as he did in 934). Because attributed to a woman, the work is written in *kanabun*—a fact prescient for the triumph of kana literature by women in the next century. The two chief emphases of the work are on travel (its beauties and rigors) and the woman's grief for the daughter who had died in Tosa. The many poems are well suited to the individuals who are supposed to have composed them, with the result that many are very simple and a number comic in their setting. Since such styles are suitable to the individual characters, it is difficult to assume, as some Japanese critics have, that Tsurayuki was turning to a simpler style late in life. It may well be, however, as others have suggested, that it was intended to serve as a hand-book of all styles of poetry, or that it is the prototype of *haibun* with verse.

Tsurayuki is unquestionably a highly gifted poet. Equally certainly, he does not belong to the transcendent few. It remains true that no other poet and theorist so radically affected not only poetry but literature over the centuries, by the important act of instituting the fundamental terms on which literature was to be understood.

KIN'YŌ(WAKA)SHŪ 金葉(和歌)集 (*Collection of Golden Leaves (of Japanese Poems)*). Late Heian royal *waka* collection (*chokusenshū*); fifth of the *nijūichidaishū* and *hachidaishū*. Ordered by Shirakawa (r. 1072–1086), with *Minamoto Shunrai as compiler, making this anthology the only collection since the first two (see Part Six) compiled solely by someone not of the Fujiwara line. Shunrai's tastes proved to be too advanced for Shirakawa, who required at least three drafts between 1124 and 1127. Although it follows the *Kokinshū* model, it does so in ten books; its 716 poems make it the second shortest of the twenty-one official collections. Shunrai's tastes prevailed at least to the extent of his emphasizing contemporary innovating poets (even if he could not always include their most advanced work) and *tanrenga*. There is no preface.

KISANJI. See Hōseidō Kisanji.

KISEKI. See Ejima Kiseki.

KISEN 喜撰. Fl. ca. 810–824. Priest, *waka* poet. He is known for one poem and for being mentioned by *Ki no Tsurayuki in the Japanese preface to the *Kokinshū*, which gave him the status of one of the *rokkasen*, even if one of the least known and least considerable as a poet. After taking orders, he first lived in a temple in Saga northeast of Kyoto, later moving south of the capital to Uji, where he lived a life of reclusion.

KISSHŪ. See Karagoromo Kisshū.

KITABATAKE CHIKAFUSA 北畠親房. 1293–1354. Nambokuchō *waka* poet, political figure. His political activity centered both on power and on the exciting art of survival. His efforts and those of his family to find place in those troubled times led to association with the ill-fated Godaigo (r. 1318–1339) and with Gomurakami (r. 1339–1368). Although he survived, a son died in the struggle. His principal work is historical, *Jinnō Shōtōki* 神皇正統記 (*An Account of Our Divine Sovereigns and True Royal Line*, rev. 1343), six parts in three divisions. The first division treats Japan as a land of divine sovereigns. The second treats of the legendary divinities and the founding of the nation. The third traces the royal line from Jimmu to Gomurakami, to the not unexpected end of showing the southern house to be the divinely appointed one. His poetry, which is in the line of the insipid *Nijō Poets, is represented in the *Shin'yōshū*. He became a priest in 1329 with the name Kakukū, and he is author of a vernacular tract (*kana hōgo*), *Shingon Naishōgi* (*The Inner Meaning of Shingon*, 1345).

KITAGAWA UTAMARO 喜多川歌麿. 1753–1806. Late Edo *ukiyoe* artist. He specialized in female beauties, especially women with "long necks," that is, with some part of the shoulders bared or even in poses disrobed to the waist. Some think that the wood-block print reached its apogee with him.

KITAMURA KIGIN 北村季吟. 1624–1705. Early Edo *waka*, *renga*, *haikai* poet; scholar of literary classics. His waka are written in the attenuated style of the *Nijō poets. He inherited from his father a profession of medicine and a taste for renga. But on going to Kyoto and studying with *Yasuhara Teishitsu and then *Matsunaga Teitoku, he became much more involved in haikai. By the time he was

twenty-four, he had published a book of haikai writings, *Yamanoi* 山之井 (*The Mountain Well*) and had emerged as a major exponent of Teimon haikai. He subsequently published a number of haikai studies or collections: *Haikai Awase* 俳諧合 (*A Haikai Match*, 1656), *Shinzoku Inu Tsukuba Shū* 新続犬筑波集 (*The New Collection of Dog Renga, Continued*, 1667), *Zoku Renju* 続連珠 (*Linked Poetic Gems, Continued*, 1676).

The scholarship of Kigin is of very great distinction. Among many fine studies, his *Kogetsushō* 湖月抄 (1673) must be given pride of place. So important is this study of *Murasaki Shikibu's *Genji Monogatari* that it continued to be the basic commentary for students well into this century. It lives on, incorporated into the commentary and interpretation of contemporary scholars. It is difficult to think of another study of the greatest work in a national literature, a study that was written about six and a half centuries after the work and that has continued to be important for another three.

Kigin did not forget the other familiarly annotated classics, as is shown by studies of the *Ise Monogatari* (1667) and *Man'yōshū* (1682–1686). In addition, he broke new ground with studies of the *Yamato Monogatari* (1653), *Tsurezuregusa* (1667), and *Makura no Sōshi* (1674). Although any of these works can be counted on to start fresh trains of thought in the modern reader, his *Hachidaishū Shō* 八代集抄 (*Study of the Collections of Eight Eras*) remains indispensable. Not only has its commentary of the *Kokinshū* and *Shinkokinshū* become part of what is thought to have been always known, but his commentary on some of the intervening collections constitutes the chief criticism to this day. In the pithy style of his commentary, he has a knack for making himself say what he means without wasted words, so being both understandable and eminently usable. He must yield to *Motoori Norinaga for scholarly originality and range, but his specific comments, especially on poems, are hardly to be excelled, and his scope is far greater than the titles mentioned can suggest.

KIYOMASA. See Torii Kiyomasa.

KIYOMITSU. See Torii Kiyomitsu.

KIYONAGA. See Torii Kiyonaga.

KIYONOBU. See Torii Kiyonobu.

KIYOSUKE. See Fujiwara Kiyosuke.

KŌ 孝. Dates unknown. Muromachi *renga* poet, included here as an example of many meritorious writers of whom little or nothing is known. In the *Anegakoji Ima Shimmei Hyakuin*, his nine stanzas equal or surpass those by such famous renga masters as *Shinkei, *Sōzei, *Chiun, and *Senjun.

KOBAYASHI ISSA 小林一茶. 1763–1827. Late Edo *haikai* writer. Like many modern writers with unhappy childhoods, he made himself his chief subject. The unhappiness he felt with his father's second wife and family led him also to sympathize with the vulnerable, whether human or animal. By 1789 he had become known as a haikai writer, of which he is the last of importance. His best writing is not to be found in sequences, however, but in *hokku* (by his time all but indistinguishable from modern *haiku*, except that they still might initiate sequences and that they still might be part of a composition in prose) and especially in *haibun*. His haibun include accounts of himself. Of these the best are *Shichiban Nikki* 七番日記 (*The Seventh Diary*, covering 1810–1818), *Hachiban Nikki* 八番日記 (*The Eighth Diary*, concluding with 1821), and above all *Oraga Haru* おらが春 (*This Year of My Life*, based on 1819). The last is one of the very few works of haibun worth setting beside those of *Matsuo Bashō and *Yokoi Yayū. In it he manages to reach concerns that both interest and include the reader.

KŌBŌ DAISHI. See KŪKAI.

KOBORI ENSHŪ 小堀遠州. 1579–1647. Early Edo tea master, garden architect. He served both Toyotomi Hideyoshi and the early Tokugawa shogunate. He was also an accomplished *waka* poet, architect, flower arranger, and artist in other media. He was extraordinarily versatile, and one of the most attractive figures of his time.

KŌETSU. See HONNAMI KŌETSU.

KOGOSHŪI 古語拾遺 (*Gleanings in Old Words*). Early Heian historical polemical work in one part, compiled by Imbe Hironari in 807, when he was almost eighty. This is a salvo in the paper and personal war fought to justify claims at court by the Imbe against the Nakatomi, who were supported by the powerful Fujiwara house descended from Nakatomi (Fujiwara) Kamatari (614–669).

KOHON SETSUWASHŪ 古本説話集. Late Heian *setsuwa* collection in two parts. The compiler is unknown, but the *kanabun* and *monogatari* character of the collection (in contrast to the more Sinified *Konjaku Monogatari* and *Uchigiki Shū*) support the view that this may have been assembled at the request of a highly placed court lady. In particular, the beginning connects with Dai Saiin (Princess Senshi).

The first part contains some diverting as well as serious stories. The comic relate to human imperfections, the serious to *waka* and, of course, religion. Given the number of poems and the light touch, this part looks somewhat like a disjointed *monogatari*. The second differs enough from the first and from usual norms to be difficult to classify. Sometimes it seems more historical than usual in this kind of literature (at least in terms of actual people dealt with); at other times it seems to resemble a Heian diary. The religious emphasis here falls on matters that would appeal to women: stories of Kannon, visits to Hasedera, and so on.

The work long existed in a unique copy from the Kamakura period and held in a family collection. After being declared a National Treasure in 1949, it has been printed a number of times and has attracted considerable interest.

KOIKAWA HARUMACHI 恋川春町. 1744–1789. Late Edo writer of *kibyōshi* and *sharebon*. A man of samurai extraction, he used this pen name (Love-river Springtown) in writing and illustrating a series of works. He was highly prolific. His first important work, *Kinkin Sensei Eiga no Yume* 金々先生栄花夢 (*Professor Clink-Clink's Dream of Glory*, 1775) helped establish the distinctive kibyōshi style, adding to prose the wit and humor found in *kyōka* and *senryū*, as well as *tsū*, a connoisseurship in what is up-to-date. Other works frequently referred to are *Kōmansai Angya Nikki* 高慢斎行脚日記 (1776), *Kotoba Tatakai Atarashi no Ne* 辞闘戦新根 (pub. 1780), and *Mudai Ki* 無益委記 (1779). He was highly influential in his illustrations as well as his stories, proving more effective with kibyōshi than with sharebon. Contemporary and later writers happily learned from him. His last work, *Ōmugaeshi Bumbu Futamichi* 鸚鵡返文武二道 (1789), met with success among his readers. But since it seemed to offer criticism of the Kansei Reform, he was summoned by the *bakufu* for examination. Whether fearing worse punishment or not, it is said that he took his life.

KOJIDAN 古事談 (*Talks about Ancient Matters*). Early Kamakura *setsuwa* collection in six parts. It is possible that a traditional ascription to Minamoto Akikane 源顕兼 as compiler is correct. The evidence for dating the collection about 1212–1215 seems even stronger. The six parts contain 461 stories of the usual kind: see *Konjaku Monogatari*. The style is not distinguished, but the heavy use of *katakana* offers a sort of transition from *kambun*. The contents also have some novelty, for although the basic orientation is toward the court, some stories in the fourth part take warriors as their subject.

KOJIKI 古事記 (*Record of Ancient Matters*). A chronicle in three parts made up of 114 brief sections. According to his preface in elegant Chinese prose, Ō no Yasumaro 太安万侶 set down the work from the recitation of memorized matter by *Hieda no Are 稗田阿礼. Yasumaro reports that Temmu asked for the work after the Jinshin War (672)—no doubt to legitimize the position he held.

Although the work was transmitted orally by Are for Yasumaro to set down, and although Are had memorized many things she had heard, it is also clear that she had access to written sources for her memorizing. These are usually characterized as two kinds: one dealing with the early divinities and their doings, leading the sun goddess, Amaterasu Ōmikami, to settle her descendants on the Land of Reed Plains, Japan; and the other something like a book of regnal annals for the successive sovereigns, beginning with the legendary first, Jimmu. The former source is usually called *Sumeramikoto no Hitsugi* (*The Sovereigns' Sun-Lineage*) or, for short, *Teiki* (*Royal Chronicles*), *Jindaiki* (*Chronicles of the Gods*), or *Senki* (*Former Chronicles*); and the second, *Sakitsuyo no Furugoto* (or Sinitically as *Sendai Kuji; Ancient Matters of Former Ages*), or *Honji* (*Fundamental Matters*), as also *Kuji* (*Ancient Matters*). It seems reasonable to assume that if Are had access to written materials, then Yasumaro did also, and that it is therefore more proper to think of him as a compiler-author than as a scribe.

The *man'yōgana* employed uses Chinese characters in the usual three ways: as Chinese writing, phonetically, and in combination. The second and third parts settle into a pattern of first presenting genealogical matter in Chinese style and then *uta* (poems or songs) and anecdotes or stories in a Japanese or mixed style. Uta particularly tend to employ the phonetic method.

In this century there have been three successive views of the *Kojiki* and *Nihon Shoki*. In the first they were venerated as national scriptures; in the second they were dismissed as worthless fabrications; and in the recent, or third period, close examination by philologists, folklorists, historians, and literary critics has yielded impressive results in all those fields. Although Kimmei, the twenty-ninth sovereign (r. 539–571), is taken to be the first who is fully historical (see Part Two above), it has been possible to work with Chinese records for comparison and verification to recognize earlier reigns back to Yūryaku (21st) and sometimes earlier. The uta included are often found in somewhat different versions in the *Nihon Shoki*, one or the other source being the older with no consistency. In both chronicles there are about 500 uta all together, including many duplications with variants. It is patently impossible for creatures who never existed to have recited uta attributed to them, but opinion has been returning to the view that often, especially later in the temporal range, some real situation is reported with its appropriate uta, even if to us today the uta seems to have been forcibly imposed. It is also evident that the *Kojiki* implies a Yamato myth, legitimizing that people's rule over such other groups as the Izumo and Kumaso, whose work is cleverly subordinated to Yamato ends.

After the age of the gods (kamiyo) dealt with in the first part (sections 1–46), the second part covers the reigns of the legendary first fifteen sovereigns, that is, from Jimmu to Ōjin (660 B.C. to A.D. 310 in the legendary history). The third part covers the reigns from Nintoku (supposedly 313–399) to the thirty-third, Suiko—her reign is of course historical (592–628).

It is generally agreed that the *Kojiki* is superior to the *Nihon Shoki* in literary terms as well as historical, except for the late portions of the *Nihon Shoki*, which not only grow more accurate than the earlier ones but also move farther on in time. In spite of its superiority, the *Kojiki* was little known for centuries, and manuscripts of it are relatively few and late. Until Edo times, references to early Japanese history or the age of the gods pertain almost always to the *Nihon Shoki*. *Motoori Norinaga and a few predecessors among the *kokugakusha* are responsible for clarifying the relationship between the two chronicles and for furthering interpretation in major respects. See *Nihon Shoki*.

KOKAN (SHIREN) 虎関 (師錬). 1278–1346. Late Kamakura Rinzai Zen priest, scholar, biographer, and *kanshi* poet. Numbered among the early representatives of *Enni's branch of the Five Mountains (*Gosan*), Kokan was a man of broad learning in Buddhist and Confucian classics and in the methods of Chinese poetry. Like his contemporary *Musō, he studied with I-shan I-ning (Issan Ichinei, 1247–1317), the Chinese monk-scholar whose introduction of literary pursuits into Zen is seen as the initial stimulus for the Gosan movement. The *Genkō Shakusho* 元亨釈書 (*The Genkō Era's History of Buddhism*, 1322) is the first Japanese chronological history of eminent monks. It is said to have taken Kokan ten years to complete, and he is said to have undertaken the project after having been embarrassed at being unable to answer questions about Japanese Buddhism put to him by I-shan. The history is still of great value to scholars. The *Saihokushū* 済北集 (*Northern Hut Collection*, after 1314) is a compilation of Kokan's Chinese poetry and prose; and his *Jubun Inryaku* 聚分韻略 (*Rhymes Classified and Explained*, ca. 1306), was a widely used Chinese rhyming dictionary.

KOKIN (WAKA) ROKUJŌ 古今 (和歌) 六帖 (*Six Quires of the Ancient and Modern [Japanese Poetry]*). Early Heian *waka* collection in six parts. Perhaps compiled by *Minamoto Shitagō or Prince Kaneakira, it was put together by 987. It is a very long collection—4,370 poems—more than half of which had appeared in the *Man'yōshū, *Kokinshū, and *Gosenshū. Others are taken from major *monogatari*, *nikki*, and *Sei Shōnagon's *Makura no Sōshi*. Essentially an anthology from other collections and works, it is a mirror of late tenth-century taste and preserves many poems in older textual versions than would otherwise be known.

KOKIN (WAKA) SHŪ 古今 (和歌) 集 (*Collection of Ancient and Modern [Japanese] Poems*). Early

Heian official *waka* collection (*chokusenshū*); first of the twenty-one anthologies compiled by royal decree (*nijūichidaishū*). Envisioned by Uda (r. 887–897) and ordered by Daigo (r. 897–930), perhaps in 905, it appears to have been completed in 914 or ca. 920, the date of the last poem presumed to be added. The compilers were *Ki no Tsurayuki, *Ki no Tomonori (who had died before completion), *Ōshikōchi Mitsune, and *Mibu no Tadamine. They chose about 1,111 poems (the number in our editions).

The conception underlying the collection no doubt reflected then existing ideas about poetry. But it realizes them so well and so influentially that to some degree all Japanese poetry before 1868 is conceivable only on its terms. For one thing, poems on the seasons are considered the most important (as noted below), a fact reflected in *haiku* to this day. For another, its idea of including the old as well as the new—"Ko-kin," as the title designates—is followed later in prose as well as verse. For poetry, this allowed for arrangement by topics, and therefore by temporal progressions in the poems through the sequence of seasonal phenomena augmented by the court calendar set forth in the annual observances (*nenjū gyōji*; see Part Seven H). Love poems were ordered to show the presumed process of a courtly love affair, with various fluctuations. Such progression and the associative relations of one poem to the next by progression make the collection the ancestor of *renga* and *haikai*. The Japanese preface by Tsurayuki also initiates Japanese criticism (see Part One). There was, in addition, a quite similar Chinese preface by Ki no Yoshimochi.

The division into twenty parts no doubt reflects such "old" models as the *Man'yōshū* and some collections of Chinese poetry. But the organization by topic is new, and was followed by all subsequent official collections, although two—the *Kin'yōshū* and *Shikashū*—scaled down the model to ten parts. The *Kokinshū* model also set two main divisions by halves, the first beginning with the most highly valued poetic topics, those on the seasons; the second beginning with the next most highly prized topic, love. The placement of other parts and the identity of some topics varied from collection to collection thereafter. Some new topics were introduced later—Buddhism, for example; and the Miscellaneous topic (in which no one element seems to predominate) became more and more important subsequently. Yet the fundamental design remained the same, and therefore should be set out here as the *Kokinshū* model:

1–2 Spring (Haru no Uta, Jō, Ge); 3 Summer (Natsu no Uta); 4–5 Autumn (Aki no Uta); 6 Winter (Fuyu no Uta); 7 Congratulations (Ga no Uta); 8 Partings (Wakare no Uta); 9 Travel (Tabi no Uta); 10 Acrostics (Mono no Na no Uta).

11–15 Love (Koi no Uta, Ichi-Go); 16 Laments (Aishō no Uta); 17–18 Miscellaneous (Kusagusa no Uta, Jō, Ge); 19 Miscellaneous Kinds (Zattei no Uta); 20 Poems from the Bureau of Poetry (chiefly traditional songs, ritual poems; Ōutadokoro no Ōnuta).

The compilers also indicated the author (if known or not desirably hidden). In addition, they specify the topic (*dai*), if known. But such topics usually describe the circumstances that prompted the poem. In other words, apart from some poems composed for screens, most of the poems reflect actual life—of course as it was beheld by eyes trained to see in certain ways. Most of the poems suggest an air of self-confidence or even witty high spirits that contrasts with the often more deeply pondered, more somber poetry on fixed, and fictional, topics in some later collections. Among its presumably older poems, there are a number of anonymous ones of great beauty. The major poets represented, apart from the compilers, include *Ariwara Narihira, *Ono no Komachi, *Ise, *Henjō, and Fujiwara Okikaze.

KOKON CHOMONJŪ. See TACHIBANA NARISUE.

KOMACHI. See ONO NO KOMACHI.

KOMA NO CHIKAZANE 狛近真. 1177–1242. Kamakura master of court music (*gagaku*) of the so-called T'ang kind 唐楽, and especially of samai 左舞. He compiled the *Kyōkunshō* 教訓抄 (*A Learner's Treatise*), a major collection and treatise in ten parts (1233).

KOMPARU ZENCHIKU 金春禅竹. 1405–? Mid-Muromachi *nō* actor, playwright, critic (see Part Five and Part Six G and K). According to family tradition, Zenchiku was the thirtieth head of his house, a position held from his early twenties. Although he has been eclipsed by his father-in-law, *Zeami, Zenchiku is only slightly less important than he. Both Zeami and his eldest son, Motomasa, praised Zenchiku, regarding him as the sole person able to maintain the true art of *sarugaku*. Their affections must have joined their judgment when Zenchiku married a daughter of their house. They can only have been deeply grateful to Zenchiku for looking so carefully after Zeami's affairs during exile in Sado.

Zenchiku was a voluminous writer. His plays include such famous ones as *Bashō, Ugetsu,* and *Tamakazura*. His criticism has become more noticed recently, and interest has risen with the discovery of a couple more texts. It is far easier to describe his intellectual affiliations than it is to give a clear, simple account of his critical ideas. His thought ranges over all that was available to a person in his time. Even if he did not know that eccentric intellectual, *Ikkyū (although it seems certain he did), he knew Ikkyū's follower Sōgen and others acquainted with the master's version of Zen Buddhism. From *Ichijō Kanera, he learned of *waka* and other classics. He also studied Shinto and Confucianism. He is credited with bringing a Confucian rationality to bear on other kinds of thought to the end of elucidating nō.

That may be, but the expectation that Zenchiku is penny plain does not survive even initial inspection. One of his central ideas is that of multiple rings (usually six, sometimes three), which came to him on contemplating the Kannon depicted at Hasedera: see his *Rokurin Ichiro no Ki* 六輪一露之記 (*A Record of the Six Rings and the One Sword*). The six rings involve a symbolism at once visual and conceptual. For example, the first ring, that of full life, is represented by a plain circle: a figure and yet an empty ring, playing on the Buddhist polarity of being and nonbeing, presence and absence (u-mu). "If we come to follow the two roads of being and nonbeing," Zenchiku wrote, "being is what we see, and nonbeing is the vessel. What expresses being is nonbeing." The other consistent element in his titles and thought is the one drop of dew (ichiro). This is a metaphor for what Buddhists depict as a sword, which is itself an emblem of the world as form (shiki) and as emptiness (*kū*). Tendai Buddhists also postulated a Mean (chū 中) between form and emptiness. Borrowing on Zeami's concept of Flower Nature (shōka) and and perhaps on the concept of the Buddha Nature (busshō) in all sentient things, Zenchiku posited nature (shō 性) as his mean between emptiness and form. And it is in that nature that we may discover the true beauty of nō (that is, kabuyūgen no hontei).

So brief an introduction to Zenchiku's first ring must suffice to give some sense of the character of his thought. It will be clear that he, like Zeami, sought to bring to bear the greatest intellectual sources available in order to explicate and elevate the art they practiced. Zeami would have been the first to give his son-in-law credit for his penetrating thought and for his grasp of the fundamental character of nō. Apparently a man of very great appeal and integrity, Komparu is one of the most attractive figures in Japanese theater, as also one who will steadily repay further study.

KONJAKU MONOGATARI (SHŪ) 今昔物語 (集) ([*A Collection of*] *Tales of Times Now Past*).

Late Heian *setsuwa* collection. That this is one of the important literary classics no one would deny. Otherwise little is agreed upon, except that it dates from the late Heian period (a time-span of nearly two centuries), that it consisted of thirty-one parts, of which existing manuscripts lack three—nos. 8, 18, and 21—as well as portions of others.

According to a number of old sources, the author was Minamoto Takakuni (1004–1077), to whom is also attributed the *Uji Dainagon Monogatari*. Quite apart from what authorship means for a collection of this kind—editorship being more to the point— there is no adequate proof of his being involved.

More recently it has become common to think of the collection as one made by priests to assist other clerics by providing materials for future writing or for preaching. But no widely acceptable solution exists to the questions of whether in the process many priests or few, or laity, were involved; whether in the end one or several people arranged and unified the collection; or whether after all Takakuni might be considered as something like a copyist-reviser.

The many stories have obviously been selected, arranged, and stylized. Each of the more than 1,200 stories begins, "Some time ago" ("Ima wa mukashi"). Each story ends, "... and this is how the story has been handed down" ("... [to nan] kataritsutacru to ya"). The separate episodes of the *Ise Monogatari* usually begin in a similar formulaic fashion ("Mukashi otoko arikeri"), and the various formulaic "to zo" or "to ya" endings of Heian *monogatari*—including the *Genji Monogatari*— imply exactly what is said at greater length for each story here. Between such formulas, each story introduces the main characters(s), identifying the person(s) by traits, lineage, or other means; then going on to relate what happened; and ending with a judgment, criticism, or moral.

The alternative endings of the title apply very well. Considered as monogatari, the work tells stories that establish a single ethos—again, much as the *Ise Monogatari* earlier and many other, later creations. Considered as a *shū*, we have very much a collection of tales from various times, although almost wholly from the past and connected, by moral comment, to the hearer's or reader's present.

The sense of collection also exists in the situation of stories in India (Tenjiku), China (Shintan), and Japan (Honchō)—as if stories originating in places over a reach of thousands of leagues have been brought together. This is not to be taken as a literal description of origin, although many of the stories can be traced back to origins or analogues farther west than India. The implication is rather that the stories represent human experience throughout the known world: from the Buddha's own land east to the Middle Kingdom and so on to the islands descended from the sun. (Korea, so important to Japanese reception of continental knowledge, is for once also included.) The conspectual aim is clear otherwise. Of all the many provinces and major islands—the collective kuni (see Part Eight C) that were considered to make up Japan—only Iwami and the islands Iki and Tsushima do not provide sites for stories.

Other evidence of purpose can easily be found. The stories are not simply thrown together. Because we do not have an entire work, no complete description is possible. But in many, many instances, the move from one story to the next is smooth and satisfying, as is the case with the arrangement of poems in the *Kokinshū* and other poetic collections antedating this collection.

The date of collection is not clear. If, as most scholars agree, it may have been the second half of the eleventh or the first half on the twelfth century, the author-compiler(s) could have drawn on more than one *waka* collection, the *Ise Monogatari*, **Genji Monogatari*, **Sugawara Takasue no Musume's Hamamatsu Chūnagon Monogatari*, numerous diaries, and other kinds of lengthier composites of diverse materials into literary wholes. The means were there, but when the act was done, and how it was done, depend in turn on one's conception of authorship, of the purpose of the whole, and so on. If we posit a Takakuni and a largely literary purpose, an earlier date seems likely. If we posit joint authorship by priests, a later date such as coincides more nearly with *renga* may be more likely. If we posit a single priest or courtier teaching or criticizing existing society, then the date depends on the individual.

Present opinions about these matters incline to a date toward the end of the eleventh or beginning of the twelfth century, and to multiple priestly collection or authorship. The style as well as the old attribution to Takakuni has led to a consensus that the authors or compilers were male. The consensus on these matters is certainly important, if not finally proved.

Such problems relate in part to a chief virtue of the work, its multifarious variety. The characters range from princes to peasants, from soldiers and priests to doctors and fishers. If that were not enough, there is a range from Bodhisattvas and native divinities to plants (the range is copied in such later setsuwa collections as *Kokon Chomonjū*). Another virtue is the constant purpose in that variety: to depict and judge lives. In some stories, depiction seems to have priority over judgment, and more often judgment over depiction, but even the compilers (or compiler) often seem to have been uncertain of their motives in choosing and rewriting a story. Certainly there is a general aim to represent experience of diverse people throughout the known world to an audience of Japanese.

And what exactly was that audience? Like so much else, the answer depends on moot answers to other questions. Yet a few things are clear. There is not expected of readers the infinitely modulated sensitivity implied by earlier Heian (and some later) literature written for court women. The stories seem quite clearly to imply that the audience will adapt the same stance as what may for convenience sake be termed the compiler. The audience is expected to take an impartial view of human nature. No matter how attractive or off-putting this or that character may be, what counts are actions, passions, and motives betrayed and laid before us for judgment (commonly judgment explicitly guided). Again and again there is didacticism. There is also a remarkable sense of all human creatures being very much at one before what may most simply be termed the Law of the Buddha. There would have been, for the original audience (as there is for us on different terms) a distancing, an otherness implied by stories from remote India or about people quite different from oneself in the stratified rank-conscious Heian society.

It has been said with great insight, although somewhat less justice, that the *Konjaku Monogatari* occupies a world and provides a transition between the worlds of the **Genji Monogatari* and the **Heike Monogatari*. Clearly, this collection does open the earlier world to daylight, to teeming variety, to the far as well as the near, to miracle as well as accustomed experience. The reduction of the lengthy parts of the *Genji Monogatari* to short units within a larger monogatari or collection can also be thought of as preparing for the *Heike Monogatari*. Yet the observation probably tells us more about the *Heike Monogatari* than this question-riddled collection, for that later *gunki monogatari* owes not a little in its brief episodes to the setsuwa concept, while keeping the world of deep sensibility, and even the tears, of the *Genji Monogatari* along with the new daylight of the out-of-doors world.

If we are to attempt a rigorously literary judgment, we probably must say that the *Konjaku Monogatari* offers a collection of stories usually with didactic intent, and therefore requiring assent to a judgment impartially passed (as such things go), but also that it has many stories of uncommon interest, as is attested by the countless adaptations of those stories not only by later setsuwa works but also by modern authors. Yet if we stand farther off, letting some of the outlines take on the shadings that are inevitable to rigorous modern scholarship—and perhaps to a mixed original intent—we are left with a literary work shot through with questions, none of which detract from the fact of its greatness.

KŌRIN. See OGATA KŌRIN.

KOTOMICHI. See ŌKUMA KOTOMICHI.

KUJŌ YOSHITSUNE. See FUJIWARA YOSHITSUNE.

KŪKAI 空海 (or **KŌBŌ DAISHI** 弘法大師). 774–835. Early Heian poet in Chinese, religious figure, founder of Shingon Buddhism. By the age of twenty he had studied at the court school and had taken orders. After that his life was marked by residence at major temples such as Tōdaiji, Tōji, and the center of Shingon Buddhism, Mount Kōya. Although he studied in China, he was not content to be an importer of, or mere commentator on, Chinese Buddhism. His powers of innovative thought led him into rivalry with a suitably able opponent, *Saichō, founder of Tendai Buddhism. His writings contain remarkably little personal information, as is perhaps appropriate to a proponent of esoteric Buddhism. But he ranged widely into Chinese poetry and other secular writings, bringing to Japan the intellectual temper of Six Dynasties and T'ang thought in original ways befitting so powerful a mind.

In 806 Kūkai returned from studying the tenets of the Chen-yen (Shingon) sect in China, and set about propagating its esoteric practices in Japan. These emphasized the use of nonconceptual means to spiritual awareness: *mandalas* (pictorial representations), *mudras* (hand gestures and body postures), and *mantras* (mystic phrases). Kūkai's brilliance and breadth of interests made him a favorite of the court, and he was successful in establishing Shingon as a major Buddhist movement in the Heian period, second only to Saichō's Tendai. In 816 he began construction of the Kongōbuji on Mount Kōya, which became the sect's administrative center; and in 823 he was appointed abbot of Tōji in Kyoto.

Kūkai's major doctrinal works include the early *Sangō Shiiki* 三教指帰 (*Indications of the Goals of the Three Teachings*, 797), in which the superiority of Buddhism over Confucianism and Taoism is argued in a novelistic setting. His literary works include *Bunkyō Hifuron* 文鏡秘府論 (*Secret Treasury of Poetic Mirrors*, 819), a collection of excerpts from Six Dynasties and T'ang poetic treatises, and *Bumpitsu Genjinshō* 文筆眼心抄 (*The Essentials of Poetry and Prose*, 820). Sometime between 830 and 835 Kūkai compiled his *Tenrei Banshō Myōgi*, an early Japanese dictionary of about a thousand Chinese characters (see Part Six Q). After his death, his disciple Shinzei collected fragments from his writings, into the ten-part (*Henjō Hakki*) *Seireishū* (遍照発揮)性霊集 (*The Collected Works of Kūkai's Prose and Poetry*), also known as the *Shōryōshū*. This is a major source of information about Kūkai's life and literary interests.

To later generations he became a great culture hero, traditionally (but doubtfully) credited with the development of the *kana* syllabary and its formulation as the *Iroha Uta*. He was also an outstanding calligrapher, as the common proverb implies: "Kōbō mo fude no ayamari," (Even Kōbō makes mistakes with his brush).

KUMAGAI NAOYOSHI 熊谷直好 . 1782–1862. Late Edo *waka* poet. Although he lived steadily in the Kyoto-Osaka area during adulthood, it was his samurai affairs that first took him to Kyoto at eighteen, and repeatedly thereafter. In 1825 he resigned his samurai status to devote himself to poetry. He left behind some personal collections, including *Ura no Shiogai* 浦の汐貝 (*Shells Left by the Bay Waves*), but he is not one of the major poets of the age.

KUMAZAWA BANZAN 熊沢蕃山 1619–1691. Early Edo Neoconfucianist. Born in Kyoto, he studied under *Nakae Tōju, from whom he learned *yōmeigaku*, the Wang Yang-ming variety of Neoconfucianism. Although he followed Nakae, he also had his own emphases, and his talents led him

to service in various places. Toward the end of his life he became disaffected with the *bakufu*, which more and more was emphasizing *shushigaku* as orthodox Neoconfucianism. He left behind some works, but appears not to have had the influence his talents seemed to promise.

KUNAIKYŌ 宮内卿 . D. ca. 1204. Early Kamakura *waka* poet. A young lady-in-waiting at the court of *Gotoba, and daughter of a woman who had similarly served Goshirakawa (r. 1155–1158), she was active as a poet during the important years when the *Shinkokinshū* was being compiled. She wrote hundred-poem sequences (*hyakushuuta*), was one of the thirty poets in the mammoth *Sengohyakuban Utaawase* (1201), and composed a congratulatory poem at the celebration for *Fujiwara Shunzei's ninetieth year. The *Shinkokinshū* and later official collections include forty-three of her poems. Her style somewhat resembles that of *Shokushi Naishinnō or *Fujiwara Shunzei no Musume in its intensity. One story has it that she died young having contracted a disease by reason of such passion in her poetry.

KUNISADA. See Utagawa Kunisada.

KUROHITO. See Takechi Kurohito.

KYŌDEN. See Santō Kyōden.

KYŌGOKU 京極 **POETS.** The sons of *Fujiwara Tameie (himself son of *Fujiwara Teika) split into three groups in dispute over inheritance, poetry, and politics. One son, Tamenori (1226–1279), established a house known from its location as Kyōgoku. This group made joint cause with the also poetically liberal *Reizei poets against the conservative *Nijō poets, their rivals. The Kyōgoku poets and others persuaded of their literary ideals produced the finest poetry of the period ca. 1240–1350.

KYŌGOKU TAMEKANE 京極為兼 . 1254–1332. Late Kamakura *waka* poet and political figure. He inherited a poetic and political allegiance opposed to the conservative *Nijō poets and allied with the more sympathetically liberal *Reizei poets. He was the foremost critic as well as the best poet of his age. Other poets either followed his example or fought with him. He was equally in the thick of political events. He was committed to *Fushimi (r. 1288–1298) as rivalries were about to split into two lines of claimants. His commitment and intrigue twice earned him banishment to Sado Island—for five years starting in 1298, and for an unknown time after 1315, although it is known that he died in Kawachi near the capital area.

His Nijō rivals were better politicians than he and had the backing of most of the sovereigns of the time. Two of the exceptions were *Fushimi and *Hanazono (r. 1308–1318), themselves accomplished poets. The first commissioned Tamekane to compile the *Gyokuyōshū, the longest of the official collections (Tamekane seems to have felt it a do-or-die chance to get the poems of his group into a chokusenshū). Hanazono later ordered the *Fūgashū, another copious anthology. In compiling the former, Tamekane did not ignore the Nijō poets (he included some good poems by them) and, following tradition, he included many poems by earlier poets. But the lion's share went to Kyōgoku and Reizei adherents.

The characteristic Kyōgoku-Reizei poetry radically distinguishes between seasonal and love poems, the one tending to consist entirely of images, the other to be free of images. Both share emphasis on an intense moment relative to the speaker, a fact that makes the love poetry and its general language very difficult. The poets also experimented with unusual diction, with complex religious allegory that looks like seasonal description, and with zō poems that often effect a mean between seasonal and love poems. Or rather, since many of the set seasonal and love topics had become worn with use, the zō or miscellaneous category was one in which they could exercise considerable freedom. In making more of this category, they may have been influenced by renga practice, in which the category is the alternative to seasonal topics. Certainly the integration of these two official collections, like the hyakushuuta and other waka sequences they wrote, added renga techniques of distant and close relation between poems in the integrated flow.

In his major poetic treatise, Tamekane Kyō Wakashō 為兼卿和歌抄 (Lord Tamekane's Poetic Treatise, ca. 1287), he invoked the *Man'yōshū as a standard in a way often misunderstood. Apart from poems in that anthology having a range of diction in some ways different from the official waka collections that followed, it shared very little else with the extremely intense poetry that Tamekane and others were propounding. The main reason for invoking the authority of that now distant collection was simply that many of Tamekane's poetic principles could not be justified by existing waka canons. The very remoteness of the Man'yōshū made it convenient to evoke, as it had been earlier and would often be later, as justification of poetic styles that share little more than an archaism or two (like the occasional use of the old exclamation, kamo). A far more important influence on Tamekane's poetry and thought came from Zen Buddhism and the more recent Sung poets (such as Su Tung-p'o) whom the Zen masters were extolling. Under such exciting and perilous circumstances, Tamekane ushered into being the last truly great period of waka.

KYŌKAI. I.e., Keikai. See Nihon Ryōiki.

KYOKU SANJIN 曲山人. D. ?1840. Late Edo author of yomihon. Beginning as a graphic artist,

Sanjin became interested about 1827 in the yomihon and kusazōshi of writers like *Kyokutei Bakin. He specialized in writing about women, as in his first major work, Onna Daigaku 女大学 (The Greater Learning for Women, 1830; see *Kaibara Ekiken), and sometimes in the subject of military houses (like the oiemono of the theater), as in Kana Majiri Musume Setsuyō 仮名文章娘節用 (1831–1834). In a manner reminiscent of *Chikamatsu Monzaemon, he made much of the issue of giri and of the pathos of lovers' suicides. He shared popularity with *Tamenaga Shunsui, with whom he seemed to have invented a new fictional world. But as other works show, such as Musume Shōsoku 娘消息 (1834–1839), he was most concerned with the lives of Edo townspeople, especially townswomen, and the mores of their time. His period of writing his lengthy stories appears to have been the late years of his life. He showed an unusual temperament for understanding the place and problems of women in a society governed by a misogynistic official Confucian morality.

KYOKUTEI BAKIN 曲亭馬琴. 1767–1848. Late Edo writer of yomihon and kusazōshi. Bakin's learning and troubled life correspond to elements in the make-up of the other great author of prose narrative at the time, *Ueda Akinari. But he was more ambitious for his family, and had ambiguous attitudes toward the very art to which he devoted his energies and his eyesight. Many of these matters have been treated in Part One. What follows concerns his authorship.

Not to speak of various casual writings, this indefatigable writer was author of haikai, sharebon, kokkeibon, zuihitsu, and imitations of Chinese as well as Japanese classics. What might be termed his apprentice years (ignoring the doings of his youth) were marked by a collection of earlier haikai, Haikai Kobunko 俳諧古文庫 (A Little Haikai Library, 1787). Four years later, he brought out a kibyōshi, Tsukai Hatashite Nibu Kyōgen 尽用而二分狂言. From about 1803 to 1807, he published his first yomihon. Among five or six principal titles there are Sumidagawa Bairyū Shinsho 墨田川梅柳新書 (The Plum and the Willow by the Sumida River, 1807); and Sanshichi Zenden Nanka no Yume 三七全伝南柯夢 (The Complete Story of Osan and Hanshichi, 1808). Bakin was in full stride.

At this time he began the first of his four major works, (Chinsetsu) Yumiharizuki (椿説)弓張月 (The Crescent Moon). Drawing on Chinese plots (as he did so often) and on the life of Minamoto Tametomo (1139–1170), he wrote and wrote, bringing out this long work in 1811. Two years later, he had printed Beibei Kyōdan 皿皿郷談 (Talk in Rural Dialect), which draws on the *Ochikubo Monogatari, in a way casting its love plot into terms of karma. Although he was already at work on his longest and most famous creation, he began Kinseisetsu Bishōnenroku 近世説美少年録 (Golden

Youths in Recent Times) in 1828, and had it published six years later. In a fashion typical of his mature writing, this work draws on both a Chinese plot and a genuine native historical setting, featuring virtuous and villainous characters (here in particular the youths referred to in the title) and a rapid agitation of plot. It is by no means a short tale.

Bakin's masterpiece is usually thought to be the last major work he completed (*Nansō Satomi*) *Hakkenden* 南総里見八犬伝 (*The Story of Eight Virtuous Heroes*), which he worked on for almost twenty-five years (1814–1832). It consists in all of nine *shū* and ninety-eight parts (*kan:* see *gōkan; shū*). He resembles Balzac in that only he can be said to have read every word he wrote, and this work is one reason why that is so. *Hakkenden* is highly moral, and the contrast between good and evil characters is one of the few guides the reader has in a plot almost explosive with new events and sudden shifts. Chinese models, Japanese history, and an extraordinary gift for invention from them characterize the work.

Bakin had the energy of *Ihara Saikaku with a cramped sense of the world deriving from his own experiences of it. The rapid fluctuation of plot testifies to a need to achieve personal freedom within the cramping, but by the time he came to devote so many years to this long work, even he could probably not say whether the compulsion to write brought a sense of freedom from his afflictions or whether it was a symptom of them. It does seem clear that his chivalric world and heightened style provided him riches that his own straitened life was far from offering him. It should be emphasized that this and other mature works do not offer easy, Trollopian plots or episodic, disjointed stories like those in Dickens's *Pickwick Papers*, but rapid, complex, integrated narrative in a style constantly heightened, agitated. Whatever the rewards Bakin may have felt such art brought him, and they do not seem to be many, the cost in effort is as impressive in result as it is appalling in what it implies of his personal life.

KYORAI. See MUKAI KYORAI.

KYŌTAI. See KATŌ KYŌTAI.

KYŪSŌ. See MURO KYŪSŌ.

KYŪZAI (KYŪSEI, KAKEI). See GUSAI.

LADY NIJŌ. See GOFUKAKUSA IN NIJŌ.

MABUCHI. See KAMO NO MABUCHI.

MANTEI ŌGA 万亭応賀. 1818–1890. *Gesaku* writer. He is included here chiefly to represent the as yet insufficiently studied writers of prose fiction who bridge the late Edo and modern periods. None of his

work has a high reputation at present, but he is seldom read for proof. His work most often referred to—*Shaka Hassō Yamato Bunko* 釈迦八相倭文庫 —was published in fifty-eight parts from 1845 to the fourth year of the reign of Meiji (1871), well showing his historical position.

MAN'YŌSHŪ 万葉集 (*Collection of Ten Thousand Leaves*, or *for Ten Thousand Generations*). The oldest extant collection of Japanese poetry and the most highly revered today. It was compiled either in late Nara or possibly early Heian times from a variety of sources, including some otherwise lost collections. The dates of its earlier poets and poems are often not ascertainable, and many of its poets are shrouded in anonymity or lost by attribution of their work to greater poets. The period most certain and best represented is that from 600 to 759 (the last datable poem is from 759). The final compiler is thought to have been *Ōtomo Yakamochi, also one of the four principal poets included. It is organized into twenty books, a practice that seems to have set the usual number for most of the later, royal collections (*chokusenshū*). Unlike those later collections, the *Man'yōshū* is not ordered by topics for individual books. Topics sometimes prevail, but an attempt appears to have been made to adjust topics to chronology and kinds of poems. The result is somewhat haphazard, especially given the very large number of anonymous poems.

Out of some unknown number of early poems, the compilers included 265 *chōka*, 4,207 *tanka*, 62 *sedōka*, 1 *tanrenga*, 1 *bussokusekika*, 4 Chinese poems, and 22 passages of Chinese prose. There is no preface. The continental influence is felt in Taoist stories, in an occasional Confucian touch, in some Buddhist emphasis in later poems, in the ancestry of poets (many of whom were of continental extraction, it now seems), and in such classifications of poems as "poems in relation to things" (*mono ni yosete omoi o noburu uta*). It is therefore something of a paradox that Japanese regard the *Man'yōshū* to be particularly Japanese. They extol its forthrightness (*makoto*), its manliness (*masuraoburi*, although there are many female poets), and its Japanese purity. There is an important sense in which such attitudes are true. No subsequent collection derives as wholly from the Yamato homeland or is so largely Shinto in cast—so relatively free of Buddhist impact. Yet the most important fact about such beliefs is that Japanese should find it desirable to hold them. A portion (some say a third) of the nobility was then of Korean stock; and the culture—the new religion, sculpture, music, architecture, along with magical beliefs—came from Korea, even if the origins were Chinese. One of the few principal poets, *Yamanoe Okura, is called by some a third-generation Korean. Not only that, many of the highly extolled anonymous poems, such as the frontier-guard poems (*sakimori no uta*) as well as other poems by the humble were in fact collected, touched up, or even in fact written by sophisticated poets such as Yakamochi.

Yet this early collection has something of the freshness of dawn. Apart from the cumbersome *man'yōgana* in which the collection is set down, the language exerts a powerful appeal on the sentiment of readers, and not only on Japanese readers. There are irregularities not tolerated later, such as hypometric lines (*jitarazu*); there are evocative place names and *makurakotoba*; and there are evocative exclamations such as "kamo," whose appeal is genuine even if incommunicable. In other words, the collection combines the appeal of an art at its pristine source with a romantic sense of venerable age and therefore of an ideal order since lost. The older character of its language assists in giving this aura: later waka is written in a language closer to modern writing morphologically, phonologically, and in vocabulary.

It is now customary to divide the poetry of the collection into four periods. The first goes back to a legendary, prehistoric (or largely unverifiable) past to sovereigns such as Yūryaku (supposedly r. 456–479), and leads into the barely historical reign of Yōmei (r. 585–587), on to still shadowy rulers like Saimei (r. 665–661), and then, with *Tenji (r. 668–671), reaching historical assurance. The era of the Taika Reform (645) and of *Fujiwara Kamatari (614–669) shows the nation in full growth. Since the named poets of this period are of the highest nobility, we must conclude either that they excited such awe as to lead to the recording of their works above all others, or that literacy and culture had not yet spread widely. Perhaps both factors were involved.

The second period includes the last two decades or so of the seventh century, so coinciding with the period of presumed flourishing of *Kakinomoto Hitomaro, one of Japan's few greatest poets. In his handling, the chōka and its tanka envoys (*hanka*) integrate in sense, as also often in a continuous syntax, to deal with a wide variety of human experience in poems relatively lengthy.

The third period covers the first three decades of the eighth century. Most of the rest of the important poets appear then: *Yamabe Akahito, *Ōtomo Tabito, Okura, and so on. Akahito remains resolutely Japanese, which in his age costs some depth to retain the purity. Tabito and Okura are much happier in borrowing and refashioning elements from the continent—Tabito chiefly Taoist elements, Okura both Buddhist and Confucian. Such interests set Okura apart from contemporary poets.

The fourth period includes about three further decades (ca. 730–759), and includes the last really great poet of the collection, Yakamochi. As an editor, he was able to give full representation to his own poems and those of his circle. Opinions vary considerably as to the significance of his work. Most critics think his poetry, or at least that of the rest

of this fourth period, somewhat attenuated. Others rate his poetry more highly. Whatever one's opinion, this period and the second are dominated by a single important poet, whereas the third has several worth mentioning with those two, and the first none. But it should be stressed that there are also many, many anonymous poems, mostly tanka, of uncertain date; and that not a few of these are among the first to come to the mind of a Japanese thinking of "Man'yō poetry."

Five of the twenty books have no discernible system of classification. Among the remaining fifteen, no one system dominates. The three most consistently used terms to classify poems are: *zōka*, a capacious category of "miscellaneous poem" largely defined as not belonging to the other two; *sōmonka*, poems of intimate feeling, commonly on romantic love, but also on such other topics as parental love; and *banka*, elegies. The three categories are taken from Chinese classifications and do not always fit intelligibly in a given instance. On the other hand, much editorial work has gone into the collection. Headnotes and endnotes are often used, the former to indicate such things as authorship, title, and poetic kind. The endnotes are used for direct comment on a poem by the editors. Both within a poem and as subsequent alternatives, editors often give variant readings or the source in some earlier collection.

Japanese critics have said very little about one of the most conspicuous features of the *Man'yōshū*. In it alone do we discover Japanese poets writing easily on public topics such as war, policy, affairs of state, the discovery of gold, and historical events of other kinds. Such poems deal with what human beings share, whereas later poetry ranges from the private to the social, emphasizing what differentiates individuals or (more usually) unites them in small groups. Like the similes of Western epics, the *makurakotoba* enact the rites of a shared realm—a realm above the action and above ourselves, unlike the lower realms typical of Western similes. The "pillow-words" enable the poet and reader to share mutually in time, in world, and in humanity. The public achievement is greatest in chōka. The shorter poems range from the private to the social, like later waka.

Another feature of the chōka poetry is a narrative element, which tanka could achieve only in the quite different methods of relating in sequences with other tanka or by provision of prose contexts. There are, then, numerous reasons to believe with Japanese readers that there is something special about this "Collection of Ten Thousand Leaves."

MARUYAMA ŌKYO 円山応挙. 1733–1795. Mid-Edo painter. Although he began by studying Kanō school styles, influences from abroad led him to a new style at once delicate and realistic. He painted many kinds of subjects—human, botanical, animal, avian—with equal skill. Study of him reveals a great deal about enduring Japanese tastes and receptivity to outside examples.

MASAFUSA. See Ōe no Masafusa.

MASAKADO KI. See *Shōmonki.*

MASANOBU. See Kanō Masanobu.

MASUKAGAMI 増鏡 (*The Larger Mirror*) Namboku *rekishi monogatari* in three parts. Authorship is uncertain. The most likely candidate is *Nijō Yoshimoto, and the date of composition, 1368–1375, can be established from internal evidence, since it effectively begins with the birth of *Gotoba in 1170.

The preface uses the device familiar from earlier "mirror" works, the *Ōkagami, *Imakagami,* and *Mizu Kagami.* The narrator has gone to worship at a temple in Saga (northwest of Kyoto) and there meets a nun aged more than one hundred. She tells of historical events and legends that continue, in *monogatari* fashion, the history left off in the *Ima Kagami* at 1180, beginning a decade later and running to 1333. The first part begins with the artistic elegance of the rule and administration (after retirement) of *Gotoba. The later parts focus particularly on the reigns of Gosaga (r. 1242–1246), Gofukakusa (r. 1246–1259) and Kameyama (r. 1259–1274). The mid-Kamakura period is depicted not in terms of the government in Kamakura but of the royal court and its elegant doings.

The concluding part is especially interesting for its account of events following Godaigo's accession (1318). Various wars break out. The Hōjō regents (who had long since held the power nominally vested in the Minamoto shoguns at Kamakura) are temporarily overthrown. Godaigo rallies forces to plot a restoration of court rule. These are defeated in turn, and Godaigo is exiled. The work ends before his return to the capital from exile. Although no effort is spared to tell of cultural activity, many individual tragedies are shown, as Japan lurches toward yet greater disorder. Coherence is going and the world is on the verge of anarchy, tyranny, or both.

The author drew on a number of historical and poetic sources, and is particularly indebted to the three "mirrors" that precede this one. As the fourth, it completes a set of four histories (shiki), a group often compared to the earlier Chinese counterpart, reminding us that history as well as lyric are included in East Asian conceptions of literature. A special feature of its style is the *renga*-like associative connections of one unit with its predecessor. There are two hundred *waka*. Without question, the *Ōkagami* and this are the finest of the four "mirrors." With the *Eiga Monogatari* they comprise the greatest rekishi monogatari of the court. They are excelled as historical writings only by the rather different *Heike Monogatari,* which had among its resources most of these works—and a superior style.

MASUMI. See Sugae Masumi.

MATSUDAIRA SADANOBU 松平定信. 1758–1829. Late Edo *zuihitsu* writer, politician. A member of a branch of the Tokugawa family and of the *bakufu*'s council of elders (rōjū), he pursued a series of activities between 1787 and 1793 intended to improve the state. At first largely intellectual, his effort became more political and economic. This Kansei Reform was a conservative and moral reaction to the libertarian but corrupt government promoted by Tanuma Okitsugu. Sadanobu was a *waka* poet and calligrapher as well as essayist, leaving behind numerous writings. The most surprising of them is, of all things, a *gesaku* piece, *Daimyō Katagi* 大名気質 (*Portrait of a Daimyo:* see *katagimono* for the strangeness of the title). Not only is this like works he was suppressing but it is also—a final paradox—excellent of its kind. It seems that Sadanobu also sought the assistance of *Santō Kyōden (who had suffered as an artist from the Kansei Reform). One explanation is that Sadanobu gradually relaxed his puritanical attitudes, coming to enjoy (whether or not approve) what he had once sought to repress. But the early date of his *Portrait* suggests a long-standing ambivalence.

MATSUE SHIGEYORI 松江重頼. 1602–1680. Early Edo *haikai* poet, one of the seven worthies of *Teimon* haikai. He lived in Kyoto as a merchant and as a poet of increasing fame. In 1633 he compiled a collection of Teimon haikai in seventeen parts, *Enoko Shū* 犬子集 (*Puppy Renga*). His *Kefukigusa* 毛吹草 (1638, 1647) contains, in addition to more than two thousand stanzas, a codification of seasonal words, instructions on *hokku, tsukeku, tsukeai,* and so on, and is a principal source for knowledge about distinctive features of Teimon haikai. His own poetry is not rated all that highly today, but these were the formative years for haikai, with developments occurring rapidly. Shigeyori had an eye for what was going on and contributed to the direction events were taking. So it is that his *Futokorogo* 懐子 (1660) includes some early *Danrin* poetry and his *Sayo no Nakayama Shū* 佐夜中山集 (1664) prints the first published poetry by *Matsuo Bashō.

MATSUKURA RANRAN 松倉嵐蘭. 1647–1693. Early Edo *haikai* poet. He was a samurai but later left service to devote himself to haikai, living in the Asakusa area of Edo. With *Enomoto Kikaku and *Hattori Ransetsu, he is one of *Matsuo Bashō's three most important Edo adherents. He followed Bashō's styles from about 1675, and in that year was published as a disciple of Bashō (Tōsei was then Bashō's pen name) in a collection of twenty solo *kasen*. He participated in kasen in *Minashiguri*, and the kasen in **Sarumino* as well as in the *hokku* section there. (See Part Six for haikai collections.) Bashō appreciated his forthright honesty and wrote a memorial on his death.

MATSUNAGA TEITOKU 松永貞徳. 1571–1653. Early Edo *waka*, *renga*, and *haikai* poet, student of earlier literature. Born in Kyoto and the son of a renga master, he studied under some of the most famous poets of the day, including *Satomura Jōha, *Hosokawa Yūsai, and Kujō Tanemichi. Although best known today as the founder of *Teimon* haikai, most of his life was spent in other occupations. He served for a time as secretary for Toyotomi Hideyoshi. After the Tokugawa regime was established, he turned to waka and its study. Without really realizing it, he laid the foundations of haikai by popularizing it, making it available to people of moderate education in the *kamigata* cities.

He had, above all, a love of words that took him at times to *kyōka* and to verbal connections (*kotobazuke*) between stanzas of linked poetry. He and his age moved together, turning to haikai in the last two decades or so of his life. From his *Gosan* 御傘 (*Haikai Usages*, 1651) onward, he propounded the canons of his style of haikai, which he exemplified in such collections as *Matsue Shigeyori's *Enoko Shū*. By his death, Teimon haikai was firmly established. The other important haikai schools (*Danrin, Shōfū*) were begun by those who started in his style and then paid him the compliment of opposition. Today the verbal play of Teimon haikai seems overdone, but by mastering words the poets of an age were able thereafter to master conception. His waka collection, *Shōyū Gushō* 逍遊愚抄 (*The Rambles of a Fool*) appeared in 1677.

MATSU NO HA 松の葉 (*Pine Needles*). Ca. 1703. One of the principal, and the first, of musical collections, chiefly of varieties of *kayō* for *shamisen*. Its five parts include song kinds such as *nagauta*, *hauta*, and *Azuma jōruri*. Compilation is credited to one Shūshōken.

MATSUO BASHŌ 松尾芭蕉. 1644–1694. Early Edo poet, critic, prose writer—Japan's best loved author. He was born at Ueno in Iga (Mie). Near the time of his father's death, he entered the service of Yoshitada, the third son of the local samurai lord and only two years older than he. They studied *Teimon* haikai and other matters under the eminent poet-scholar, *Kitamura Kigin. From 1666, when Yoshitada died, Bashō's doings are uncertain for about six years, but he did become familiar with *Danrin* haikai. Very probably he spent time in the capital. Some say that, while in Kyoto, he lived with a woman known by her later religious name Jutei,

who later visited him in Edo with a child or two that may or may not have been his.

He moved to Edo about 1672, seeking to make his way as a poet. By 1680 he gained recognition when he had published a solo *kasen* each by "Twenty Disciples of Tōsei," Tōsei being the pen name he used at the time. The twenty include *Enomoto Kikaku, *Sugiyama Sampū, and *Matsukura Ranran. Among other activities that year, he settled into his first Bashōan, or Banana-Plant Hut, from which he derived the style by which he is best known. In 1682, this hut in Fukagawa was suddenly swallowed in flame and he barely escaped with his life. Although it was later rebuilt on the spot, many attribute to this event a lasting seriousness, and a growing tendency to write of life in relation to death. For that or other reasons, his poetry steadily took on greater depth. And although he never rivaled the Teimon or Danrin schools in popularity, his seriousness was widely recognized.

In 1683 appeared the first major collection of the Bashō school, Shōfū, or Shōmon. This collection was *Minashiguri* 虚栗 (*The Hollowed Chestnuts*), one of seven of what might be called the canonical collections of the school (see Part Six F). This was very much an Edo collection in the identity of its poets, especially in the lively figure of Kikaku, Bashō's first and greatest follower—if the honor for greatness does not go to *Nozawa Bonchō. Bashō's literary interests at the time are also more evident than they would be later. These include *Saigyō and *Sōgi among earlier Japanese poets, and with them Tu Fu, Po Chü-i, Li Po, and "Han-shan" among Chinese. Tu Fu and the prose *Chuang-tzu* then provided by far the most important Chinese writings for him.

In 1684–1685 he visited his native Iga Ueno. This led to one of the travel accounts in which he excelled, *Nozarashi Kikō* 野ざらし紀行 (*The Moor-Exposed Skeleton Diary*) or *Kasshi Ginkō* 甲子吟行 (*Journey of Haikai Composition in 1685*). From there he continued his journey, stopping in Nagoya, which was then a major cultural center rivaling, if at a little distance, *kamigata* and Edo. In a short while during the winter of 1684, he and a number of Nagoya poets composed a number of sequences. On the evidence of the five kasen selected to make up his next major collection, *Fuyu no Hi* 冬の日 (*A Day in Winter*), this was one of the most fruitful moments of his career. Going back to Edo, he was soon restlessly off on various journeys, including those recorded in *Oi no Kobumi* 笈の小文 (*Essay from a Traveler's Book-Satchel*, 1687) and *Sarashina Kikō* 更科紀行 (*A Journey to Sarashina*, 1688). The later is wonderfully written. The former holds particular interest for its comment on his art of haikai and what he terms diaries of the road (michi no nikki), explicitly setting these prose works interspersed with *hokku* in the tradition of poetic diaries going back to *Ki no Tsurayuki's *Tosa Nikki* (ca. 935). By the autumn of 1688, he was again in Edo. Early the next year, another major collection was published, *Arano* 阿羅野 (*The Uncleared Fields*). In the spring he set out on the longest of these foot journeys, accompanied much of the way by Iwanami Sora.

A major part of this trip is covered by his greatest prose writing, *Oku no Hosomichi* 奥の細道 (*The Narrow Road through the Provinces*).This deals with the journey from Edo northward up the Pacific coast, across the inland mountains to the Japan Sea coast, south along that coast, and then again across the island. Bashō actually continued much farther, but the account ends with him in Mino (Gifu), thinking of Ise. (His habit of revising extended from poetry to prose in this instance, and only death really brought an end to the process. The work was not published till eight years after his death, 1702). Sora kept a more factual diary, comparison with which has shown how Bashō heightens, omits, changes, or simply makes things up. Although no one would wish away any part of this splendid work, everyone agrees on certain passages as highlights: the opening prose poem on time, the sections on Matsushima, Hiraizumi, Kisagata, and that on the prostitutes at Ichiburi. This last is entirely fictional. It is now clear that the design underlying this work is that of a *kasen*, so that the fictional encounter with prostitutes corresponds to love stanzas that might be expected at that point. The passage on Hiraizumi is rich with historical resonance and poetry, both fusing in the recollection that Saigyō had been there five centuries earlier. At Japan's greatest beauty-spot, Matsushima, Bashō says that he will write no *hokku*. Actually he did, but it is not up to the prose or the place, so that he omitted his verses and drew instead on the haikai conception of a blank or space (ma): a so-to-speak nonpoem poem to celebrate the place.

Perhaps with some suggestions from Bashō himself, *Mukai Kyorai divided the last fourteen years of Bashō's career into three periods. The first began with the famous hokku on a crow perching on a withered branch. This period ended, Kyorai said, with the journey of *Oku no Hosomichi*. The second period began in 1689, with yet another visit to Iga Ueno. From there he went to the capital, staying first with Kyorai in Saga and then in the Ōmi (Shiga) area. Early in 1690, he walked off once more to his old home, then again to Ōmi, composing the while poetry included in *Hisago* ひさご (*The Gourd*, 1690), another important collection. One of his followers, Suganuma Kyokusui, had inherited from an uncle the Unreal Hermitage (Genjūan) in Ishiyama near Lake Biwa. Bashō more or less made the place his headquarters during the latter half of 1690, a very satisfying period to him. He traveled around the area, visiting famous places. He stayed a while with Kyorai, as recorded in his *Saga Nikki* 嵯峨日記 (*A Saga Diary*, 1691). There was a steady stream of visitors, some from far away, especially to

the hermitage in Ishiyama. During this time, Kyorai and Bonchō (with Bashō also involved) were compiling what would become the most famous collection of the school, *Sarumino* 猿蓑 (*The Monkey's Straw Raincoat*, 1691).

These first two periods, a total of ten years (1680–1689), were governed primarily by an ideal Bashō termed *sabi*. One major explanation holds that the sabi ideal implies stillness; another that it involves deterioration. Perhaps both are involved, and with them, or as part of them, the posing of one element against another that is different, typically something relatively high in estimation, such as we expect from *waka* and *renga*, against something lower or humbler than they provide. It is an ideal producing an art that is very difficult to achieve, and yet more difficult to maintain. That may be one reason why Bashō altered his style in his last period (1691–1694).

The new style is referred to as having lightness, *karumi*, a metaphor for which there has been no great agreement as to signification, beyond the fact that it implies a release of some of the tension, a greater simplicity. It seems likely that this may represent a further move from Danrin styles (especially in their use of allusion, both *honkadori* and *honzetsu*), perhaps less irregularity in sequences (that is in stanzaic connection, *tsukeai*), but principally reduction of the complex tensions of the hokku. Bashō's fame had so grown in these later years that he found himself composing far more sequences than he had earlier. A simpler art made the business easier. Another way of putting it, however, is that the karumi ideal is predominantly a kasen ideal. Or that the sabi ideal had been one for which hokku, kasen, and prose were each striking claimants.

In 1692 the third Bashō-an was built. The next year Bashō retired to it for a time to get some rest. Long seclusion was impossible, however, since there were many who wanted to talk with the famous old poet. There were also his own irresistible urges. Everywhere he went, he was the great poet, the Old Master. And almost everywhere he was expected to participate in writing sequences. So it was that two more collections appeared quickly: *Fukagawa* 深川 (1693) and *Sumidawara* 炭俵 (*A Sack of Charcoal*, 1694).

This brings us to the last year of his life. Kikaku and Bonchō—his two greatest followers—had now deserted his school. Bonchō's motives are not wholly clear. Kikaku did not take at all to the *karumi* ideal, and maybe the long absences from Edo simply encouraged him to go his own way. But Bashō had no lack of admirers. In this last year he met many of them as he set out on what he thought would be his longest trip, perhaps even to southern Kyushu. As always, he was ready to die on the road, and this time he did. He got no farther than Osaka where, on the twelfth of the eleventh month his journey in this world ended. By the end of the year, his followers past and present prepared a memorial volume, *Kareobana* 枯尾花 (*Withered Pampas Plumes*). In 1698 the last of the seven major shōfū collections appeared. This was *Zoku Sarumino* 続猿蓑 (*The Monkey's Straw Raincoat, Continued*), and like the memorial volume it was edited by Kikaku, who obviously retained warm memories of the Old Master.

Bashō's reputation has had its vicissitudes. But in the generations since his death, Japanese of all persuasions and conditions have constantly held him in highest esteem and affection. Like Saigyō, he has often been sentimentalized and distorted. In spite of certain limitations in him or his work, and in spite of misplaced admiration, his place is secure. His work is not as copious as one might expect, since he kept revising to perfect and often reused a given hokku (for example) in different contexts. This desire to make right sets him off from major figures in the rival schools, and is part of his total seriousness in respect to his art. The deterioration of haikai immediately following his death shows that his own greatness was a necessary source of the greatness in others. In an age of political rigidity and control, his sense of time, suffering, and death led him to combine—with a skill no other lyric poet has shown—the high and the low, the objective with the subjective, the commonplace with the tragic. These combinations are well suggested by his remark that he was half priest and half layman. Much of our knowledge about him derives from Kyorai and *Hattori Dohō. Much of our knowledge of our world and ourselves may be derived from *his* writing.

MIBU NO TADAMINE 壬生忠岑. Fl. 898–920. Early Heian *waka* poet, compiler, one of the thirty-six worthies of waka (sanjūrokkasen), father of the almost homophonous Tadami. Tadamine emerged as an important poet in one of the early poetry matches, *Koresada no Miko no Ie no Utaawase* 是貞親王家歌合 (*The Poetry Match at Prince Koresada's Residence*, by 893). Thereafter he was involved in the poetic developments of his age, culminating in his participation in the compiling of the first official collection, the *Kokinshū.

There are various versions of his personal collection, *Tadamine Shū*, running from 60 to 185 poems, making the canon uncertain. A work called *Wakatei Jusshu* 和歌体十種 (*The Ten Waka Styles*) or *Tadamine Juttei* 忠岑十体 (*Tadamine's Ten Styles*) appeared in 945 and exercised considerable influence on subsequent Heian criticism. He is an accomplished but not a great or prolific poet (as far as his known canon attests)—one of the second rank among the poets represented in the *Kokinshū*.

MICHICHIKA. See TSUCHIMIKADO MICHICHIKA.

MICHIKATSU. See NAKANOIN MICHIKATSU.

MICHINAGA. See FUJIWARA MICHINAGA.

MICHITOSHI. See FUJIWARA MICHITOSHI.

MICHITSUNA NO HAHA. See FUJIWARA MICHITSUNA NO HAHA.

MICHIZANE. See SUGAWARA MICHIZANE.

MIKOHIDARI POETS. See FUJIWARA SHUNZEI.

MINAMI SHINJI 南新二. 1835–1895. Although chiefly regarded as an early modern writer of "novels" and as a theater critic, the humorous dimension in some of his work exemplifies the retention of Edo fiction in the new age.

MINAMOTO SANETOMO 源実朝. 1192–1219. Early Kamakura *waka* poet. While yet a child, he lost his father, Minamoto Yoritomo, first shogun of the Kamakura *bakufu*. In 1203, on the death of his brother Yoriie, he became the third shogun. With the death of his father, however, the government was riven with division exploited by the Hōjō family, which, in the name of advisors, came to rule the shoguns and the country. There were signs of trouble in the provinces as well. Sanetomo seems to have turned from such frustrations to find relief in the court and its arts (as well as in drink). During 1218 and 1219 he acquired a series of ever more impressive court titles. He married into a court family and took up waka, court music, and court kickball. At only twenty-seven, he was assassinated by political rivals.

Sanetomo's waka has been so extravagantly praised in Japan that balanced assessment is difficult. In any event, his personal collection is the *Kinkai Wakashū* 金槐和歌集. One version has 663 poems, another 53 more. From other sources more poems can be added to a total of 753, a good-sized collection. One analysis divides these into 60 in the style of the *Man'yōshū*, 662 in the style of the later official collections, and 27 in his own style. The first group has been given unrestrained praise, the second reproof. Both are pretty insipid, with occasional signs of experimentation and infrequent signs of success. His real poetry comes with the small last group, showing that his assassination cut short the promise of very fine poetry, and such a loss seems wholly of a piece with his tragic life.

MINAMOTO SHITAGŌ 源順. 911–983. Early Heian *waka* poet, scholar; one of the *sanjūrokkasen*. In contrast to his middling career at court, he became well known as a scholar and poet. While only in his twenties, he compiled the *Wamyō* (*Ruijū*) *Shō* 和名 (類聚) 鈔 (ca. 931–937), which combines features of a dictionary and an encyclopedia, the first such work to appear in Japan. In 952, he was included among the Five Men of the Pear-Jar Room, who compiled the second official collection, the *Gosenshū*. His poems appear there, in various later *chokusenshū*, and in his *Minamoto Shitagō Shū* (by 983). He was also an important early scholar, a student of the *Man'yōshū*, and a composer in Chinese, getting pieces into *Honchō Monzui* and other collections. A number of works have been ascribed to him, although his authorship of them is no longer accepted: *Kokinrokujō*, *Utsuho Monogatari*, and *Ochikubo Monogatari*. His waka are not without appeal, more for their diction than their conception. He is part of a generation that consolidated the new poetry of the *Kokinshū* and the systematic poetics by *Ki no Tsurayuki.

MINAMOTO SHUNRAI (or TOSHIYORI) 源俊頼. ?1055–?1129. Late Heian *waka* poet, critic, compiler. Like his father, *Minamoto Tsunenobu, he was a major force in the practice and acceptance of new descriptive styles in the face of conservative opposition. Unlike his father, he did not rise to high rank, and was eccentric.

The first four decades of his life were spent in Kyushu, where his father was governor. Around 1094, he joined the court of Horikawa (r. 1086–1107) as musician and poet. In the ten years following his father's death in 1092, he led a group of innovative writers at Horikawa's court, taking a strong stand against his archrival, *Fujiwara Mototoshi. He participated in, and judged at, various poetry matches. About 1104 he completed his *Horikawa Hyakushu* 堀河百首 (*A One Hundred-Poem Sequence of The Horikawa Palace*). From the age of about fifty-five to his death, he faithfully promoted his literary ideals, often clashing with Mototoshi, as at the *Naidaijin no Ie no Utaawase* 内大臣家歌合 (*A Poetry Match at the Palace of the Minister of the Center*), where the two were judges. Some of his poems really are odd, and sometimes he did not behave as people expected. But he was a genuine poet, and so great a critic as *Fujiwara Shunzei looked on Shunrai even more than on Shunrai's father as his most important predecessor.

His persistence won him the reward of a commission by Horikawa to compile a *chokusenshū*, the *Kin'yōshū*, but the two found trouble in agreeing. Three versions in four years were required, and at that there are but 716 poems in ten books. His own collection, *Samboku Kikashū* 散木奇歌集 (*Irregular Poems by a Useless Man*) is longer: ten books with 1,622 poems. Both the official and the private collection have humdrum pieces; but both also contain the most original, the truest poetry of the time, and his poetic treatise, *Shunrai Zuinō* 俊頼髄脳 (*Shunrai's Poetic Essentials*, ?1115) is of great importance.

MINAMOTO TAKAKUNI. See *Konjaku Monogatari*.

MINAMOTO TOSHIYORI. See Minamoto Shunrai.

MINAMOTO TSUNENOBU 源経信. 1016–1097. Late Heian *waka* poet, critic. From his late title as Acting Governor of Kyushu (Dazaifu no Gon no Sochi) and his court title (Dainagon), he was known as the Grand Counsellor Governor (Sochi Dainagon). This explains why his two personal collections are titled *Dainagon Tsunenobu Shū* 大納言経信集 and *Sochi Dainagon Shū* 帥大納言集. As the titles, and his long life, suggest, he was active in court affairs over a long period. He was variously as well as greatly talented. He had unusual musical ability, excelling on the lute (biwa) and in playing wind instruments, as well. He was skilled in Chinese composition, participating in the *Eijō Rokunen Jishin Shiawase* 永承六年侍臣詩合 (*The 1051 Match of Chinese Poems by His Majesty's Attendants*) and other matches of Chinese poems.

Although he gave it up late in life, his best work was in waka, where his style of description, rich in suggestion, was the most original of his time. He was quite at odds with the conservative and choleric *Fujiwara Michitoshi, and attacked Michitoshi's official collection, the *Goshūishū*, in his *Nan Goshūi* 難後拾遺 (*Faulting the Goshuishū*, 1097). He also left behind a diary, *Sochiki* 帥記 (*The Tsukushi Governor's Diary*). Few of his poems were included in contemporary official collections, but as tastes caught up with his own, his poems were often included in later collections and praised especially for their loftiness of conception and style. It is difficult to think of any other person so well suited as he to be the ideal of a late Heian courtier.

MINAMOTO YORIMASA 源頼政. 1104–1180. Late Heian poet, military figure. His contemporary reputation as a poet—a gift by which he is said to have gained his high status in the third court rank—has not survived, although (or because) we do have his personal collection, (*Minamoto*) *Genzammi Yorimasa Kyō Shū* 源三位頼政卿集 (*The Collection of Lord Minamoto Yorimasa of the Third Rank*). The most famous anecdote concerning him is that of his ridding the court of an infestation of birds called "nue" (one translation is "tiger thrush"), whose night call, "Hyō-hyō," was thought extremely depressing. Similar success did not attend his political and military ventures, and he left this world by taking his own life.

MINAMOTO YOSHITSUNE 源義経. 1159–1189. Not to be confused with *Fujiwara Yoshitsune. Late Heian, early Kamakura military figure and legendary hero. It is difficult to separate history from legend. But it is clear that he was one of the greatest generals in the *Gempei wars, defeating the Heike forces at Ichinotani, Yashima, and Dannoura. In the *Heike Monogatari* these exploits are related from the Heike-Kyoto perspective. The story is told with a Genji emphasis in the *Gikeiki*, taking it to Yoshitsune's defeat and suicide along the Koromo River at Hiraizumi. *Matsuo Bashō recalls this ending in a famous section of *Oku no Hosomichi*, and the Yoshitsune legends—including his loyal retainer Benkei and his mistress Shizuka— became topics for *nō, jōruri, kabuki*, and narrative retellings. From one of his offices, Yoshitsune was known as *hōgan* and, given his affecting story, the term *hōgan biiki* ("sympathy with the Lieutenant") has been used to describe the Japanese penchant to identify emotionally with the failed hero—a category that also includes such individuals as the mythical Yamato Takeru, *Sugawara Michizane, Shizuka, Kusunoki Masashige (d. 1336), and Saigō Takamori (1827–1877). No one has ever thought of applying the term to his successful brother, Minamoto Yoritomo, who is more or less an off-stage villain in most accounts centering on Yoshitsune.

MINASE SANGIN HYAKUIN 水無瀬三吟百韻 (*A Hundred Stanzas by Three Poets at Minase*). Mid-Muromachi hundred-stanza *renga* sequence composed in the early spring of 1488 at Minase. The three poets are *Sōgi (hokku)*, *Shōhaku (waki)*, and *Sōchō (daisan, ageku)*. The sequence was composed for presentation at the shrine of *Gotoba, who had come to be venerated as a protecting divinity of poetry. Sōgi's opening stanza beautifully alludes to Gotoba's most famous poem, on a spring evening at Minase. Although this is the most famous renga sequence, Sōchō mars it at several points by a subjectivity that is moralizing or sentimental. His language has an aural beauty like that of *waka*, something that may be thought a more venial offense. The splendid work by Sōgi and Shōhaku have given the sequence its fame (along with some few excellent stanzas by Sōchō). Stanzas 1–8 and 51–78 are of outstanding excellence, exemplary of the sequential art of renga.

MINCHŌ 明兆. 1352–1431. Early Muromachi priest, painter. He worked in the styles of Sung and Mongol dynasty painting, doing a great deal of work at the temple Tōfukuji. Also called Chō Densu 兆殿司.

MITSUKUNI. See Tokugawa Mitsukuni.

MITSUNE. See Ōshikōchi Mitsune.

MITSUHIRO. See Karasuma Mitsuhiro.

MIURA BAIEN 三浦梅園. 1723–1789. Mid-Edo intellectual. Born in Bungo, he crossed Kyushu to Nagasaki for study of Neoconfucian and Western thought. He sought a logic that would explain the order of the cosmos, and among his voluminous writings, he treated philosophy, ethics, religion, education, history, politics, economics, medicine, and other subjects. Those other include even literature, but he is really more a polymath than a literary figure.

MIURA CHORA 三浦樗良. 1729–1780. Mid-Edo *haikai* poet. A leader among Ise haikai poets, he is a quite prolific example of the poets associated with the Haikai Revival, which is usually thought in terms of poets more able than he—*Yosa Buson, *Takai Kitō, *Katō Kyōtai, and so on.

MIYAKO NO NISHIKI 都の錦. B. 1675. Early Edo *ukiyozōshi* writer. After going to Kyoto for study, he moved to Osaka, where he worked on ukiyozōshi under *Nishizawa Ippū. Early in the eighteenth century he brought out a series of stories, among them *Genroku Taiheiki* 元禄太平記, *Genroku Soga Monogatari* 元禄曽我物語, *Gozen Otogi Bōko* 御前御伽婢子. Not without skill, the stories show his knowledge of earlier literature (Genroku era redoings of the *Soga Monogatari* and *Taiheiki*), and give him a place in the development of Edo fiction. But his work is marred by tendencies to disorganization, pedantry, and self-advertisement. Finding literature a stern mistress, he moved to Edo in search of a better life. The end of his life is obscure where it is not depressing.

MIYAMOTO MUSASHI 宮本武蔵. D. 1645. Early Edo swordsman and painter. His style of fencing was variously referred to, usually as the Nitō style, but later he was regarded as founder of the Niten school. He traveled around Japan in search of lore and to inculcate his ideas, acquiring a reputation also for his painting, an art for which he had considerable talent. His modern fame is fortuitous, resting both on the very long novel with his name as title by the popularizer of military heroes, Yoshikawa Eiji (d. 1962) and on publication of his book on military matters, *Gorinsho* 五輪書 (*A Book of Five Rings*), as if it were a handbook to business success.

MIZU KAGAMI 水鏡 (*The Water Mirror*). Late Heian or early Kamakura *rekishi monogatari* in three parts. Possibly by (Fujiwara) Nakayama Tadachika (藤原)中山忠親 (1131–1195). Modeled on the *Ōkagami* and *Ima Kagami*, this work does not, however, present a historical sequence beginning, as might have been expected given the sequence of composition, where the *Ima Kagami* stops. But in effect it provides a context for the earlier works by going back to the legendary first sovereign, Jimmu, and on to the death of the fifty-fourth (and historical) Nimmyō (r. 833–850).

The style is very literary, and once more is told by a prodigiously aged teller. This one was born in the age of the gods: Jimmu supposedly reigned 660–585 B.C. The scene of telling is again near Hasedera. The technique has grown more annalistic, as if to offset the fundamental incredibility of such a narrator. The tone is highly idealistic. The combination works, as numerous implicit and explicit criticisms further show, to set off the wondrous past from the present, when the court's power is being taken by warrior houses infiltrating it or dominating the provinces.

MOKUAMI. See KAWATAKE MOKUAMI.

MOMOSUMOMO もゝすもゝ (*Peaches and Plums*). A mid-Edo collection of two thirty-six-stanza *haikai* sequences. Each was written by *Yosa Buson with *Takai Kitō; there is a preface by Buson. The two *kasen* are *Botan Chitte no Maki* 牡丹散っての巻 (*Peony Petals Fell*) and *Fuyu Kodachi no Maki* 冬木だちの巻 (*The Wintry Wood*). The sequences are exceptional in having been composed over a period of eight months in 1780 rather than at single sittings. A few stanzas had been used before. In both stanza sequences, as in Buson's preface, there is no lack of wit and humor. Moreover, the individual stanzas are of uncommon brilliance, even when low in tone or formal impressiveness. But the stanzaic connectedness (*tsukeai*) tends to be minimal, showing a breakdown in the spirit of haikai as sequential poetry, even in the hands of the most gifted of eighteenth-century Japanese poets, Buson.

MONZEN 文選. A Chinese collection (*Wen Hsüan*) covering a millennium of writing beginning with the Chou dynasty. It was known comparatively early in Japan, and provided models for composition in prose, rhyme prose or fu 賦, and verse. Although it is not integrated on the aesthetic principles of Japanese anthologies, its categories were influential, and it sometimes served as a model collection, as obviously for *Fūzoku Monzen.*

MORITAKE. See ARAKIDA MORITAKE.

MORONOBU. See HISHIKAWA MORONOBU.

MOSUI. See TODA MOSUI.

MOTONOBU. See KANŌ MOTONOBU.

MOTOORI NORINAGA 本居宣長. 1730–1801. Late Edo *waka* poet and, above all, the greatest *kokugaku* scholar. Born in Ise, he moved here and there as result of family changes and, having decided at last to make a living as a doctor, he went to Kyoto for study in 1752. Although the details of those years would make a novel, the dry facts are that in addition to pursuing amusement and medicine he found time for Confucianism and the *Keichū kind of

kokugaku. He made the important decision of picking literature as his special interest. In 1757 he returned to his birthplace, Matsuzaka in Ise, to practice medicine. How he found time to teach, much less to study, remains something of a mystery—but he did. At first the students drawn to his lectures were mostly from that cradle of learning, Ise. They heard him on the *Genji Monogatari*, *Man'yōshū*, *Kokinshū*. *Shinkokinshū*, *Ise Monogatari*, as well as much else.

He was so prolific that we can only assume that he, like Aristotle, published the results of work done by him with his students' aid, a custom still alive in Japan. But he was the magnet that came to draw serious people from all over Japan, and by the time he died he had five hundred followers. He stamped his work not so much by learning, although he had that, as by the originality of his questions, his approach. In fact, he was unusual in often teaching through questions rather than by lecture. After his death, students brought out an example of his dialectical method, *Suzunoya Tōmonroku* 鈴屋答問録 (*A Compilation of Norinaga's Answers*, 1835), "Suzunoya" being the name for the family business; this name also entered into the title of the best known of his poetic collections, *Suzunoya Shū* 鈴屋集 (1798). He is not so important as a poet, and it goes without saying that many of his works are not read today and that most of us come to our knowledge of him second-hand. It is enough to say that 260 volumes on ninety-one subjects are credited to him. Years after his death, his books—completed by others—continued to appear. A few of his best-known studies may be mentioned.

His *Isonokami Sasamegoto* 石上私淑言 (*Murmurings of Old Things*, 1692) is a poetic treatise presented in dialogue, or spoken, form. He contrasts Japanese with Chinese poetry, concerns himself with diction and calligraphy, examines the treatment of love in *waka*, the relation between waka and virtue, and so on. *Kotoba no Tama no O* 詞の玉の緒 (*Beads of Jeweled Words*, composed 1779) deals chiefly with the *hachidaishū*, the first eight royal waka collections, from which the practice of earlier linguistic usage is defined.

Two studies deal with the two most important of the royal collections and were completed in 1792: *Kokinshū Tōkagami* 古今集遠鏡 (*A Long View on the Kokinshū*) and, with its difficult title, *Shinkokinshū Mino no Iezuto Dō Orisoe* 新古今集美濃廼家苞同折添. Norinaga's methods in the two studies differ as much from each other as from approaches by earlier scholars. The *Kokinshū* provided the conspicuous model for poetic language, but it was now so "distant," as his title says, that it required nearer reflection. As part of that enterprise, he discussed all that collection except the Chinese preface and the *chōka* that appear in part 19. But above all, he offered for the first time paraphrases in the ordinary language of his time. In the *Shinko-*

kinshū study (printed 1795), he selected six hundred poems for commentary, ranging through other collections for evidence and, in unprecedented fashion, presented his own commentary without attention to his predecessors.

In *Genji Monogatari Tama no Ogushi* 源氏物語玉の小櫛 (*A Little Jeweled Comb of the Genji Monogatari*, written 1793–1796), he concerns himself at length with correction of earlier scholarship. But the first two of the nine parts are devoted to his positive interpretation, explaining the work in terms of *mono no aware* (see also *Murasaki Shikibu), a thesis propounded earlier in *Shibun Yōryō* 紫文要領 (*Essentials of Murasaki Shikibu's Writing*, 1763).

Uiyamabumi 初山踏 (*First Steps up the Mountain*, completed 1798) is that rare thing, a Japanese book on methods of study, offering as well the principles of a great teacher. The idea for the treatise apparently occurred to Norinaga as he was finishing some early portion of *Kojikiden* 古事記伝 (*Commentary on the Kojiki*, fully published only in 1822). His usual method is to begin with general or miscellaneous remarks, then go on to a full range of textual, linguistic, and other matters. Nothing on such a scale had been known in kokugaku before.

Yet another posthumous work, *Tama Katsuma* 玉勝間 (*The Beautiful Basket*, 1801; pub. 1812) is more often known first hand and probably represents the peak of his literary creation. It is a relaxed miscellany of hundreds of shorter or longer units for which *zuihitsu* is the inevitable, agreeable Japanese label. For once Norinaga puts his own thoughts (rather than the works of others) at the center, allowing himself a prose style of a consistent beauty he had not shown otherwise. The humanity as well as beauty of this work is probably the most attractive tribute he left to the world, and to himself.

MOTOTOSHI. See Fujiwara Mototoshi.

MUJŪ 無住. 1226–1312. Mid-Kamakura priest, author of *setsuwa* and *kana hōgo*. Scion of the ill-fated Kajiwara family, Mujū took the tonsure in his teens under Tendai auspices. After broad exposure to the varieties of Buddhist thought and practice, he allied himself with Rinzai Zen, following a brief encounter with the eclectic *Enni. Doctrinal accommodation is a major theme of his writings. From 1262 until his death, Mujū lived at the Chōboji, a small temple near Atsuta Shrine in what is now Nagoya. His popular didacticism is illustrated with commonplace, often humorous, anecdotes. The setsuwa collection, *Shasekishū* 沙石集 (*Sand and Pebbles*, 1279–1283), is his earliest and best-known work. Late in life he composed *Zōtanshū* 雑談集 (*Casual Digressions*, 1305) and two vernacular tracts, *Shōzaishū* 聖財集 (*Collection of Sacred Assets*) and *Tsuma Kagami* 妻鏡 (*Mirror for Women*, 1300).

MUKAI KYORAI 向井去来. 1651–1704. Early Edo *haikai* poet. Born in Nagasaki, he moved to Kyoto and studied the martial arts. But in his twenties he "threw away the bow and arrows" to devote himself to poetry. An important year in his life came in 1686, when he met *Matsuo Bashō, and when he and his sister Chine, also a haikai poet of some merit, made a trip to Ise recorded in his *Ise Kikō* 伊勢紀行 (*Record of an Ise Journey*). Later he was in Edo, composing sequences with Bashō and others, as they did later near Kyoto, where he had bought his hermitage, the Rakushisha, which Bashō and other friends visited from time to time. He and *Nozawa Bonchō compiled the most prestigious of haikai collections, *Sarumino, in 1691 (see *Matsuo Bashō and Part Six F). He was closely associated with Bashō during the next and last three years of that poet's life. Bashō placed him in charge of the thirty-three western provinces for matters of the school, as he did *Sugiyama Sampū for the eastern thirty-three. In 1694 Kyorai hurriedly took a night boat from Kyoto to Osaka to be present at Bashō's fatal illness. He had supported Bashō's late style of lightness (*karumi*) against *Enomoto Kikaku and others and, after the master's death, he modestly set about to edit various works, including Bashō's *Oku no Hosomichi* and the haikai collection, *Ariso Umi* 有磯海 (*The Etchū Seacoast*), 1695). From his *Kyorai Shō* 去来抄 (*Kyorai's Recollections of Bashō*, 1702–1704) and *Hattori Dohō's *Sanzōshi* we derive much of our knowledge about Bashō's life, personality, and poetic principles. Seldom a writer of striking *hokku*, he was excellent in sequences. His wife Kana(jo) was also a haikai poet, as were individual members of his Nagasaki family.

MUMYŌZŌSHI 無名草子 (*The Untitled Book*). Not to be confused with the *Mumyōshō* by *Kamo no Chōmei. Early Kamakura critical, semi-fictional work in one part. The work purports to be by a woman of long service at court and now over eighty. It is suspected to be by a woman closely known to *Fujiwara Teika and Fujiwara Takanobu. Some have thought it is by *Fujiwara Shunzei no Musume, who would qualify, but the evidence is inadequate. Various details in the book show that it was written between 1196 and 1202.

The opening is highly effective. The aged nun totters, as it were, into the room, posing to the younger ladies of the house the question, what is the most precious thing in the world? Answers vary from sutras to the moon, from letters to dreams. The correct reply is at last given: *monogatari*, so leading into the main concern of the work. *Murasaki Shikibu's masterpiece is discussed extensively, part by part, detail by detail. Other monogatari are taken up in turn: *Sagoromo Monogatari, *Sugawara Takasue no Musume's *Hamamatsu Chūnagon Monogatari*, *Yoru no Nezame, *Torikaeba ya Monogatari*, etc. The practice is to identify the best features, along with any defects. Recurrent terms of praise are "it is moving" ("aware naru"), "it has a charming beauty" ("en aru"), and "it is of great import" ("midokoro aru").As everyone knows, there are comments on prose narrative in the "Fireflies" chapter of the *Genji Monogatari*, but this work provides the first extended criticism, the first detailed discussion of individual works. It is of inestimable importance, not simply for giving us an early view of these monogatari but also because its judgments have stood the test of time. The *Genji Monogatari* is the greatest, *Sagoromo* is the second *Genji* (*nisei Genji*), and so on.

The work closes with discussion of the great Heian female writers, particularly poets, beginning with *Ono no Komachi, including of course *Sei Shōnagon, *Izumi Shikibu, *Murasaki Shikibu, and others. For them, the high praise is "splendor" ("medetasa"). The work clearly shows that by Kamakura times women had become aware of *their* literary inheritance. Monogatari were always written for women (men actually liked them and read them but on the sly—they openly read *Genji Monogatari*—until the Kamakura period), and after Murasaki Shikibu were certainly written by women. The work deals primarily, then, with literature by and for women—and it is easy to see in the later examples of monogatari examined that the authors were wholly aware of the fact. The work also deals with the outstanding women who wrote in genres that men as well might practice: *waka* and *zuihitsu*. The author takes obvious pride in the established tradition of great women writers. In Asian terms, this is radically different from China and Korea; and no woman in any other language could validly make this claim, least of all at the turn of the twelfth and thirteenth centuries.

MUNENAGA SHINNŌ 宗良親王. B. 1311. Namboku *waka* poet. The Genkō War of 1331 and its aftermath found him first in political straits and then banished to Sanuki in Shikoku. But after three years he was allowed to return to Kyoto and resume his place as a prince. He spent time in travel to places such as Yoshino, and many of his trips involved his alignment with interests of the southern dynasty. Between about 1381 and 1389 he put together his personal collection, *Rikashū* 李花集 (*Plum Flowers*). His poems are also found in other personal collections and in the *Shin'yōshū* (1381), which he compiled on the order and scale of a *chokusenshū*, making it a collection tantamount to the southern court's official collection (see Part Six A) In it he has ninety-nine poems with his name, with another ninety-six designated Anonymous, making him much the most fully represented contributor. His poetry not unnaturally resembles the collection as a whole—insipid when in the style of the *Nijō poets, fresh when it has touches of a warrior's experience and other elements of his tempestuous life as son of the foolhardy sovereign, Godaigo.

MUNETAKA SHINNŌ 宗尊親王. 1242–1274. Mid-Kamakura *waka* poet. At the age of ten he was sent to Kamakura as nominal shogun, remained there for about fifteen years, then returned to Kyoto. When his father, Gosaga (r. 1242–1246) died in 1272, he took orders, and died still young only two years later. He sponsored or participated in a number of poetry matches and other literary gatherings. His poems appear in various personal and official collections. About three thousand are extant. Most of his poems are not very impressive. There is much greater interest in those he wrote after returning to Kyoto and had false charges brought against him. The improvement near the end of his short life and the similarity of their abilities justify the comparison sometimes made between him and *Minamoto Sanetomo.

MURAKAMI 村上. R. 946–967. Although no special literary figure himself, his reign was sometimes idealized—in the *Genji Monogatari*, for example—as a glorious age for the court.

MURASAKI SHIKIBU 紫式部. D. ?1014. Mid-Heian writer of *monogatari*, *waka*, and *nikki*. Very little is known of the author of the greatest work of Japanese literature, the *Genji Monogatari*, although numerous attempts have been made to use her diary and *kashū* to reconstruct her life. These efforts are natural enough, but both the diary and the poetic collection are more emphatically literary than autobiographical. For all the devoted study, very little that is certain has been added to the information about the author.

She was born into one of the houses that had turned more and more to literary study as a few other houses of the Fujiwara got power into their hands. She showed an early talent for literature, including study of Chinese poetry which, according to the account so well attested, she learned more quickly than her brother at a time when Chinese study was nominally a male preserve. In 999 she married Fujiwara Nobutaka, who was so much her senior that he had a son older than she. The details of her marriage are not at all clear. She was widowed two years later.

In 1006 or 1007 she went into the service of one of the consorts of Ichijō (r. 986–1011). This was Shōshi, better known by her later name, *Jōtō (or Shōtō) Mon'in. The court of Shōshi and of Teishi, another consort of Ichijō, were then the centers of literary culture. At Teishi's, *Sei Shōnagon—also well versed in Chinese—provided a witty genius all her own. At Shōshi's, Murasaki Shikibu was part of a glittering array of talent, including also *Izumi Shikibu, the greatest poet of the time, *Akazome Emon, and others. Murasaki Shikibu's "name" as we know it derives from the heroine of the first two parts of the *Genji Monogatari*, Murasaki (no Ue), and from her father's position at the Bureau of Rites (Shikibu). Although little else is known, she left three works—none of them entirely free from suspicion of revision by later hands. The works will be discussed in the order of her diary, poetic collection, and the *Genji Monogatari*.

The *Murasaki Shikibu Nikki* (*The Diary of Murasaki Shikibu*) is one of the four major Heian diaries. A diary only in the wide sense of *nikki*, it does not use daily entries, and in fact covers only a brief period, from the early autumn of 1008 to the beginning of 1010. There seem to be three major blocs of revised composition, and much of what they contain appears to have been revised yet further to make an integral unit, although there are one or two major breaks. The whole original diary, if there was one, would constitute a major literary recovery. The cadenced opening suggests that there was a rewriting that would establish the diary as a separate literary creation. Portions of the *Eiga Monogatari* show that other parts of the diary once existed. How many and in what form are questions that cannot be answered.

The diary deals chiefly with a gifted woman's reponse to events at Shōshi's court during fifteen months or so. Its public events can be verified from other sources. These include the lying-in of Shōshi, *Fujiwara Michinaga's joy over the child (his grandson and assurance of continuing power in the court), parties, illnesses, priests, ladies, and the ever-present courtiers, tipsy or sober.

The diary does include other, more personal elements. There are memorable moments such as Ichijō's request for the diarist's story of Genji. His comment, that the author must have read the *Nihon Shoki*, suggests that he read it as a court history. There is an incident when *Fujiwara Kintō approaches the area for the ladies-in-waiting, asking if there were any Murasakis present (referring to the "Waka Murasaki" of the *Genji Monogatari*). The author's reply: how can there be if there are no Genjis? Her great work is referred to as the *Genji no Monogatari*, which strictly or pedantically speaking should be its title. There are also other glimpses of her place at Shōshi's court. She taught her mistress poems by Po Chü-i more or less on the sly, and she would return home only be to be summoned back to court before long. As might be expected, she reveals great sensitivity to seasonal phenomena. But her greatest interest is in people, especially her mistress, Michinaga, and attendant members of court. What they say and do, how they dress and behave—these are prime concerns. Everyone is struck by her comments on a few important individuals at the court. Murasaki Shikibu is sharp-tongued about what she considers the loose life of Izumi Shikibu: was there also some jealousy over that woman's greater poetic gifts? Sei Shōnagon's knowing look annoys her. Her great consolation was undoubtedly Lady Saishō, her confidante and sensitive friend.

The diary contains a number of poems, and there are almost 800 poems in the *Genji Monogatari*. Selections from these and other sources (with considerable omissions) make up her *Murasaki Shikibu Shū* (*The Poetic Collection of Murasaki Shikibu*). It contains only just over 120 poems, a fraction of those in her masterpiece. It is difficult to say just what this collection represents, especially since besides the usually presented version there is another or rival one. As has been said, the collection is now often used to biographical ends. It really does not help serious investigation that its selective nature suggests that it was designed as a private collection to give a portrait of its author, because whether the poems included are in their order of composition or whether Murasaki Shikibu is the compiler are both issues that are not easily determined. It is clear that she is no match for Izumi Shikibu as a poet pure and simple. Her poetry is at its best in prose contexts like those supplied by the dairy and the *Genji Monogatari*. Those contexts give the poetry a degree of normative control and irony (the two qualify each other to a degree almost of bafflement). And if the normative control is that of the Buddhism of her time and the attitudes are of a rather strait-laced observer of others, the potentialities are realized, or rather transcended, by her greatest work.

The *Genji Monogatari* 源氏物語 (*The Tale of Genji*) is a *tsukurimonogatari* in fifty-four parts, a long work. Theories of other authorship or of completion by another or other writers founder on traditional ascription and on the unquestioned greatness of the work as it exists. The present arrangement of chapters has also been questioned, and with similar conclusion, that no other order would make as much sense as the present sequence of parts. Since we last see the hero, Hikaru Genji, in the forty-first part ("Maboroshi") and then move on to other characters, it was sometimes postulated that there was a missing chapter, "Kumogakure" ("Lost in the Clouds"). That testifies to readerly curiosity more than to anything else, as do efforts to provide a sequel to the ending of the work. The best attempt of a few is "Yamaji no Tsuyu" ("Dew on the Mountain Path"), which has been thought of well enough to have been attributed to *Kenrei Mon'in Ukyō no Daibu. But there can be no doubt that, taken as we know it, the *Genji Monogatari* is a complexly integral work of a difficulty surpassed only by its greatness.

Taking the work as we have it, we observe that obvious break between the forty-one parts dealing with Genji and the thirteen that follow. Of these thirteen, the final ten are normally called "the ten Uji parts" ("Uji jūjō"), after the location where much of the action takes place. The dominant characters in these ten (or indeed the last thirteen) parts are three people. They include Kaoru, Hikaru Genji's putative son, who is so important (with whatever other reservations) as to give this section the title of the "Kaoru Monogatari." The other principal male character is the philandering Prince Niou, Genji's grandson and a close associate of Kaoru's. The third central figure is Ukifune, who finds herself entangled in love affairs with both Kaoru and Niou. Because the story comes inreasingly to focus on her, it is common to think of an "Ukifune Monogatari" within the "Kaoru Monogatari."

Beyond the simple ordering into Genji- and post-Genji portions of the story, there is an analysis by Ikeda Kikan that has defined all subsequent study. He argued that the *Genji Monogatari* is "a work with three divisions." That is, "there are three phases of life—glory and youth, conflict and death, and transcendence of death. To be specific, the first phase consists of the parts from 'Kiritsubo' to 'Fuji no Uraba' [1–33]; the second phase from 'Wakana (Jō)' to 'Maboroshi' [34–41, ending with the disappearance of Genji]; and the third made up of the ten Uji parts [45–54]. These three divisions are unified by a concern with human fate [karma]. This unified view of human life is to be found precisely in its portrayal of humanity and the world." Although accepted by Japanese critics, this view omits assigning of parts 42–44 to any division. Since the three are among the most doubtful as to authorship, some Japanese scholars along with Ikeda simply omit consideration of them. It has become increasingly common, however, to treat them as part of the third division along with the ten that follow. No other explanation rivals in consent Ikeda's division. It gives us three integers of increasing size: the fifty-four parts, the three divisions, and the whole.

The wide cast of characters in the story is sufficiently numerous as to receive a section in handbooks on the *Genji Monogatari*. Almost all we see of humanity is devoted to the small elite taken to matter (the "yoki hito"). Exceptions do occur—in "Yūgao," "Akashi," and "Ukifune." A special problem in reading or translating the work concerns "names." There are two notable Ukons, and a large number of Menotos (wet-nurses). No character is known by names in the Western sense of personal designations inherited from and given by parents. Hikaru Genji (the radiant Genji, or simply Genji) is a "name" deriving partly from his charisma and partly from the name of the nonroyal family to which his father assigned him to avoid court intrigues against him: the Minamoto, or Genji in another version. (Since "Minamoto" is his assumed surname, and since royalty lacked surnames, he is not the prince that he is often called.) The women derive their names from place, rank, or office, or more usually from a poem, the latter being the case for one or two male characters (principally Yūgiri, Genji's son). Since women so often derive their "names" from poems, their appellations are also usually titles for parts (Yūgao, Murasaki, Tamakazura, Ukifune, and so on). Others derive their names from relation in a family, as with Ōigimi and Nakanokimi, the two elder, full sisters in the Uji chapters. Other women derive their names from court ranks, as with Nyosan no Miya, or from their

place of residence and status, as with Rokujō no Miyasu(n)dokoro (the Lady Rokujō of translations). With women, and even more with men, there are burdensome complications as characters change rank or as others take their place in the former positions. Of these the most important is Genji's friend and foil, the man we first meet as Tō no Chūjō, a rank in the palace guards. By "Tamakazura" he is a high minister of state. As all this implies, the characters belong to a highly rank- and status-defined society, and the miracle is that the characters are so individualized, whatever their appellations and our confusion over them.

Genji's absence from the last thirteen parts has as its counterpart his presence in the first forty-one. In these, there is not one in which he is not present—something that cannot be said of the other characters. The women in his life appear serially, as it were, not together, unless his gathering of them into his Rokujō palace be considered a spatial togetherness that is not honored by the episodes of the story. Kaoru and Niou dominate the last thirteen chapters and often appear together. This befits a pair that represents in halves Genji's wholeness. Kaoru has Genji's sensitivity, but is solipsistic and indecisive. Niou indeed acts, but in amatory terms that reveal him to be culpable. Of all the characters other than Genji, the most normative are Murasaki, who has to put up with a great deal in Genji's attention to other women, and Ukifune. Ukifune is the one character who moves from involvement with the larger world of other characters to a retired life that she preserves by taking religious vows, in spite of inducements to rejoin full contact with the world.

In the second part, "Hahakigi," Uma no Kami leads a long discussion of the kinds of women one may encounter, and much of the work plays out such distinctions of individuality, rank, and kind among the noble women. Murasaki prefers spring, Akikonomu autumn. As early as the fourth part, "Yūgao," Genji is involved in a number of women who set each other off. The haughty, unbending Aoi (Genji's wife) has a foil in the gentle, yielding Yūgao. The spirited and proud Rokujō no Miyasudokoro is evoked in the first phrase of "Yūgao," and by the end her jealous spirit has destroyed Yūgao as it will Aoi later. Genji is also in touch with two other women. Nokiba no Ogi is comically licentious. Utsusemi who continually resists Genji. Yūgao is not licentious like Nokiba no Ogi. Yet by the mores of the time, when she or one of her women sends out to Genji a poem with some gourd flowers (yūgao, evening faces), he is entitled to pursuit. This summary hardly suggests the complexities.

Genji and his ladies, along with the Tō no Chūjō character, constitute the normative level of attention in the story. Above them are the reigning or retired sovereigns, their consorts, and their princely children. The sole incursion from the dominant group into that higher realm is Genji's remarkable affair with Fujitsubo, his father's loved lady-in-waiting. Yūgiri's sight of Murasaki during the typhoon offers a very mild, and Kashiwagi's seduction of Genji's last official wife, Nyosan no Miya, a much more serious incursion from the first group below to the normative group.

Various kinds of characters and names, or functions, are represented in the yet lower characters. Koremitsu, Genji's much employed attendant, is replicated in the retainers of Kaoru and Niou. The wet nurses (menoto) so important in life are also of consequence in the story: it is after visiting his that Genji chances upon Yūgao. There is also a kind of woman who is older than her mistress, devoted and worried, the Ukons we find next to Yūgao and Ukifune. There is a more highly placed, sophisticated female attendant (the nobility waited on their superiors) who is younger than the normative group. This Chūjō figure first appears with Rokujō no Miyasudokoro and recurs at Genji's Rokujō palace. Such patterning of figures has its counterparts in the figures above the normative group and serves to characterize a society by representative characters who individualize the social order and embody its values. And the human recurrences, like the return of the seasons, lend the story a temporal intelligibility beyond that of mere pattern, reminding us not just of time but also of the three-part development posited by Ikeda.

The Uji section differs in character relation as it does in its locations, usually away from the capital. We now discover female equals together, first the two elder daughters of Prince Hachi, Ōigimi and Naka no Kimi. After Ōigimi dies, Kaoru (who has never consummated his love for her) passes on Naka no Kimi to Niou, an act as baffling to him as to the reader. Ukifune, a half-sister of these two, appears first on a visit to the now married Naka no Kimi. The result is the Ukifune Monogatari within the other of Kaoru—something that could not exist in the first forty-one parts, where Genji dominates all.

Religious characters now matter more. The nun Imōto replays the Ukon figure to Ukifune to some degree, but she is also a mother who has lost her daughter, at once a version of the Akashi Lady as also of Genji, who lost his mother. Her brother, Sōzu, so saintly and efficacious, is the finest of all the good priestly figures, from Koremitsu's brother to the priest come to administer the tonsure to Genji. (Sōzu and Ukon are modeled on *Genshin and his sister, the Nun Ganshō.) It is Sōzu who cuts Ukifune's hair, administering nun's vows. Her religious strength does not assure her worldly happiness, but it offers a vision of that transcendence that Ikeda posited. What Ukifune offers is much needed by the reader, just as are the occasional comic characters—Suetsumuhana of the red nose and Ōmi no Kimi (the foil to Tamakazura), with her rapid clatter of tongue, lovely hair, and low brow

like her father, the grand minister who had entered the story as Tō no Chūjō. Not only these but other characters as well make up a highly patterned social elite that yet holds individuals always distinct from each other. Characterization represents in one crucial respect the pantoscopic genius of the author.

If the narrator is not precisely a character, she does play crucial roles, whether of intrusion (her closing remarks in "Yūgao" are the most famous) or of seeming to disappear or merge with the thoughts of her characters. Certain signs indicate an act of narrating even when the narrator is otherwise hard to identify. Perfective constructions are among the signs, as are certain narrative formulas. "Sono koro" (about that time) designates a narrative shift to new characters and action, as "to ya" or "to zo" are formulaic endings suggestive of a narrator's gesture to credit others with her information ("they say"). The difficulties of following the narrative are far greater to us than they seem to have been to Heian readers. Heian ladies somehow read a wholly unpunctuated text, one lacking any indentation throughout a whole part, except to indicate poems. The syntax is a rack of vagueness to readers beginning with it, and many modern versions that supply marginal indications of who thinks what of whom increase ease of reading with some sacrifice of polysemous writing.

The narrative grows more complexly subtle beginning with part thirty-four, "Wakana," and yet more so again as the Uji chapters get underway. In each case there is a lessening of the strength of the narrator's point of view and an increase in the point of the attention of the narrator, and the reader, in the minds of characters. The ambiguity is pliable enough, then, to yield a very subtle, complex subjectivity that is the more moving for involving the reader with the narrator and the characters.

Given the complexity of narratorship, it is not surprising that the attitudes induced by the narrating are also complex. Whether the problem be considered solely in terms of the narrator, the response of the reader, or otherwise, the issue of the tone of the work is finally referrable to the author and the reader dealing with a "story," "text," or literary creation. Recent criticism has stressed increasingly the ironies of the work. An example occurs in one of the most famous episodes, the discussion of the art of monogatari in "Hotaru." Hikaru Genji is having some difficulty in keeping his amorous hands away from Tamakazura, his lovely, sensitive daughter—or so the world thinks, although she is really the former Tō no Chūjō's lately recovered daughter. (Yūgao was her mother.) After Genji's jest and earnest about monogatari, he proposes that they make an unexampled love story (tagui naki monogatari). The brazen suggestion reduces her to tears. Poems are exchanged, Genji is embarrassed, and the dangerous moment passes. The narrator intervenes to say that Tamakazura was safe for the moment but also to ask, after what had occurred, what could lie ahead for her? Then there is a sudden cut or shift. The next words are, "Murasaki also ..." ("Murasaki no Ue mo ..."). The stark contrast makes one catch one's breath.

The ironic criticism directed toward Genji begins early and intensifies, although readers differ greatly on its pervasiveness, limits, and import. The Uji parts constitute the author's ironic masterpiece, because in them failed communication and failed understanding wreck the lives of attractive people. But Genji is in many ways the crucial instance. The greatest artist of human life created in world literature, he has faults enough to blemish any lesser character and that, given his sensitive intelligence, can only be termed moral—unfashionable as the term is in discussions of Japanese literature. Important as this ironic criticism of the central figure of the work may be, it is accompanied by a countervailing irony: no other character approaches his status, and in the Uji parts we are led to revise our opinion of him favorably as we see lesser versions of him in Kaoru and Niou. It is not just a question of merit but yet more of awe. The more we see of others after him, the more we realize his extraordinary centrality and importance to the world depicted.

Earlier monogatari seem quite certainly to have been written for women by men. The shift from male to female authorship is easy to get wrong, since the femaleness of the author is finally transcended by her genius. One rude example will be found in monogatari endings. Early works had ended happily. If we accept Ikeda's division into three parts, we can only say that the first ends happily, but that the second and third do not. For that matter, later monogatari— mostly written by women—show an authorial (and no doubt readerly) inclination for happy endings. It might be argued that Ukifune shows in her religious determination what should be termed positive. But the context, including Kaoru's much muddled thoughts that conclude the story, shows that Murasaki Shikibu will not allow facile solutions to her very complex issues.

There are also histories implied by the story and histories of the work's reception. Numerous and sometimes contradictory historical exemplars have been proposed for her hero: in reverse historical order, the supposed models include *Fujiwara Michinaga, *Arıwara Narihira, and *Shōtoku Taishi. It seems clear that the opening—"In which reign was it?" ("Izure no ōntoki ni ka")—sets the story in some earlier reign, whether that of Uda (r. 887–897), Daigo (r. 897–930), or *Murakami (r. 946–967), the last half century or so before the work is written. Centuries of devoted study have identified fictional sovereigns with real ones, even if fictionalized history does not obey whatever rules attend dynastic history. In any event, it is agreed that if Genji were alive when the story ends, he would be about seventy-four years old. But he is not

alive, and the loss as well as the fact are apparent in the story as also, by implication, in the fictional world of the story and whatever it implies of the author's conception of her own age.

It is now generally recognized that although women were the chief audience for monogatari, the *Genji Monogatari* provides a partial exception. It was clearly written for women and clearly spoke to their hearts, as the response of *Sugawara Takasue no Musume shows. But if men read later (and possibly earlier) monogatari on the sly, the *Genji Monogatari* was something of an exception. As we have seen, Ichijō and Kintō read it, probably before it was complete. It is therefore not really true that 150 years passed before men appreciated it, although the late date of extant manuscripts does seem to imply that the work was not at once granted the primacy it has had since the twelfth-century. Certainly it was the standard by which later Heian and Kamakura monogatari were judged, and the model (especially in its Uji parts) on which they were written.

The revaluation establishing primacy was led by twelfth-century male readers. One reaction was the historical one of Ichijō, with the difference that the work was held to be a kind of history of its age—a reminder that East Asian poetics included history with lyric as the two major constituents of literature (Chinese wen, Japanese bun, fumi, and so on). *Fujiwara Shunzei propounded literary reasons of a kind we can recognize more readily. In one judgment at the *Roppyakuban Utaawase*, he declared in effect that one could not be a poet without knowledge of the poems in the work. His son, *Fujiwara Teika, is responsible for copying the work in what is usually considered the best available text. In later times, handbooks were prepared—sometimes giving plot outlines, with or without poems—and some of these were of great importance to writers of renga and nō. In fact, however gifted a renga poet might be, and none more so than *Sōgi, their status in the culture of their times was proved by lectures like his on this work and on the *Ise Monogatari*.

This prominence was naturally put in question by the Neoconfucianists with their somewhat simplified practical moral emphasis and their low opinion of women. By then there was a legend that Murasaki Shikibu had been damned for writing lies (even as another tale held her to be an avatar of the Bodhisattva Kannon; see kanzen chōaku and kyōgen kigo. In the main, however, the work has justified the words about monogatari that Murasaki Shikibu gave to Genji in the "Hotaru" part. A writer of monogatari, she said, would treat widely various experience, the bad as well as the good, so that there would not be a time when people would not know of what was important to her. The result fulfilled her ambitions. It has made Japanese literature one whose greatness is referrable to a single work, like the *Aeneid* in Roman literature, the *Divine Comedy* in Italian, or *Don Quixote* in Spanish. A lady of a lesser Fujiwara house of whom we know very little produced, for a small circle of an elite class and especially for female readers, one of the handful of masterpieces of world literature. That much is clear, and that much makes Murasaki Shikibu and Japanese literature unique among the literatures of the world. And yet none of those things matters as much as the complex artistry of the work, an artistry giving us a sense of the close relation between art and life, and giving us also versions of our own lives that at times arouse our laughter or bring our tears, but an artistry that transcends both to a fuller understanding of the limits and capacities of human life.

MURATA HARUMI 村田春海. 1746–1811. Late Edo *kokugaku* scholar, *waka* poet. Born in Edo, he studied under members of his family and the important kokugaku scholar, *Kamo no Mabuchi. His many writings include poems, a few of which are still well regarded.

MURO KYŪSŌ 室鳩巣. 1658–1734. Early Edo Confucian scholar. Born into a doctor's family, his acquired Neoconfucian learning of the *Shushigaku* kind led him to serve three generations of Tokugawa shoguns. His emphasis on the role of human feelings and of the lives of the people mark him off from the standard moralizers and more abstract thinkers typical of Japanese Neoconfucianism. He published voluminously.

MUSASHI. See MIYAMOTO MUSASHI.

MUSHIMARO. See TAKAHASHI MUSHIMARO.

MUSŌ 夢窓. 1275–1351. Late Kamakura-early Ashikaga Rinzai Zen prelate, political adviser, landscape designer, and poet. Musō was one of the most influential religious and cultural leaders of his age. Although, like *Enni, he favored a syncretic Zen, his political maneuverings—first with Godaigo and then with the Ashikagas—brought him into conflict with the Tendai establishment. In 1345 he was appointed abbot of the Tenryūji, a temple in the western suburbs of Kyoto built by the Ashikaga military regime to commemorate the death of Godaigo. Musō's famous *Muchū Mondō* 夢中問答 (*Questions and Answers in a Dream*, 1344) is a three-part work on the principles of Zen. His writings also include the *Musō Kokushi Goroku* 夢窓国師語録 (*The Record of National Teacher Musō*), a compilation of shorter works composed between 1325 and 1351. Several hundred of his waka are included in the *Shōgaku Kokushi Wakashū* 正覚国師和歌集 (*Musō's Waka*), the *Musō Kokushi Goeisō* 夢窓国師御詠草 (*Musō's Poetry*), and in many royal collections.

MUTSU WAKI 陸奥話記 (*An Account of Mutsu*; also other, similar titles). Late Heian *gunki mono-*

gatari in one part. An account of the Zen Kunen no Eki, or War of Nine Years Ago, part of a twelve-year struggle that concluded in 1062. This story had predecessors and is not taken as one of the great military tales. Its style is said to be heavily Japanified *kambun*.

MYŌE 明恵. 1173–1232. Early Kamakura Kegon reformer, recluse, polemicist, and poet. Because of his dedication to the study of Kegon theory and esoteric practice, Myōe was commissioned by *Gotoba in 1206 to restore the Kōzanji on Mount Toganoo as a center for Kegon's rejuvenation. His reform movement lacked popular support, and his theoretical works are of less historic interest than various popular writings. He was a poet of some lunacy, and his favorite topic was the moon. Although he did not frequent the fashionable literary circles of his day, about two dozen of his poems can be found in royal collections. There is a later collection (1248) the *Myōe Shōnin Wakashū* 明恵上人和歌集 (*The Venerable Myōe's Waka*), and he frequently appears in popular literature as the pious recluse. He is the subject of the *nō, Kasuga Ryūjin* 春日龍神 (*The Dragon God of Kasuga*).

NAGATA TEIRYŪ 永田貞柳. 1654–1734. Early Edo *kyōka* poet. Born into an Osaka confectioner's household, he studied *haikai* while very young, as his father had done, and soon thereafter kyōka, which he was precociously composing by fourteen. His younger brother, *Ki no Kaion, and others flourished in kyōka under his aegis, and he came to have many followers. With Kaion's urging, he developed a serious interest in *waka*, to the point of studying *Kokindenju* with *Keichū. Later in his life, again thanks to Kaion, he was on close footing with *kabuki* people. When the family shop burned in 1724, he turned the business over to Kaion, retiring to a hermitage to devote himself to his chief love, kyōka. In 1729, his *Kyōka Iezuto* 狂歌家づと (*Mad Poems as Gifts for Home*) was published, followed by other collections. As he said, his humor specialized in the juxtaposition of the elegant with the vulgar. He affected a large number of writers and gave waka a perverse new life appropriate to an age of haikai.

NAGAWA KAMESUKE 奈河亀輔. Dates unknown; latter half of eighteenth century. Mid-Edo playwright. Beginning in *jōruri*, he turned to *kabuki*, writing over fifty works. He is granted a place in the history of jōruri's effect on kabuki, but his own plays have not been highly rated.

NAGAYA NO Ō(KIMI) 長屋王. 684–729. Yamato prince, political figure, poet of *kanshi*. During the reign of Genshō (715–724) he rose to high office, especially after the death Fujiwara Fuhito (659–720). In the struggle against the Fujiwara domination of the court, and among rival royal factions, he became Minister of the Right in 721 and Minister of the Left in 724. But the Fujiwara managed to embroil him in intrigue, and obtained a royal edict requiring Nagaya, his wife, and their children to take their lives.

Prince Nagaya was not a great poet, but he played a crucial role in enabling members of the court and other learned people to obtain command of the elaborate styles of late Six Dynasties and early T'ang poetry. During his years of eminence he held what has been described as a salon in his residence, holding poetry parties along the lines of famous Chinese gatherings, so fostering an atmosphere in which Chinese verse could become naturalized in Japan. Under his aegis, Japanese met with learned Korean immigrants and visitors to compose impromptu lines or to offer more elaborate compositions. It is clear that *Yamanoe Okura was among the visitors. Okura's Chinese style is, however, highly idiosyncratic, and none of his poems is included in the later monument to Nagaya's poetic achievements, the *Kaifūsō.

NAHIKO. See KATORI NAHIKO.

NAKAE TŌJU 中江藤樹. 1608–1648. Early Edo Neoconfucian scholar. He is taken as the founder of *Yōmeigaku* in Japan, Neoconfucianism of the school of Wang Yang-ming, opposed to the *Shushigaku* (orthodox Confucianism because of its support by the *bakufu*). It should be observed that Yōmeigaku is, then, not a late development in Edo Japan but one substantially contemporary with its official rival. *Kumazawa Banzan and others followed Nakae Tōju's lead, so strengthening Edo intellectual life even if it did not find official favor.

NAKAMURA FUMIKUNI 中村史邦. Dates unknown. Early Edo *haikai* poet. Born at Inuyama, near Nagoya, he was a physician who served for a time at the palace in Kyoto. When he took up haikai is not known, but *Mukai Kyorai introduced him to *Matsuo Bashō. He is represented in both the *hokku* and *renku* sections of *Sarumino* (see Part Six F).

NAKANOIN MICHIKATSU 中院通勝. 1558–1610. Very early Edo poet, critic. He had a considerable reputation as a poet and for learning, but his poetry as we have it (there is no personal collection) is in the tired line of *Nijō poets, and his literary studies show no great originality. Some of his fame derives from a connection on his mother's side with *Sanjōnishi Sanetaka and from his acquaintance with *Hosokawa Yūsai, whom he joined when he fell out with Goyōzei, writing a still useful commentary on the *Genji Monogatari.

NAKARAI BOKUYŌ 半井卜養. 1607–1678. Early Edo *kyōka*, *haikai* poet, physician. He played a part in the redefinition of haikai, having 171 stanzas included in *Matsue Shigeyori's collection, *Enoko Shū*. He also acquired a name for himself in prose. But he wrote kyōka early and late. His haikai collection, *Yakko Haikai* 奴俳諧 (*Haikai in Slave Language*, 1667) preceded his kyōka collection, *Bokuyō Kyōkashū* 卜養狂歌集, which apparently came out within a few years of his death. The haikai is light-spirited and is esteemed for mellifluousness. His kyōka are meant to astonish. He gained considerable success as a physician serving the *bakufu*.

NAKATOMI YAKAMORI 中臣宅守. Dates unknown. Nara *waka* poet. Because of a scandal, he was exiled to Echizen in 739. While there he participated in seventy-three poems of exchange (forty being his own) that more or less fit together like an *uta monogatari* (see *Man'yōshū*, 5), and wrote Chinese verse included in the *Kaifūsō*. When allowed to return to Nara, he seems to have given over poetry for official duties.

NAKATSUKASA 中務. Ca. ?920–980. Mid-Heian *waka* poet. Daughter of *Ise, who was an intimate and favorite of Daigo (r. 897–930), she was a poet in her own right. We owe to her preparation the survival and probably the ordering of her mother's personal poetic collection. Her own *Nakatsukasa Shū* survives, and she is one of the *sanjūrokkasen*. Although not as intense a poet as her mother, and apparently not as prolific as some of her contemporaries, she is one of the band of court ladies who wrote with ease at the Heian court.

NAMBOKU. See TSURUYA NAMBOKU.

NAMBŌ SŌKEI 南坊宗啓. Dates unknown. Azuchi-Momoyama tea master. He is known for being elder brother of *Sen no Rikyū (Sōeki), and for a treatise on tea, *Nambō Roku* 南方録, in nine parts, the last two of which were completed by another hand.

NAMIKI GOHEI 並木五瓶. 1747–1808. Late Edo *kabuki* playwright. Born in Osaka, he was known as a playwright by the time he was twenty-five. Thereafter he produced a steady output of well-regarded plays. In 1794 Sawamura Sōjūrō III invited him to Edo as house playwright, and there he remained till his death. A witty, self-indulgent man, he was said to have spent half his time in tea-houses, drinking and sporting with the maids. As representative plays from Osaka and Edo, we may take *Kimmon Gosan no Kiri* 金門五山桐 (1789) and *Sumida no Haru Geisha Katagi* 隅田春妓女容性 (1794)—see *katagimono*. He produced one of the few good treatises on kabuki, *Kezairoku* 戯財録 (1801), and is said to have practiced *haikai* late in life. Later undistinguished playwrights bore his name for two generations.

NAMIKI SHŌZŌ 並木正三. 1730–1773. Mid-Edo *jōruri*, *kabuki* playwright. Devoted to playwriting from an early age, he wrote *jōruri* under *Namiki Sōsuke, but after his master's death he changed to *kabuki*. He produced about one hundred plays and is best known for his skill in use of sets and machinery.

NAMIKI SŌSUKE 並木宗輔 1695–1751. Mid-Edo *jōruri* playwright. At about the age of twenty-nine he appears in records as a playwright at the Toyotakeza in Osaka, collaborating with *Nishizawa Ippū and Yasuda Abun. As a house playwright thereafter he produced plays with Abun and his own apprentice playwrights. In 1741 he left Osaka for Edo, from which he shortly returned to write *kabuki* as well as *jōruri*. In 1745 he changed to the Takemotoza. His best plays were written in rivalry with—and often on the same topics as—plays written by *Takeda Izumo I and II. These include such famous titles as *Sugawara Denju Tenarai Kagami* 菅原伝授手習鑑 (*Sugawara's School of Calligraphy*, 1746), also called *Terakoya* 寺小屋 (*The Little Temple School*), *Yoshitsune Sembonzakura* 義経千本桜 (*Yoshitsune and the Thousand Cherry Trees*, 1747), and *Kanadehon Chūshingura* 仮名手本忠臣蔵 (*The Treasury of Loyal Retainers*, 1748). He fell fatally ill while writing another *jidaimono*. He was prized for his skill in building up the tension and pace of action, and for making good theater in other ways.

NAMPO. See ŌTA NAMPO.

NANKAKU. See HATTORI NANKAKU.

NAONOBU. See KANŌ NAONOBU.

NAOYOSHI. See KUMAGAI NAOYOSHI.

NARIHIRA. See ARIWARA NARIHIRA.

NARISUE. See TACHIBANA NARISUE.

NATSUME SEIBI 夏目成美. 1749–1816. Late Edo *haikai* poet. Born in Edo, he was on easy terms with such contemporary poets as *Kaya Shirao and *Ōshima Ryōta, but he identified himself with no particular school. In addition to a volume of his verse, *Seibi Kashū* 成美家集, he published a number of critical writings. Among Japanese, he is best known for the support he gave to *Kobayashi Issa.

NICHIREN 日蓮. 1222–1282. Mid-Kamakura religious figure, founder of the sect which bears his name. Like most of his fellow reformers, Nichiren began his religious career as a Tendai monk. Although in his later teachings he continued to share Tendai's belief in the primacy of the *Lotus Sūtra* (see Part Six O), he left Mt. Hiei in 1253 to found a movement that emphasized the invocation of its title (*daimoku*): "Praise to the Sūtra of the Lotus Blossom of the Fine Dharma" ("Namu Myōhō Renge Kyō")—a practice analogous to the Pure Land *nembutsu*. Nichiren's fiery and uncompromising personality has been an inspiration to his followers into modern times. His *Risshō Ankokuron* 立正安国論 (*The Establishment of Legitimate Teaching for the Security of the Country*), presented to Hōjō Tokiyori in 1260, criticized *bakufu* policy. This, and his intolerance of all other sects, led to a near escape from execution and eventual exile to Itō and later to Sado (1272). After being pardoned, he devoted the last decade of his life to the propagation of his ideas. Among his many writings, his letters hold enduring personal and literary appeal, being adapted to the recipient and yet always showing the writer's mind. Nichiren is portrayed as *waki* in the *nō Ukai* (*The Cormorant Fisher*), in which he saves a fisherman from hell through the merit of the *Lotus Sūtra*.

NIHON (KOKU GEMPŌ ZEN'AKU) RYŌIKI (or **REIIKI**) 日本（国現報善悪）霊異記. (*Miraculous Stories of Karmic Retribution of Good and Evil in Japan*). Early Heian *setsuwa* collection in three parts, and perhaps the first example of the kind. Said to be compiled by Keikai (or Kyōkai, dates uncertain), a monk of the temple Yakushiji, Nara, ca. 823. The preface (like the full title) makes clear that the collection is designed to show the workings of karma, using solely Japanese examples. There are 116 stories (including some that involve things that happened to the author) that are supposed to represent the 116 era names of the fifty-three sovereigns, including the last year of the Kōnin era (of Saga, r. 809–822). Some of the stories are ancient, remote. Others give valuable insight into daily life in the Nara period. They are adapted to provide explanations of matters in sutras, with pains taken to put matters in a clear Chinese style. Some are retold in later *setsuwa* collections such as the *Konjaku Monogatari*.

NIHON SHOKI 日本書紀 (also **NIHONGI** 日本紀). Nara-period compilation of many elements in the guise of history, largely to justify the line of sovereigns. In 720 it was set down by order of Genshō (r. 715–724) in thirty books and another of genealogy (which has not survived), partly to preserve lore that had previously been transmitted orally, partly to emulate Chinese dynastic histories, and partly to claim legitimacy. The work was compiled chiefly by *Toneri Shinnō, but from accumulated materials. The personages dealt with are mostly divinities and sovereigns. The material covered is very much like that dealt with in the *Kojiki. That work is more accurate until late portions, but the *Nihon Shoki* is of special value for continuing longer in time and for fuller treatment of the more recent matters. The two accounts share a number of the same poems, often in differing versions, with neither work consistently giving older or newer versions. Because the *Kojiki* was set down in the difficult man'yōgana but this was written in prestigious *kambun*, the *Nihon Shoki* was far better known and exists in far older manuscripts. Today there is a general literary preference for the other work, but the two are essential to understanding early Japan. Together they are referred to as "kiki" from their last two characters (the same in sound but different in the left elements) and their poems "kiki kayō." See *Kojiki* and *Rikkokushi*.

NIJŌ, LADY. See GOFUKAKUSA IN NIJŌ.

NIJŌ 二条 POETS. In disputes over property, poetry, and politics, the descendants of *Fujiwara Tameie (himself son of *Fujiwara Teika) split into three rival groups. The eldest son, Tameuji (1222–1286), gained most of the property and established the Nijō house, named after its location. This group was very scholarly, but apparently so much in awe of Teika and their grand poetic progenitor, *Fujiwara Shunzei, that they did not venture much beyond the safe, conservative, and tepid in poetry—a conservative stance that put them at odds with their more liberal family rivals, the *Kyōgoku poets and *Reizei poets. Surnames for individuals of the house sometimes are "Fujiwara," sometimes "Nijō."

(FUJIWARA) NIJŌ TAMEYO (藤原)二条為世. 1251–1338. Late Kamakura poet and a good representative of the conservative *Nijō poets. He compiled the *Shingosenshū and *Shokusenzaishū. As might be expected, he was a strong opponent of *Kyōgoku Tamekane.

NIJŌ YOSHIMOTO 二条良基. 1320–1388. Namboku official, *waka* and *renga* poet. He was of the nobility just below the royal house and, like his father, held the highest court titles. These then carried less power than formerly, but they still gave status, and he advised three shoguns. To have power and survive in those days was virtually impossible. Somehow he did, even while finding time to locate in literary art an inheritance he prized and a coherence for his worldly life.

His waka follows the pale style of the *Nijō poets (no relation), which he studied under *Ton'a. These two produced a poetic treatise by question and answer, and Yoshimoto went on to a waka treatise of his own. He also participated in poetry matches such as The *Nenjū Gyōji Utaawase 年中行事歌合 (*Poetry Match on the Annual Observations*, 1366) and numerous waka sequences (*hyakushuuta*).

It is renga, however, for which he is known. His father encouraged him, and Yoshimoto's practice was important enough for *Shinkei to call him a holy man (hijiri). Renga occupied him to the end of his life. He began it at ten, and a decade or so later was formally taught by *Gusai. He was recognized as an authority before he was thirty—an astonishing feat in that art, where to be forty was usually still to be a novice. In 1356–1357 he compiled the immensely influential *Tsukuba Shū* 菟玖波集 (a title adapted from a poem in the *Kojiki), after which renga was called the way of Tsukuba (Tsukuba no michi), and "Tsukuba" signified "renga." This large selection gives the chosen stanza along with its predecessor (*maeku*).

The appearance of renga under the sponsorship of Yoshimoto helped make its reputation. In 1372 he provided renga poets with his ideas of the rules in *Renga Shinshiki* 連歌新式 (*A New Handbook for Renga*, 1372; also known as *Ōan Shinshiki*, 応安新式 *New Handbook for the Ōan Era*). He was a voluminous writer. His critical-miscellaneous works include: *Renri Hishō* 連理秘抄 (*The Secrets of Renga Composition*, 1349); *Tsukuba Mondō* 筑波問答 (*Renga Dialogues*, 1357–1372); and *Kyūshū Mondō* 九州問答 (*Dialogues with the Governor of Kyushu*, done 1376). A sample of his renga will be found in *Bunna Senku* 文和千句 (*A Thousand Stanzas in the Bunna Era*, 1355) and *Ishiyama Hyakuin* 石山百韻 (*A Hundred Stanzas at Ishiyama*, 1385). There is also his renga match with Shūa: *Yoshimoto Shūa Hyakuban Rengaawase* 良基周阿百番連歌合 (*A Renga Match in One Hundred Rounds between Yoshimoto and Shūa*, date uncertain). And there is much more. In *Sōgi's periodization, Yoshimoto brought the first period of renga to its close. Another way of describing his role is that he acted as regent till renga attained its majority.

NINAGAWA CHIUN or **CHIKAMASA.** See CHIUN.

NINSEI 仁清. Dates unknown. Early Edo potter, most of whose known work was done ca. 1661–1673. Although he made many kinds of goods and worked in Kyoto and elsewhere, he is most famous for tea bowls using gold and colored designs.

NISHIYAMA SŌIN 西山宗因. 1605–1682. Early Edo *renga* and *haikai* poet, founder of the *Danrin* school. Born in Kumamoto, he went to the *kamigata* area where, after being introduced to renga in his teens, he devoted himself more and more to the practice of it in the style of the Satomura school. One of the best-known sequences he participated in was *Ogura Senku* 小倉千句 (*The Ogura Thousand Stanzas*, 1665). Like so many poets before and after him, he was a traveler who wrote up his visits to famous places, as in *Matsushima Kikō* 松島紀行 (*Record of Travel to Matsushima*, 1662–1663).

Sōin thought of himself as a renga poet, but he began to pay more attention to its haikai version as he grew older. Earlier he had looked on haikai almost wholly as a pastime. The transition was easy for one who could write: "Even if the words are all those of renga, a fundamental conception that is diverting (okashi) will make it haikai."

He turned to haikai at just the propitious moment. Many poets thought that *Teimon* haikai had reached a dead end. Sōin organized the resistance and articulated its aims. He allowed a new freedom of language and emphasized stanzaic connection by conception (*kokorozuke*) rather than by words (*kotobazuke*). Danrin style also uses frequent allusion (*honkadori*, *honzetsu*) and playful wit emphasizing "narrative" connections and learning. Such was the appeal of the new style that it attracted writers of the stature of *Ihara Saikaku and *Arai Hakuseki.

Achievement came quickly. The school is represented by *Ōsaka Dokugin Shū* 大阪独吟集 (*A Collection of Solo Sequences at Osaka*, 1676) and *Danrin Toppyakuin* 談林十百韻 (*Ten Hundred-Stanza Sequences of the Danrin School*, 1676). Sōin himself shows well in his *Saiō Toppyhakuin* 西翁十百韻 (*Ten Hundred-Stanza Sequences by Old Sōin*, 1672), the achievement of which may be represented by one of the ten *hyakuin*. All hundred stanzas of *Hana de Soro no Maki* 花でそろの巻 (*I am Called Flower*, 1671) offer a variant of haikai in being devoted to the subtopic of love (*koi no haikai*). Using his haikai pen name of Saiō, he composed this highly interesting sequence, starting with a witty brief preface and a very humorous *hokku* that introduces a flower stanza in a highly unorthodox way. The nature of love varies from courtly to sordid, comic to serious. It is an excellent example of Danrin haikai in its heavy use of allusion, its use of conceptual and narrative elements of connection (*tsukeai*), and its preference for the hundred-stanza sequence. All in all, Sōin planned well, and the Danrin school became the most prosperous and longest lasting of the haikai styles.

NISHIZAWA IPPŪ 西沢一風. 1665–1731. Early Edo writer of *ukiyozōshi* and *jōruri*. A bookseller and publisher in Osaka who dealt especially with plays, he began writing late. In 1698 appeared his *Shinshiki Gokansho* 新色五巻書 (*New Stories of Love in Five Parts*), one of many ukiyozōshi inspired by *Ihara Saikaku (in this case *Kōshoku Gonin Onna*). These stories that lead to suicide are realistic enough, but they lack Saikaku's verve and style. Ippū does approach the master more nearly than anyone else, however, and he wrote more than twenty narratives in many kinds. Some are historical romances: for example, *Gozen Gikeiki* 御前義経記 (*Yoshitsune's Story Told before His Excellency*, 1700). As with Saikaku, the element of parody was highly congenial, although more explicitly with him: *Fūryū Ima Heike* 風流今平家 (*Today's Modish Heike*, 1693); *Ima Genji Utsubobune* 今源氏空船 (*Present-Day Genji and the Empty Boat*, 1716); and *Midare Hagi Sambon Yari* 乱脛三本鑓 (1718). Shortly thereafter he turned to jōruri, succeeding *Ki no Kaion as a popular dramatist. His biggest hit appears to have been *Hōjō Jiraiki* 北条時頼記 (1726), a tale centered on the life of the Hōjō regent, Tokiyori (1227–1263).

It seems altogether fitting that this very talented bookseller should cap his career with the first history of the jōruri theatre, *Ima Mukashi Ayatsuri Nendaiki* 今昔操年代記 (*Chronicles of the Puppet Theater Past and Present*, 1727). This includes many valuable observations drawn from personal experience in addition to the fruits of his research.

NŌAMI 能阿弥. 1397–1471. Muromachi *renga* poet, artist, incense master, etc. Founder of the three generations of "Ami's": see *Geiami and *Sōami. Nōami deserves more than a few words as a representative of the many talented people of low origin who rose to prominence in the fifteenth and sixteenth centuries, not least of the group whose talent was fostered by the Ashikaga shoguns. For these men to do so, many had to take real or nominal orders and, under the Ashikaga *bakufu*, also take on a name ending in -ami, reflecting the Amidist emphasis in Buddhism at the time. Many of such people rose from being mere temple servants to dōbōshū, artists or otherwise cultured attendants on Ashikaga potentates and their emulators. Most were highly versatile, like Nōami, who perfected his accomplishment in many areas. Their many-sidedness distinguishes them from such other figures as *Kan'ami and *Zeami, who excelled in but one art, *nō*, although in the end the latter have greater claim on our attention.

NŌIN 能因. 988–?1058. Mid-Heian *waka* poet, priest. A poet of some powers, he was even more a literary and personal figure. It is said that he fell in love with a woman who bore him a child, and that on her death in 1013 he took orders. Other stories tell how he impersonated another person in order to take part in a poetry match, how he secretly tanned himself in order to show some travel poems he had written at home in Kyoto, and so on. His poems appear in the **Goshūishū* and later royal collections (see Part Six A), in *Fujiwara Teika's *Hyakunin Isshu*, and other personal anthologies. His personal collection, *Nōin Hōshi Shū* 能因法師集 (*Priest Nōin's Collection*) is thought to have been compiled by him, and he also made a personal anthology, *Gengenshū* 玄々集 (*The Mysterious Collection*), selecting 167 poems by 91 poets from about 990 to 1045.

Certain works were attributed to him, but even with his name in the title it is doubtful whether they can be added to those already named. The attribution suggests a certain reputation, and if he did nothing else he established in Japan the figure of the poetic traveler: his poem on the Shirakawa Barrier was one of the prototypes of works to follow by

*Saigyō, *Sōgi, *Matsuo Bashō, and many others: "At the capital,/I departed as companion/Of the haze of spring,/And now the autumn wind blows here—/ The Barrier of Shirakawa" (*Goshūishū, 9: 518).

NONOGUCHI RYŪHO 野々口立圃. 1595–1669. Early Edo *haikai* poet, one of the seven worthies of the *Teimon* school. He studied under *Matsunaga Teitoku, but quarreled with another leading member of the school, *Matsue Shigeyori, over the latter's important collection, *Enoko Shū*, and gradually drew apart from the school. He was a leader as well as a quarreler, and had a large number of followers. He also worked on renga and earlier Japanese studies. Apart from a large number of anthologies, he has his own work in *Haikai Hokku Chō* 俳諧発句帳 (*An Album of Opening Stanzas for Haikai*, 1633).

NONOMURA NINSEI. See NINSEI.

NORINAGA. See MOTOORI NORINAGA.

NOZAWA BONCHŌ 野沢凡兆. D. 1714. Early Edo *haikai* poet. Born in Kanazawa, he went to Kyoto, where he practiced medicine. About 1688 he joined the western branch of the school of *Matsuo Bashō, along with *Mukai Kyorai, *Nakamura Fumikuni, and Esa Shōhaku. The next year, two of his stanzas appeared in *Arano* (see Part Six). His talents developed with astonishing rapidity. In *Sarumino* (see Part Six), edited by him and Kyorai, his forty-one *hokku* exceed by one even those by Bashō. And next to Bashō, he is clearly the best of the poets participating in the *kasen* included in *Sarumino*. The first three of these are regarded as the apex of Bashō-style haikai, so that Bonchō has a very important place. His wife, Tome, better known by her name as a nun, *Ukō, was also a gifted poet.

Around 1690 he began to withdraw from Bashō for reasons that are not clear. By the end of the century, he was living in Osaka. Some say that the close of his life was spent in poverty, but he continued to bring out poetic collections. It is generally agreed that his late poetry does not match that he wrote while associated with Bashō, although since that is also in general true of the others, what it really means is that he was a great poet for just two or three years, then equaling or perhaps excelling even *Enomoto Kikaku, both in hokku and *renku*.

Japanese school children are taught two hokku as representatives of "haiku"—one being Bashō's on the frog leaping into the old pond. That is given as a poem with an element of the slightly comic. The other, by Bonchō, is given as example of the serious: "On and on it goes/the river making one dark line/ across snowy fields" (*Sarumino*, 1: 73).

NUKATA (or NUKADA) NO ŌKIMI 額田王. B. 630. Yamato *waka* poet. She seems the best poet of

her time, writing with assurance on public and private topics alike, making Chinese elements seem wholly native. Judging from her connections with various sovereigns, councillors, and factions as well as her survival of the intrigues involved in the Jinshin War (672), she must also have been astute in political matters and have been assisted by her role as shaman (miko), revealing the intentions of Shinto divinities.

OCHIKUBO MONOGATARI 落窪物語 (*The Tale of Ochikubo*). Mid-Heian *monogatari*. Neither date nor authorship is known, but opinions concur that it dates from the later tenth century, before *Murasaki Shikibu's *Genji Monogatari*. It is therefore a *mukashi monogatari* as well as a *tsukurimonogatari*. Like other mukashi monogatari, this is thought to have been written by a man for female readers, although the present version may be of an original altered over the years by copyists-revisers. Critics divide somewhat on the extent to which the prominent element of the story is its tale of love or its depiction of a mistreated stepdaughter (see *Sumiyoshi Monogatari*). There is no doubt that Ochikubo is mistreated, but later her stepmother is also. Much of the usual detail of the mistreated stepdaughter stories is simply assumed or present at the outset, whereas the care devoted to the romance of the heroine and her lover has little in common with the Cinderella kind of story, in which amatory matters are largely perfunctory. The happy ending is typical of mukashi monogatari, if not always in the widespread way of this genial though not profound tale. It is difficult in considering this work to believe that the *Genji Monogatari* was about to be written.

ŌE NO MASAFUSA 大江匡房. 1041–1111. Late Heian *waka* and *kanshi* poet. Born into a learned family, he had read some Confucian classics by the age of seven. He was greatly admired for his learning, and employed to use it by five sovereigns, beginning with Goreizei (r. 1045–1068). He became known as the "Prestigious Lord of Past and Present." He was, with *Fujiwara Akihira, one of the two greatest exponents of Chinese literature in late Heian times, but he did not restrict himself to ancient China. He commented on parts of the *Man'yōshū*, compiled *Wakan Rōei Gōchū* 和漢朗詠江注 (*Ōe's Notes on the Wakan Rōeishū*), wrote waka on many topics and in many styles, and is credited with the setsuwa, *Gōdanshō*. In his *Gōki* 江記 (*Ōe's Own Record*), he records the affairs of his house along with innovations taking place in government. He sums up many admirable traits of a Heian courtier and foretells certain kinds of study that would become practiced with distinction later.

ŌGA. See MANTEI ŌGA.

OGATA KENZAN 尾形乾山. 1663–1743. Mid-Edo potter. After studying pottery with various masters, calligraphy with his father, and painting with his brother, *Ogata Kōrin, he practiced a fresh style of pottery. His wares became highly favored by tea masters for shape, color, glaze, and combination of paintings with calligraphy. Later in life he introduced the techniques of Kyoto raku pottery to Edo.

OGATA KŌRIN 尾形光琳. 1658–1716. Mid-Edo painter. After a period studying the Kanō styles of painting, he shifted to work with more innovative artists like *Sōtatsu. His work combines a sense of fidelity to nature with a height of decoration that makes it at once recognizable and impressive. His many gifted followers seem not to have been able wholly to grasp the secret. Perhaps it was genius rather than technique, and so incommunicable.

OGAWA HARITSU 小川破笠. 1663–1747. Mid-Edo artist, haikai poet. An Ise man, he studied *haikai* under *Matsuo Bashō and others. Although proficient in poetry as well as in painting, he most excelled in lacquer work. Besides his genius for fresh design, he was an innovator in such techniques as ceramic inlay, for which he was the finest as well as one of the first artists.

OGURA HYAKUNIN ISSHU. See *karuta*; FUJIWARA TEIKA.

OGYŪ SORAI 荻生徂徠. 1666–1728. Early Edo Confucian scholar, *kanshi* poet. Born in Edo, in his early life he had much to endure. Persevering, he began to attract attention for his learning in the mid-1690s. About 1705 he became involved in composing Ming-style poetry, making the techniques known to a wide audience.

The fame he was acquiring as leader of a new intellectual movement is testified to by an Edo *hokku* on his opening his school.

Ume ga ka ya   The plum fragrance—
tonari wa Ogyū   next door to Ogyū
Sōemon.   Sōemon.

His studies ranged widely and influenced diverse social groups. His interpretation of Confucianism and attention to public affairs attracted the attention of the most powerful men of the time: particularly the *bakufu* senior counsellor, Yanagisawa Yoshiyasu (1658–1714) and, through him, the fifth Tokugawa shogun, Tsunayoshi (1646–1709). Under another sobriquet, Ken'en 蘐園, Sorai organized a literary house or school, the Shibunsha 詩文社 which found favor with many samurai and *chōnin*.

In his *Sorai Sensei no Gakusoku* 徂来先生学則 (*Master Sorai's Regulatory Principles*, 1715), he begins by positing the places where the Confucian Sage may be sought. The Sage does not appear in Japan to the east or in the various countries to the west. The sage exists solely in pristine Chinese poetry, prose, rites (or etiquette), and music. This

seems daunting. But since Sorai practiced *gagaku* to gain insight into the Sage, it is clear that by the right principles and method, one does have access to the wisdom of the Sage.

His reasoning is shown by one of his arguments. He distinguished between poetry and prose as transmitted by words (*kotoba*) and rites (*rei*) and music as transmitted by practice (okonai). Moreover, he attributed to the teaching of the Sage in rites and music the transcendent beauty of high art or *fūga*—in *Sorai Sensei no Tōmonjo* 徂来先生答問書 (*Master Sorai's Response to Questions*, 1724). In other words, although distinguishable by their media of transmission, rites and music belong, equally with poetry and prose, to the Way of the Sage. This distinction between differing means and common ends has come to hold increasing interest to students of Edo culture. (But see *hōben*.)

Beyond these matters, there are complexities that have led to different accounts of Sorai. It is clear that he was not orthodox in Edo Confucian terms, supporting neither the orthodox Neoconfucianism, *Shushigaku*, nor its major alternative, *Yōmeigaku*. He is one of the major proponents of *kogaku*, study of the presumed true, old, pristine learning. The problem is that, in closing Japan from intercourse with other nations, the bakufu prevented Japanese, Sorai included, from learning Chinese in China. As a result, all Edo interpretation of Confucianism was dealt with in terms of a dead language. Yet Sorai maintained not only that the pristine meaning must be found, but also that he had devised the method to do so.

In the spirit of kogaku, it was first necessary to free the Confucian truth from encrusted error. As a counterpart to *Itō Jinsai's kogigaku (semantics of the classics), Sorai offered kobunjigaku (philology of the classics). He began by rejecting the whole method of Japanese reading of Chinese, including means such as *okurigana* and *kunten*. As he said, that system produced a "dialect" of "what language I do not know" (*Yakubun Sentei* 訳文筌蹄 *Translation as Method*, ca. 1715). Instead, he said, one must ascertain the true meaning of words. To further this enterprise, Sorai produced two quasi dictionaries, the *Yakubun Sentei*, and *Kun'yaku Jimō* 訓訳示蒙 (*Guide to Translation*, date uncertain). Unlike familiar Chinese or Japanese dictionaries, these are not organized by entries according to graphic appearance or by sound, but by meaning. His philological purpose is to distinguish what may be confused, as his end is removal of false interpretations in order to justify true meanings. These lexicographic or philological methods and purposes were furthered in two other major studies: *Bendō* 弁道 (*Explanations of the Way*) and *Bemmei* 弁名 (*Explanations of Terms*, both pub. 1740).

Sorai anticipated the idea of the "hermeneutic circle" known in the West from the historian Wilhelm Dilthey: the need to know the part (to Sorai, the word or phrase) in order to understand the whole (the work or even the Way), and yet the need to know that whole in order to understand that part. To deal with the matter, Sorai urged thorough philological study of a methodical kind. One must go through the Chinese classics carefully, culling words and phrases, writing them down, and sorting them into containers distinguishing between historical periods and individual styles. Along with this directive to painstaking work, Sorai offered great optimism over the ease with which pristine meanings could be recovered. He reminds one of the Protestant faith in "literal" hermeneutics and of the adage that practice makes perfect.

Sorai's optimism enlisted able followers like *Hattori Nankaku and Dazai Shundai. They became teachers in their own right, so extending Sorai's influence. Although Edo Confucianism has been thought an arid, fruitless matter in much of modern times, many have recently come to discover—and in particular, in Sorai—serious attention to problems that endure. In terms of the discussion here, which has slighted so many of his activities, he raises in serious terms problems of interpretation. How are we to account for the relationship, or meaning, of the world, what writers write about it, what readers make of the writings and the world, and what the connections between these matters may be? As Edo studies advance, the Chinese poems of his *Sorai Shū* may be similarly revalued. The poems are certainly central to his total enterprise, one large facet among many. For intellectual breadth, energy, and lasting interest, Sorai's only Edo rivals in his sphere are probably *Motoori Norinaga and *Hiraga Gennai.

OKADA YASUI 岡田野水. 1658–1743. Early Edo *haikai* poet. A Nagoya man, he was probably better known at the time for this practice of tea. During the stay by *Matsuo Bashō in Nagoya in the winter of 1684, Yasui participated in composing *kasen* later published in *Fuyu no Hi* (see Part Six F). He is sometimes said to have a narrative element in his style, meaning that his stanzaic connection (*tsukeai*) tends to look backward to a greater degree than usual, incorporating—and advancing—major elements of a situation in the preceding stanza. He is one of the principal Nagoya representives of Bashō's school, along with *Yamamoto Kakei and *Tsuboi Tokoku.

ŌKAGAMI (also *YOTSUGI MONOGATARI*) 大鏡 (世継物語) (*The Great Mirror* [*The Tale of Yotsugi*]). Late Heian (ca. 1119) *rekishi monogatari* in three, eight, or (as is usual) six parts. The 176 years covered (850–1025) involve the glory of the court, in particular of the branches of the Fujiwara family with power, and as exemplified by *Fujiwara Michinaga. In this coverage, the work follows the *Eiga Monogatari* in choice of subject.

The literary treatment differs. Instead of the indirection of narratorship such as is usual in a *mono-*

gatari or history, this work gives a specific narrative situation and narrator, however fictional. The introductory section involves a person telling of his attendance at a religious service held at the Unrin Temple at Murasakino (Kyoto) during the fifth Month of 1025. He encounters two figures whose talk makes up the work—(Ōyake) Yotsugi and (Natsuyama) Shigeki, the one 190 and the other 180 years old. Other characters, less important, and less mature, also appear. Yotsugi and Shigeki do not tire in speaking of the splendors of royalty, even as they (such radical fictions themselves) earnestly seek to separate fact from legend, the genuine from the spurious. The effort of the author through such fictions has been sufficiently successful for the work to be a major historical source, and many of its judgments are thought to be sound. Yotsugi's aged wife provides a less formal, more intimate view of life at court as she knew it over the century since she was eleven.

Religious matters are more important than in the *Eiga Monogatari*, which is some manner of inspiration for it. But this work gives a stronger sense of the great days lie in the past, especially in the fourteen reigns dealt with, and more particularly in the twenty Fujiwara potentates who ruled in the name of the royal aegis. As the account nears its end, and more recent times, there is less focus. The historical panorama seems gradually to dissolve, until the fiction once more returns us to the situation at the Urin Temple.

The range of characters is impressive, including many kinds of individuals who are by no means all highly placed or powerful. The naturalness of the conversation contributes greatly to the literary quality of the work. Unity is obtained by the dominance of the incredibly old men, whom we come to accept as voices like those in a Platonic dialogue. Japanese feel that the style of presentation is more masculine than is the case with the great Heian monogatari, including the *Eiga Monogatari*.

The author, whoever it was, clearly was well possessed of learning in historical, Buddhist, and poetic matters, in addition to having a clear sense of life at court. This work initiates—and is the best exemplar of—a sub-kind called *kagamimono* ("mirror works"). It is a matter of some comparative interest that the concept of mirror does not introduce Western conceptions of mimesis, or medieval ideas of a moral "speculum." This and the other "mirrors" provide a means of seeing from afar, of looking into the past. The Western counterpart would later become the metaphor of the telescope or perspective.

OKANISHI ICHŪ 岡西惟中. 1639–1711. Early Edo *haikai* poet. About 1669 he became acquainted with *Nishiyama Sōin, thereafter becoming an important *Danrin* figure. A few titles suggest his wide ranging interests: *Haikai Sambushō* 俳諧三部抄 (*A Treatise on Haikai in Three Parts*); *Kinrai Haikai*

Fūteishō 近来俳諧風躰抄 (*On the Styles of Recent Haikai*, 1679); and *Zoku Mumyōshō* 続無名抄 (*The Nameless Treatise Continued*; 1700: see *Kamo no Chōmei).

ŌKUMA KOTOMICHI 大隈言道. 1798–1868. Late Edo *waka* poet. His efforts as a poet received little recognition in his lifetime. Discovery by Sasaki Nobutsuna in 1898 effectively began his reputation. Kotomichi's adult life started out well as a teacher and a scholar, but he moved restlessly about, never quite getting established in the world. There is in his poetry that freshness that is repeatedly claimed as an ideal by Edo waka poets and equally often far to seek. In terms of poetic quality, he is the last poet worthy to be named with *Ryōkan and *Kobayashi Issa.

OKURA. See YAMANOE OKURA.

ŌKURA TORAAKIRA 大蔵虎明. 1597–1662. Early Edo *kyōgen* actor, critic, and commentator. He is best known today as author of *Warambegusa* 童子草, ca. 1660, a collection of anecdotes and remarks, in eighty-nine parts, on the nature of kyōgen as a comic art. See Part Six H, for further comment on him, and Part Five B, for more on kyōgen.

ŌKYO. See MARUYAMA ŌKYO.

ŌNINKI 応仁記 (*The Record of the Ōnin War*). A *gunki monogatari* in two parts; author and date unknown. It deals with the devastating Ōnin War (1467–1477), which ravaged the capital.

ONITSURA. See UEJIMA ONITSURA.

ONO NO KOMACHI 小野小町. Fl. ca. 833–857. Early Heian *waka* poet, one of the *rokkasen*. It is impossible to recover the historical woman from the veils of legends depicting her as a woman of passion, a beauty, a lover, and, at her sad end, a hag. Like *Ariwara Narihira, if differently, she has fed the imaginations and perhaps the desires of many a daydreamer. Her poetry justifies the legends to the extent that it is the most intense example of the passionate woman poet. There are also some playful or gallant exchanges with some of her contemporaries—*Fun'ya (Bun'ya) Yasuhide, *Henjō, and *Ōshikōchi Mitsune.

She is by no means the sole poet in the *Kokinshū* to make use of *kakekotoba*, but no other poet uses the technique as often, or as effectively. There are only some 110 poems in her personal collection, *Komachi Shū*, but many of them, and especially those shared with the *Kokinshū*, are of such remarkable intensity that their impact is all out of proportion to their number. Most readers come to prefer other waka poets, but she is one of the very best with

whom to begin, and the impression she first makes is indelible. For dramatic versions of her legends see, among *nō*, *Sōshiarai Komachi, Kayoi Komachi, Sekidera Komachi*, and *Sotoba Komachi*.

ONO NO TAKAMURA 小野篁. 802–852. Early Heian *waka, kanshi* poet. Although of distinguished ancestry, it was only by reforming his eccentric ways that he gained recognition by Saga (r. 809–823). In his own time his reputation depended not a little on his poetry in Chinese, examples of which appear in *Keikokushū, Honchō Monzui*, and *Wakan Rōeishū*. Contemporary accounts refer to his great gifts, as they also do to his growing insane for a time. He became known as "Yakyō" 野狂—a learned, punning, Sinified way of using a part of his name to say he was mad.

In 837 he was appointed to the Chinese embassy under Fujiwara Tsunetsugu. Feigning illness, he did not board the ship and later wrote ironically about embassies to China. For his offense, he was banished to Oki Island, where he composed poems, including the seventy bewailing his plight in *Takukōgin Shichijūin* 謫行吟七十韻.

A highly romanticized version of his life appears in a work variously titled *Takamura Monogatari, Takamura Nikki*, and *Takamura Shū*: a tale, diary, or collection. Its two parts treat first his anguished, frustrated love for his half-sister, and then his triumphant rise and marriage. Whoever its author, it is not an outstandingly important work, and he is not a stellar poet. But such a life and literary reputation make him a suitable subject as well as writer.

Ō NO YASUMARO. See *Kojiki*.

ORIBE. See FURUTA ORIBE.

ŌSHIKŌCHI MITSUNE 凡河内躬恒. Fl. 898–922. Early Heian *waka* poet, one of the *sanjūrokkasen*. He was governor of Kai, Izumi, and Awaji over a period of years, and on his return to Kyoto he became one of the compilers of the *Kokinshū*. He distinguished himself at poetry matches and in writing poems to go with pictures on folding screens. He ranks with *Ki no Tsurayuki as one of the chief poets of the day, for although he never quite seems to transcend talent, he also holds to a standard of quality that was immediate and admired: he has no fewer than 193 poems included in the official collections, a very large number for someone of his time. He also has a personal collection, *Mitsune Shū*.

ŌSHIMA RYŌTA 大島蓼太. 1718–1787. Mid-Edo *haikai* poet. Although he studied haikai in Edo, his place of birth is uncertain. Among the thirty journeys he is said to have taken to compose poetry on the way, there is one following the footsteps of *Matsuo Bashō as recorded in *Oku no Hosomichi*. Since he gathered more than 3,000 followers, he must have been a very attractive person. His poetry is another matter. From being plain in nature, it degenerated into the less than mediocre. He did compose *renku*, giving him insight into Bashō's genius, as he showed otherwise in his important *Bashōō Shichibu Sagashi* 芭蕉翁七部捜 (*Gleanings from the Seven Collections of Old Master Bashō*, 1761). The Haikai Revival seems to have brought out the best in him as a person and critic without blessing him with greatness.

ŌTA NAMPO 太田南畝. 1749–1823. Late Edo writer of *kyōka*, *kyōshi*, and various prose kinds. Born in Edo, he followed his father in *bakufu* appointments, leading a kind of double life as official and as comic writer—a fact that suggests something of the strains (and possibilities) of life at the time. Because of his lengthy and various career, he had occasion for an unusually large number of pen names: Neboke Sensei, Shihō Sanjin, Yomo no Akara, Shoku Sanjin, and so on.

It was as Neboke Sensei that he first made his name, as early as 1777, when he was twenty-eight. His *kanshi* collection, *Neboke Sensei Bunshū* 寝惚 先生文集 (*Professor Sleepy Head's Poems*), revealed gifts for comic writing so fresh as to make him the leading writer of that kind in his time. Two years later, with whatever help or encouragement from his friend, *Karagoromo Kisshū, he published his first *kyōka* collection, *Ameuri Dohei ga Den* 売飴土 平伝, which showed an acute eye for what a Marxist would term the contradictions of feudal society. By the time he was twenty, he had published so much that was well recieved—and so varied—that he was a literary figure of importance and influence. He wrote *kokkeibon*, *hanashibon*, and *kibyōshi* among kinds of prose narrative, often giving them absurd titles. Moreover, if any collection of kyōka can be said to have established its popularity, it was Nampo's *Manzai Kyōkashū* 万載狂歌集 (*A Thousand Centuries of Kyōka*, 1783).

Nothing seemed to stop his writing, not even appointments in Osaka and Nagasaki (and back in Edo). He is quite unusual as a popular writer in leading the tastes of the time without having been absorbed into the literary establishement. Of course he had his literary friends, and he went out of his way to promote those he admired, such as *Yokoi Yayū. There is something difficult to assess in Nampo. What was the motive of his compulsion—or was it a serious dedication—to write? And even if compelled or dedicated, where could he have got the inspiration to avoid the repetition from which the work of a *Jippensha Ikku suffers? It is remarkable for a comic writer that his works most esteemed today include two from the end of his life. Of these, his *Shokusan Hyakushu* 蜀山百首 (1818) is of course a collection of one hundred kyōka; "Shokusan" is a pen name he had adopted in Osaka, it being identified with the coppersmith (*dōza*) trade he had

engaged in there. Some say that the poems were selected by one or more of his followers, but all agree as to its centrality as a kyōka collection. The other, *Ichiwa Ichigen* 一話一言 (*One Talk, One Word*, apparently composed 1779–1820), is a collection of prose jottings normally assigned to the *zuihitsu* category. It contains miscellaneous writings by others as well as himself. Like his other work, it is addressed to the quick-witted and intellectual reader.

Few writers in any literature have been so versatile and successful without being thought truly great. One of Nampo's titles, a characteristic Edo fabrication, (*Kankoku Mutai*) *Koitsu wa Nippon* (漢国無躰) 此奴和日本 (1784), labels a work that well represents Nampo's limits as well as his talents. But Edo literature is steadily being revalued, and critics may find ere long some serious purpose in his work—perhaps by relating it to his double life and his peculiar engagement with his world, that is, to his lasting, fertile effort to come to grips with those factors.

ŌTOMO KURONUSHI 大伴黒主. Fl. 885–897. Early Heian *waka* poet, one of the *rokkasen*, or six poetic sages. Little is known of him, and from the poetry by him in the *Kokinshū* and a later collection or two it is not easy to understand why he should be included among the rokkasen along with *Ariwara Narihira and *Ono no Komachi.

ŌTOMO SAKANOE NO IRATSUME 大伴坂上 郎女. B. 695–701; d. ca. 750. Nara *waka* poet. She attracted the attention of several men, including one by whom she is known to have had children. She has a considerable number of poems (eighty-four) in the *Man'yōshū*: six *chōka*, seventy-seven *tanka*, one *sedōka*. The explanation might be taken to be the fact that *Ōtomo Yakamochi, presumed last editor of the collection, was her half-nephew and son-in-law. But there is reason in the poems themselves. About two-thirds of them are love poems, and although it is impossible to say whether they deal with real or fictional events, they help make the tradition of the passionate female poet that was to continue throughout Japanese literature: besides certain male poets who wrote fictionally, there are *Ono no Komachi, *Izumi Shikibu, *Shokushi Naishinnō, and others.

ŌTOMO TABITO 大伴旅人. 665–773. Nara *waka* poet, father of *Ōtomo Yakamochi. His family had a distinguished military past, but it was being eased out of power to lesser functions of administration and to learning. In his post at Dazaifu (Kyushu), Tabito made the place a literary center. His poetry has a historical importance to a degree that its subjects may not seem to suggest. The "Preface" in elegant Chinese and poems on an excursion to the Matsura River (*Man'yōshū*, 5: 853–60; assuming this to be his) and his poems on sake (3: 338–50) show how Taoist ideas could be naturalized in Japanese poetry. His plum blossom banquet (see 5: 815–46) was a recollection of a Chinese one, and in the great adjustment of Chinese literature to Japanese—and the reverse as well—Tabito, along with his friend *Yamanoe Okura, took a conspicuous lead. In another poem (5: 810–11) he tells how a Japanese zither made of paulownia wood appears to him in a dream and speaks to him. This degree of fictionality, like the degree of assertion of his own personality in the sake poems, marks a distinct phase of development in Japanese literary awareness. Tabito also has the distinction of producing a yet more gifted poet as son, Yakamochi, whose entry follows.

ŌTOMO YAKAMOCHI 大伴家持. D. 785. Late Nara *waka* poet, a compiler of the *Man'yōshū*, son of *Ōtomo Tabito. His 479 poems (including 46 *chōka*) make up over 10 percent of the whole collection. He lived at Dazaifu during his father's service there, returned when his father died, and then studied at the court school (daigaku). After service at the court of Shōmu (r. 724–749), he held posts as a provincial governor. He particularly disliked service in Etchū (Toyama), so far from the capital, but he developed as a poet there; about 220 poems can be assigned to those years. Such remoteness also saved him from being embroiled in political turmoils in the capital.

Many of the poems written in Etchū describe flowering plants and trees, but he also wrote letter-like longer poems to friends in the capital. Most of the love poems exchanged with various ladies cannot be reliably dated, and for that matter it is not clear whether or not they were so seriously meant. In any event, when in 751 he returned for a seven-year stay in the capital, his poems grow more somber. The bitter court rivalries in Nara led him to reflect on the uncertainty of life. In 758 he left for about a year as governor of Inaba, and he later held other, similar posts, none of them commensurate with his sense of his family's historical importance and prestige.

Everyone agrees that he is one of the four principal poets of the *Man'yōshū* with *Kakinomoto Hitomaro, *Yamanoe Okura, and *Yamabe Akahito. There is less agreement as to where Yakamochi stands in relation to them. All would place him after Hitomaro, but the question is how far. Compared with Hitomaro, and even Okura at his best, Yakamochi seems lacking in intensity. But as we reread him, and what is very nearly the same thing, as we age, he comes to seem much more important than Okura or Akahito, capable of some things that even Hitomaro does not achieve. His poetry is as various as it is extensive, and he is as skillful with separate *tanka* as with *chōka*, something that cannot be said of Hitomaro. Some of his poems are highly public, some very inward and subjective. His appeal grows

as one encounters, like him, some of the disappointments and learns some of the more modest enthusiasms that come with time.

OZAWA ROAN 小沢蘆庵. 1723–1801. Late Edo *waka* poet. He was from a household of military retainers in Owari province, but he chose to live in Kyoto until, at about thirty-four, he decided to lead a retired life in Okazaki (back near Nagoya). He studied waka early on under Reizei Tamemura. He extolled certain poets of the Edo period over earlier ones, and opposed the *kokugaku* school of *Kamo no Mabuchi. Although no Edo waka poet truly recaptures the greatness of earlier times, Roan comes as close as any. He wrote: "Poetry consists in expressing just what you presently feel, using your own language and the motives you sense." And his best poems reflect a concern for strong frankness and a freshened diction, each in its way a sign of his devotion to his art.

RAI SAN'YŌ 頼山陽. 1780–1832. Late Edo Chinese scholar, historian, *kanshi* poet. Born in Osaka, he was descended from tradespeople and Confucianists. His father's obligations of service entailed considerable moving about. Family traditions of learning led him to study in Edo in 1797, and shortly he pursued the same goal in Osaka and Kyoto. In 1800, while his father was on duty in Edo, he resigned his samurai status without permission. He hid out in Kyoto, but was discovered and punished with house arrest. During the next three years or so of constricted life he wrote his masterpiece, *Nihon Gaishi* 日本外史 (*The Extra History of Japan*). Released from his house arrest in 1803, he studied here and there, until in 1810 he opened his own school in Kyoto. From time to time he made trips, but he died still fairly young while straining himself to complete the manuscript of his *Nihon Seiki* 日本政記 (*A Record of Japanese Government*).

He was at once versatile and strong-willed. He chanted the *Heike Monogatari* to the lute, had ability in military matters, carved name seals excellently, wrote very well in verse and prose—whether Japanese or Chinese—and of course studied Confucianism, especially its historiography. His *San'yō Shishō* 山陽詩鈔 (*San'yō's Verse and Prose*) in eight parts gives a sample of many kinds of writing, including travel accounts, a native genre that he practiced with distinction, and poems in Chinese.

His renown rests, however, on *Nihon Gaishi* (published 1836). It is an extra history (gaishi) in that it deals, not with sovereigns, annals, or the state as a basis, but with the vicissitudes of military houses from the Taira and Minamoto to the Tokugawa. It is written in such heightened style, pointedness of description, and such memorable observations that it continued to be popular into modern times. Today its stylistic virtues may pose some difficulties, and modern historians have leveled heavy criticism of its derivative character and its many errors. Yet its youth and verve make it a classic.

As in China, so in Japan, concepts of literature included history: the *Kojiki, *Nihon Shoki, and *Fudoki belong to such a concept of letters (bungaku) as much as do lyrics. The historical lines in fiction and drama are comparably strong (see jidaimono, rekishi monogatari). There was a Japanese tradition of writing history in Chinese as well. With history served so well by literary works and by Chinese, works recognizable in Western terms as "pure" history appear late, and San'yō has a very important place in such writing. His Nihon Gaishi no doubt has the faults attributed to it. But it is recognizable, outstandingly written history—in Chinese—by a young man in his twenties.

RANRAN. See MATSUKURA RANRAN.

RANSETSU. See HATTORI RANSETSU.

RAZAN. See HAYASHI RAZAN.

REIZEI 冷泉 POETS. The sons of *Fujiwara Tameie (himself son of *Fujiwara Teika) divided into three groups in dispute over inheritance, poetry, and politics. A wife of Tameie's, *Abutsu Ni (as she is known by her religious name) persuaded Tameie to deed some property to her elder son, who became known as *Reizei (or Fujiwara) Tamesuke. Tamesuke and his adherents were more innovative in poetry than the *Nijō poets led by his elder brother, Fujiwara (Nijō) Tameuji. The Reizei group was on good terms with a third branch, the *Kyōgoku poets, descended from yet another son of Tameie's, Tamenori. The Reizei group managed to gain possession of many important manuscripts by Teika, handing over forgeries to the Nijō house, thus giving them a kind of poetic capital, much of it known about but not publicly acknowledged until about 1980. Over the centuries, however, as the Reizei house gained poetic dominance, it became even more ossified than the Nijō. The surname used was usually "Reizei," sometimes "Fujiwara."

(FUJIWARA) REIZEI TAMEHIDE (藤原) 冷泉 為秀. D. 1372. Late Kamakura waka poet. He belonged to the liberal line of *Reizei poets descended from *Fujiwara Teika. His poems (ten of them) first appear in the *Fūgashū. Some few more appear in later collections.

REIZEI TAMESUKE 冷泉為相. 1263–1328. Late Kamakura waka poet. Grandson of *Fujiwara Teika, son of *Fujiwara Tameie and *Abutsu Ni, he was founder of the school of *Reizei poets. He made cause with *Kyōgoku Tamekane and other *Kyōgoku poets in seeking a more liberally conceived poetry than that promoted by their common rivals, the *Nijō poets. Tamesuke's mingled poetic

and political ambitions led him to try to obtain influential friends among the warrior houses to the east of the capital, near the bakufu in Kamakura. Although not the best poet of his house, he kept alive the principle of original conception advocated by his grandfather and great-grandfather, *Fujiwara Shunzei. His personal collections include the Shūi Fūtei Wakashō 拾遺風体和歌抄 (Gleanings of Waka, compiled ca. 1303) and Ryūfū Wakashō 柳風和歌抄 (The Wind in the Willows, 1310). In addition to valuable copies he made (or had made) of important earlier works, he also seems to have composed late in life a renga treatise, Fujigayatsu Shikimoku 藤谷式目 (The Wisteria Valley Handbook).

RIJŌ. See RYŪTEI RIJŌ.

RIKKOKUSHI 六国史 (The Six National Histories). Nara or early Heian compilation of largely dynastic histories. The title therefore means "Six National Histories" rather than "The History of Six Countries" (or provinces). The six histories can be designated by name, length, and periods covered:

1. *Nihon Shoki (Nihongi). See the separate entry.
2. Shoku Nihongi 続日本紀 (The Nihongi Continued). Forty parts dealing with the reigns of Mommu (697–707) to part of that of Kammu (781–806), stopping in 791.
3. Nihon Kōki 日本後紀 (Later Records of Japan). Also in forty parts, running from 792 to the end of Junna's reign (824–833).
4. Shoku Nihon Kōki 続日本後紀 (Later Records of Japan Continued). Twenty parts, covering Nimmyō's reign (833–850).
5. (Nihon) Montoku (Tennō) Jitsuroku (日本) 文徳 (天皇) 実録 (Actual Records of Montoku [Tennō] [of Japan]). Ten parts, covering Montoku's reign (850–858).
6. (Nihon) Sandai Jitsuroku (日本) 三代実録 (Actual Records of Three [Japanese] Reigns). Fifty parts, covering the three reigns of Seiwa (858–876), Yōzei (876–884), and Kōkō (884–887).

As might be expected, more material is available for later reigns, so that successive volumes devote greater length to shorter periods of time. The placing of the Nihon Shoki as the first of these histories probably reflects the fact that it was far better known than the *Kojiki, although they include much of the same matter. The familiarity can be seen in the *Genji Monogatari as well as other important literary works. The Rikkokushi are written in kambun.

RIKYŪ. See SEN NO RIKYŪ.

ROAN. See OZAWA ROAN.

ROKUJŌ SAIIN BAISHI NAISHINNŌ NO SENJI 六条斎院禖子内親王宣旨. ?1022–1092. Late Heian monogatari writer, waka poet. The writer is also variously called Saiin Baishi Naishinnō no Senji, Saiin Rokujō no Senji, etc., and for our purposes may be termed simply Senji. She has not always been thought author of the *Sagoromo Monogatari*. The work was formerly ascribed to *Murasaki Shikibu's Daughter, Daini no Sammi, as if the author of the "the Second Genji" should be the daughter of the author of the first. The appropriateness has yielded to various evidence pointing to Senji. A number of women seem to have been conflated with her at various times, but she is taken to be daughter of Minamoto Yorikuni, and said to have first married Fujiwara Takasada. She was divorced from Takasada when he was banished to Hitachi for the death of Minamoto Sadasue. She later became a wife or concubine of Minamoto Takakuni, who was close to Fujiwara Yorimichi, in those days a figure of great power (and the model for the Horikawa Chancellor, Sagoromo's father). Such connections served to get her service with Princess Baishi when, in 1046, the seven-year-old Baishi became Kamo Shrine Priestess. Senji seems to have served the princess for thirty years or so, well accounting for the appellation by which she is known, Waiting-Lady to Princess Baishi.

The *Sagoromo Monogatari* 狭衣物語 (*The Tale of Sagoromo*) and poems in various *utaawase* and other sources make up Senji's known oeuvre, and it is the *tsukurimonogatari* that exercises greatest claim. It is divided into four lengthy parts without titles, and it is taken to have been written between 1058 and 1092, probably between 1069 and 1072. The story takes Sagoromo through a period of eleven years, during which he rises from a decent rank for a young man to the position of sovereign. Modeled on *Murasaki Shikibu's Genji, he and his world have not a little of the flavor of the Uji chapters concluding the *Genji Monogatari*. The hero's story is to a major degree the continuo for the sad melodies of the lives of the women he knows. He is the son of the imagined Horikawa Chancellor (kampaku) of his day, a hero suitably ideal in person and gifts. His female counterpart, Genji no Miya, never fulfills the love they share, and to which she at least remains steadfast.

Much of the action of the first part is taken up with the inability of Sagoromo and Genji no Miya to realize their love for each other, and with the unhappy love that arises from Sagoromo's chance encounter with Asukai no Onnagimi. In the second part, he loses Onnagimi and becomes attached to Onna Ni no Miya, a princess whose mother announces herself pregnant to hide the fact of her daughter's condition. The princess bears a son looking for all the world like his father (cf. the result of the liaison between Genji and Fujitsubo). Tiring of the world, the princess subsequently takes orders. Genji no Miya is appointed Kamo Shrine Priestess. Sagoromo restlessly visits various temples, at one of which he learns from an itinerant ascetic (yama-

bushi), brother of Asukai no Onnagimi, that she has drowned herself (cf. Ukifune's attempt in the *Genji Monogatari*).

The third part complicates matters in a way befitting this stage of a story. Hearing that his daughter by the dead Asukai Onnagimi frequents the palace of Ippon on Miya, he visits it in disguise. Here the plot complicates. There is a triangular affair centered on the princess, featuring a rival for Sagoromo, much as in the Uji chapters of the *Genji Monogatari*. Then with Sagoromo's father proposing for him, the hero marries the princess. Unfortunately, he is not that interested in her. When he sees Genji no Miya at the Kamo Festival and then Onna no Miya in nun's habit, he determines to renounce the world for the priesthood.

In the last part, however, Sagoromo's father, the Horikawa Chancellor, learns by a dream of Sagoromo's intent and forbids it. On hearing that Saishō Chūjō no Imōtogimi resembles Genji no Miya, Sagoromo becomes involved with her (cf. Kaoru's attraction to Naka no Kimi and Ukifune because of their resemblance to his dead Ōigimi). A year or so later, after a heavenly revelation, the sovereign abdicates in favor of Sagoromo, who offers to make Ippon no Miya his royal consort. When she declines, he introduces into the palace as his bride the pregnant Saishō Chūjō no Imōtogimi. She takes on the title of Fujitsubo no Nyogo and delivers a son. Ippon no Miya takes orders and later dies. Nothing more comes of the lasting love between Genji no Miya and Sagoromo.

Such a world, such a romance owes much to the *Genji Monogatari*, substituting for its metaphysical riches a deep awareness of wrongdoing and a certain worldly realism: here pregnancy is the common effect of the hero's love affairs. It will be obvious that the plot is not uniformly realistic: not even monogatari heroes are usually permitted to dream of becoming sovereign. In fact, this accession was criticized in the *Mumyōzōshi*, which otherwise has very many good things to say about the work. To those we can add, in spite of that one event, a remarkably good plot, good in its telling and even better in its intrinsic interest. This seems to have been the judgment of contemporary readers also. There are not only numerous manuscripts but also extraordinary verbal variations among them, showing that the story was thought to be the thing rather than its verbal realization.

So little is certain about so much concerning this work that it is difficult to know how far to press speculations by Japanese editors. (For a work with such a reputation as this, there is surprisingly little criticism.) It seems clear that in writing about the earlier reigns of Reizei to Ichijō, the author wrote to some extent of the reigns she lived in. How far we are meant to pursue such identification is not clear, but it would assist in accounting for the unusual popularity of the work.

Perhaps the readiest focus that can be given the issue is attention to the heroine, Genji no Miya. It seems clear that she is modeled on Senji's mistress who, like Genji no Miya, served as Kamo Shrine Priestess (saiin). And her love for Sagoromo is taken to allude to the relations between Saki no Saiin [sic] Kenshi and Minamoto Toshifusa. The fact that her royal mistress later took Buddhist vows probably need not bear on the date of the story's composition. For although Genji no Miya also does that, it is a standard Heian solution to the world's problems.

It is rather more interesting to observe what a shadowy figure Genji no Miya is. We take her status as heroine pretty much on faith. The author seems, in fact, almost to have gone out of her way to make a mystery of her heroine (because modeled on the princess?). There are very few scenes at the royal palace, where Genji no Miya might have appeared at utaawase and other events like those that brought her historical model before the court. It is telling that of the just over two hundred poems in the work, only eight are by the heroine, and precious few in response to Sagoromo. Given such bloodless heroineship through so much of the work, the reader suddenly discovers that there really is a loving, passionate woman in Genji no Miya. In a few pages of the last part, she responds to three poems that Sagoromo sends—now that it is in effect too late for her avowal to do her any good. Here are the first two, obviously responding to poems by him and to the autumnal scene:

> If your moon itself
> Were not separated from me
>   By a bank of clouds,
> I would wish each night to bring
> Its light reflected on my sleeve.

Nothing, given the indirection of the time, could be clearer than that. Sagoromo's next poem uses much the same imagery, and she replies with another surprisingly open avowal of her love.

> My deepest feelings
> Go with yours and autumn moonlight
>   Unfamiliar with my sleeve,
> So it is not from some sky gazing
> That my sleeves reflect the light.

That is, my tears are not those in response to lonely autumn sensations but to unsatisfied love of you. Within five and a half pages of that, Sagoromo is sovereign of the land.

The important monogatari from *Murasaki Shikibu's masterpiece on are written by women for women readers (although men also were eager to read them unofficially, as it were). There is no parallel for this in another traditional society, and we find it difficult to come to grips with the significance of that literature. It does seem to matter that although Sagoromo may have his problems and may shed tears of sensibility, it is the women in his life who really know what suffering is. Sagoromo

provides, as it were, the motion of the work, and the women he impinges upon provide the meaning. The sudden flowering into life of Genji no Miya tells us how deeply some quiet female streams must have been running. And that the passion is shown too late tells us something of the hard lot that women experienced, even when they were gifted and of the high aristocracy.

The passion and the suffering of Genji no Miya set an example for important female characters in other important monogatari. Like Genji no Miya's creator, later authors turned to the Uji chapters of the *Genji Monogatari*, and particularly to Ukifune, for versions of human (and especially female) experience. In *Sugawara Takasue no Musume's Hamamatsu Chūnagon Monogatari*, there is a more obvious version of Uji in the Yoshino frequented by Chūnagon (hereafter the usual rank of the hero), a device used also in *Torikaebaya Monogatari*. But the most interesting redefinition of the Uji chapters via the *Sagoromo Monogatari* occurs in *Yoru no Nezame*. Nezame has the passion of Ukifune and Genji no Miya but seems both aware of it and confident in it. She is also made central to the whole story. Each of the later versions has things to offer that Senji's story does not, but none is as energetically and smoothly told.

It is difficult to say assuredly what else the *Sagoromo Monogatari* should be said to signify. Everyone seems to notice the Buddhist diction (given that Senji's mistress was a Kamo Shrine Priestess, some have held that that showed she could not be author). Japanese critics do not seem to think that the Buddhist diction involves a Buddhist theme: after all, Sagoromo decides against taking orders and gains the throne. There are religious figures and details in the story, but not in a way comparable to Ukifune's situation. It is hard to resist the conclusion that Senji set herself three chief aims: the telling of an engrossing tale, the use of a second Genji for the coherence of the story and milieu, and a range of women to convey her most serious concerns. Some might posit a fictionalizing of her own times. Certainly, in showing that the *Genji Monogatari* could be put to new and quite independent use, Senji showed the way to a number of successors.

ROKUJŌ SAIIN MONOGATARI UTAAWASE 六条斎院物語歌合. This is perhaps the earliest of monogatari awase, matchings of poems or other elements in *monogatari*. It may have been inspired by the first match inclusive of pictorial versions of monogatari in the "Eawase" chapter of Murasaki Shikibu's *Genji Monogatari*. It is a precursor of various later works, in particular of the *Mumyōzōshi*, and it is remarkable for having been compiled within a half century of the completion of the *Genji Monogatari*. See also *Fujiwara Shunzei.

ROPPYAKUBAN UTAAWASE 六百番歌合 (*The Poetry Match in Six Hundred Rounds*). Convened in

1193 by *Fujiwara Yoshitsune, this match in 600 rounds involved six poets on each side writing a hundred-poem sequence (*hyakushuuta*) on set topics—1,200 poems in all. In part it was seen to be a match between the conservative Rokujō house of the Fujiwara family, and the innovative Mikohidari house. Fujiwara Shunzei was judge, and his recorded comments are of great critical interest. His son, *Fujiwara Teika, and nephew, *Jakuren, were among the men and women who took part.

RYŌJIN HISHŌ 梁塵秘抄 (*Songs to Make the Dust Dance on the Beams*). Late Heian (ca. 1169) collection of songs and poems in ten books, from which only about a tenth survives. In kind the songs resemble the *kagura*, *saibara*, *fūzoku*, *azumaaso-biuta*, and other sorts known from ancient times. Whatever the resemblances, the songs included went under the capacious category of *imayō*, and therefore were conceived of as popular or current.

These popular songs were gathered from various provinces, and were probably associated with female performers such as *shirabyōshi*, *kugutsu*, or prostitutes. Some songs are Shinto in nature, some Buddhist, some secular. Some appear to have had origins at, or associations with, posting stations, and some with ports. Classifications of some songs include those of divinities (*kamiuta*), songs of Ashigara Shrine (*Ashigara*), plain imayō (*tada no imayō*), and such other hardy kinds as rice-planting songs (*taueuta*).

Whatever their origin or kind, it is clear that they exercised wide appeal, including court circles. In fact it was the loss of many good tunes and texts that led Goshirakawa to join the *Kashishū* 歌詞集 (*Song Texts*) and *Kudenshū* 口伝集 (*Collected Teachings*) to have the present collection made. When it was rediscovered in 1911 after being lost for about six centuries, some admirers considered it a second *Man'yōshū*. That seems excessive by any standard, yet this collection does give a sense, even in its present fragmentary version, of life and of a people's amusements.

RYŌKAN 良寛. 1758–1831. Late Edo poet, priest. Born the eldest son of a family in Izumozaki near Niigata, he forsook a promised succession to his father as village headman and at twenty-one took orders in Sōtō Zen Buddhism. He was followed into the religious life by three brothers and three sisters. While he was performing travel austerities in 1795, his father (who proved quite incompetent for village government, as did a brother thereafter) committed suicide in Kyoto. By this time Ryōkan's travels had taken him as far as Shikoku. He returned to Izumozaki in 1804, setting up in a hermitage on Mt. Kugami. From there he would go down to beg food or play with children, and in his hut he practiced devotions and literature.

In both Japanese and Chinese his poetry is at once heavily indebted to earlier writers and wholly his own. By the standards of then accepted poetic practice, his poetry was bizarre. His idiosyncratic combinations are, however, recommended by the freshness and commitment they possess. It more and more seems that he is superior to *Kobayashi Issa, his better-known contemporary.

He published none of his work, except for including poems in letters. At the age of sixty-eight he met a beautiful twenty-eight-year-old nun, Teishin, with whom he formed a close attachment. Whatever its nature, it was expressed in fervent poems by both. She brought out the first selection of his poems, *Hachisu no Tsuyu* 蓮の露 (*Dew on the Lotus*) in 1835. Choosing the otherwise tired *waka* and Chinese poetry as his means, he is a singular example of a much influenced and uninfluential poet who wrote the most original poetry of his age.

RYŌSHUN. See IMAGAWA RYŌSHUN.

RYŌTA. See ŌSHIMA RYŌTA.

RYŌUN(SHIN)SHŪ 凌雲(新)集 (*A [New] Collection from Above The Clouds*). A collection of Chinese poems in one part. Ordered by *Saga as the first official collection of Chinese poetry, *chokusen-shishū*, written by Japanese, it was compiled by Ono no Minemori 小野岑守 and others about 814, so recognizing the absorption of the continental new learning in Japan. The poems collected were written between 782 and the compilation. The original had ninety poems by twenty-three poets. Three sovereigns are included—Heizei, Junna, and Saga himself. His twenty-two poems are the most by any poet; the chief compiler and Kaya no Toyotoshi each have thirteen. There are some ten topics distinguished in Chinese fashion. Irregular prosody is to be found along with the 7- and 5-character lines. The collection shows that in court circles, the scholars, ministers, and rulers had absorbed their Chinese lore.

RYŪHO. See NONOGUCHI RYŪHO.

RYŪTEI RIJŌ 滝亭鯉丈. D. 1841. Late Edo *kokkeibon* writer. His two best-known works were published after his death: *Hanagoyomi Hasshōjin* 花暦八笑人 (written 1820; published 1848); and *Kokkei Wagōjin* 滑稽和合人 (1823; 1844). Lively in their fashion, these works do show a deterioration of the tradition well practiced by *Shikitei Samba and others.

RYŪTEI TANEHIKO 柳亭種彦. 1783–1842. Late Edo writer of prose fiction and drama. Born in Edo, he came from a samurai family. He esteemed learning, the martial arts, and the life of a writer, including *kyōka* and prose fiction. The *gesaku* writing he began about 1804 represents a departure. His newer ventures included: *Yama Arashi* 山嵐 (*A*

Mountain Storm), a *sharebon* (1808); and *Kakesu no Saezuri* 懸鳥囀, a *kokkeibon* (1815).

Tanehiko was really more at home on the stage and in longer works. His contemporary reputation began with work in *jōruri* and especially with his realistic *Shōhon Jitate Shohen* 正本製初編 (1815). Thereafter he tried his hand at *haikai* and various sorts of fiction until, in 1829, he had published his best-known work, *Nise Murasaki Inaka Genji* 修紫田舍源氏 (*The Fake Murasaki and Country Genji*). This is no adequate response to the *Genji Monogatari*, but neither is it a crude parody. To some extent he emulated stories using Chinese fiction— situating the action in an earlier period— Muromachi times. He had evidently been reading his contemporary, *Kyokutei Bakin. The main plot concerns the love of the hero (the country Genji), Mitsuuji, and gives a good sense of the atmosphere of a military household. He was not really a master of characterization, however, and much of the book's popularity relies on the illustrations by *Utagawa Kunisada. A nice later edition came out just before his death—an end caused by illness, according to some accounts, by his own hand according to others.

His strength lay in conception, ordering, and atmosphere—the idea more than the execution of character. A gifted writer, he does not measure up to Bakin.

SADAIE. See FUJIWARA TEIKA.

SADANOBU. See MATSUDAIRA SADANOBU.

SAGA 嵯峨. 786–842. Early Heian *kanshi* poet, sovereign (r. 808–823). In addition to ordering various collections such as the *Ryōun Shū*, he composed some one hundred Chinese works (including shih and fu) as well as individual lines in styles reminiscent of Six Dynasties and T'ang poetry. He was venerated for his learning, which perhaps he valued as much as his rule.

SAGOROMO MONOGATARI. See ROKUJŌ SAIIN BAISHI NAISHINNŌ NO SENJI.

SAICHŌ 最澄 (or **DENGYŌ DAISHI** 伝教大師). 767–822. Early Heian religious leader who, in 788, founded the Enryakuji on Mount Hiei northeast of Kyoto. This was the origin of a great monastic center that was to exert a powerful influence upon the religious and civil life of the nation until the temple's destruction in 1571 by Oda Nobunaga. In 804 Saichō went to China for a year to study the doctrines and practices of the T'ien T'ai sect, and was also initiated into esotericism (*mikkyō*) and the Niu-t'ou (Gozu) tradition of Ch'an (Zen). The Tendai sect that he founded on his return to Japan was scripturally based on the *Hokkekyō* (Lotus Sutra, see Part Six O), especially as interpreted by the third Chinese patriarch of T'ien T'ai, Chih-i, whose *Maka Shikan* is the basic exposition of the sect's meditation practices. Saichō's Tendai was a synthesis of many influences, reinforced by the Lotus Sutra's doctrine of the Buddha's accommodation (*hōben*) to human diversity and needs. His *Shugo Kokkaishō* 守護国界章 (*The Defense of the Nation*, 818) was Saichō's major apology for Tendai against the attacks of the Nara establishment. His *Hokke Shūku* 法華秀句 (*The Excellent Phrases of the Lotus*, 821) comments on that sutra. In his time Saichō did not enjoy the popularity of his younger contemporary *Kūkai, but Tendai was to become the Mother Church of Japanese Buddhism.

SAIGYŌ 西行. 1118–1190. Late Heian-early Kamakura *waka* poet, priest. He was born into a house that for generations had produced soldiers, a family apparently trusted by the court but restricted to the relatively low status of warriors at the time. He studied waka chiefly with *Minamoto Shunrai, *Fujiwara Shunzei, and members of Shunzei's circle. Considering that he is one of the three best-loved poets in Japan, he wrote a considerable amount of conventional poetry, most of it on the set topics of the day. Some of such poems are highly attractive, but his distinctive approach was to compose poems either on immediate experience or on topics that relate to it. None of his efforts would have meant that much to his poetic career, however, if he had not taken orders (in 1140), becoming Saigyō after being Satō Norikiyo.

There is evidence to show that, like most serious people in the court period, he had often thought and written about the desirability of "throwing away the world" (tonsei, yosute). As legends began to grow about him, particular motives were assigned to his becoming a priest: such experiences as an unhappy love affair, or distress over the political difficulties of Sutoku (r. 1123–1141). Whether it is motive or result, one matter is clear: by becoming a priest, Saigyō became able to treat with people of all social conditions and free to move about the country. In this his career came to parallel that of *Nōin, whom he often recalls, but his own example is the more famous. Many men and women after him took orders for the freedom it gave, the easy social access it brought, and the opportunities for travel and poetry that it provided.

In the years immediately following his taking the tonsure, he resided at various temples and hermitages near the capital, attracting notice as a poet by writing hundred-poem sequences. On returning from his first trip to the reaches of the north, he became a Shingon priest and resided on the venerated mountain of the sect, Kōya.

The ensuing years (ca. 1148–1168) make up a distinct period of his life. He attracted increasing attention as a poet, but he also knew sorrow and straitened circumstances. He seems to have arranged poems written during his earlier northern tour, so that parts of the miscellaneous (zō) section of his poetic collection (see below) read like a poetic travel diary. On a later visit to Shikoku (1168), he managed much the same feat, now extending the prose introductions to his poems. He had kept in correspondence with Sutoku (d. 1164) in banishment to Sanuki (Shikoku), so that his Shikoku trip was something of an act of fealty, as also a means of urging Sutoku to strict Buddhist observance. Earlier, when the Hōgen War had broken out in 1156, he left his quiet on Mount Kōya for the dangers of strife-torn Kyoto. A human and complex individual, his motives perhaps mingled simple humanity with a desire to see what was going on that was natural to a person from a military house. He held to his religious vocation, even while sometimes doubting that it suited with his role as a poet. He also perserved in his poetry, and during these years formed a poetic circle at Ohara, north of the capital, where he wrote *renga* as well as waka, and where he is remembered at a temple by virtue of one of the many cherry trees afterwards called "Saigyōzakura." (There is a *nō* of that title.)

When he returned to Mount Kōya, he had acquired fame as a poet and as a priest. In 1186, he set off eastward on the Tōkaidō toward Musashi, and at Kamakura was detained by Minamoto Yoritomo, victor in the *Gempei* wars and founder of the Kamakura regime. Their talk is known to have included warfare and court kickball, in which Saigyō was highly proficient. Surely they also spoke of poetry, since Yoritomo had some pretensions as a waka poet.

It is not known when he put together his poetic collection, but sometime during his last ten years seems most likely. In 1187, after his return from the east to Kyoto, he sent to *Fujiwara Shunzei and *Fujiwara Teika for their judgment his thirty-six-round poetic matches with himself, or *jikaawase*, *Mimosusogawa Utaawase* 御裳濯川歌合 (1187) and *Miyagawa Utaawase* 宮川歌合 (1189) (*The Poetic Match at the Mimosuso River* and *The Poetic Match at the Miya River*). In the former he pit himself as "Visitor to the Mountain Hut" against himself as "Master of the Path across the Fields." Some poems during these last fifteen or so years feature an understanding of war unavailable to poets of different background.

His reputation rests on 2,090 *tanka*. (Ten of his renga stanzas are also extant.) His chief collection, compiled by him, is the *Sankashū* 山家集 (*The Mountain Hut*). The first of its three parts treats poems on the four seasons, and the third is devoted to miscellaneous poems. Some of the best-loved seasonal poems are on autumn topics, but even more are on his favorite flower, the cherry, whose beauty depends on its early fragility. Many of these poems on cherry blossoms are situated in his much-loved Yoshino, where he seems to have had one or more hermitages. The poems assisted in the gradual shift from the plum to the cherry as the ideal Japanese flower. The miscellaneous poems might be expected, because he often wrote about immediate experience (like the poets of the *Kokinshū*) rather than on the fictional topics dear to other poets of the age. It is less clear why he should have made his second book from love poems—why he wrote so many. Perhaps in this, as in some other respects, he anticipated *Matsuo Bashō, to whom love stanzas were crucial in conveying the agitation, longing, and uncertainty of life. Perhaps he was following convention, and perhaps he had been in love.

Two shorter collections have been recovered in this century: *Kikigaki Shū* 聞書集 (*Jottings of What I Have Heard*) and *Kikigaki Zanshū* 聞書残集 (*Remaining Jottings of What I have Heard*) These are also of uncertain date. But since neither duplicates in its poems the other or the *Sankashū*, it is presumed that they are sequels, as collections if not as to dates of composition. The last collection he is presumed to have made, *Ihon Sankashū* 異本山家集 (*Another Version of the Mountain Hut*), takes almost 450 poems from the three earlier collections (including 428 from the *Sankashū*) and adds 139 poems that had not been collected before. Many in this last group are especially fine, and they provided an important source for the compilers of the *Shinkokinshū*, in which he is represented by ninety-four poems, by more than any other poet.

Saigyō is a very rare example of a poet highly regarded in his time and who has never suffered serious loss or oblivion in his reputation. Bashō has been consistently the poet most loved by Japanese, but both in his time and later dissident voices have been raised. *Kakinomoto Hitomaro has always been admired when known; but the writing system of the *Man'yōshū* made him inaccessible for a time, and today his language is harder for modern readers to understand. Legends and sentiment have invested Saigyō with some unfounded attractions, but he is a poet of great talent, and he was a major poet in the descriptive style that has been so congenial to Japanese readers. There is a seeming paradox in his representing ideals highly prized by Japanese because they are rare in their lives: sophisticated doubt with genuine religious devotion; rejection of the secular world with full knowledge of it; more than lip service to quiet, seclusion, and independence; and the conviction that one should say what one really feels rather than what is expected of one. He struggled hard and imperfectly to achieve such aims. Since he was so much more successful than most people, since he could translate his struggle into moving poetry, and since his struggles, as well as his ideals, are familiar to us all, the high Japanese regard for him is justly shared by readers everywhere. See also *Senjūshō.

SAIKAKU. See Ihara Saikaku.

SAIONJI TAKEMUKI. See Hino no Takemuki.

SAKAI HŌITSU 酒井抱一. 1761–1828. Late Edo painter, priest, son of a daimyo. He took orders and advanced to high ecclesiastical rank at Nishi Honganji in Kyoto, but he went to Edo, and in seclusion lived a highly unconventional life. He had studied painting in the style of *Ogata Kōrin, which he greatly adapted to eccentric ends.

SAKANOE NO IRATSUME. See Ōtomo Sakanoe no Iratsume.

SAKIMARO. See Tanabe Sakimaro.

SAKURADA JISUKE 桜田治助. 1734–1806. Edo *kabuki* dramatist. Born in Edo of a *chōnin* family, he spent some time in *kamigata* after conceiving a liking for theater, and on returning to Edo began to compose plays for the Moritaza from late in 1764. He wrote, or collaborated in, 120 plays during his last four decades of life. For a time the most popular playwright, he lost public esteem after about 1800. He specialized in unusual theatrical elements accompanied by agile dialogue. His popular plays include *Yoshiwara Suzume* 吉原雀 (1768), *Date Kurabe Okuni Kabuki* 伊達競阿国戯場 (1778), and *Keisei Azuma Kagami* 傾情吾嬬鑑 (1788). As the leading playwright, he had many disciples. Three later and less distinguished playwrights bore his name.

SAMBA. See Shikitei Samba.

SAMPŪ. See Sugiyama Sampū.

SANDAISHŪ 三代集. The first three royal collections (*chokusenshū*) of the twenty-one in all (*nijūichidaishū*): the *Kokinshū, *Gosenshū, and *Shūishū. These were taken by *Fujiwara Teika and others to provide the formal models of poetic diction.

SANETOMO. See Minamoto Sanetomo.

SANJIN. See Kyoku Sanjin.

SANETAKA. See Sanjōnish: Sanetaka.

SANJŌNISHI SANETAKA 三条西実隆. 1455–1537. Late Muromachi *waka* and *renga* poet, scholar. Of a rank just below the highest nobility, he served Gotsuchimikado (r. 1465–1500) and Gokashiwabara (r. 1500–1526). The Ashikaga shoguns Yoshimasa and Yoshihisa, as well as Hosokawa Takakuni, esteemed him greatly. Meanwhile he found time to study literature, in which he was accounted the foremost authority of his time. Turning over his public affairs to his son, Kin'eda—who also came to be learned in literary matters and a patron of *Satomura Jōha—he spent his last two decades in literary and pious pursuits. He left behind two personal collections of waka: *Setsugyokushū*

雪玉集 (*Jewels of Snow*) and *Chōsetsushū* 聴雪集 (*Sanetaka's Collection*), as well as a late poetic diary, *Saishōsō* 再昌草, and a more important ordinary diary, *Sanetaka Kō no Ki* 実隆公記 (*Sanetaka's Public Record*), which is a gift to historians, because it runs from his nineteenth to his eighty-first year.

His most important contribution to literature came indirectly, not through what he wrote so much as what he enabled others to write. He was well versed in Chinese studies, especially the poetry of Tu Fu, which he was taught by the monks of the *Gosan temples. In spite of his public work, Chinese studies, and poetry writing, in spite as well of the devastations of the Ōnin War and the tumults that followed, he managed his most important work, making known the Japanese classics.

Even today his writings remain in many parts of Japan on poem cards (tanzaku), with raised lacquer work, and other similar media. He was acquainted with *nō* figures, and above all with the renga master, *Sōgi, and his associates. From Sanetaka, Sōgi learned the essentials of such classics as the *Ise Monogatari* and *Genji Monogatari*. To him Sōgi owed much else in the way of personal, literary prestige that enabled him to rise so far in the world, just as Sōgi was able find financial support for his noble friend. It would be difficult to find a parallel for this busy, learned nobleman, and difficult also to imagine what that tumultous period might have yielded without him. To him and a few others it was left to ensure that the inheritance of Japanese literature be passed on to a different social group. He seems to have represented coherence as well as continuance in a time of confusion, revolution, and protracted human suffering.

SANO NO CHIGAMI NO OTOME 狭野茅上娘子. Nara *waka* poet. She is known from an exchange of love poems with *Nakatomi Yakamori in part 15 of the *Man'yōshū*. She is given twenty-three of the sixty-three poems exchanged. Her best-known poem (15: 3,724) expresses her desire to burn up the road he must take from her and so prevent his departure.

SANTŌ KYŌDEN 山東京伝. 1761–1816. Mid-Edo writer of various kinds of *gesaku*, and an artist. He was born in Edo, the eldest son of a pawnbroker. A younger brother was also a writer of popular fiction. He became talented and thoroughly acquainted with the manners of the town by devoted study of writing, music, *ukiyoe*, and the Yoshiwara pleasure quarters. He had an acute way with words and pictures for catching details by which people expose themselves. Although not at all vicious or even pessimistic, he spared no feature of his characters and the Edo world. He was equally at ease with exaggeration and diminution, and above all with comedy, linguistic fun, and the details of Edo life. His attention to real features of the life of his time, in fact, makes it difficult to distinguish between what should be thought real and what distortion in his writing and art.

He began writing *kibyōshi* while still in his teens. He matured as an illustrator earlier than as an author, and under the name of Kitao Masanobu 北尾政演 he illustrated a number of books by *Koikawa Harumachi and others. After some initial success, he wrote in 1785 the second book to take the town and the kibyōshi for which he is best known today. Written by Santō Kyōden and illustrated by Kitao Masanobu (one and the same, but of course neither his real name—Iwase Sei), this has one of those crazy Edo titles, *Edo 'Umare* [although written *Mumare*] *Uwaki no Kabayaki* 江戸生艶気樺焼, which has been skillfully rendered as *The Playboy Grilled, Edo Style*. The would-be uwaki-mono, or playboy, Enjirō, is the one born in Edo and who more or less gets broiled like an eel (kabayaki) in the course of his attempt to cut a figure. He has enormous wealth behind him, and in episode after episode he devotes no little of it to the effort to prove himself a proper lady-killer. These include such things as hiring a prostitute to be jealous of him as a woman at home should be of an irresistible rake; hiring news hawkers to gossip about him around town, hiring ruffians to beat him, and even staging a double suicide—all things that he hears are expected of a real playboy. His knowledge is gained as much from plays as from the town itself, and he proves as empty in the head as full in the purse.

The episodes are printed from blocks that give not only the text but the picture, and there is simply no way of understanding the one adequately without the other. The pictures by Kitao Masanobu may claim the text by having writing near the character speaking the words, by the triangular nose given Enjirō, or by such striking effects as his ten-meter-long silken loincloth in the mock double suicide scene. But the text by Santō Kyōden also claims the pictures by explaining what is going on, by making the illustrations literary by such devices as a bookcase holding the *Genji Monogatari* and *Ise Monogatari* (with their genuinely knowing amorous heroes), or by signs and pictures within the pictures that offer literary allusion in other ways.

Much in the story is also related to drama. That is not simply Enjirō's closest access to reality but also an inspiration for the dominant method of relation in the episodes: first by a narrator such as we encounter in *jōruri* and then by dialogue. To such an extent, the work resembles the *eiribon* that were popular earlier. The ending also seems to promise a dramatic stagelike reconciliation, especially of the kind made popular in Edo *jidaimono* combined with *sewamono*. Enjirō's experience teaches him as strong a lesson as he is capable of learning. For more detail, see Part One.

At one point Kyōden describes the oddly shaped nose drawn for Enjirō as a peony nose ("botan no hana," punning on "flower" and "nose"). This matter of the nose became better and better known, reflecting on the author-painter, who gained the nickname, Kyōden the Nose (Kyōden Hana). Two principal later works by this spirited artist are a *sharebon*, *Tsūgen Sōmagaki* 通言総籬 (1787); and a *yomihon*, *Sakura Hime Zenden Akebono no Sōshi* 桜姫全伝曙草紙 (1805). In his later years he pursued various investigations that interested him, leaving behind a row of publications and printings. Not surprisingly, when he turned to poetry, he wrote *kyōka*. In his age of voluminous writers, he did not write more pages than anybody else. But he found numerous kinds of expression, sometimes in words and sometimes in pictures, and he was still writing six hours before he died.

SANUKI NO SUKE 讃岐典侍. Dates unknown. Late Heian diarist. Daughter of Fujiwara Akitsune, who was something of a poet, and could look to other talented connections as well. At court, she and Horikawa (r. 1086–1107) became deeply attached to each other, and at his death she suffered greatly. After a time she entered the service of Toba (r. 1107–1123), where she got on well until she suffered from a mental disorder in 1118. Late the next year, she moved to the establishment of her brother, Fujiwara Michitsune, after which nothing is known of her. Her diary, *Sanuki no Suke Nikki*, covers about two years, the last of the reign of Horikawa and the first of Toba. It records deep love ending with an illness and death, followed by grief and recollection.

SAN'YŌ. See RAI SAN'YŌ.

SARASHINA KIKŌ. See MATSUO BASHŌ.

SARASHINA NIKKI. See SUGAWARA TAKASUE NO MUSUME.

SARUMINO(SHŪ) 猿蓑(集). (*The Collection of*) *The Monkey's Straw Raincoat*. This is the fifth and most important of the seven *haikai* collections associated with *Matsuo Bashō, the (*Bashō*) *Shichibushū* (芭蕉)七部集. Known for its importance as the *Kokinshū* of haikai, it was compiled in 1691 by *Mukai Kyorai and *Nozawa Bonchō, with Bashō's active interest and advice. Its organization testifies to careful deliberation in a fashion involving haikai change, *haikaika*. For example, the hokku in parts 1–4 are not ordered in the usual manner beginning with spring, but in the sequence of winter, summer, autumn, spring. The four *kasen* are similarly ordered (on the seasons specified by their *hokku*) and end with one that is a mess after three of the greatest in which Bashō took part. We have argued elsewhere that such gestures betoken a kasen design (parts 1–4 being ordered so as to produce flower stanzas at a point equivalent to the crucial 35th stanza, etc.; and part 5 using the messy last kasen to fulfill a *jo-ha-kyū* rhythm for the four kasen; with other measures of like nature throughout). Other gestures distinguish the collection. One hokku is labelled "Anonymous," as if this collection were indeed a *Kokinshū*. A stanza by one poet is included under another name. These examples of haikai change reflect the pleasure Bashō and his associates experienced in the Kyoto-Ōmi area during 1690–1691, following the trip celebrated in *Oku no Hosomichi*. See Part Six F for information about the divisions of this and other haikai collections.

SATOMURA JŌHA 里村紹巴. ?1524–1602. Momoyama *renga*, *waka* poet, critic, scholar. Like most of the great renga poets before him, Jōha came from humble origins. Against great odds he achieved success by effort, talent, and luck. During his life time, renga became established into houses like waka.

Although he now is seen as a person of great importance, both as a poet and critic, he has been little studied until recent years, and even now his very large canon has discouraged systematic study. From 1563 he was the central renga figure of his day. Two of his best-known sequences are thousand-stanza works composed alone, one on the death of his father, the other on the death of his patron and friend, Sanjōnishi Kin'eda (1487–1563): *Bōfu Tsuizen Dokugin Senku* 亡父追善独吟千句 (1555) and *Shōmyō In Tsuizen Dokugin Senku* 称名院追善独吟千句 (1563). The *Mōri Senku* 毛利千句 (1594) was a more typical joint composition. Three of his critical works may also be mentioned: *Renga Shihō-shō* 連歌至宝抄 (*The Greatest Renga Treasure*, 1585) *Renga Kyōkun* 連歌教訓 (*Renga Teachings*, 1587), and *Shikimoku Hishō* 式目秘抄 (*Handbook of Secrets*, 1587). He makes more explicit than earlier critics had the importance of the concept of *hon'i* to renga and other kinds of literature.

Jōha seems to have lacked the taste, or the necessity, for travel that distinguishes his predecessors. But he did do some, especially in the company of Kin'eda, and he records his travels to the east in *Fujimi Michi no Ki* 富士見道記 (*A Diary of a Visit to Mt. Fuji*, 1567). Like his predecessors, he had to prove himself by lecturing on major classics, and his *Ise Monogatari Jōha Shō* 伊勢物語紹巴抄 (*Jōha's Commentary on the Ise Monogatari*, 1580) shows he could meet the requirements.

He seems to have had only a decade's training in renga. He began with Shūkei two years before the poet's death (1544), and then spent another eight with Shōkyū (1510–1552). Simple as this sounds, and short though the period seems for renga, complicated rivalries were involved. Renga was enormously popular in the sixteenth century. Both Jōha and Sōyō (1526–1563) saw the financial and social possibilities. Sōyō set out to be the first renga poet of his time, and his chief rival was Jōha's teacher, Shōkyō, who died young as renga poets go, leaving an eleven-year-old son, Shōshitsu (1541–1603), totally unable to offer rivalry to Sōyō. This meant either disaster for Sōyō's house or opportunity for Jōha. He did the right thing by becoming a kind of renga regent for the child, tutoring him as he grew older. By then, Jōha had acquired such fame that the renga method he taught was known as Satomura style, and ultimately Jōha headed its northern school as Shōshitsu did its southern.

To achieve such eminence, the support of the Sanjōnishi family was crucial, and Jōha benefited greatly from it. By good fortune, he had been able to succeed his first teacher, Shūkei, as renga master for the household. This may smack of opportunism and luck, but nobody ever achieved success unsought or without some opportunity. In fact, Jōha appears to have known a good thing when he saw it but to have behaved honorably, gaining the trust of Kin'eda and then of Shōshitsu's family.

He was also quite simply an outstanding poet, the last of the great renga masters and different from his predecessors. Although not distinguished for famous *hokku*, he wrote some that are remarkable. Like *Sogi in his different way, Jōha was chiefly concerned with stanzaic connection (*tsukeai*) and sequence integrity. Above all, he developed a style that emphasized ceaseless, rapid progression or fluctuation. This emphasis is, of course, especially evident in his solo *hyakuin* which, as we noticed, he wrote by the tens on his father's and Kin'eda's death. At the same time, he assisted in that institutionalizing of renga into houses that made it impossible for others like him to emerge from humble beginnings to poetic and social preeminence. But such tendencies had begun before him and were later insisted on by the social roles into which the Edo *bakufu* sought to place everyone. In sum, Jōha showed that even in such an age of increasing rigidity it was possible (with genius and good fortune) to be something of a free agent and give renga its last really great hour.

SEAMI. See ZEAMI.

SEGAWA JOKŌ 瀬川如皐. 1806–1881. Late Edo, early modern *kabuki* writer. Born in Edo, he served apprenticeship as a theater writer and came to write a number of *oiemono* and *kizewamono* for Ichikawa Kodanji IV, among them *Yowa Nasake Ukina no Yokogushi* 与話情浮名横櫛 (1853). He had an eye for detail, but his work was repetitive. After about 1857 he was eclipsed by *Kawatake Mokuami.

SEIBI. See NATSUME SEIBI.

SEIGAN. See YANAGAWA SEIGAN.

SEIHAKUDŌ GYŌFŪ 生白堂行風. Dates unknown. Early Edo *kyōka* poet, editor. Very little is known of him. He does seem to have studied *waka* with *Matsunaga Teitoku, and it is thought that thereafter he may have studied *renga* or *haikai*. By 1665 he was living in Osaka and thereafter published the hefty kyōka collections for which he is best known. These include: *Kokin Ikyokushū* 古今夷曲集 (*Rustic Poems from Former and Present Times*, 1666) and its sequel, *Gosen Ikyokushū* 後撰夷曲集 (*A Later Selection of Rustic Poems*, 1672), both in ten parts; as also *Gin'yō Kyōkashū* 銀葉狂歌集 (*A Collection of Silver Leaves of Mad Poems*, 1678). With these titles, cf. *Kokinshū*, *Gosenshū*, and *Kin'yōshū*. The three collections assisted the vogue for "mad waka."

SEI SHŌNAGON 清少納言. Mid-Heian author of *zuihitsu*, *waka*. Although her dates are uncertain, she may have been born about 966, and the last contemporary reference to her seems to be one of 1017. In other words, she is a contemporary of the two other great female writers of the time, *Murasaki Shikibu and *Izumi Shikibu, a trio without precedent or later example. Like them, she served at the court of a royal consort, in her case that of Teishi (or Sadako), a consort of Ichijō Tennō.

The name by which she is known takes the Sinified reading of the first character of her family name, Kiyowara 清原 (as was common for court ladies), and the "Shōnagon" specifies a court rank. She was of a once powerful family that had been increasingly edged from power into learned pursuits. Her education included training not only in waka but in Chinese. It is no longer possible to maintain that all Heian ladies possessed no knowledge of Chinese, and in her case the topic becomes one of lively debate over some of her sources.

In 983 she married Tachibana Norimitsu, an event that seems to have done little to decrease her liveliness or presence in the world. In the same year and in 986 she distinguished herself in public literary appearances. When her mistress, Teishi, died in 1000, she seems to have left the court and, at some date soon thereafter, to have become a later wife of Fujiwara Muneyo, known as the former governor of Settsu. Either that event or her taking of orders late in life appears to have enabled her to travel, since she left behind a number of legends in different places.

Among the stories that grew up about her is one that she lacked real beauty. If so, she was no Izumi Shikibu, though she had a better reputation. Murasaki Shikibu confided in her diary that she could not abide Sei Shōnagon's knowing look (shitarigao). One can well believe that she presented a knowing air, since she was signally uninhibited in passing judgment on whatever or whoever she observed. She had ample opportunities to make her witty discriminations in the status-conscious circles in which she

moved and from the age's emphasis on response to natural detail. She also had the genius to make her discriminations universally memorable.

Her surviving waka number no more than fifty, although one was included in the *Hyakunin Isshu* by *Fujiwara Teika.

Her masterpiece, *Makura no Sōshi* 枕草子 (*The Pillow Book*), is fundamentally impossible to categorize. Modern Japanese consider this "Pillow Book" the prime exemplar of zuihitsu (see Part Six E), a category as difficult to characterize as is this greatest of its exemplars. Of course certain kinds of description are feasible. Her masterpiece is a work in prose that includes sixteen waka and is divided into various kinds of short parts—the jottings presumed to be made into the book at her bedside. A three-kind distinction is often made. On this view, the first includes her lists of matters: for example, "Distasteful Things" (nikuki mono) or, more elaborately, "Things that look pretentious when written in Chinese characters" (such as "Doctor of Literature"!). The second kind is more diarylike, given to temporal flow and the author's subjective exploration. In the third, the outer and inner worlds are poised. This common distinction has its uses, given the unusual character of the work. But it fails to make clear Sei Shōnagon's extraordinary ability to invest the most objective set of things with her subjective presence, or her capacity to speak of *what* is moving without lapsing into sentiment. A reader may be forgiven for thinking hers the only dry eye, or at least hers the only dry sleeve, in Heian Japan.

When faced by so anomalous a masterpiece, scholars inquire into sources. One theory holds that she borrowed her categorical lists from Chinese writings. This seems wholly possible, since she did read Chinese, but no one has been able to prove (understandably enough at so great a gap in time) that she read specific Chinese works or (what is a weakness in the theory) just how they explain her art. Diary literature (*nikki bungaku*) offers an obvious kind of source, as do proverbs. But once again there is a transformation by her highly individual insight. It is altogether appropriate that one of the most gifted of *kokugakusha*, *Kitamura Kigin, should have made a study of this work, his *Makura no Sōshi Shunshoshō* 枕草子春曙抄 (*A Spring Dawn Study of the Makura no Sōshi*, 1674; twelve parts). The appropriateness includes the scholar's critical desire to come to terms with so rich and unprecedented a work. But there is more to it than that. Kigin's interest in *renga* and *haikai* must surely have led him to inquire into a work made up, like a *chokusenshū*, of a sequence of short units. Although in the end attention to the organizing principles of her work in terms of progression and association may yield only more questions, those seem to be more fruitful for literary criticism than have been the source studies. Analysis is made more difficult by the fact that the work is known to us in two textual lines that differ in ordering and in constituent units.

At the end of the Kamakura period, a picture scroll was made, *Makura no Sōshi Emaki*, in one part.

Like so much else about the work, its impact on later literature is difficult to define. Did *Kenkō or *Kamo no Chōmei, the other principal authors of zuihitsu, really know it? Yet nobody can appreciate later literature without attention to such parts as her opening, describing the time of day most moving in each season: "For spring it is dawn," and so on. Neither there nor anywhere else would one claim her to be a profound metaphysician, but in another meaning of that word she is among the healthiest diagnosticians in literature. This woman about whom so much is uncertain, whose masterpiece we grope to characterize, manages to catch, to make memorable major features of our lives and world. After worrying over the obscurity of Izumi Shikibu's poetry or getting lost in the mazes of Murasaki Shikibu's prose style, it is always a pleasure to rediscover the essential clarity of mind that characterizes the *Makura no Sōshi*. If Sei Shōnagon did not exist, there would be no one to invent her.

SENGOHYAKUBAN UTAAWASE 千五百番 歌合 (The Poetry Match in Fifteen Hundred Rounds).

This grand poetry match was convened by *Gotoba in his palace and held in 1201 as a means of getting excellent contemporary poems for the *Shinkokinshū*. Gotoba commissioned thirty poets to write hundred-poem sequences (*hyakushuuta*). There were ten judges, with Gotoba on hand as a kind of supreme arbiter. Because each poet was required to present one hundred poems in the presence of Gotoba, the match was also called *Sentō Hyakuban Utaawase* 仙洞百番歌合 (*A Poetry Match in One Hundred Rounds in the Royal Presence*). The poets included *Fujiwara Teika (who also served as one of the judges) and such women as *Fujiwara Shunzei no Musume and *Kunaikyō. Next to the *Shinkokinshū*, this was the most spectacular of a number of literary events Gotoba arranged.

SENJUN 専順. 1411–1476.

Namboku-Muromachi *renga* master. What renga training he had is unclear—perhaps he studied under *Bontō or *Sōzei. His first known poetry appeared in 1443. About 1447 he participated with *Sōzei *Shinkei, and other major poets in the *Anegakōji Imashimmei Hyakuin*. He has various collections such as *Senjun Gohyakku* 専順五百句 (*Senjun's Five Hundred Stanzas*) and *Renga Hyakkuzuke* 連歌百句附 (*A Renga Linking One Hundred Stanzas*), as well as a treatise on composition, *Katahashi* 片端 (*Just One Topic*). Although not one of the greatest renga poets, he was admired both by contemporaries and by later poets.

SENJŪSHŌ 撰集抄 (Selected Stories).

An early Kamakura *setsuwa* collection in nine parts. Because compilation was formerly attributed to *Saigyō (1118–1190), and because it is sometimes printed in editions of his works, this has long been a popular collection. It is impossible to say that the tradition has no basis in fact, but present versions date from after about 1200. Texts differ in running from 58 to 117 parts.

The attribution may derive from attractive features of the work. It is easier to read than many such setsuwa compilations, and if it shares many stories with such other collections as the *Konjaku Monogatari*, those are good ones. Moreover, its aims are plainly literary as well as religious. The didactic end of such collections is highly qualified by a reflective and critical emphasis as well as in the depiction of people as people rather than as moral examples. Such being the case, it is difficult to find the dominance of a Buddhist sense of evanescence (*mujō*) that some critics emphasize.

Nō such as *Eguchi* and *Ugetsu*, otogizōshi such as "Suzuriwari," and the story "Shiramine" from *Ueda Akinari's *Ugetsu Monogatari* represent a range of adaptations of parts of the collection.

SENKAKU 仙覚. B. 1203.

Early Kamakura scholar of the *Man'yōshū*. Born in Hitachi, he first became interested in the *azumauta* of the collection (some of which pertain to his province). As his interests and fame grew, he was able (with various influential support—for example by Kujō Yoritsune—of a financial and social kind) to make a considerable scholarly advance by collation of various manuscripts. Until he was nearly seventy, he pursued his painstaking work. His best known study is *Man'yōshū Chūshaku* 万葉集注釈 (*Man'yōshū Commentary*, 1269).

SEN NO RIKYŪ 千利休 (or SŌEKI 宗易). 1522–1591.

Azuchi Momoyama tea master. His service to the potentates of the time is famous, as is his having to commit suicide at the wrath of one of them, Toyotomi Hideyoshi. The most famous tea master of Japan, he founded three lines of tea ceremony, including Omote Senke, Mushanokōji (Senke), and Ura Senke. He was famous for the various arts and crafts associated with tea.

SENZAI(WAKA)SHŪ 千載(和歌)集 (Collection [of Japanese Poems] of a Thousand Years).

Late Heian royal *waka* collection (*chokusenshū*); seventh of the *nijūichidaishū*. Ordered in 1183 by Goshirakawa (r. 1155–1158), although there is evidence that the compiler, *Fujiwara Shunzei, had begun work ca. 1171–1175. Official presentation was held up by the confusion of the *Gempei* wars, but took place in 1187 or, more probably, 1188. Modeled on the *Kokinshū*, it has twenty books, 1,287 poems. Shunzei wrote the Japanese preface.

His catholic tastes are evident, so that in one respect the anthology summarizes the previous six collections. In another, however, the greater emphasis given to living poets brings to attention the styles he advocated and that would dominate the *Shinkokinshū*. The 235 poets included outnumber by ten times those in the *Shikashū*, and Shunzei's stated aim of "considering the poem, not the poet," led to including one poem (anonymously) by *Taira Tadanori of the defeated Heike house, one by a prostitute and, what really caused a sensation, more poems by the eccentric *Minamoto Shunrai than by the redoubtable but hidebound *Fujiwara Mototoshi. See Part Six A.

SESSHŪ 雪舟. 1420–1506. Late Muromachi priest, painter. Probably the most famous Japanese painter, he entered Shōkokuji at an early age and there studied with *Shūbun. In 1467, he went to Ming China for two years, studying the latest styles of the northern Sung and Mongol dynasties in ink wash, and returning to Japan to produce a series of excellent landscapes. He also worked with smaller scenes of birds and flowers. His combination of economy, elegance, and sublimity have given him fame throughout the world.

SESSON 雪村. B. 1504. Late Muromachi priest, painter. Although he worked in the style of *Sesshū—in Sung-Mongol dynasty ink wash—he was from Hitachi, and spent his career in a series of provincial locations producing highly regarded works, particularly of scenery.

SETSUBOKU RYŌGIN SUMIYOSHI HYAKUIN 雪牧両吟住吉百韻 (*A Hundred Stanzas on Sumiyoshi composed by Chōsetsu and Sōboku*). A late Muromachi hundred-stanza renga sequence composed in 1532. Unlike most renga sequences jointly written, this was not composed at a single sitting but over a period of five or six days. The two poets, the second characters of the names for whom give the first two characters of the title, are Chōsetsu 聴雪, which is to say *Sanjōnishi Sanetaka, and Sōboku.

The sequence illustrates for the most part the usual practice of renga. Occasionally the language seems inauspicious for a sequence associated with the Sumiyoshi Shrine, locus of the divinity of Japanese poetry. Other signs of latitude with the rules include an unusually small use of travel subtopics and an unusually large number of allusions (*honzetsu*)—six—to the *Genji Monogatari*. The beauty of the six opening stanzas is dazzling.

SHADŌ. See HAMADA CHINSEKI.

SHARAKU 写楽. Dates unknown. Mid-Edo *ukiyoe* print artist. Sometimes known by another artistic name, Tōshūsai 東洲斎. Almost nothing is known about him. One story holds that he had been

a *nō* actor, but there is no verification. His known prints seem to have been done entirely in 1794–1795, and they consist mostly of heads of actors and sumo wrestlers in a curiously strained, caricature-like, and yet not malicious style. The distortions do not fit usual Japanese conventions very well, and he probably would have been ignored had it not been for Western fascination with his work.

SHIGETANE. See SUZUKI SHIGETANE.

SHIGEYORI. See MATSUE SHIGEYORI.

SHIINOMOTO SAIMARO 椎本才麿. 1656–1738. Early Edo *haikai* poet. A samurai from Yamato, he resigned his status to devote himself to poetry. After study with one haikai master, he worked under *Ihara Saikaku. In 1677 he went to the Edo area. After becoming familiar with some writings by the school of *Matsuo Bashō he altered his style from features of the *Danrin* style learned from Saikaku. After 1689 he settled in Osaka. He compiled two collections of his poetry.

SHIKA(WAKA)SHŪ 詞花(和歌)集 (*Collection of Verbal Flowers [of Japanese Poems]*). Late Heian royal *waka* collection (*chokusenshū*); sixth of the *nijūichidaishū*. Ordered in 1144 by Sutoku (r. 1123–1141), completed in 1151. The compiler, Fujiwara Akisuke, produced the shortest of the twenty-one anthologies, with only 411 poem in ten parts and by only twenty-three named poets. The title was criticized for its first syllable, the "shi" meaning "diction" but being homophonous with the word for "death," and for other reasons. Yet, for all his conservative inclination, Akisuke was relatively catholic in taste, including innovative work by *Minamoto Shunrai and *Sone no Yoshitada, along with what he no doubt thought was the tried and true. There is no preface. See Part Six A.

SHIKISHI NAISHINNŌ. See SHOKUSHI NAISHINNŌ.

SHIKITEI SAMBA 式亭三馬. 1776–1822. Late Edo writer of various kinds of *gesaku*. Son of a printer and himself full of enterprise, he entered into various businesses connected with books. At one time he sold various patent medicines, including a concoction of his own, "Edo no Mizu" ("Edo Water"). The best known among his many books are two *kokkeibon*: *Ukiyoburo* 浮世風呂 (*The World at the Bath-House*, 1809–1813) and *Ukiyodoko* 浮世床 (*The World at the Barber Shop*, 1813–1814). By the device of a public bath in the one and a barbershop in the other, he managed to create in each a meetingplace and microcosm of the ordinary Edo townspeople whose common dispositions he liked to treat. Readers must have felt that he knew their neighbors inside and outside. They enjoyed his catching of Edo language and his splendid humor.

There is no question but that he excels in the recreation of the conversation and behavior of his time. Yet his work is also very learned. Throughout its extent, *Ukiyoburo* uses many allusions to, and parodies of, the Japanese classics. The third part begins by reproducing the famous opening of *Sei Shōnagon's *Makura no Sōshi*, only to lapse into flat Edo talk halfway through. The fourth part begins with a *Kokinshū* poem. He also touches on the works of *Utagawa Toyokuni and *Utagawa Kunisada.

At one point in the third part, two learned Edo townswomen appear, Kamoko and Keriko. ("Kamo" is a poetic exclamation in *Man'yōshū* poetry; -keri is a classical verb inflection; the two are also homophonous with words for "wild duck" and "wild goose"). This pair in the bathhouse quote the *Genji Monogatari*, consider what *Kamo no Mabuchi's latest ideas are, and go on to discuss *Motoori Norinaga's *Genji Monogatari Tama no Ogushi* and *Katō Chikage's recent *Ukeragahana*. One can otherwise find in this wonderful miscellany much on the theater and specific plays and, above all, a sense of Edo language and townspeople's lives—for which the work remains a superlative introduction.

Edo culture reaches one kind of peak in Samba's work, and, although he is often paired with *Jippensha Ikku as a quintessential writer of *kokkeibon*, Samba is more consistent and inventive in showing us the side of life behind the offical front. Without question he makes that hindside seem the more real.

SHIKŌ. See KAGAMI SHIKŌ.

SHIMIZU HAMAOMI 清水浜臣. 1776–1824. Late Edo *waka* poet, *kokugaku* scholar. Born in Edo, he followed his father in medicine for a time, then devoted himself to study and writing. He became a follower of *Murata Harumi, and was on close terms with *Katō Chikage. He devoted himself to philology, study of the native past, and poetry. He also took part in a new, fashionable kind of study, applying the methods of *Kamo no Mabuchi. Not a very seminal figure, he was, however, extremely well liked by others in the literary circles of his day. When he died under fifty, he had a host of friends, the closest of whom felt a deep grief not felt on the passing of many greater figures.

SHINCHOKUSEN(WAKA)SHŪ 新勅撰(和歌) 集 (*A New Royally Ordered Collection [of Japanese Poems]*). Early Kamakura royal *waka* collection, ninth of the *nijūichidaishū*. Ordered in 1232 by Gohorikawa (r. 1221–1232) and completed the year after his death, that is, in 1235. The compiler, *Fujiwara Teika, also furnished the Japanese preface. Modeled on the *Kokinshū*, it has twenty

books. Its 1,374 poems reflect an adjustment of Teika's taste in his late years, adding to styles of the immediately preceding collections an emphasis on relatively simpler poetry. Court contemporaries remarked with some hostility on the inclusion of a relatively large number of poets from military houses. It seemed to rivals that he was currying favor with the Kamakura *bakufu*, which had prevailed in the Jōkyū War of 1221. There must have been truth in that, but Teika saw that survival of court culture was at stake and that accommodation would serve court interests better than simple opposition. See Part Six A.

SHINGOSEN(WAKA)SHŪ 新後撰(和歌)集 (*New Later Collection [of Japanese Poems]*). Late Kamamura royal *waka* collection (*chokusenshū*); thirteenth of the *nijūichidaishū*. Ordered in 1301 by Gouda (r. 1259–1274), completed in 1303. Compiled by *Fujiwara Tameyo of the conservative *Nijō poets. On the *Kokinshū* model, it has twenty books, 1,606 poems, mostly of the Nijō persuasion. There is no preface. See Part Six A.

SHINGOSHŪI(WAKA)SHŪ 新後拾遺(和歌)集 (*New Later Collection of Gleanings [of Japanese Poems]*). Late Kamakura official *waka* collection (*chokusenshū*); twentieth of the *nijūichidaishū*. Ordered by Goen'yū (r. 1374–1382, of the northern court) at the request of the shogun, Ashikaga Yoshimitsu. Compilation was begun by Fujiwara Tametō and completed by Fujiwara Tameshige, both of the line of conservative *Nijō poets. First completed in 1383, revised in 1384. On the model of the *Kokinshū*, it has twenty books and includes 1,554 poems. The poetry is of the court in decline, but the Japanese preface by *Nijō Yoshimoto is worth attention. See Part Six A.

SHINKEI 心敬. 1406–1475. Mid-Muromachi *waka*, *renga* poet, priest. He learned the style of waka practiced by the *Reizei poets from *Shōtetsu. It is not clear how he learned renga, since he seemed to have made his name in it suddenly when he was in his fifties. In 1463, he left Kyoto for Kii (Wakayama), writing about the journey and his art in a much-praised account, *Sasamegoto* さXめごX (*Whisperings*). Three years later he identified himself enough with renga to put out a collection of his stanzas, *Shingyokushū* 心玉集 (*Shinkei's Own Selections*). In 1467 he joined the many people who left Kyoto during the storms of the Ōnin War (1467–1477), moving about frequently during the period. During the following years, his life was one of traveling, writing renga and waka, and publishing various treatises. Somehow, he also fulfilled his ecclesiastical duties during his lifetime and rose to high preferments.

He shares with Shōtetsu and a few members of the nobility the passing on of the finest of court literature to a new age. Opinions vary as to whether he or Shōtetsu is the finer waka poet, but he is very much more complex, and to some of us he seems a greater poet, particularly in renga. He is much the most difficult of waka and renga poets in his time, a factor that may have debarred full appreciation of his gifts. Even contemporaries complained of the obscurity of some of his poetry. Yet his stanzas are the most brilliant in renga history, and if he is not the first poet in the art, it is because the very brilliance of his stanzas (as well as some inexplicable lapses into triviality) makes sequential integration difficult. His glorious failure in renga involved his bringing to bear of the most intense, brilliant, compact elements of waka into renga. As he is better studied, he may come to occupy a place vis-à-vis Sōgi corresponding to that of *Yosa Buson in relation to *Matsuo Bashō. For if he does not have Buson's genius as a painter or the same uniform excellence, he has a counterpart in his waka and in his distinguished criticism. In a remark often quoted from *Sasamegoto*, he says, "If you were to ask one of the great poets of the past how to compose waka, the answer would be pampas grass on a withered moor and the moon disappearing into the sky at dawn." This resembles the answer to a Zen Buddhist kōan or riddle. Or as he adds, "This involves understanding the wisdom [*satori*] of that which is chilled and withered [*sabitaru*]." To be sure, the second remark reminds us more of Bashō than Buson, which no doubt shows the fruitlessness after all of comparing really important writers.

Among collections of his poetry, there is a second of renga, *Shinkei Sōzu Hyakku* 心敬僧都百句 (*One Hundred Stanzas by Bishop Shinkei*). Also two waka collections: *Gondaisōzu Shinkei Shū* 権大僧都 心敬集 (*Acting Archbishop Shinkei's Collection*) and *Shinkei Sōzu Juttai Waka* 心敬僧都十体和歌 (*Bishop Shinkei's Waka in Ten Styles*). Although his poetry and criticism have received devoted study by some critics and scholars, they remain rich mines for further exploration.

SHINKOKIN(WAKA)SHŪ   新古今（和歌）集
(*New Collection [of Japanese Poems] of Ancient and Modern Times*). Early Kamakura royal *waka* collection; eighth of the *nijūichidaishū*. Ordered in 1201 by *Gotoba (r. 1183–1198) and compiled by *Fujiwara Teika, *Fujiwara Ariie, *Fujiwara Ietaka, *Jaturen, Minamoto Michitomo, and *Fujiwara Masatsune. *Fujiwara Shunzei had started preparation earlier, as had Gotoba in a sense by commissioning a large poetry match, the *Sengohyakuban Utaawase*, whence a number of the poems are taken. Gotoba also took an unusual degree of interest in compilation, including supervision and disagreement with Teika; he even took the collection to exile in Oki, where he prepared a somewhat shorter version more to his liking. On the model of the *Kokinshū*, it has twenty books. The

title claims it to be a new version of that collection, and it is usually esteemed as either the best after it or, more usually, the finest of the twenty-one official collections. Its 1,978 poems made it the longest anthology to date, and like its model it included poets from the *Man'yōshū* to contemporaries—101 of them—with an unprecedented representation of the new, featuring 94 poems by *Saigyō and 92 by his fellow priest, *Jien. The collection perfected the progressive and associative methods of integration begun by the *Kokinshū*, so that the whole may be read as substantially a single work of nearly 10,000 lines. Although the prefaces read as if they had been written by Gotoba, the Japanese one was written by *Fujiwara Yoshitsune and the Chinese by Hino Chikatsune—this being the first collection since the *Kokinshū*, and one of the very few among the twenty-one collections, to have prefaces in both languages. See Part Six A.

SHINRAN 親鸞. 1173–1263.
Early Kamakura religious figure. Ordained a priest by Tendai's *Jien in 1181 while still a child, Shinran became a disciple of Hōnen two decades later (1207), severing his ties with Mt. Hiei. Whereas *Hōnen had attempted to accommodate the sole-practice (senju) *nembutsu* with traditional Buddhism, Shinran detailed the implications of the popular Amidist movement and in 1224 founded the True Pure Land sect (Jōdo Shinshū). The central issue was the value of faith versus good works during the period of the Latter Days of the Law (*mappō*). Total reliance on the Other Power (tariki) of Amida's Original Vows (hongan) to lead to his Pure Land those who called upon his name (*nembutsu*) was contrasted to the Self Power (jiriki) of the traditional practices, which Shinran viewed as useless self-assertion. Shinran's position is epitomized in the famous statement in the *Tannishō* 歎異鈔 (*Collection Inspired by Concern over Heresy*; compiled by a disciple, ca. 1264–1282): "If even a good man can be born in the Pure Land, how much more so a wicked man!" Shinran's major work, the *Kyōgyōshinshō* 教行信証 (*Teaching, Practice, Faith, Attainment*, 1224) is a reply to *Myōe's *Saijarin* 摧邪輪 (*An Attack on the Bad Vehicle*, 1212), which had been directed at Hōnen's *Senjaku Shū*. Shinran married, perhaps several times, and was a major force in the establishment of a married clergy. Devotion to the Buddha Amida had long been part of the Mahāyāna tradition. But the new emphasis on the sole power of faith evoked widespread popular response that we find reflected in the nō, in Chikamatsu's plays, and in Issa's *haiku*—to name but a few of its literary manifestations.

SHINSENZAI(WAKA)SHŪ 新千載（和歌）集 (*A New Collection [of Japanese Poems] of a Thousand Years*).
Namboku royal *waka* collection (*chokusenshū*); eighteenth of the *nijūichidaishū*. Ordered by

Gokōgon (r. 1352–1371, of the northern line) as the first of two he commissioned, at the request of the shogun Ashikaga Takauji. Completed in 1359 by the compiler, Fujiwara Tamesada of the conservative Nijō house. On the *Kokinshū model, it has twenty parts; its 2,364 poems make it the largest official anthology apart from the *Gyokuyōshū. But its tastes are quite conservative, and with this collection we see the steadily declining status of the court and its culture. There is no preface. See Part Six A.

SHINSHŌ 信生. Fl. ca. 1225. Early Kamakura poet, priest. Under his secular name, Utsunomiya Tomonari (or Asanari) 宇都宮朝業, he served *Minamoto Sanetomo. On Sanetomo's assassination in 1219, he seems to have been attracted to a religious life, which he entered in 1225. Alternating between reclusive life and travel, he spent time in Kyoto for ascetic training, although his background was that of an eastern (Kantō) warrior. Part of his Shinshō Hōshi Shū 信生法師集 (Priest Shinshō's Collection) is devoted to a trip back and forth between these points, and in general a large portion of his poetry turns on Buddhist topics. It was included in chokusenshū from the *Shinchokusenshū on. Attention has come to him relatively recently, in part as an example of a cultivated warrior, in part for the appeal of much in his collection. In its first half, for example, Shinshō portrays a moving conflict between religious dedication and worldly attachment to his family.

SHINSHOKUKOKIN(WAKA)SHŪ 新続古今 (和歌)集 (New Collection [of Japanese Poems] of Ancient and Modern Times Continued). Nambuku royal waka collection (chokusenshū). Twenty-first and last of the nijūichidaishū. Ordered by Gohanazono (r. 1429–1464) in 1433 at the request of the shogun Ashikaga Yoshinori, completed in 1439. Compiled by Asukai Masayo, who was related to the *Nijō poets and their school of conservative poetry. Modeled on the *Kokinshū, this collection has twenty books and 2,144 poems, a large collection. One of the few points of interest today is its prefaces in Japanese and Chinese by *Ichijō Kanera, who was a major factor in disseminating court culture to renga poets. With this collection, the twenty-one official collections end in an age of splendor that lapsed into bloodletting and anarchy. Perhaps appropriately, its title echoes that of the first collection, with two of the usual prefixes for later collections, "Shin/shoku." See Part Six A.

SHINSHŪI(WAKA)SHŪ 新拾遺(和歌)集 (New Collection of Gleanings [of Japanese Poems]). Late Kamakura-Nambuku royal waka collection (chokusenshū); nineteenth of the nijūichidaishū. The second such collection ordered, this one in 1363, by Gokōgon (r. 1352–1371, of the northern court) at the request of the shogun, Ashikaga Yoshiakira, and completed in 1364. Compilation was begun by Fujiwara Tameaki and completed by *Ton'a, both adherents of the conservative *Nijō poets. On the *Kokinshū model, it has twenty books, and 1,920 poems. There is no preface. See Part Six A.

SHINTŌSHŪ 神道集 (Shinto Stories). Nambuku setsuwa collection of fifty stories in ten parts. It is written in hentai kambun, although some stories have kana glosses. The work is said to have been compiled about 1358–1361 by one or more of the preachers at the Tendai temple, Agui 安居院. Most of the collection deals with Shinto and related animistic stories, but nine have Buddhist or other non-Shinto subjects. The majority involve Shinto legends, particularly those connected with shrines in eastern Japan. It is a largely non-Buddhist setsuwa collection and a syncretistic work of the shimbutsu dōtaisetsu 神仏同体説 kind, adapting Buddhist figures to Shinto ones.

SHIN'YŌ(WAKA)SHŪ 新葉(和歌)集 (Collection of New Leaves [of Japanese Poems]). Nambukuchō poetic collection, ordered in 1381 by Chōkei (r. 1368–1383). This is a would-be chokusenshū in twenty parts, compiled by *Munenaga Shinnō, who wrote a large portion of its poems, which total 1,420, so making a good-sized collection. Although most of the poetry is in the insipid styles of the *Nijō Poets, there is also a fresh tinge of warrior interests.

SHIRAO. See KAYA SHIRAO.

SHITAGŌ. See MINAMOTO SHITAGŌ.

SHŌHAKU 肖柏. 1443–1527. Mid-Muromachi renga, waka poet, priest, sometimes known by another pen name, Botange 牡丹花. Unlike most other poets accomplished in renga, he came from a princely family. He is occasionally dismissed as dilettante because of his expressed love for peony flowers (hence his "Botange"), the fragrance of sweet flowering daphne, and sake. Such was his personal response to an age of nearly constant disorder, seeking in matters aesthetic some kind of controlled meaning. He led a retired life, although not at first taking orders, and at his Muan hermitage near Ikeda (modern Osaka), he escaped much of the havoc endured by the capital during the Ōnin War (1467–1477), although he remained near enough to visit it when required, unlike most who fled far away if they could. Like *Sōgi he learned from *Ichijō Kanera, and he kept invaluable notes on Sōgi's lectures concerning important classics such as the *Genji Monogatari.

His waka poetry is not without interest, but his fame derives from renga. His first known sitting was in 1470, for a hundred-stanza sequence. In 1488, he took part in the most famous of renga sequences, the *Minase Sangin Hyakuin*, and three years later in the sequence now deemed superior, the *Yunoyama Sangin Hyakuin*. Both were written with Sōgi and *Sōchō, although the former is marred by Sōchō's inability to match the other two in creating a fully integrated, impressive sequence. Shōhaku's own performance in both leaves nothing to be desired.

Sōgi included thirty-three of his stanzas in his *Shinsen Tsukuba Shū*. Shōhaku issued his own collection of renga stanzas, *Shummusō* 春夢草 (*Plants of a Spring Dream*) in 1515–1517. In 1517, he moved to Izumi, where he died ten years later. Although he will never be ranked with Sōgi, he will figure more highly in the history and criticism of renga as he is better known.

SHOKUGOSEN(WAKA)SHŪ 続後選(和歌)集
(*Later Collection [of Japanese Poems] Continued*). Mid-Kamakura royal *waka* collection (*chokusenshū*); tenth of the *nijūichidaishū*. Ordered in 1248 by Gosaga (r. 1242–1246), completed in 1251 by the compiler, *Fujiwara Tameie of the conservative *Nijō poets. On the *Kokinshū* model, it has twenty books, 1,368 poems. This and the next three collections (see Part Six A) show a distinct falling-off in quality from the preceding collections. There is no preface.

SHOKUGOSHŪI(WAKA)SHŪ 続後拾遺(和歌)集
(*Later Collection of Gleanings [of Japanese Poems] Continued*). Late Kamakura royal *waka* collection (*chokusenshū*); sixteenth of the *nijūichidaishū*. Ordered in 1323 by Godaigo (r. 1318–1339), it was completed in 1325. Compilation was begun by Fujiwara Tamefuji and completed by Fujiwara Tamesada, both conservative *Nijō poets. Modeled on the *Kokinshū*, this has twenty books and 1,347 poems, with a few by the innovative poets of other houses. There is no preface. See Part Six A.

SHOKUKOKIN(WAKA)SHŪ 続古今(和歌)集
(*Collection [of Japanese Poems] of Ancient and Modern Times Continued*). Mid-Kamakura royal *waka* collection (*chokusenshū*); eleventh of the *nijūichidaishū*. Ordered by Gosaga (r. 1242–1246) in 1259 and completed in 1265. The compilers included *Fujiwara Tameie, with Fujiwara Motoie, Fujiwara Ieyoshi, Fujiwara Yukie, and Fujiwara Mitsutoshi, all conservative *Nijō poets. On the *Kokinshū* model, it has twenty books, 1,925 poems. It is uncertain who wrote the Japanese and Chinese prefaces. The poems are mostly of the mediocre Nijō kind. See Part Six A.

SHOKUSENZAI(WAKA)SHŪ 続千載(和歌)集
(*Collection [of Japanese Poems] of a Thousand Years Continued*). Late Kamakura royal *waka* collection (*chokusenshū*); fifteenth of the *nijūichidaishū*. Ordered in 1318 by Gouda (r. 1274–1287) and completed in 1320 by the compiler, *Fujiwara Tameyo,

of the conservative *Nijō poets. On the *Kokinshū* model, it has twenty books. Its 2,159 poems make it a long collection, perhaps to rival its predecessor, the *Gyokuyōshū*. Although some Kyōgoku-Reizei poets are included, most of poems conform to the conservative line of Tameyo's house. There is no preface. See Part Six A.

SHOKUSHI (or SHIKISHI) NAISHINNŌ 式子内親王.
D. 1201. Early Kamakura *waka* poet. Daughter of Goshirakawa (r. 1155–1158) and at one time Kamo Shrine Priestess, she was at the center of much of the cultural life of the court. Although only 388 of her poems survive, their consistently high quality establish her as one of the first poets of her day. She was a gifted descriptive poet, especially in the *yōembi* style instituted by *Fujiwara Teika. She was unexcelled in her time for her love poetry of intense passion, rarefied beauty, and rich allusiveness. She brought to new life the ancient and continuing poetry of the passionate woman, transforming or heightening it by indirection and descriptive symbolism. Given the brilliant realization of her poetry, it is not surprising that it was sometimes read as autobiography, and so, as with *Ono no Komachi, legends of her arose. The best known concerns a love affair between her and Teika. They did share dedication to poetry of the highest quality. Her own often combine seasonal and love elements when writing on either topic, and she is one of the most skillful users of *honkadori* among all *waka* poets. What evidence exists shows that she was personally thoughtful, whether to a grand old poet like *Fujiwara Shunzei, or to women in her service.

SHOKUSHŪI(WAKA)SHŪ 続拾遺(和歌)集
(*Collection of Gleanings [of Japanese Poems] Continued*). Mid-Kamakura royal *waka* collection (*chokusenshū*); twelfth of the *nijūichidaishū*. Ordered, probably in 1276, by Kameyama (r. 1259–1274), completed in 1279 by the compiler, Fujiwara Tameuji of the conservative *Nijō poets. On the *Kokinshū* model it has twenty books and includes 1,461 largely undistinguished poems. There is no preface. See Part Six A.

SHŌKYŪKI. See JŌKYŪKI.

SHŌMONKI (or MASAKADOKI) 将門記 (*An Account of Masakado*).
Mid-Heian (940) *gunki monogatari* in one part. The work covers the rebellion of Taira Masakado, an episode beginning in 935 and known as the Masakado War. A disagreement that began in a single family gradually involved more and more principals until most of the Kantō area was in arms. Matters finally ended with Masakado's death in 940. It is said that at the end of the work there is the date equivalent to, "sixth Month, 940," making the account unusual for a

monogatari of any kind in treating events as they were happening. The writer is unknown but is said to be sympathetic enough with the rebel protagonist to be thought a partisan, although certain features may indicate that the author was from the capital. The style with eccentric or *hentai kambun*, jargon of the time, and odd similes is said to make reading difficult. For the literary student the interesting question posed is how such factuality under the label of monogatari suits with definitions of "literature," as it clearly does by Japanese views.

SHŌSAN. See Suzuki Shōsan.

SHŌTETSU 正徹. 1381–1459. Early Muromachi *waka, renga* poet, priest. An extraordinarily prolific, often outstanding, and still insufficiently studied poet, he offers a major transition (along with *Shinkei) between the court and the social world that followed. By about 1395 he had come to know the *Reizei poets and *Imagawa Ryōshun, whose student he became. In 1414 he attracted notice by a hundred-poem waka sequence. From 1418 he has left a travel account of his journey to the east and north in *Nagusamegusa* なぐさめ草 (*Consoling Plants*). He continued to write waka, participating in poetry matches and other similar activities with cultivated members of the warrior nobility and in gatherings at his own retreat in Higashiyama. This hermitage was destroyed by fire in 1432, taking with it over 20,000 poems that he had written. For some reason, he incurred the wrath of the Ashikaga shogun, Yoshinori, who prevented inclusion of Shōtetsu's poems in the *Shinshokukokinshū. After Yoshinori's sudden assassination in 1441, he returned to poetry as his preoccupation, gathering about him a group of poets who shared his dislike of the bland styles of the *Nijō poets. These students included Shinkei and the renga poet *Takayama Sōzei, with whom he practiced renga as well as waka.

His principal critical work is *Shōtetsu Monogatari* (from 1448). In it he declared that those who criticized *Fujiwara Teika would not only fail to enjoy divine favor but be visited by punishment. He severely reprehended members of the nobility for signs of corruption in their poetry (such criticism is itself a sign of changing times). His personal waka collection, the *Sōkonshū* 草根集 (*The Roots of Plants*) is not least remarkable for containing over ten thousand poems. This has a preface by *Ichijō Kanera. For a poet so very prolific, he seems to have maintained a high standard, although most critics have done little more than sample his large canon.

SHŌTOKU TAISHI 聖徳太子. 574–622. Yamato prince, regent, political figure, religious and philosophical scholar. Prince Umayado, known to history as Crown Prince Shōtoku, was regent during the reign of his aunt, Suiko. He was a member of the

Soga clan, which had defeated its rivals, chiefly the Nakatomi (liturgists) and the Mononobe (armorers), in the struggles for political dominance as Japan began to coalesce into a centralized state in the late sixth century. Shōtoku, one of the great leaders of early Japan, was a scholar of the Confucian classics, a supporter of Buddhism, and a patron of the arts. The famous *Jūshichijō Kempō* 十七条 憲法 (*Seventeen-Article Constitution*) of 604, recorded in the *Nihon Shoki*, is no longer thought to have been of his writing, although he may have given advice for it. It is a set of moral injunctions for good government based largely on Confucian principles tempered with Buddhism. It includes (Article VI) the earliest Japanese statement of the principle of *kanzen chōaku* ("Chastise that which is evil and encourage that which is good"), which became the motto of Confucian didacticism, especially during the late Edo period.

Shōtoku is traditionally credited with composing commentaries on three sutras (*Sangyō Gisho*) and although some modern scholars doubt that he was their author, he does seem to have been author in some major degree. They are the *Shōmangyō Gisho* 勝鬘経義疏 (*Commentary on the Sūtra of Queen Srīmāla*), the *Yuimakyō Gisho* 維摩経義疏 (*Commentary on the Vimalakīrti Sūtra*), and the *Hokkekyō Gisho* 法華経義疏 (*Commentary on the Lotus Sūtra*), one extant manuscript of which may be in Shōtoku's own hand. He initiated diplomatic missions to China in 607, the same year in which he founded Nara's Hōryūji, where he had his own private chapel, the Yumedono (Hall of Dreams). Later generations revered Prince Shōtoku as an incarnation of the bodhisattva Kannon, and depictions of him are to be found in various temple statues and pictures. They include a very famous one, old although of uncertain date, held by Hōryūji until modern times, when it was taken over for the royal collection.

SHŌTŌ MON'IN. See Jōtō Mon'in.

SHŌZŌ. See Namiki Shōzō.

SHŪBUN 周文. Dates unknown. Mid-Muromachi painter and priest who flourished in the former half of the fifteenth century. His very great reputation remains for his skill in Sung and Mongol Dynasty ink wash. He had traveled to Korea, and held important appointments at Shōkokuji in Kyoto and under the Ashikaga shogunate, and he taught the next generation of great painters, including *Sesshū. Unfortunately, little or no authenticated work is known.

SHŪI(WAKA)SHŪ 拾遺(和歌)集 (*Collection of Gleanings of [Japanese Poems]*). Mid-Heian royal collection of *waka*; third of the *nijūichidaishū*. Ordered by *Kazan (r. 984–986)—it is not clear when, and several other circumstances of compilation are also unclear. It appears that Kazan played played an unusually interested, direct role in the putting together of this anthology, but *Fujiwara Kintō seems to have been the chief agent for compiling. The work appears to have been done at some time between 1005 and 1011. Modeled on the *Kokinshū*, it has twenty parts, 1,351 poems, most reflecting the taste for the safe and bland certainly held by Kintō. It is, with *Gosenshū*, one of the least interesting of the first eight official anthologies, no doubt in part because it favors earlier poets, already pretty well combed, rather than a number of interesting contemporaries. There is no preface. See Part Six A.

SHUN'E (or SUN'E) 俊恵. B. 1113. Late Heian *waka* poet, priest. He was son of *Minamoto Shunrai, a very gifted poet if somewhat eccentric person. Shun'e inherited little of these qualities. He entered Tōdaiji at an early age and appears to have held important ecclesiastical posts. He was held in high estimation as poet and critic by many contemporaries, gathering about him a poetic circle known as the Karin'en 歌林苑 (Garden in the Poetic Woods). That had three dozen or so prominent poets as members, and its activities led to a few collections. Although his poetic career seems not to have been lengthly, about 1,100 of his poems survive. They appear generously or singly, as in such famous collections as *Fujiwara Teika's *Hyakunin Isshu*.

As an arbiter of taste in his time, he was a natural figure for *Kamo no Chōmei to use as dialoguist, or pronouncer, in his *Mumyōshō*. If that work represents (as seems wholly likely) Shun'e's ideas as well as Chōmei's own, Shun'e stressed *sugata* and *kotoba*, total effect and language (as opposed to the third major poetic principle, *kokoro*, conception). On the same presumption, he gave to Chōmei one of the best accounts of *yūgen* and some of the most interesting anecdotes about poets of the time, as well as a major discussion of allusion (*honkadori*) and its management. His own poetry is tranquil, his diction skillful without mannerism. These qualities lend his poetry its appeal, but the relative lack of consideration of kokoro in his poetics is significant: he is neither very intense nor original, unlike his disciple, Chōmei.

SHUNRAI. See Minamoto Shunrai.

SHUNSUI. See Tamenaga Shunsui.

SHUNZEI NO MUSUME (SHUNZEI'S DAUGHTER). See Fujiwara Shunzei no Musume.

SŌAMI 相阿弥. D. 1525. Late Muromachi painter, flower arranger, incense master; third of the "3 Ami's" (see *Nōami). Such was his skill that he was not only patronized by Ashikaga Yoshimasa but

had schools named after him in the arts of flower arranging and incense compounding.

SŌCHŌ 宗長. 1448–1532. Late Muromachi *renga* poet, priest. Apparently from Suruga (Shizuoka), he wrote that he was a son of a smith. He took orders at seventeen, probably as a Shingon priest, and spent time in the provinces during the Ōnin War (1467–1477). After many travels, perhaps as an intelligence agent and certainly as negotiator for his great patron, Imagawa Ujichika, and others, he settled into the capital around 1471, having made acquaintance with *Sōgi about five years earlier in Suruga. When he was not away from Kyoto, he was on close terms as well with the eccentric priest, *Ikkyū. Although he belonged to a celibate sect, he formed relations with a woman and had two children. Everything known of him shows he had a capacity to invoke interest and trust among diverse people.

He wrote in the usual kinds of the renga masters: for example, a collection of renga stanzas, *Nachigomori* 那智籠 (*Secluded at Nachi*, 1515–1516); a book on composition, *Amayo no Ki* 雨夜の記 (*Record of a Rainy Night*, 1519); and travel diaries like *Utsunoyama no Ki* 宇津の山の記 (*Record of Utsunoyama*, 1517) and *Sōchō Shuki* 宗長手記 (*Sōchō's Recorded Experiences*, 1527; for other travel diaries, see Part Six C). He is best known as a poet today for his participation with *Sōgi and *Shōhaku in one hundred-stanza renga sequences. In one, *Minase Sangin Hyakuin* (1488), his stanzas are overly subjective and have an aural smoothness too much like *waka*. In the other, *Yunoyama Sangin Hyakuin* (1491), he is seen at his very best. Contemporaries complained about the quality of his stanzas, but his personality appears to have alleviated deficiencies found in him as a poet. Moreover, in his emphasis on conceptual connection in *mushin* renga, in which he excelled, he influenced the major *haikai* principles of *Nishiyama Sōin. He was a distinctly odd person and a gifted if uneven poet.

SOGA MONOGATARI 曽我物語 (*The Tale of the Soga Brothers*). A *monogatari* whose ten-book Chinese version was completed in the late Kamakura period and twelve-book Japanese version in early Muromachi. What follows concerns the Japanese.

No sooner had the victorious Genji established their government in Kamakura after the *Gempei* wars than the Soga brothers executed their long-sought revenge on Kudō Suketsune, whose retainers had killed their father. Their act was done on the night of the twenty-eighth of the fifth Month, 1193, at the hunting grounds at the foot of Mt. Fuji. Soon the Kanto area buzzed in excitement over the event, which apparently remained a dear subject for talk among samurai circles for generations. It seems that the spirits of the two brothers were thought to be abroad, and the writing of the story may have been an act to propitiate them.

Although the monogatari neglects nothing of the story, its handling is marked by an unusual degree of didactic comment—an element difficult to assess. Perhaps the preachiness shows that the story was developed by itinerant priests. Perhaps the author(s) who developed it saw religious meaning in it. Perhaps with the rise of Neoconfucianism in warrior and official circles, such people desired a moral dimension to the story. Each possibility seems real, but it is no longer possible to assess the weight of any.

The pronounced didacticism distinguishes the work from the *Heike Monogatari, although the first part of the Soga Monogatari draws on the opening section of the earlier work ("Gion Shōja"), and the second on the added story of Kenrei Mon'in added at the end of the story of Heike ("Kanjō no Maki")—these two sections being the most explicitly religious in the earlier story. The connection suggests the contrast. Where the earlier story was oriented toward the Heike and the west of Japan, this is directed toward the Genji and the east. Where the former was imbued with court and poetic understanding, the latter is founded on military and didactic principles. In fact the Soga Monogatari is difficult to classify. It has elements of the gunki monogatari, of denki monogatari, of setsuwa—as also of heroic literature separable from any given kind.

The story is usually divided into three sections. The first (parts 1 and 2) shows the origin of the brothers' revenge, back to "matters from the beginning of the age of the gods." The second (parts 3 into 10) treats the revenge by the brothers after numerous episodes and vicissitudes, and their deaths. The third (from 10 to 12) deals with later events. There is in this a strong resemblance to the jo-ha-kyū rhythm of renga and nō.

The characters who stand out the most are obviously the brothers, Jūrō (Sukenari) and Gorō (Tokimune). Fatherless from youth, they are reared by their mother with thoughts of revenge. Other important characters besides their mother include, in the third section, Jūrō's beloved, the courtesan Tora, and Shōshō with whom the mother and lover tour various provinces on pilgrimages. Toward the end, Shōshō preaches at their request, and Tora dies enlightened. This highly popular story was afterwards adapted to kōwakamai, nō, jōruri, and kabuki —as well as ukiyozōshi and kusazōshi. With Chūshingura (the story of the forty-seven rōnin), it has endured as one of the two most popular Japanese tales of revenge.

SŌGI 宗祇. 1421–1502. Late Muromachi renga poet, critic. As with so many renga masters, his background is obscure, and although there are two main traditions about his area of origin, there is no certainty. It is clear that by genius, longevity, and luck he survived the devastations of the Ōnin War (1467–1477) to become the greatest poet of his age. As renga continues to be studied more fully and be appreciated more widely, he will probably be joined to the small roster of the greatest Japanese poets— with *Kakinomoto Hitomaro, *Ariwara Narihira, *Saigyō, *Fujiwara Teika, *Matsuo Bashō, and *Yosa Buson.

He seems to have studied Buddhism at the Zen temple, Shōkokuji, in Kyoto, and to have spent time as a begging priest. His poetic studies probably began about the age of thirty, with study of waka in the school of the conservative *Nijō poets (whose precepts he interpreted generously), and of renga under *Takayama Sōzei and *Shinkei. He later divided renga into three periods, the first culminating with *Nijō Yoshimoto, the modern beginning with Sōzei.

Like others who could, he left Kyoto during most of the Ōnin War. As a priest, he was able to travel freely, and he associated with various warrior lords and commoners. From his Azuma Mondō 吾妻問答 (Eastern Dialogues, 1467, 1470), it is clear that he developed close friendships with provincial persons in the eastern domain of Musashi, where he sat with Shinkei in 1470 to participate in the Kawagoe Senku 河越千句 (A Thousand Stanzas at Kawagoe, 1470). About this time he composed alone his Mishima Senku 三島千句 (A Thousand Stanzas at Mishima) as a ritual offering for cure of the grievous influenza of a son of Tō no Tsuneyori, one of his most consistent patrons.

Tsuneyori (who also benefitted, financially) gave Sōgi invaluable teaching concerning Kokin denju and works other than the Kokinshū—along with social influence that enabled him to get on in the world, especially as other renga poets were dying in the turmoil of the times. During this uncertain period for transmission of court culture, men of humble origins like Sōgi played a crucial role almost out of necessity, since a renga poet had to give proof of talent not merely by linked poetry but yet more by knowledge of the *Kokinshū, *Genji Monogatari, and *Ise Monogatari. By 1474, Sōgi was teaching these classics, and from surviving notes kept by his follower, *Shōhaku, it is clear that his discussions broke new ground: instead of fussing over details, as was traditional, he considered classics, especially the Genji Monogatari, as integral in their wholes and ordering.

He returned to Kyoto when conditions settled somewhat, establishing himself in a well-appointed hermitage, the Shugyokuan, where, by 1473, highly placed people attended his lectures on the classics. Later he was discussing the Ise Monogatari before princes, and in 1487 he gave lectures on these classics to the nobility as well as his own followers at none other than Shōkokuji, where he had once been among the lowlier priests. He gained his highest appointment in 1488, when the Muromachi *bakufu* appointed him renga supervisor at the Kitano Shrine. He had earned this highest honor for a renga poet by demonstrating classical learning as much as by his renga poetry. Since he was not born either to court culture or poetry, his position was gained by genius, hard work, and strong patronage. His holistic approach to the classics derived not merely from his adaptation of Sung aesthetics (gained from teaching by the Zen monks?) but from literary insight and his greatness as a renga poet.

His teaching survives in but sketchy form. His enduring reputation therefore rests on his prose and, of course, his poetic creations. His wanderings prompted him to works in travel diary kind. *Nōin, *Saigyō, and other traveling poets lie behind his *Shirakawa Kikō* 白河紀行 (*A Diary of Travel to Shirakawa*, 1468), *Tsukushi Michi no Ki* 筑紫道記 (*A Record of Travel to Tsukushi*, 1480), *Oi no Susami* 老のすさみ (*Play in Old Age*, 1479), and similar writings.

The last named is more miscellaneous and critical, adapting elements taken from one of his major renga collections, *Chikurinshō* 竹林抄 (*The Seven Poets of the Bamboo Grove*, 1476), which included stanzas from seven poets he particularly prized. He had already collected renga stanzas in a personal collection, *Wasuregusa* 萱草 (*Plants of Forgetfulness*, 1474). This run of anthologies was officially crowned by the *Shinsen Tsukuba Shū* 新撰菟玖波集 (*A Newly Selected Renga Collection*, or *A Newly Selected Tsukuba Shū*, 1495), compiled with *Sanjōnishi Sanetaka and others as a deliberate reprise, in twenty books, of *Nijō Yoshimoto's *Tsukuba Shū*. In these collections, his arrangement more or less followed that of the *chokusenshū*, and each stanza selected was given its predecessor (*maeku*), because a given renga stanza (*ku*) was taken (unless a *hokku*) to exist as a poetic unit only with its predecessor.

Sōgi would have an important place in literary history on the basis of such writings and collections. But his greatness truly rests on his poetry. Much of what he wrote has been lost, and no complete, annotated edition of his copious extant writing exists. Yet his standing as a poet would be clear if only on the evidence of three one hundred-stanza sequences now widely available. These include the most famous of all renga sequences, *Minase Sangin Hyakuin*, the superior *Yunoyama Sangin Hyakuin* —both written with *Shōhaku and Sōchō—and a solo sequence deserving separate attention.

Taking his time and pleasing himself in the fashioning of a masterpiece, Sōgi spent four months in 1499, three years before his long life ended. The result was his *Sōgi Dokugin Nanihito* (or *Nanikara*) *Hyakuin* 宗祇独吟何人（唐）百韻 (*A Hundred Stanzas Related to "Person" ("China") by Sōgi Alone*). Many subtle features show that the poet sought to make this his crowning achievement. There are also obvious signs of divagation. There are the usual four flower stanzas, but one comes in the *hokku*, and there is none on the fourth sheet (*nagori*). There are ten moon stanzas instead of the usual seven. There is a much higher proportion of seasonal stanzas than the usual half, and there are at least twenty love stanzas, an extraordinarily high proportion. Sōgi obviously sought, and equally obviously achieved, unusual richness. His presence is felt in other ways. His explicit and implicit concern with the sufferings of his bellicose time is remarkable, as is also his concern for ordinary people in it. He represents himself as near the Buddha's age at departure from the world (at eighty; Sōgi was seventy-nine—both by Japanese count) and also about to die (stanzas 83, 100). The sequence shows the utmost reach of renga. Not only are individual stanzas of uncommon attractiveness; more than that, the handling of stanzaic connection (*tsukeai*) and of sequential rhythm (*jo-ha-kyū*) are above praise.

Sōgi mastered the three principal features of renga: stanzaic composition, stanzaic connection, and integration of the whole. His individual stanzas are often highly impressive: he is especially given to lovely stanzas involving haze, to others involving human affairs, and to yet others combining particulars with universals. He also made more of ground (*ji*) stanzas than did his contemporaries in order to achieve sequential variety and integrity. In all this, his personal tastes are clear, as in his almost eccentric liking for the humble plant, wild yellow roses (yamabuki). The fourth stanza of his *Wasuregusa*— Yo ni furu mo/ sara ni shigure no/ yadori kana:

> Even as time falls
> so more in this world the drizzle
> at a grass-thatched hut—

was so famous that *Matsuo Bashō violated the principal rule for a hokku in echoing Sōgi's stanza without specifying a season in his own stanza. Sōgi's drizzle is commonly taken as a metaphor for the sufferings in his war-torn age. From that anguish was born the beauty of his art, and in those terms did he practice, and evoke in others, a genius for linked poetry. In doing these things, he brought into currency what was often only implicit in earlier Japanese literature.

SŌI 宗伊. 1418–1485. Muromachi *renga* master, military figure. Apart from various military studies, he worked with *Ikkyū to learn Zen Buddhist practices and renga. After the death of his wife, he took orders (1480). *Sōgi held him in esteem, choosing him as one of the seven poets represented in *Chikurinshō*—by 209 *tsukeku* and 25 *hokku*. Some say that there is a Chinese cast to his stanzas (because of some parallelism?). Like *Chiun, he was a warrior who was also a poet, and with even better artistic success.

SŌIN. See NISHIYAMA SŌIN.

SŌKEI. See Nambō Sōkei.

SOKŌ. See Yamaga Sokō.

SONE NO YOSHITADA 曽禰好忠. Active last quarter of the eleventh century. Mid-Heian *waka* poet. Like *Minamoto Shunrai, Yoshitada was an uneven but highly gifted poet whose styles were so in advance of his time that he suffered from contemporary criticism but was hailed by later poets. Unlike Shunrai, he was not of sufficiently high social status to require recognition in social terms. He longed in vain to be freed from provincial service in Tango in order to return to the capital and gain success as a poet. He was in touch with *Fujiwara Kintō and *Minamoto Shitagō, but they seem not to have been able to help him move or to have been very enthusiastic about his poetry. This has the fluency of earlier and contemporary styles with a new tautness, and a new freedom of conception. His occasional lapses in taste may have confirmed the doubts of the Kintōs. But after his death his reputation grew steadily among those who observed his freshness and intensity. As a result he was increasingly included in collections from the *Goshuishū* to the *Shinkokinshū*. And his personal collection, *Sotanshū* 曽丹集 (*The Collection of Sone the Tango Official*; also *Sone no Yoshitada Shū*) excels most such collections in its quality, and particularly in two of its constituents. One, the *Yoshitada Hyakushu* convincingly expresses the agonies he felt over his thwarted ambitions without becoming tedious or mawkish. The other, the 360 poems of his *Maigetsushū* 毎月集 (*The Twelve Months*) represent a year in the old calendar, so constituting a novel poetic diary. Yoshitada is one of the waka poets still too little appreciated. Study of his personal collection offers one of the best means for proper appreciation of his special gifts.

SORAI. See Ogyū Sorai.

SOSEI 素性. Active 859–897. Early Heian *waka* poet, one of the thirty-six Poetic Sages (*sanjūrokkasen*). Of very high social status, he took orders like his father—*Henjō—before him. Although lost today in the shadows of *Ariwara Narihira and *Ono no Komachi, his contemporary reputation was very high. Some sixty poems, a large number for a poet of his time, are included in collections beginning with the *Kokinshū*. There is a personal collection, *Sosei Hōshi Shū*.

SŌSUKE. See Namiki Sōsuke.

(TAWARAYA) SŌTATSU (俵屋) 宗達. Dates unknown. Early Edo painter, designer. He was remarkable both for ability and versatility. In illustrating scrolls, he revived traditional kinds of painting. He also introduced new elements into ink wash painting, designed superior screens, used gold and silver to great effect, etc. One of his most famous works is a screen illustrating the *Genji Monogatari*.

SŌZEI. See Takayama Sōzei.

SUGAE MASUMI 菅江真澄. ?1754–1815. Late Edo writer of travel literature. Born in Mikawa, he devoted the latter half of his life to writing of his travels, especially about village life in the "snow country" region of Japan. *Akita No Karine* 齶田 濃刈寝 (*A Brief Sleep in Rural Akita*, 1784) is one of many such writings. In recent times, he has been revaluated and, especially with the praise of Yanagita Kunio (1875–1962), has come to be thought the outstanding folklore scholar of the Edo period.

SUGAWARA MICHIZANE 菅原道真. 845–903. Early Heian court figure, poet in Chinese. Born into a scholarly family, Michizane proved brilliant at an early age, rapidly advancing from elementary subjects into Chinese and historical learning. He received the rare degree of Doctor of Letters in 877, rejoicing his family, since he was the third in his house to do so in as many generations. He prospered with appointments by Uda (r. 887–897), attaining ever greater influence at court. This led to alarm on the part of Fujiwara potentates and the jealousy of scholarly rivals. With the accession of Daigo (r. 897–930), his fortunes gradually waned. In a few years he was effectively exiled to Kyushu, where he died two years later. A series of natural calamities thereafter led many to assume that Michizane's wronged and angry spirit was at large. He was accorded numerous posthumous honors and, in popular belief, became the divinity of learning. Apart from historical writings, he is best known for his collections of Chinese composition: *Kanke Bunsō* 菅家文草 (*Sugawara Poems*, probably 900) and *Kanke Kōshū* 菅家後集 (*A Later Sugawara Collection* by 902). Over the centuries, he has held the reputation of one of the few most gifted of Japanese poets in Chinese, as well as acquiring fame as a representative of learning.

SUGAWARA TAKASUE NO MUSUME 菅原孝 標女. B. 1008. Late Heian diarist, writer of *monogatari*; the Daughter of Sugawara Takasue. Born into what was then perhaps the most learned family, she was descended paternally from *Sugawara Michizane, and male members of her house usually headed the court school (daigaku) and honored as doctors of letters, a rare title. Although her father was not greatly inclined to letters, other relatives were. Her mother's elder sister was *Fujiwara Michitsuna no Haha, author of the *Kagerō Nikki*. Her stepmother was not only something of a poet but was also related to the daughter of *Murasaki Shikibu. So it is no wonder that she was an avid reader from her youth or that she should wish to write.

Much of what we know of her life derives from her *Sarashina Nikki* 更級日記 (*The Sarashina Diary*). This is one of the four major court diaries, along with those of *Murasaki Shikibu, *Izumi Shikibu, and *Fujiwara Michitsuna no Haha. In some ways it is the most enjoyable of the four to read. Its prose style is more natural, at least easier, than Murasaki Shikibu's; we do not find the tone of grumpiness that there is in the *Kagerō Nikki*; and the author is more like us than is the lady of the *Izumi Shikibu Nikki*. Quite apart from when it may have been written or reshaped, it is, in effect, one of the very few early Japanese literary autobiographies that cover substantially a whole life. It begins in the autumn when she was twelve, and goes on for a year or so after her husband's death, to some time in her fifties or perhaps to sixty. Her avid reading of monogatari while a girl has often been quoted. Her particular delight is the *Genji Monogatari*, and in it the sad stories of Yūgao and Ukifune. She seems to have acquired a copy about 1021, perhaps from the author's daughter. Given the textual problems of that work and the lack of any text anywhere near as old, recovery of this "association copy" of the *Genji Monogatari* would be the literary find of centuries in Japan.

About 1040 she married Tachibana Toshimichi, and from this time the suffering depicted in monogatari began to be replicated in life, inclining her— as age inclines us everywhere—to see the vivacity of the commonplaces of the race, for her particularly those of Buddhism. From time to time she seems to have served at the court of Princess Yūshi but to have found no close feeling with the princess. In her late thirties and forties, she occupied herself with rearing her son, Nakatoshi, and took intermittent pilgrimages to temples. She reported that in 1055 she had a trustworthy dream of the coming of the Amida Buddha to welcome the spirits of the dead, and as her writing shows, the world of dreams was deeply significant to her. In 1057 her husband was posted to the provinces for a year. Shortly after his return he died, leaving her in very straitened circumstances.

Her talents were so well recognized that numerous works were attributed to her. On his copy of her diary, *Fujiwara Teika ascribed to her not only it and her *Hamamatsu Chūnagon Monogatari* (which he called *Mitsu no Hamamatsu*) but also *Yoru no Nezame, Mizukara Kuyuru, Asakura*, and other writings. The last two works have not survived; *Yoru no Nezame* is now believed to be by another, unknown author; and there is no certainty that she wrote the first named (see below). But Teika's ascription conveys, at the very least, his view that she was in the front rank of Heian authors. About ten poems from her diary were selected for various official collections.

Hamamatsu Chūnagon Monogatari 浜松中納言物語 (originally *Mitsu no Hamamatsu* みつの浜松 from a poem by the hero; *The Tale of Hamamatsu*).

Late Heian *tsukurimonogatari, gikomonogatari* in six parts, the first now lost, although some poems are extant and, with their headnotes and details in the extant parts, the outline of the lost part is clear.

There are those who doubt the traditional ascription of authorship. One poem appears to allude to a poem by another hand datable to ca. 1064. That seems to some critics a time when the author was probably deep in religious devotions and unlikely to be writing fiction. In fact, she may even have been dead by then. But the evidence of tradition resembles, more or less, that for the *Genji Monogatari* and the *Izumi Shikibu Nikki*, the arrangements of the *Makura no Sōshi*, and much else in Heian literature. The woman who, at age forty-seven, had a perfect vision of the Amida Buddha is not the least likely author of *this* work. There is also the correspondence between this work and her diary in the conspicuousness of dreams: eleven in the diary and thirteen in the monogatari (counting two in the lost first part).

The plot is not difficult to follow, but it is unusually necessary to our understanding of the work. For that reason an exceptional summary is offered here.

Part 1 (inferred). Son of a prince, Hamamatsu lost his father while yet a boy. His mother married a widower with two daughters, the elder of whom, Ōigimi, he intends to marry to the profligate Prince Shikibukyō, who will surely be appointed heir to the throne. Hamamatsu comes to share a strong romantic attachment with the elder. They manage to control their passion. Hamamatsu has, however, a dream in which he learns that his father has been reborn as Third Prince of the T'ang, and filial piety requires a visit to China. As he is about to leave for his permitted three years, the sorrow of parting leads Hamamatsu and Ōigimi to one night's consummation of their love. He goes off to Tsukushi (northern Kyushu) for departure for China, not knowing that his beloved is pregnant, her father upset by the disruption of his plans, and she now in the state of a nun. (Note: Japanese count of "chapters" usually designates the following as Part 1, etc.)

Part 2. In China Hamamatsu impresses all with his extraordinary beauty and abilities. He meets everyone of importance, including the Third Prince, and a large number of women. Quite contrary to historical fact, Chinese women are depicted more in the public light than Japanese. Hamamatsu manages even to meet the Third Prince's mother. She is a replication of Yang Kuei-fei and the Kiritsubo mother of Genji in being the most favored concubine of the sovereign and hounded by the jealousy of other women and their families. Moreover, she is the daughter of a Japanese princess and a Chinese ambassador. To avoid trouble she has gone to Hoyang and is known as the Hoyang Consort. Hamamatsu has a momentary love affair with her, not knowing at first who she is. With effort and help, he makes the discovery, receives the son she bore him, and sees her briefly again before returning to Japan.

Part 3. On arrival in Tsukushi with his son, Wakagimi, and his Chinese escorts, he hears the news of Ōigimi. Full of thoughts of her and of the Hoyang Consort, he rejects for a time the offer by a lord, Daini, of his daughter as concubine. Her attractions, and his, lead to some bond between them. He departs for the capital, taking care of Wakagimi in hiding. He visits court; and he establishes a brother-sister relationship with Ōigimi. Looking at the letter the Hoyang Consort has asked him to deliver to her Japanese mother, he senses her agony when he reads that she cannot expect ever to visit Japan unless she is reborn there.

Part 4. The Hoyang Consort's mother is a nun living at Yoshino, looked after by a monk and looking after her other daughter, Yoshinohime. He conveys the letter from China, staying some unspecified lengthy time at Yoshino, looking after the material needs of those there. Meanwhile, Daini has come to the capital with his wife and daughter. Since Hamamatsu seems established otherwise, he marries off his daughter as second and younger wife to Emon no Kami, Hamamatsu's uncle. Back in the capital, Hamamatsu swears to Ōigimi that although they cannot be husband and wife, he will never marry while she is alive. Soon, however, the sovereign tells Hamamatsu that he wishes to bestow the Fourth Princess on him. The part ends with the hero's going again to Yoshino.

Part 5. Hamamatsu puts off the royal offer by reporting that his next three years are the most dangerous in his life and that he must hold off marriage until he has survived that period. While he is at Yoshino, the pious nun dies and, as a great fragrance arises, it is clear that she has been taken to paradise. From the monk he learns of Yoshinohime's karma: her life will be disastrous if she knows a man sexually before she is twenty. The news comes in time for him to control his relations with her, which might now have been intimate. He tells her about his time in China, including information about her half-sister, the Hoyang Consort. He takes her to the capital and puts in her charge the young Wakagimi, who calls her "Mother" and adores her. Hamamatsu is pleased by this and the thought that Yoshinohime is under his prudent care, safe from the philandering Shikibukyō. A sudden voice from the sky thrice states that the Hoyang Consort has left this world for paradise. Installed in Hamamatsu's mansion, all goes well for Yoshinohime until she falls seriously ill. To improve matters, Hamamatsu takes her to Kiyomizu Temple, where he leaves her in charge of her ladies. (He cannot be with her because of a directional taboo.) The prince hears of the whereabouts of the woman he thinks

Hamamatsu's mistress. The narrator wonders what will occur next.

Part 6. Shikibukyō abducts Yoshinohime, leaving the unsuspecting Hamamatsu distraught. We learn that Daini's daughter is pregnant by Hamamatsu. He dreams that the Hoyang Consort will be reborn as the child Yoshinohime is carrying. Moving to retrospection, the narrator tells of Yoshinohime's abduction and her comatose state. In desperation, the prince asks whom she wishes to see: the hero. The prince calls him, he goes, and they take her back to Hamamatsu's mansion in a precarious condition. The prince and Hamamatsu spend nights together watching her, and she does begin to improve. Hamamatsu tells the prince and others falsely that she is his half-sister by a common father. He has some difficulty in repressing amorous inclinations toward the still pregnant Yoshinohime. His relations with Ōigimi continue as before, and the story ends with news from China confirming some details of his dream about the Hoyang Consort.

The summary serves to show certain matters. One is the overwhelming debt of the story to the Uji section of the *Genji Monogatari*. An episode in *Torikaebaya Monogatari* drawing both on Murasaki Shikibu's masterpiece and this shows that Yoshino is simply a longer word for the Uji of Kaoru, Niou, and Ukifune. The many resemblances testify both to an extraordinarily detailed memory of the earlier work and to transformation, in a very different counterpart or situation, of everything used.

Another matter implied by the summary would hold even if the other principal or mentioned characters (upwards of thirty in all) were included. Almost everybody is related somehow. Hamamatsu's father is (now) the son of the Hoyang Consort, as is Wakagimi, making Hamamatsu, as it were, stepfather to his father, and so forth. Curiously, in spite of this, the author manages to avoid the near brush with incest that we find Genji involved in.

The final matter deducible from the summary takes us next to the heart of the work. This monogatari is not so much impossible, although it may be that, as incredible in its plot or events. Further details would heighten that impression, and yet knowing the whole work does away with the judgment. Once we have the full story in all its descriptions, actions, talk, dreams, and ideas we have an entire, integral, and moving work.

The work omits much of what its great predecessors—the *Genji Monogatari* and *Sagoromo Monogatari*—lovingly provide. Leaving apart the complex thematic treatment of time implied by transmigrations, it is remarkable how little attention is paid to the seasons, the atmosphere of the time of day, the intersection of time, character, and place. The story is very perfunctory about Hamamatsu in

China, and the more it is suggested to differ from Japan the more it seems the same. A character in the *Mumyōzōshi* found features of the treatment of China unconvincing or unreal (makoto shikarazu). The remark may be limited to some such thing as the Hoyang Consort's mixed ancestry, but readers today will discover that Hamamatsu is an unreal Japanese Chūnagon in an unreal China—until he begins to react with other individuals. Then his rank, his nation—and those of the person he deals with—simply do not matter. Human relations are what count in this story. It is as refreshing as it is astonishing in a Heian writer to discover such indifference to the ranks of the hero and others. The author might, however, have considered promoting Hamamatsu several notches in order to do the decent thing for a monogatari hero—and to make credible the tennō's offer of the Fourth Princess. (Such seeming indifference may be explained by the fact that the author's family was of the zuryō, low or provincial governors' order of the nobility, and was not well acquainted with the court.) These are really venial matters. It is more difficult to judge another criticism made in the *Mumyōzōshi*, that the transmigration of the Hoyang Consort to Yoshinohime's child is not credible. The point turns not on transmigration, of course, or on yet another astonishingly close-range coincidence of far-separated things, but on a doctrine that the special blessed state to which the Consort had been taken should last centuries. The objection is not to the fact itself: in this lies the key to the unusual power held by the work in spite of its tall tales.

The author's lapses over details testify to her earnest concern with what does matter to her. She wishes to delineate the ultimately unfathomable nature of human personality, the mystery of human relationships in this world, and to account for those matters by grounding human experience in Buddhist metaphysics. The Buddhism seems to be a syncretic Tendai kind ranging from its esoteric (mikkyō) to the overt teaching of emptiness (*kū*) and on to Amidism. But above all, there is karma, which is to say human action and its results, causality from one existence to another. It is not clear that this should be termed fatalism, but it is clear that it is more a cause of our insight and wonder than of pessimism. If we are to term the causality fate, it must be understood in the Buddhist sense that what happens now is the result of action in a prior existence (*sukuse*, shukuen*), and of course the many dreams aid this understanding. In her diary, Izumi Shikibu speaks of yielding to her karma (sukuse ni makasete) when she finally decides to go to the prince's palace. What is isolated or implicit in that diary and the *Genji Monogatari* is prominent and explicit here, particularly in matters having to do with the hero. He may not get things as he wishes them for himself, but for others he is repeatedly treated as the Buddha's

expedient (*hōben*) in bringing comfort. His benefits to the nun at Yoshino, for example, include the inestimable one of enabling her to cut attachments with this world and achieve birth in paradise.

It is certainly true that the author's religion is manifest at every turn. The turns include odd twists, paradoxes, strange coincidences, extraordinary accidents, feats of chance. These resemble the contrivances of Providence and God's mysterious ways in Christianity, and it is impossible to read this work without the conviction that these matters constituted the weave of life to its author. That being the case, it is also significant that the story received no criticism on these grounds, because it transcends them. It is also worth remarking that the story makes less of pollutions, directional taboos, and other magical matters than do most other Heian works.

A final criticism from the *Mumyōzōshi* also illuminates. The work is faulted because its hero never develops a happy relation with a woman—that is, one that is in some sense both ideal and normal, and that the work does not end happily. The allegation is fundamentally just, but not the implication: that it is a fault. The author's view of experience is the highly tenable one that relations may be normal and under special circumstances ideal, but not both. The two most ideal relations in the work include Hamamatsu's with the Hoyang Consort, which can exist ideally only for two brief moments and otherwise produce only frustrated longing. The ideal moment is a proximate cause of ensuing suffering. The other ideal relation is, of course, that of the hero and Ōigimi after his return from China. It is ideal only on the premise that it is sexless—clearly something as abnormal as it is unideal to the author and the standards of her age.

In these matters as in so much else, the author is heavily indebted to the stories from the *Genji Monogatari* recalled in her diary as the most moving—those of Yūgao and Genji and of Ukifune and Kaoru. It does lack the happy ending of the usual monogatari (the *mukashi monogatari*, *Sagoromo Monogatari*, *Torikaeba ya Monogatari*, and so on), although it does not end with the human failure of the *Genji Monogatari*, either. We are left with a profound sense of regret for what might have been but will not be. The theme is not restricted to this work, and it is not a conviction restricted to Japanese literature. It is nonetheless important, moving. Causality enters into this experience, especially because we never know when a cause will exert an effect and often do not know that it exists till there is an effect. The dreams also enter. They are all reliable, if sometimes not immediately clear.

The author offers in all this a fresh version of the Heian duality of dream and reality (yume, utsutsu), making mature and attractive truths integral to the action and religion in her work. We must understand ourselves, others, and the world. The farther our understanding progresses, the more we appreciate two things. One is our responsibility for what we do. No other Heian monogatari or diary makes this so clear, and those who think that moral judgment is suspended in Heian writing such as the *Genji Monogatari* will have to deny the existence of this story. Hamamatsu repeatedly shows awareness of his responsibility, as does Prince Shikibukyō in the end. How there could be karmic causality without responsibility is not easily explained, as this work shows. The other thing is that the further we understand ourselves, our world, and others, the more dreamlike, imperfect, and insubstantial those entities become in any other than a religious explanation. (One standard meaning of yume or dream is utsutsu, reality: and vice versa.) In fact, on one view the author and her work are superstitious, credulous. On another view, they are rare for her time in offering a version of Buddhism in which ontology and epistemology are no more important than faith. For this work, knowing is not more important than believing, a hint taken (like so much) and independently developed (like all else taken) from the Ukifune story of the *Genji Monogatari*. It is no accident that its well over one hundred poems are highly allusive to poems in the *Genji Monogatari* and the principal anthologies, or else use gestures (the play on "ama" as "nun" and "fisherwoman") that recall Ukifune. The poems lack that inevitable fit with occasion that Murasaki Shikibu's possess in her masterpiece, and there is not the same resonance between and among them. But the poems, like all else, fit better with the guiding ideas that the author takes such pains to make clear. It seems quite just that the *Mumyōzōshi* should list this monogatari with the *Genji Monogatari* and *Sagoromo Monogatari* as one of the three greatest.

SUGITA GEMPAKU 杉田玄白. 1733–1817. Mid-Edo physician, student of foreign learning. He was surgeon for the Obama domain in Wakasa (present Fukui). Credited with founding Dutch learning, *rangaku*; by its means he acquired a then unusual knowledge of foreign science, particularly medicine, winning a *bakufu* appointment as medical officer. He was one of the seven translators involved in the first medical treatise translated into Japanese from the West, *Kaitai Shinsho* 解体新書 (*A New Treatise of Anatomizing*, 1774). But his most famous work was *Rangaku Kotohajime* 蘭学事始 (*A Primer to Dutch Studies*, 1815).

SUGIYAMA SAMPŪ 杉山杉風. 1647–1732. Early Edo *haikai* poet. Born in Edo into a wealthy mercantile house, he practiced haikai in the *Danrin* style until meeting *Matsuo Bashō in 1672. His support of Bashō included provision of a hermitage, the first Bashōan, from which the master took his best-known pen name. An early and lifetime sup-

porter of Bashō, he has poetry in all seven of the major collections of the school (see Part Six F). Bashō appointed him arbiter for his school in the thirty-three eastern provinces, as *Mukai Kyorai of the thirty-three western.

SUMIAKI. See TOYOHARA SUMIAKI.

SUMIYOSHI MONOGATARI 住吉物語 (*The Tale of Sumiyoshi*). Early Kamakura *giko monogatari* in two parts, an immensely popular story of no great literary merit. It tells how (once upon a time) a certain middle councillor had two wives. The heroine, daughter of one of them, loses her mother at seven and thereafter is persecuted by her nasty stepmother (see *Ochikubo Monogatari*). Our hero, Shōshō, son of a grand councillor, hears of the heroine's plight and becomes interested. Learning of this, the evil stepmother pretends that her younger daughter is the one involved and marries her to Shōshō. He, later realizing that he has been duped, finds that he can do little but repine. Meanwhile, and so on. The heroine is at last rescued by the hero from her refuge in Sumiyoshi (hence the title), they marry, and they live happily ever after.

Nearly seventy distinct manuscripts survive, an astonishing number. They vary in the fluctuations of episodes centered on poems. It appears from various Heian accounts that there had been a version, now lost, that differed in its second half (something similar having occurred earlier with the *Taketori Monogatari*). Earlier versions seem to have had pictures that could be used with the text to savor the vicissitudes of the heroine, or perhaps to be looked at while the text was read aloud. The changes in the text are surmised to have come gradually, with popularity bringing constant small alterations until there were major differences from early versions.

Like its predecessor, the *Ochikubo Monogatari*, this anticipates the Cinderella story. It is said to have influenced the similar *Akizuki Monogatari*, just as its version of the trials of love influenced *Koke no Koromo* and other later stories.

SUZUKI HARUNOBU 鈴木春信. 1725–1770. Mid-Edo *ukiyoe* artist. He was a master of the technical as well as artistic features of wood-block printing. Before him, colors consisted of red and green added to black. He found processes that allowed for as many as ten. This, with his somewhat ethereal portrayals of female beauty, transformed the art.

SUZUKI SHIGETANE 鈴木重胤. 1812–1863. Late Edo *kokugaku* scholar. Born in Awaji, into a family that had furnished village headmen for generations, he benefited from his father's interests in learning. He traveled for study throughout the area between Kyoto and Edo, and first settled down to study with a branch of the school of *Hirata Atsutane. On Atsutane's death, he seems to have associated with a slightly revisionist group. He wrote voluminously. Probably his most famous work was *Nihon Shoki Den* 日本書紀伝 (cf. *Motoori Norinaga's *Kojikiden*). A strikingly fresh feature of his work lies in his interest in the Ainu and in Korea, topics usually entirely ignored by kokugakusha scholars and other classical Japanese writers.

SUZUKI SHŌSAN 鈴木正三. 1579–1655. Early Edo *kanazōshi* writer. In his eventful life, he first followed his Mikawa samurai traditions, fighting for Tokugawa Ieyasu at Sekigahara and Osaka Castle. Later he took orders as a Sōtō Zen priest, and in his zeal worked to repress Christianity, publishing in 1661 a work urging extirpation of the alien religion, *Ha Kirishitan* 破吉利支丹 (*Destroy Christianity*). Publication of this and others of his works was delayed till after his death. Those include *Bammin Tokuyō* 万民徳用 (*The Significance of Everybody's Activities*, printed 1651) among his sermons; as also *Inga Monogatari* 因果物語 (*The Tale of Karma*, printed 1661) and *Ninin Bikuni* 二人比丘尼 (*The Two Bikuni*, printed 1663) among his literary. The last is his best known, partly for its readability, partly because it was one of the works drawn on by *Ihara Saikaku. For depiction of a bikuni, see Part Ten E.

TABITO. See ŌTOMO TABITO.

TACHIBANA AKEMI 橘曙覧. 1812–1868. Late Edo *waka* poet. After priestly studies, he turned to history and literature. His work involved contact with the schools of *Rai San'yō and *Motoori Norinaga. But he is known today as a poet. If we set aside outstanding waka poets like *Ryōkan and *Ōkuma Kotomichi, Akemi probably wrote the best waka of the century, often integrating sets of poems in interesting ways.

TACHIBANA NARISUE 橘成季. Dates unknown. Kamakura literary and musical figure, governor of Iga. He was famous as a biwa player, although his literary fame resides mostly in a major *setsuwa* collection in twenty parts, *Kokon Chomonjū* 古今著聞集 (*Stories Heard from Writers Old and New*, 1254). Following the practice of the *Konjaku Monogatari*, it has a general preface in *kambun*, a list of contents, and an afterword in *kanabun*. Its 726 stories are divided into thirty sections, each having a brief preface, and the sections are grouped in largely chronological order.

Although its style is not superlative, the interest of its stories places it with (but after) the *Konjaku Monogatari* and *Uji Shūi Monogatari* as one of the three great *setsuwa* collections. The title suggests emulation of the former collection and perhaps recalls the *Kokinshū* as well. In any event, Narisue's preface makes clear that he had intended a lavish production, with illustrations, before other occupations intervened. His organization shows his care. The first two sections—distinguished as Shinto and Buddhism—are classified by topics such as appear in some royal *waka* collections (*chokusenshū*). Other topics—food and plants—are more typical of set-suwa collections.

The classifications do not obscure the emphasis upon human actions and motives so important to setsuwa. Love and courage, with less attractive traits, are well shown. Some critics see in the collection a decline of court atmosphere, a transition to the world of soldiers and commoners. Yet one virtue of the setsuwa collections all along had been their inclusiveness of so many kinds of people. In the end, the stories are what matter, and if Narisue failed to dress up his collection as he had wished, he accomplished the main thing in making his stories worth reading.

TADAMINE. See MIBU NO TADAMINE.

TADANORI. See TAIRA TADANORI.

TAIGA. See IKE NO TAIGA.

TAIHEIKI 太平記 (*The Record of the Great Peace*), Namboku *gunki monogatari* in forty parts, written by many people in various stages—particularly, it seems, by priests favoring the southern dynasty, and perhaps given its final version by Priest Kojima in 1372. According to *Imagawa Ryōshun's criticisms in his *Nan Taiheiki*, Priest Gen'e produced a thirty-book version on order from Ashikaga Tadayoshi, who found it so full of errors that he had it thoroughly revised. Because Gen'e's and Tadayoshi's deaths are recorded by part thirty as we have the work, much reworking was done.

This narrative covers the five decades (1318–1367) of recurrent war following Godaigo's efforts to rally groups disaffected with the Kamakura *bakufu* run by the Hōjō regents in his vain hope to restore power about the sovereign in Kyoto. The vicissitudes of these years are well shown. The early part of the work deals especially with the wars of the Shōchū and Genkō eras (1324–1326 and 1331–1334), culminating in the brief recovery of power by the court during the Kemmu Restoration (1334–1336) (parts 1–12). But Godaigo's triumph was short-lived. He was out of touch with the new realities of fractious military houses. Various temporary allegiances split, regrouping in dynastic terms about the rival northern and southern courts (parts 13–21). As a consequence, forces identified with the Ashikaga regime had been able to regroup, only to discover its own divisions as power was reacquired. With more bloodshed—including the deaths of the shoguns Tadayoshi, the brilliant if corrupt Takauji, and then

Yoshiakira—the stage was set for the stewardship or regency of Hosokawa Yoriyuki over the child Yoshimitsu and government left no more stable than it had been (parts 22–40).

The later books appear to be more critical of the Ashikaga regime, and one line of interpretation holds that the work as we have it is governed by social criticism. Another, religious, interpretation discovers the theme of karma working throughout. Both are plausible, but we may also read the title (which reads oddly for those events, even if taken as *The Record of the Great Pacification*) less to indicate the irony of a social critic or the worldly illusion posited by priests than as a vain but persistent desire for peace in an age whose diverse rivalries and violent tragedies continued to frustrate natural human hope.

The style offers a lively version of *wakan konkōbun*, and the description of Godaigo's death is an example of how fine the work is. For if the story is no serious literary rival of the **Heike Monogatari*, it is a vehicle that clearly presents an extraordinarily complex and often obscure rough-and-tumble, see-saw plot of violence and intrigue. The means of achieving such clarity involve debts to Chinese sources, to court monogatari, to diary literature, and to *rekishi monogatari*. The debts attest to literary intent as well as realization, and they were in turn repaid by the work's subsequent influence. *Hachi no Ki* (*nō*), *Chūshingura* (*jōruri*), and **Kyokutei Bakin's Hakkenden* (*yomihon*) were influenced by the *Taiheiki*. For it to do so can only betoken a major achievement.

TAIRA TADANORI 平忠度. 1144–1184. Late Heian poet, general, known from presentation in the **Heike Monogatari* and *nō*. As the Heike cause seemed doomed, he visited **Fujiwara Shunzei to ask that a poem of his be included in the official collection (**Senzaishū*) that Shunzei was assembling. Tadanori was slain at the battle of Ichinotani, and, given the Genji triumph, Shunzei did what he could, including one poem entered as "anonymous."

TAIRA YASUYORI. See *Hōbutsushū*.

TAKAHASHI MUSHIMARO 高橋虫麻呂. Dates unknown; fl. ca. 730–735. Nara *waka* poet. Little is known of him. His family traditionally served as table-stewards of sovereigns, although his own career seems to have involved provincial service. He is well represented in the **Man'yōshū* by comments and poems. The poems include thirteen *chōka*, eighteen *tanka*, and a *sedōka* said to be taken from a Takahashi Mushimaro collection. The poems usually selected have made him best known for treating travel and legends. The relation of legends (as about the woman, Mama no Tekona) recalls other Man'yō poets such as **Ōtomo Yakamochi and **Yamabe Akahito, although his narrative approach more resembles that of **Kakinomoto Hitomaro. He is not the equal of any of those poets, but his work is distinctive in subject, style, and tone.

TAKAI KITŌ 高井几董. 1741–1789. Mid-Edo *haikai* poet. Like his master, **Yosa Buson, he studied *Danrin* haikai, specifically under Yahantei Sōa in Kyoto. It was there that he met Buson, whose most important follower he became. In 1780 they composed the two-*kasen Momosumomo*. On Buson's death three years later, Kitō vainly sought to keep alive the principles and practices of his teacher. Although he could compose striking stanzas, apparently his gifts did not include those of the leadership that Buson possessed.

TAKAMURA. See ONO NO TAKAMURA.

TAKARAI KIKAKU. See ENOMOTO KIKAKU.

TAKAYAMA SŌZEI 高山宗砌. D. 1455. Namboku-Muromachi *renga* master. He studied *waka* and the *Genji Monogatari* under **Shōtetsu, and renga with **Bontō. By 1427 he had written enough to have a collection of his work. In 1433 he participated in a ten-thousand renga sequence sponsored by the shogunate—the *Kitano Manku* 北野万句—and in a sequence of equal length in 1436. With his reputation made, he was called upon to move about from a hermitage in which he had established himself by 1432. He must have written his treatise, *Kokon Rendanshū* 古今連談集 (*Talks Old and New on Renga*) in the 1430s or 1440s. In 1447 he participated as the senior figure with other important poets of the time, in the **Anegakoji Imashimmei Hyakuin*, and in the next year was given the highest official appointment available a renga poet, supervisor of the art by *bakufu* appointment to the Kitano shrine. He was associated with the major poetic figures of his day, including **Shinkei and **Ichijō Kanera. Besides his involvement in numerous important sequences of the time, he published collections of his stanzas, such as *Sōzei Kushū* 宗砌句集 (*Sōzei's Stanzas*, 1454). Although his earlier style has been criticized for its verbal play, the closely observed seasonal detail of his later work is highly esteemed. **Sōgi often praised him, saying that the third or modern period of renga began with him. He was also one of the seven poets whose stanzas Sōgi included in *Chikurinshō*.

TAKEBE AYATARI 建部綾足. 1719–1774. Mid-Edo author. Among his abundant writings are *yomihon, haikai*, and accounts of his extensive travels. He criticized **Matsuo Bashō, otherwise shared many tastes with **Yosa Buson, and was associated with **Kamo no Mabuchi. But his work is not highly regarded, and he is commonly dismissed as a merely "representative" writer.

TAKECHI KUROHITO 高市黒人. Dates unknown, but he seems to follow shortly after *Kakinomoto Hitomaro; fl. ca. 700. Early Nara poet. There is confusion over the authorship of eighteen *tanka* in the *Man'yōshū* attributed to Kurohito—or Furuhito: perhaps they are one person. It is easy to exaggerate the importance of these poems, but the immediacy with which they express what is seen has appealed to Japanese over the centuries. Like Hitomaro, there is something of the professional poet about him.

TAKEDA IZUMO 竹田出雲. D. 1747. Mid-Edo *jōruri* playwright, *haikai* poet. By 1705 he had become the chief playwright for the Takemotoza in Osaka, and is best known today for his version of *Terakoya, Sugawara Denju Tenarai Kagami* 菅原伝授手習鑑 (*Sugawara's School of Calligraphy*, 1746), but his fame was eclipsed by the second writer to use the name.

TAKEDA IZUMO II 竹田出雲二代目. 1691–1756. Mid-Edo *jōruri* playwright. He was the most famous dramatist of his time, bringing new luster to the Osaka Takemotoza. He had a hand in at least twenty-eight plays, including three of the most famous subjects. With his predecessor, *Takeda Izumo I, he wrote a *Terakoya*. With others he wrote a *Yoshitsune Sembonzakura* 義経千本桜 (*Yoshitsune and the Thousand Cherry Trees*, 1747) and a *Kanadehon Chūshingura* 仮名手本忠臣蔵 (*The Treasury of Loyal Retainers*, 1748). Such joint composition was characteristic of the time, making artistic roles differently defined from Western ideas. The fact is, however, that under his aegis the plays produced led the Takemotoza to flourish as never before or after.

TAKEMOTO GIDAYŪ 竹本義太夫. 1651–1714. Early Edo *jōruri* reciter or chanter. Although students of literature are apt to think of jōruri in terms of great playwrights like *Chikamatsu Monzaemon, the reciters of the narrative and dialogue were considered far more important, and were paid accordingly. (See Part One, concerning Chikamatsu.) Gidayū not only established the great Takemotoza in Osaka but was so famous that *gidayū* has become a common noun for recitation as well as reciters. In terms of Japanese *theater* his name belongs with those of the few most famous actors and dramatists for making drama a living, flourishing practice.

TAKEMUKI. See Hino no Takemuki.

TAKETORI MONOGATARI 竹取物語 (*The Tale of The Bamboo Cutter*). Early Heian *monogatari*. Given the central figure of the story, it should properly be called "Kaguya Hime Monogatari," but from early times it has been known as "Taketori" (sometimes pronounced "Takatori"), "Taketori no Okina," or "Taketori Okina Monogatari." Because it is "the parent and first to come out of all tales," as a famous passage in the *Genji Monogatari* says, there has been more thorough scholarship and extensive speculation than the work itself may seem to deserve.

The old bamboo cutter of the title discovers a very tiny maid in a bamboo stalk, and other parts of bamboo yield him all the gold anyone would need. She grows to be the loveliest of young women, is wooed by noblemen, and captivates the reigning sovereign. Yet, since she is a heavenly creature, she must fly back to her native sky. The distraught sovereign sets fire to her letters and other mementos, so producing the smoke that has come from Mount Fuji ever since (at least as of the time when the story was written). One theory of date holds for a time before ca. 920, the other for a later date; but it is generally accepted that the present version dates from about 960. It evidently has had some changes subsequently, since in the *Genji Monogatari* ("Hotaru") Tamakazura recalls events not in the existing version.

Folklorists have postulated the existence of a Taketori *setsuwa*, something distinctly likely, since Japanese folklore abounds with encounters between a human and a divine figure. But evidence shows that this story originally came to Japan in Chinese and that it exists throughout Asia in many versions. This version is taken to have been written by a man (many candidates have been unconvincingly proposed) who was familiar with *waka*, Chinese learning, and popular tales. From some early point the story also spread among lower classes.

TAKIZAWA BAKIN. See Kyokutei Bakin.

TAMEHIDE. See Reizei Tamehide.

TAMEIE. See Fujiwara Tameie.

TAMEKANE. See Kyōgoku Tamekane.

TAMENAGA SHUNSUI 為永春水. 1790–1843. Late Edo author of *ninjōbon*. Although he seems to have been from Edo, the first half of his life is obscure. He apparently learned various features of storytelling from *Ryūtei Tanehiko and *Shikitei Samba. In 1819 he made something of a debut with *Akegarasu Nochi no Masayume* 明烏後正夢. After his masterpiece, (*Shunshoku*) *Umegoyomi* (春色) 梅児誉美 The (*Love-Tinted*) *Plum Calendar*, 1832–1833), he vainly tried to repeat his achievement in several stories, all having titles beginning *Shunshoku*.

Umegoyomi, as it is usually called, deals with the vicissitudes of love in terms that were at once very familiar and fresh. The hero, Tanjirō, is in love with a Yoshiwara courtesan from the Koigakubo house,

Yonehachi; and also is loved by the more proper Ochō. Tan, or Tan-san as they call him, greatly resembles the amorous males in some of the *sewamono* plays by *Chikamatsu Monzaemon, being if anything more amorous, gentle, and sweet to the point of weakness. Shunsui combined this with features of *jidaimono*: persecution of a lord's son (Tanjirō, it turns out, is no less), devotion by a loyal retainer, a stark villain or two, a missing treasure (duly recovered), and a happy ending. We close with the restoration of the errant son to his family domain, his marriage to Ochō, and his keeping Yonehachi as a concubine. The happy outcome deprives the story of the seriousness of Chikamatsu and the energy of *Ihara Saikaku. But in a lively style punctuated by verse and moralizing comments we find a pungency tempering the sweetness and an ingenious tiered narrative technique. There are also windows opened on the Edo world that the happy ending does not altogether close. See also Part One.

TAMESUKE. See REIZEI TAMESUKE.

TAMEYO. See NIJŌ TAMEYO.

TANABE SAKIMARO 田辺福麻呂. Dates unknown. Nara *waka* poet, associated in the *Man'yōshū* with an event in 748. In parts six and nine of the collection, a collection bearing his name is referred to as the source of the poems given. Like *Kakinomoto Hitomaro, *Kasa no Kanamura, and *Yamabe Akahito, he was a celebrator of the court to which he was attached, and at his best he managed to recall them.

TANCHI 湛智. 1163–1237. Kamakura composer and performer of music connected with Buddhist services, author of *Shōmyō Mokuroku* 声明目録 (*Classification of Buddhist Service Music*, 1224) and *Shōmyō Yōshin Shū* 声明用心集 (*Collection of Music for Buddhist Services*, 1233). His musical style was used for Tendai services, which follow his principles to this day. He was also a composer.

TANEHIKO. See RYŪTEI TANEHIKO.

TANI BUNCHŌ 谷文晁. 1763–1840. Late Edo painter. He worked on various well-regarded book illustrations, including those for *Ishiyamadera Engi*, legends about Ishiyama Temple. He infused the southern style (*nanga*) with other Chinese elements, showed his skill with native traditions (*yamatoe*), and foreign styles. He became well known for realistic depiction in some excellent portraits as well as for travel scenes in various provinces.

TANIGUCHI BUSON. See YOSA BUSON.

TANKEI 湛慶. 1173–1256. Kamakura sculptor. Like the work by his father, *Unkei, his is Buddhist, including images of the Buddha, Kannon, and so on. He often worked with his father at such temples as Tōdaiji, and he is considered one of the greatest of known Japanese religious sculptors.

TANOMURA CHIKUDEN 田能村竹田. 1777–1835. Late Edo literati painter (of *bunjinga*). Going to Edo, he studied Confucianism and Chinese poetry as well as painting, and came into contact with *Rai San'yō and other important contemporaries. His style is thought to have an element of elevation and light elegance. He was esteemed as a theorist of his art.

TAN'YŪ. See KANO TAN'YŪ.

TEIKA. See FUJIWARA TEIKA.

TEIRYŪ. See NAGATA TEIRYŪ.

TEISHITSU. See YASUHARA TEISHITSU.

TEITOKU. See MATSUNAGA TEITOKU.

TENJI 天智. 626–671 (r. 668–671). Yamato *waka* poet, sovereign. A *chōka* and three *tanka* by him survive in the *Man'yōshū*, as does a tanka in the *Nihon Shoki*. Although he touched literature in a variety of ways, his life was more remarkable in the political and general cultural spheres. He was the son of two tennō, Jomei and Saimei (for this and other details following, see Part Two B) and he had a rival brother, also son of Saimei but by a different father. During the two reigns of Saimei (the former as Kōgyoku) and the intermediate reign of Kōtoku, Tenji played a public role of growing prominence. The major work of drawing up and instituting the Taika Reform (645) was done by him and Fujiwara Kamatari (614–669), founder of the fortunes of that family. In 661, he was set to accompany his mother on an invasion of Korea, a purpose frustrated by various events, including the death of Saimei. Thereafter began a struggle for power between Tenji and his half-brother, later Temmu, and Temmu's redoubtable wife, also usually known by her regnal name, Jitō. Properly speaking Japan was without a sovereign between the reigns of Saimei (655–661) and Tenji (668–671). But not long after his mother's death, Tenji set up court at Ōmi, on the southwestern side of Lake Biwa.

The Ōmi Tennō, as he came to be known, attracted respect even from those who opposed him. Among the cultural matters for which he is well known, there were his establishment of a court school (daigaku), his welcoming of Korean immigrant intellectuals, his encouragement of composition in Chinese, and his equation of literature with wise rule. On his death in 671, he was succeeded by his son, Kōbun. In the following year, forces despatched by Temmu razed the Ōmi palace in the brief but decisive Jinshin War. It was recorded that numerous valuable papers were lost, including, it is thought, prepatory work for what would have been a *Kojiki celebrating Tenji as the present version does Temmu.

Poems by *Kakinomoto Hitomaro give the Temmu version of that struggle in the royal house. In his poem on the death of Prince Takechi, son of Temmu, Hitomaro writes of the victory in battle of Temmu's forces over those of the Ōmi court (*Man'yōshū, 2:199–201). And another poem purports to relate his emotions "On Passing the Ruined Capital of Ōmi" (ibid., 1, 29–31). At one point he shows his Nara bias:

What purpose was there
To leave Yamato to cross the hills of Nara,
    Rich in colored earth,
To establish a new capital in a land
    Beyond the horizon,
To found a palace out in the country?

Before long, however, he is speaking with awe of Tenji, and in the close of his *choka* writes the epilogue of the Ōmi court in terms universally understandable, giving its epitaph:

Though they relate how at this site
    There rose a palace,
Though they insist high halls stood here,
    Now wild grasses grow
In a springtime of profusion
    And haze-streamers float
Across the mild spring sun, misting over
    The ruins of a palace
Built on foundations many-layered,
And just to look upon it makes me grieve.

Often highly praised in literary histories and familiar in selections from the *Man'yōshū*, Tenji is of chief interest for showing how ancient is the relation between poetry and Japanese sovereigns.

TOBI NO HA MO NO MAKI 鳶の羽もの巻 (*Even the Kite's Feathers*), also known as *Hatsushigure* 初時雨 (*Early Winter Rain*). An early Edo thirty-six-stanza *haikai* sequence (*kasen*) composed in the winter of 1690. The four poets are *Matsuo Bashō, *Nozawa Bonchō, *Mukai Kyorai, and *Nakamura Fumikuni (dates unknown). The sequence was later included in *Sarumino* (see Part Six). Kyorai wrote the *hokku* in the "host" position, Bashō the *waki* in the "guest" position, Bonchō the *daisan*, and Fumikuni the *ageku*. The first six stanzas (the jo of the *jo-ha-kyū*) are somewhat irregular, but otherwise this sequence is very regular, wonderfully conceived, and deservedly famous, especially for stanzaic connection (*tsukeai*).

TODA MOSUI 戸田茂睡. 1629–1706. Early Edo *waka* poet. In a life of many ups and downs, Mosui was in trouble with the authorities and then pardoned. He took a position only to resign it. He opposed the two lines of poetry still dominating waka, those by the *Reizei poets and the *Nijō poets. He declared: "since we compose poems in Japanese, we should compose them in words such as people speak." Like most before and since, he followed such a ringing—and conventional—slogan with poetry of a more or less conventional and insipid kind. He did compile collections such as *Tori no Ato* 鳥の跡 (*The Birds' Footsteps*, 1702) and *Sazareishi* さざれ石 (*Pebbles*, 1703) that give useful if not altogether breath-taking views of Edo waka of the time.

TOJŪ. See NAKAE, TŌSU

TŌKAN KIKŌ 東関紀行. Mid-Kamakura travel account. Authorship is unknown, and ascriptions to *Kamo no Chōmei, Minamoto Mitsuyuki or his son Chikayuki are now rejected. The author describes himself as "in age nearly half a hundred" and as back in Kyoto for nineteen years after the journey described in the *Kaidōki. So now he undertook another trip to the eastern barrier (tōkan), traveling during the eighth month of 1242. In something between ten days and a fortnight he traveled to Kamakura, where he had been earlier, and where *Abutsu was to go in 1280. This account is not as attractive as his earlier one, partly for reasons of style, partly because it lacks the Buddhist overtones that impart seriousness to the earlier work. In fact, this is much more restricted to being a travel account. But with the earlier account and Abutsu's, it is one of the three principal accounts of the period to describe journeying along the Tōkaidō road. It is said to have had some influence on the *Heike Monogatari and *Gempei Jōsuiki (although given the nature of the growth of the *Heike*, perhaps the influence went the other way). The contrast with *Jippensha Ikku's *Hizakurige* gives some idea of the difference in outlook after six centuries would pass.

TOKOKU. See TSUBOI TOKOKU.

TOKUGAWA MITSUKUNI 徳川光圀. 1628–1700. Early Edo daimyo, scholar, writer. As second head of the Mito domain, he had many official affairs to conduct. But he is remembered as the founder of *Mitogaku*, for his Neoconfucianism, his knowledge of Ming affairs, his philosophical and practical interest, and as a convener of learned men for discussion. His *Dai Nihonshi* 大日本史 (*History of Japan*) finally included thirty parts. They began to appear as his work in 1656 and were continued by generations of Mito scholars, finally ending in 1906. Among other works, he left behind a personal *waka* collection under the pen name Bairi 梅里, after the famed plum plossoms of his domain. To others in his time he was well known as Mito Kōmon 水戸黄門, "kōmon" being the Chinese equivalent of his court rank, chūnagon. His lively travel stories probably constitute his most popular work today.

TOMINAGA NAKAMOTO 富永仲基. 1715–1746. Mid-Edo independent thinker. A native of Osaka, Tominaga was born into a merchant family and his ideas reflect the values of the townspeople. He is noted for his iconoclastic critique of traditional thought: of Confucianism, Buddhism, and Shinto in his *Okina no Fumi* 翁の文 (*Writings of an Old Man*, 1738), and of Buddhism in particular in his *Shutsujō Kōgo* 出定後語 (*Words after Enlightenment*, 1744). Tominaga saw all ideas as relative to their historical and cultural backgrounds and advocated a humanistic ethic of conventional common sense.

TOMONORI. See Kı no Tomonori.

TON'A 頓阿. 1289–1372. Late Kamakura *waka* poet, critic, priest of the Amidist Ji sect. He emerged as a poet in *Ōchō Hyakushu* 応長百首 (*A Hundred-Stanza Sequence of the Ōchō Era*, 1311). He was on close terms with the conservative *Nijō poets, representing their principles better than they did. He participated in many poetry matches and wrote more sequences like that named. After first appearing in the *Shokusenzaishū, he is represented in most of the six remaining official collections. In fact, he completed the *Shinshūishū when the compiler, Fujiwara, deceased. The strong point of the Nijō poets was learning, and Ton'a seems to have played an important part in *Kokinshū studies or *Kokin denju* for the house. He also practiced *renga*, and nineteen of his stanzas appear in *Nijō Yoshimoto's collection, *Tsukuba Shū*. Late in life he retired to a hermitage at temple Ninnaji in Kyoto.

TONERI SHINNŌ 舎人親王. 676–735. Nara historian, political figure. Prince Toneri was the fifth son of Temmu (see Part Two B and *Tenji). He was the chief compiler of the *Nihon Shoki*, and perhaps it is to him that we owe its continuation beyond the point where the *Kojiki* leaves off. He was important enough in politics to earn the posthumous title of prime minister (dajō daijin).

TORAAKIRA. See Ōkura Toraakira.

TORII KIYOMASA 鳥居清倍. 1694–?1716. Mid-Edo *ukiyoe* artist, second in the Torii house, after Kiyonobu. Following his father's craft, he made actors' pictures for theater posters and illustrated theater programs. He also made some attractive separate block prints.

TORII KIYOMITSU 鳥居清満. 1735–1785. Late Edo *ukiyoe* artist. The third in the Torii house, he was well known for his depiction of actors, but he

also specialized in female nudes, of which he has left a number of highly esteemed examples.

TORII KIYONAGA 鳥井清長. 1752–1815. Late Edo *ukiyoe* artist. From Sagami, he went to Edo and studied under *Torii Kiyomitsu, and like him made a number of prints of actors. He gradually shifted to depictions of beautiful women, often in groups. Their poise and postures led to the distinct Kiyonaga beauty.

TORII KIYONOBU 鳥居清信. 1664–1729. Mid-Edo *ukiyoe* artist, founder of the Torii house of artists. Born in Osaka, where he studied under his father, he moved to Edo. By adding elements from older Japanese kinds of painting (Kanō, Tosa) to the ukiyoe style of *Hishikawa Moronobu, he created what was recognized to be a new, distinct style. Much of his work depicts actors for theater posters or programs, but he excelled in depicting beautiful women as well as actors, whether in paintings or prints.

TORIKAEBAYA MONOGATARI とりかえばや 物語 (*The Changelings*). Late Heian *tsukuri-monogatari*, *giko monogatari*. Authorship unknown. In three parts. The *Mumyōzōshi* discusses two versions, one now generally referred to as the old, *Ko Torikaebaya*, and the other as the new or present, *Ima Torikaebaya*. In the view of the *Mumyōzōshi*, there are few things to praise and much to object to in the old version, but much to praise and little to criticize in the new. Given the improvement effected by the revision, or imitation, few argue that the extant version derives from the old. The major theories hold that the extant version is an amalgamation of the old and the new; that it descends in a textual line from the new; or is yet another stage after the old and the new. Since both those versions are lost, evidence turns on comparison of what the *Mumyōzōshi* says with the extant version, and of poems in the present version with those said to be from the work and included in the *Fūyōshū*. The evidence is sufficient only for speculation, as is also true for evidence on authorship and on the sex of the author. It was probably written between 1115 and 1170, given the works it seems to echo and the works echoing it.

In many respects the work is a standard Heian *monogatari*. The scene is laid in the court and its environs, the characters are of the nobility, and much is made of amorous involvements and rise in court ranks. Above all, we move from an initial situation through increasing complications to a happy ending. The story's initial conception, and a source of some notoriety, is the exchange of sexual roles by a daughter and a son—extraordinarily like each other and handsome in looks—born at much the same time to different wives of the same man. When the girl begins to behave like a boy (including participating in outdoor sport) and the boy like a girl (including playing with dolls), the father utters the wish that gives the monogatari its (Japanese) title: "If Only They Could Be Exchanged." The change is effected by narrator fiat, when, at one point, she (to express a guess as to the narrator's sex) says she will follow the world's error and speak of the girl as the son and the boy as the daughter. She then leaps ahead in time to a point at which court titles will indicate the pretended sex of each of the pair. The "son" becomes a Middle Counsellor (Chūnagon—the standard beginning rank of a hero since the *Sagoromo Monogatari*), the "daughter" a Lady in Waiting (Naishi no Kami) to the Crown Princess. At the age of sixteen, we are told, the Counsellor marries the Fourth Daughter, aged nineteen, of the Minister of Rites. This strange situation can remain stable only as long as the "son" does not come sexually to life, as long as the Fourth Daughter does not object to an unconsummated marriage, and as long as no one else enters the picture. Of course the point is that the story should not remain stable.

Things begin with a certain Saishō Chūjō's seduction of the Fourth Daughter, discovering to his surprise that the wife of his acquaintance, Chūnagon, was a virgin. Meanwhile, the Counsellor has gained the acquaintance of the priestly and learned Third Prince—who had been to China, had married there, had been widowed, had brought his two daughters to Japan (it was a rare favor for women to be allowed ocean passage), and who had retired to Yoshino when factions at court misrepresented him. This Yoshino situation manages to combine elements of *Murasaki Shikibu's Genji Monogatari* (the Uji section tells of a priestly prince with daughters at Uji) and of *Sugawara Takasue no Musume's Hamamatsu Chūnagon Monogatari* (developing from the same portion of the *Genji* a transfer from Uji to Yoshino, a voyage to China and back with a child or children). The Counsellor becomes friends with the Prince's two daughters, and "he" suffers enough from uneasiness about "his" personal identity so as to consider closely the standard Heian solution to life's problems, taking orders. One of the debated episodes in the story then occurs when the Third Prince prophesies (he has learned the Counselor is a woman) that "he" is destined for great things and so should go back into the world. The seemingly irreligious advice from a character idealized for piety has seemed contradictory to many critics. It appears to be partly a vestige of a magic, prophetic mirror in the old version and even more a recollection of a prophetic dream by Sagoromo's father in the fourth part of the *Sagoromo Monogatari*.

Meanwhile, Saishō Chūjō has been visiting the Fourth Daughter frequently in her "husband's" absence, with the result that she has become pregnant. On hearing the news, the father of the exchanged children (who knows nothing of the Chūjō) reflects with astonishment on "this very odd and unanticipated" development. There are a number of these delightful comic touches. Some are reprises of the *Genji*. For example, the Counsellor (the "son") visits the Third Prince's daughters, chats, and then marches behind the screen of the elder sister with an enterprise typical of Genji—although by her being in fact a woman the brisk act has no result. Or, Chūjō spends the night beside the Lady in Waiting, like Kaoru not consummating love with an Ōigimi figure. The Lady is, of course, male, a fact unknown to him.

The plot enters a new phase when on a warm evening Chūjō visits the house of the Counsellor and the Fourth Daughter. Naturally he must call on the "husband" rather than the wife (This replays the scene by The Lady in Waiting). The light clothes of the Counsellor suggest her real sex, and her beauty leads Chūjō to make advances that end in consummation. Before long the Counsellor is pregnant. Chūjō wishes "him" to become a woman and his wife, with the Fourth Daughter as second wife. Questions have been raised about Chūjō's morality. Obviously the more seriously we consider the story the more we must consider his responsibility. One reply is that Genji and Sagoromo are in fact more amorous. But perhaps the best answer is that Chūjō's ambitions not only further the issues of the transferred sexual roles but also forecast the future triumphs of the male Lady in Waiting.

The first part ends with the pregnant Counsellor continuing "his" duties at court, including a heartfelt imagined last musical performance that draws the artistic and, it seems, erotic attentions of the tennō—and earns a promotion. We learn early in Part Two that this "hero" has turned nineteen. Clearly the first third of the story concentrates on the daughter playing a man's role.

Attention shifts to the Lady in Waiting when "her" supposed brother disappears: "he" has gone to Uji to lie in. "She" resolves to disguise "herself" as a man and seek out "her" "brother." Since "he" has been so fond of Yoshino, "she" thinks of looking for "him" there. In the hot weather, the disguised Lady in Waiting, who may now be designated "'he,'" catches a glimpse of "'his'" beautiful sister and is seen by "him," but "'he'" leaves without a full encounter. Attention shifts to Uji long enough for the "brother" to bear a son and then returns to the "sister."

In a prophetic dream (another recollection of the *Hamamatsu*), the father of the role-exchanged children learns they will "change" to the social roles identified with their biological sexes. In this second stage of the story, the work brings to its height the dream and reality (yume, utsutsu) emphases of the work. When the two children meet, the "brother" teaches the "sister" socially considered male activities. At one point the two grow quite confused as to who is she and who he, and there are points when the reader is equally at sea—which is obviously part of the fun and theme. But the change is made, and the children are reconciled with their overjoyed father.

Part Three involves working out the important change in terms of the relations of the sister and brother to other characters in the story. When the real sister takes up the position of Lady in Waiting it turns out that before leaving to search for his "brother," disguising himself as a man, the male Lady in Waiting had got the Princess pregnant, as he shortly does the astonished Fourth Daughter as well. The brother's plot is gradually resolved in good monogatari fashion. He acquires the Princess, the elder Yoshino Princess, and the Fourth Daughter as wives, whom he installs in a new mansion, recalling Genji's Rokujō Palace via Hamamatsu's mansion. By the end of the story, he is Minister of the Left and regent for the new, young tennō, a role not unlike Genji's. This series of events is interwoven with the story of the sister and other characters. The reigning tennō has always liked the looks of the Lady in Waiting to his daughter (even when "she" was the male look-alike) and at last beds her, perplexing himself only in discovering that she is not a virgin. This gives him pause and the story suspense. Will he reject her or love her all the same? It takes time, but she ends as royal Consort, so fulfilling the prophecy of the Yoshino Prince. The former Chūjō, now well advanced in rank, is married off to the younger Yoshino princess by our now openly male hero, but the new husband is denied information of the whereabouts of his former "male" friend the Counsellor, now royal Consort.

This monogatari manages its difficult plot very adroitly, although its greatest technical success comes from keeping credible (and very interesting) what is obviously unbelievable in realistic terms. The occasional comedy and the uncertainty of dream or reality in the middle of the work testify to an assured control of the action and of the milieu of the story. Little matters are handled with an attention to which the author of Hamamatsu is sometimes maddeningly indifferent: rank and changes in it, clothes, weather important to those experiencing it, pregnancy that seems real with morning sickness, virginity or its absence.

Comparing it with its three great predecessors on their grounds would lead to the conclusion that it is a little Genji, a little *Sagoromo Monogatari, a little *Hamamatsu. Its plot is more like that of Sagoromo than those of the other two, particularly in outcome. One looks in vain for the Buddhist language of Sagoromo and the Buddhist themes so pervasively implicit in the Genji and explicit in the Hamamatsu. In a way not to the good, Torikaebaya secularizes its predecessors.

Yet if we inquire into the work on its own, or in modern terms, we see that its basic conception is more than a device for an erotic, suspenseful plot. It

also raises questions as to just what maleness and, more particularly, what femaleness is. It seems unlikely that any other than the Heian period in a traditional literature could raise the issue of the basic nature of human sexuality as a determinant of personality. Certainly it and related issues are dealt with more profoundly than by Shakespeare or Ben Jonson, who had boy actors play women disguised as men. The fullness with which the psyche of the female Chūnagon is explored implies to us that the author of the present version was either a woman or a man with uncanny insight into women's hearts. The sister's life receives more attention than the brother's, although he and the Chūjō are fully treated and characterized. The work suggests that there must have been men and women at the time who wondered what it was like to be of the other sex, and perhaps even some who would have liked a try at change. The work goes no small distance in showing how society defines maleness or femaleness on bases termed sexual but actually social. If the old question of what is due to nature and what to nurture can never be answered, it can be explored, as this work does with brilliance, aplomb, and a twinkling-eyed narrator. Only a country whose greatest writer is a woman could have produced this lesser but still impressive monogatari so many centuries ago.

TOSHINARI. See Fujiwara Shunzei.

TOSHIYORI. See Fujiwara Shunrai.

TOYOHARU. See Utagawa Toyoharu.

TOYOHARA SUMIAKI 豊原統秋. 1450–1524. Late Muromachi gagaku musician. Perhaps the most famous of performers on the shō (a reed-wind instrument in gagaku), he wrote extensively on music, as in his highly regarded Taigenshō 体源鈔, in twenty parts. He also studied waka under *Sanjōnishi Sanetaka.

TOYOHIRO. See Utagawa Toyohiro.

TOYOKUNI. See Utagawa Toyokuni.

TSUBOI TOKOKU 坪井杜国. ?1657–1690. Early Edo haikai poet. A Nagoya rice dealer, he matured as a poet remarkably early. His brief career was spent in the school of *Matsuo Bashō, with whom he traveled from Ise on the journey recorded in Oi no Kobumi. Bashō was very fond of Tokoku. During Bashō's brief stay in Nagoya in the winter of 1684, Tokoku joined him and other poets in composing the kasen for Fuyu no Hi (see Part Six F). The quality of his haikai there equals the best of the age; his early death was a great loss to poetry, as also a personal loss to Bashō, who mourned him in the Saga Nikki.

TSUCHIMIKADO MICHICHIKA 土御門通親. 1149–1202. Early Kamakura political figure, historian, diarist, poet. In the past, Michichika was often lost in the faint praise of comparison of works by him to masterpieces. His *Takakura In Itsukushima Gokōki* 高倉院厳島御幸記 (1181) was compared with the **Heike Monogatari*, and his *Kōzan ni Gishi Sōdō o Mosuru no Ki* 擬香山摸草堂記 to **Kamo no Chōmei's *Hōjōki*. More recently, these works have been found to have merits of their own. The *Gōkoki* is not merely a prosaic gesture: Takakura is mourned in poetry that seems heartfelt. The *Kōzan ... no Ki* is modeled on the *Ts'ao-t'ang Chi* by Po Chü-i (771–846), and it contributed to the growth of an elegant way of life by recluses in their "grass huts."

TSUGA TEISHŌ 都賀庭鐘. 1718–1794. Mid-Edo writer of *yomihon*. He wrote a few stories of note: *Hanabusa Sōshi* 英草紙 (1749), *Shigeshige Yawa* 繁野話 (1750), and the late *Hitsujigusa* 莠句冊 (1786). In addition, he engaged in such other enterprises as collecting *kyōshi*. His major compilation was *Kyōshisen* 狂詩選 (*A Selection of Kyōshi*, 1763). He also made one of the revisions of the *K'ang-hsi* dictionary (see Part Six Q): *Kōki Jiten* 康熙字典 (first published in 1716), a dictionary of over 40,500 characters, making it of greater utility to Japanese readers. It is also said that **Ueda Akinari studied medicine with him. Although he is not one of the greatest of Edo authors, it is clear that he had wide interests that led to a varied achievement in literature and scholarship.

TSUNENOBU. See Mɪɴᴀᴍᴏᴛᴏ Tsᴜɴᴇɴᴏʙᴜ.

TSURAYUKI. See Kɪ ɴᴏ Tsᴜʀᴀʏᴜᴋɪ.

TSURUYA NAMBOKU 鶴屋南北. 1755–1829. Late Edo *kabuki* playwright, writer of prose narratives. Born in Edo to a family of dyers, he became acquainted with **Sakurada Jisuke about 1775. In the ensuing quarter century he wrote a number of things that attracted attention, but he is best known now for works after 1800. Of these a few may be mentioned with their witty titles. In 1811 he had performed his *Nazo no Obi Chotto Tokubē* 謎帯一寸徳兵衛, and in 1813 *Osome Hisamatsu Ukina no Yomiuri* 於染久松色読販. His best-known plays are *Toki mo Kikyō Shusse no Ukejō* 時桔梗出世請状 (1808) and *Tōkaidō Yotsuya Kaidan* 東海道四谷怪談 (1825). He specialized in the astonishing, combining a host of theatrical effects, sometimes to the point of melodrama, as with the last named, a ghost play or *kaidan(mono)*. See Part One.

TSUTSUMI CHŪNAGON MONOGATARI 堤中納言物語. *The Tales of the Tsutsumi Middle Counsellor*. Late Heian collection of ten short tales and a fragment. Ca. 1055. Although certain features of this collection are still obscure, it has become clear that it is a product of the flourishing of *monogatari* during the mid- and late- eleventh-century at three courts presided over by royal women. They include Goreizei's consort, Kanshi (daughter of the Fujiwara chancellor of the time, Yorimichi), Princess Baishi, and Baishi's elder sister, Princess Yūshi. Some sense of the talent convened at those courts can be judged from the fact that at Baishi's there served **Rokujō Saiin Baishi Naishinnō no Senji, author of the *Sagoromo Monogatari*, and at Yūshi's, **Sugawara Takasue no Musume, author of the *Sarashina Nikki* and, it is supposed, of the *Hamamatsu Chūnagon Monogatari*. It is easily imagined that there was a spirit of competitive cooperation among these three salons to excel and to make the familiar fresh. (Men also took part in these stories.)

In 1055, Baishi convened a poetic match known as **Rokujō Saiin* [i.e. *Baishi*] *Monogatari Utaawase*. Eighteen ladies who had written stories paired on the usual two sides to match poems selected from their stories. Among the participants were Senji, author of the *Sagoromo Monogatari* and a Koshikibu who is little known, although from her poem she must be the author of one of the lively stories in the present collection, "Ōsaka Koenu Gonchūnagon" ("The Acting Middle Counsellor Who Couldn't Make It to Love"). This parodies an episode in **Murasaki Shikibu's *Genji Monogatari*, in which Kaoru spends the night beside Ōigimi without consummating his love. The same episode is parodied in another fashion in **Torikaebaya Monogatari*, suggesting that to these witty ladies it was memorable and more or less comic, at least in potential. In "Hanazakura Oru Shōshō" ("The Lesser Captain Seeking a Cherry Bough"), the man who anticipates leading a beautiful young woman to his pleasure turns out, in the effective ending, to have an aged nun in tow.

The examples show that the ladies took freedom with male desires and notions of self-importance. It may be that the amusing wit directed against men provides a hint to the meaning of the title of the collection, which means *The Tales of the Tsutsumi Middle Counsellor*. As late Heian monogatari show, the rank of chūnagon (middle counsellor) is the one frequently used for heroes. The fact is that no counsellor named as in the title is the hero of any of the ten stories. It rather seems that these witty women manufactured an imaginary hero for an imaginary monogatari, and it would have been entirely in character if the name they chose was their nickname for some contemporary young lord with airs. In any event, it is striking that the term "monogatari" is applied to the collection rather than to individual stories. In modern terms, each of the stories is a short monogatari (*tampen* monogatari), and there is a kind of counterpart of the title in that of the **Konjaku Monogatari Shū*. Yet there the *Collection*

(*Shū*) rather than stories (*monogatari*) defines the whole.

These stories are of a length resembling the religious exempla (*setsuwa*) that are so important in Japanese literature, but their comic tone differs greatly. In fact, such short monogatari are hardly to be found otherwise, whether because they were not written or were not esteemed and so were lost. This fact makes it unlikely that, as some have wished to claim, stories like these, or these very stories, are the ancestors of short Edo and modern fiction. It seems more likely that this work represents an experiment that succeeded well enough not to need doing again, and that if we are to inquire into its ancestors, they are to be found in *utamonogatari* like the *Heichū Monogatari*, which appears to have occasionally been drawn on by authors of these ten stories. Something may also be assigned to a new taste for shorter narrative as found in the setsuwa that emerged as a major interest at this time. Above all, the brief collection shows the high spirits of cultivated, leisured ladies of the court in the heyday of Yorimichi, son of *Fujiwara Michinaga—days that would later be longingly recalled in the *Eiga Monogatari* and *Ōkagami*. Obviously there were lively successors of *Jōtō Mon'in and Murasaki Shikibu.

UCHIGIKI SHŪ 打聞集 (*Stories Heard*). Late Heian *setsuwa* collection, ca. 1111. The compiler is unknown, but the title and other signs point to priestly use for inculcating religious points by interesting examples. The single present part is thought to be one of two or three. Its twenty-seven stories may be classified in terms such as those used by the *Konjaku Monogatari*, with which it shares twenty-one tales. It shares eight with the *Uji Shūi Monogatari*, and four with each of those two collections, and another two with the *Kohon Setsuwashū*. Such overlappings have offered opportunity for scholarly comparison. Whether because of a somewhat outdated style or for some other reason, the collection seems not to have been widely known.

UEDA AKINARI 上田秋成. 1734–1809. Mid-Edo writer of *ukiyozōshi* and *yomihon*; also a *kokugaku* scholar. (See Part One.) Born in Osaka, he suffered from severe, crippling illness in his youth, and thereafter his life was one of continuing misfortune into adulthood. At twenty-six he found some happiness in marrying Tama, a peasant woman from Kyoto adopted into an Osaka family. His mind was eager, and he developed a taste both for *haikai* and *gesaku*, as well as for those Japanese and Chinese classics that would play so important a role in his later writings. His kokugaku studies were directed by various masters, including Katō Umaki (1721–1777). Among the important studies prosecuted for Umaki, Akinari edited, with commentary, *Ki no Tsurayuki's Tosa Nikki*. Under his haikai pen name Muchō 無腸, Akinari issued a study, *Ya Kana Shō*

也哉抄 (*A Study of Cutting Words*, 1774), an examination of *kireji* such as ya, kana, and ka. The work had the added distinction of a preface by *Yosa Buson.

Akinari is best known, however, for his prose narratives. One of the first of his stories was *Seken Tekake Katagi* 世間妾形気 (1767). In spite of this treatment of "worldly concubines," erotic subjects did not really interest him. Perhaps too much misfortune had befallen him. Certainly a sense of suffering as well as learning in native and Chinese classics went into the making of his masterpiece, *Ugetsu Monogatari* 雨月物語 (*Tales of Moonlight and Rain*) a yomihon (1768). Each of its five parts except the fourth has two stories, nine in all. The manner of telling involves a colloquial style and elements of narrative derived from *setsuwa* and, of course, from *monogatari*, perhaps especially some of the more heated Kamakura examples. But the plots are taken from specific works of Chinese fiction. As *Murasaki Shikibu had pointed out long before, Chinese tastes run much more to the supernatural and astonishing than do Japanese, although from the *Taketori Monogatari* onward, there is also such a line in Japanese writing. For Akinari, the strangeness of the fictional "Chinese" world served to assuage what he found wrong with his own, giving him a feverish idealism with a dark sense of the mysterious and perverse. His own restlessness and fresh trials continued to agitate him, but even while he sought to make a livelihood in medicine and other activities, he kept writing. To his masterpiece he added three other major works. A yomihon, *Harusame Monogatari* 春雨物語 (*A Tale of Spring Rain*, 1808), dropped the use of Chinese sources. He relied instead on setsuwa literature, as a model at least, and his ten new stories gave the central character a larger role. The atmosphere does not engulf the character quite so much, although the combination of Buddhist and supernatural elements can be taken to be more Chinese than close examination shows. If he had not written *Ugetsu Monogatari*, this would be his master work. Another work of 1808, *Tandai Shōshinroku* 胆大小心録, is a *zuihitsu* in 160 parts, dealing with the human faults and failures with which his own life had made him abundantly familiar.

His earlier *Kuse Monogatari* (or *Kusemono Katari*) 癇癖談 (1791) also deserves notice to show that Akinari could write with a lighter touch. Parodies seldom maintain interest beyond a page or so, but this is sufficiently distinguished work so that it can be read in innocence of the existence of the *Ise Monogatari* and the romantic figure of *Ariwara Narihira. Of course few readers are such innocents, and they have been amazed by the subtle fidelity of the parodic version. Perhaps it is not too much to say that parody describes the feat less than "haikai change" (*haikaika*), the deliberate lowering of the world of the original to the commonplace world of late eighteenth-century Japan. Although we have become aware of many more prose writers than were formerly considered seriously, it is still difficult to dispute the old truism that, with *Kyokutei Bakin, Akinari is the greatest writer of prose fiction between *Ihara Saikaku and the finest modern novelists.

UEJIMA (or KAMIJIMA) ONITSURA 上島鬼貫. 1661–1738. Early Edo *haikai* poet. Born into a distiller's household, he spent much of his adult life in the *kamigata* area. His first poetry was of the *Teimon* kind, but he later switched to the *Danrin*. He wrote a best seller in *Hitorigoto* 独言 (*Talking to Myself*, 1718), an important haikai treatise stressing the roles of *sugata* and *kotoba*. He was one of the most important poets between the school of *Matsuo Bashō and that of *Yosa Buson, introducing a greater degree of colloquial language with an exactness of observation that was important to Buson.

UJI SHŪI MONOGATARI 宇治拾遺物語 (*Stories Gleaned at Uji*). Early Kamakura *setsuwa* collection (ca. 1190–1242), in extant versions consisting of 197 stories in two, four, or eight parts, although it is known that lost versions (as late as 1659) had fifteen parts. (The question appears to be one of dividing a set number of stories.) With the *Konjaku Monogatari*, it is highly prized for the quality of the stories it includes (some with counterparts in China or farther west), even if the purpose of collection is pretty clearly for priestly, didactic use. But the stories are well chosen, and the colloquial touches suggest a readership at court or perhaps writing partly adapted for less learned readers. Although the stories are too various to classify easily, the compiler(s) had an interest in common humanity that still holds appeal for their discernment of human motives and limitations as well as for intermittent humor. The title should perhaps be rendered *Stories Gleaned by the Uji Great Counsellor*, that is, Dainagon Minamoto Takakuni (1004–1077), who is traditionally associated with this collection as well as the *Konjaku Monogatari*. Nothing is certainly known, however, as to the identity of the compiler or, therefore, as to the significance of the the title.

UKŌ 羽紅. Dead by 1735, perhaps as early as 1716. Early Edo *haikai* poet. Her lay name was Tome, and her husband was *Nozawa Bonchō. Born in Kyoto, she lived in Osaka much of the time. She took orders as a devotional means of overcoming ill health and probably for another reason that led men to take on the cloth: freedom of movement and association. When *Matsuo Bashō was staying in Kyoto at the Rakushisha hermitage of *Mukai Kyorai, her care was such as to elicit Bashō's grateful comments in his *Saga Nikki*. Even earlier, in the collection *Arano*

(see Part Six F), she had had poems collected under her lay name.

Although not the poetic equal of her husband, she is one of the few best represented by *hokku* in *Sarumino* (see Part Six), and she is the finest female poet of the age. She shows that even in a time of official subjection of women, their poetic talents found some outlet and recognition, although their cultural achievement in the Edo period is too little investigated.

UNKEI 運慶. D. 1223. Early Kamakura sculptor. His strong, rather realistic style had considerable influence on later Kamakura sculptors, and his work is still found in a few major temples in Nara, such as Kōfukuji and Tōdaiji.

URAGAMI GYOKUDŌ 浦上玉堂. 1745–1820. Late Edo literati painter (of *bunjinga*). He took pleasure in the lute as well as painting; to these and other ends he traveled up and down the land. He is esteemed for the poetic feeling he imparted to his paintings.

UTAGAWA KUNISADA 歌川国貞. 1786–1864. Late Edo *ukiyoe* artist. Best student of *Utagawa Toyokuni, he later styled himself Toyokuni II, although in fact the third. While still Kunisada, he did a famous series of illustrations for *Ryūtei Tanehiko's *Nise Murasaki Inaka Genji*.

UTAGAWA TOYOHARU 歌川豊春. 1735–1814. Mid-Edo *ukiyoe* painter, artist, founder of Utagawa school. The distinct nature of the school was its use of Western painting and detail to a new degree.

UTAGAWA TOYOHIRO 歌川豊広. 1773–1828. Late Edo *ukiyoe* artist, pupil of *Utagawa Toyoharu. Besides doing beautiful women, he illustrated many *kusazōshi* and *yomihon*.

UTAGAWA TOYOKUNI 歌川豊国. A style for late Edo *ukiyoe* artists. The first, who specialized in actor prints, lived 1769–1825. The second, earlier called Toyoshige 豊重, lived 1777–1835. The third was *Utagawa Kunisada, although he also styled himself the second.

UTAMARO. See KITAGAWA UTAMARO.

UTSUHO (or UTSUBO) MONOGATARI 宇津保物語 (*The Tale of the Hollow Tree*). Early Heian *tsukurimonogatari* in twenty parts, an important predecessor of the *Genji Monogatari*, and so by definition a *mukashi monogatari*. The work is vexed with problems of authorship, date, text (these three matters much entwined), interpretation, and evaluation. The text comes in versions that differ widely and with indecipherable passages, because of words or passages lost (and differing from one manuscript to another) as well as other uncertainties. These are not the product of complexity but of downright uncertainty as to what the text should read and how it is to be taken.

The oldest attribution of authorship designated *Minamoto Shitagō; the next oldest in effect denies that. A number of alternatives to Shitagō have been proposed, each dismissed by subsequent study. There is general agreement that the work dates from the late tenth century; that it precedes the *Ochikubo Monogatari (and therefore the Genji Monogatari); and that it follows the other mukashi monogatari.

The work has twenty lengthy parts, amounting to well over half the length of the Genji Monogatari. It is, therefore, the first chōhen or lengthy monogatari, at least among those extant. There is a remarkable difference in conceptions of what the world is like between the marvels of the first and last parts and the terrestial nature of parts 2–18. There are variances in style that do not correspond solely to those divisions, evidence of interpolation and change, and for other reasons of atmosphere, differences so great as to suggest multiple authorship as a distinct possibility. Given these considerations, it is perhaps a reasonable presumption (although no more) that Shitagō wrote some part or parts and that other, unknown hands were involved with the rest.

In the first part and the last two (19–20) the secret of performing celestial music on magical zithers (kin) is central, to the quite unhistorical extent of presuming that musical gifts would assure success at the Heian court. (Perhaps it is significant that the central family involved is basically Kiyowara rather than Fujiwara.) Between the beginning and ending, the bulk of the work (parts 3–18) deals with a world far more like that known in Heian times. But for reason of distinct changes in plot and prominent characters, it is probably best to accept a four-section interpretation. Despite the space required to accommodate it, an account of the plot, curtailed as far as possible, therefore seems necessary.

The first section (part 1) may be termed the Toshikage monogatari. It deals with the remarkable adventures of Kiyowara Toshikage in a dimly perceived Malaysia and nearer parts. He has conspicuous encounters with a number of otherworldly beings, including the Buddha, and he receives knowledge of musical performance that is quite beyond ordinary human powers. He returns to Japan with twelve zithers, including two of supernatural effect for an adept in the art. Entering service at court, he advances speedily in rank, has a daughter born to him, and retires to teach her his celestial art of musical performance. Toshikage's daughter survives her father. She has a son, Nakatada, by the young lord Kanemasa, who is unaware of that fact and of the poverty to which the mother and son are reduced. These straits lead the mother to take her son into the woods, where Nakatada's filial piety (a virtue that Shitagō, with his knowledge of

Chinese, would presumably have ranked very high) induces bears to leave their lair, a hollowed place in a great cedar tree (the origin of the title). The magical music of the zithers brings Kanemasa to his beloved and their son. He takes them back to the capital, where Nakatada advances rapidly in favor and rank. This part stretches the imagination and credibility, but is a romance of three generations. Its seeming completeness, and the fact that the title refers to this part alone suggests that perhaps the original story consisted solely of this part. It shares not a little with the *Taketori Monogatari in terms of presumptions of the range of the feasible in fiction, and it reminds one of some passages in the Chinese Journey to the West (Hsi-yu Chi, J. Saiyūki; sixteenth century).

By contrast, the second section (parts 2–12 in this discrimination) has more of ordinary possibility about it. It is based on the motif known throughout the world—the competing suitors (another connection with the Taketori Monogatari). Some sixteen rivals pay court to the lovely Atemiya (Princess or Lady Surpassing) until she at last becomes a wife of the heir apparent. The plot is much less beset with sudden turns and miraculous music (that occurs but once). The connection between this second and the first part is, however, tenuous. It involves Nakatada, who (as we have seen) does not get the princess.

The third section distinguished by plot analysis comprises parts 13–18. It deals with struggles over naming an heir apparent. The two contenders, or sides, are wives and families of the wives of the crown prince: an earlier wife, Nakatada's half-sister, and the former Atemiya. For a time Atemiya seems to fade away, but in the end her son is declared heir apparent by the tennō, and Nakatada's sister's son third in succession. Nakatada is appointed a kind of tutor or regent for the designated heir. This section is said to be based on the intrigue over succession to Reizei (r. 967–969) in 967. This is potentially real political stuff of the Heian court, and as such seems to be designed for a different readership, or aspect of human experience, from the preceding two sections, especially from the first.

The concluding section combines features of the first (magical music) and the preceding two section (a court focus). Nakatada's daughter Inumiya (Princess or Lady Dog, a very strange name for a woman) is instructed at very tender years by her father and grandmother in the art of the zithers, including the magical ones. The three adepts conclude the work at a plenary audience of the court. The two wondrous instruments cause the celestial realm to vibrate and dance. This, along with kindred effects, understandably holds the attention of the court.

This summary of the plot may suggest that the work is best read for reasons other than its story. But the characters lack flesh and blood, the descriptions do not arrest attention (except for their incredibility), the talk of the characters tends to be wooden, and the style is plain to the point of being humdrum. So plot and its embellishments do seem to offer a reader today the greatest interest. There are a couple of mildly amusing boors among the suitors in the second section and a heavy would-be blocking character in the third. The embellishments include the supernatural elements, much that is irrelvant, and almost one thousand poems (by comparison with the nearly eight hundred of the *Genji Monogatari*). The poems are sufficiently uninteresting not to be included in the standard compendium of *waka*, *Kokka Taikan* (pre-1983 version).

One way of regarding the work is to assign parts 1 and 19–20 to the heritage of the *Taketori Monogatari* (although *Sugawara Takasue no Musume would make something much finer of such miraculous elements in the *Hamamatsu Chūnagon Monogatari*), and to take the long middle and its constituents as models for what would and would not do in the mind of *Murasaki Shikibu as she sat down to write the *Genji Monogatari*. Yet, when it appeared, the work was taken to be an exciting one. In her *Makura no Sōshi*, *Sei Shōnagon mentioned it more frequently than any other monogatari (she did not know the *Genji Monogatari*). That cannot have been due simply to the fact that she was a Kiyowara, both because few minds were more independent than hers and because her work shows that others at court were debating fine points in the work. As usual, we may best trust the subtle art of Murasaki Shikibu. In "The Picture Match" ("Eawase") part of the *Genji Monogatari*, there is a match preliminary to the main competition. The Left side (which we are led to favor) introduces illustrations for the venerable *Taketori Monogatari* and the Right those for the *Utsuho Monogatari*. The Right wins. This work is indeed an advance over the *Taketori Monogatari* in the direction of depicting credible human life (in parts 2–18), but it is only worth conceding to the side with inferior tastes.

WATANABE KAZAN 渡辺華山. 1793–1841. Late Edo southern-style (*nanga*) painter. After studying Confucianism and taking up Dutch learning (*rangaku*), he studied painting with *Tani Bunchō and others, gaining an independent style by addition of Western elements to traditional nanga. Along with usual subjects such as scenery, he left sharply drawn, realistic portraits. He wrote a book criticizing the exclusionary policy of the government, which earned him banishment to his native place, where he died by his own hand.

WEN HSÜAN. See *Monzen*.

YAKAMOCHI. See Ōtomo Yakamochi.

YAKAMORI. See Nakatomi Yakamori.

YAMABE AKAHITO 山部赤人. Fl. 724–737. Nara *waka* poet. Almost nothing is known of him apart from his poems. These include thirteen *chōka* and thirty-seven *tanka* (some of which are *hanka* envoys). His poems are associated with places extending from Naniwa (modern Osaka) in the west to present Chiba prefecture in the east. His best poems show an acute sense of place recreated by representative details, mellifluousness, and Shinto elements. The details selected are the finest and purest—ladies trailing skirts along the shore or birds singing by a riverside. The Shinto purity makes it seem that Buddhism had never been taught in Japan of *Man'yōshū* times.

He shares his Shintoism and role as a court poet with *Kakinomoto Hitomaro. In his preface to the *Kokinshū*, *Ki no Tsurayuki found it difficult to put Akahito below Hitomaro. The judgment is understandable only on the terms it was probably made—by comparing their tanka poetry. Hitomaro integrates his when used as hanka to the chōka, and those that are separate are not as impressive as Akahito's. Even Akahito's hanka seem separable, as for example those with the chōka on the Yoshino palace (6: 923–25). In intelligence and contact with wide human experience, however, he is a distinct fourth, behind not only Hitomaro but also *Ōtomo Yakamochi and *Yamanoe Okura.

YAMADA KENGYŌ 山田検校. 1757–1817. Late Edo musician and composer, founder of the Yamada school of koto performance. He was also famous for his beautiful singing voice. He left behind numerous compositions as well as a style of performance.

YAMAGA SOKŌ 山鹿素行. 1622–1685. Early Edo scholar of Confucianism and martial arts. He began by studying the Neoconfucianism made orthodox by the Edo *bakufu*. Later, with the publication of *Seikyō Yōroku* 聖教要録 (*Essential Military Teaching*, 1665), he advocated a return to pristine Confucianism, *kogaku*. After studying Hōjō military principles, he wrote *Bukyō Zensho* 武教全書 (*A Compendium of Military Teachings*, 1656), using a sufficiently independent view to set up his own school. Although not genuinely seminal, he had degree of originality that extended to his late blend of the Confucian and military in *Chūchō Jijitsu* 中朝事実 (*Japanese Truths*, 1681).

YAMAMOTO KAKEI 山本荷兮. 1648–1716. Early Edo *haikai* poet. Born in Nagoya of a doctor's family, he began haikai in the *Teimon* style, joining the school of *Matsuo Bashō when Bashō visited Nagoya in 1684. That city then enjoyed a flourishing cultural life, as is testified to by the *kasen* composed in a brief period of winter during Bashō's visit. Kakei collected for *Fuyu no Hi* (1684), just as he was also compiler of the next two important *shōfū* collections: *Haru no Hi* (1686) and *Arano* (1689;

see Part Six F). As this shows, he was a mainstay of the school at a crucial time. He later fell out with Bashō and separated from the school. In whatever school, he is an excellent *renku* poet, although not of the grat promise of his fellow townsman, *Tsuboi Tokoku.

YAMANO(U)E OKURA 山上憶良. 660–ca. 733.
Nara poet in *waka* and *kanshi*, writer of *kambun*. Although we know less of him than we would wish, one influential opinion holds Okura to have been of recent Korean stock. One of the three or four principal poets (some would say the second after *Kakinomoto Hitomaro) of the *Man'yōshū*, he is represented in it by ten *chōka*, sixty-two *tanka* (many of them *hanka* to the *chōka*), a *sedōka*, and writing in Chinese. His poems are chiefly concentrated in book 5. He compiled a now-lost waka collection, *Ruijū* (or *Ruiju*) *Karin* 類聚歌林 (*Forest of Classified Poems*).

In 701 he went with a T'ang embassy to China, and he has a very Japanese poem of longing for home while abroad (1:63). Fortunately he made it home safely, unlike *Abe no Nakamaro. His trip to China and ability to speak Chinese were apparently the reasons why he was invited into the poetry circle of *Nagaya no Ōkimi. But from two kinds of evidence he appears to have been wholly out of sympathy with the flowery style of Chinese then practiced in Japan in emulation of late Six Dynasties and early T'ang poets. One is the absence of poems by him in the *Kaifūsō*. Another is the verse and prose in Chinese included in the *Man'yōshū*. Both are in a style that seems of Okura's own devising, based on sutras rather than elegant poets. It must have been intolerable to Prince Nagaya.

In fact, Okura's Japanese style is also hardhitting, crabbed, jerky—unmistakable and in general extremely effective. He is at his worst when he combines moralism and sentiment—as in the envoys to chōka with a dialogue between a poor and a destitute man (5: 892–893) and to another on the instability of human life (5: 804–805). But the chōka are in a vein that no other *Man'yōshū* poet uses. The dialogue is inspired by Confucian poetry of social criticism, and centuries would pass before anything like it would be seen again in some *renga*. The poem on instable human life is Buddhist, perhaps the first clear sounding of that note of *mujō* that thereafter would reverberate in Japanese literature like a temple bell.

It is very clear that Okura was a self-aware artist. He names himself in one poem (3: 337). The dialogue poem mentioned creates two fictional speakers, a man who is poor but has something to wear, eat, and drink, and a destitute man who is on the brink of starvation. In another poem he writes fictionally as if he were Ōtomo Kumakori lamenting his approaching death (5: 886–891). There are also a number of poems preceded by Chinese prefaces—that (5: 794–799) mourning a wife's death—with four

lines of Chinese verse as well as prose; that yearning for his children (5: 802–805); and that on his sufferings as well as his loss of his children (5: 897–903), prefaced by a long Chinese essay. There is also an essay in Chinese lamenting his illness (after 5: 896), and another important example that will be mentioned shortly. Since the combination of Chinese and Japanese composition was then novel, not only must we assume that Okura was aware of what he was up to but also that he was in an intellectual vanguard that was experimenting with various ways of adapting to Japanese experience the resources of continental philosophy and art. In this we see something of a division of labor between *Ōtomo Tabito, who was finding ways to use Taoism to his ends in Japanese poetry, and Okura, who adapts the more moral Confucian strain and the Buddhist religious air. Then there is another poem with a Chinese preface in prose (5: 800–801), a remonstrance to a person derelict in Confucian filial piety, lacking in duty to the state—a man at once proud and useless. There is evidence that Okura has set himself up as Professor Confucian Moralist in this poem in mock outrage at Tabito's setting himself up as Professor Taoist Disdain. So read, the poem shows the great sophistication that had been achieved in Japanese poetic circles in a generation or two.

This is not to suggest that Okura was insincere, but that he was a genuine intellectual, the poet in the *Man'yōshū* who above all deserves that title. Yet he is also—and he seems to know it—very human and vulnerable. Somehow, the most potentially disastrous poetic subject—one's own children—finds him in top form. There may be those who do not appreciate his downright, homely imagery—

> Eating a melon
> I think of my children;
> Eating chestnuts,
> I think of them more—

but then such readers will not have worried over children (5: 802–805). This poet who would write about legends (5: 813–814) or—one of the most delicious situations in the whole collection—write a farewell poem to the Chinese embassy chief but *in Japanese* (with a Chinese echo or two; 5: 894–896): truly this was no ordinary poet. We can be sure that his technique was deliberate, and we can be sure that the technique will continue to move readers, when with a typical fragmentation of language, he laments his dead son Furuhi in the hanka to a chōka (5:904):

> Since he is so young
> He will not know the road to take.
> I will pay your fee.
> O take him there upon your back,
> Courier from the land below.

In poems like this, Okura is not particularly Confucian or Buddhist, but particularly human.

YAMATO MONOGATARI 大和物語 (*Tales of Yamato*). Heian *utamonogatari*. With the **Ise Monogatari* earlier and the **Heichū Monogatari* later, one of the three principal examples of the kind. The authorship, date, and significance of the title are all unclear. Among possible authors, Ariwara Shigeharu and **Kazan (r. 984–986) have been mentioned. Some suppose a court lady as author. It has also been speculated that someone at the earlier court of Uda (r. 887–897) or Daigo (r. 897–930) was responsible. Although a time after 950 would accommodate all the historical individuals mentioned, composition may have begun as early as 938 and have ended as late as 1011. That is, the work seems so loosely organized that multiple authorship over a long period is distinctly possible, although uncertain.

The title seems to postulate Yamato as a contrast to the Ise of the *Ise Monogatari*, but it is not clear why Yamato is better than some other part of Japan. Some have speculated that Yamato is opposed to China (Kara). Others relate the title to *waka* (*yamatouta*) or some person. It is quite uncertain.

Over 170 poetic episodes are included, concentrating in the reigns of Yōzei (r. 876–884), Uda, and Daigo. Typical characters besides those sovereigns include lords and ladies near them, as also priests and dancing girls who frequented the court. As in the *Ise Monogatari* and *Heichū Monogatari*, love is the dominant subject. Although this collection is not as unified as the other two, it provides a far wider range of experience. A parent's longing for a dead child, a person mourning a dead friend, courtiers fretting over lack of advance—these are newer topics. Toward the end yet another kind appears, introduced from folk lore. There are: "Otomezuka," which is related to the "Ikutagawa" story in the **Man'yōshū*; "Obasute," which has numerous later versions, including a *nō*; and "Ashikari," retold in modern times by Tanizaki Jun'ichirō. Such variety has a bit of the air of a *setsuwa* collection, and it probably suggests that less revision has been done to stories than in the *Ise Monogatari*. But if speculation be allowed, further study may show that the work is organized in terms not unlike the love poems of a *chokusenshū* in a manner anticipating *renga*.

YAMAZAKI ANSAI 山崎闇斎. 1618–1682. Early Edo Neoconfucianist, scholar of Shinto. Born in Kyoto and the son of a masterless samurai, he entered Myōshinji, becoming a priest. Later he moved to another temple, where he came upon the Neoconfucianism of the *shushigaku* variety. After studying it, he moved to Edo, taking part in governmental matters. In his early fifties he received instruction in Shinto, a study he pursued on his own thereafter, specializing in "the age of the gods" (jindaiki) in the **Nihon Shoki*. His combination of Neoconfucianism and Shinto is strikingly irregular—possible because the two are in the mind of a Buddhist priest? But it

must have had great appeal, since he was credited with six thousand followers, including some of the famous men of his time.

YAMAZAKI SŌKAN 山崎宗鑑. Dates unknown. Late Muromachi *renga* and *haikai* poet. He flourished in the late fifteenth and the sixteenth centuries, but for someone so important the lack of biographical certainty is strange. Five or more traditions exist as to his death date (1534–1577) and age at death (72 to 89). With **Arakida Moritake, Sōkan is taken to be one of the two founders of real haikai—that is, of haikai no renga as opposed to *mushin* renga. His fame today rests chiefly on his highly influential collection (compiled ca. 1532–1546), known under several titles, the most frequent of which are *Haikai Renga* 俳諧連歌 and *Haikai Renga Shō* 俳諧連歌抄. But its more familiar title, (*Shinsen*) *Inu Tsukuba Shū* (新選)犬筑波集 (*Dog Renga* [*Newly Selected*]), connects the anthology with famous renga collections made by **Nijō Yoshimoto and **Sōgi. The titles prevailing in its time tell of the origins of haikai and suggest the decided shift to haikai from renga that occurs about this time.

YANAGAWA SEIGAN 梁川星巌. 1789–1858. Late Edo poet of kanshi. After a period of study with different masters, he traveled about various parts of Japan before settling for a time in Edo to teach Chinese poetry. Later he moved to Kyoto, altering to a patriotic style that he held to be old and pure. His *Seiganshū* 星巌集 in thirty-two parts was published 1841–1856.

YASHIRO HIROKATA 屋代弘賢. 1758–1841. Late Edo *kokugaku* scholar. Born in Edo, he studied under various masters, including **Hanawa Hokinoichi, whom he assisted on the monumental *Gunsho Ruijū* 群書類従. He also had a collector's instinct, bringing together folk materials in a number of collections.

YASUHARA TEISHITSU 安原貞室. 1610–1673. Early Edo *haikai* poet. Born into a paper merchant's house in Kyoto, while yet in his teens he was attracted to haikai by **Matsunaga Teitoku. Until 1650 or so he was a principal supporter of *Teimon* haikai. But he aspired to more attention, so breaking off to establish himself on his own. His effort was not wholly successful, since he did not have the originality or vision possessed by Teitoku.

YASUI. See OKADA YASUI.

YASUTANE. See YOSHISHIGE YASUTANE.

YATSUHASHI KENGYŌ 八橋検校. 1614–1685. Early Edo koto composer, performer, founder of the Yatsuhashi school. Leaving Edo for Kyoto, his studies there and his abilities led him to set up his own popular school. He was famous as a performer on the shamisen and kokyū (an instrument resembling the shamisen but played with a bow).

YAYŪ. See YOKOI YAYŪ.

YŌFUKU (or **EIFUKU**) **MON'IN** 永福門院 . 1271–1342. (Although "Eifuku" is the more familiar pronunciation, "Yōfuku" now appears to be the correct one.) Late Kamakura-Namboku *waka* poet, like her husband, *Fushimi. Both were attracted by the innovative poetic ideals and practice of *Kyōgoku Tamekane. She appeared in a number of *utaawase* of Tamekane's group, as for example the *Jūgoya Utaawase* 十五夜歌合 (*Poetry Match of the Full Moon*, 1297) and *Sentō Gojūban Utaawase* 仙洞五十番歌合 (*Poetry Match in Fifty Rounds in the Royal Presence*, 1303). She also wrote a hundred-round poetry match with herself, *Yōfuku Mon'in Hyakuban Jikaawase* 永福門院百番自歌合 , ca. 1335? Her poetry attracted warm contemporary interest, so appearing in a number of unofficial collections made by others. Her poetry is best known, however, for its heavy representation in the last two important royal collections, the *Gyokuyōshū* and *Fūgashū*. Like others of the Kyōgoku-Reizei schools, she wrote seasonal poems in a highly particular, imagistic style and love poems in an even more intense but almost image-free and very complex style. To these common styles of the group, she added an element from the tradition of the passionate woman poet—and above all a talent that makes her, with Tamekane, one of the two greatest waka poets of her time.

YŌFUKU (or **EIFUKU**) **MON'IN NAISHI** 永福門院内侍 . Ca. 1264–1347. Late Kamakura *waka* poet and, as her title indicates, a lady serving *Yōfuku Mon'in. She was a gifted poet in the style of the *Kyōgoku poets and the *Reizei poets. She participated in the poetry matches of those houses and wrote one-hundred-poem sequences. She first appears in the *Gyokuyōshū* among royal collections and has twenty-nine poems in the last really important of these *chokusenshū*, the *Fūgashū*.

YOKOI YAYŪ 横井也有 . 1702–1783. Mid-Edo *haikai* poet. He was from an old Nagoya (Owari) family with distinguised ancestry and served the home fief of the Tokugawa family. His grandfather had studied with *Kitamura Kigin, and his father was a haikai poet. He grew up in an unusual atmosphere of affluence, samurai position, and devotion to haikai. He fell ill in his forties, and in the autumn of 1754 retired to a hermitage south of Nagoya castle, becoming like *Ryōkan one of the last of Japanese poets to lead the life of a retired person (inja), recalling such predecessors as *Kamo no Chōmei *Kenkō, *Saigyō, and *Shinkei as well as the itinerant *Matsuo Bashō.

Even before his retirement, Yayū had shown his talents as a writer. His works include *hokku*, sequences mingling Chinese and Japanese verse (*wakan renku*), haikai sequences, and other kinds of artistic cultivation including painting and music. But his masterpiece is *Uzuragoromo* 鶉衣 (*Rags and Tatters*), a deliberately modest title, since both in Chinese and Japanese a "quail's robe" is a metaphor for poor and tattered things—like a quail's feathers.

The composition and compilation of *Uzuragoromo* is very complex. It was not published till after his death (in units, 1787–1823), but it is known that some version of the work was in existence when Yayū was thirty-seven. Matters can be simplified somewhat by a description of the work as it is known today. There are four major units, each divided into three parts and containing pieces of prose, often with poems at the end (whether hokku, *tanka*, or renku). The four units with the numbered pieces are:

Early Part (Zempen). 1–48
Later Part (Kōhen). 49–106
Continued Part (Shokuhen). 107–80
Gleanings (Shūihen). 181–228

In a very *haibun*-like account, *Ōta Nampo, wrote that he had been so taken by reading the delightful twenty-fourth piece, "Karimono no Ben" (ben is a category nominally devoted to the sorting of facts or truth) that he asked Yayū's devoted friend, Ki no Rokurin, to send a collection for printing. Actually, Nampo seems to have had on hand at least the first two units. In one manuscript he designates the four parts Spring, Summer, Autumn, and Winter. Such labels suggest a collection of hokku. But the learning of the people involved was such that earlier precedents were also no doubt on their minds—sequences of court poetry such as *hyakushuuta*, or even the royally commissioned collections, *chokusenshū*. This is to say that Yayū, with whatever help from others such as Rokurin or Nampo, ordered the selections with the usual care of compilers of Japanese collections. Nampo's point is really that *Uzuragoromo* is, like the precedents specified, an ordered or integrated collection. The various parts have a variety of prefaces and postscripts. The first has a preface by Yayū with another by Shoku Sanjin (that is, Nampo). The fact that Yayū wrote a preface suggests that he must be credited with the conception of an ordering of selections of his writing on the model of *Fūzoku Monzen*, whose twenty-one classifications it draws on, adding a few more.

Putting aside the textual complications and the matter of arrangement, we have in *Uzuragoromo* a work of a highly miscellaneous and uneven character well deserving attention for the delight afforded by its best compositions. It is one matter that Yayū's other works are scarcely regarded. It is another that high-school students in Japan read selections from *Uzuragoromo* along with *Bashō's *Oku no Hosomichi* as the second major exemplar of haibun. It is yet another that the most adult experience of the world enables one to esteem his compositions—particularly in the first part (Zempen)—as some of the most natural, attractive prose writing in Japanese. Among those read by Japanese students there are the ninth, a narrative piece on demons (oni), and the lengthier twenty-fourth, which deals with various insects.

An adult reader, or at any event a reader whose mind is stocked with earlier literature and experience of the world, will find numerous other pieces to hold appeal. The twenty-seventh, on love, combines with the stated topic on travel, and the reader of *waka* or *renga* will not be surprised, although pleased, by the easy grace of the combination. The tenth, on sleeping late into the morning, has some light erotic touches with many of the allusions that Yayū introduces with great ease. The eighteenth, on dreams, resembles the twenty-seventh in taking a central topic of Japanese poetry and handling it with a relaxed assurance of the resonances of the conceptions of classical literature that shows Yayū in entire mastery of his art. Every reader will have favorite examples, but it is difficult to believe that anyone would exclude from highest praise the thirtieth piece, on the forgetful old man. This turns inside out the disadvantages of faulty memory (in a piece much given to remembering), so that the fault we all know too well becomes a merit: if the old man forgets in the morning what he read at night, the pleasure of rereading is like that of first discovery. The piece ends with a poem echoing *Shokushi Naishinnō, as earlier it had recalled the *Heike Monogatari* with proper haikai change, so that the old man's thoughts while urinating are part of the picture of fallible human life. Yayū's style is some kind of miracle of ease with complex allusiveness. The author emerges as a person of great self-composure, a man one regrets not having known oneself as a visitor to his hermitage. No doubt there are greater works in Japanese literature. No doubt the Bashō so much admired by Yayū is much more profound. Yet there is also no doubt that the author of *Uzuragoromo* is one of the most attractive and, as it were, comfortable, friendly writers in any literature.

YORU NO NEZAME 夜の寝覚; also *YOWA NO NEZAME* 夜半の寝覚 or simply *NEZAME*. A late Heian (probably end of twelfth century) *monogatari, giko monogatari* in five extant parts. Author unknown. Some speculate that the five-part version extant is a late Kamakura adaptation of an original in as many as twenty parts or more. The present text has two principal omissions: one lacuna at the end of the second and beginning of the third parts; the other at the end of the fifth. What happens in the lost sections can be pieced out from many references to the work. But given the unusual, absorbing nature of the work, the loss is real.

The story is distinctive among monogatari in several respects, all bearing in some fashion on the fact that the central female figure, Nezame (a "name" derived from an early incident) gives the work its title: Awake (Nezame) at Night (Yoru no) or at Midnight (Yowa no). The unknown author clearly learned from *Rokujō Saiin Baishi Naishinnō no Senji, author of the *Sagoromo Monogatari*, that the vicissitudes of female experience were the real subject for work written by women for women, and she learned also that the great well-spring for later fiction was the Uji section concluding *Murasaki Shikibu's *Genji Monogatari*, and yet more particularly the heroine of that section, Ukifune. Its other sources include poems by *Izumi Shikibu, a major resource in making Nezame into so full-blooded and passionate a character. Whether its use of prophecy is to be associated with the *Utsuho Monogatari* seems doubtful. There were more proximate precedents, if not as numerous, in the *Genji Monogatari* (the Korean soothsayers early on) and in the *Sagoromo Monogatari* (near the end). And many of the dreams in *Sugawara Takasue no Musume's *Hamamatsu Chūnagon Monogatari* are either prophecies or similar versions of revealing intelligence. *Yoru no Nezame* is in a very good lineage and otherwise stands in the best company of the time. But it is also a distinctly different creature.

Most monogatari feature a hero who is at least the nominal subject of the work. As the *Sagoromo Monogatari* shows, the convention could be given full credit and yet be made a means of revealing female experience. *Yoru no Nezame* certainly does not drop men—that would have made the real experience of women impossible. But the story has as its center for both plot and meaning the heroine, Naka no Kimi, middle daughter of the prime minister. Given the various titles of the work, we may call her Nezame.

The story begins in what seems the standard way, with focus on the chief male character, known as so often as Chūnagon. He is son of the Chancellor-Minister of the Left. The shift to Nezame is effected by what is infrequent in a gikomonogatari, a use of a material element from a *mukashi monogatari*. The author borrows from the *Utsuho Monogatari* the idea that characters may possess a celestial ability in music. That is Nezame's charisma at this point. Drawn by her extraordinarily lovely music, Chūnagon visits her quarters on night, managing to sleep the night with her. He has no little of Prince Niou's amatory enterprise in the *Genji Monogatari*. It is very difficult to communicate what happens thereafter and throughout the first two parts, precisely because so little occurs, and yet the tension is very high. There is clearly one plot issue: will Chūnagon and Nezame be able to get together? (At the opening, the problem seems chiefly that of the hero.) There are many obstacles that seem to exist, but from time to time the hero and heroine also seem to meet. One obstacle to their meeting is Chūnagon's marriage to Nezame's elder sister. This occurs in spite of Nezame's having had a child by him, a fact kept secret from the world and given to the reader, like everything else, not so much as an item of plot but as another feature of the scenery. Scarcely a breeze seems to turn. Actions do not so much occur as get explored in the minds and hearts of the central characters. All this moves very slowly while a radical shift is being made from the mono-gatari defined, as usual, by a hero to a new one defined by the heroine.

The fact is fully realized with the beginning of the third part. One cannot say that from this point one reads the story for its plot, as one certainly can the *Sagoromo Monogatari*. But Nezame has become a character who can act as well as feel and think. The emphasis remains strongly psychological, and the characters' foreheads remain feverish, but the causes of heat and tension—and even their fruits—are better known. Nezame becomes a strong character. She discovers, more properly she admits, her physical passion. She likes her good looks. She is not averse to manipulating people. From his point Chūnagon matters mostly as an agent or extension of Nezame. He has to put up with the tennō as a rival. One incident is without parallel in the known monogatari literature. Like many a monogatari hero, Nezame finds that events force her into a marriage of convenience. In marrying a lord much older than she, she seems—with her passion and enterprise—about to cause an explosion. No such thing happens. She finds that a woman can put up with the attentions of an older man, and in fact when he dies she feels a genuine sorrow, even while Chūnagon remains her idea of a lover.

It is difficult to know what to make of the theories that the parts extant represent only a portion of the work. Since there is that gap at the end of the fifth and last of the extant parts, it is very hard to decide what might have been added or, for that matter, if anything was. The one thing certain about the story is its daring presentation of a woman as central figure, or rather perhaps the making a woman into as passionate and as active a figure as a man. This, of course, does not mean that life is all cozy and sweet for Nezame—she has many reasons to know why the world is called a place of suffering. But she exerts a claim—as central character—on readers such as no other monogatari female does. We are not asked to take her as an ideal figure like Murasaki in the *Genji Monogatari*, and there is not the same art used to delineate her life as there is for Ukifune. But the *assumption* of the characterization (only Nezame is fully portrayed) and of the narration (which comes to rest most securely only in her mind) is radical.

The story seems to have exerted little influence on subsequent monogatari. Various reasons have been, and can be, offered. One theory is that the mutilated condition of the work precluded influence. But we do not know how much is missing. Another expla-

nation holds, in effect, that the radical feminizing of the story holds the explanation. Yet another set of reasons seems more convincing. Like *Torikaeba-ya Monogatari*, this is a late Heian exploration of female experience in a manner dependent on the *Genji Monogatari* or, more properly, on its legacy. The woman who created Nezame was one of the last gifted writers of tsukurimonogatari. The course of events in prose narrative was shifting, as were those in politics, and the new energies found expression in men's literature, especially in military tales. (The *Heiji Monogatari* dates from this period.) All in all, it is useless to speculate on what might have been if the story ran to ten books, or why it had no great impact on subsequent writers. It is enough that in the prose narrative line of women's literature (*joryū bungaku*) the potential of monogatari for dealing centrally with a woman's experience was at last realized in a way that would have gratified Izumi Shikibu, who was generous enough probably to have thought that the author of *Yoru no Nezame* had succeeded—even to an extent she had not her-self in her diary—in sustaining the woman's view as that central to the world created. This is not to say that *Yoru no Nezame* has the fineness of *The Diary of Izumi Shikibu*, but that it is a descendant of that earlier work in spirit as much as it is of *The Tale of Genji* in narrative resources. No mere copy of either, this heated, remarkable story is the full realization of what the women's literature of the Heian period implied for prose narrative.

YOSA (or **TANIGUCHI**) **BUSON** 与謝（谷口）蕪村. 1716–1783. Mid-Edo *haikai* poet, painter in the *bunjinga* style. Born Taniguchi, he is sometimes referred to by that surname, but more often by his later one, Yosa, which properly speaking should be pronounced "Yoza." He used a number of artistic and poetic styles. Born in Settsu (Hyōgo), he went to Edo about age nineteen, studying haikai in one of the many branches of *Danrin* style haikai. When his teacher in art and haikai died in 1742, he left Edo, and for the next decade lived a free life in parts of the Kantō and Tōhoku regions. In 1751 he settled down in Kyoto, but during the three years thereafter, he once more went traveling, returning again to Kyoto, finally adopting it as his home.

During the decade from 1756 to 1765, he was highly productive as a painter. Landscapes, an-imals, portraits—all were his subjects, whether in an admirable variety of *nanga* or *haiga* styles. From 1762, he was chief poet in his Yahartei school. And he continued to show his fluency in Chinese verse and prose.

Voicing the slogan, "Back to Bashō!" Buson showed his fundamental independence from Danrin and other schools, his desire to initiate a more serious art. His efforts to do so led to the name, the Haikai Revival, for the period from 1743 to his death. These decades coincided with a rare moment of liberalization by the Edo *bakufu*. Buson represents the peak of literary talent, the best result of the new (and temporary) freedom.

The exact meaning of his slogan is not clear, but a comparison between Buson and *Matsuo Bashō is one of the standard critical exercises in Japan. To the extent that comparison is confined to *hokku* and other individual stanzas, Buson is more brilliant, more prolific, and more consistent in level of creation. At his best, Bashō is more profound and much greater a poet in *renku*. Buson sometimes tends to pay too much attention to writing a striking stanza rather than to making integral sequences, whereas the more attention Bashō bestows—and he was a compulsive bestower—the more profound his work becomes.

Buson is one of those great artists who do so many things so very well that they are harder to appreciate adequately than a person who excels in just one or two. He was one of the greatest painters as well as certainly the greatest poet of his age. He was a master calligrapher, an adept in Chinese. His *Shin Hanatsumi* 新花摘 (*New Flower-Picking*, 1777) offers a sample of his talents. Basing his conception on *Enomoto Kikaku's *Hanatsumi*, he covers sixteen days following the memorial services for his mother. The entries consist of ten units that combine prose, pictures, and hokku. Actual composition was extended over a longer period. In some ways this is Buson's most impressive work involving haikai, and no other writer could have produced a work that so combined allusion and narrative, irony and precept, prose, poetry, and graphic art. It is his counterpart to Bashō's *Oku no Hosomichi* (a work for which he painted screen pictures that are justly famous). Among his best-known renku are two *kasen* composed over several months with his most able follower, *Takai Kitō. These are a summer and a winter sequence, along with a witty preface and the deliberately irrelevant and odd-sounding title, *Momosumomo* (桃李 although written as a palindrome in kana: ももすもも; *Peaches and Plums*). Both trees are associated with spring, not the season of either sequence. The individual stanzas in the two sequences are consistently impressive, but they are almost isolated creations, commonly having connection (*tsukeai*) only by the accident of juxtaposition. Yet the other principles of sequence are well observed, and these two kasen alternate humor with seriousness, the beautiful with the low, with additional elements in brilliant fashion. Other sequences show Buson knew the art of haikai thoroughly, and we may expect further study to reveal his mastery of normal haikai sequentiality.

Buson's excellent hokku are too numerous to identify. We should probably conclude that his "Back to Bashō!" meant return to a high standard of poetry, certainly not that he was in any sense an imitator. When Bashō writes a weak stanza, as he does from time to time, it is usually not clear. Something important has been attempted and failed. When Buson writes a weak stanza—but who can remember any? His level of quality is astonishingly high. He is not only a brilliant artist and the greatest poet of the eighteenth-century but an inspirer of poetry in others such as his wife and Kitō. See *Botan Chitte mo no Maki* and *Fuyu Kodachi no Maki*.

YOSHIDA KANEYOSHI. See KENKŌ.

YOSHIMOTO. See NIJŌ YOSHIMOTO.

YOSHINO SHŪI 吉野拾遺 (*Stories Gleaned at Yoshino*). A Namboku *setsuwa* collection dating from about 1358. It is considered to be in two parts, although three- and four-part versions also exist. Numerous men have been named as the possible compiler, but the matter cannot be determined. The collection is made up of anecdotes about a large number of people, especially those associated with the Yoshino court during this era of rival courts. People are treated in literary terms for their human rather than historical characters. Much of the material seems indebted to such works as the *Shin'yōshū, *Taiheiki, and *Masukagami, but many matters are fabricated at variance from ascertainable historical fact. This may suggest that some later author adapted sources in the attempt to create the aura of a court he did not know personally.

YOSHISHIGE YASUTANE 慶滋保胤. Ca. 931–1002. Mid-Heian scholar of Chinese studies. His inclination for Po Chü-i and his veneration of Buddhism make him central to the tastes of his age. He founded a group to promote studies of such poetry and the religion, including in it *Minamoto Shitagō, Tomohira Shinnō, and others. The Anna Affair (Anna no Hen, 969) ushered in Fujiwara hegemony by the institution of regency and chancellery to exercise the power of the court and control the sovereign. Yasutane viewed such developments critically, referring to the ills of the time in his *Chiteiki* 池亭記 (*Record of the Pond Pavilion*, 982), which may have had an impact on *Kamo no Chōmei's *Hōjōki*.

In 986 he went to Mount Yokawa to take the tonsure at the hands of *Genshin. He later dwelt at a temple in Higashiyama, from which he set out on numerous pilgrimages. His learning led to a number of publications. One of his most learned, although largely inspired by Genshin, was his *Nihon Ōjō Gokuraku Ki* 日本往生極楽記 (*An Account of Japanese Births in Paradise*, ca. 983) concerning the lives of forty-five priests, from *Shōtoku Taishi on. Yasutane's contribution had some influence, as in shown by its provision of some things for the *Konjaku Monogatari*, part 15. His prose is represented in *Honchō Monzui*, his *waka* in the *Shūishū*.

YOSHITADA. See SONE NO YOSHITADA.

YOSHITSUNE. See FUJIWARA YOSHITSUNE; also
MINAMOTO YOSHITSUNE.

YUNOYAMA (or *YUYAMA*) *SANGIN HYAKUIN*
湯山三吟百韻 (*A Hundred Stanzas by Three Poets
at Yunoyama* [*Yuyama*]. A mid-Muromachi *renga*
sequence in a hundred stanzas, composed at
Yunoyama (Arima hot springs in today's Kobe) in
the winter of 1491. This *hyakuin* is probably the
most highly esteemed renga sequence composed at
one sitting, and by more than one poet. The three
poets are: *Shōhaku (*hokku, ageku*), *Sōchō (*waki*),
and their master, *Sōgi (*daisan*). Three years earlier
they had composed *Minase Sangin Hyakuin*, but
Sōchō shows to much better advantage here. The
poets used considerable freedom with renga canons.
There are nine moon stanzas instead of the usual
seven. In stanza 66, Sōgi violates a rule by continuing cultivation imagery to a third stanza. Some
important topics get fewer stanzas than the rules
call for: for example, 50 and 59 (only one each
on love) and 99–100 (only two on autumn). The
pace is leisurely, the tone one of suffering as much
as is allowable within the beauty indicated by the
auspicious place. The suffering is represented by
the unusual repetition of "ushi" (miserable) seven
times, and the beauty by the supernumerary moon
stanzas.

This sequence has not been as long studied as has
the *Minase Sangin Hyakuin*, perhaps because its
hokku does not have the evocative power of Sōgi's
in the earlier sequence. And anyone who has read
the *Sōgi Dokugin Nanibito Hyakuin* will probably
agree with the judgment that renga could be no finer
than that. But if *Yunoyama* does not have so striking
a hokku, it is not marred by Sōchō's frequent lapses
in *Minase*. And if it does not have the unity of
mature vision of Sōgi's *Dokugin*, it has greater nor-
malcy. That is, it is truer renga, a sequence composed by more than one poet at a single sitting. Such
conditions allow for natural movement, constant
interplay. The trick was, of course, to make the
conditions of composition work to poetic advantage. In *Yunoyama* they do to a degree no less astonishing for being handled with such seeming ease.

YŪSAI. See HOSOKAWA YŪSAI.

YŪSHŌ. See KAIHŌ YŪSHŌ.

ZEAMI 世阿弥 (or KANZE MOTOKIYO 観世元清).
Ca. 1364 ca. 1443. Early Muromachi *nō* actor,
playwright, critic. (See Part Five A and Part Six G
and K.) Following his father, *Kan'ami, he became
the second head of what had become Yamato *sarugaku*. His father seems to have had the genius to
combine diverse elements into a synthesis that can
be identified as *nō*, although performances then

varied from modern ones in being much more rapid.
Zeami's achievements include the social one of
making his art acceptable to the most powerful
house of the time, the Ashikaga shogunate, which
ruled the country insofar as anybody could be said
to do in those times. Put another way, his father was
a mere actor, a strolling player. Perhaps Zeami was
so also to many of the time, but for many others his
career showed that sarugaku had changed from an
entertainment to an elegant (*ga*) art.

The first and last decades of Zeami's life are obscure. The most decisive turn in his fortunes came at
the age of eleven when, in 1375, he was seen in
performance by Ashikaga Yoshimitsu, the shogun,
six years older than the actor. Zeami's beauty and
ability alike appear to have captivated the young
shogun. Thereafter till Yoshimitsu's death in 1408,
Zeami enjoyed the capricious patronage of the high-
born. The Ashikagas were splendid if unpredictable
patrons who knew more about the fine arts than the
rude one of government. Zeami's name implies service to the Ashikaga household because, in those
Amidist times, artists retained by the Ashikagas
were expected to take on such -ami names (see
*Nōami).

When Kan'ami died in 1384, the twenty-year-old
Zeami was responsible for the fortunes of the Kanze
troupe. He had rivals for the attention of Yoshimitsu, who commonly preferred his rival from Ōmi
sarugaku, Inuō (or Dōami). All the same, Yoshimitsu's death (1408) brought Zeami more difficulties than it eased. He had won high estimation,
but an acting house depends on patronage. Under
Yoshimitsu's successor, Yoshimochi, he was not
wholly without favor, even if the golden days must
have seemed long past. In some ways his best fortune in these years came when *Komparu Zenchiku
married one of his daughters. He was a great admirer of Zenchiku's art, and he had every reason to
become more and more grateful for the generous
fidelity of his son-in-law. About 1422 Zeami took
orders. Certainly his affairs did not prosper, as they
once seemed they would. The shogun, Yoshinori,
preferred Zeami's nephew, Motoshige, and put
Zeami in a much lower position. When Motoshige
had become leading Kanze actor, Yoshinori was
angered by Zeami's refusal to assist his nephew.
Other problems followed. In 1430, his second son,
Motoyoshi, took orders out of grief for his lack of
skill as an actor, and his eldest son, Motomasa—
who was then rated more highly than Zeami as an
actor—suddenly died in Ise. In effect, the Zeami
line of the Kanze school was gone, and it was
Motoshige's that came to be one of the four
approved by the Edo bakufu and that, in its
descendants, is most prosperous today.

For reasons not clear, at age seventy Zeami was
exiled to Sado Island. He certainly spent two years
there; if and when he returned from exile is not
certain. In the meantime, Zenchiku carefully looked

after Zeami's financial and artistic interests. That was one bright element in the shadows of his last years, when his glory at eleven must have seemed long since faded. One tradition has it that he died in a Zen temple back from exile.

Zeami the actor can only be imagined from writings, since the pace of nō acting today is so much slower. He obviously had great talent, and being a person of the theater, he would have adapted his art according to the preferences of his powerful patrons. He would have taken what he liked from Zenchiku or Inuō, as they would from him. Beyond that is conjecture.

Zeami's stature as a playwright is of course bound up with methods of acting that cannot be recovered, and as with the theater everywhere, he often adapted rather than originated a play, or wrote on subjects such as others had chosen. It is certain that his plays continue to act well, and that they have consistently greater literary interest than the plays of any other nō dramatist. His concept of rich beauty (*yūgen*) is apparent throughout his work, and it has been said that one can distinguish—even identify—his plays by their unity or harmony of imagery. About fifty plays are attributed to him. From them, anyone would wish to include certain favorites in a short list: *Takasago, Oimatsu, Matsukaze, Tadanori, Kiyotsune, Atsumori, Sanemori, Yorimasa, Kinuta, Izutsu* (often considered his greatest), *Nue*—the problem is where to stop. See Part Six G.

Although his criticism (Part Six M) is inconceivable without his experience as an actor, as a dramatist, and as a manager, the criticism is by itself enough for a high reputation. His first treatise, one of his most important, is *Fūshikaden* (*Teachings in Style and the Flower*, 1400–1402). The basic problem is the meaning of "flower" (*hana*, ka), an element so recurrent in his critical titles. It is clear that from *renga* the flower is the most important, precious image. But the usage here also involves his transmittal of his father's art or flower, which Zeami does not alter so much as adapt to traditional poetics (see Part One A). In no other treatise does he make so much of *monomane*—imitation, miming.

In his redefinition, monomane comes to mean something like acting a role or a play—as a katsura*mono* is a wig-role or a woman's part; and as a waki-nō*mono* is a play of the first group in nō. In all this, he was careful to fit his art into the canons of *waka*.

The *Fūshikaden* shows Zeami adapting *Ki no Tsurayuki's terms *kokoro* and tane in the opening of the preface to the *Kokinshū*. Tsurayuki had said that Japanese poetry takes the human heart or mind (kokoro) as its seed or effecting cause (tane). Zeami posited that for nō the seed-cause was art or performance (*waza*), and that the flower derived from, or was, the kokoro. His elusive style is the despair of translators, but by hana he appears to have meant art, art in terms of its possible beauty and in terms of its effect on the audience. Certainly we discover him at the outset seeking to present a general theory that will account for his father's teaching within the prestigious terms of waka and renga criticism.

His later critical writings include a good deal of instruction for actors, along with refinements and enlargements of the early criticism. Of the other twenty treatises now established to be by him (with some overlapping as shorter works sometimes became part of longer), the most important are usually assumed to be *Shikadō* 至花道 (*The True Path to the Flower*, 1420); *Kakyō* 花鏡 (*A Mirror of the Flower*, 1424); a work sometimes titled *Nōsakusho* 能作書, and sometimes *Sandō* 三道 (*The Three Elements in Composing a Play*, 1423); and *Sarugaku Dangi* 申楽談儀 (*Zeami's Reflections on Nō*, dated 1430), which Motoyoshi compiled from his father's teachings.

There have been many actors who have been great dramatists (Sophocles, Shakespeare, Molière). There have been playwrights who have been great critics (Jonson, Corneille, Dryden). But there is not another to equal Zeami for excellence as an actor, dramatist, and critic. Such genius is present today, six centuries later, in a continuous tradition of acting, in extant plays, and in the critical means of understanding he provided.

ZENCHIKU. See KOMPARU ZENCHIKU.

PART FOUR Literary Terms

The terms are entered under their Japanese names, because it is not feasible to give translations that are at once brief and adequate. For readers with little or no Japanese, and as a quick guide to others, a brief preliminary Glossary by category is given. By no means all important terms are included, but it is difficult to proceed otherwise without presenting too much information.

The most important terms are italicized *in the Glossary*. (Many of these are more general entries and lead out to related terms.)

Within the long list of literary terms itself, the words italicized under one heading will be found elsewhere in the list, but such a word is italicized only on first appearance. Titles or names preceded by an asterisk will be found in Part Three.

Further information and cross-references will be found in: Part 1: A Brief History; Part 3: Major Authors and Works; Part 5: Theaters (for details of stages, etc.); Part 6: Major Collections; and the Index.

GLOSSARY

POETRY (SEE ALSO SONG)

Waka (uta, yamato uta)

KINDS

Azumauta	hanka	nagauta
bussokuseki no uta	iroha uta	sedōka
chōka	kata uta	*tanka*
darumauta	komponka	

TOPICS AND CATEGORIES: *dai*

aishōka	*koi*	shakkyōka
banka	mono ni yosete	sōmonka
daiei	omoi o noburu uta	ushintei
ga no uta	mono no na	*zō*
jingi	oriku	zōka
kinuginu	sakimori no uta	

PARTS: *kami no ku*, kotobagaki

COLLECTIONS AND SEQUENCES

chokusenshū	*kashū*	sanjūrokkasen
goshū	nijūichidaishū	shisenshū
hachidaishū	rokkasen	*utaawase*
hyakushuuta	sandaishū	zenshū
jūsandaishū		

Renga

STANZAS

ageku	hiraku	waki
daisan	*hokku*	

LENGTHS

chōrenga	senku	tanrenga
hyakuin	shoori	yoyoshi
iisute		

CANONS

dai	kireji	shikimoku
furimono	kokorozuke	sobikimono
fushimono	kotobazuke	*shinku*
ji	*mushin*	tenja
jo-ha-kyū	nigeku	*tsukeai*
jōza	*sarikirai*	tsukeku
kidai		

Haikai (in addition to terms for renga)

Danrinfū	hosomi	ryūkō
fueki	*kasen*	sabi
haibun	maekuzuke	shiori
hankasen	mikasazuke	*Shōfū*
hokku-waki	nigeku	*Teimon*

Other kinds

kyōka	kyōshi	senryū
kyōku	*renku*	wakanrenku

SONG (SEE ALSO POETRY)

Kayō

eikyoku	*imayō*	kamiuta
enkyoku	kamiasobiuta	*nagauta*

Other terms

gagaku	kamiasobiuta	*rōei*
kagura	kosaibari	saibara

NARRATIVE

Prose Fiction

biwa hōshi	kaiwabun	*nikki bungaku*
akabon	kanabon	ninjōbon
amakusabon	kanazōshi	otogizōshi
aohon	katagimono	*rekishi monogatari*
dangimono	ki	sagabon
denki monogatari	kibyōshi	*setsuwa* (*bungaku*)
eiri yomihon	*kikō bungaku*	sharebon
ezōshi	kōhon	shinnaigo
gesaku	kokkeibon	*sōshi*
gunki	kōshokubon	sōshiji
gunki monogatari	kotoba	tanryokubon
hanashibon	kurohon	*ukiyozōshi*
Heike biwa	*kusazōshi*	utagatari
Heike bushi	kyōgenbon	*uta monogatari*
Heikyoku	*monogatari*	yomihon
ji	*Naraehon*	

Other

kambun	karon	*zuihitsu*

THEATER (SEE ALSO PART FIVE)

Nō (see also *kyōgen*)

aikyōgen	maejite	*serifu*
dengaku	*michiyuki*	*shimai*
hayashi	*monomane*	*shite*
jiutai	*mondō*	*tsure*
kamiuta (shinka)	men	*utai*
katarimono	nanori	utaibon
kogaki	sangaku	*waki*
kuse	*sarugaku*	*yōkyoku*

Kyōgen (see also *nō*)

ado	*serifu*	Tarōkaja
kouta	*shigusa*	*tsure*
sarugōwaza	*shite*	*waki*

Jōruri (see also under *kabuki*)

ayatsuri	impon	shinjōruri
daihon	*jidaimono*	*shinjū*
eiribon	*kojōruri*	shūgen
eirikyōgenbon	*serifu*	tanryokubon
Gidayū	*sewamono*	*tayū*
Gidayūbushi		

Bunraku (see *jōruri*)

Kabuki (see also under *jōruri*)

aragoto	kagura	*nagauta* (2)
ba	kabukikyōgen	*nuregoto*
buyōgeki	kaomise	*onnagata*
dan	katarimono	*otokogata*
engeki	kouta	shosagoto
hayagawari	mie	

Other (see also dance and performing arts)

kōwakamai	Mibu kyōgen	kagura

Dance and Performing Arts (see also preceding)

bugaku	*manzai*	*rakugo*
heikyoku	nagauta (2)	sangaku
kabu	nembutsu	sekkyō
mai	*odori*	utamai

Entertainers, Performers

bikuni	etoki	goze

Instruments

fue	ōtsuzumi	*shamisen*
kotsuzumi	sasara	taiko

TECHNICAL AND CRITICAL CONCEPTS (SEE ALSO EARLIER ENTRIES)

azumaasobiuta	*hon'i*	*kami no ku*
dai	*honkadori*	karumi
en	*honzetsu*	*kokoro*
engo	jiamari	*kotoba*
fūryū	*jo*	*makoto*
ga	kaibunuta	*makurakotoba*
gago	*kakekotoba*	*miyabi*

mondō	*sama*	*utakotoba*
monoawase	sakimori no uta	waza
mono no aware	*sharefū*	*yōembi*
mono no na	*sugata*	*yojō*
mumon	taketakashi	*yūgen*
mushin	*umon*	zae
musubidai	*ushin*	zoku
sabi		

LANGUAGE AND WRITING SYSTEMS

benreitai	kanji	wabun
kambun	kyōshi	wakan
kana	mana	*wakan konkōbun*
kanabun	*Man'yōgana*	yūrigo
kanshi	semmyō(tai)	

SOCIAL AND RELATED MATTERS

chōnin	kataribe	nyobo kotoba
joryūbungaku	*nenjūgyōji*	onnade
kabane	*giri*	otokode
kamigata	*ninjō*	*tonseisha*

ASSOCIATIONS WITH OTHER ARTS

biwa hōshi	Heike bushi	shamisen
emaki(mono)	Naraehon	*Yamatoe*

RELIGION AND PHILOSOPHY

Shinto

harai	norito	semmyōgaki

Buddhism

hakanasa	*mujō(kan)*	*satori*
kū	nembutsu	shikan
michi	*nori*	*sukuse(musubi)*

Christianity

Christian (Kirishitan) Bungaku

Confucianism

giri   *jugaku*   *shushigaku*
kogaku

National Studies, etc.

Kokin denju   *rangaku*   shingaku
kokugaku   Sagabon

LITERARY TERMS

Ado 迎合. In *kyōgen* a role supporting the chief character, *shite*.

Ageku 挙げ句. The last stanza (in 7-7 syllables) in a *renga* or *haikai* sequence.

Aikyōgen 間狂言. (1) Also called ai, *kyōgen*, or kyōgengata; a player of kyōgen who appears in *nō* in a bit part as a lower social character, or who relates the play's narrative during the interval of a two-act play, especially of the first or "god" category. (2) Humorous interludes between the acts of three-act *jōruri*.

Aishōka 哀傷歌. Laments. A *dai* (topic) for *waka*; a category as for poems in *chokusenshū* or other collection; one of the possible books in a *chokusenshū*.

Akabon 赤本. Red-covered books of about ten pages from ca. 1675–1764. Stories mostly for children: "Shitakiri Suzume," "Momotarō," etc. See *gesaku*.

Akashi. See *mei*.

Aohon 青本. Green-covered books of popular stories, ca. 1745–1770. Ten-page units, but up to ten units or more might be gathered. See *gesaku*.

Aragoto 荒事. Rough, bold business. The style of *kabuki* acting favored in Edo. Started by *Ichikawa Danjurō I, probably from an earlier stage of the puppet theater, kimpira *jōruri*. This style favors striking effects, spectacular acting, as opposed to *nuregoto*.

Ate 貴. Majesty, courtliness, poise.

Atojite. See *nochijite*.

Aware. See *mono no aware*.

Ayatsuri 操り. Manipulation. Ayatsuri theater (ayatsuri kyōgen, ayatsuri shibai, ayatsuri ningyō) involves manipulation of puppets. The manipulation was at first by one person, but the number grew to three as the mechanisms grew more complex. The puppets, a meter or more tall, are used in the *jōruri* theater, now called *bunraku*.

Azumaasobiuta 東遊歌. Songs for the eastern dances. Thirteen extant songs sung at Shinto festivals. Although of varying ages and forms, they are more primitive than the *azumauta*.

Azumauta 東歌. Eastern poems. A classification of songs and poems in the *Man'yōshū* and *Kokinshū*, designating those with elements showing origins east of Yamato or Kyoto—for example, areas such as modern Tokyo.

Ba 場. In *kabuki*, equivalent to a scene, as *dan* is to an act.

Bakufu 幕府. Shogunal government, in particular the Minamoto government at Kamakura, the Ashikaga government in Kyoto, and the Tokugawa government in Edo.

Ban 番. A "round" in an *utaawase* or other, similar match in which rival entities are entered competitively from two sides, the left (senior or first) and the right. See *monoawase*.

Banka 挽歌. A poem of mourning. A poetic topic in *waka* or a classification for a book of them in a *chokusenshū*, etc. With *sōmonka* and *zōka*, one of three major classifications in the *Man'yōshū*.

Benreitai 駢儷体. Also bembun 駢文, benreibun 駢麗文. Decorative, rhythmical prose. A Chinese Six-Dynasties elaborated prose style that impressed Nara intellectuals, who used it. It employed a pattern of 4- and 6-character rhythm in some form of alternation, normally with occasional different units to vary the flow.

Bikuni 比丘尼. Also etoki bikuni, Kumano bikuni (from Kumano Shrine), and kanjin bikuni (when raising funds for a shrine or temple). In Kamakura and Muromachi times, nuns who traveled to perform by explaining religious pictures (see *etoki*), or who recited long narratives, such as the *Soga Monogatari*. These they softened by removing misogyny, by emphasizing religious and amatory confessions, and by proclaiming enlightenment to important characters. The emphasis on the amatory appears to have assisted in the degeneration of bikuni to prostitutes in the Edo period. See Part Ten E for an illustration.

Biwa hōshi 琵琶法師. Lute priests. From the Heian period there were itinerant reciters/singers of texts. They became best known as reciters of the *Heike Monogatari*. See *heikyoku*.

Buga 舞歌. (1) Dance and song, in much the same sense as *kabu*. (2) In particular, for *nō*, a designation of what was, with *monomane* (imitation, representation) the art of acting.

Bugaku 舞楽. Dance art. (1) In the Nara period and somewhat later, kinds of dance and music introduced from various continental sources. Such kinds as tōgaku and komagaku are now extinct, but *gagaku* (which relates these two kinds) has survived. (2) A kind of gagaku, to distinguish it from kinds in which dance is not used.

Bungaku 文学. The modern word often thought of as the translation of "literature"; it implies, however, literary study, Literaturwissenschaft, as well. See the next entry.

Bungei 文芸. Literature, art. A modern term encompassing both words: hence, respectively, closer to German Dichtung and Kunst than to English terms, or than to Literaturwissenschaft, as suggested more by *bungaku*.

Bunjinga 文人画. Literati painting, a style (initiated in China) popular in the eighteenth century, and represented by *Yosa Buson.

Bunraku 文楽. The modern name for a kind of *jōruri*, after the Bunrakuza established in Osaka.

Bussokuseki no uta (or **bussokusekika**) 佛足石の歌. Poems of the Buddha's foot-print stones. Twenty-one poems carved on stone at Yakushi Temple in Nara. The poems, which praise the Buddha and the Buddha's teaching, are written as in *Man'yōgana*, and are like *tanka* except for having a sixth line in seven syllables at the end. A minor kind within *waka*.

Buyō 舞踊. Dance. A generic term, combining the characters for *mai* and *odori*.

Buyōgeki 舞踊劇. Dance drama, a general *kabuki* category distinguished from the more dramatic, *engeki*.

Chabyōshi 茶表紙. Another term for *sharebon*.

Chariba 茶利場. A comic scene in *jōruri* or *kabuki*.

Chōhen 長編(篇). A lengthy work of verse or prose, especially the latter. A modern term, going with *chūhen* for middle length and *tampen* for short length. The terms are relative, of course. After first being applied to modern prose narrative, they have been used in discussing older literature, designating the *Utsuho Monogatari* as a chōhen *monogatari* and the stories in the *Tsutsumi Chūngagon Monogatari* as tampen monogatari.

Chōka 長歌. Long poem, also pronounced *nagauta* (1). With *tanka*, short poem, one of the two principal kinds of *waka*. It consists of lines of five and seven syllables in alternation, concluding with a couplet of sevens. The longest example in the *Man'yōshū* consists of 149 lines. To chōka might be added one or more *hanka* as envoys. Chōka were practiced after the *Man'yōshū*, but never with true distinction.

Choku 直. Rightness, exactitude; undeviating in poetic art.

Chokusenshū 勅撰集 Collections compiled by order of a sovereign. (1) In the widest and loose sense, any major collection of *waka* (chokusenwakashū), *kanshi* (chokusenshishū), waka and kanshi, and even other kinds of poems or prose. (2) In the usual sense, the *nijūichidaishū* compiled by royal order. These waka collections of twenty-one eras are often grouped into two prestigious groups and one less favored group. The *sandaishū*, collections of three eras, are the first three (especially the *Kokinshū*), and set the standard for later poetic diction, for poetic topics or *dai*, and for ordering of the collections. The *hachidaishū*, collections of eight eras, are the first eight and are esteemed especially for the inclusion of the *Shinkokinshū*. The *jūsandaishū*, collections of thirteen eras, complete the twenty-one; these are less often read today, except for the *Shinchokusenshū*, *Gyokuyōshū*, and *Fūgashū*. Properly speaking, "waka" should be included in these names: chokusenwakashū, *Kokinwakashū*, etc. But they are also further abbreviated, especially for adjectival purposes: for example, *Kokin, Shinkokin*. See Part Six A, Principal Collections, for more detailed information.

Chokusenwakashū 勅撰和歌集. See *chokusenshū*.

Chokusho 勅書. A royal rescript. See *shōsho* and *semmyō*.

Chōnin 町人. Townspeople. City-dwellers, chiefly of Osaka, Kyoto, and Edo; therefore, especially merchants, shopkeepers, artisans; also used to describe the literature they favored. Opposed to kuge (court people), shi or bushi (warriors), and nō (peasants).

Chōrenga 長連歌. Long *renga*. As opposed to *tan-renga*, it means extended sequences. The same as *kusarirenga*. Renga as usually conceived.

Chōten 長点. Long mark. A line drawn above or along side an example to distinguish outstanding *waka*, *renga*, *haikai*, etc. or their parts. Such symbols are still used, including the batten or "x" for faulty work, a small circle (maru) for something worthy of notice, and so on.

Christian (kirishitan) bungaku 切支丹文学. Christian literature flourished ca. 1590–1610 as Western priests and Japanese converts published a variety of books: works of proselytizing, didacticism, religious discipline, saints' lives, and so on. *Amakusabon* was a name for one kind of volume so produced. The publications varied, since Japanese Christians included some luminaries (as from the Konishi family) and many humble people. The *de contemptu mundi* literature well fitted with certain Buddhist ideas (e.g. *mujō[kan]*) and sustained many of the numerous martyrs. The *Dottrina Christiana* introduced elements of Greek and Thomistic philosophy, and the *Isoho Monogatari* brought a new parabolic narrative. This literature first acquainted Japanese with roman letters. There was even a *romaji Heike Monogatari*.

Chūhen 中編（篇）. Of middle length. See *chōhen*.

Chūbon 中本. Middle-sized book; chiefly *kokkeibon* and *ninjōbon*.

Chūko sanjūrokkasen. See *sanjūrokkasen*.

Dai 題. Topics. In *waka*, categories for composition or classification of poems. The chief are the four seasons, beginning with spring (haru, natsu, aki, fuyu). These open a *chokusenshū*, occupying six of the usual twenty books. Next in importance is love (*koi*), some books on which open the second half of a collection. Over a period of time a miscellaneous (*kusagusa no uta*) category became increasingly important, usually closing the books of a collection. For waka, kusagusa no uta designates a poem in which no single topic predominates, although sometimes classification proved more complex. Waka collections typically include, among other topics: travel (*tabi*), laments (*aishō*), elegies (*banka*), grievances (*jukkai*), felicitations (*ga no uta*), Buddhism (*shakkyō*), Shinto (*jingi*), parting (*wakare no uta*), etc. In *renga* and *haikai*, dai are either one of the four seasons or *zō*, with such others as love or travel demoted to subtopical status.

Daiei 題詠. Topical composition. Composition of a poem on a certain topic (see *dai*), a more formal kind of verse than that composed on the spur of the moment or from immediate circumstances. Topics came to be handed out or chosen for *hyakushuuta* and other sequences, as also for *utaawase*. Daiei is therefore inherently fictional, as opposed to the immediately autobiographical. See *kotobagaki*.

Daihon 台本. (1) Scripts for *kabuki* or *jōruri*. (2) Published versions of jōruri and kabuki, giving just the script and actors' names written above their dialogue.

Daimoku 題目. The "title" of the Lotus Sutra, chanted by followers of the Nichiren sect: "Praise to the Sutra of the Lotus Blossom of the Fine Dharma" ("Namu Myōhōrengekyō"). The invocation is sometimes found in literary contexts instead of the familiar Pure Land *nembutsu*, as in the suicide scene of *Chikamatsu Monzaemon's *Shinjū Kasane* (see Part One).

Daisan 第三. The third stanza in a *renga* or *haikai* sequence.

Daitsū 大通. A man with outstanding command of *tsū*, or connoisseurship, particularly in detailed knowledge of fashionable arts associated with the demimonde and its culture. See Part Ten, Fig. 93.

Dammari だんまり. Silent, miming action by characters in *kabuki*. Includes jidaidammari, involving stereotyped roles in *jidaimono*, that is, robbers or evil women wearing set, conventional costumes; and sewadammari, *sewamono* roles involving less stereotyping and stage action.

Dan 段. (1) In *jōruri* and *kabuki*, equivalent to an act, as *ba* is to a scene. In *nō*, the designation for a part of the text. (2) Individual entries or episodes in *utamonogatari* and *zuihitsu* such as *Sei Shōnagon's *Makura no Sōshi*.

Dangimono (also dangibon) 談義物. Instruction. A type of *yomihon* in the Edo period, taking its name from Buddhist instruction. One was to read aloud a text that was not religious in the voice of a reciting priest for the comic effect.

Danjo (nannyo) utaawase 男女歌合. A *waka* match between men on one side and women on the other.

Danrin (or Danrinfū) 談林（風）. Danrin style. The most popular school of *haikai*, established by *Nishiyama Sōin and long continued. Opposed to *Shōfū* and *Teimon*.

Darumauta 達磨歌. "Zen" or nonsense poems. A term of opprobrium in the twelfth and thirteeth centuries for what was thought poetic obscurity or abuses of language.

Dengaku 田楽. Field music. At first dengaku involved planting rituals, for which it provided music, song, and rhythm for the women putting out seedlings; in the Heian period dengaku was made a kind of performance by individuals called dengaku hōshi. In Kamakura and Nambokuchō times, it was a rival with *sarugaku*. When sarugaku underwent rapid development into *nō*, it took over some features of dengaku, which then went into gradual decline, being performed chiefly at shrines and temples.

Den(ki) 伝 (記). Biography. As the last element in a title, -den may also convey the sense of method or commentary. See also *hongi*.

Denki monogatari 伝奇物語. "Traditional tales." Marvelous or supernatural stories, best represented by works of *Ueda Akinari.

Dokugin 独吟. A *renga* or *haikai* sequence composed by one person.

Eawase 絵合. A painting match, one kind of *monoawase*. (1) A competition by two sides matching paintings, or paintings inscribed with poems. (2) The title of a part in the *Genji Monogatari* in which such a match features.

Eikyoku 郢曲. Recited songs. A kind of *kayō* popular in late Heian-early Kamakura times. Many kinds of traditional songs might be brought together (*imayō*, *rōei*, etc.). The selection made would reflect the purpose or occasion.

Eiribon 絵入本. Published versions of *jōruri* or *kabuki* texts, especially popular in *kamigata*; the texts were novelistic in incorporating speakers and dialogue signs (unlike *eirikyōgenbon*) with pictures of actors in their roles.

E'irikyōgenbon 絵入狂言本. Published *jōruri* or *kabuki* texts with pictures of actors or scenes.

E'iri yomihon 絵入読本. Illustrated reading books. Distinguished from the nonillustrated variety that began to appear about 1820–1830, as in the *ninjōbon* of the time.

Emaki(mono) 絵巻 (物). Illustrated scroll narratives. In general, these show episodes of *monogatari* and similar literature depicted in sequence on a scroll. Certain chapters in the *Genji Monogatari* (e.g., "Hotaru") show that there was much copying of monogatari, so that at least three persons were responsible for emaki: the author of the literary text, the painter, and the calligrapher of the writing or *kotobagaki* accompanying the painting. One of the pictures in the *Genji Monogatari Emaki* shows a

further step ("Azumaya" picture): one woman reads aloud while others look at pictures, and one has her hair combed.

En 艶. Charm, beauty. This may designate a style more lovely than profound or a central principle of aesthetic beauty. See *yōembi* and *sama*.

Engeki 演劇. (1) Dramatic kabuki plays featuring dialogue, *serifu*, as opposed to *buyōgeki*, featuring dance. (2) Drama in general.

Engo 縁語. Verbal association. Words thought to associate by meaning, convention, or sound, as yume (dream) and mi- (see). Such association might unify the halves of a *tanka*, connect poems in a *chokusenshū* or *hyakushuuta*, or join stanzas in *renga* and *haikai*.

Enkyoku 宴曲. A kind of *kayō* (also called sōga, light song) popular among the nobility, higher warriors, and priests; flourished in the Kamakura and Muromachi periods. Its light-hearted tempo suited feasting and celebrations.

Ennen no nō 延年の能 (or **mai** 舞, or **ennen**). From the Heian period to its height in the Kamakura and Muromachi periods, this was a kind of *nō* (1) performed at certain large temples. The name suggests a performance to extend life.

Etoki 絵解. Picture explainers (also the words or explanation). From the late Heian period, performers who developed moving explanations of pictures of the Buddha, of hell, of temples and shrines and divinities worshiped at them, and of important priests. Some were male, etoki hōshi, and some female, etoki *bikuni*. It is debated whether or not they used biwa or lutes, and whether they were blind, like *Heike hōshi* and *goze*.

Ezōshi 絵草子・絵双子. Also ehon. Short (ca. four pages) illustrated publications reporting events of the time, sometimes in journalistic, sometimes fictional fashion, or both. A version of kinds with colored covers. See *sōshi* and *gesaku*.

Fue 笛. Flute. See *hayashi*.

Fueki 不易. Changelessness. A polar term with *ryūkō* in *Matsuo Bashō's *haikai*, the two constituting the bases of *fūga* or true art.

Fūga 風雅. (1) Two of the six kinds of Chinese poems designated by the Great Preface to *The Book of Songs* 詩経 (*Shih Ching*; J. *Shikyō*). (2) The art of writing in poetry or prose. (3) *Haikai* in *Matsuo Bashō's definition of his art, on a par with *waka* and *renga*. (4) That which is equivalent to *miyabi*, *fūryū*.

Fūgetsu 風月. The wind and the moon. 1. A fresh wind and a bright moon. 2. Natural scenery. 3. The prime subjects for Chinese and Japanese poetry; the essential matter of art.

Fujiwara style 藤原スタイル. A modern term, designating competent but listless achievement in *waka*, a style mastering *utakotoba*, *utamakura*, and poetic skill but without genuine originality.

Furimono 降物. Falling things. A *renga* motif category for such phenomena as rain, snow, dew, and so on. Opposed to *sobikimono*, rising phenomena such as clouds, haze, smoke, and so on.

Fūryū 風流. Stylishness; style or conduct of an admired, artistic kind. A native version of Chinese feng-liu, during the Heian period the term meant something like *miyabi*, with overtones of *kokoro aru* and imamekashi (up-to-date). Later the term came to represent either artistic endeavor in general, or the stylish in particular, as with *iki* and *sui*.

Fushimono 賦物. Directives. In early *renga*, a term directing composition and relating to some specific word in the first stanza. Thus, kuro or black would call for darkness, hair, and so on. In later renga, the directives were largely or purely formal, and might be added later, as a kind of title. The usual form of specification is nani-, with nanibito, some person, the most common.

Fūzoku (uta); also **fuzoku** 風俗 (歌). A variety of *ōuta*, or court song, highly popular at banquets and social gatherings in Heian times. They were usually accompanied by the Japanese zither (wagon). They are mostly provincial in origin, with special representation from the eastern provinces.

Ga 雅. The elegant, truly artistic, as gabun is such writing. Although at first the term was simply one of approbation, it came to be used in contrast to *zoku*. The polar terms more or less divided various kinds of literature into the true (or official) on the one hand and the common (or not worth considering) on the other. In practice, that which deserved being termed ga was that with ample precedent, particularly *waka* and other literature written entirely or mostly in *wabun* (or Chinese), or as time passed and precedents became more numerous (and older literature was revalued), also *monogatari*. Some later writers might claim more or less in vain (except for themselves and their followers) that their art was true, ga work. *Matsuo Bashō is an example, since most of his contemporaries would have thought his *haikai* undeserving of such status. As that example shows, and as does that of monogatari, what was once thought zoku might come to be thought true art. This historical alteration of view has continued into modern times, as revaluation has led, for ex-

ample, to many kinds of Edo literature thought lesser in status than haikai being considering true literature. This dynamic is part of the history of Japanese literature. It follows that certain kinds can be described at different moments as taken to be ga in status or ga-zoku, zoku-ga, or zoku. Confusing as this kind of classification may be, it is crucial to Japanese views of literary history and taste. Bashō used the term fūga, which is akin to *fūryū*. See also *ushin*.

Gagaku 雅楽. Elegant music. In ancient China, a kind of ritual music. Brought to Japan in later guise from China, or Korea, in the early Nara period, it came to be music by instruments used variously at court, long after the continental prototypes had disappeared. It is still performed. It had a three-part rhythm of *jo-ha-kyū* very important in influence on *renga*, *nō*, and *haikai*. See also *bugaku*.

Gago 雅語. Elegant words. The right readings, freed from dialect, later corruption, and so on; sought chiefly by Edo *kokugakusha* in older texts by use of philological and other resources.

Ga no uta 賀歌. Congratulatory poems, auspicious poems. Also a poetic *dai* or topic and a book of such poems in a *chokusenshū* or similar poetic collection.

Gempei 源平. An abbreviation for Genji (Minamoto clan) and Heike (Taira clan). In a series of bloody wars from mid-twelfth to late twelfth century, the Genji replaced the Taira as military rulers in late Heian times. The subject of the *Heike Monogatari* and numerous other writings, dramatic as well as nondramatic. Because the Genji carried white flags and the Heike red, the term also designates that contrast in color.

Genzainō 現在能. A *nō* piece in which the role played by the main character or *shite* is a person of the present, presently alive. This class of play is opposed to *mugennō*, but the opposition is not rigorous in terms of definition so much as convention. See also *gobanmemono* and Part Five A.

Gesaku 戯作. Popular literature in the Edo period including especially *yomihon*, *kibyōshi*, *sharebon*, *kokkeibon*, and *ninjōbon*. See Part One D3 for an account of such kinds.

Gidayū 義太夫. Strictly speaking, the word designates *Takemoto Gidayū, the reciter of *jōruri* in Osaka. Also, such a *kamigata* style of reciter or recitation; as also such reciters, recitation in general. See also *gidayūbushi*.

Gidayūbushi 義太夫節. Gidayū reciting. Recitation by *Takemoto Gidayū, by members of his school, or in his manner. The practice is therefore associated with Osaka *jōruri*, where it greatly assisted the popularity of plays by *Chikamatsu Monzaemon and others. Other schools, such as Takemoto and Toyotake, developed from it.

Gikobun(tai) 擬古文（体）. (1) Prose style imitative of older styles; prose so written. (2) Writing *ga* in nature. (3) In particular, Edo-period imitations of Heian prose by *kokugakusha* such as *Kamo no Mabuchi, *Motoori Norinaga, and so on.

Giko monogatari 擬古物語. *Monogatari* of the Kamakura period, most of them indebted to *Murasaki Shikibu's *Genji Monogatari* and to *Sagoromo Monogatari* (which, however, is usually also included in this class). The sense of modeling is suggested by this modern term, which means something like "monogatari emulating older ones." For distinctions, see *monogatari*.

Giri 義理. Principles of good; duty. (1) Proper conduct. (2) The particular obligations incurred from one's relations with others. In general, the bond of obedience, service, and self-abnegation owed to superiors and family during the Edo period. Sometimes in conflict with *ninjō*, sometimes its complement.

Gō 碁, 棊. A game for two imported from China. Black and white stones or pieces are moved toward a victorious formation on a board with a grid of 19 by 19 lines and 361 crossings.

Gobanmemono 五番目物. The five classes of *nō* conventionally distinguished (a few pieces are classified differently in the lists of the various schools, and the system was fully devised only in the Edo period). When nō was practiced before the Edo period, the pace of playing was much faster than since, and a formal, full-scale performance might well include one play from each of the five classes. To the extent that that formal ideal was realized, it sustained the *jo-ha-kyū* rhythm, with the first representing a stately jo, the last a rapid kyū, and the middle 3 the agitated ha. In each of the categories, the term -banmemono is exchangeable with the name set forth in Chinese characters.

Ichibanmemono. Wakinō 脇能, deuteragonist nō; also kaminō 神能, god-pieces.
Nibanmemono. Shuramono 修羅物. Asura pieces.
Sambanmemono. Kazuramono 鬘物. Wig pieces; that is the *shite* plays a woman; although see the next.
Yobanmemono. Kyōjomono 狂女物. Madwoman pieces.
Gobanmemono. Kirinō 切能. Concluding pieces.

In most lists of selected or best plays, the second category has the fewest examples, and the fourth the most. Many critics think, however, that the third category provides the essence of nō. See *mugennō*, *genzai nō*; Part Five A, Six G.

Gōkan 合巻. Popular illustrated stories and romances, prose narrative succeeding *kibyōshi*, and flourishing sometime after 1807. By combining three or four *sōshi* into one gōkan unit, much longer stories were possible. See *gesaku*.

Gomaten 胡麻点. Sesame points. Variously shaped marks, about the size of a sesame seed, used to point emphasis, etc., and entered along the right side of a line of text for *nō*, *jōruri*, and so on.

Gosan (gozan) bungaku 五山文学. Literature of the five temples. Literature produced by Zen priests during the late Kamakura to the Muromachi periods at the major Zen temples in Kamakura and Kyoto. The literature (and non-literary writings) might be in Japanese, Chinese, or various combinations.

Goshū 後集. Later collection. Japanese or Chinese poems or other compositions made into a collection after the death of the author(s). Opposed to *zenshū*.

Goze 瞽女. From the Muromachi period forward, blind female performers of lengthy narratives such as the *Soga Monogatari*, folk songs, and popular songs. Pictured reciting to self-accompaniment on a *kozutsumi* or hand drum, they are female counterparts (more or less) of *biwa hōshi*.

Gunki 軍記. Military record. A subject classification for *monogatari* and other kinds of writing: soldiers and warfare, often with such other elements as scenes at court, love plots, and so on.

Gunki mono 軍記物. Martial stories and subjects, especially: (1) war stories of the Edo period; (2) *gunki monogatari*.

Gunki monogatari 軍記物語. Martial tales. One of the principal kinds of late Heian literature and following. The stories take, of course, military matters as their subject, with or without additional romantic or historical elements. A title usually names a specific house, as does the *Soga Monogatari*, or a historical incident, as does the *Hōgen Monogatari*. The masterpiece of the kind is the *Heike Monogatari*. For distinctions, see *monogatari*.

Hachidaishū 八代集. The collections of eight eras. See *chokusenshū*.

Haibun 俳文. Haikai writing. Prose composition, usually with *haikai* stanzas, by a haikai poet. Normally with an autobiographical or theoretical interest, it could treat many kinds of experiences. When it treats a journey, it becomes a species of *kikō*. See also *nikki(bungaku)*.

Haiga 俳画. Painting and drawing by a *haikai* artist or having some other connection with haikai.

Haikai 俳諧. Nonstandard, comic, or improper. Originally 誹諧. (1) As *haikaika*, a tanka with usual features, But usually (2), nonstandard *renga*, that is, haikai no renga or haikai renga. This was at first an amusement (as renga had also been) but it took on seriousness with the evolution of the *Teimon*, *Danrinfū* and *Shōfū*, the first associated with *Matsunaga Teitoku, the second with *Nishiyama Sōin, and the last with *Matsuo Bashō. Haikai sequences, like those of renga, were of various lengths including the minimal *hokku-waki*, but more usually the *hyakuin*, *kasen* (most favored by Bashō), and *hankasen*. See *renga* for further details.

Hai(kai)ga 俳(諧)画. *Haikai* pictures. Painting or drawing accompanying, or in the spirit of, haikai poetry. They might be simple or detailed, humorous or serious.

Haikai jittetsu 俳諧十哲. The ten haikai sages. These are most familiar when from a single school: e.g., Shōmon 蕉門 jittetsu, the ten most famous followers of *Matsuo Bashō. Among them are *Enomoto Kikaku, *Hattori Ransetsu, and *Mukai Kyorai; but the exact membership has been disputed for all ten. The specification is something of a haikai counterpart of the *rokkasen* or *sanjūrokkasen* (six or thirty-six sages) of *waka*.

Haikaika 俳諧化. *Haikai* change. The principle, practice, or fact of altering a subject to make it suitable for treatment in haikai. This usually involves deflation or lowering of something grand, without yet rendering it negligible or distasteful.

Haikaika 誹諧歌. Also occasionally read hikai no uta. Poems grouped in the 19th part of the *Kokinshū* and considered indecorous or humorous because of deficiencies (or excesses) in language or conception. See also *haikai*.

Haiku 俳句. An abbreviation of haikai no ku, and a term seldom met in classical literature, although *hokku* were increasingly composed in ways highly similar. See *haikai*.

Hairon 俳論. Treatises on *haikai* theory, practice, canons. A specific variety of *haisho*.

Haisho 俳書. Writings about *haikai*. A general term, more inclusive than *hairon*.

Hakanasa 果無さ(はかなさ). Transience, lack of stability, evanescence. The Japanese noun (adjective, hakanashi) for the human and natural world

in time, as also for the Buddhist idea of the flux of worldly phenomena. See *mujō(kan)* and *kū*.

Hana 花. Flower. *Zeami's term for the highest realization of expressive and affective art in *nō*. See Part 1, p. 13.

Hanashibon 話本(咄本). Collections of short humorous stories in the Edo period. See *sōshi*, *gesaku*, *sharebon*.

Hanja 判者. A judge in a poetry match.

Hanka 反歌. Envoy. One or more of these were commonly added to a *chōka* (long poem) in the five-line kind of *tanka* (short poem). Also called kaeshiuta.

Hankasen 半歌仙. Half *kasen*. An eighteen-stanza *haikai* or, rarely, *renga* sequence.

Hanka(tsū). See *Tsū*.

Hanshi (or **hankotoba**) 判詞. (1) A pronouncement on the qualities or worth of a poem or stanza (*ku*). (2) In particular, a written judgment at a poetry match, *utaawase*.

Hanshibon 半紙本. A half book. Another term for *yomihon*.

Harai 祓. Shinto ritual purification. As a religion of ritual pollution and, even more, of purification, Shinto is deeply imbued with a sense of purity gained from contact with natural things such as water, hills, and so on and their individual kami or divinities. This element is prominent in poems on the *dai* of *jingi*, but it also deeply affects Japanese literature and aesthetics in numerous less obvious ways.

Hashikotoba 端詞. The same as *kotobagaki*.

Hayagawari 早替り. Quick change. A rapid costume change of a spectacular kind during a single scene of *kabuki*.

Hayashi 囃. (1) The music or musicians for *nō*, *nagauta*, *kabuki*, and some other performed arts. In *nō*, the small orchestra includes a *fue*, transverse flute; *kotsuzumi*, an hour-glass-shaped hand drum held on the right shoulder and struck by the right hand; *ōtsuzumi*, a larger such drum held at the left thigh; and sometimes a *taiko*, a large drum struck with sticks in either hand. In kabuki, there will also be *shamisen*, gongs, and so on. (2) Musical playing at informal recitals of nō.

Heike biwa 平家琵琶. The kind of biwa or lute used for recitation of the *Heike Monogatari*.

Heike bushi 平家節. The particular chant or song used for reciting the *Heike Monogatari*.

Heikyoku 平曲. The sung version of the text of the *Heike Monogatari*, or similar kinds of delivery.

Hentaigana 変体仮名. Nonstandard syllabary. A modern term (Meiji period), it was devised to refer to other kinds of syllabaries or characters when *hiragana* was standardized. The kinds thereafter considered nonstandard were as a rule less simple than those chosen. Previously, all kinds had been termed hiragana and were possible in *onnade*, *waka*, etc.

Hikiage 引上. Brought forward. In *renga* and *haikai*, a moon or flower stanza (such as hikiage no hana) appearing earlier than its appointed place or *jōza*. See also *kobore*.

Hikiuta 引歌. Recollection, especially in *monogatari*, of a famous poem. The quotation or allusion is normally of a small part, perhaps of a part preceding the actual allusion. Also such a recalled poem. Cf. *honkadori*.

Hiraku 平句. Ordinary stanzas. Usually means those in a *renga* or *haikai* sequence after the first three (*hokku*, *waki*, *daisan*), but also not the last (*ageku*); sometimes all stanzas except the first one.

Hōben 方便 (Skt. upāya). Expedients, accomodations. A term expressing the pervasive Mahāyāna doctrine that the Buddha devises innumerable means to adapt his teaching to differing sentient beings. The term is used to designate elements of plot and character in *Sugawara Takasue no Musume's Hamamatsu Chūnagon Monogatari*, and is incorporated in the discussion by Genji of *monogatari* in the "Fireflies" chapter of the *Genji Monogatari*. The parables in the *Lotus Sūtra* (see *Myōhōrengekyō*, Part Six O) encouraged the use of fiction as hōben, providing a Buddhist justification for literature against straitlaced moralists. See *kyōgen kigo*.

Hōgan biiki 判官贔屓. Partiality or favor for one who, like *Minamoto Yoshitsune (hōgan was one of his titles), is a "sincere" hero who meets misfortune. By extension the term applies to the sympathy felt for a weak hero. Like other peoples, Japanese may feel sympathy with those who fail in great efforts. But it may go farther with them, as is shown by the weak yet attractive *irogonomi* heroes of many *jōruri*, *kabuki*, and *ninjōbon*.

Hokku 発句. The opening stanza of a *renga* or *haikai* sequence, three lines of 5-7-5 syllables sometimes composed independently, like a modern *haiku*. See *ku*.

Hokkuwaki 発句脇. A two-stanza *haikai*, often used by *Matsuo Bashō. See *hokku* and *waki*.

Hommondori 本文取り. Borrowing or taking over more or less as it is a passage from an older work. Chiefly used for Edo levies on older stories in prose narrative. It is distinguished from *hon'an* (which is more adaptive), from *honkadori* (which involves allusions in a poem to an older poem), and *honzetsu* (which is poetic use, allusion to a motif or episode in an earlier narrative). See also *hikiuta*.

Hon'an 翻案. Adaptation of what an earlier writer had written. A term used in modern criticism of prose narrative. See *hommondori*.

Hongi 本紀. Biographies of figures of the royal house, a term borrowed from China. With it went seika 世家, biographies of the nobility and other such exalted figures; and retsuden 列伝, biographies of commoners. See *den(ki)*.

Hon'i 本意. Essential character. An aesthetic principle, especially of *renga*, conventionally entailing the character of certain things. For example, love (*koi*) entailed unrequited longing (unless sometimes love meetings, au koi); travel (*tabi*) entailed suffering and travel in some direction other than to the capital; flowers (hana), spring unless otherwise qualified; the moon (tsuki), autumn unless otherwise qualified; spring rain (harusame) implied gently falling rains. In reality, life or nature provided other possibilities, but the codified versions were considered especially poetic. The essential versions derive from ancient Shinto beliefs, from the annual observances of court (nenjūgyōji), from Chinese principles, and from various literary formulations such as *Sei Shōnagon's in the opening section of her *Makura no Sōshi*. *Renga* codified such essential characteristics and passed them on to *nō*, *haikai*, and other literary kinds. Adopted from Chinese pen-i.

Honkadori 本歌取り. Allusive variation. A later poet would take some diction and conception from an earlier "foundation poem" (honka) and vary it (-tori, -dori) with a new conception, perhaps making a spring poem of a summer foundation poem, or a love poem of a spring original. A major resource of later poetry, it had various canons, such as avoidance of language from the most famous poems. See *hikiuta*, *hommondori*, *hon'an*, *honzetsu*.

Hōnōka. See *hōraku*.

Honzetsu 本説. Allusion. Unlike *honkadori*, which involves allusive variation on earlier *waka*, this entails allusion to Chinese poems, situations in *monogatari*, and so on: for example, use of the *Ise Mono-*

gatari or **Genji Monogatari* by *renga* poets, or of the *Genji Monogatari* and Chinese poetry by *Matsuo Bashō in *Oku no Hosomichi*. See *hikiuta*.

Hōraku 法楽. Votive *waka*, *renga*, or *nō* composed for presentation to, or expressive of, the wishes of the gods—or, for nō, also the Buddha. For waka, *hōnōka* is also used.

Hosomi 細み. Fineness. One of the *haikai* ideals, with *sabi* and *shiori*, of *Matsuo Bashō. It suggests a depth of meaning in a stanza along with subtlety of expressive intent.

Hosshitan 法師譚 or **shukketan** 出家譚. Stories about taking orders. Most of these are told in the first person and have some likeness to Western conversion literature. An individual is made aware of spiritual faults more or less suddenly, the awareness leading to amendment of life and taking orders. Examples include some stories in part 19 of the *Konjaku Monogatari and *Kamo no Chōmei's *Hosshinshū*.

Hyakuin 百韻. A *renga* or *haikai* sequence of one hundred stanzas.

Hyakushu(uta) 百首(歌). A sequence or composite poem of one hundred poems. One of a number of lengths of sequences of *tanka*, whether by one, several, or one hundred people, in which last case the compiler would usually be another person, as for the *(Ogura) Hyakunin Isshu* (see *Fujiwara Teika.) A distinctive kind of sequence, integrated by associative and progressive techniques, flourished in the Kamakura period, often using as model all or part of a *chokusenshū*, so producing in a hyakushuuta a poem of five hundred lines. In number and in techniques of joining poem to poem, it helped define *renga*.

Hyōbanki 評判記. An Edo term for writing dealing with, or evaluating, the persons and skills of geisha or actors.

Ihon 異本. Another or variant text. A lesser, later, or otherwise alternative text.

Iisute 言ひ捨て. An irregular and not large number of stanzas for a *renga* or *haikai* sequence, usually a casual production not felt worthy of recording.

Iki 粋. The stylish, smart, or elegant, a term used between 1804 and 1840 and identified with Edo, especially with usage by the Fukagawa or downtown (shitamachi) geisha. A counterpart of the earlier *kamigata* term *sui*, and opposed to *yabo*. It is also closely associated with connoisseurship of what is in vogue, *tsū*.

Imayō 今様. Present-day songs. (1) Newly popular songs. (2) Especially popular songs of the middle of the Heian period, usually sung by female entertainers such as *kugutsu*(shi) and later by *shirabyōshi*. Thus, a variety of *kayō* and, when accompanied by dance, of *utamai*.

Imikotoba 忌詞. Taboo words. (1) Words banned on occasions such as New Year's or weddings. (2) The words used in lieu of those in (1) for euphemistic purposes.

Insei 院政. Government by cloistered sovereigns. In an effort to recapture power from nonroyal ministerial houses, Shirakawa (r. 1072–1086) began the practice of early abdication from the onerous ritual duties of the nominal ruler in order to exercise power in retirement. While reigning, a given figure—*Gotoba, for example—would be styled Gotoba Tennō 天皇 and, after abdication, Gotoba In 院. It is usual to use the later designation to identify the figure. The insei system had some success, and certainly eased the lives of those who abdicated. But efforts to gain substantial power were usually vain or successful only briefly, as Gotoba's own case shows. The insei system is one of the many manifestations of Japanese ways of governing, involving manipulation of charismatic sovereignty so that a person (usually persons) other than the nominal, ritual sovereign held power. See *bakufu*; see Part Nine C.

Irogonomi 好色(色好). The characters are also read *kōshoku*. (1) In Heian times, matters concerned with love, or persons who understand its nature. (2) In plays and fiction of the Edo period, especially an amorous male of a gentle, passive kind. (3) The same as *kōshoku* (2).

Iroha uta 伊呂波歌. Before the two syllabaries, katakana and hiragana, were arranged in the modern fashion (a-i-u-e-o, etc.), a poem was made using forty-seven, or most, of the syllables: "n" is the conspicuous omission. This poem became a child's first step in *tenarai*. By memorizing the poem, the child learned as it were the alphabet; and the order of the syllables became the basis for arranging compiled information: see Part Six Q, Dictionaries. The poem follows in six versions.

Katakana	Hiragana
イロハニホヘト	いろはにほへと
チリヌルヲ	ちりぬるを
ワカヨタレソ	わかよたれそ
ツネナラム	つねならむ
ウヰノオクヤマ	うゐのおくやま
ケフコエテ	けふこえて
アサキユメミシ	あさきゆめみし
ヱヒモセス	ゑひもせす

Transliteration	Modern Romanizing
I-ro ha ni-ho-he-to	Iro wa nioedo
Chi-ri-nu-ru wo	Chirinuru o
Wa-ka yo ta-re so	Waga yo tare zo
Tsu-ne na-ra-mu	Tsune naran
U-wi no o-ku-ya-ma	Ui no okuyama
Ke-fu ko-e-te	Kyō koete
A-sa-ki yu-me mi-shi	Asaki yume miji
We-hi mo se-su.	Ei mo sezu.

Usual Japanese

色は匂へど
散りぬるを
我世誰ぞ
常ならむ
有為の奥山
今日越えて
浅き夢みじ
酔もせず

Translation

Although flowers glow with color,
    They are quickly fallen,
And who in this world of ours
    Is free from change?
The mountain of mundane illusion
    Must be crossed today,
Parting from our shallow dreaming,
    Never drunk again.

Traditionally ascribed to *Kūkai, this poem is now believed to date from the mid-Heian period.

Ji 地. (1) Plain. In *renga* and *haikai*, less impressive stanzas, as opposed to mon 文 more impressive ones. Intermediate kinds can be distinguished: ji-mon or plain-design, and mon-ji or design-plain. One important element of sequential art is varying the degree of impressiveness. See *renga*. (2) The chorus in *nō*; that is, an abbreviation of *jiutai*. See also Part Five A.

Jiamari 字余り. Hypermetric lines. In *waka*, *renga*, and *haikai*, a line might easily have more than five or seven syllables. Hypometric lines (jitarazu) were not allowed after very early poetry. Usually the superfluity is of but one syllable, and often involves elided vowels. But a famous *hokku* by *Matsuo Bashō has two (or three) extra in its second line: Kareeda ni / karasu no tomarikeri [tomaritaru ya]/aki no kure.

Jidaidammari. See *dammari*.

Jidaimono 時代物. Classification for *jōruri* and *kabuki*: plays dealing with subjects in earlier periods; opposed to *sewamono*. Further distinguished into *ōdaimono*, plays dealing with the court nobility and their time of flourishing; and *oiemono*, plays dealing with the houses of daimyō and/or samurai. See Part Five I.

Jiguchi 地口. Punning talk or other word play.

Jikaawase 自歌合. A poetry match with oneself. A late 12th-c. ff. version of *utaawase*. A poet would set topics and compose rival poems, often by fictional authors, or simply by "left" and "right" sides. The result was usually submitted to someone respected for judgment at utaawase; for example, *Saigyō, *Mimosusogawa Utaawase*, submitted to *Fujiwara Shunzei.

Jindai moji 神代文字. Divine script; written characters of the age of the gods. It was once mistakenly believed that Japan possessed such a writing system before the end of the third century or so, when Chinese characters were introduced. *Hirata Atsutane was one of those who argued for their existence.

Jingi 神祇. Shinto. A topic for poems or classification in a collection. See *dai* and *chokusenshū*.

Ji (no bun) 地(の分). Narrative, narrated portions. The term has developed for criticism of the *Genji Monogatari* to designate normal third-person narrative as distinguished from characters' dialogue or speech (*kotoba*), characters' inner thoughts (*shinnaigo*), narrator's comments (*sōshiji*), or authorial intrusion (*sakusha no kotoba*).

Jitarazu 字足らず. Hypometric line. See *jiamari*.

Jiutai 地謡. The *nō* chorus, given to speaking the words or thoughts of *shite* characters rather than participating as a character. Also abbreviated to *ji* (2).

Jo 序. Preface. (1) The introductory parts of a work or volume. (2) The use of some lines in a *waka* to prepare for a later idea or word(s); also called jokotoba, joshi. The point of juncture may involve simile, sound, or logical connection. See also the next entry.

Jo-ha-kyū 序破急. Preparation-development-fast finale. A sequential rhythmic principle begun with *gagaku* and subsequently developed metaphorically for "pace" in *renga*, which bequeathed the principle to *nō*, *haikai*, and other kinds of literature. The jo tends to be elevated or smooth; the ha (more literally "breaking") to be more agitated and various; and the kyū to be climactic, quickly successive, or given to other resolution, although it normally ended in poise or rest—completion.

Jōruri 浄瑠璃. A large variety of kinds of performance go under this name, including kinds of *heikyoku*. They have in common musical accompaniment of the related plots. In somewhat later kinds, the *shamisen* became the instrument of accompaniment. Although the subject matter continued to vary widely, after the old jōruri, *kojōruri*, three versions have dominated discussion. (1) Performance with puppets (ningyō *jōruri*, ningyō geki), which required three crucial human functions—playwright, reciter, and puppet manipulator, with the reciter counted most important. (2) Stage performance by actors (*kabuki* jōruri). (3) Casual performances in a hall or street. Kind (1), with *Gidayū* relation, is the idealized kind. Early kinds (see *kojōruri*, *kyōgen*) were longer and had interludes. Subsequently the five-act kind dropped to three (see *aikyōgen*), and later the five- and three-act kinds were maintained without interludes. The plays came to be distinguished by the nature of the period dealt with—the past or present (*jidaimono* in five acts; *sewamono* in three), although other distinctions were also made and the two kinds later were sometimes merged. *Kabuki* proper would have been impossible without the development of jōruri. See Part Five D.

Joryū bungaku 女流文学. Literature by women. Although men often wrote *monogatari* for women up to the eleventh century and other kinds of work thereafter, in Japan women have been esteemed as writers since ancient times. From the tenth century, and even later, to the dominance of society by warriors, women produced much of the greatest Japanese literature. For representative major writers, see: *Ono no Komachi, *Murasaki Shikibu, *Sei Shōnagon, and *Izumi Shikibu. The term is sometimes taken to be dismissive, pejorative—as if literature by women is not quite literature normatively considered.

Joshi 序詞. See *jo*.

Jōza 定座. Appointed place. The formally stipulated places in *renga* and *haikai* for moon and flower stanzas to appear, as hana no za.

Jugaku 儒学. Confucianism, Confucian studies. See *kogaku* and Part Six P.

Jūsandaishū 十三代集. The collections of thirteen eras. See *chokusenshū*.

Kabane 姓. In ancient Japan, appellations of court office or rank. The Yamato court had dozens, of which the chief were: omi 臣, muraji 連, miyatsuko 造, kimi 君, atai 直, fubito 史, agatanushi 県主, and suguri 村主. In 684, after the Taika Reform, Temmu reorganized the offices or ranks within a yakusa 八色 no kabane. In descending order, these were: mahito 真人, asomi 朝臣, sukune 宿彌, imiki 忌寸, michinoshi 道師, omi 臣, muraji 連, and inagi 稲置. Kabane gradually faded away; first kabane became the hereditary rights of given clans (uji 氏), then the clans themselves divided into families (ie

家), which in turn divided according to an individual's succession of ranks at court. See Part Nine A. The full designation of familiar *Man'yōshū* poets is, then, Kakinomoto no Asomi no Hitomaro, Ōtomo no Sukune no Yakamochi. In the course of time most of the titles disappeared, but a few were kept in usage, even if under different pronunciation (asomi became ason) and with differing meaning (ason came to designate noble males). The simplest translation for all the kabane when they were in full use is probably "lord" or "lady."

Kabu 歌舞. Song and dance. Performances involving singing and dancing of various kinds. Also a general term for such elements combined, and opposed to such things as fully developed drama that may also use these elements. See *utamai*.

Kabuki 歌舞伎. Originally, strange song and dance; the present third character was fixed ·in the Meiji period. Various seemingly strange—perhaps with overtones of the erotic (hence kabuki, or the verb kabuku) combinations of dance, theater, and song began to appear well before the Edo period. Several places, at first religious, were involved, but Kyoto became the first center. Young women with hair cut short might act men's roles with swords and male garb, singing *kouta* and dancing *odori*. This became traditionally identified with an actress, Okuni, who set up a troupe along the Kamo River in Kyoto: in 1603, according to one account. But the name seems to have designated a succession of women. The entertainment spread around the country. In 1629 the government banned it, charging the women with loose morals. Young men replaced them, till another ban in 1652 for similar reasons. At last men became actors (adult male sexuality seems to have bothered authorities less). In developing to what is known today, kabuki drew on many *nō* for stories but chiefly on *jōruri*. As with the stories by *Ihara Saikaku, kabuki expressed the milieu, concerns, and amusements of townspeople, *chōnin*. Osaka and Edo were the two major centers. Various subjects are treated: the legendary or supernatural (*Kokusen'ya*, *Tsuchigumo*), the military (*Kanjinchō*, *Chūshingura*), current happenings (*Sonezaki Shinjū*, *Shinjū Ten no Amijima*) and the celebratory (*Sambasō*). Above all, kabuki is an actors' theater, and the players have made individual plays into vehicles for their own styles and personality. See Part Five E.

Kabukikyōgen 歌舞伎狂言. The older, formal name for *kabuki*, individual examples or parts of which may still be termed kyōgen. See Part Five E.

Kachō(ga) 花鳥(画). Flowers and birds. Painting of natural scenes of a somewhat small focus. The flowers are commonly those of trees, and in poetry there are some specific association, as of the warbler (uguisu) with the plum. Butterflies, other insects, animals, or plants may be included. **Kachō fūgetsu** 風月: literally, flowers and birds, wind and moon. 1. The most beautiful scenery, as in nature or in painting, or imagined in literature. 2. Elegant pastimes; *furyū* activities. **Kachō gessetsu** 月雪. Flowers and birds, moon and snow. The essentially seasonal elements of each of the four seasons; therefore also the seasons themselves. See *sansui*, *sōmoku*.

Kaeshiuta 返歌. The same as *hanka*.

Kagamimono 鏡物 Mirror works. Historical works, *rekishimonogatari*, with "kagami" in their titles: conspicuously, **Ōkagami*, **Imakagami*, **Mizukagami*, and **Masukagami* (but usually not **Azuma Kagami*).

Kagura 神楽. Gods' music. (1) Also kamiasobi, gods' dances. A dance with music by three instruments and later sometimes a fourth used in Shinto rites. (2) A version of (1), also called satokagura. (3) Adaptations for *kyōgen* and *kabuki*.

Kahei. See uta no yamai.

Kaibunuta 回(廻)文歌. A poem that is a palindrome.

Kaidan(mono) 怪談(物) See *sewamono*.

Kaiwabun 会話文. Speech or dialogue elements in a narrative. A modern term, the same in meaning as *kotoba* (3). See *ji*.

Kakekotoba 掛詞. Pivot word. Use of a series of sounds to mean two things: for example, "Hono-bono to / *Akashi* no ura no," where "akashi" means the place, Akashi, and to "dawn," so meaning something like, "Faintly, faintly *dawn* / *Breaks Akashi Bay*."

Kakushidai 隠題. Concealed topic. In *waka* or *renga*, various means of incorporating a topic or a message into a poem. The first syllables of lines might be used to yield a word (like "iris"-ka-ki-tsu-ha[ba] ta); or the word might be represented by the last syllables of lines; or by syllables bridging successive lines; or one might use the first syllables down of the lines of a poem and the last syllables up, etc. In the **Kokinshū* these acrostics are termed mono no na 物名 (book 10). See *oriku*.

Kambun 漢文. Composition, by Japanese, of prose in Chinese. To facilitate reading such composition, or prose by Chinese, Japanese have developed systems of marks, *okurigana*, etc., enabling them to adapt Chinese syntactic order to Japanese. See *wabun*, *wakan konkōbun*, *kanshi*.

Kambun kundoku 漢文訓読. Reading of Chinese prose in the fashion of Japanese syntax, etc.

Kamiasobiuta 神遊歌. Songs in *kagura*.

Kamigata 上方. The Kyoto-Osaka area; or designation of works produced there during the Edo period.

Kaminō. A class of *nō* pieces; see *gobammemono* and Part Five A.

Kami no ku 上の句. Upper stanza, lines. In *tanka*, the initial three lines in 5-7-5 syllables, in distinction to the shimo no ku, or lower stanza, that is, two lines, in 7-7 syllables; in *haiku* the first, 5-syllable line. See *ku*.

Kamiuta 神歌. Divinities' songs. (1) A poem in such *kayō* as *imayō* and treating Shinto matters, or a similar composition. (2) The words in *nō* by an Old Man (okina), but for such purpose the characters are usually pronounced "shinka."

Kana 仮名. Phonetic syllabary. Two types developed out of *kanji*, the Chinese characters. Katakana is the more angular, and today is used (though not formerly) for foreign words, telegrams, and special emphasis; and hiragana, the more cursive, which is used today in place of *kanji*, for particles, inflections, and certain kinds of stress. Modern hiragana is a descendant of various earlier versions now usually called hentaigana. Kana were the basis of a considerable literature (*kanabungaku*) in the Heian period, either by women or written for them by men, or writing of like kinds. See *iroha uta*.

Kanabun 仮名文. *Kana* writing. Writing entirely or mostly in syllabic characters as opposed to writing making exclusive use of Chinese characters, *kanji*. Also things written in *kana*. Therefore especially the literature written by women in the Heian period. See *onnade*.

Kana hōgo 仮名法語. Vernacular tracts. In contrast to the formal sermons (hōgo), usually composed in Chinese by eminent Buddhist priests, the vernacular tracts are in the standard written Japanese of their day. Although the word *kana* (cf. *kanazōshi*) suggests that these works employed the syllabary exclusively, they did in fact maintain the usual proportion of characters to kana. These popular tracts began to appear prominently in the Kamakura period, along with the new movements of Buddhism. When stories were used to illustrate the argument they approached the form of Buddhist tale literature (*bukkyō setsuwa*), but they are distinguished from that genre by a higher ratio of sermon to anecdote.

Kanahon 仮名本. Books in *kana*. Stories of the Edo period, written entirely or mostly in hiragana (see *kana*) for people with little education in reading and mostly given to entertainment. Numerous kinds followed each other in popularity. For contrast, see *yomihon*.

Kana(no)shi 仮名 (の) 詩 or **Washi** 和詩. A bizarre, minor kind of poetry in which the five- or seven-character (or other lines) of Chinese poetry are emulated in *kanabun* so as to write a "Chinese" poem in Japanese. It is an invention (among others) of the very eccentric *Kagami Shikō.

Kanazōshi 仮名草子. Books in the vulgar script. Books or shorter stories more or less easily read, being written for children and the poorly lettered. Preceded *ukiyozōshi*.

Kanji 漢字. Chinese written characters. See *kana*.

Kanshi 漢詩. Composition, by Japanese, of Chinese poetry.

Kanzen chōaku 勧善懲悪. Poetic justice; moral improvement; didacticism. Commonly abbreviated to kanchō, using just the first and third characters. The phrase kanchō shōsetsu (didactic prose narrative) was first used by Tsubouchi Shōyō (1859–1935), although in other contexts it dates from the age of *Shōtoku Taishi and Chinese writing. The very cumbersomeness of the longer term testifies to Japanese disfavor for the didacticism and moralizing long popular in China and Korea. But the *yomihon* of *Kyokutei Bakin provide lengthy and impressive examples from classical literature.

Kaomise 顔見世. Showing the face. The first run of the annual *kabuki* season, beginning on the first of the eleventh Month (lunar calendar). For other runs, see Part Five E.

Karon 歌論. Poetic discussion. Criticism, practical or theoretical, related to *waka*. At first it was more or less a counterpart of Chinese poetics (shigaku), which continued to influence Japanese poetics. But with *Ki no Tsurayuki's preface to the *Kokinshū (905), an indigenous poetics was formed by adapting Chinese poetics to Japanese literature, as the Romans did the Greeks, as the moderns did the ancients, and so on. Japanese are specially given to insisting on the uniqueness of their language, culture, and people—in past times and now.

Karumi 軽み. Lightness. A stylistic ideal of a lighter, less tense, or simpler kind of *haikai*, especially for *hokku*, advocated by *Matsuo Bashō in his last years.

Karuta カルタ or sometimes 歌留多. (1) Any of a number of card games involving matching of one part of a poem or element with another or an entirety. Varieties include utakaruta, irohakaruta, hanagaruta, etc. (2) In particular, a game of the kind

of (1) specifically involving the one hundred poems of *Fujiwara Teika's model collection, *Hyakunin Isshu*. The pastime is associated with, but by no means confined to, New Year's and family participation.

Kasen 歌仙 Poetic sage or sages. 1. A poetic sage, famous poet: see *rokkasen* and *sanjūrokkasen*. 2. A *haikai* sequence of thirty-six stanzas, the name being derived from the sanjūrokkasen.

Kashū (1) 歌集. Also written in a way that may be read as ie no shū 家集; also similar to *shikashu*: private collection. In contrast to a *chokusenshū* or *shisenshū* that collects poems by many writers, this gives, or purports to give, poems by a single author. One of the earliest is the (*Kakinomoto) Hitomaro *Kashū*, although extant examples raise problems of its authenticity. The most beloved by Japanese is no doubt *Saigyō's *Sankashū*. The distinctions between a kashū and a *nikki* or *monogatari* are not always clear, and some works are variously classified (such as *Ise Monogatari, *Ono no Takamura Monogatari, *Izumi Shikibu Nikki, *Kenrei Mon'in Ukyō no Daibu Shū—see under author's names). Works variously classified tend to have a single central figure, with numerous poems by that person and perhaps others exchanged with that person, and some prose context. A poetic diary is thought of as written sequentially about events by the person whose poems are included, and a monogatari as written in the perfect aspect by someone other than the person(s) to whom the poems are attributed. Kashū are thought of as having been made by the poet and focus on the poems, without a presumption of sustained plots. Kashū commonly have the poet's name with (ka)shū added: (such as *Ise Shū), but fancier titles, like Saigyō's, are not uncommon; see Part Six A. And for distinctions, see *monogatari*. (2) 花修. Preparation for the flower. A term of *Zeami's, designating means toward realizing his artistic ideal.

Katagimono 気質物. A species of story dealing with humbler people and their doings, popularized by *Ejima Kiseki.

Katari 語り. Relation, particularly of prose narative, but applied more generally. See *monogatari*.

Kataribe 語部. Reciters. From preliterate into literate times, a group that memorized and recited events or compositions of traditional importance. See *kabane*.

Katarimono 語物. Narrated matters. Those parts of a drama that are narrated, as distinguished both from those parts that are presented in natural exchange of dialogue and those that are highly songlike. See *kayō* (2).

Kataudo 方人. Persons constituting a side. In *utaa-wase* and matches of other kinds, the left or the right group or side seeking to outmatch the other.

Katauta 片歌. Half poem. A minor kind of *waka*, using as it were the *kami no ku*, upper stanza, of a *tanka* (5-7-5 syllables) as an entire poem. It is most important for use in song texts in *gagaku* and its dance.

Kayō 歌謡. Songs. (1) Poems of a melodic kind, and especially those sung aloud or those made expressly for singing. (2) A more melodic part in drama, opposed to narrative elements, *katarimono*. (3) Specific examples of the above, making a corpus of songs so labeled, as kiki kayō, songs from the *Kojiki* and *Nihongi*.

Kazuramono 鬘物. A class of *nō* pieces; see *goban-memono* and Part Five A.

Kei 軽. Lightness. In *Matsuo Bashō's haikai* terminology, a stanzaic connection in which verbal and conceptual elements provide only a remote connection with the preceding stanza. The same as *so*; see *shinku*.

Ki 記 or sometimes 紀. (1) Historical or factual account; records—either with or without a distinction between this kind and literature. The usual character is the last in the title, *Kojiki*, and the less usual is the last last for *Nihon Shoki*. Cf. kiroku, kikō. (2) (the first character) One of several categories of writing (fu 賦 den 伝, etc.) taken by Japanese from the Chinese collection, *Monzen* (*Wen Hsüan*; *Poetic Selections*) and used in *Fūzoku Monzen* and *Yokoi Yayū's Uzuragoromo*, etc.

Kibyōshi 黄表紙. Yellow-covered books with popular stories, but for adults, unlike earlier colored-cover books. Some accounts say they were popular 1770–1805, others from 1804 on. Their illustrations were sometimes colored. See *gesaku*, *sōshi*, and Part Ten, Fig. 91.

Ki(chiku)mono 鬼(畜)物. Specter plays. The same as *gobanmemono* and *kirinō*, the fifth category of *nō*. See Part Five A.

Kidai 季題. Seasonal topic, a modern term. In *renga* and *haikai*, stanzas are distinguished as to topic either by having a kidai or being *zō*, miscellaneous. The seasonal topic is indicated by use of seasonal words, kigo. Thus, "kasumi" (haze) designates spring, "yūsuzumi" (evening cool) summer, and so on; see *hon'i*.

Kikō(bungaku) 紀行(文学). Travel (literature). Most generally, writing in prose (Japanese or Chinese) that expresses feelings, thoughts, or details of travel, with appreciation of famous places, *uta-makura*. More particularly, an account in prose or prose with verse of a particular journey. *Ki no Tsurayuki's Tosa Nikki* is the first of such classics in Japanese. *Matsuo Bashō's Oku no Hosomichi* (in prose with *haikai* stanzas and a few *tanka*) is no doubt the greatest. Bashō also wrote kikō without poems. See *nikki bungaku*, *haibun*, and *tabi no uta*.

Kinuginu 衣衣, 後朝. Morning parting. In early marriage practice and in amours and courtly love lore, a man visited a woman in the evening. The pair slept under their piled robes, which each severally put on in the morning as the man prepared to part. The act of preparation, the parting, and the (very early) morning are all referred to by the term. After returning home, the man was expected to send the woman a kinuginu no fumi (文) whose bearer was a kinuginu no tsukai (使). In the letter there would probably be a poem, and from the practice arose kinuginu no *koi* as a fictional love topic. In a love sequence, this stage follows au koi, love meetings.

Kireji 切字. Cutting words or syllables. In *renga* and *haikai*, expressions ending a stanza or line, such as kana, -keri, ran, ya, etc. Certain stanzas (such as the first and third) were supposed to employ them, and other stanzas doing so were expected to be *kami no ku*. *Matsuo Bashō* insisted for haikai that even the *hokku* (first stanza) might be a kireku (cut stanza) without using kireji.

Kirinō. A class of *nō* pieces; see *gobanmemono* and Part Five A.

Kirishitan bungaku. See *Christian bungaku*.

Kirokugaki 記録書. Record abbreviations. Simplified characters used in lieu of complex ones for ease in making records.

Kiyose 季寄. Seasonal index, a modern term. A listing of seasonal topics and words indicating the topics for use in *haikai* composition: also called saijiki.

Kiyoshi. See *sei*.

Kizewamono 生世話物. See *sewamono*.

Koado 小アド. The second *ado*, that is, supporting role, in *kyōgen*. Cf. *omoado*.

Kōan 公案. Paradoxical questions for illumination. Rinzai and Ōbaku Zen sects use kōan, a so-to-speak catechetical question whose aura is an impossibility or so great a simplicity as not to seem to need an answer, the purpose being to stimulate the process of enlightenment.

Kobore-こぼれ 零れ etc. Spilled over. In *renga* and *haikai* a moon or flower stanza (e.g., koborezuki) that appears later than its appointed place, *jōza*. See *hikiage*.

Kogaki 小書. Little writing. Textual variants between one school or another of *nō* and *kyōgen*.

Kogaku 古学. (1) Pristine Confucianism. This is something of an assorted variety of Edo Neoconfucianism. Some thinkers sought to overcome what they considered the limitations of Neoconfucianism of the orthodox *Shushigaku* and its main rival, *Yōmeigaku*. The kogaku proponents argued that it was necessary to go back to older, more reliable sources to reform the corruptions that had grown. As so often happened in Japan and China (and the Protestant Reformation), so for these thinkers: the advocacy of the pristine was a means of advocating the new. Among the most important of these revisionists are *Yamaga Sokō, *Itō Jinsai, and *Ogyū Sorai—although many might wish to put the last in a category by himself. (2) *Kokugaku*, second sense.

Kohitsugire 古筆切. Old writing by sheets. A particularly elegant style of writing that flourished in the Heian and Kamakura periods. Only a few lines would be written per page. Much favored by tea masters subsequently.

Kohon 小本. Small book; another term for *sharebon*, *kusazōshi*, or *ninjōbon*.

Kohon 古本. Old book. In textual scholarship, early versions of a work.

Kōhon 校本. Edited text. A modern term for an editor's text established by collation of various textual versions and lines.

Koi 恋. Love. A principal topic for poems and classification for collections. In *chokusenshū*, the second half invariably begins with a few books on this topic, and in *renga* and *haikai* (where it is a subtopic of a season or miscellaneous, *zō*), it agitates the sequence. It is normally taken to mean unrequited yearning, not being loved, and becomes darker in tone in later times, although even in *renga* one of the many versions, au koi, or a love meeting, may have a momentary joy that sets off the misery that precedes or follows. Books of love poems are especially agitated and given to variance in tone. See *dai*, *chokusenshū*, and *hon'i*.

Kojōruri 古浄瑠璃. Old *jōruri*. That up to and including the early practice of *Chikamatsu Monzaemon and *Takemoto Gidayū, with whom jōruri proper begins. In the mid-fifteenth century there appeared a rhythmic version of the sad story of

Ushiwaka (young Minamoto Yoshitsune) and his lover, Jōruri Gozen, whose name provides the traditional origin of jōruri.

Kokindenju 古今伝授. *Kokinshū* learning. Teaching of the *Kokinshū* as the first and most esteemed, in classical times, of the *chokusenshū*. Disciples were to write down the main points from their master's transmittal of secret lore. Too often such learning degenerated into pedantry over small points learned at high fee. Yet important people were involved: *Fujiwara Shunzei and his son, *Fujiwara Teika, as well as *Sōgi among poets; *Tō no Tsuneyori and *Sanjōnishi Sanetaka among learned noblemen, and *Hosokawa Yūsai among learned warriors.

Kokkeibon 滑稽本. Humorous, witty, or similarly stylish stories of the later Edo period by writers such as *Shikitei Samba. See *sōshi* and *gesaku*.

Kokoro 心. Heart, mind, spirit, conception. (1) In *waka* and later criticism, a polar term with *kotoba*. Kokoro represents the capacity for being affected, the conception resulting, and the informing cognitive element. See *kotoba* and *sugata*. (2) Sensibility, right conception, as in reference to a person or poem (kokoro aru), or a classification of such features (*ushin*).

Kokorozuke 心付. Conceptual connection. In *renga* and *haikai*, the relation of one stanza to the former in a sequence by intellectual, cognitive connection rather than verbal association. Opposed to *kotobazuke*.

Kokubungaku 国文学. National literature, i.e., Japanese literature, not to be confused with *kokugaku*. A modern term, coined in line with European conceptions, it suggests study of Japanese literature, and its closest counterpart is probably Nationalliteratur Wissenschaft. Cf. *bungaku* and *bungei*.

Kokugaku 国学. National studies. Studies and institutions of various kinds have been so named, including: (1) learning taught elsewhere than the capital; (2) a special school set apart for various studies (this ended in the late Heian period); more especially, (3) a line of specifically Japanese studies opposed to those of Chinese, Confucianism, Buddhism, and other foreign learning. The third sense refers particularly to a great Edo achievement, with representative kokugakusha that included *Keichū, *Kamo no Mabuchi, *Motoori Norinaga, and so on down to *Hirata Atsutane. Kokugaku flourished to the end of the classical period, laying the foundations of Japanese scholarship to the present, even as it developed out of medieval commentaries and concerns as in sense (2). Kokugaku often dealt with texts such as the *Kojiki*, *Man'yōshū*, or *Genji Monogatari*, or with topics such as language, Shinto, and fief study (hangaku).

Komponka 混本歌. Meaning unknown. This is one of the prosodic kinds mentioned in the Chinese preface to the *Kokinshū*. Some think it designates a kind repeating a *shimo no ku* (which would make it a *sedōka*), or others that it involves a repeated *kami no ku*.

Konnyakubon 蒟蒻本. Another term for *sharebon*.

Kosaibari 小前張. Part of the latter half of a *kagura*, whether mostly sung or instrumental; textually the oldest portion of these Shinto rites.

Kōshoku 好色. 1. The same as *irogonomi* (2). 2. A character or kind of writing devoted to sexual activity, as in writings by *Ihara Saikaku and other *ukiyozōshi* writers.

Kōshokubon 好色本. Books with erotic or at least prominent amatory emphasis. Some of the stories first imported from China and some last written in the Edo period belong to this category, as do in part classics such as the *Genji Monogatari* and much especially of the writing by *Ihara Saikaku and *ukiyozōshi* in general. Such stories are everywhere. In Japan they have flourished in times of peace and isolation, and have often disappeared during times of struggle and feverish importation of the foreign.

Koten 古点. Old markings. (1) Marks to assist in reading old Chinese or Buddhist writing. (2) Similar marks, devised in the Heian period to assist in reading the *Man'yōshū*. Also called *kunten*.

Koten 古典. A modern term for the classics or the classical; contrasting with gendai or modern, it designates the span of literature covered in this book, that is, from the beginnings to 1868.

Kotengeki 古典劇. Classical drama. A somewhat vague modern term, usually designating the chief kinds of classical theater—*nō*, *kyōgen*, *jōruri*, *kabuki*—as well as their various antecedents.

Kotenpon 古点本. A book marked with *koten* or *kunten*.

Kotoba 詞(言葉). Words, diction, subject matter. (1) In *waka* and subsequent criticism, a polar term with *kokoro*. Kotoba represents that which has been expressed by an affected poet—language, materials, subjects; so also the literary expression. See *kokoro*, *sugata*. (2) In picture scrolls (*emaki*), the writing or legends accompanying the pictures. (3) Characters' speech or dialogue in a narrative; also called kaiwaibun. In derivation and early usage, matters are far more complex, involving relations between a number of Chinese characters used for "koto" or "kotoba," and widely variant meanings. The usage here is a specialized one; cf. *ji*.

Kotobagaki 詞書. Headnote. A statement of the circumstances of composition or of the topic (see *dai, daiei*) of a poem. The former tends to be less formal, the latter more. But a given headnote might combine the two possibilities: "Composed at my son's house on the topic, 'A Distant View of the Sea.'" Some kotobagaki are long enough to present a mini-narrative element, like the prose parts of the *Ise Monogatari*; in some instances in *chokusenshū* they seem to be fictional or otherwise made up by compilers.

Kotobazuke 言葉付. Word connection. In *renga* and *haikai*, the relation of one stanza to the former in a sequence by verbal or sound associations. Opposed to *kokorozuke*.

Kotodama 言霊. The word spirit. In early times it was believed that great power, for good or ill, dwelt in words, and that the power might be released by appropriate, or even accidental, recital. The result of an activated kotodama was called a kotoage 言挙. By the time of the *Man'yōshū*, the concept seems to have been softened to designate only a power to do good. In the *Kojiki* the powers to harm are also evident. The idea has counterparts around the world, and is particularly closely related to that of the supernatural power (mana) resident in persons or things in the beliefs of various Pacific people.

Kotsuzumi 小鼓. Drum. See *hayashi*.

Kouta 小歌. Short songs. (1) Songs of various and now uncertain kind distinguished at the Heian court from others kept in the Bureau of Traditional Songs (*ōutadokoro*). (2) In the Muromachi period, songs of popular origin taken on by higher classes. (3) One of the kinds of song in *kyōgen*. (4) An exceptional kind of song chanting in *nō*, probably taken from (2). Also 小唄: (1) Early Edo popular songs. (2) Short popular songs accompanied by the *shamisen*. (3) A late Edo kind of popular song.

Kōwakamai 幸若舞. Developed in the Muromachi period, a kind of drama featuring military stories, like those in the *Heike Monogatari*, mimed with dance by actors to the accompaniment of music and a chanted narrative, with some parts marked as speeches (*kotoba*). Descended from kusemai of *nō*, it is akin to *Mibu kyōgen* and a precursor of *jōruri*: see Part Five C.

Ku 句. Line(s), part, or stanza. The sense of stanza developed in *renga* and *haikai* and was extended to include a separate *hokku* or a *haiku*. For the sense of part, see *kami no ku*. Japanese do not emphasize lines as much as do Westerners, especially the Greeks, who tended to identify poetic kinds by the prosody of lines. But ku does designate line(s), as various evidence shows. Such is the usage for lines of Chinese poetry and (in similar fashion) sūtras. There are also some usages meaning "lines" in classical criticism, such as *Komparu Zenchiku's phrase on "matters of 5-7, 5-7 lines" ("go-shichi, go-shichi no ku no koto"). Thus *kami no ku* means both the upper lines and the upper portion of a *tanka*.

Kū 空. Skt. Śūnya, śūnyatā: the Void, Emptiness, Relativity, Interdependence, Nothingness, etc.; also (from the Japanese reading of the character), sora, "sky," which can be used as its symbol. Such celestial imagery in *waka* sometimes has figural implication.

In order to explain the fact of impermanence (*mujō*) in the phenomenal world, early Buddhists (such as the Sarvāstivādins, represented by the Japanese Kusha sect; see Part Six N) postulated the existence of ultimate psychophysical elements called dharma (hō 法). The gross forms (people, dogs, houses, etc.) of the phenomenal world arose and subsided in time according to the principle of Dependent Origination (engi 縁起; Skt. pratītya-samutpāda). Since all persons and things were mere congeries of dharmas, they were without permanent self or substance (muga 無我; Skt. anātman); at the same time, Buddhism as the Middle Way sought to steer a course between the denial of continuity (and hence of moral causality), and the assertion of a permanent substance or soul.

The Mahāyāna, however, viewed Dependent Origination not as a principle of temporal sequence but as the essential dependence of things on each other, as their ultimate Emptiness (kū, śūnyatā). The Void is not an entity apart from this world but the same reality as phenomenal appearance: the world of transmigration (rinne 輪廻, saṃsāra), when properly understood is itself Nirvāṇa. Viewed as arising interdependently, all persons and things are Void, Empty of all persisting, static form; but the provisional reality (ke) of this same world is also a truth not to be denied. Hence the famous statement in the *Hannyashingyō* (Heart Sūtra; see Part Six O): "Form is no other than Emptiness, Emptiness is no other than Form" ("shiki soku ze kū, kū soku ze shiki"). To realize Emptiness (not merely conceptually with the head but experientially with the heart) is to have wisdom (chie, prajñā), which, with compassion (jihi, karuṇā), defines the Mahāyāna religious ideal, the Bodhisattva (Bosatsu). (See, for example, the definition given in the *Kongō-kyō*, the *Diamond Sūtra*.)

This central concept of Mahāyāna Buddhism, with Hīnayāna antecedents, uses negative terminology to indicate that the Absolute is ultimately devoid, empty, of all determinate characteristics. But Buddhist philosophers have always been careful to warn critics that its negative language does not argue for nihilism, for the denial of existence; rather, it uses a via negativa to lead us to the positive Ground of all

things, what in another tradition would be called the Godhead.

Kudai waka 句題和歌. Poems on famous Chinese verses or, much less frequently, on *waka* from early *chokusenshū*. A single verse or couplet would be chosen from Chinese poems or extracts (Po Chü-i was especially popular as a source in Heian times) to paraphrase, adapt, or otherwise use in writing a Japanese poem. See *dai* and *daiei*.

Kugutsu 傀儡. Small puppets and their manipulators. (1) The puppets. (2) Their manipulators (sometimes designated by the addition of "mawashi") who recited appropriate stories, and who were commonly pleasure-women. (3) Hence, such women.

Kumadori 隈取. Make-up for *kabuki* actors, sometimes amounting to little more than accentuation of human features, sometimes greatly altering facial features by the lines and colors used.

Kunten 訓点. Japanese markings. Markings of Chinese and *kambun* works so they are legible to Japanese readers. See *koten*.

Kun'yomi (or **kundoku**) 訓読. The Japanese reading as opposed to the Sinified. The character for *east*, 東, is normally read "higashi" (earlier, "himukashi," "hingashi") in kun'yomi and "tō" in the Sinified or *on'yomi* version. Also designated wakun 和訓.

Kurai 位. (1) Rank, especially court ranks. (2) The degree of dignity in a *nō* performance. See Part Nine and *kabane*.

Kurohon 黒本. Black-covered books of popular stories, ca. 1744–1751. See *gesaku*.

Kusagusa (no uta) 雑の歌. Miscellaneous poems. Also pronounced zō(ka). (1) In the *Man'yōshū* a category for poems not classified as *banka* or *sōmonka*. (2) From the *Kokinshū* onward, the term has the meanings discussed under *dai*.

Kusarirenga 鎖連歌. Chain *renga*. As opposed to *tanrenga*, it is renga properly so considered, in a sequence of some length of stanzas. The same as *chōrenga*.

Kusazōshi 草双紙. In the widest sense, illustrated fiction such as *akabon*, *kurohon*, *kibyōshi*, and *gōkan*; in the narrow sense, *gōkan*. One to six satsu of five folded sheets each; printed in large numbers for popular audience. See *gesaku*, Part One D.

Kuse 曲. One of the divisions of a *nō*, occurring near the end as part of the climax. Kusemai is the dance part of the kuse.

Kutsukaburi 沓冠. Syllable acrostics. A kind of *oriku* in which the first and last syllables of lines combine in a series to make an acrostic.

Kyō 狂. Madness. The general literary sense is that which is witty or humorous (see the following entries), when it is not used literally (as it may be in *nō*) to describe a deranged individual.

Kyōgen 狂言. Mad words. In spite of the meaning, the term came to have several important implications: (1) Drama in general. (2) That kind also known as *nōkyōgen*. This grew up with *nō*, with which it was performed, and its present character was defined in the Edo period. It usually has two or three characters, such as a daimyo and servant, or two priests, and so on. It deals as much with the earthy present world, as *nō* is apt to be concerned with another world. It admits far more action, often of a farcical kind, and its style is appropriately prosaic. (3) The character also known as *aikyōgen* or *kyōgengata*; a *nō* character, somewhat more realistic than the others, appearing in certain *nō*. (4) Interludes between acts of a five-act *kojōruri*, which would culminate with an auspicious *shūgen*. These additional parts were subsequently done away with. (5) *Kabuki* when qualified as *kabukikyōgen*. See Parts Five B, Six H.

Kyōgenbon 狂言本. Mad-word books. Illustrated books about actors, etc. circulating during the Genroku era.

Kyōgen kigo 狂言綺語. Wild words and fancy language. The characters are taken from what is no doubt the prose statement by Po Chü-i most famous in Heian and later Japan: "I have long cherished one desire, that my deeds on this earth and the faults occasioned by my wild words and fancy language shall be transformed, for worlds to come, into a factor extolling the Law and a link to the preaching of the Buddha's word. May the myriad Buddhas of the Three Worlds take heed" (*Hakushi Monju*, part 71). By itself, the phrase has been taken to depreciate literature, but in context it is usually interpreted to mean that literature is one means of extolling the Law, one means of enlightenment. This is very much what Genji concludes in the "Fireflies" chapter of *Murasaki Shikibu's Genji Monogatari*. See *hōben*.

Kyōjomono 狂女物. A class of *nō* pieces; see *gobanmemono* and Part Five A.

Kyōka 狂歌. Mad poems. *Waka* with a humorous or witty cast of language or thought. Word plays involving several meanings were especially popular. See *kyōku*.

Kyōku 狂句. Mad verse. (1) Poems using word play or low language to appeal to a popular audience. (2)

A generic term for various kinds such as *kyōka*, *kyōshi*, *senryū*, etc. (3) *Mushin* (nonstandard) *haikai*.

Kyōshi 狂詩. Mad verse. A kind of *kyōku* in Chinese verse. See *kyōku*.

Maejite 前仕手, 前ジテ. In a two-part *nō*, the disguised role taken on by the main character, *shite*, before turning to the actual role in the second part. Also maeshite. Cf. *nochijite*.

Maeku 前句. (1) In *renga* or *haikai* the preceding stanza, that is, the one to which an added stanza, *tsukeku*, is joined. In renga collections of striking added stanzas, the maeku was given with the tsukeku to make the art of the tsukeku clear. (2) In *maekuzuke*, the foundation stanza, whether in 7-7-syllable stanzas, as was usual, or in 5-7-5; to this was added a tsukeku of the alternative stanzaic length. The maeku was set by a judge (*tenja*), who furnished both the foundation stanza and judgments on attempts to join stanzas.

Maekuzuke 前句付. Connection with a preceding stanza. (1) In general, the connection of a stanza with its predecessor in a *renga* or *haikai* sequence. (2) In particular, a variously described poetic pastime in which one person, usually a master charging a fee for setting and criticizing, would provide a stanza to which one or (some say) more persons would add some four or five others. Descriptions vary as to whether the *maeku* had independent *tsukeku* added or whether the *tsukeku* were added in succession to make a brief sequence, and as to whether the *maeku* was in the *hokku* version of 5-7-5 syllables or the *waki* of 7-7 syllables. But the initial setting of a waki seems to have been usual practice. See *Karai Senryū and *Kei Kiitsu.

Magana 真仮名 (字). The same as *Man'yōgana*.

Mai 舞. Dance. Various kinds of dance, most no longer extant, usually associated with a degree of representation or presentation. Formally distinguished from *odori* in that mai involves lifting of feet and legs as a crucial feature. See also *kuse*.

Makoto 真・誠・実. Truth, sincerity, immediacy or genuineness of response, lack of art or guile. A recurrent artistic and ethical ideal, usually in response to what is deemed artificial, sophisticated. Thought to be particularly well exemplified by the poems in the *Man'yōshū*. Sometimes merely an excuse for the sentimental or platitudinous, but one of the most meaningful ideals to Japanese, in art and life.

Makurakotoba 枕詞. Pillow word. A word or phrase conventionally fixed by meaning, association, or sound to one or more words: as chihayaburu (mighty they are) for kami (the gods); or shirotae no (of white bark cloth or hemp) for sode (sleeves). Although a particular resource for poems in the *Man'yōshū* and other early writings, they continued to be coined and used into this century. See also utakotoba and utamakura.

Mana 真名・真字. Chinese characters or composition, as opposed to *kana, kanabun*, Japanese characters or composition.

Mandara 曼荼羅. Mandala, a symbolic representation of religious beings or attributes, usually portrayed as a geometrical pattern and used as a focus for meditation or ritual. In Japan the term mandala usually refers to a genre of painting—the genzu 現図 or iconographic mandala—employed in esoteric practices (mainly of the Shingon and Tendai sects; see Part Six O). The term was extended thence to include nonesoteric configurations, including diagrams of Shinto-Buddhist correlations and visions of paradise, especially as seen through the Pure Land movements.

The two basic mandalas of Japanese esotericism, the Diamond (Vajradhātu, Kongōkai 金剛界) and the Matrix (Garbhakośadhātu, Taizōkai 胎蔵界), symbolically represent, respectively, the knower and the known, by whose integration the devotee becomes the Buddha Mahāvairocana (Dainichi Nyorai 大日如来): one thus "attains Buddhahood in this very body" (sokushin jōbutsu 即身成仏). In both mandalas the main Buddha of the central constellation is Mahāvairocana. The Diamond assembly shows him surrounded on the four directions by four Buddhas, notably Amitāyus (Muryōju 無量寿) in the west. In the Matrix assembly he is surrounded by a somewhat different group of Buddhas, but with Amitābha (Muryōju 無量寿) also in the west (cf. Part Six O, Jōdo Sect). In all, the Diamond assembly represents 1,461 deities in nine groups; the Matrix represents 414 deities in twelve halls. The complexity of the various mandalas provided a special challenge to the religious craftsman, and the esoteric art of the Heian and Kamakura period is a great treasure from those times.

There were also prevalent pictures, such as the Kasuga Miya Mandara 春日宮曼荼羅 (Nezu Museum), which represented Shinto shrines and deities as local manifestations (suijaku 垂迹, traces) of various Buddhas and Bodhisattvas who were conceived of as their "Original Ground" (honji 本地).

The Pure Land hensōzu 変相図 (pictorial visions of paradise), borrowing the designation from their esoteric counterparts, are commonly referred to as mandalas. They include three famous examples: the Heian Chikō 智光 Mandala, the silk tapestry Taima 当麻 Mandala of the Nara period (possibly imported from T'ang China), and the Shōkai 清海

Mandala, also from the Heian period. In early Kamakura Pure Land devotees, including *Hōnen, were castigated by *Myōe, Jōkei and other members of the religious establishment for circulating the so-called Sesshu Fusha Mandala 摂取不捨曼陀羅 (Mandala Embracing All and Forsaking None), which depicted only those who practiced the *nembutsu* being saved. A variety of lesser-known religious paintings were also loosely referred to as mandalas.

The literary implications of this symbolism have yet to be fully studied. But see the reference to a mandala in "Suzumushi," ch. 36 (missing from the Waley translation) of *Murasaki Shikibu's Genji Monogatari, and *Zeami's Taema, with its relation to the Taima mandala.

Man'yōgana 万葉仮名. *Man'yōshū* characters. The first system of Japanese writing, preceding the *Man'yōshū* (having been used from the *Kojiki* on, and probably adapted from Korean means of using the Chinese characters). Characters are variously used: (1) to represent words—that is, they were used logographically; (2) to represent Japanese syllables phonetically; (3) to represent Japanese in a combination of (1) and (2). The method of (2) was later developed into the simplified versions of katakana and hiragana: see iroha uta, kana. The combination of (1) and (2) in the sense of modification in kana evolved into the modern written language of Japanese. An alternative, magana 真仮名(字), may be preferrable in many ways, but it does not have the same currency.

Manzai 万歳. Ten thousand years. (1) A new year's performance or performer, involving costume and drum, plea for an auspicious year, and a dance; also called senzu manzai. (2) Comic, rapid-patter dialogue of a traditional kind involving two speakers in earthy, angry, and other such scenes; presently associated mostly with the Kansai area, especially Osaka. See rakugo.

Mappō 末法. The Decline of the Law. Indian Buddhist literature includes scattered references to the notion that after the death of Shakamuni (Śākyamuni, Gautama Buddha) his teaching would gradually disappear, eventually to be succeeded by the Law of the next Buddha, Maitreya (Miroku 弥勒). During the interval immediately after the death of Shakamuni, known as the Period of the True Law (shōbō 正法), people would have the capacity both to comprehend and to practice the Buddha's teaching. In the subsequent Period of the Imitative Law (zōbō 像法), people would be able to understand the theory of the teaching but not to implement it in practice. And during the final period of the Decline of the Law (mappō 末法), they would be capable of neither. Variations in the time allotted to the three periods led to numerous interpretations, the most common in China being that the True Law lasted for 500 years and the Imitative Law for 1,000. There was general agreement that the final period would endure for 10,000.

The reasons for the currency of the idea vary enormously, but in Japan they were given currency by the popularity of the *Mappō Tōmyōki* 末法灯明記 (*The Record of the Lamp during the Latter Days*), a Heian forgery attributed to *Saichō: it is noteworthy that neither *Kūkai nor *Dōgen propounded the notion. But the work convinced many that the shōbō ran from the death of Shakamuni in 949 B.C. to a millennium beyond, and that the following second millennium of the zōbō would lead to the mappō beginning in A.D. 1052. To the pessimistic, there were many signs validating the calculation—the burning of the Hasedera and other calamities. Influenced by this thought, Fujiwara Yorimichi (990–1074) converted his villa at Uji into the temple known today as the Byōdōin or Phoenix Hall. Many associate the currency of the idea with the decline of the court, and others have seen it as a deepening of a sense of *mujō*, of transience and the vanity of human wishes.

Yet not all were so pessimistic: *Genshin, for one, wrote of means for hope. And the Pure Land movements seized on the idea to discredit older sects: yes it was about to be, or was, the period of the Decline of the Law, and therefore devotion to Amida and recitation of the *nembutsu* were required for—and would guarantee—place in the Western Paradise. So it was that the Heian forgery that dispirited many could be the grounds for hope in the Pure Land preaching of *Hōnen and *Shinran, as well as in the Lotus teaching of Nichiren.

Masuraoburi (or-gokoro) ますらおぶり（ごころ）. Manly style (spirit). A modern term used to characterize the supposed masculinity of the *Man'yōshū*.

Medetasa めでたさ. A term of praise used in discussions of *monogatari* in the *Mumyōzōshi*, designating outstanding writing. The range of meaning includes the outstanding, the splendid, the accomplished.

Mei (or akashi) 明. Brightness, truthfulness.

Meisho. See *utamakura* (2).

Meishoki 名所記. Accounts of famous places, guide books. A subclass of *kanazōshi*.

Men 面. Masks. Masks were used in *gagaku*, some Shinto rites, and were later taken up by *nō*, where they are worn by the *shite* characters. They are classified in various ways. Shikisamba is one of the oldest and is used for congratulatory pieces. Other male masks include okina; and female masks include koomote. The fact that little can be seen

through the masks helps explain why nō is slow in performance. The best have an extraordinary expressive range and are true works of art.

Mibu kyōgen 壬生狂言. A kind of pantomime theater presented annually at the Mibu Temple in Kyoto. See Part Five C.

Michi 道. The way. The term usually was taken to represent the way of the Buddha, although there were also the other ways: those of the native divinities (Shinto), Taoism, and Confucianism. In the Kamakura period and somewhat later, there were those who held that enlightenment was possible by devout exercise of one's own calling. Thus there was the uta no michi, the way of *waka* poets, the Tsukuba no michi, the way of *renga* poets, and so on. See *satori*.

Michiyuki 道行. Going on the road. A literary set piece, taking its name and settled kind in *nō*, as the entered *waki* gives an account of his journey to the place with which the play opens. But the convention exists in primitive song and some *Man'yōshū* poems. It later found its way into prose literature (such as *Heike Monogatari*) and works by authors such as *Ihara Saikaku. The most distinguished dramatic examples following *nō* are in plays by *Chikamatsu Monzaemon, as when lovers travel to their suicide, *shinjū*. On constituents of nō, see Part Five A.

Mie 見え. Manipulation of the eyes as part of a striking pose by a *kabuki* actor.

Mikasazuke 三笠付. A variety of *maekuzuke* in which three people participated, each writing one of the three lines of a *hokku*.

Minori 御法. See *nori*.

Mitogaku 水戸学. An Edo school of study originating in the Mito domain (han) and with *Tokugawa Mitsukuni. Its combination of *kokugaku*, historical, and Shinto study with Neoconfucianism proved highly influential. Some of its practitioners wrote poetry, but the school is more distinguished for its historical writings and influence on the Meiji Restoration.

Miyabi 雅. Also pronounced "ga." Courtly beauty, elegance. The aesthetic ideal of art and life during the court period, exemplified by the hero of the *Genji Monogatari*. It entails fundamental good taste, sound language and responses, and avoidance of the low or ugly. A more Japanese version of *fūryū*. See also *ga*, *kokoro*, *sama*, and *ushin*.

Mon 文. See *ji*.

Mondō 問答. Question and answer, dialogue, whether in verse or prose; cf. *serifu* for the stage. (1) In verse, the *Man'yōshū* has characteristic examples, sometimes in the two halves of a *sedōka* or in *tanrenga*. The latter lasts on, often shading off to capping of verses. The finest example of verse dialogue is *Yamanoe Okura's in *Hinkyū Mondō* (*Man'yōshū*, 5: 892–93). (2) In prose, the *renga* masters make conspicuous use of it. (3) A section of a *nō*: see Part Five A. (4) Zen dialogue between master and student to elicit an intuitive, nonconceptual response.

Monoawase 物合. A match of things. The general term for a competition involving matching pairs of things by two sides, *kataudo*, left and right. Primarily a Heian court practice. The things might be pictures (*eawase*), roots, particular flowers, and so on. See also *utaawase*.

Monogatari (bungaku) 物語（文学）. Relating of things; narrative (literature). Tales or prose narratives of various kinds, often including poems; traditionally began with the *Taketori Monogatari*, called "the parent and the first to come out of all monogatari." "Monogatari" has two meanings: to relate (*kataru*) things (*mono*), and a person (*mono*) who relates (*kataru*). History as part of literature and oral recitation are also involved. Most works thought of as monogatari use the term in the title, but there are exceptions such as *Yoru no Nezame*. Also, some works often designated monogatari may also, or more usually, be termed *nikki*, *kashū*, or *setsuwa*. And some works all but defy classification, as does *Gofukakusa In Nijō's *Towazugatari*.

On one view, however, the concept of monogatari is very simple in being the classical Japanese term for narrative: *katari* also served to that end, and in modern times the somewhat stilted joji 叙事 was invented. But Japanese taxonomies are no neater than those of other countries. Sometimes usage is simply confusing or contradictory, although usually it is clear if we think of the function presumed. Monogatari are works taken to be about someone other than the author. *Setsuwa* (sometimes termed monogatari) are usually compilations of anonymous, traditional stories. If a mostly prose work has as its function concern with its author, it is a *nikki*, or diary, in its various kinds. If a combination of prose and poems has as its chief function the presentation of the poems, it is considered an *utamonogatari*; or, if such a work is dominated in function by the poems, with less prose, it is a *kashū*. Because the function of a given work is often conceived differently, many works come with various titles. Modern criticism makes other distinctions. There are *utamonogatari* like the *Ise Monogatari* that take poems as their chief reason for being, and *tsukurimonogatari* like *Murasaki Shikibu's *Genji*

Monogatari in which the prose matters more. The mukashi monogatari are those preceding *Murasaki Shikibu's *Genji Monogatari*; monogatari indebted to, or like that work and following it (and also in some distinctions the *Sagoromo Monogatari*) are termed today *giko monogatari*. All these are further classed as tsukurimonogatari, from the mukashi monogatari to giko monogatari. Jitsuroku monogatari are those emphasizing actual, historical events; *denki monogatari* deal with marvels. Later kinds are distinguished by subject matter from those mentioned: *rekishi monogatari* deal with history, and *gunki monogatari* deal with martial matters, a distinction making better historical than logical sense. Distinctions are also made in terms of length: the long or *chōhen*, the middling or *chūhen*, and the short or *tampen*—as for the modern *shōsetsu*, a term frequently applied anachronistically to the works referred to here. The customary modern English rendering of monogatari is "tale"; the term is less than satisfactory and seems to derive from Arthur Waley's translation of the *Genji Monogatari* as *The Tale of Genji*.

Monomane 物真似. Imitation, representation. In *nō*, the practice and principle of representing a character by action; therefore mime, as opposed to *buka*, dance and words. As a general conception, a central feature of *Kan'ami's *sarugaku* aesthetic.

Mono ni yosete omoi o noburu 寄物陳思. Things as matter for poems. In the *Man'yōshū*, parts 11 and 12, poems are often classified as being concerned with (not similes for) certain phenomena: kumo (clouds) ni yosuru, and so on.

Mono no aware 物の哀. Or aware. The deep feelings inherent in, or felt from, the world and experience of it. In early classical times "aware" might be an exclamation of joy or other intense feeling, but later came to designate sadder and even tragic feelings. Both the source or occasion of such feeling and the response to the source are meant.

Mono no na 物の名. Names of things. Acrostic poems, or a book of such poems in a *chokusenshū*. See *kakushidai*.

Mugennō 夢幻能. A *nō* piece in which the role played by the main character or *shite* is that of a spirit, a divinity, or the soul of a dead person. The characters for "mugen" designate dream and mystery. This class is opposed to *genzainō*, but the opposition is not rigorous in terms of definition so much as of convention. See also *gobanmemono* and Part Five A.

Mujō(kan) 無常（感）. The inconstancy, transience of the phenomenal world; Skt., anitya. The three characteristic marks of the Buddhist teaching (sam-bōin) are (1) that all conditioned things are impermanent (shogyō mujō, as it is stated in the opening lines of the *Heike Monogatari* and in the Nirvāṇa Sūtra, *Daihatsunehangyō*); (2) that all phenomena are without self or substance (shohō muga; see *kū*); and (3) that the religious goal is the peace of nirvāṇa (nehan jakujō). Although Buddhism proposes a *solution* to the problem of worldly suffering, its formulations often emphasize the desolation of the unenlightened state and the dangers of attachment to what is transient. This outlook gave deep seriousness to writing between the Heian and Edo periods. (The earlier court literature had its counterpart also in *hakanasa*.) Many Japanese find the view best expressed in *Saigyō's poems on the fragile beauty of cherry blossoms and in his poem (*Shinkokinshū*, 4: 362), "Kokoro naki/ Mi ni mo aware wa ..." and in *Matsuo Bashō's mature style. But it runs through Japanese literature with Buddhist influence, so distinguishing it from the less Buddhist Chinese literature. See *hakanasa*, *sabi*, and *yūgen*.

Mukashi monogatari 昔物語. See *monogatari*.

Mukojo kyōgen 聟女狂言. Domestic *kyōgen* with a wife, adopted son, or son-in-law as the main character.

Mumon 無文. Designlessness, artlessness. (1) In *waka* or *renga*, great simplicity; unadorned writing. (2) In *Zeami's usage, an art that is superficially very plain but essentially very rich. Cf. *umon*.

Mushin 無心. Nonstandard, without *kokoro*. (1) In *waka*, nonserious or nonstandard poems; and so *hai-kaika*. (2) A variety of renga distinguished from its serious versions. See *haikai*, *ushin*, *kokoro*.

Musubidai 結び題. Compound topic. Employs two or more substantive elements, such as "A Mountain Village in Snow" or "Love on a Spring Night." Often given in Chinese characters and syntax, so resembling *kudaiwaka*. See *dai*.

Nagauta (1) 長歌. Long poems or songs. The same as *chōka*. (2) 長唄. A kind of song or music for separate performance or *kabuki*. In *kamigata* a kind of music distinguished by length and other features from differing kinds of music. In Edo, much the same but with the *shamisen* essential. The Edo variety developed out of kamigata *jōruri* and kabuki, but in its own way became the essence of musical development of this general kind, particularly for kabuki.

Nagori no ori 名残の折. See *shoori*.

Nakairi 中入り. Temporary exit. In a two-part *nō*, the *shite* plays an assumed role in the first part. A brief exit is required for a costume change, when the shite returns for the climactic conclusion. See *aikyōgen*, *maejite*.

Nanga 南画. Southern pictures, painting of the Southern Sung. It came to be used as a descriptive term for painting in that and associated styles by Japanese artists.

Nanori 名告(乗)り. Giving the name. The literary meanings of the term include: (1) that initial part of a *nō* or *kyōgen* in which the newly entered character says who he is; (2) in stories like *gunki monogatari*, the practice of warriors loudly and proudly announcing who they are, with whatever additional flourishes.

Naoshi. See *choku*.

Nara ehon 奈良絵本. The reason for the Nara designation is uncertain. Typical examples involve illustrations of narratives, sometimes religious and sometimes secular in nature, sometimes sumptuously and sometimes crudely done. Works illustrated and represented include those like the *Sumiyoshi Monogatari* and *Genji Monogatari*, as well as many *otogizōshi*. Flourishing in Muromachi to early Edo times, these works were broadcast throughout the land by a number of kinds of male and female performers, providing literature to a very wide audience and influence on subsequent kinds of literature as well as on later combinations of narrative with pictures.

Nashitsubo no gonin 梨壺の五人. The five men of the Pear Jar Room. The five learned men appointed by *Murakami in 950. They studied *Man'yōshū* and compiled the *Gosenshū*. They are *Minamoto Shitagō, Sakanoe Mochiki, Ki no Tokibumi, Ōnakatomi Yoshinobu, and Kiyowara Motosuke. Also called Nashitsubo no Gokasen.

Nembutsu 念佛. Recital of the Buddha's name (in particular the seven syllables of "Namu Amida Butsu"), a central precept of various Amidist sects. To assist their proselytizing, Amidist priests developed elements of entertainment on their travels, including a dance, nembutsu odori. Sometimes the term therefore took on overtones of certain kinds of performed entertainment. Cf. *daimoku*.

Nenjūgyōji 年中行事. Annual observances. The celebrations, feasts, and duties at court (and later in other versions) as codified throughout the months of the year; for example, the picking of young greens, the presentation of "blue" horses to the tennō, the changing of seasonal clothes (koromogae), and so on. Some of these were taken into poetry as *dai* and helped develop the temporal progressions of *chokusenshū*. See Part Seven H.

Nigeku 逃句. Escaping stanza. (1) In *renga* and especially *haikai*, a stanza that follows one difficult to connect with, and so composed so as to make connection easier for the composer of the next stanza. (2) Since the situation of (1) involves a departure from the preceding stanza, the term also designates a stanza distant or light in relation. See *yariku*, *shinku*, and *kei*.

Nijūichidaishū 二十一代集. The collections of twenty-one eras; the collections or anthologies of *waka* compiled by royal command. See *chokusenshū*; and see Part Six A for specific titles.

Nikki(bungaku) 日記（文学）. Diary literature, a relatively new term for a phenomenon as old as Tsurayuki's *Tosa Nikki*. Since subsequent examples often drop daily entries, the result amounts to works that record or recreate some portion of a person's life. This tendency led to overlapping of nikki with *kashū* and *monogatari*. (For distinctions, see *monogatari*.) Hence the *Ise Monogatari* is also called *Zaigo Chūjo Nikki*; the *Ono no Takamura Shū*, also *Takamura Nikki* and *Takamura Monogatari*; and the *Isayoi (Izayoi) Nikki*, *Abutsu's *Roji no Ki*. A major example is *Matsuo Bashō's *Oku no Hosomichi*. He designated the category *michi no nikki* (diaries of the road), including *Abutsu's work and others. The Japanese have continued to be diarists in literary and nonliterary kinds. In the Heian period and later men often kept diaries in *kambun* Chinese prose, but these are not included in diary *literature*. Often concerning travel and so called *kikō* (*bungaku*). See Part Six C.

Ninjō 人情. Human feeling. (1) The fellow feeling or compassion owed other people. Paired with *giri*, that is, obligations owed superiors, family, and so on. Ninjō might mean therefore the obligations owed one's inferiors or strangers, or (2) the natural workings of human passion and feeling, and therefore sometimes in direct conflict with *giri*.

Ninjōbon 人情本. Books of human feeling or passion. Developing in sense from *ninjō* (2), this refers most broadly to prose narratives on love published during the Edo period, and more particularly to one kind that developed from the *sharebon*.

Ni no ori 二の折. See *shoori*.

Nō 能. (1) Performance (of a combination of dramatic situation, song, and dance) as in *sarugaku no nō*, *dengaku no nō*, and *ennen no nō*. (2) About the end of the Namboku era and the beginning of the Muromachi era, this kind of theater took on its distinctive nature from various miming, song, dance, and literary elements that had been long practiced in different parts of Japan, although chiefly in the Yamato and Kyoto areas. Properly speaking it was called *sarugaku no nō* by

*Zeami and others. Sarugaku had been comic as late as the Kamakura era. Another similar kind, *dengaku* or field music, was also a principal forerunner. *Kan'ami, Zeami's father, was in large measure responsible for combining such elements into Yamato sarugaku. In addition to his Kan'amiza, predecessor of the Kanze school, there developed others: the Emaiza 円満井座, later the Komparu 金春 school; the Sakadoza 坂戸座, later the Kongō 金剛 school; and the Tobiza 外山座, later the Hōshō 宝生 school. The Kita 喜多 school is the most recent. All preserve their own versions of the texts and traditions of acting. In all schools, although for reasons unclear, nō acting slowed considerably in the course of the Edo period. The principal artistic constituents of nō are: *utai*, the recitation of texts; *yōkyoku*, the texts recited and another name for nō; *mai* or *shimai*, the movements and especially the dance; music by the *hayashi*; and chanting by the *jiutai* on behalf of the *shite*. The principal characters are the shite, the protagonist; the *waki*, or secondary character, commonly a traveling priest; their tsure (-zure) or accompanying acters; and *aikyōgen*, lower characters who make brief appearances in some plays. Some 2,000 nō are extant, most from the Edo period. Standard lists of titles, as of 100, etc., exist, although some are rarely performed. See Parts Five A, Six G.

Nochijite 後ジテ. Also called atojite. The term refers to the return of the *shite*, in true character and changed clothes, in a two-part *nō*. The *tsure*, if any, is or are also therefore called nochizure.

Nori 法 or **minori** 御法. The Law of the Buddha; the Buddhist teachings, especially of karma. "Minori" is the thirty-ninth chapter of the *Genji Monogatari* in which Murasaki dies and Genji decides to remounce the world. See *sukuse*.

Norito 祝詞. Texts, upwards of thirty in number, derived from ancient times, used in Shinto rites, and much vexed as to explanation. The auspicious openings of some of the *chōka* by *Kakinomoto Hitomaro resemble some of these texts.

Nuregoto 濡れ事. Wet matters. Plays of passion. The style of acting favored in *kamigata*. (Moisture contains erotic as well as lachrymose associations in Japan.) Nuregoto plays featured plot, character, and dialogue rather than the spectacular effects of *aragoto*. Also called wagoto.

Nyōbō kotoba 女房言葉. Ladies' language. In the Muromachi era, diction used by court ladies for food, clothes, and so on. It was gradually taken up by women in the shogun's service and from them extended to the houses of townspeople and to men.

Ōdaimono 王代物. See *jidaimono*.

Odori 踊. Dance, Normally accompanied by music or percussion, it is a livelier, more various and popular kind of dance than extant kinds of *mai*. It is said to differ in that odori does not involve lifting a foot from the ground or stage; but that is variously inappropriate. See also *buyō*.

Ōgi 奥義. Deep learning. The last stages of learning in the fine or martial arts. Often, especially in *nō*, treated as secrets handed down to only one or two people.

Ōgiri 大切. The last act or offering of a *kabuki* program. Cf. *kirinō*.

Oiemono 御家物. See *jidaimono*.

(Ō)in (押)韻. Rhyme.

Ōjōden 往生伝. Also called *ōjōsetsuwa*. Spiritual biographies; in particular, accounts of ways individuals achieved birth (ōjō) in a Pure Land, usually Amida's or Miroku's. Seven such biographies survive, including the *Nihon Ōjō Gokuraku Ki* of *Yoshishige Yasutane; see also *Genshin. Originally, birth in a pure land was considered a lesser accomplishment than complete enlightenment, but it might be all that one could hope for as human abilities weakened during the Decline of the Law (*mappō*). But with the rise of the popular Amidist movements in the Kamakura period, the distinction gradually collapsed. Cf. *hosshintan*.

Okashi おかし. (1) Humorous, foolish; odd, unusual; dubious, suspicious. (2) Delightful; interesting; tasteful; outstanding; beautiful. (3) A term used in *Zeami's time to designate *kyōgen* within *nō*.

Okiji 置字. Auxiliary words in Chinese unavailable to articulation in Japanese reading.

Okototen ヲコト点. A system of dotting in fixed positions about a character in Chinese prose so that its equivalent inflection in Japanese would be clear and the text therefore legible. For example, with 引, a dot in one place indicates the reading 引きて, and in another 引くに. The term derives from the first three dots, reading down from the top right, signifying ヲ, コ, ト.

Ōkukazu 大句数. (1) The title of a *haikai* collection including the 1,600 stanzas composed by *Ihara Saikaku himself in twenty-four hours in May 1677. (2) Thereafter any such solo feat of stanza production in twenty-four hours. This is also termed (ō)yakazu(haikai) (大)矢数(俳諧).

Okurigana 送りがな. Accompanying *kana*. (1) Small katakana syllables attached to the lower right of Chinese characters to represent Japanese inflections and syntactic order. (2) Also in colloquial

usage, kana syllables placed *after* kanji to indicate inflections, thus complementing furigana, which are frequently attached to the right side of a character to indicate its reading.

Omoado 主アド. When more than one *ado*, or supporting player, is present in *kyōgen* this one is chief. Cf. *koado*.

Omoshiroshi おもしろし. Delightful; pleasing; interesting; elegant; lovable.

Oniyamabushi kyōgen 鬼山伏狂言. *Kyōgen* with the main role that of a spirit or pilgrim.

Onnade 女手. Female hand. (1) Handwriting by a woman. (2) Writing in Japanese, especially *kana*.

Onnagata 女形. In *kabuki*, female roles as opposed to male or *tachiyaku*. See Part Five E for details.

On'yomi (or **ondoku**) 音読. Reading for sound, that is, the Sinified pronunciation of a character as opposed to the Japanese, *kunyomi* (or kundoku). They are classified according to the supposed place or time of origin; thus, Kan'on (Han pronunciation), Go'on (Wu pronunciation), frequently used in Buddhist contexts), Tō'an (T'ang pronunciation), and so on.

Ōraimono 往来物. Model letter books, text books. In the Heian period, collections of model letters. Thereafter, textbooks for writing in a wider sense, as at *terakoya*.

Oriku 折句. *Tanka* or *haikai* with hidden topics, such as those in conundrums, charades, and acrostics. The usual trick was to guess the connection between the topic given before the poem and that represented by the poem. See *kakushidai*.

Otogizōshi 御伽草子. Shorter prose narratives, stories flourishing from Muromachi to early Edo times. "Otogi" suggests the comforting or interesting; various kinds exist: (1) early tales on the lives and loves of the nobility, such as *Sakura no Chūjō* and *Wakakusa Monogatari*; (2) Buddhist stories, often with didacticism, such as *Ashibiki* and *Sannin Hōshi*; (3) literature about warriors, such as *Rashōmon* and *Onzōshi Shimawatari*; (4) literature for farmers, artisans and townspeople, such as *Issun Bōshi* and *Saru Genji Sōshi*. This literature is anonymous, a sign that it was meant for entertainment. But the shifting subject matter suggests changing audiences and a gradual change from the *monogatari* to the literary kinds of Edo times. See *Nara ehon*, *setsuwa bungaku*, and *sōshi*.

Otokode 男手. Men's hand, men's writing, as opposed to women's, *onnade*. (1) In general, writing or works written by men. (2) More particularly, writing using Chinese characters in more or less high proportion; or *kambun, kanshi.*

Ōtsuzumi 大鼓. Drum. See *hayashi.*

Ō(n)uta 大歌. Great songs. Songs used at court for certain ceremonies, rites, and pleasures. In one section of her *Makura no sōshi,* *Sei Shōnagon mentions two kinds as particularly appealing. Among songs, fūzoku (that is, fūzoku uta) are what she most prefers, but *kagura* are also interesting. The former were least tied to court events (see Part Seven H, annual observances), and were songs from various provinces, especially the eastern ones. They were favored at banquets and similar less formal social activities of the court. See *Kinkafu, kouta,* and the next entry.

Ōutadokoro no ōnuta 大歌所の御歌. Songs from the Bureau of Traditional Song. Traditional songs and poems read or sung on special court occasions and represented in *Kokinshū,* book 20.

Rakugo 落語. Comic monologue, ending with a witty push or ochi 落ち. Said to have begun in early Edo times when *Anrakuan Sakuden parodied daimyo in dramatic skits. Although not solely an Edo or Tokyo entertainment by any means, it tends to have such associations as opposed to *manzai* (2). Historically it was also called otoshibanashi, karakuchibanashi.

Rangaku 蘭学. Dutch studies. During the Edo period, only the Dutch were allowed to trade with Japan—on a limited scale at Nagasaki. Beginning in effect with the support of the eighth shogun, Tokugawa Yoshimune (1684–1751), men were assigned to study Dutch as a means to foreign learning. At first the fields of study were largely medicine, the calendar, and related subjects. Aoki Kon'yō (1698–1769), who held a scholarly appointment at the Edo *bakufu,* and *Sugita Gempaku were among the founders of this learning. In the course of time, studies turned more to the physical sciences and technology, including the military, although botany and other subjects were not neglected. To the popular imagination, something exotic was found in this study, which perhaps explains why *Ihara Saikaku was called Oranda (Dutch) Saikaku. The main aesthetic influence of the new learning came in the graphic arts, where perspective and other Western conventions caused great interest.

Rei 麗. Stately and beautiful to sight or hearing; splendid.

Rekishi monogatari 歴史物語. Historical tales. A *monogatari* like the *Ōkagami* that is largely historical in its subject matter. See *monogatari* for a fuller context.

Renga 連歌. Linked poetry. It developed from a pastime in the twelfth century into serious art. In effect, successive *kami no ku* (5-7-5 syllable stanzas) and *shimo no ku* (7-7 syllable stanzas) of *tanka* were joined in sequence so that each made an integral poetic unit with its predecessor (and therefore its successor) but without semantic connection with any other stanza in the sequence made of such alternations. Hence, called *kusarirenga* or linked, chain renga. The sequences were of various length: see *tanrenga, kasen, yoyoshi, hyakuin, senku, iisute.* They were composed by varying numbers of people, typically one to three: *dokugin* (1), *ryōgin* (2) *sangin* (3), etc. Apart from other elaborate rules, there were requirements for a certain number of moon stanzas (one per side of paper sheets) and flower stanzas (one per sheet). See *sho-ori.* Canons governed the ever-changing combinations of such matters and the alteration in impressiveness (see *ji*) and closeness of stanza connection (see *shinku*). Stanzas were classified by topics: see *dai.* Topics involved language and conception, and often conventional ideas of poetic essence: see *hon'i.* Some stanzas had names: first, *hokku;* second, *waki;* third, *daisan;* last, *ageku.* The rest were *hiraku.* The sequence was also governed by a rhythm: see *jo-ha-kyū.* Haikai adapted these canons, in general with somewhat greater freedom.

Rengashi 連歌師. Renga masters. Often real or nominal priests.

Renku 連句. The modern name for a *haikai* sequence. As 聯句—also pronounced "rengu"—this was an early term designating stanzaic successions of Japanese or (more usually) Chinese verse, without canons of linking.

Rensaku 連作. Connected compositions, works with some degree of associated commonalty or sequentiality.

Retsuden. See *hongi.*

Rizoku 離俗. "Abstain from the low"—a *haikai* maxim of *Yosa Buson.

Rōei 朗詠. Recitation of poems and other compositions in a fashion such as chanting or singing; also one kind of song. It was taken from a manner of delivering Chinese poetry, and thereafter provided the basis for reciting *waka, nō,* and other texts, subsequently having a major influence on *heikyoku* and similar kinds of chanted delivery.

Rokkasen 六歌仙. The six poetic sages, so called because they were the six modern (but not contemporary) poets singled out for comment by *Ki no Tsurayuki in his Japanese preface to the *Kokinshū.* They include: *Ariwara Narihira and *Ono on Komachi, by far the most important of the six; also, *Henjō, *Ōtomo Kuronushi, *Fun'ya Yasuhide, and *Kisen. See *kasen, sanjūrokkasen*.

Rufubon 流布本. The most widely circulated, accepted text. Although applicable very widely, the term is especially useful and familiar in scholarship on the *Heike Monogatari*, whose many variants and great popularity led to popular texts at variance from others (in Chinese prose style, for example). After printing came into use, well-esteemed examples became, as it were, standard editions, even if not always the best versions textually.

Ryōgin 両吟. A *renga* or *haikai* sequence composed by two people.

Ryūkō 流行. Change; the current, or popular. A polar term with *fueki* or the changeless in Bashō's *haikai* theory, the two constituting the grounds of *fūga*, true art.

Sabi 寂. The desolation and beauty of loneliness; solitude, quiet. It was introduced as a positive ideal for *waka* by *Fujiwara Shunzei, and thereafter developed variously by subsequent writers, notably *Matsuo Bashō. Some posit stillness as the basis, others deprivation and attrition. There is usually one or the other to a striking degree, but also the presence of an added element to intensify and qualify the experience. Cf. Bashō's *hokku*: "Shizukasa ya / iwa ni shimiiru / semi no koe" and its context in *Oku no Hosomichi*. See *yūgen*.

Sachū 左注. Notes printed to the left side of a page (with the characters in vertical columns read from right to left); afternotes, footnotes.

Sagabon 嵯峨本. Saga books. Books of *kokugaku* studies made in the late sixteenth, early seventeenth centuries at Saga (near Kyoto) from movable wooden type. Also called *kōetsubon*, *sumi no kurabon*.

Sai. See *zae*.

Saibara 催馬楽. Horse-readying music, colt music. In the Nara period, a kind of folk music. In the Heian period, it was influenced by *gagaku* and became more courtly. The music was supplied by several instruments, and the texts were often old.

Saijiki 歳時記. See *kiyose*.

Sakasakotoba さかさ言葉. Edo slang term for tricks with words: pronouncing "hamaguri" as "gurihama" or using a word to mean its opposite, and so on.

Sakimori no uta 防人の歌. Poems of the frontier guards. *Tanka* grouped in books 19 and 20 of the *Man'yōshū*, by—or ostensibly by—men who had to leave for frontier duty in Kyushu. Some were composed by court poets, and the category derives from a similar Chinese classification. Cf. *azumauta*.

Sakusha no kotoba 作者の詞. Authorial speech, intervention. See *ji*.

Sama 様. Style. *Ki no Tsurayuki gave the word currency in his preface to the *Kokinshū*, designating elements of *fūryū* or *miyabi*. It was also used in its Sinified reading, -yō, as in *taketakaki yō*. Later critics tended to use -*tei* (or -*tai*). The presumption is that although one style may be best or all styles may rest on one fundamental style (see *ushintei*), there are several distinct styles. *Zeami's distinctions of various kinds of flower, *hana*, represent a variant conception.

Sandaishū 三代集. The collections of three eras. See *chokusenshū*.

Sangaku 散楽. (1) Originally a kind of Chinese music that entered Japan in Nara times and became associated with *dengaku* and other kinds of performance. (2) In connection with (1), it later became another name for *sarugaku*.

Sangin 三吟. A *renga* or *haikai* sequence composed by three people.

Sanjūrokkasen 三十六歌仙. The thirty-six poetic sages. The poets selected for special regard by *Fujiwara Kintō, including the major poets of the *Man'yōshū* and earlier royal collections. One kind of painting subject was portrayal of individual members, usually in a series of all thirty-six, and each represented with the exemplary poem chosen by Kintō. Although personal likeness is out of question, the painting and calligraphy are often of great beauty, Subsequently various imitations were devised; for example; chūko sanjūrokkasen 中古 三十六歌仙, the more recent thirty-six poetic sages; nyōbō sanjūrokkasen 女房三十六歌仙, the thirty-six female poetic sages. Besides the individual poets, then, this set includes thirty-six exemplary poems, which came to be widely known and diversely depicted. So familiar was it that it took on the abbreviated name of "kasen," and in that guise came later to mean a *renga* or *haikai* sequence of thirty-six stanzas.

San no ori 三の折. See *shoori*.

Sansui 山水. Mountains (or hills) and waters (usually rivers or seas) Landscape painting of some breadth of prospect. Just as in Chinese poetry connections can be made by paralleling mountain and water imagery, so in connecting *waka*, *renga*, and *haikai* in sequences, one of the elements may be used to connect with the other. See *kachō* and *sōmoku*.

Santai 三体. The three principal *shite* roles in *nō*: the old person, the woman, the soldier.

Sarik(g)irai 去り嫌い. Also kuzari. Suspensions. Chiefly a canon in *renga*, to some extent in *haikai*. After a given usage (or number of usages) in a sequence, a word or topic (see *dai*) should be suspended, or was technically forbidden to reappear for a stated number of stanzas. Some examples follow: once used, "yume" (dream) should not appear again for seven stanzas. "Mushi" (unnamed insects as opposed to named, na no mushi) should appear only once in one hundred stanzas and therefore not at all in a sequence of lesser length. "Onna" (woman, women, female) should appear but once in ten thousand stanzas, and therefore not at all in a *hyakuin*. The principle was that the more powerful or impressive the element the less frequent should be its use. The concept of suspension also involved other, very complex principles of *tsukeai* and *hon'i*.

Sarugaku 猿楽. Also written 散楽 and 申楽, its original meaning and etymology are unclear. Like *dengaku*, it developed into a form of entertainment to provoke laughter. By Kamakura times, it becomes sarugaku (no) nō, or *nō*, inclusive of *kyōgen*. See Part Five A and B; also *sangaku*.

Sarugōwaza 猿楽態. Although "sarugō" is another pronunciation of the characters for *sarugaku*, sarugōwaza is a major forerunner of *kyōgen* rather than of nō, and as such it is mentioned in the Muromachi period, or later as having been acted at various places.

Sasara 筤. A generic term for a variety of clappers, rattles, or scrapers associated with folk music, *sekkyō*, *dengaku*, and so on.

Satokotoba 里言葉. The same as *yūrikotoba*, brothel language.

Satori 悟り. Enlightenment, wisdom, illumination. Intuitive awakening to the truth of experience rather than a conceptual understanding of its principles. Seeing into one's own nature to realize that it is identical with that of the Buddha (kenshō jōbutsu); the immediate awareness of Emptiness (*kū*). A Buddhist counterpart of "being reborn," satori is seen by the Zen sect as a sudden experience in contrast to the gradual attainment of other forms of meditation. The highest level is the unexcelled enlightenment of the Buddha (mujō bodai; Skt., anuttarā samyaksaṃbodiḥ). The moon unsullied and bright is sometimes a figural image for satori, by which Consciousness is free of all discrimination. Birth in a Pure Land (Amida's, Maitreya's, etc.) was originally considered to be a lesser attainment,

but in time became identified with the realization of Buddhahood, with enlightenment. See *nori*, *kū*, *shikan*, *nembutsu*, and *daimoku*.

Sedōka 旋頭歌. Head-repeated poem. One of the kinds of *waka*, practiced chiefly in the **Man'yōshū*, **Kojiki*, and **Nihon Shoki*. It consists of six lines, repeating the last three lines of a *tanka*; 5-7-7, 5-7-7.

Sei (or **kiyoshi**) 清. The clear, the pure in poetic practice.

Seika. See *hongi*.

Sekkyō 説経. In the Heian and Kamakura periods, this was a formal, solemn commemorative service performed by monks. Beginning with ornate Chinese prose, it included explanation of a portion of a sutra—often using allegory—and closed with more ornate prose in Chinese. In Muromachi times, the practice was popularized and secularized. Gestures and special vocal delivery were devised. Before long it became a performance accompanied with *sasara* by performers (sekkyōshi) tonsured like priests who sat on a mat under an umbrella put up at popular religious and secular public places. The stories were meant to affect the audience to tears. Two texts, *Sanshō Dayū* and *Karukaya*, have survived from seventeenth-century transcription. By 1700 it had become a species of old *jōruri*, emphasizing Buddhist elements but using puppets, *shamisen*, and recitation. Later it was absorbed into jōruri.

Semmyō(tai) 宣命（体）. A royal order, edict, rescript; and the style in which it was written. As opposed to its *kambun* counterpart, *chokusho*, semmyō were written in Japanese syntax and in a fashion otherwise Japanese except for the presence of Sinified diction and other Sinifications. Use of the style gradually spread from the tennō to other members of the royal family, and by Heian times to the nobility, Shinto priests, and others. It is the origin of the *wakan konkōbun* that is fundamental to all common forms of spoken and written Japanese.

Senryū 川柳. The kind of poetic form of pungent observations on human life that is known by this name today is but one kind of *maekuzuke*, *zappai*, or *haikai*—to give increasingly broader terms. Usually conceived as 5-7-5-syllable stanzas, senryū were originally composed as a stanza attached (*tsukeku*) to a foundation stanza (*maeku*) or topic (*dai*) set by a master like **Karai Senryū* or **Kei Kiitsu*.

Serifu 台詞（科白）. Dialogue. Used for the spoken words of various kinds of drama and, in *kyōgen*, opposed to *shigusa*, stage action. It is true stage speech, as opposed to *mondō*.

Setsuwa 説話. Brief narratives, in practice collected into fairly large compilations. But the term is also used in a more abstract sense to designate stories like those in such major collections as the *Konjaku Monogatari*. Setsuwa differ from *utamonogatari* in not requiring poems and in not coalescing in a single issue or climax narrowly defined, having either none or more than one. The great setsuwa collections date from the Heian and Kamakura periods, although their influence has been great on subsequent prose narrative in classical and modern times. See Part Six D for examples. The term is also used to designate a story or motif: the Hagoromo setsuwa, the Cinderella setsuwa, etc.

Sewadammari. See *dammari*.

Sewamono 世話物. Classification for *jōruri* and *kabuki*: plays dealing with present-day or domestic subjects; opposed to *jidaimono*, although the combinatory classification sewajidaimono is sometimes used. Between 1780 and 1850 there grew up a variant, kizewamono, "living" or melodramatic kabuki of two kinds: kaidanmono, spectral or mystery pieces; and shiranamimono, rogues' and villains' pieces.

Shahon 写本. A hand written text, whether the original or a facsimile.

Shakkyō no uta. 釈教歌. Buddhist poems. A poem or stanza on a Buddhist topic; a book of such poems in a *chokusenshū*. See *dai*.

Shamisen 三味線. A three-stringed, lutelike instrument, whose strings are plucked by a large plectrum, picks, or the fingers. See Part Five D.

Sharebon 洒落本. Clever, "smart" books. Popular ca. 1764–1788. Stories mostly about the licensed quarters, but also about other subjects involving people's passions, preoccupations, and customs. See *gesaku* and Part One D.

Sharefū 洒落風. Witty style. A *haikai* style devised by *Takarai Kikaku after the death of *Matsuo Bashō. Lively wit and impressive technique figure in the display, which was especially congenial to Kikaku.

Shigusa 仕種(草). In many kinds of stage presentation, the action; in *kyōgen* a term for stage action as opposed to *serifu*, dialogue.

Shiika 詩歌. Poetry. A modern word encompassing poetry of all kinds and nations. See *waka* and *kanshi*.

Shikan 止観. Cessation and insight; Skt., śamatha vipaśyanā. Stopping discriminations and concentrating on an object in order to attain insight into one's self-nature. Several varieties of meditation codified by the Tendai philosopher, Chih-i in his Maka

Shikan (See Part Six N, O) and differing from later Ch'an (Zen) practices. It was adapted to poetic composition by *Fujiwara Shunzei and others. Sometimes a term used to designate Tendai Buddhism.

Shikashū 私歌集. Private collection; one made by a private individual or of an individual's poems. It should be distinguished from the homophonous *Shikashū*, sixth of the *nijūichidaishū*. See also *kashū*, *chokusenshū*.

Shikimoku 式目. Rules, or a rulebook, for *renga* or *haikai* composition.

Shimai 仕舞. Dance. See *nō*.

Shimo no ku 下の句. Lower stanza, lines. See *kami no ku* and *ku*.

Shingaku 心学. Study of the heart. (1) Confucian study of moral culture—Teishugaku (or Sōgaku) and *Yōmeigaku*. (2) Study originating with Ishida Baigan (1685–1744) in Kyoto in the first half of the eighteenth century, a popular, humanistic teaching that flourished especially among *chōnin*. This also appealed to many people in all groups for its espousal of the idea that fundamental humanity is not a matter of social class.

Shinjōruri 新浄瑠璃. New *jōruri*. That practiced after the earlier work of *Chikamatsu Monzaemon and *Takemoto Gidayū.

Shinjū 心中. Lovers' double suicide, as in plays by *Chikamatsu Monzaemon and others.

Shinku 親句. Also *shin* for the fact. (1) In *waka*, a poem whose upper part, *kami no ku*, is closely related by words and conception to its lower, *shimo no ku*; as opposed to *soku* 疎句 (so) poems in which the relation is distant or not apparent. (2) In *renga* and *haikai*, it designates the same kinds of relationship between successive stanzas, also with intermediate relations of shin-so or close-distant and so-shin or distant-close. *Matsuo Bashō tended to classify shinku as heavy, jū 重, and soku as light, kei 軽. An essence of sequential art is varying such relation. See *renga*.

Shinnaigo 心内語. Characters' reported inner thoughts in a narrative; sometimes translated "free indirect discourse," which it sometimes is. Cf. *ji*.

Shinwa 心話. Interior monologue, indirect representation of speech, free indirect speech, and so on. A modern term for which there are many variants, the alternatives (like this term) being unstable or various in significance.

Shiori しおり or 撓. That in the configuration of a *haikai* stanza which seems spontaneously to reveal sensitive observation of the human or the natural. A major term in the school of *Matsuo Bashō.

Shirabyōshi 白拍子. Although a hyōshi is one kind of percussion instrument that these performers must have once used, the term came to designate performers of various kinds of song and dance, *kabu*. In particular, they were female performers in late Heian and Kamakura times. Wearing male clothes, they would sing *imayō* and dance. Although they were basically pleasure-women in social class, they were popular at court and among the military aristocracy of the period, as references in the *Heike Monogatari* and other works show.

Shiranamimono 白浪物. See *sewamono*.

Shisenshū 私撰集. A poetic anthology. (1) This most closely approximates Western anthologies. Unlike a *chokusenshū*, it did not require royal ordering, and often is made by one person. Well-known examples include: the *Man'yōshū*, *Kokin Rokujō*, and *Ogura Hyakunin Isshu*. Outside *waka* there are: the *Tsukubashū* for *renga*, the *Inu Tsukubashū* for *haikai* (both for individual stanzas with their predecessors) as well as *Sarumino* for whole *haikai* sequences as well as *hokku*. A shinsenshū should not be confused with the *Shinsenshū*, Part Six A. See *chokusenshū* and *kashū*.

Shite 仕手 (シテ). The principal character in *nō* and *kyōgen*; in *nō* sometimes accompanied by one or two *tsure* (shitezure); opposed to *waki* and, in some plays, *aikyōgen* as other characters. In many *nō* the shite first appears in disguise and later in true character. For such two-part plays, *maejite* and *nochijite* or *atojite* designate the shite in earlier and later appearances. The shite therefore is the character to use *men*, masks.

Shitezure 仕手連 (シテヅレ). See *tsure*.

Shōfū 蕉風. Bashō style. *Haikai* in the styles of *Matsuo Bashō in his mature years. Also the styles of his closest followers. Opposed to the kofū (older styles) of *Matsunaga Teitoku (*teimon*) and *danrinfū*. The Bashō school often used the characters 正風 (also shōfu, right style) among themselves, as did adherents of other schools.

Shōgi 将棋. Japanese or Asian chess. A variant of the game found around the world, this also involves a board, pieces of different rank and capability, and victory through checkmate.

Shōhon 小本. Another term for *sharebon*, as are other readings of the same characters, kobon and kohon.

Shōmono 抄物. A book of excerpts of *waka*, Chinese poetry or prose, or Buddhist texts; in particular, during the Muromachi period selections made from Chinese sources, including translations of sutras, by priests of the *gosan* temples.

Shoori 初折. The first of four sheets (written on front and back) for a *renga* or *haikai* sequence of one hundred stanzas, *hyakuin*. The next three sheets are: second, *ni no ori*; third, *san no ori*; fourth, *nagori no ori*. When only two sheets are used, as for a *kasen* of *haikai*, they are called shoori and nagori no ori.

Shosagoto 所作事. Essentially the same as *buyōgeki: kabuki* featuring dance as a major element.

Shōsetsu 小説. Fictional narrative in prose. A modern term. The Chinese hsiao-shuo (same characters) designates very different kinds of writing. "Shōsetsu" was adopted as the word to render English "novel," French "roman," and so on. The term is also used to designate modern Japanese prose stories, although to call them novels may be misleading at times. Japanese often use the term loosely for earlier kinds of prose narrative: *monogatari*, *otogizōshi*, *ukiyozōshi*, and so on.

Shōsho 詔書. A royal edict.

Shū 集. Collection, compendium. Collections are so central a feature of Japanese literature that many important titles should have, though they commonly do not have, this word in their titles: for example, *Konjaku Monogatari (Shū)*, *Sarumino (Shū)*. Other works not normally thought of as collections are or were sometimes referred to as shū, such as *Matsuo Bashō's Oku no Hosomichi*. Given the pervasive impulse to make collections, many works have been given alternative titles ending in shū, *monogatari*, or *nikki*. The royal collections included both early ones of Chinese poetry (chokusenshishū) and later of Japanese poetry (chokusenwakashū). See *chokusenshū*. Nonroyal or personal poetic collections might also be of poetry in Chinese (shishū 詩集) or in Japanese (kashū 歌集). There were also *renga* and *haikai* and other poetic collections (such as *kyōku*, *kyōshi*, and *senryū*). Some collections in these various kinds omitted "shū" from their titles: *Kaifūsō*, *Sōgi's Wasuregusa*, etc. See part Six for major exemplars.

Shūgen 祝言. The auspicious conclusion to a five-act *kojōruri*, corresponding in a sense to the *kyōgen* (4)—interludes between the preceding acts. Such additional parts were later done away with.

Shūka 秀歌. An outstanding *waka*; a model poem for emulation.

Shukke 出家. Leaving the family. Religious retirement or devotion, involving taking partial or full vows and at least nominal departure from secular activity.

Shukke zatō kyōgen 出家座頭狂言. A *kyōgen* whose main figure is a priest, a lay priest, or is blind.

Shūku 秀句. (1) An outstanding line, especially of Chinese poetry. (2) In *karon*, a line or lines so famous in an old *waka* that they may not be used in allusion (*honkadori*); sometimes also called "words with a master" (nushi aru kotoba). (3) An outstanding *renga* or haikai *stanza* printed with its predecessor (*maeku*) in a collection of stanzas. (4) Clever phrasing, as in word play—see the *kyōgen*, *Shūku Daimyō*.

Shukuse 宿世. See *sukuse*.

Shuramono. A class of *nō* pieces; see *gobanmemono* and Part Five A.

Shushigaku 朱子学. Study of Shushi, that is, of Chu Hsi (1130–1200). This is one of the principal schools of Neoconfucianism and, in Japan, the one thought orthodox in Edo times by the *bakufu*'s support of it alone. The one who established it in Japan is usually said to be *Hayashi Razan. Other figures of importance are *Fujiwara Seika, *Kaibara Ekiken, *Matsudaira Sadanobu, *Muro Kyūsō, and *Yamazaki Ansai. See *Yōmeigaku*, *kogaku*, and Part Six P.

Sobikimono 犨物. See *furimono*.

Sōga 早歌. See *enkyoku*.

Soku 疎句. See *shinku*.

Sōmoku 草木. Plants and trees. The natural constituents of a landscape scene, whether in painting, poetry, or other conception.

Sōmoku kokudo shikkai jōbutsu 草木国土皆成仏. "The plants, trees, and the earth itself will all attain Buddhahood." The phrase originates in the *Nirvāṇa Sūtra* (*Daihatsunehangyō*, Part Six O), and is most familiar to Japanese as "sōmoku jōbutsu." Although it was common Mahāyānist doctrine that all sentient beings had the Buddha-nature and thus might obtain Buddhahood, the Japanese made much more of the idea that "plants, trees, and the earth itself" might also do so. Plants and inanimate matter are not included in traditional Buddhist grouping of sentient beings into six (sometimes ten) realms. For traditional thinkers, the phrase must have been a hyperbole. To those who took it literally, it expressed a major doctrinal shift. In the *Nihon Shoki* it is said that in the land that would be called Yamato "bases of boulders, tree trunks, and leaves of plants also have the power of speech." The

animism that so marks Shinto must have played an important role in the unusual Japanese development of this line of thought. The phrase, "sōmoku jōbutsu," occurs in *Bashō* and other *nō*.

Sōmonka 相聞歌. Relationship poems. One of three major categories of poems in the *Man'yōshū*, including also *banka* and *zōka*. Most such poems deal with love, but relations between friends or between parents and children are also treated.

Sōrōbun 候文. Sōrō writing. Developing from Kamakura speech, this became a style of prose writing using the verb, "sōrō" ("saurahu," "sahurahu") as a single verb or an auxiliary and with inflections. It emerged in Kamakura prose of distinction, is familiar today from usage in *nō* prose passages, and lasted into this century as a polite style.

Sōshi, -zōshi 草子, 冊子, 草紙, 双紙. (1) From ancient times, paper for composition. With printing, they were sewn together to make a thin book. These could be gathered into kan, and those into shū for longer works. (2) A generic term for such books. See Part One D for an account of various kinds.

Sōshiji 草子地. A term that varies in meaning in classical and modern usages, but in general applies to a narrator's or author's comment. In classical usage, it implies an identification of author and narrator, whereas in modern usage distinctions may be implied between author and narrator, and the term may designate the "voice of the work" or "the voice of the text," sometimes expressed in the alternative phrase, sōshi no kotoba 草子の詞. In classical usage, sōshiji is generally taken to be distinguished from normal relation, *ji*, and in modern usage from character dialogue, *kaiwa no bun*. Although implications vary historically and from critic to critic, in classical times sōshiji commonly represents authorial intrusion, *sakusha no kotoba*, or intrusion, comment, or reflection by the narrator. See *ji*.

Sōwa 挿話 An episode, a unit of plot or action, as in a *monogatari*. For drama, *ban* and *dan* are the long-established terms.

Sugata 姿. Configuration. In *waka* and later criticism, the cognitive outlines of a poem, so expressing in a metaphor of form some of the features of *kokoro* and *kotoba* but implying also a constituent whole. It designates the individual poetic result in terms of the classical affective-expressive poets. See *kokoro*, *kotoba*.

Sugoroku 双六. A game for two, somewhat like backgammon. It is played with pieces or counters on a board divided into twelve rows to the left and the right. Moves are determined by dice throws. The game has been traced to Indian origins.

Sui 粋. (1) Thorough acquaintance with human feeling (2) Particularly, natural ability to behave knowingly in the pleasure quarters or more generally in the arts. Both meanings are of seventeenth-century *kamigata* origin. See *iki* and *tsū*.

Suki 好. Aesthetic liking, desire. (1) A deep desire to follow an aesthetic way of life, usually in reclusion or travel; hence the expression suki no *tonseisha*. (2) *Irogonomi*, first sense. (3) An affection for *waka*; or, waka itself.

Sukuse(musubi) 宿世 (結び). Also shukuse, shu-kuen, inga. Karma. Causation of events in one existence from those in an earlier. A central Buddhist concept, or the essential feature of the Law—*(mi)nori*—or of Buddhist teaching, *Shakkyō*. See *kū*, *mujōkan*, and *satori*.

Tabi 旅. Travel. A topic for poems or classification in a collection. Conceived of normally as a rigorous, lonely journey to some destination other than the capital (to which one returned). See *dai*, *choku-senshū*, and *hon'i*.

Tabi no uta 羇旅歌. Travel poems, poems, or poetry. Often called kiryo no uta, kiryoka. Besides being such a poem, the word may also refer to the class of poem, its topic, or a classification in a collection or sequence. See *dai*, *tabi*.

-Tai 体. Style. See *sama*; also pronouced "tei."

Taiko 太鼓. Drum. See *hayashi*.

Taketakaki yō 長高き様. Lofty style. A representative of the many styles of *waka* distinguished by critics, this lofty style involves broad, unencumbered conception, decorous and auspicious diction. It has long seemed to represent a kind of elevated beauty particularly Japanese. See *sama* and *ushin*.

Tampen 短編 (篇). Of brief length. See *chōhen*.

Tanka 短歌. Short poem. With *chōka*, one of the two principal kinds of *waka* poetry. (*Sedōka* constitute a very poor third.) After the *Man'yōshū* period, tanka became the major waka kind. It is short, consisting of five lines (5-7-5-7-7 syllables). Tanka were also used as envoys, or *hanka* for chōka; as such they are, by convention, numbered separately in the anthologies.

Tanrenga 短連歌. Short *renga*. An old version of renga, in fact being capped verse of the parts of a *tanka*, with one person adding a *shimo no ku* to another's *kami no ku*.

Tanryokubon 丹緑本. Red and green books. One kind of Edo book, used ca. 1625–1700, for publishing *kōwakamai, kojōruri, kanazōshi*, and so on.

Tanzaku 短冊 短籍 短尺. Short paper. A piece of paper for poems or pictures. Originally paper of no great length for writing poems and, at times, attaching to an object: a poem on lilies might be attached to a fine specimen of the flower and be sent to a friend. Use of paper resembling the modern version, measuring about 36 by 6 centimeters, had apparently begun by the Kamakura period. Since then, they have been used for *waka*, for *hokku* of *haikai*, and for *haiku*. The practice of writing the hokku of haikai on tanzaku was well known in the seventeenth century, and seems to attest to the slow process by which hokku evolved into modern haiku.

Taoyameburi たおやめぶり or 手弱女振. Ladies' style. The supposed feminine character of the *Kokinshū* and other royal collections. Cf. *masu-raoburi*.

Tarōkaja 太郎冠者. A typical servant in *kyōgen*. The first (Tarō) among kaja or kanja servants, often appearing with his junior, Jirōkaja.

Tayū 太夫. (1) The reciter in *jōruri*, and a component of the names of the most famous, as *Takemoto Gidayū (1651–1714). (2) The head of a performing group.

-Tei 体. Style. See *sama*. Also pronounced "tai."

Teihon 定本. (1) A text established by collation and emendation; an accurate or scholarly text. (2) 底本 The copy text for an edition.

Teimon(fū). 貞門 (風). Teitoku style or school. That of *Matsunaga Teitoku and his followers. Opposed to *Shōfū* and *Danrinfū*.

Tenarai 手習. Writing practice. (1) Working to improve one's calligraphy. (2) Writing out famous poems or one's own lines to express one's feelings and ideas at the time. See the so-titled fifty-third chapter in *Murasaki Shikibu's *Genji Monogatari*.

Tenja 点者. (1) A judge in *renga, haikai, senryū*, or *maekuzuke* competitions. (2) In modern times the official at the royal poetry competitions held annually; on him falls responsibility for approving initial selections.

Tenjobito 殿上人, otherwise **tōshō** 堂上. Higher-ranking people of the court, in particular those of the fifth rank (go-i) and above as also the recorders of the sixth rank, who were admissible into the presence of the sovereign and the highest-ranking nobility. Effectively those, other than priests and nuns, who were able to appear at court. See Part Nine A.

Terakoya 寺子（小）屋. Originally a school for children of a temple, by Edo times it had become the mainstay of elementary education, used to teach reading, writing, and calculation to most students and more advanced subjects to those who were to become Buddhist or Shinto priests or doctors. From a scene set at such a school, the *jōruri* and *kabuki* versions of *Sugawara Denju Tenarai Kagami* are familiarly known as *Terakoya*.

Tonseisha 遁（遯）世者. (1) Originally, Buddhist ascetics (e.g., *Myōe) who "abandoned the world." (2) Aesthetic recluses. Priests, especially of the late Heian and Kamakura periods, who defined their lives both by reclusion in their grass huts (*sōan*) and by attachment to aesthetic practice. They were also associated, in many cases, with travel. Major exemplars include *Nōin, *Kamo no Chōmei, and *Saigyō. In more than one sense, some later writers—*Matsuo Bashō and *Yokoi Yayū—may be said to follow in their steps.

Tōrimono 通り者. A man with full knowledge of the pleasure quarters, a frequent character in *sharebon*. See *tsū*.

Tsū 通. Connoisseurship, full knowledge of a subject; also the person possessing the knowledge. An Edo (and Modern) term, it suggests full acquaintance with the details of some matter (especially some up-to-date matter), special vocabulary, attention to detail, and innate taste. In the Edo period the usual subject was the pleasure quarters, their arts, languages, and styles, as well as other achievements such as *haikai*. The knowing person was also termed tsūjin 通人: see Part Ten, Fig. 93. A hanka(tsū) is one who wishes to be thought or to become a tsūjin but fails to make the grade, a kind of figure *Santō Kyōden enjoyed portraying: see Part Ten, Fig. 91. See *daitsū*, *iki*, *sui*, *tōrimono*, and *yabo*.

Tsukeai 付合. Joining. In *renga* and *haikai*, the art of relating a joined stanza, *tsukeku*, to its preceding stanza, *maeku*.

Tsukeku 付句. Joined stanza. See *tsukeai*.

Tsukinami 月並. A *haikai* association meeting monthly. It flourished during the Tempō era (1830–1844), lasting on through various changes to become a *haiku* movement of widespread popularity in the early years of the modern period.

(Tsukinami) Manku Awase （月並）万句合. A kind of *maekuzuke* version of *haikai*, it involved composing *hokku*-like stanzas for a *maeku* in 7-7-syllable form. Five or six-sheet units were involved, and these could be gathered into larger amalgamations, in this instance providing the basis for the important *senryū* collection, *Yanagidaru*, 1765; see Part Six K. In all this, we find the move from haikai to senryū encapuslated, although serious haikai continued to be written.

Tsukurimono 作物. Constructions. Stylized Stage properties used in *nō* and *kyōgen*.

Tsukurimonogatari 作物語. See *monogatari*.

Tsure 連（ツレ）. Or -zure, as in maezure, nochizure, shitezure, wakizure. In *nō* and *kyōgen*, a role of someone who accompanies the *shite* or *waki*. In a two-part nō, the role is that of maezure in the former and nochizure in the latter.

Ukiyo 憂き世; 浮（き）世. The painful world, this world; the amatory world. (1) The first version given in Japanese was a Heian term designating the suffering existence of this life, the painful amatory relations between men and women, and the indeterminate nature of one's present life. Later the term came to designate the nature of human society, this world. (2) From late Muromachi times, the second Japanese version (usually with the "ki" supplied) came to mean this world's unstable nature. (3) The second Japanese version, with or without the "ki" designated the present time, as in ukiyouta 浮世歌, poems of this age. (4) The second version came to mean sensuality, as in expressions like uikyogurui 浮世狂, and in the seventeenth century this concept was applied to a prose literature dealing with a "floating world," amorous life, *ukiyozōshi*, whose greatest practitioner was *Ihara Saikaku.

Ukiyoe 浮世絵. This-worldly, contemporary, or amatory pictures. (1) A kind of pictorial art practiced from about 1660 to the end of the Edo period. The main subjects included actors and theater scenes, female beauties, geisha of various classes, the pleasure quarters, landscapes, famous places, and birds with flowers. (2) Pornographic pictures. (3) In modern usage, pictures by artists associated or identified with wood-block prints.

Ukiyozōshi 浮世草紙（子）. *Sōshi* of the floating world. Prose stories popular in *kamigata* from about 1682 for a century. Chiefly about townspeople (*chōnin*) and deep human feeling (*ninjō*). See *sōshi* and *Ihara Saikaku.

Uma (or Muma) no hanamuke 餞 or **hanamuke** はなむけ. A formal seeing off of someone journeying, involving wishes for safe travel, presents, and commonly poems. See *wakare no uta*.

Umon 有文. (1) That possessing design, art. (2) In *waka*, *renga*, and *haikai*, skillful technique. (3) In

*Zeami's usage for *nō*, an art that conveys beauty by its rhythmical features of voice or gesture. See *mumon*.

Ushin 有心. Possessed of proper conception. (1) *Waka* of the standard or proper kind. (2) For *renga*, the serious version that developed from a pastime, to distinguish it from the *mushin* variety that was the earlier pastime, or from later nonstandard kinds that used word-play, Chinese words, sexual innuendo, and so on, and that developed in time into *haikai*. See *kokoro*.

Ushintei (-tai) 有心体. A style possessed of proper heart or conception. *Fujiwara Teika came to distinguish this as at once a fundamental style of all poetry and as a separate style. The idea dates from features of *Ki no Tsurayuki's preface to the *Kokinshū* and other Heian writing; it influenced *renga* and *haikai* poets later. See *sama*, *kokoro*, and *ushin*.

Uta 歌. Poetry, song. Although often used synonymously with *waka* (as with *Yamatouta*), its relation to the verb "utau" suggests, in many contexts, singing or reciting. See *waka*, *kayō*, *utai*, and *rōei*.

Utaawase 歌合. Poetry match, a variety of *monoawase*. Originally a pastime or game, like matching such things as roots, shells, or pictures. With the *Kampyō no Ōntoki Kisai no Miya no Utaawase* (ca. 890) the matches take on seriousness as a major occasion for composing formal poems. Competitors were divided into *kataudo*: a left (senior or first) and a right (second) side to compete on set topics at first handed out, later distributed in advance. A judge or judges decided win, draw, or lose for each round (*ban*). Chinese verses, or mixtures of Chinese verses and Japanese poems, or *renga*, *haikai*, and so on, could also be matched.

Utagaki 歌垣. Poetic exchange. In very old times (see *Nihon Shoki*), a kind of mating ritual; young men and women met at a gathering, exchanging poems of proposal and rejection or acceptance. Somewhat later versions were stylish exchanges in which the mating was fictional.

Utagatari 歌語. *Waka* tales or traditions. Oral traditions about individual waka circulating among lords, ladies, and men of letters from the ninth through the twelfth centuries, When written down, these became *utamonogatari*.

Utagoto no monogatari 歌事の物語. A recent term devised to account for the *setsuwa* elements in what are normally termed *utamonogatari*. Setsuwa features are present in the three major exemplars: *Ise Monogatari*, *Heichū Monogatari*, and *Yamato Monogatari*, particularly in the last. Strictly speaking, *utagatari* coalesce the poems in a single narrative climax, whereas setsuwa may have none or more than one such element. Most utamonogatari consist largely of utagatari in this sense but also contain few or more setsuwa *dan*, which explains this recent, finer distinction.

Utai 謡. Chanting. Especially the rhythmical recitation of *nō* texts by an actor or the chorus (*jiutai*) on stage, or by an individual for practice or pleasure. See *uta*, *nō*, and *rōei*.

Utaibon 謡本. A book for *nō* recitation, *utai*, or for following such recitation during performance, or for reading.

Utakotoba 歌詞. Poetic words. The proper diction of poetry. In general, until *haikai*, this excludes words not strictly Japanese (*kun'yomi*). At its most restrictive, the term meant the words actually appearing in the first three of the *chokusenshū*, the *sandaishū*. It also might mean, more broadly, expressions especially typical of poetry. See *makurakotoba* and *utamakura*.

Utamai 歌舞. Song-dance. A general term for the combinations of song and dance that have so many versions in classical Japan. See *kabu*, which uses the same characters in Sinified reading.

Utamakura 歌枕. (1) Originally, words, phrases, and images codified for poetic use. They were commonly of five or seven syllables so as to fill a line: nubatama no, hototogisu, haru no akebono, Ōsaka no seki, and so on. The basis of classification varied. The seasons might be used, with flora, fauna, and other details such as the legendary (as of the goddess Saohime) or human customs associated with the annual observances (nenjūgyōji; see Part Seven H). The months might be used, with the same matter given in greater detail. *Makurakotoba* might be compiled. Or the details classified might be famous places (meisho 名所). (2) The more particular and dominant later usage is restricted to names of famous places. See Part Eight K.

Utamonogatari 歌物語. Stories of *waka*. Brief prose narratives centering on one or more poems, a written or literary form that developed from its oral counterpart or predecessor, *utagatari*. The three great exemplars are: *Ise Monogatari*, *Heichū Monogatari*, and *Yamato Monogatari*. The first was long considered, with *Murasaki Shikibu's Genji Monogatari*, as an epitome of court literature. Because all three, and particularly the *Yamato Monogatari*, contain *setsuwa* elements, a modern term, *utagoto no monogatari*, has been devised to refine the distinction between utagatari and setsuwa. Brief examples of utamonogatari (such as individual *dan* in the *Ise Monogatari*) also have counterparts in those poems with lengthy headnotes in royal collections like the *Kokinshū*. The distinctions may bewilder, but there is no question of the centrality of utamonogatari to court and subsequent literature.

Uta no yamai 歌の病. The diseases of poetry. A chiefly Heian term referring to some number of faults or blemishes in *waka* composition; also pronounced kahei.

Wabi(shi) わび(し), 佗(し). A feeling of powerlessness; a sensation of great loneliness, or its cause; painfulness; shabbiness, wretched appearance.

Wabun 和文. Composition in more or less exclusively Japanese diction and readings of Chinese characters. See *kambun* and *wakan konkōbun*.

Wagoto. See *nuregoto*.

Waka 和歌. Japanese poetry. In the widest sense, all Japanese rather than foreign poetry, especially Chinese. Hence the word is a component in titles of *chokusen(waka)shū*. In the more usual restricted sense, it designates Japanese poetic kinds predating *renga*: *chōka*, *sedōka*, and especially *tanka*. Given the dominance of tanka over the centuries, it is often synonymous with that. See *Yamatouta*, *uta*, and *shiika*.

Wakan 和漢. Combinations, or alternations, of Japanese and Chinese composition so that (for example) wakan *utaawase* would match Japanese poems against Japanese, and Chinese verses against Chinese, in some succession, and *wakan renku* linking verse in the two languages in alternation.

Wakan konkōbun 和漢混淆文. A style mingling Japanese and Sinified readings of characters, words, and elements, as opposed to *wabun*, which uses more or less exclusively Japanese readings and diction. The mixed style is represented most beautifully in classical literature by the *Heike Monogatari*, but in effect this mixed style is the basis of much classical writing and of modern Japanese. See *wabun*, and *kambun*.

Wakan renku 和漢聯句. Linked Japanese and Chinese poetry. These sequences used both Chinese verses and Japanese stanzas begun with a Japanese *hokku*, continuing with stanzas in Japanese (*kami no ku* and *shimo no ku* in *renga*-style alteration) or in Chinese lines of five-character verse. This was a pastime of *Gosan bungaku*.

Wakare no uta 離別歌. Poems on parting, departure. Also pronounced ribetsu no uta, ribetsuka. A category and topic of poetry codified in the *Kokinshū*, 8. As 別れの歌, see *kinuginu*. See also *dai*, *uma no hanamuke*.

Waki 脇. (1) The second stanza in a *renga* or *haikai* sequence: 7-7 syllable line. (2) The secondary character of a *nō*, a priest or other traveler appearing at the outset of a play.

Wakinō. A class of *nō* pieces; see *gobanmemono* and Part Five A.

Wakizure 脇連. See *tsure*.

Wakun 和訓. The same as *kun'yomi*.

Warizerifu 割ぜりふ. Divided dialogue. In *kabuki*, speech so divided among two or more characters that sense is made only by completion of the syntax by a latter or last character.

Washū 和習. (1) Japanese traditions, customs. (2) The Japanese temper or character manifested in composition of Chinese verse or prose.

Watarizerifu 渡ぜりふ. Alternating dialogue or lines spoken by two or more characters in *kabuki*, each line or speech making integral sense; cf. Western stichomythia.

Waza 技. Although its usual meanings designated action or behavior, the word also specifically meant artistic work, art.

Yabo 野暮. The lack of elegant, stylish knowledge, or the person so deficient. The opposite of *tsū*.

Yakazu. Also ōyakazu, yakazuhaikai; the same as *ōkukazu* (2).

Yamatoe 大和絵. Japanese painting. (1) A term current into Kamakura times to distinguish Japanese from Chinese painting: cf. *yamatouta*. (2) A kind of Japanese painting influenced by Chinese but depicting the human and ordinary, a contrast made in the *Genji Monogatari* ("Hahakigi," "Eawase"). This kind began in the Heian period, flourished through the Kamakura period, and developed into the Tosa school. The *Genji Monogatari Emaki* is the most famous, but a not altogether typical, example. (3) A generic term for numerous kinds of premodern painting.

Yamatokotoba 大和言葉，大和詞 (1) The Japanese language. (2) Japanese words. (3) "Pure" Japanese as opposed to inclusion of Sinified pronunciations or readings of Chinese characters. By extension, the pure diction of *Yamatouta* or *waka*.

Yamatouta 大和歌. Japanese poetry. The same as *waka* in its widest sense: Japanese rather than Chinese or other foreign poetry. It is the first word of the Japanese preface to the *Kokinshū*. See *waka*, *shiika*.

Yōembi 妖艶美, or **yōen**. Ethereal beauty. A style expressive of the delicate, of the ethereal, of romance, and using complex techniques as well as a subtle or magical aura. Especially associated with the early mature poetry by *Fujiwara Teika.

Yojō 余情. Remaining feeling, after-meaning. The affective and cognitive richness lingering after one has finished reading or reciting a poem, often because a poem is taken to imply more than its surface statement, predication.

Yōkyoku 謡曲. The recitation, *utai*, of *nō*; hence also designates the text for such recitation and nō itself.

Yōmeigaku 陽明学. Study of Yōmei, that is, of Wang Yang-ming 王陽明 (1472–1529). This is one of the principal schools of Neoconfucianism. It attracted a number of adherents in Edo Japan, including *Nakae Tōju and *Kumazawa Banzan. But it never found favor with the *bakufu*, and so was more or less heterodox. See *Shushigaku* and *kogaku*.

Yomihon 読本. Reading book. A substantial book in five or six kan or more (see *sōshi*), popular ca. 1750–1867. With plots using imaginary elements to didactic ends of Buddhist or Confucian kinds.

Yomikudashibun 読み下し文. A Chinese text read as if Japanese in syntax, and so on.

Yo(n)gin (or **shigin**) 四吟. A *renga* or *haikai* sequence composed by four people. "Shigin" is the pronunciation most analagous with *sangin*, but the frequent dislike of the "shi" sound seems to have led to "yogin," and thence to "yongin" as easier or nicer to say.

Yoriaizuke 寄合付. Stanza connection in *renga* by use of *engo*, word association.

Yoyoshi 四十四, 世喜, 世吉. A forty-four-stanza *renga* or, rarely, *haikai* sequence.

Yūgen 幽玄. Mystery and depth. One of the most enduring but changing ideals in Japanese poetry and aesthetics. It was introduced positively by *Fujiwara Shunzei, who associated it with *sabi* and a deep, mysterious beauty accompanied by sadness or deprivation. In *renga*, *nō*, and *haikai* aesthetics, it comes to mean something more like ideal beauty. Its earlier overtones were darker, more religious. See *sabi* and *mujō(kan)*.

Yūrigo 遊里語. Brothel language. Any of a variety of special kinds of diction used in one gay quarter or another: for example, kuruwakotoba 廓詞.

Zae (also **sai**) 才. Talent in a certain practice, art, or study; also any of those itself. Honzae 本才 meant study of Chinese writing for Heian men, and Karazae 唐才 meant either that or a talent for it. In the "Eawase" ("The Picture Match") part of *Murasaki Shikibu's *Genji Monogatari*, the term is used for efforts ranging from backgammon (*sugoroku*) to Japanese painting (*yamatoe*), to other arts, and to Chinese study.

Zappai 雑俳. Miscellaneous, irregular, or low *haikai*. Toward the end of the seventeenth century various kinds of popular poetic amusements gradually took on competitive if not quite serious earnestness, chiefly—although not exclusively—in Edo. The best known of these today is *senryū*, which, however, historically is but one kind of added stanza (*tsukeku*) to a foundation stanza (*maeku*). These included *maekuzuke* of different kinds, along with *oriku*, kasazuke, kutsuzuke, mojirizuke, kasenzuke, Genjizuke, and so on. Sometimes the stanza was attached to (that is, composed on) a given topic (*dai*) instead of a maeku. The popularity and potential profitability of these pastimes led the *Danrin* and *Teimon* poets to participate as judges (*tenja*). *Matsuo Bashō regarded these amusements with contempt. They were not worthy of the true art of haikai but merely something "that a peasant could enjoy, hoe in hand." See *Karai Senryū and *Kei Kiitsu.

Zatō 座頭. In Kamakura times, there were four ranks of blind entertainers: in descending order, kengyō 検校, bettō 別当, kōtō 勾当, and zatō. Tonsured zatō performed on the lute (biwa), shamisen, and zither (sō); they sang and told stories; and they practiced massage and acupuncture. For some reason the zatō rank of these entertainers caught the attention of *kyōgen* playwrights, as in the remark in *Saru Zatō*, "No—there's a zatō engaged in flower viewing"—a tasteful but impossible occupation for one who is blind.

Zattei no uta 雑体の歌. Miscellaneous poetic forms. A category for non-*tanka* poems in *Kokinshū*, 19. Often pronounced zōtai no uta or zōtaika.

Zenshū 前集. Earlier collection. As opposed to *goshū*, a later collection, this was a collection made by the author(s) before death.

Zō 雑. Miscellaneous. In *renga*, a classification for a stanza that has no seasonal topic (*dai*). Also [especially as zō no uta or zōka) a *waka* classification, the same as *kusagusa no uta*.

Zōka 雑歌 See *kusagusa no uta*.

Zoku 俗. Common, low, not true art. A polar term with *ga*, designating kinds of writing that were not thought to measure up to standards of genuine art because of inappropriate subject matter, audience, or diction. Thus, *jōruri* and *kabuki*—however seriously written—were considered zoku, along with other new kinds of Edo literature, whereas *waka*, *renga*, and *nō*—even *kyōgen*—were accorded ga status, no matter how stereotyped. In general, waka was the exemplar above all of ga. *Haikai*, various kinds of prose literature as well as dramatic, were thought to be of zoku status. In the course of time estimations of a given kind might rise, a course of development continuing to this century and marking stages in Japanese history as well as alterations in the sense of the fundamental literary canon. See *ga*, *haikai*, and *mushin*.

Zōshi 草子（紙）. See *sōshi*.

Zōtai no uta. See *zattei no uta*.

Zuihitsu(bungaku) 随筆（文学）. Following the writing brush. A loose or miscellaneous prose kind of various guises to set down observations, reflections, or feelings in an apparently casual way. In concept, it is like the Western essay or "attempt." *Sei Shōnagon's *Makura no Sōshi* and *Yoshida Kenkō's *Tsurezuregusa* are the most famous examples, but the loose category is very congenial to Japanese and is exemplified by many kinds of writing to this day. See Part Six E.

Zuinō 髄脳. The marrow or essentials of an art, particularly *waka*; a term given currency by *Fujiwara Kintō's *Shinsen Zuinō*.

PART FIVE

Theaters

The major kinds of Japanese theater—*nō*, *kyōgen*, *jōruri*, and *kabuki*—are so complex in development and sufficiently different from major Western kinds as to require more explanation than is feasible in the terms set by Parts One and Four. What follows provides brief characterizations along with figures to illustrate the stages used.

Dance is, with song, probably the art most universally performed by individuals, and although the role of a dancer is prescribed, it leaves him or her freer as a creator than any other performer. Dance also suits well with song and with representation, and thereby has a strong potential for lyric, dramatic, and narrative enrichment. The combinations may vary as numerous social, religious, and entertainment needs are fulfilled, and certainly not all kinds of Japanese dance have led to dramatic creation. But beginning with the story in the *Kojiki (1, 17) that the Sun Goddess was tempted out from her cave by a dance that amused the other gods, we can see that dance, representation, religion, and much else have been involved in the various dramatic and quasi-dramatic kinds of performance in Japan, as is shown by the various kinds of *bugaku*, *kagura*, and other performance (see Fig. 5-1.)

So numerous are they that only general reference is feasible, but no small element in the history of the evolution of drama in Japan involves development dependent on dance and then away from it, with numerous returns.

A. Nō

Nō was the first kind of drama to acquire the esteem that enabled it to influence the course of classical Japanese aesthetics, as we have seen in Part One A. This priority derived, in no small measure, from the lyric cast of nō poetics as well as from the verse passages of its text. It also has an unusually strong tendency to narrative. The elements of narrative and lyricism distinguish nō from Western drama, but the body movements of nō actors are quite properly classified as *shimai*, performance-dance. The ritual effect conveyed by nō has much to do with shimai, especially in the slowed-down versions of performance known to us today.

As nō gained prestige in Muromachi times, it was still a much more mimetic (involving *monomane*, imitating things) and rapidly performed art than that practiced today. Where formerly five main plays were typically performed along with *kyōgen* interludes, today the slow presentation allows for but one, two, or three, normally accompanied by a forepiece or interlude from kyōgen or by intervals of shimai.

Nō plays are distinguished in certain traditional ways that involve the kind of character represented by the main actor, *shite*. This holds true especially for the distinction between two kinds of plays: mugennō and genzainō. "Mugen" suggests dream and mystery, that is, the other world. In these dramas, the shite plays a spirit, divinity, or soul of a dead person. "Genzai," by contrast, deals with a "presently living" person: that is, the shite—the central determinant in nō—is of the same time or period as the *waki*. The plays are further distinguished, again chiefly on the basis of the character played by the shite, but also to some extent by subject matter and the manner of representation (for example, with or without masks). An example follows of each kind.

1. Wakinō 脇能, kaminō 神能. The shite is a divinity and the piece therefore has a celebratory, auspicious tone. *Takasago*.

2. Nibanmemono 二番目物, shuramono 修羅物. The shite is likely to be a hero from the *Gempei* wars and the subject is his suffering or refinement. *Sanemori*.

3. Sambanmemono 三番目物, katsuramono 鬘物. The shite is usually a beautiful young woman. With little action but idealized beauty, this kind is thought essentially nō-like in character. Not surprisingly for a male-acted theater, many of the most beautiful masks have been made for this kind. *Izutsu*.

4. Yobanmemono 四番目物, including kyōjomono 狂女物, genzaimono, etc. The shite is a mad person (male or female); or from "modern" times, in which case masks are almost never worn. This group is the largest and the most actively dramatic. *Sumidagawa*.

5. Gobanmemono 五番目物, kirinō 切能, ki(chiku)mono 鬼(畜)物. The shite tends to be a supernatural character. The action moves with relative despatch, generally requiring a two-part sequence. *Funa Benkei*.

The mnemonic for the five is, then: God-Warrior-Woman-Mad One-Devil. It should be said that different schools of nō classify some of the plays differently, and that the play with oldest roots, *Okina*, stands apart from the classification. And it must be added, moreover, that the division of works into these five kinds was a feat of the eighteenth century. With whatever antecedents, the division is one made after nō had long since seen its prime. Even the issue of which plays are in the repetoire of a given house is subject to change: the present head of the Komparu school has recently redefined the canon of his house. And yet some effort must be made to describe nō in terms that one encounters in Japan.

See Part Six G for two lists of nō by title and by groupings, and with an alphabetical finding list offering variant titles.

Nō took on a distinct character during the lifetime of *Kan'ami (1333–1384). In the first half of the fourteenth century, a number of troupes of proto-nō existed, whether of the *sarugaku* (or *sangaku*) or *dengaku* kind, particularly in the Kyoto-Nara areas (see Fig. 5-2). These two kinds were not wholly unlike, but by the second half of the century sarugaku (or sarugaku no nō), particularly that working from temples and shrines near Nara, eased out most competitors and provided the beginnings of four of the five main shite schools today: Kanze, Komparu, Hōshō, and Kongō. The fifth, Kita, emerged early in the 1600s. Of these the Kanze school has had the most prestige from the outset by virtue of its patronage by the Ashikaga shoguns and the genius of Kan'ami and *Zeami. The Kanze school has not monopolized talent, however, and in addition to having produced famous actors and playwrights, the other four have maintained certain textual variants (*kogaki*) as well as different traditions of performance of individual plays. In addition, there are waki schools with their own important textual variants although less prestige. Both shite and waki (and their *tsure* or accompanying characters, if any) wear white mitten-toed socks (tabi), unlike the *ai* (*kyōgen*) actor, who wears orange (originally deerskin).

Some plays employ only a shite (main character) and waki (secondary role) as actors, along with the musicians (*hayashi*) and the chorus (*jiutai, ji*), both groups of whom come from the shite schools. Masks are often worn, according to the class of play and example of the class, but only by the shite or a *shitezure* in a woman's role, spirit role, and the like. For plays divided into two parts, the characters played by the shite and shitezure may change from the apparent to the real person, so that critics distinguish fore- and after-shite and tsure (maejite, maetsure; nochijite, nochizure). Other roles are sometimes distinguished, such as kokata, a child actor, who sometimes, however, plays adult characters. The waki normally gives entry to the world of the play by announcing his identity in a part termed *nanori*, and recounting the foot journey to the scene in a *michiyuki*. The shite role comes to dominate—to define—the play and, with help from the chorus, enacts the climax in a "dance" part known as *kuse* or *kusemai* and, with the chorus as surrogate, is the last speaker in the play. Waki, shite, and ai(kyōgen) have specified home areas on the stage (see Figs. 5-3 and 5-4).

The stage also has set areas for the chorus and the musicians. The chorus consists today of eight chanters. They take on the words of the shite during dances, moments of deep emotion, and so on. The musicians almost always consist of but three or four, of whom the most important plays a transverse flute, *fue*. Another beats an hour-glass-shaped hand drum, *kotsuzumi*, held by the left hand on the right shoulder. A third beats a slightly larger drum of like shape, *ōtsuzumi*, held at the left side. Sometimes there is a fourth who uses a stick in each hand to strike a large drum, *taiko*, on a stand. The musicians also utter a number of emphatic, rhythmic sounds that initially disconcert a Westerner but that contribute effectively to the complex of musical, dance, and other rhythms.

Amateurs often practice features of nō to understand performance better and to participate in the training of the schools. The most popular of such pastimes are the chanted recitation, *utai*, and the patterned motion or dance, shimai. Some amateurs engage in actual performance after a lengthy period of training. Audiences usually find it difficult to follow recitation, especially by masked actors, since the masks are made for visual effect rather than vocal projection. For such reason, it is common either to purchase in the theater the texts of the day's plays, or to carry to the theater an edition of plays, *utaibon*, that will include the 100 most popular plays (hyakuban) from the 250 or so commonly presented (more than 2,000 are extant, the majority from early Edo times). But many in the audience simply have plays memorized from utai recitation or other experience. (*Yōkyoku* is utai, strictly speaking, but is often used to designate the texts or nō itself.)

Like other kinds of premodern Japanese drama, nō is first and last a theatrical art. The texts do exist and often have great beauty, but one could hardly infer the nature of performance from a bare text. Modern editions help in visualizing by including stylized figures of the actors, stage directions, and so forth. Editions also often include specification of the parts of a play and divide them into sections. Some of the terms are modern, and even the most important may be difficult to understand. For example, the sections referred to are called *dan*, which in the case of jōruri and kabuki correspond well to the Western notion of act. In nō, however, there is in one sense never a shift in scene. That is, if there is one, as in the two-part *Takasago*, the waki "takes us" to the second place by means of another michiyuki. The mae and nochi or ato parts of a two-part play correspond most closely to acts, since at least the exit and reentrance of the shite will be involved.

In what follows, the basic features of a nō text are described, beginning with language, which is basically of two kinds, depending on whether a passage is written in prose or verse. The prose is a variety of *wabun* that uses Sinified pronunciations and *sōrōbun* (verbal terminations like -sōrō, -sōrae). The verse is characterized by a language close to waka and a prosody using a 7-5-syllable composite measure, with the variations accommodated by shortening or lengthening in delivery. The manner of delivery involves a range of chanting (from near speech to near singing) that varies from shite to waki to *jiutai*, from prose to verse, and from kind of unit to kind of unit.

The rich visual and auditory experience of nō renders full explanation in words infeasible. But because even rudimentary descriptive accounts are very difficult to find in Japanese, and because little consistency is to be found between accounts, we offer in the ensuing pages a reasonably complete and consistent explanation of the order and the constutuents of works of nō. To enable a reader to understand a description abounding in Japanese terms, ours moves in stages of detail. We begin with the *jo-ha-kyū* rhythm as used in nō. That is followed by general structural distinctions. We then turn to an account in outline of a two-part nō, followed by a detailed description of the constituents of a two-part nō, with attention to major variations. We conclude with a reduced description of a one-part nō. This order leads from the simpler to the complex, from the more regular to the more irregular.

The jo-ha-kyū rhythm governs nō generally and in almost every detail—in theory at least. Not only is a given work divided into the pattern of jo or introduction, ha or agitated development, and kyū or fast close (as will shortly be set forth); but it is further held that the jo, the ha, and the kyū themselves each have their jo, ha, and kyū. Ideally speaking, all else is so governed. A given subpart (*mondō*, ageuta, rongi, and so on) should be governed by the same three-part rhythm. Even a given gesture—for example, the shite's raising the right hand slowly toward the eyes of the downward inclined face as a gesture of weeping—should be governed by the jo-ha-kyū rhythm. In considering such details, we perhaps do best by considering the rhythm an ideal with which the actor imbues his art, having made—through his practice and interpretation of a given work—the rhythm second nature and a feature of aesthetic habit in performance of parts and the whole.

Students will wish to know the Japanese characters for the terms sprinkled so heavily in what follows. Rather than disfigure an already diagrammatic text with them, we offer them here (terms in Part Four are not included).

fukushikinō　複式能	sashi　サシ
tanshikinō　単式能	kuse　クセ
nakairi　中入リ	ageha　アゲハ
shidai　次第	iguse　居グセ
nanori　名ノリ	maiguse　舞グセ
ageuta　上歌	aigatari　間語リ
tsukizerifu　着ゼリフ	machiutai　待謡
serifu　セリフ	kakeai　掛合
issei　一声	kakeri　カケリ
sageuta　下歌	jo no mai　序の舞
mondō　問答	naka no mai　中の舞
shodō　初同	kyū no mai　急の舞
katari　語リ	kamimai　神舞
nakanoriji　中乗地	hayamai　早舞
hiranori　平乗	ōnoriji　大乗地
rongi　ロンギ	*Yashima*　八島
kuri　クリ	*Ashikari*　芦刈

The order is that of the appearance of the terms in the discussion.

The structure of nō has been determined with very great precision by recent Japanese criticism, and essentially the analysis is the same as that given by *Zeami in treatises on nō composition such as *Nōsakusho* (also *Sandō*) and *Fushizuke Sho*. Zeami distinguished between two-part and one-part nō. Contemporary critics further differentiate the former between double pieces (fukushikinō) and single pieces (tanshikinō). Because double nō are more complex, we begin with them and then offer a brief account of single nō.

The term "double" refers to the two appearances on stage by the shite. Between the two, the shite actor returns to the dressing room. The shite of the earlier part, the maeshite, is the ghost or specter of a person involved in events long ago at the imagined site of the action who appears in the guise of a quite ordinary contemporary of the waki. The shite of the later part (nochijite, atojite), reappears as a vision in a dream to the waki and, now in the proper role of the shite, revives from the past the circumstances of the older time. Because the two guises of the shite differ so radically in the roles impersonated, there is a mysterious air in its disappearance that goes beyond a mere exit to change costume. This disappearance, from the view of spectators, is a temporary exit (nakairi). During this interval, the kyōgen actor (normally in the guise of a person of the locality) is in charge and relates circumstances from the past at the request of the waki. As this relation ends, the recostumed shite reappears and the second part begins.

The jo-ha-kyū rhythm involves dividing a play into five units, for as Zeami wrote, the jo constitutes one phase (dan), the ha three, and the kyū one. In what follows the units defining each phase are set forth with comment as to their constituent natures.

Constituents of a Two-Part Nō

FIRST APPEARANCE

1. A. Jo. The waki enters, telling why he has come to the dramatic location.

2. B. Ha, first section. The shite enters and chants, in an emotionally charged fashion, hints of this character's past.

3. C. Ha, second section. The waki and shite engage in talk, discussing past events at the location.

4. D. Ha, third section. The shite relates past occurrences at the location of the action. (This is usually chanted in the rhythm termed kuse, and is accompanied by dance.) The chanting completed, the shite disappears from the stage.

5. Temporary exit. Since the kyōgen actor is in charge, the jo-ha-kyū principle is not involved. During the kyōgen actor's narration, the matter is termed an interval (ai) or kyōgen interval (aikyōgen).

SECOND APPEARANCE

Kyū. The shite enters a second time, reenacting events from the character's past. The basic feature is a dance or mime. When this is complete, all the characters leave the stage.

The second appearance is over so quickly that, although Zeami treated it as a distinct unit, modern accounts treat it as a repetition, in curtailed form, of the first appearance. In such a view, this brief last section may also be subdivided in a way corresponding with the units of the first appearance.

6. A′. First part. The waki awaits the shite's reappearance. (Corresponds to the waki's entry and the jo of the first appearance.)

7. B′. Second part. The shite reenters. (Corresponds to the shite's entry in the first appearance: first section of the ha.)

8. C′. Third part. The encounter (kakeai) of shite and waki. (Corresponds to the dialogue [mondō] between shite and waki in the first appearance: second section of the ha.)

9. D′. Fourth part. The renactment of occurrences in the past (corresponds to the relation of past matters in the first appearance: third section of the ha.)

The end of the second appearance repeats the disappearance of the shite at the end of the first. Because this structure of the second appearance has been fundamentally honored since Zeami's time, it is certain that nō authors wrote with awareness that the second appearance repeats the first in abbreviated fashion. But when nō is staged, and when the second appearance is enacted at a pace like that for the first appearance, the whole gives a sense of integrated relaxation, which leads people to regard the second appearance as a single, fifth part.

The two appearances are made up from combination of briefer and well defined constituents called subparts (shōdan) by some scholars. The subparts involve combinations of various kinds of verbal and musical composition, and each is designated by a given term. Certain scholars have made extremely precise distinctions as to the nature of the subparts, but the following explanation employs terms for the subparts that are used in common among the schools of nō. (The terms are designated in small capital letters.)

FIRST APPEARANCE

Jo

SHIDAI. Consists of two composite 7-5 syllable verses. Since the former of the two is repeated, the actual total is three. There may be variants like 8-5 or 7-4, but these are changed by vocal syncopation or elongation so that their rhythm accords with the 7-5.

NANORI. In prose and spoken. The waki introduces himself and explains why he has come to the location.

AGEUTA. Beginning with a 5-syllable verse, this is chanted in measures of 5-7 composite verses (again with variants). It has the same rhythm as the shidai, but is chanted in a more heightened tone. For the most part it is the waki's descriptive account of the places passed in journeying to the site of the action.

TSUKISERIFU. In prose and spoken. The waki relates his arrival.

Ha, first section

ISSEI. Chanted in a 3-verse measure of 5- and 7-syllable verses. Before and after the issei, a SASHI prose unit is chanted. The sashi has a much greater measure of recitation than tsukiserifu, but it is not prosodic and falls into no set rhythm. A lengthy vibration of the voice is used to extend the ending of each unit.

SAGEUTA. Two or three composite 7–5 verses chanted in a middle and a lower tone, ending in a lower. Rhythmical. In content it forms a set with the next unit in describing the scenery of the location where the waki has arrived.

AGEUTA. The same properties as the waki's earlier ageuta.

Ha, second section

MONDŌ. Exchange of dialogue between waki and shite. In prose.

SHODŌ. In verse much like an ageuta. With a rise in feeling in the dialogue between the waki and shite, the *jiutai* (chorus) takes over, chanting an

AGEUTA. During this interval, the kyōgen actor appears, sitting at the kyōgen position on the hashigakari (see Fig. 5-4).

Ha, third section

This part is the showpiece of the first appearance, taking on many forms. The two most frequently observed kinds are given here.

TYPE A

KATARI. Prose without rhythm. It involves, however, a more solemn recitation than serifu, and mime often accompanies it.

NAKANORIJI. This is an ageuta chanted by the jiutai. Because it does not have a 7–5 measure, it differs in rhythm from the ageuta of the shite and waki (which are classified as hiranori rhythm).

RONGI. An exchange of chanting between the shite and jiutai in a rhythm using the 7–5 measure. A heightened tone is essential, but the rhythm differs slightly in nature from that of an ageuta.

TYPE B

KURI. Although a less rhythmical recitation, there is a heightened tone and the rhythm used is attractive. The tone must be lyrical, since this provides an introduction to the next two following.

SASHI. A prose unit, like the sashi in ha, the first section. Although ending with some chanting, it is mostly near speech—a kind of subsection ha.

KUSE. The jiutai is in charge. Begins in a lowered tone, but at the point where the shite chants a 5-syllable verse (called ageha), a high tone dominates. The contents are the same as in Type A, a relation of what happened in former times at this place, but instead of using the narrative features of Type A, the kuse is lyrical. There are two kinds of kuse:

1. IGUSE. While the jiutai chants the kuse, the shite sits in center stage, not in action.

2. MAIGUSE. The shite rises and, in time with the jiutai, performs a simple dance.

(Kuri, sashi, and kuse constitute a series of subparts, none of which may be cut.)

Temporary Exit (NAKAIRI)

When the shite leaves stage by the hashigakari and is once more inside, the waki calls to the local person (the kyōgen actor) at the kyōgen position and inquires about doubtful matters heard in dialogue with the shite. The kyōgen actor gives an AIGATARI or narration of what happened in the past at the site. This is more colloquial than the shite's account in Type A, and since it gives just a bare outline of events in an accent typical of kyōgen, there is little sense of repetition.

SECOND APPEARANCE

Kyū

MACHIUTAI. The waki is in charge. An ageuta whose contents involve the expectation of a dreamlike meeting with the character (formerly the ghost, though not really known to be so by the waki) in the first appearance.

ISSEI. In verse, as in the first appearance. This involves a striking impression as the shite now appears in its proper guise from the past. Lyrical.

MONDŌ. In prose. Serifu is sometimes used, but a sashi is more common. Now in a dream state, the waki engages in conversation with the shite.

Since in a KAKEAI the shite and the waki divide between them the relation of a single passage, it is appropriate that the contents be in the charge of the jiutai.

It may happen that the jiutai will continue with an AGEUTA or the like; it is usual to go directly from an ISSEI to the MAI (dance).

Since what follows is the central feature of the second appearance, there are many forms used. The two most common are set forth.

TYPE A

KURI. In musical terms, the same as for the maeshite (first appearance, type B).

SASHI. In musical terms the same as for the maeshite (first appearance, type B). It is usual to have a KAKEAI between the shite and the jiutai.

KUSE. In musical terms, the same as for the maeshite (first appearance, type B). But it is not an iguse. (At this point the shite may also do a KAKERI—a type of action only involving circling the stage following a rhythm.)

KAKEAI. The shite and the jiutai chant an ageuta that is not set to a rhythm.

NAKANORIJI. In musical terms, the same as for the maeshite (first appearance, type A). Although the jiutai is in charge, the chanting of the shite may also be involved here and there. Or, there may be a shift to some other element such as a RONGI.

TYPE B

MAI. It is usual to make central a JO NO MAI (introductory dance) or NAKA NO MAI (middle dance). But a KYŪ NO MAI (fast close dance), KAMIMAI (god dance), or HAYAMAI (rapid dance) may also be used. It also happens that a HA NO MAI (development dance) will accompany the jo no mai. These various dances are distinguished chiefly in terms of their speed.

ŌNORIJI. The jiutai is in charge, but it may happen that the shite will also chant a bit. Since an ōnoriji has one sound per beat, its rhythm will also be found in Western vocal music. The ōnoriji differs from the nakanoriji of Type A just preceding in the greater irregularity of the nakanoriji. The ōnoriji is not just more regular, however, but will also involve some chanting by the shite within the dominant chanting by the jiutai.

After this, the shite's concluding beat (a single stamp of the foot as a sign of ending) sounds, and the whole play is over. Starting with the shite, all performers leave the stage.

The preceding describes the established structure of nō works, a structure perfected a short time after Zeami. There are not many works that provide complete examples, and the model given is therefore idealized. *Yashima* is a good example of the perfected structure, but most nō lack one part or another. Certain other differences exist, especially in short pieces.

In what follows there is an outline of a one-part nō. Since all the terms have previously been explained, they will not be explained here. For one-part nō, genzaimono are the most common.

Jo

SHIDAI——NANORI——AGEUTA——TSUKISERIFU. The sequence is the same as for two-part nō, and the waki is in charge. It sometimes happens just after this that there will be a mondō between the waki and a kyōgen actor.

Ha, first section

ISSEI——SASHI——SAGEUTA——AGEUTA is the sequence. This is the part in which the shite appears on stage.

Ha, second section

MONDŌ——SHODŌ is the sequence. The mondō occurs between the waki and the shite; it may also happen that the jiutai will shift to ageuta, sageuta, or rongi.

Ha, third section

KAKEAI——AGEUTA——MONDŌ——KURI——SASHI——KUSE is the usual sequence, but there are other kinds.

Kyū

RONGI——ISSEI——MAI——ŌNORIJI is the sequence. With the shite's concluding stamp of the foot, the performers leave the stage.

As an example of a single-part nō akin to the two-part pieces, there is *Ashikari*. But since the one-part pieces are so often genzaimono, their theatrical character differs, and they are much more given to variation than are two-part nō.

The historical development of nō resembles its elusive art in certain complexities of detail not always easily kept in the mind. By the Edo period, nō had achieved (with kyōgen) the status of an art worthy of support by the military aristocracy. In that tidying way favored by the Edo *bakufu*, four houses were recognized as "the four companies with one style" (shiza ichiryū). The four are named in various orderings but include Kanze, Komparu, Hōshō, and Kongō. The Kita school was omitted from that recognized group, but it has its own respected traditions as a shite school.

B. KYŌGEN

Consideration of *kyōgen* allows for a further analogy between *renga* and *nō*. Renga began as a kind of amusement, an entertainment, a pastime, and only gradually developed as a serious literary art claiming kinship with.*waka*. Even in so becoming *ushin* or serious, however, renga had its *mushin*, nonstandard or comic counterpart. Nō had also begun as a kind of dramatic performance meant to elicit laughter from the onlookers, only later becoming sufficiently serious for *Zeami to claim it as an element in "the central artistic tradition." As it became serious, nō had its comic sister in the "wild words" of kyōgen—which is more properly styled nō no kyōgen or even sarugaku no nō no kyōgen. Nō and kyōgen share the same stage, just as the ai or *aikyōgen* may appear in the interval of the two parts of various nō. In much the same fashion, kyōgen has historically alternated with, or provided interludes for, the five pieces of a full nō performance. It is generally agreed that in Zeami's time the two arts resembled each other more than they do today, when nō has been slowed and otherwise altered. In both its origins and in its historic role, kyōgen has been an integral part of the experience of nō.

In other words, although kyōgen may be formally regarded as an equivalent of *kyōka* to waka, a comic version of a serious model, kyōgen is more than that. It is a genuine counterpart, a second half of a single drama that bears in it more of its origins than the other half does. In an important sense, comedy is more essentially dramatic than tragedy, since it is freer of ritual origins and social rites. Certainly, kyōgen is one of the most universally accessible of all kinds of Japanese drama and a spiritual home of the Japanese comic imagination.

The origins of this drama are so mixed as to be obscure. The early Edo master *Ōkura Toraakira wrote in his *Warambegusa* (or *Kyōgen Mukashigatari Sho*) that kyōgen had long been a kind of variety show. That is, he said it consisted of such things as little dances (komai), narrative, and other such elements until the Namboku writer Gen'e (d. 1350) had brought unity to such constituents. Whether Gen'e played so material a role may be doubted, but the variety-show nature of early versions seems definite. We need only recall that before kyōgen emerged in its recognizable form, *sarugaku* was itself comic, along with much of *dengaku*, *kōwakamai*, and such other early performances as engikabuki. In a sense, these quasi-dramatic performances—and many others practiced by priests and nuns, jongleurs and minstrels, reciters and entertainers—all existed before drama proper, before plays were regularly presented on permanent stages. Such predrama has ancient roots, as was observed of nō. There is no cause for surprise that Fujiwara Akihira (d. 1066) should write in his *Shinsarugōki* that this "new sarugaku" was a kind of entertainment with such enduring comic staples as the rustic's visit to the capital (cf. the kyōgen, *Kanazu*).

One distinction seems possible. It appears that public storytelling-recitation and what Japanese term *kabu* (song-dance) or enacted entertainments developed separately before both kyōgen and nō brought together, each in its own way, elements of both into sarugaku no nō and sarugaku no kyōgen. For the latter, this coalescence appears to have taken definite form around 1400, with a predecessor called *sarugōwaza* providing the stimulus.

The problem of accounting for the development of later kinds probably rests more with nō than kyōgen, with the development of high seriousness rather than the comic spirit. A famous account of sarugaku as late as 1423 tells of three character types common to the performances: the exhausted noble character, monkeys, and the bumbling priest. Characters in such guise provide obvious comic material. That date represents a time when both nō and kyōgen had assumed something like their mature, full status. It therefore suggests the extent to which "sarugaku" continued to be a term comprehending both as a single dramatic art, just as they continued, and still continue, to use the same stage. The distinction between these two kinds of sarugaku surely involves the efforts by Zeami to bring nō into the waka-renga aesthetic, and by such means to obtain social recognition for a serious art. Yet just as Zeami was patronized by Ashikaga Yoshimitsu, so was Ōkura Toraakira by Toyotomi Hideyoshi and Tokugawa Ieyasu.

The strongly emergent decorum that distinguished the two kinds of sarugaku marks that tidying-up which Edo authorities brought in with their stabilizing, conservative, and feudal mentality. As performances of nō have slowed and as kyōgen has ceased to be performed in the four intervals of five nō plays, we have come to share the mental outlook of the Edo shogunate. We too wish to separate nō into the category of the quiet, serious, reminiscent, allusive, and aristocratic; and kyōgen into another of the bumptious, funny, this-worldly, social, and common. Zeami himself would have been surprised at so radical a distinction. Even today, that unclassifiable nō, *Okina*, with its black-masked Sambasō resembles celebratory kyōgen more than it does first-category nō.

Zeami's sympathy with the comic art of his colleagues finds expression in his remark that kyōgen "embraces the joyful amid its laughter" (*Shūdōsho*). With some exceptions, kyōgen leads us to a laughter without cruelty, even if our "sudden glory" leads us to a sense of safe removal from the plights of the characters whose comedy discomfits them. As the sufferings of the people in nō are bearable in tragic fashion because they involve personages exalted or otherwise remote from our times and experience, the situations of characters in kyōgen are easily tolerated because they so palpably exist on their own terms in their own preoccupied world of hunger, thirst, greed, and other fundamentally human, absorbing preoccupations.

Kyōgen may sometimes include dance, masks, and much else that reminds us of nō. But its fundamental character, its comic understanding of human life, derives from two quite distinct aesthetic components that can be termed language and stage action. Viewed in one way, the language is of course less exalted than that of its solemn sister. It developed from versions of actual Muromachi speech as subsequently modified. To that flavor of an older time, but of a time more recent than the language of nō, it adds the tang of a syntax and verve much closer to actual speech, and indeed to modern Japanese. But the "language" comprehends far more. Records from the fifteenth century show that "kyōgen" was a term often applied to the performances of storytelling priests and especially to rapid-patter stories (hayamonogatari). The association between rapid talk and comedy is an enduring one in Japan, uniting the egregious Ōmi Lady in the *Genji Monogatari* with the *manzai* we associate with *kamigata* comedy and with television skits to this day. In this sense, "language" involves comic delivery and fun with words ranging from puns and wit to a sense of what will take with audiences. But "language" also has a yet more fundamental role in making kyōgen a distinct kind of sarugaku.

As a counterpart of the stage action (*shigusa*) of kyōgen, dialogue (*serifu*) provides the basis for an internationally accessible kind of drama. The dialogue shows that nō rather than kyōgen is the theatrical exception. As we have seen, one of the shōdan 小段 or elements of nō is mondō 問答, "dialogue." Yet mondō is less dramatic, an essentially narrative answer to a dramatic question. In fact, nō is far more narrative in cast than is any other major dramatic kind in the world. The dialogue (serifu) of kyōgen, on the other hand, is recognizable theatrically as verbal human interchange, as dynamic question and answer, as remark and rejoinder, as a dynamic process whereby one thing leads to another and a series of speeches directs us to a climax. The action (shigusa) is stylized, as the stage requires, but it is not stylized into narrative and lyric such as mark nō. In a word, kyōgen is more dramatic. In this respect, although nō bequeathed stories and motifs to jōruri and kabuki, the words and actions of kyōgen bequeathed the dramatic temper itself. It is no accident that kabuki is properly styled kabukikyōgen.

In its early stages as a distinct kind, kyōgen appears to have involved a good deal of the impromptu and ad lib. This again reminds us of kabuki. There is in the Tenshō Kyōgenbon a late sixteenth-century tendency to set down texts of plays for reading, and that implies that plays were becoming fixed in their "language." But since the texts so presented vary from their present counterparts, the spirit of improvisation must have lasted on. Just before 1650, Tokugawa Iemitsu sought to have nō and kyōgen settled into proper feudal houses or guilds, and players were so organized and recognized. In view of what happened when waka and renga earlier became the property of rival houses, this institutionalizing of kyōgen probably marks the date from which standardizing began for the acting texts (daihon) of kyōgen.

Iemitsu's regularizing led to the recognition of a number of kyōgen schools, including the three principal ones: Ōkura 大蔵, Sagi 鷺, and Izumi 和泉. Texts for yet other schools were published in a series after 1660: Kyōgenki 狂言記, Kyōgenki Gai 狂言記外, Zoku Kyōgenki 続狂言記, and Kyōgenki Shūi 狂言記拾遺. But the texts most familiar today derive from the roughly 200 of the Ōkura canon and the roughly 250 of the Izumi school. A few of these plays appear in one school's canon but not the other's. See Part Six H for a list of kyōgen titles.

Like the many plays of nō, those of kyōgen are classified into groups or types. There are seven, not the five of nō as distinguished by Zeami and later—although it does appear that nō also once had seven kinds. In any event, the kyōgen groups can be set forth with their names, some brief description of grounds for distinction, and a famous example of plays in each category:

1. Waki Kyōgen 脇狂言. These are celebratory. (See first-category nō.) Daikoku Renga.
2. Daimyō Kyōgen 大名狂言. The shite plays a daimyo's part. Utsubozaru (one of many plays involving the rascally Tarōkaja).
3. Shōmyō Kyōgen 小名狂言. The shite usually plays the role of Tarōkaja, sometimes of Jirōkaja. Kirokuda.
4. Muko Onna Kyōgen 聟女狂言. Although in two instances the shite plays

the woman's role in these comedies about couples and domestic life, usually the waki does. *Futaribakama*.

5. Oni Yamabushi Kyōgen 鬼山伏狂言. This corresponds somewhat to nō dealing with demons (fifth-category) and yamabushi. *Asahina*.
6. Shukke Zatō Kyōgen 出家座頭狂言. Originally this involved ridicule of the blind, but changing sensibilities have led to making such characters more sympathetic. *Kanazu*.
7. Atsume Kyōgen 集狂言. Miscellaneous plays. Many of these resemble Daimyō Kyōgen. They involve such subcategories as thieves and strife. *Akutagawa*.

If it is impossible not to admire and ponder the high art of nō, it is very easy to give one's heart to kyōgen. Because it has never had a Zeami to claim these plays as a part of "the central artistic tradition" of Japan, it seems impossible to expect any such criticism at this late hour; the only real kyōgen criticism is that by *Ōkura Toraakira. But since so much of the world's high literature, including that of Japan, seems to post a warning, Laughter Not Permitted, kyōgen offers a welcome reminder that our lives do not consist solely of the solemnity with which the French regard food, we regard Shakespeare, and the Marxists economics. In its relative lack of theory and High Seriousness, kyōgen is not entirely the loser.

The schools of kyōgen actors do not have recorded histories as long as those of nō schools. The three main schools seem to have begun to take on definition in the Kamakura and Muromachi periods, but there are no adequately annotated texts of plays that can be traced back so far. Thereafter, however, the Ōkura, Sagi, and Izumi schools received official recognition and maintained separate traditions as well as somewhat variant texts. There are at present few texts accessible, printed in modern type and annotated. Those commonly so presented are really reading versions. As texts are now being published in seventeenth-century acting versions, kyōgen begins to gain something of its proper theatrical and literary status. Unfortunately, during the Meiji period the Sagi school and its resources were lost. The then head of the school taught kyōgen principles to a kabuki actor. So incensed were the samurai-born sponsors of kyōgen that they withdrew all support. This illustrates what was said at the outset, that kyōgen is really nō no kyōgen, something far above the pretensions of the kabuki theatre and its kabukikyōgen. We may deplore the attitude, but the kind of thought involved is highly informative, and it lends no little credence to the *ga* and *zoku* distinctions traditionally made for different kinds of literature.

C. Mibu Kyōgen 壬生狂言 and Kōwakamai 幸若舞

Any effort to give a clear account of the performed arts in classical Japan can only distort a most complex period of evolution. A very large number of kinds of performance existed, many of them designed for the lower classes, and many originating from such classes. They survived by virtue of the Japanese instinct to preserve and by taking on characteristics of the higher culture and the social organization emerging after the internecine strife of sengoku times (1476–1568).

There are many, many terms to describe various sorts of performance. Often the same thing is given different names. Often the same name comes to designate quite different things in the course of time. *Mibukyōgen* and *kōwakamai* may be taken as examples of performances that have just barely survived. Moreover, they offer us some sense of the kind of performance existing about *nō* and *kyōgen*, and possess features that made *jōruri* and *kabuki* possible.

Mibu kyōgen is also termed Mibu sarugaku and Mibu nembutsu (*nembutsu*, or recitation of the Buddha's name, having led to various kinds of performance earlier). A standard dictionary defines it as "one of a number of kinds of folk drama of the sarugaku line" (*Kōjien*). It is still performed annually at Mibu Temple in Kyoto for a few days in the latter half of April by people who have inherited the costumes, roles, and site. For our purposes, it is especially significant that its action is extremely vigorous. Perhaps it shows us what nō or at least sarugaku once was like, although it is not humorous. The action is performed to the accompaniment of a temple gong, a flute, and a large drum. As a performance ends, there is a ritual breaking of simple dishes by pushing them down to the grounds beneath the stage. The audience also sits in an elevated position, regarding the players across a gulf of space, with broken dishes lying below from the preceding performance. The plays include, for example, *Tsuchigumo*, on the huge earth spider, and the actor for the role has a great time casting webs about. This topic was, of course, used also by nō and kabuki in their ways. The Mibu kyōgen version differs from those others in that it, like all its performances, is purely pantomime, without a word of text. This may lead us to infer that the art is closely related to religious ritual, but its present version is distinct from any sectarian emphasis.

Kōwakamai has been more thoroughly studied. As might be expected, that has made matters more complex. The art has continued to be performed only in the village of Ōe in Fukuoka. However, fifty texts have survived from the seventeenth century, and the titles of another sixty-odd are known. Of those fifty, forty deal either with figures from the *Gempei* wars or with the Soga brothers' revenge. Comedy and romantic attachments are rigorously excluded in this male depiction (for male audiences?) of the heroic era. The scripts are in prose, and performances take two to three hours.

Unlike Mibu kyōgen, kōwakamai does not consist solely of miming, though it does include mime with dance elements that involve stamping of feet. The texts have no dialogue but rather recitation. There are also passages designated "kotoba." These words are spoken by individual players rather than by the reciter, although most of the play is given to the reciter. It is as if the chorus in nō handled most of the text and the shite or waki said just a bit now and again. The characters have nō-like designations: tayū 太夫 (*shite*), *waki*, and *tsure*.

The rest remains open to varying description. The pieces have usually been termed kōwaka bukyoku 幸若舞曲, or dance pieces, and there are many records praising early performers for their dances. It is not clear whether the foot-stomping, which is about all that constitutes dance in performance now, was considered especially appealing or whether several other kinds of movement have been lost. The texts also show up in places that may seem natural or unexpected. It is not surprising that they should be included among "old jōruri" (*kojōruri*), but it is another matter to find them among *otogizōshi* and *ukiyozōshi*.

Those who acted kōwakamai were often called shōmyō, which strictly speaking refers to Buddhist liturgical musicians or chanters. But such people had long since taken on the role of entertainers to propagate the faith, so the title could have purely secular overtones; performers, much like nominal or actual nuns (*bikuni, etoki* bikuni), traveled about the country performing by explaining religious pictures or reciting long narratives. The actors were also sometimes referred to as senzu manzai, after the performers of auspicious rites at New Year's. The names are not as important in themselves as the glimpse they give of a welter of kinds of performance in pre-Edo Japan.

The heyday of kōwakamai was relatively brief. According to legend, it was founded by Momonoi Naoakira, whose dates are variously given. Whether or not he had anything to do with the development of the art, the dates assigned are those of the fifteenth century, and it does seem likely that that much is right. This kind emerged, then, a half century or so after *sarugaku*-style nō and kyōgen had taken on their distinct character. About the middle of the sixteenth century, its texts were set down and seem to have remained fixed thereafter. During the following fifty years kōwakamai flourished and thereafter declined. Various explanations have been given for the decline. The most likely seems to be that as the performers achieved status as samurai when the nation settled down, they no longer thought acting worthy of their status.

Mibu kyōgen shows that lively action or pantomime was part of the Japanese sense of drama. Kōwakamai shows how drama could develop with action explained by recitation. Both features were to be taken up by the major subsequent kinds that developed during the Edo period, and in *jōruri* we discover a kind of drama whose genius was like that of kōwakamai, if also far greater.

D. JŌRURI

Very numerous kinds of entertainment have been termed *jōruri*, some old and some late: for example, kabukijōruri properly designates *kabuki* music. For something of the variety, see the jōruri entry in Part Three. What follows concerns one line, that involving puppets.

Although it shares very much in its development with numerous other kinds of performance, *jōruri* (today termed *bunraku*) is different from other kinds of Japanese drama, and probably from all other important kinds in the world, in being a theater using puppets. The elimination of actors placed greater importance on other elements, which came to include the following four in decreasing order of importance:

recitation	*tayū*	太夫
music	*shamisen*	三味線
manipulated puppets	*ayatsuri ningyō* (or ningyō)	操人形
text	*daihon*	台本

Modern ideas have come to rate the author of the text more highly than did the practitioners of jōruri in its heyday, but it remains quite clear that for actual theater the other three are still crucial to performance.

What may be termed proto-jōruri is a kind of puppet entertainment. Puppet manipulators, *kugutsu*, were functioning as early as the Nara period, at first men but later women also. The puppets they used were small, after the fashion of Western kinds, and were made from wood or pottery. Early puppet shows seem to have concentrated on representing dance or fights. A more sophisticated manipulation appeared with the ebisukaki 恵比須舁 group of kugutsu. This developed in Nishinomiya (Hyōgo prefecture) and became a type of performance.

About the Muromachi period, proto-jōruri had many resemblances with *heikyoku, sekkyō, kōwakamai* and other kinds of performance, and even at later stages of development it retained features from these other kinds. For a long time its performers, including the ebisukaki, were as much strollers as were the performers of heikyoku and so forth. Yet the ebisukaki gradually attached themselves to temples and shrines, and acquired a degree of respectability and interest. By the middle of the sixteenth century, courtiers had taken notice of them. Ono no Otsū 小野お通, a female attendant of Oda Nobunaga, composed her *Jōruri Jūnidan Sōshi* 浄瑠璃十二段草子 (*A Jōruri Book in Twelve Acts*), so suggesting some degree of interest among the Azuchi–Momoyama authorities. By the mid-fifteenth century, jōruri seems to have enjoyed special popularity in Mikawa province (near modern Nagoya). During this time it resembled other kinds of performance in being essentially a kind of mimed narrative accompanied by music, but it differed in using puppets. Yet, as this account also shows, the identification of jōruri with puppets is a later stage.

The old jōruri (*kojōruri*), as it is called, came about with the adoption of what is now termed the shamisen, a three-stringed lute- or banjo-like instrument plucked by fingers or a plectrum. Like the French horn among wind instruments, this is a very expressive invention and very difficult to play truly well. The instrument arrived in Japan from China via the Ryukyu Islands about 1555 to 1570. Between about 1595 and 1625, it was adapted to Japanese tastes, so that the sanshin or jabisen at last became the shamisen. The instrument is light enough and small enough to be easily portable. But there is something about it that has led Japanese to use it in preference to other instruments for performance on the popular classical stage. In this sense, its adoption by jōruri signifies a potential for performance in theaters rather than by strolling minstrels.

Old jōruri seems to have begun in Kyoto, but by the second quarter of the seventeenth century was flourishing more in Edo. Thereafter its history is one of the rivalry between theaters in three centers—Kyoto, Osaka, and Edo—and with *kabuki*. In the middle of the century, popularity shifted to Kyoto, where at last the lines of great reciters began to emerge, and this may be thought the crucial period for the development of the art as it is usually known. With the emergence about 1677 of the most famous of reciters, *Takemoto Gidayū, the old jōruri was established as an independent art, at once popular and worthy of separate aesthetic consideration. With the addition of the literary genius of

*Chikamatsu Monzaemon, the art realized its potential. From the appearance in 1685 of *Shusse Kagekiyo*, written by Chikamatsu for Gidayū, Japanese scholars date the new jōruri (shinjōruri). The date is somewhat arbitrary, and in fact certain kinds of jōruri have continued to be called *Gidayūbushi*. (The rest of the development is properly the part of history in Part One.)

Many discriminations (and even more names) have been made over the centuries, one of which involves the distinguishing of three kinds of jōruri. The kind that concerns everybody most is ningyōgeki, which includes old jōruri, Gidayūbushi, and new jōruri. A second joins jōruri with kabuki. And a third involves domestic performance.

A more important distinction, one passed on to kabuki, is that between two kinds of plays: *jidaimono* or period pieces and *sewamono* or contemporary pieces. The former was itself subdivided:

ōdaimono	dealing with courtly matters
jidaimono	dealing with older matters
oiemono	dealing with daimyo or samurai matters

These categories are obviously not fully parallel or exclusive. Sometimes a simpler distinction is drawn between military pieces, *gunkimono*, and others. This would seem to suggest the primacy of jidaimono. But the existence of that which is called sewajidaimono seems to suggest the opposite, that sewamono exerted influence on the period pieces. (For plays exemplifying such kinds, see the next section, on kabuki.)

Both kinds are usually divided into *dan* and *ba*, for which "act" and "scene" are accurate enough (meaning as they do different things in Italy, France, and England). The old jōruri seems to have taken on a five-act sequence:

1. Sambasō   三番叟
2. kyōgen   狂言
3. kyōgen
4. kyōgen
5. shūgen   祝言

Sambasō (as we saw in connection with *Okina* in nō) and shūgen are felicitous, offering an auspicious beginning and ending, at least in name. The three middle acts are those of the action proper. Later, Gidayū also distinguished five acts, but his categories obviously signify a quite different kind of play:

1. love (koi)   恋
2. battle (shura)   修羅
3. offense (shūtan)   愁嘆
4. travel piece (*michiyuki*)   道行
5. dialogue (*mondō*)   問答

This seems quite arbitrary, an adaptation from nō. These two five-act distinctions were thought characteristic of jidaimono, whereas sewamono were divided into three acts. (Nobody knows where these five- and three-act divisions came from, but they are also most common in the West, where their origins are equally obscure.)

Chikamatsu distinguished for sewamono a three-act or three-part sequence:

1. opening (kuchi) 口
2. middle (naka) 中
3. end (kiri) 切

The same divisions may in fact be made for jidaimono, as can be shown variously but most simply in terms of the divisions in old jōruri: Sambasō, three kyōgen, shūgen. This makes the middle portion much longer than the other two. This sorts well with Japanese senses of proportion. In fact, whether deliberately or simply out of a sense of fitness, Chikamatsu was obviously distinguishing something very like the *jo-ha-kyū* rhythm of *gagaku*, nō, *renga*, and *haikai*.

A jōruri stage can be set up in a kabuki theater or on a Western stage. As the audience enters, it faces the stage where the puppets are manipulated. (See Figs. 5-8 and 5-9.) To the right (stage left) and jutting out toward the audience are places for two men to sit. The one closest to the audience is the reciter (tayū, Gidayū, etc.). At his right (nearer the stage) sits the shamisen player. The puppets of jōruri kugutsu were once small enough to be carried in a box suspended from the shoulders, while the hands manipulated two puppets from behind and the manipulator could comment or relate. Being of about the half-human size they are today, the puppets are now more than one manipulator can handle. Also, since the facial features can be moved, elaborate dances be staged, and puppets be made to seem to smoke a pipe or throw and catch fans, the three manipulators have specialized parts of the body to deal with, and must be extremely skillful. The puppets may have their own stage, as it were (perhaps a domestic interior), but essentially the manipulators stand behind a boarded area that covers the lower parts of their bodies. The audience can see the manipulators from the waist up, including heads and arms. They are dressed in black and covered with a kind of black gauze. So skillful is the handling that, in fact, one is caught up in the acting.

The shamisen used to accompany the action and reciting, as also to give some music on occasion, is of a heavier kind than that used in kabuki or to accompany dances (*odori*). It has a wonderful strength of tone and a range of effect that requires hearing to appreciate. The reciter (in Edo-style clothes) sits before his text rack and gives the only speaking voice (or voices) heard. All that is narrated or spoken by the characters derives from him. A soldier boasting of his name and threatening his enemy blusters through the reciter. A couple weeping last vows for the next world as they go to double suicide do so in the shaking voice of the reciter. It may be that in theory three such dissimilar elements should not make up effective theater, yet they do. Although kabuki has a range beyond that of jōruri, the theatrical spirit is purified to a degree in jōruri that enables us to understand why it could exceed kabuki in popularity over periods of time. And it seems likely that no other Japanese theatrical art holds the same interest as jōruri for theories of dramatic possibility.

E. KABUKI

Kabuki is the grand, at times the irresponsible or spendthrift, heir of the many kinds of performance that led to its birth in the early seventeenth century. Like *jōruri*, its immediate parent, it is a drama for everyone, regardless of social condition, although it emerged as a theater for city people (*chōnin*), flourishing in Kyoto, Osaka, and Edo. Like *nō* and *kyōgen*, it can be very serious or comic; but it also can be tear-jerking, melodramatic, noisy, silent—whatever seems to be most effective. From *nō* it has adapted many stories. From *kyōgen* it has taken the comic spirit and its official name, *kabukikyōgen*. Unlike *jōruri*, it uses live actors. Unlike *nō*, it counts on being heard distinctly, and so it features makeup rather than masks. Unlike *nō* and even *kyōgen*, it displays great dynamism in the acting, and it has had a marked capacity to adapt to changing tastes.

The present characters for kabuki, 歌舞伎, are sometimes made much of, as meaning song-dance-drama. Of these the second and particularly the third tell most of its nature, although the characters have been used only since recent times and, until the Meiji period, the third character was 妓. The word originally derived from a verb signifying to be different, erotic, or abnormal. It was perhaps the words kabukimono, kabukionna (strange man, woman) that led to its designation as kabukikyōgen. At least that supposition sorts with the existence of both male and female troupes near the end of the sixteenth century. The no doubt justified suspicion of immorality, and perhaps the avowed feudal aim of subjugating women, allowed authorities to forbid women from acting. This brought about a change of focus in kabuki plots from women to a contrast of women and men as well as of evil and good characters.

Although the various kabuki troupes have borrowed with a free hand what seemed to work on the stages of rival companies, a basic distinction is felt to exist between *kamigata* and Edo plays. In Kyoto and Osaka, the speciality was *nuregoto*, stories of passion; in Edo it was *aragoto*, spectacular action. Nuregoto plays dwell more on plot, dialogue, and individualizing of characters. Aragoto plays feature stage business, pose, dance, and attitudes struck by the actor. To the extent that the distinction holds, nuregoto exploits more of the features of jōruri sewamono and aragoto more of the jidaimono.

Improved communication between Edo and Osaka in the eighteenth century led to assimilation by Edo kabuki of many features of kamigata jōruri. This suggests something of its continuing development. The many illustrations of theaters at the time show that they were far smaller than those today, so that the scale must have resembled a nō theater much more nearly. In 1758, the Osaka playwright, *Namiki Shōzō (1730–1773) invented the revolving stage, so essentially making the theater what it is today (see Figs. 5-8 and 5-9.) Kabuki was also becoming institutionalized by the establishment of houses of actors and musicians. The former included the Ichikawa 市川, Sawamura 沢村, Matsumoto 松本, Segawa 瀬川, and Nakamura 中村. The jōruri music schools of Tokiwazu 常磐津, Tomimoto 富本, and Kiyomoto 清元 were given new vitality with kabuki, and *nagauta* was perfected for stage purposes. Most of the plays performed today had ruder precursors in this period.

Kabuki achieved full development between 1780 and 1850—along with some signs of decadence in dwelling on the lurid and melodramatic rather more than previously. Yet the Iwai and, particularly, the Onoe houses of actors had also made their mark. All the main kinds of kabuki came to full development, and what we know of kabuki today is essentially what was known then (although contact with the West and more recently with film and television has left marks on the older entity).

As kabuki matured, it brought into being plays that have been variously distinguished. The most general distinction is that between *buyōgeki* (i.e., *shosagoto*) and *engeki*. The former are dance plays by name, although they involve as well action and dialogue. The dancing is accompanied by singing and above all by *shamisen* playing. This combination uses nagauta or jōruri music. Engeki are dramatic plays emphasizing dialogue (*serifu*). Another distinction is taken over from jōruri. For *jidaimono*, the same subcategories were distinguished as for the puppet theater. For *sewamono*, an extra category of *kizewamono* ("living," that is, melodramatic domestic plays), including both *kaidanmono* (spectral or mystery pieces) and *shiranamimono* (rogues' and villains' pieces). This general category was developed by one of the last great kabuki playwrights, *Kawatake Mokuami (1816–1893). A title like *Shiranami Gonin Otoko* reminds us of *Ihara Saikaku, who would have liked these plays.

Before this dramatist there were many others of high importance, such as *Tsuruya Namboku. Their position—relative to other people involved in the plays—was in general superior to that of their counterparts for jōruri. But just as that theater had been dominated by the reciter, kabuki has always been dominated by actors. The playwright would have to change what would not show off an actor's talents to best effect, and an actor might improvise as the idea struck him. But literary students must understand that such are more or less the conditions of living theater throughout the world, and one might go farther still to say that audiences control even the actors, since what will not bring people to the theater will not long be played.

The types of roles became more and more specialized. In general, actors earned their careers by being able to play numerous kinds of parts, but it was no doubt inevitable that the special talents required have led some actors to specialize in women's roles, *onnagata*, some men's, *otokogata*, and within these groups other roles such as comic, romantic, or heavy characters. Actors often make their debuts as young children and gradually work their way along to playing old men and women. It must be remembered, however, that many of the most esteemed performances of young women's parts have been by older actors. The following categories of actors are usually distinguished.

OTOKOGATA 男形. Male Roles

TACHIYAKU 立役. In general, leading male roles; more particularly, good characters

WAGOTO 和事. Attractive men, often lovers, whether samurai or of ordinary class

JITSUGOTO 実事. Straightforward men

ARAGOTO 荒事. Great heroes; bold, bustling men
BUDŌ(GATA) 武道(方). True warriors

KATAKIYAKU 敵役. Villains, contrasted with tachiyaku

JITSUAKU 実悪. Downright evil characters, usually samurai
IROAKU 色悪. Amorous villains
OYAJIGATA 親仁方. Old villains
TEDAIGATAKI 手代敵. Villainous managers or servants in mercantile houses
DŌKEGATA 道化方. Comic men, fools
HANDŌ(GATAKI) 半道敵. Comic male villains

ONNAGATA 女方. Female Roles

WAKAONNAGATA 若女方. Women about twenty or so

TAYŪ 太夫. Courtesans of high rank in the licensed quarters
MUSUMEGATA 娘方. Young women of ordinary class
AKUBA 悪婆 or DOKUFUGATA 毒婦方. Villainous women
KASHAGATA 花車方(形). Old women

MISCELLANEOUS

WAKASHUGATA 若衆方. Young men or boys

OYAJIGATA 親仁方. Old men (cf. kashagata)

KOKATA 子方. Children, especially boys

Other roles, such as those of the nobility, spirits, and even animals also exist, but those specified here pertain to the kinds that the government wished, in its feudal and bureaucratic way, to classify, and in fact did manage to control to some extent until there was a relaxation in the nineteenth century. It has been remarked with great penetration that "modal beauty" rather than merely particularized or realistic portrayal is the essential quality of kabuki, and, more provocatively, that this lies most essentially in the art of the onnagata. There are some who hold that when the onnagata disappear from the stage, kabuki will be no more.

The acting houses took on various characteristics, including names in a hierarchy of esteem, acting techniques, and favorite plays that have become part of the traditions of the theater. Some of us will never forget the great onnagata Onoe Kikugorō VI 尾上菊五郎 (1876–1949) playing the title role in *Musume Dōjōji* at the age of seventy-one, making the dancing girl come to graceful life. For a generation, then, a given actor of a given house may seem to define a specific role or kind of role. One symptom of this tendency has been the definition of semi-official lists of prime plays by a given actor for a given school. These include *Shinko Engeki Jusshu* 新古演劇十種, ten plays selected by Onoe Kikugorō V (1844–1903) from those made most famous by his acting and that of his predecessors. This group was subsequently altered. Another selection, the *Shin Kabuki Jūhachibanshū* 新歌舞伎十八番集 selected by Ichikawa Danjurō IX (1838–1903), includes both dramatic and dance pieces in which he starred. As this name suggests, there was before it the most famous collection of all, *Kabuki*

Jūhachiban, said to have been compiled by Danjurō VII (1791–1859), which included plays especially suited to the Ichikawa aragoto style.

Perhaps one of the readiest ways of showing something of the nature of kabuki (and also jōruri) plays is to run through all eighteen of the Kabuki Jūhachiban plays with various comments.

1. *Fuwa* 不破 (1680). Jidaimono. Rivalry over a courtesan between Fuwa Banzaemon and another samurai.

2. *Narukami* 鳴神 (1684). Jidaimono. The priest named in the title as the divinity of thunder raves in anger after having given himself to the enchantments of a beautiful woman. Like *Fuwa,* not among the enduring favorites.

3. *Shibaraku* 暫 (1697). Jidaimono. "Just a Moment." The title comes from the word rung out by the hero, a good samurai who rescues another from a tyrant lord. This is performed each *kaomise* and is one of the most famous of all.

4. *Fudō* 不動 (1697). Jidaimono. The title refers to the Fire Divinity, to represent the distraught jealousy of a woman.

5. *Uwanari* 嫐 (1699). Jidaimono. Also about female jealousy. The title means "The Mistress."

6. *Zōbiki* 象引 (1701). Jidaimono. This "Plundering an Elephant" is an ancient moralizing story. An imperiously proud nobleman rides to view plum blossoms on an elephant. A righteous warrior punishes him and takes the elephant. Edo people were hardly familiar with live elephants, and the staging of this must have been spectacular as well as exotic.

7. *Kanjinchō* 勧進帳 (1703). Buyōgeki. An adaptation of the nō, *Ataka,* "The Subscription List," and one of the kabuki favorites. Benkei, the retainer of Yoshitsune, uses various ruses to get his master past the Ataka Barrier. The acting, dancing, and posturing make this a wonderful spectacle.

8. *Sukeroku* 助六 (1713). Sewamono, named after the hero, lover of the high-ranking Yoshiwara courtesan, Agemaki. Although a commoner, Sukeroku defeats the samurai villain who is trying to get the woman by force. This has a fine Edo sewamono plot, and is a long-time favorite.

9. *Oshimodoshi* 押戻 (1714). Buyōgeki. The "Pushing Around" of the title refers to the superhero of the play, who quells many monsters and evil spirits. Real aragoto.

10. *Uirōuri* 外郎売 (1718). Buyōgeki. "The uirō seller" does little more than give a long mountebank speech, with dance, on the miraculous curative powers of his ware. Tour de force.

11. *Kan-u* 関羽 (1737). Jidaimono. Pretending to be the legendary Chinese warrior, Kan-u, the hero lays bare the machinations of evil samurai.

12. *Ya no Ne* 矢の根 (1729). Jidaimono. One of the many Sogamono 曽我物, or stories of the Soga brothers and their revenge, this tells how Gorō, while polishing the arrowhead of the title, falls asleep, dreams of Jūrō's plight, and rushes off to assist him. The dream presentation on stage makes the play.

13. *Kagekiyo* 景清 (1739). Jidaimono. The heroic Kagekiyo, who appears in nō and other later plays, here frees himself from confinement.

14. *Nanatsumen* 七ツ面 (1740). Jidaimono. Story of a nō mask maker and the seven masks of the title.

15. *Kenuki* 毛抜 (1742). Jidaimono. Wrongdoers are discovered and put to death by the strange means of the hair tweezers of the title and a magnet.

16. *Gedatsu* 解脱 (1760). Jidaimono. Another Kagekiyo play, this time involving the "Deliverance" of the title of a warrior's soul through earnest prayer.

17. *Jayanagi* 蛇柳 (1763). Sewamono. "The Snake Willow." Kiyohime, a dead young woman, comes back as a specter, possessing a fool in order to express her jealousy.

18. *Kamahige* 鎌髭 (1774). Another Kagekiyo play. The disguised Kagekiyo falls into argument with a swordmaker whom he encounters on his travels. "The Beard-Sickle" of the title refers to the swordmaker's ruse to shave Kagekiyo with a sickle. He intends to cut off his head, but Kagekiyo has impermeable skin. More splendid aragoto.

Some other plays are as noteworthy and famous as even *Shibaraku*, even if not as consistently performed. Just a few may be noted, beginning with three adapted from jōruri. *Kokusen'ya Kassen* 国性爺合戦, *The Battle of Coxinga*, is adapted from a play with the same title by Chikamatsu (opened 1715). The hero's role is aragoto at an extreme. *Shinjū Ten no Amijima* 心中天網島, or more simply *Koharu Jihē* 小春治兵衛 after the two central characters, tells of "The Double Suicide at Amijima," and is taken from a sewamono by Chikamatsu that opened in 1720. *Sonezaki Shinjū* 曽根崎心中 deals with another double suicide, at Sonezaki, and also was written by Chikamatsu. It was performed in 1703, and is a sewamono.

Meiboku Sendai Hagi 伽羅先代萩 or *Sendai Hagi* was originally written for jōruri by collaborators, and as "The Disputed Succession of the Date Family," is probably the finest of the Date plays. It involves conspiracies and features children playing highly affecting roles. An oiemono variety of jidaimono.

Yoshitsune Sembonzakura 義経千本桜 or *Sembonzakura*. Jidaimono. The jōruri version by *Takeda Izumo and others was performed in 1745; the kabuki version of this "Yoshitsune and the Thousand Cherry Trees" appeared the next year. Yoshitsune's valor had helped establish his brother, Yoritomo, as ruler of Japan. But now the brother has accused Yoshitsune of sending false heads for the three Taira generals he was supposed to do away with. This complicated play deals with Yoshitsune's wanderings, his encounters with the three Taira, his chivalric treatment of them and, above all, with his mistress Shizuka. She is given a wonderful *michiyuki* and dance with a magic drum. She is united with Yoshitsune at Yoshino, famous for its cherry flowers, and so on, and so forth.

Soga no Taimen 曽我の対面. This "Revenge of the Soga Brothers" is one of a half dozen or so plays on this enduringly popular story. Jidaimono.

Kanadehon Chūshingura 仮名手本忠臣蔵 or *Chūshingura*. Originally a hit jidaimono in jōruri by *Takeda Izumo and others, it is one of the all-time favorites on the kabuki stage as well. It deals with the forty-seven masterless samurai (rōnin) who carefully bide their time to avenge their lord, who was disgraced and made to commit ritual suicide. The full kabuki version runs to many, many hours. It is sometimes played entire, although as usual with kabuki today, the tendency is to excerpt favorite scenes.

(*Kyō Kanoko* or *Kyōganoko*) *Musume Dōjōji* (京鹿子)娘道成寺, *Musume Dōjōji*, or *Dōjōji* is a nagauta shosagoto that has been popular since its appearance in 1753. Dōjō Temple is about to have a new bell dedicated on a day when women are barred from the precincts. A young woman appears (the ghost of Kiyohime, a former *shirabyōshi*), and pleads to enter. The priests refuse, but yield to her request that at least she dance. As she does so, a loud sound is heard. She disappears during the confusion. The bell has fallen. The priests pray, the bell rises, and a serpent is seen inside—a manifestation of Kiyohime.

Kuruwa Bunshō 廓文章. A sewamono adapted from Chikamatsu's *Yūgiri Awa no Naruto* 夕霧阿波の鳴渡, this "Tale of the Licensed Quarter" was played in Edo in 1808. The revision well illustrates Edo tastes in sewamono. Izaemon, now disinherited from the Fujiya for his love of the Shimmachi courtesan Yūgiri, arrives in winter at the licensed house where she lives. Although she has a new patron and he is reduced by poverty to a paper kimono, they are reconciled. At the right moment a messenger arrives with familial forgiveness, consent, and the money to buy Yūgiri out of her bond.

Kagamijishi 鏡獅子. Shosagoto. Strictly speaking, this belongs to modern literature, having first been produced in 1893. But this "Lion Mirror" has a spectacular dance that well represents the spirit of one kind of kabuki.

Ichinotani Futaba Gunki 一谷嫩軍記 Jidaimono. One of a number of plays involving the valiant Kumagai Naozane and the young Atsumori. In this, Kumagai is ordered by his lord to bring Atsumori's head if at all possible. He captures the young man but, because the lad's mother had once saved his life, lets him go. He therefore presents his own son's head to his lord, takes the tonsure for a life of austerities, and leaves a grieving lord, suffering wife, and his own heroic past. The final scene on the *hanamichi* is one of the most moving and tragic in drama, although only half a dozen words are spoken.

Sambasō 三番叟. A shosagoto adapted, ca. 1650, from the nō and joruri. One of several auspicious plays of similar nature: see also *Shikisambasō* and *Ayatsuri Sambasō*.

Sugawara Denju Tenarai Kagami 菅原伝授手習鑑, better known as *Terakoya* 寺子(小)屋, "The Temple School." Jidaimono, adapted from a jōruri play by Takeda Izumo and others presented in 1746. One of the great favorites, this shows a loyal retainer offering his son to be killed in place of his lord's, intrigue, and so on.

The kabuki season began on the first day of the eleventh month (all dates by the lunar calendar) with the kaomise, face-showing performance. The newly reconstituted troupe would offer itself to the public. In the kabuki year ensuing, actors would perform about two hundred days in the various subseasons. These include spring, haru, starting on the fifteenth of the First Month. The yayoi run began on the third of the Third Month and the satsuki on the fifth of the Fifth Month. The bon run, beginning the fifteenth of the Seventh Month, was so named for starting at about the time of the bon festival of the dead. There was also an onagori or keepsake run, a farewell production, beginning on the ninth day of the Ninth Month.

A typical kaomise production would consist of two parts, a jidaimono followed by a sewamono. But "parts" is ambiguous, since it was something of a medley, with the jidaimono normally a version of *Shibaraku* redone by various playwrights in the house. In outline, the production might run as follows.

First Piece (ichibanme kyōgen: jidaimono)
1. opening (jobiraki) 序開, a comic introduction
2. second part (futatateme) 二立目
3. third part (mitateme) 三立目
4. fourth part (yotateme) 四立目
5. fifth part (itsutateme) 五立目
6. sixth part (mutateme) 六立目

Second Piece (nibanme kyōgen: sewamono)
7. sewa part (sewaba) 世話場
8. grand finale (ōgiri 大切: often a dance performance at dusk)

The fifth and sixth parts might be omitted, or they might be used as a big ending (ōzume 大詰) of the jidaimono. In general the sewamono was thought more important. Various modifications were made for other runs.

The kabuki theater evolved so continuously that it is difficult to describe except in a given period. Today's versions are theaters of some size with a proscenium arch—an importation from the West, as are the chairs for the audience. Today the musicians usually sit behind lattice work to audience left (stage right front), and from a point just to audience right of them a ramp or causeway, the hanamichi, runs out from the stage into the audience. The audience is divided into a small group on the left of that ramp and a much larger group on the right. Some ramps go straight to the back, but the usual way today is to have them go off at an angle to the audience's left side of the theater, where there is an exit door. The ramp running straight is a vestige of the early kabuki stage, in which an actor could take the ramp straight into the audience, turn 90° left and walk horizontally across the theater, make another left turn and walk back to the stage along the audience-right side of the theater. The revolving stage (mawashi), first invented in Japan, has grown increasingly sophisticated, and sometimes more than one will be used for spectacular effects (see Fig. 5-12).

The actors dress in clothes more or less appropriate to the period in which the play is set, as also to the sex, social class, and so on of the characters. Onnagata have whitened faces and wigs in an appropriate style for the character. Many plays require large casts; others small. In such matters, kabuki is so much more various than its predecessors that general characterization is not possible. But certain things are distinctive: the brown, black, and green stripes of the curtain, colors also associated otherwise with kabuki; the wooden clappers (hyōshigi 拍子木) announcing the opening of the play in a beat of increasing rapidity; and the kabuki enthusiast who will cry out just the right word at the right time from somewhere at the back of the audience.

Plays are performed today in the Kabukiza, the National Theater (Kokuritsu Gekijō), and elsewhere in Tokyo; at the Minamiza in Kyoto; at the Shinkabukiza in Osaka; at the Misonoza in Nagoya; and at other theaters.

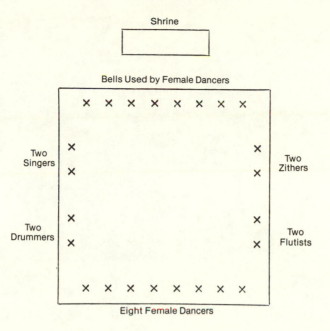

FIGURE 5-1. Design of a Kagura Stage. Adapted from Frank Alanson Lombard, *An Outline History of Japanese Drama* (London: Allen, 1928).

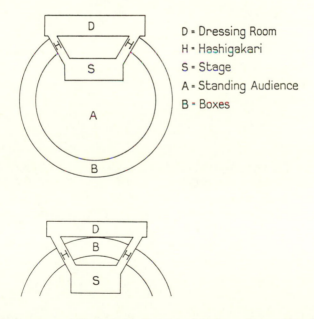

FIGURE 5-2. Reconstructed Design of a Dengaku Nō Stage from a Description Dated 1349. In a, one possibility; in b, another. From Peter Arnott, *The Theatres of Japan* (London: Macmillan, [1969]).

FIGURE 5-3. A Modern Nō Stage. From Koyama Hiroshi, et al., eds., *Yōkyokushū* (Shōgakkan, 1973).

FIGURE 5-4. The Nō Stage in Outline. Upper portion from Koyama, *Yōkyokushū* (Shōgakkan, 1973); lower from P. O'Neill, *A Guide to Nō* (Hinoki Shoten, [1954]).

1. Curtain between *hashigakari* and dressing-rooms
2. *Kyōgen's* place
3. Stage assistants
4. Side exit
5. Third pine
6. Second pine
7. First pine
8. *Shite's* pillar
9. *Taiko* drum
10. *Ōtsuzumi* drum
11. *Kotsuzumi* drum
12. Flute
13. Flute pillar
14. Naming place
15. Chorus
16. Chorus leader (Hōshō, Komparu, Kongō and Kita schools)
17. Chorus leader (Kanze school)
18. Gravel surround
19. Guide pillar
20. Steps
21. *Waki's* pillar

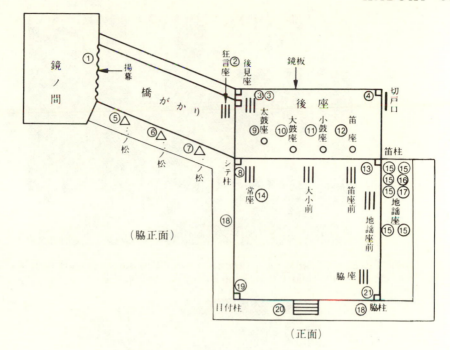

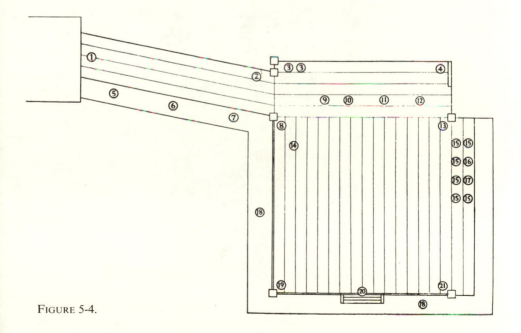

Figure 5-4.

FIGURE 5-5. Kyōgen. *Ko Nusubito* (*The Kidnapper*). The kidnapper finds himself taken by the charms of the child. From Geinō Kenkyūkai, *Kyōgen* (Heibonsha, 1970).

FIGURE 5-6. Kyōgen. *Bōshibari*. To prevent them from drinking his sake, the master ties Tarōkaja's arms to a pole and the arms of the other servant, Jirōkaja (not shown), to his body. With some cunning and work, they manage to get the drink. Actor: Nomura Manzai. From Geinō Kenkyūkai, *Kyōgen* (Heibonsha, 1970).

FIGURE 5-7. Early Itinerant Puppeteers. From Andō Tsuruo and Charles Dunn, *Bunraku* (Dankōsha, 1967).

FIGURE 5-8. Jōruri in a Late Edo Depiction. Shows puppets, puppeteers (the lesser ones covered with black cloth, as today); to the right, the tayū and shamisen player. From Andō and Dunn, *Bunraku* (Dankōsha, 1967).

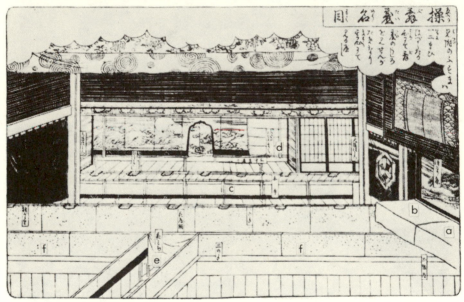

FIGURE 5-9. The Jōruri Stage in Edo Times. From Yokoyama Tadashi, ed., *Jōrurishū* (Iwanami Shoten, 1971).

a. place of reciter (Tayū)
b. place of shamisen player
c. area for puppeteers and puppets
d. back stage to which puppets can be taken: here an indoor scene
e. passageway for taking puppets among the audience (cf. the hanamichi or ramp for kabuki, Fig. 13)
f. audience.

FIGURE 5-10. A Modern Bunraku Version of Chikamatsu Monzaemon's *Sonezaki Shinjū* (*The Love Suicides at Sonezaki*), Adapted. Compare with the next. From Sasahara Nobuo, *Bi to Aku no Dentō* (Ōfūsha, 1969).

FIGURE 5-11. A Modern Kabuki Version of *Sonezaki Shinjū*. This is the moment before the final curtain is drawn. Compare with the preceding. From Sasahara Nobuo, *Bi to Aku no Dentō* (Ōfūsha, 1969).

FIGURE 5-12. The Nakamura Kabuki Za Interior (1785). Note the hanamichi or ramp from stage right to audience left. This still survives in kabuki theatres. The narrower ramps from stage left to audience right and across the audience have not, although the one on audience right may be put up for some special occasion. From Urayama Masao and Matsuzaki Hitoshi, ed., *Kabuki Kyōhonshū*, 1 (Iwanami Shoten, 1960).

PART SIX Collections, Kinds, Criticism; Buddhism and Confucianism; Dictionaries

The fourteen sections of this part provide information that concerns, in one way or another, titles by groupings relating to literature along with titles relating to religious and philosophical matters. Since there are so many sections, it will be of use to letter them here in the order of appearance:

The lettered titles here are simplifications but should enable a reader to find labeled material, and somewhat more. In keeping with the emphasis of this *Companion*, Chinese works are treated less copiously than Japanese.

Titles and authors with asterisks will be found in Part Three, Major Authors and Works. Italicized words, other than titles, will be found in Part Four, Literary Terms. Extra dates and Chinese characters have been supplied when not generally available elsewhere in this book. Short narrative sections are given to explain various matters.

A. WAKA

Over the centuries, *waka* was taken as the most representative example of literature. History did matter, and other kinds came to matter also. But certain kinds of history were not deemed literary, and every other kind began as a pastime until it was subsequently elevated to literary status. Yet it is also remarkable that the poetry so often sorts well with prose, and in fact many important works go under alternative titles designating poetic collections (-shū, *kashū*), diary (*nikki*), and narrative (*monogatari*). In what follows, usual Japanese classifications are followed.

1. The *Man'yōshū and Twenty-One Royal Collections

The most prestigious series of waka collections consist of one completed in the late eighth century and twenty-one compiled between the early tenth and the mid-fifteenth centuries. The twenty-one are known as *chokusen(waka)shū*, officially or royally commissioned anthologies, and also as the *nijūichidaishū*, the collections of twenty-one reigns. Within this group, the first three are referred to as the *sandaishū*, collections of three reigns. The first eight are known as the *hachidaishū*, collections of eight reigns. And the last thirteen make up the *jūsandaishū*, collections of thirteen reigns. The first three provided the model of language; in formal poetry thereafter, a poet was expected to use that word hoard (although of course innovations were made). The first of the twenty-one set the organizational principles for the rest. The remarks about it, the eighth, the fourteenth, and the seventeenth in Part Three may be consulted. In what follows, usual Japanese usage is employed: for example, *Kokinshū* rather than *Kokinwakashū*. Fuller information about these collections will be found in Part Three. The purpose here is to set down in one place the entire series.

The Early Collection
  Man'yōshū (ca. 759)
The Collections of Twenty-one Reigns

1. *Kokinshū*, ca. 905–920	12. *Shokushūishū*, 1278 ff.
2. *Gosenshū*, 951 ff.	13. *Shingosenshū*, 1303
3. *Shūishū*, 1005–1011	14. *Gyokuyōshū*, 1312–1313
4. *Goshūishū*, 1086	15. *Shokusenzaishū*, 1320
5. *Kin'yōshū*, 1127	16. *Shokugoshūishū*, 1325
6. *Shikashū*, 1151–1154	17. *Fūgashū*, 1349
7. *Senzaishū*, 1188	18. *Shinsenzaishū*, 1359
8. *Shinkokinshū*, 1216	19. *Shinshūishū*, 1364
9. *Shinchokusenshū*, 1235	20. *Shingoshūishū*, 1383
10. *Shokugosenshū*, 1251	21. *Shinshokukokinshū*, 1439
11. *Shokukokinshū*, 1265	

2. Waka: Unofficial and Exemplary Collections

Various other collections were made to different ends, sometimes to compile a rival to the official collections (such as the *Shin'yōshū*, below) or at other times to provide exemplary poems for aspiring poets (such as *Fujiwara Teika's *Kindai Shūka*, also below). Since these unofficial collections are privately made anthologies, they are known as *shisen(waka)shū* 私選(和歌)集 or simply as *shū*. Properly speaking, the *Man'yōshū* (see the preceding section) should begin this listing, but the place accorded it is too like that of the royal collections to justify following technicalities. It is worth mentioning, however, for the reminder that the editors of that collection often refer to earlier collections that they draw upon. We cannot go back historically to an age in Japan without poetic collections of one kind or another.

Many of these titles are noticed in Part Three. When they are entered there under the title, the title is given an asterisk here; when they are entered there under their compiler's name, that name is given an asterisk here. When no name is given, the compiler is uncertain or unknown. Dates are given at the end.

The border between unofficial and exemplary collections is an uncertain one, but it will be treated as a distinction here. Since most of the unofficial collections are not referred to in Part Three, characters are given for them here, usually omitting "waka" from the title.

Unofficial Collections

    Shinsenshū 新撰集, *Ki no Tsurayuki, 930–934

    *Kokin Rokujō 古今六帖, *Fujiwara Kintō, 976–987

    Genzon Rokujō 現存六帖, *Fujiwara Michitoshi, ca. 1090?

    Ruijū Koshū 類聚古集, Fujiwara Atsutaka, before 1120

    Shoku Shikashū 続詞花集, *Fujiwara Kiyosuke, ca. 1165

    Rin'yōshū 林葉集, *Shun'e, 1179

    Tsukimōde Shū 月詣集, 1182

    Nara no Ha Shū 楢葉集, 1237

    Mandaishū 万代集, Fujiwara (Kinugasa) Ieyoshi, 1248

    Shinwakashū 新和歌集, ca. 1259

    Tōsen Rokujō 東撰六帖, Gotō Motomasa, 1249–1269?

    *Fūyōshū 風葉集, 1271

    Ijinshū 遺塵集, 1301

    Shoku Man'yōshū 続万葉集, 1305

    *Fubokushō 夫木抄, 1308

    Ryūfūshū 柳風集, 1310

    Tōyōshū 藤葉集, Ogura Sanenori, ca. 1345

    Nihachi Meidaishū 二八明題集, *Imagawa Ryōshun, ca. 1390?

    Man'yōshū Ichiyōshō 万葉集一葉抄, *Sanjōnishi Sanetaka, 1486–1489

    Shoku Gomeidaishū 続五明題集, Imagawa Ujichika, 1515

    *Kanginshū 閑吟集, 1518

    Kōyōshū 黄葉集, *Karasuma Mitsuhiro, publ. 1669

    Ichiji Onshō 一字御抄, 1690

Exemplary Collections

    Since the titles appear in Part Three, characters are not given here.

    Shin Sanjūrokunin Kasen, *Fujiwara Mototoshi, Publ. 1260

    Shinsen Rōeishū, ibid., 1106–1120

    Korai Fūteishō, *Fujiwara Shunzei, 1197

    Kindai Shūka, *Fujiwara Teika, 1209

    Eika (no) Taigai, ibid., 1216

    Nishidaishū, ibid., 1234–1235

    Hyakunin Shūka, ibid., 1229–1236

    Hyakunin Isshu, ibid., ca. 1235

Many private or "house" collections (*kashū* 歌集, 家集) were also compiled. Many of these are noticed in Part Three under author entries. For a fuller listing, including poems, see *Zoku Kokka Taikan*, 2 vols. (Kigensha, 1925–1926; several reprintings), which includes over one hundred such collections as well as the texts of certain poetry matches. As this *Companion* was in press an excellent new version began to appear: *Shimpen Kokka Taikan*, 5 vols. (Kadokawa, 1982—).

B. MYTHICAL AND DYNASTIC HISTORIES

In Japan, as in China, history was considered a part of literature, or at least of bun, fumi 文. The earliest Japanese historical examples precede the poetic collections and contain songs of earlier date (but how much earlier or how altered no one knows). The combination of songs and myth make these justifications of Yamato hegemony more literary, more fictional than are histories as we usually conceive of them. Since the characters are given in Part Three, they are not entered here; and since details about the chronicles are given in Part Three, they are omitted here.

The Chronicles
  Kojiki, 712 (in Japanese)
  Nihon Shoki (or *Nihongi*), 720 (in Chinese)

The Six National Histories (*Rikkokushi; in Chinese)
  Nihon Shoki (as above)
  Shoku Nihongi, 797; covers 697–791
  Nihon Kōki, 840; covers 792–833
  Shoku Nihon Kōki, 869; covers 833–850
  (Nihon) Montoku (Tennō) Jitsuroku, 875; covers 850–858
  (Nihon) Sandai Jitsuroku, 901; covers 858–871

As can be seen, the last five histories recount Japanese events in historical times, so giving history in a more modern sense. Of course, like the various *fudoki* mentioned in Part One, these histories often combine legends and other elements that make them less than fully reliable, but their loss would have been a disaster for our knowledge of early Japan. The chronicles are also read for their literary merits and, in a sense, may be thought to be revived in the *rekishi monogatari* (Section D, below).

C. DIARIES AND TRAVEL ACCOUNTS

It seems that Japanese have kept diaries since they adopted writing. In construing what is diary literature (*nikki bungaku*), certain kinds of writing are commonly excluded, especially men's daily records set down in a kind of Chinese prose and other accounts thought to be too financial, prosaic, or given to record (kiroku). That distinction is accepted here. It is also conventional to distinguish diaries (*nikki*, properly niki for the earliest examples) from travel writing (*kikō*).

The distinction is of some help, but in fact it is arbitrary, as the first "diary"—*Ki no Tsurayuki's *Tosa Nikki*—shows. The distinction comes down to little more than a tendency for early accounts to be written by women, who were less likely to travel, and for later to be written by men, who were more given to the road. Yet even such relatively later women as *Gofukakusa In Nijō and *Abutsu wrote of their travels. The distinction is therefore not followed here. It must be added that works with nikki in their titles seldom have daily entries, and some have titles or other elements that could lead to classification as *monogatari* or *kashū*. But all the examples given are admitted to the class of nikki or kikō: that is, they are taken to be about their author rather than someone else as is supposed for monogatari, and they are dominated by the narrative present rather than past tense (i.e., perfect aspect).

The list is not exhausitive. When the asterisk precedes a title, the title is the basis of entry in Part Three; when the asterisk precedes the author's name, the name is the basis of entry. Where there is no asterisk, there is also no entry.

Tosa Nikki, *Ki no Tsurayuki, 935
Kagerō Nikki, *Fujiwara Michitsuna no Haha, ca. 974
Takamitsu Nikki, ca. 962
Murasaki Shikibu Nikki, *Murasaki Shikibu, ca. 1010
Sarashina Nikki, *Sugawara Takasue no Musume, ca. 1060
Sanuki no Suke Nikki, *Sanuki no Suke, ca. 1127?
Kenshun Mon'in Chūnagon Nikki (or *Tamakiwaru*), *Kenshun Mon'in Chūnagon, 1219
Kaidōki, 1223
Kenrei Mon'in Ukyō no Daibu Shū, *Kenrei Mon'in Ukyō no Daibu, ca. 1232; this is more of a *kashū*
Tōkan Kikō, 1242
Ben no Naishi Nikki, *Gofukakusa In Ben no Naishi, 1252
Mumyō no Ki, *Asukai Gayū, ca. 1269
Mogami no Kawaji, ibid., ca. 1269
Saga no Kayoi, ibid., 1269
Miyakoji no Wakare, ibid., 1277
Haru no Miyamaji, ibid., 1280
Isayoi Nikki, *Abutsu, 1280
Fushimi In Nakatsukasa Naishi Nikki, *Fushimi In Nakatsukasa Naishi, 1292
Towazugatari, *Gofukakusa In Nijō, ca. 1312
Takemuki ga ki, ca. 1349
Michiyukiburi, *Imagawa Ryōshun, 1371
Rokuon In Dono Itsukushima Mōde no Ki, *Imagawa Ryōshun, 1389
Nagusamegusa, *Shōtetsu, 1418

Sasamegoto, *Shinkei, 1463; more a poetic treatise
Masahiro Nikki, *Ichijō Kanera, date unknown
Shirakawa Kikō, *Sōgi, 1468
Tsukushi no Michi no Ki, ibid., 1480
Shōkō Niki, Matsushita Shōkō, 1473
Hokkoku Kikō, Gyōe, late Muromachi: ca. 1500?
Sōgi Shūenki, *Sōchō, 1502
Azumaji no Tsuto, ibid., 1509
Utsuyama Ki, ibid., 1517
Sōchō Shuki, ibid., 1527
Tsuyama Kikō, *Nishiyama Sōin, 1652
Matsushima Kikō, ibid., 1662–1663
Saikoku no Michi no Ki, ibid., 1665
Kōya Kikō, ibid., 1674
Azuma Nikki, *Ikenishi Gonsui, pr. 1681
Nozarashi Kikō (or *Kasshi Ginkō*), *Matsuo Bashō, 1684
Kashima Kikō, ibid., 1687
Oi no Kobumi, ibid., pr. 1709
Sarashina Kikō, ibid., 1688
Oku no Hosomichi, ibid., pr. 1702
Genjūan no Ki, ibid., 1690
Saga Nikki, ibid., 1691
An Nikki, *Hattori Dohō, 1688–1699
Ise Kikō, *Mukai Kyorai, pr. 1850
Hanatsumi, *Enomoto Kikaku, 1690
Shin Hanatsumi, *Yosa Buson, 1777
Shichiban Nikki, *Kobayashi Issa, 1810–1818 (obviously others preceded)
Oraga Haru, ibid., 1819
Hachiban Nikki, ibid., 1821

D. Monogatari and Setsuwa

Because there was no traditional word for "narrative" other than katari/*monogatari*, "monogatari" has been used in titles for works that may seem closer to *kashū* or *nikki*, although a monogatari should be about someone other than oneself, and be told in the past tense (that is, perfect aspect).

Once again, the list is neither scientifically categorized nor exhaustive. The Japanese distinctions run as follows:

utamonogatari	works with poems at center
mukashi monogatari	tsukurimonogatari (see the next) preceding the *Genji Monogatari*
tsukurimonogatari	works with the emphasis on prose narrative
giko monogatari	Kamakura (and other) period tsukurimonogatari emulating earlier tsukurimonogatari, especially *Genji Monogatari*
rekishi monogatari	works relating historical and social matters
gunki monogatari	works narrating military stories, matters of power
setsuwa monogatari	works of shorter tales, commonly Buddhist and didactic, legendary; sometimes folklore

Obviously the two last categories are not logically exclusive, and the second and fourth are in some ways unnecessary. Yet the distinctions have proved useful to Japanese and will be followed here by the notice at the end of each entry as to its kind: uta, mukashi, tsukuri, giko, rekishi, gunki, setsuwa.

From the Kamakura period alone more than a hundred titles have been preserved, but of that number, only some of the stories have survived. No one can say whether chance, or selection of those thought best, has determined survival.

Once again asterisks designate the entry in Part Three, whether by title or author.

Nihon Ryōiki, Keikai, ca. 823; setsuwa

Taketori Monogatari, 2 dates; before or after 900; mukashi

Ise Monogatari, 2 dates: before or after 905–920; uta

Shōmonki, 940; gunki

Yamato Monogatari, 951?; uta

Heichū Monogatari, ca. 957; uta

Utsuho Monogatari, ca. 982; mukashi

Sambō Ekotoba, 984; setsuwa

Ochikubo Monogatari, ca. end of 10th c.; mukashi

Genji Monogatari, *Murasaki Shikibu, ca. 1010–1014; tsukuri

Eiga Monogatari, ca. 1028–1037; rekishi

Honchō Hokke Genki, Chingen, 1040–1043; setsuwa

Hamamatsu Chūnagon Monogatari, *Sugawara Takasue no Musume, 1053–1058; tsukuri

Sagoromo Monogatari, Rokujō Saiin Baishi Naishinnō no Senji, ca. 1069–1077; tsukuri

Gōdanshō, *Ōe no Masafusa, 1111; setsuwa

Konjaku Monogatari, traditionally ascribed to Minamoto Takakuni, ca. 1120?; setsuwa

Ōkagami, ca. 1119; rekishi

Uchigiki Shū, ca. 1111–1134; setsuwa

Ima Kagami, 1170?; some say 1045–1053; rekishi

Mizu Kagami, 1170–1195; rekishi

Yamaji no Tsuyu (continuation of *Genji*

Monogatari), ca. 1180; giko
*Tsutsumi Chūnagon Monogatari, by 1180?; giko
*Yoru no Nezame, by 1180?; giko
*Kohon Setsuwashū, by 1180?; setsuwa
*Torikaeba ya Monogatari, by 1180?; giko
*Senjūshō, two dates: 1183, after 1199; setsuwa
*Hōgen Monogatari, after 1185?; gunki
Waga Mi ni Tadoru Himegimi, ca. 1190?; giko
*Uji Shūi Monogatari, 1190–1242; setsuwa
Iwade Shinobu, 1190–1201; giko
Matsura no Miya Monogatari, *Fujiwara Teika?, ca. 1193; giko
Hasedera Reigenki, ca. 1200?; setsuwa
*Heiji Monogatari, ca. 1200?; gunki
*Hōbutsushū, ca. 1200?; setsuwa
Ama no Karu Mo, ca. 1200?; giko
*Kojidan, 1212–1215; setsuwa
Hosshinshū, *Kamo no Chōmei, 1214–1215; setsuwa
Kankyo no Tomo, sometimes ascribed to *Jien but now thought to be by Keisei, 1222; setsuwa

*Jikkunshō, perhaps compiled by Rokuhara Nirōzaemon, ca. 1252; setsuwa
Kokon Chomonjū, *Tachibana Narisue, 1254; setsuwa
Koke no Koromo, ca. 1255; giko
*Sumiyoshi Monogatari, 13th c.?; a Heian version lost; giko
Godai Teiō Monogatari, 1259; rekishi
Iwa Shimizu Monogatari, 1271; giko
Shasekishū, *Mujū Ichien, 1279–1283; setsuwa
*Gempei Jōsuiki, ca. 1335? some say ca. 1260; gunki
*Baishōron, ca. 1349; rekishi
*Heike Monogatari, 1371 for Kakuichi version; others from early 13th c.; gunki
*Yoshino Shūi, ca. 1358; setsuwa
*Shintōshū, ca. 1358–1361; setsuwa
*Taiheiki, ca. 1372; gunki
*Masukagami, ca. 1374; rekishi
*Soga Monogatari, ca. 1400?; gunki
*Gikeiki, ca. 1400; gunki
Jizō Bosatsu Reigenki, ca. 1500?; some say there was a Heian original; setsuwa
Shinobine Monogatari, before 1528; giko

During the fifteenth and sixteenth centuries, Japan lapsed into strife and anarchy. Narrative of the kinds considered gave way to travel accounts and *renga*. In 1593, Christian missionaries introduced an *Esopo* (Aesop) *no Fabulas*, printed with type. As printing gradually caught on, and the nation settled down, the volume of books grew. Both because of volume and lack of classification or even knowledge of so many stories, this account of narrative cannot be continued into the Edo period. In Part Four, see: *sōshi*; *ukiyozōshi*; *gesaku*.

E. Zuihitsu

There is no adequate way to translate the *zuihitsu* into English. Until the Meiji period, the term was used in a sense like that of its Chinese originators, meaning a learned compilation. Today it is a means of including into classical Japanese literature a few of the best-loved classics, typified by Sei Shōnagon's work, given below. Significantly enough, a *Matsushima Nikki*, which is only eighteen pages long, was once included among zuihitsu simply because it was (mistakenly) ascribed to Sei Shōnagon.

In dealing with zuihitsu, one is forced to define it—and definers then discover that a great many works must be mentioned, and that categories keep coming unbuttoned. Or one may say that the term refers to a certain number of literary works and, tautologically, that a certain number of literary works belong to zuihitsu. The latter, and therefore a short list, is the decision taken here.

Chiteiki, *Yoshishige Yasutane, 982
Makura no Sōshi, *Sei Shōnagon, ca. 1000?
Hōjōki, *Kamo no Chōmei, ca. 1212
Tzurezuregusa, *Kenkō, 1330–1331
Moritake Zuihitsu, *Arakida Moritake, date unknown

Nigiwaigusa, Sano Shōeki, pr. 1682
Oi no Tanoshimi, Ichikawa Danjūrō II, pr. 1803
Sundai Zatsuwa, *Muro Kyūsō, 1732
Kagetsu Sōshi, *Matsudaira Sadanobu, 1769–1803

Perhaps the list should be abbreviated further by removing the first title and also the last five, though that would be hard on Moritake and the rest.

F. Renga and Haikai Collections

Linked poetry was "published" in various ways. The simplest was to present an individual with a sequence composed at a sitting and usually recopied on good paper by a fine hand. Another was publication and distribution of a sequence or group of sequences, multiplying copies by scribal means of printing. A third, which applies mostly to *renga*, involved selection, arrangement, and compilation of individual stanzas by earlier and perhaps also contemporary poets, after the manner of a *chokusenshū*. When this was done, whether scribally or, later by print, the prized *tsukeku* or *shūku* was printed with the preceding stanza (*maeku*), but whole sequences were not normally printed in this fashion. On the other hand, a long and impressive set, as with a *senku* for a special votive occasion, might be written out in several copies. Yet a fourth means, which applies mostly to *haikai*, involved publication of what was more or less official, canonical recent work of a given school or poet.

These last two kinds make up the examples following. Unfortunately, very few collections of linked poetry are in print, and most of those that are suffer from being incomplete, minimally annotated, out of date, or all the preceding. The recovery of linked poetry is a recent matter; we may expect better things of the future.

To compensate for the paucity of titles in the first list, the second will note the contents of the most famous collections. Asterisks designate the entry in Part Three.

Renga
  Tsukuba Shū, *Nijō Yoshimoto, 1356–1357
  Shinsen Tsukuba Shū, *Sōgi, 1470
  Chikurinshō, *Sōgi, 1476

Haikai
  Shinsen Inu Tsukuba Shū, *Yamazaki Sōkan, ca. 1523–1532
  Enoko Shū, *Matsue Shigeyori, 1633 (his *Kefukigusa* of 1645, 1647 is part collection, part treatise)
  Sayo no Nakayama Shū, *Matsue Shigeyori, 1664
  Shinzoku Inu Tsukuba Shū, *Kitamura Kigin, 1667
  Bashō Shichibushū, the seven canonical collections of the Bashō school, 1684–1698, detailed in the next list

Kareobana, *Enomoto Kikaku, 1694
Ariso Umi, *Mukai Kyorai, 1695
Shundei Kushū, *Yosa Buson, 1777
**Momosumomo*, *Yosa Buson, 1780
Kansei Kuchō, *Kobayashi Issa, 1794
Bunka Kuchō Hoi, ibid., 1804–1808
Kabuban, ibid., 1812 (and many other collections)

Parts of Certain Collections
All the following appear in the preceding list.

Tsukuba Shū, 20 parts
Preface
  1–2 Spring renga (haru no renga)
    3 Summer renga
  4–5 Autumn renga
    6 Winter renga
    7 Shinto renga (*jingi* no renga)
    8 Buddhist renga (*shakkyō* no renga)
 9–11 Love renga
12–16 Miscellaneous renga
   17 Travel renga
   18 Congratulatory renga (*ga* no renga)
   19 Miscellaneous forms of renga (zōtai no renga, including haikai, i.e., *mushin* renga)
   20 Opening stanzas (*hokku*)

Shinsen Tsukuba Shū, 20 parts
Preface
  1–2 Spring renga
    3 Summer renga
  4–5 Autumn renga
    6 Winter renga
    7 Congratulatory renga
 8–10 Love renga
11–12 Travel renga
13–17 Miscellaneous renga
   18 Shinto renga
19–20 Opening stanzas

Chikurinshō, 10 parts (one of several arrangements)
Preface
   1 Spring renga
   2 Summer renga
   3 Autumn renga
   4 Winter renga
 5–6 Love renga
   7 Travel renga
 8–9 Miscellaneous renga
  10 Opening stanzas

Shinsen Inu Tsukuba Shū (various titles), 7 parts
 1 Spring
 2 Summer
 3 Autumn
 4 Winter
 5 Love
 6 Miscellaneous
 7 Opening stanzas: spring, summer, autumn, winter

Bashō Shichibushū
1. *Fuyu no Hi*, comp. *Yamamoto Kakei, 1684
   Five *kasen* (36-stanza sequences)
2. *Haru no Hi*, comp. *Yamamoto Kakei, 1689
   Three kasen
   One *iisute* (fragment: 6 stanzas)
   Thirty-three *hokku*
3. *Arano(shū)*, comp. *Yamamoto Kakei, 1689
   Preface by Bashō
 1 Cherry blossoms (hana), hototogisu, moon, snow (symbols of the four seasons)
 2 New Year's Day; Early, Mid-, Late Spring
 3 Early, Mid-, Late Summer
 4 Early, Mid-, Late Autumn
 5 Early, Mid-, Late Winter; Year's End
 6 Miscellaneous
 7 Famous Places (*meisho*), Travel, Complaints (*jukkai*), Love, Evanescence (*mujō*)
 8 Buddhism (shakkyō), Shinto (jingi), Felicitations (iwai)
   Nine kasen
   One half-kasen (*hankasen*; 18 stanzas)
4. *Hisago*, comp. *Hamada Chinseki, 1690
   Five kasen

5. *Sarumino(shū)*, comp. *Mukai Kyorai, *Nozawa Bonchō, 1691
   This is the most famous of haikai collections—"the *Kokinshū* of haikai." What follows is, therefore, yet more detailed:
   Preface by *Enomoto Kikaku
   1 Winter hokku (1–94)
   2 Summer hokku (95–188)
   3 Autumn hokku (189–264)
   4 Spring hokku (265–382)
   5 Four kasen
      Tobi no Ha no no Maki
      Ichinaka wa no Maki
      Akuoke no no Maki
      Ume Wakana no Maki
   6 Various compositions
      Bashō, *Genjūan no Ki* (*A Record of the Unreal Hermitage*, concluding with a hokku)
      Shinken, Chinese prose and verse in praise of Bashō
      Kiyū Nikki (*A Diary at His Side*—35 hokku, making 36 or a kasen number, with Bashō's mentioned above)
      Postscript by Jōsō
6. *Sumidawara*, comp. Shida Yaba (1627–1704), Koizumi Kooku (unknown), and Ikeda Rigyū (unknown); 1694
   Preface
   1 Two kasen, one *hyakuin* (one-hundred stanza sequence, the sole example in these 7 collections), hokku
   2 Hokku, one 32-stanza sequence (san-jūniin), three kasen
7. *Zoku Sarumino*, comp. Hattori Sempo and *Kagami Shikō (1665–1731); 1698
   1 Five kasen
   2 Hokku

G. Nō

The many collections of *nō* by school and purpose may differ in canon, text, title, and classification. There are both *shite* and *waki* schools, each with its own textual traditions. In what follows, emphasis falls on the Kanze (a shite) school, which theatergoers today encounter the most often. Two main ways of classifying and collecting exist: either by sequence according to the traditional order for a school, or by classifications of plays according to the system of five kinds of pieces or "numbers" (-bammemono). For the first, the classification "wakinō-mono" is commonly substituted for the number, which is used here for convenience sake (see also Part Five).

I   Divinities, Felicitations (wakinōmono)
II   Spirits of Warriors
III   Spirits of Women, etc.
IV   Deranged Women, Warriors, etc.
V   Demons, etc.

In the second series given here, it will be clear that category IV plays are much the most numerous in the 250-play collection, and category II plays the fewest. That does not necessarily indicate popularity or quality. The first series represents, as it were, one school's first choice from among the second, although some of the most famous plays are not to be found in the first hundred.

There are a number of anomalies involved with the two lists. The Kanze hundred plays actually contains a hundred and one, counting the unnumbered first work, and the collection of 250 plays actually includes 253. There are differences between titles of plays in the two series, and yet other commonly met titles that are not used today by either of the two collections. For these reasons, we begin with an alphabetical listing by title. With the title there is also the number in the *KH* (*Kanzeryū Yōkyoku Hyakuban, Kanze Canon of the First Hundred Nō*) and/or in the *YN* (*Yōkyoku Nihyakugojūbanshū, The Collection of Two Hundred and Fifty Nō*). If no number is given, see the other title.

TITLE	KH	YN	TITLE	KH	YN
Adachigahara	33	236	Gekkyūden: Tsuru Kame		
Aioi, Aioi no Matsu:			Gempuku Soga	—	172
Takasago	1	2	Gendayū	—	19
Aizomegawa	—	131	Genji Kuyō	—	101
Akogi	24	140	Genjō (Kenjō)	95	245
Ama	39	246	Gen Sammi Yorimasa:		
Aoi no Ue	65	148	Yorimasa		
Arashiyama	70	34	Genzai Kumasaka: Eboshiori		
Aridōshi	—	180	Genzai Nue	—	235
Ashikari	63	159	Genzai Shichimen	—	201
Asukagawa	—	120	Genzai Tomoe	—	195
Atago Kūya	—	229	Giō	—	97
Ataka	51	170	Goi no Sagi: Sagi		
Atsumori	64	58	Gojō Yūgao: Hashitomi		
Awaji	—	5	Go no Yōkihi: Kōtei		
Aya no Taiko: see next			Hachi no Ki	60	156
Aya no Tsuzumi	—	145	Hagoromo	61	83
Bashō	—	66	Haku Rakuten	—	14
Bijinsō: Kōu			Hanagatami	43	118
Chikubujima (-shima)	22	28	Hana Ikusa	—	126
Chōbuku Soga	—	202	Hanjo	4	121
Chōryō	—	240	Hashi Benkei	73	190
Chūjō Hime: Hibariyama			Hashitomi	—	69
Daibutsu Kuyō	80	188	Hashitomi Yūgao: see prec.		
Daie	—	217	Hatsuyuki	—	125
Dairokuten	—	216	Hibariyama	78	119
Dampū	—	211	Higaki	—	105
Dōjōji	62	149	Higaki no Onna: see prec.		
Dōmyōji	—	23	Himuro	—	29
Ebira	68	46	Hiun	—	231
Ebira no Ume: see prec.			Hōjōgawa	—	12
Eboshiori	81	212	Hōka: see next		
Eguchi	3	73	Hōkasō (-zō)	96	178
Eguchi Yūjo: see prec.			Hotoke no Hara	—	64
Ema	—	41	Hyakuman	47	110
Enoshima	—	26	Ikari Kazuki	—	239
Fue no Maki	—	191	Ikkaku Sennin	—	242
Fuji	—	78	Ikuta: see next		
Fujidaiko	44	127	Ikuta Atsumori	—	59
Fujisan	—	25	Iwafune	—	36
Fujito	29	141	Izutsu	11	61
Funabashi	—	144	Jijū Shigehira: Senju		
Funa Benkei	48	238	Jinen Koji	—	175
Fushimi: Kinsatsu			Kagami: Zenji Soga		
Futari Giō: Giō			Kagekiyo	30	153
Futari Shizuka	32	76	Kagetsu	72	177

TITLE	*KH*	*YN*	TITLE	*KH*	*YN*
Urokogata	—	42	*Yoroboshi*	94	152
Utaura	—	179	*Yoshino Shizuka*	—	91
Utō	56	139	*Yoshino Tennin*	79	98
Wakana: Motomezuka			*Youchi Soga*	41	189
Yamahime	—	96	*Yūgao*	—	70
Yamamba	46	249	*Yuki*	—	71
Yamauba: see prec.			*Yuki Kazuraki: Kazuraki*		
Yanagi: Yugyō Yanagi			*Yugyō Yanagi*	28	85
Yashima	37	45	*Yumi Yaw(h)ata*	—	3
Yatate Kamo: Kamo			*Yūrei Nue: Nue*		
Yōkihi	15	72	*Yuya*	27	94
Yorikaze: Ominaeshi			*Zegai*	—	214
Yorimasa	10	53	*Zenji Soga*	—	197
Yōrō	18	10			

Kanze Canon of the First Hundred Nō (Kanzeryū Yōkyoku Hyakuban)

Each entry has the title in roman letters, the classification number (see p. 308, and then the Chinese characters for the title.

Kamiuta (Okina) 神歌（翁）

1. *Takasago*, I   高砂
2. *Tamura*, II   田村
3. *Eguchi*, III   江口
4. *Hanjo*, IV   班女
5. *Ukai*, IV   鵜飼
6. *Kanehira*, II   兼平
7. *Senju*, III   千手
8. *Momijigari*, V   紅葉狩
9. *Oimatsu*, I   老松
10. *Yorimasa*, II   頼政
11. *Izutsu*, III   井筒
12. *Miidera*, IV   三井寺
13. *Tenko*, IV   天鼓
14. *Sanemori*, II   実盛
15. *Yōkihi*, III   楊貴妃
16. *Tamakazura*, IV   玉葛
17. *Tōru*, V   融
18. *Yōrō*, I   養老
19. *Kiyotsune*, II   清経
20. *Kayoi Komachi*, IV   通小町
21. *Kosode Soga*, IV   小袖曽我
22. *Chikubujima*, I   竹生島
23. *Tomonaga*, II   朝長
24. *Akogi*, IV   阿漕
25. *Ohara Gokō*, III   大原御幸
26. *Tadanori*,   忠度
27. *Yuya*, III   熊野
28. *Yugyō Yanagi*, III   遊行柳
29. *Fujito*, IV   藤戸
30. *Kagekiyo*, IV   景清
31. *Kakitsubata*, III   杜若
32. *Futari Shizuka*, III   二人静
33. *Adachigahara*, V   安達原
34. *Kamo*, I   加茂
35. *Shunkan*, IV   俊寛
36. *Matsukaze*, III   松風
37. *Yashima*, II   八島
38. *Kazuraki*, IV   葛城
39. *Ama*, V   海士
40. *Kurama Tengu*, V   鞍馬天狗
41. *Youchi Soga*, IV   夜討曽我
42. *Sumidagawa*, IV   隅田川
43. *Hanagatami*, IV   花筐
44. *Fujidaiko*, IV   富士太鼓
45. *Sakuragawa*, IV   桜川
46. *Yamamba*, V   山姥
47. *Hyakuman*, IV   百万
48. *Funa Benkei*, V   舟弁慶
49. *Ominaeshi*, IV   女郎花
50. *Miwa*, IV   三輪
51. *Ataka*, IV or V   安宅
52. *Tōhoku*, V   東北
53. *Semimaru*, IV   蝉丸
54. *Shōjō*, I   猩々
55. *Morihisa*, IV or V   盛久
56. *Utō*, IV   善知鳥
57. *Sesshōseki*, IV or V   殺生石
58. *Nonomiya*, III   野宮
59. *Tōsen*, IV   唐船
60. *Hachi no Ki*, IV   鉢木
61. *Hagoromo*, III   羽衣
62. *Dōjōji*, IV   道成寺

63. *Ashikari*, IV   芦刈
64. *Atsumori*, II   敦盛
65. *Aoi no Ue*, IV   葵上
66. *Seiōbo*, I   西王母
67. *Tsunemasa*, II   経正
68. *Ebira*, II   箙
69. *Tomoe*, II   巴
70. *Arashiyama*, I   嵐山
71. *Makiginu*, IV   巻絹
72. *Kagetsu*, IV   花月
73. *Hashi Benkei*, IV   橋弁慶
74. *Kumasaka*, V   熊坂
75. *Kogō*, IV   小督
76. *Rashōmon*, IV or V   羅生門
77. *Kanawa*, IV   鉄輪
78. *Hibariyama*, IV   雲雀山
79. *Yoshino Tennin*, III   吉野天人
80. *Daibutsu Kuyō*, IV or V   大仏供養
81. *Eboshiori*, V   烏帽子折

82. *Tsuru Kame*, I   鶴亀
83. *Shun'ei*, I   春栄
84. *Tsuchigumo*, V   土蜘蛛
85. *Kokaji*, V   小鍛冶
86. *Shakkyō*, V   石橋
87. *Kappo*, V   合甫
88. *Sōshiarai Komachi*, III   草紙洗小町
89. *Ōeyama*, V   大江山
90. *Shunzei Tadanori*, II   俊成忠度
91. *Kinuta*, IV   砧
92. *Mochizuki*, IV or V   望月
93. *Shichiki Ochi*, IV or V   七騎落
94. *Yoroboshi*, IV   弱法師
95. *Genjō*, V   絃上
96. *Hōkasō*, IV   放下僧
97. *Kochō*, III   胡蝶
98. *Matsumushi*, IV   松虫
99. *Kuzu*, V   国栖
100. *Shōkun*, IV or V   昭君

The Collection of Two Hundred and Fifty Nō (*Yōkyoku Nihyakugojūbanshū*)

1. *Okina (Kamiuta)*   翁（神歌）

I WAKINŌ

2. *Takasago*   高砂
3. *Yumi Yaw(h)ata*   弓八幡
4. *Shiga*   志賀
5. *Awaji*   淡路
6. *Mimosuso*   御裳濯
7. *Shironushi*   代主
8. *Matsu no O*   松尾
9. *Saoyama*   佐保山
10. *Yōrō*   養老
11. *Taiten*   大典
12. *Hōjōgawa*   放生川
13. *Oimatsu*   老松
14. *Haku Rakuten*   白楽天
15. *Tsuru Kame*   鶴亀
16. *Tōbōsaku*   東放朔
17. *Shirahige*   白髭
18. *Ōyashiro*   大社
19. *Gendayū*   源太夫
20. *Nezame*   寝覚
21. *Umatsuri*   鶴祭
22. *Rinzō*   輪蔵
23. *Dōmyōji*   道明寺
24. *Naniwa*   難波
25. *Fujisan*   富士山
26. *Enoshima*   江島
27. *Kamo*   賀茂
28. *Chikubujima*   竹生島
29. *Himuro*   氷室
30. *Mekari*   和布刈

31. *Sakahoko*   逆鉾
32. *Kuse no To*   九世戸
33. *Kanameishi*   要石
34. *Arashiyama*   嵐山
35. *Kinsatsu*   金札
36. *Iwafune*   岩舟
37. *Tamanoi*   玉井
38. *Seiōbo*   西王母
39. *Kureha*   呉服
40. *Ukon*   右近
41. *Ema*   絵馬
42. *Urokogata*   鱗形
43. *Uchito Mōde*   内外詣

II SHURAMONO

44. *Tamura*   田村
45. *Yashima*   八島
46. *Ebira*   箙
47. *Tadanori*   忠度
48. *Shunzei Tadanori*   俊成忠度
49. *Tsunemasa*   経正
50. *Michimori*   道盛
51. *Kanehira*   兼平
52. *Tomoakira*   知明
53. *Yorimasa*   頼正
54. *Sanemori*   実盛
55. *Kiyotsune*   清経
56. *Tomonaga*   朝長
57. *Tomoe*   巴
58. *Atsumori*   敦盛
59. *Ikuta Atsumori*   生田敦盛

III KAZURAMONO

60. *Nonomiya* 野宮
61. *Izutsu* 井筒
62. *Tōboku* 東北
63. *Ume* 梅
64. *Hotoke no Hara* 仏原
65. *Uneme* 釆女
66. *Bashō* 芭蕉
67. *Sumizomezakura* 墨染桜
68. *Minobu* 身延
69. *Hashitomi* 半蔀
70. *Yūgao* 夕顔
71. *Yuki* 雪
72. *Yōkihi* 楊貴妃
73. *Eguchi* 江口
74. *Teika* 定家
75. *Senju* 千手
76. *Futari Shizuka* 二人静
77. *Mutsura* 六浦
78. *Fuji* 藤
79. *Kakitsubata* 杜若
80. *Oshio* 小塩
81. *Urin'in* 雲林院
82. *Seiganji* 誓願寺
83. *Hagoromo* 羽衣
84. *Ochiba* 落葉
85. *Yugyō Yanagi* 遊行柳
86. *Saigyōzakura* 西行桜
87. *Kazuraki* 葛城
88. *Tatsuta* 竜田
89. *Miwa* 三輪
90. *Makiginu* 巻絹
91. *Yoshino Shizuka* 吉野静
92. *Sumiyoshi Mōde* 住吉詣
93. *Matsukaze* 松風
94. *Yuya* 熊野
95. *Sōshiarai Komachi* 草紙洗小町
96. *Yamahime* 山姫
97. *Giō* 祇王
98. *Yoshino Tennin* 吉野天人
99. *Kochō* 胡蝶
100. *Sagi* 鷺
101. *Genji Kuyō* 源氏供養
102. *Ohara Gokō* 大原御幸
103. *Sekidera Komachi* 関寺小町
104. *Ōmu Komachi* 鸚鵡小町
105. *Higaki* 桧垣
106. *Obasute* 姨捨

IV KYŌJOMONO, ETC.

107. *Miidera* 三井寺
108. *Sakuragawa* 桜川
109. *Kashiwazaki* 柏崎
110. *Hyakuman* 百万

111. *Tamakazura* 玉葛
112. *Ukifune* 浮舟
113. *Mitsuyama* 三山
114. *Rōdaiko* 籠太鼓
115. *Rōgiō* 籠祇王
116. *Sumidagawa* 隅田川
117. *Semimaru* 蟬丸
118. *Hanagatami* 花筐
119. *Hibariyama* 雲雀山
120. *Asukagawa* 飛鳥川
121. *Hanjo* 班女
122. *Kamo Monogurui* 賀茂物狂
123. *Minazuki Harae* 水無月祓
124. *Murogimi* 室君
125. *Hatsuyuki* 初雪
126. *Hana Ikusa* 花軍
127. *Fujidaiko* 富士太鼓
128. *Umegae* 梅枝
129. *Torioibune* 鳥追舟
130. *Take no Yuki* 竹雪
131. *Aizomegawa* 藍染川
132. *Minase* 水無瀬
133. *Kinuta* 砧
134. *Motomezuka* 求塚
135. *Sotoba Komachi* 卒都婆小町
136. *Ominaeshi* 女郎花
137. *Kayoi Komachi* 通小町
138. *Koi no Matsubara* 恋松原
139. *Utō* 善知鳥
140. *Akogi* 阿漕
141. *Fujito* 藤戸
142. *Matsumushi* 松虫
143. *Nishikigi* 錦木
144. *Funabashi* 船橋
145. *Aya no Tsuzumi* 綾鼓
146. *Koi no Omoni* 恋重荷
147. *Kanawa* 鉄輪
148. *Aoi no Ue* 葵上
149. *Dōjōji* 道成寺
150. *Ugetsu* 雨月
151. *Tokusa* 木賊
152. *Yoroboshi* 弱法師
153. *Kagekiyo* 景清
154. *Shunkan* 俊寛
155. *Settai* 摂待
156. *Hachi no Ki* 鉢木
157. *Tsuchiguruma* 土車
158. *Kōya Monogurui* 高野物狂
159. *Ashikari* 芦刈
160. *Morihisa* 盛久
161. *Kogō* 小督
162. *Shun'ei* 春栄
163. *Nakamitsu* 仲光
164. *Shigemori* 重盛

H. KYŌGEN AND MIBU KYŌGEN

Kyōgen emerged in the Muromachi period as a companion of *nō*. Since nō was then performed more rapidly than later, a program of five nō would have kyōgen interludes performed on the same stage. In addition, kyōgen actors appear in certain nō. Hence it was formerly known as *sarugaku*kyōgen or nō kyōgen, and later simply as kyōgen as it assumed more or less separate existence—although today a kyōgen is often performed as a forepiece to a nō. Ancient versions of nō (sarugaku, dengaku, etc.) were apparently comic, but as nō writers sought high seriousness, the comic elements were taken over by kyōgen, making it rare in Japanese literature as a traditional, esteemed, and consistently comic art. In many plays there is a country daimyo with a rascally servant or two: Tarōkaja and Jirōkaja. But the characters may be two priests, husband and wife, and so on.

Three schools of kyōgen developed: Ōkura, Sagi (no longer in existence), and Izumi (大蔵, 鷺, 和泉). The Izumi is usually considered the best in its versions of the plays. Existing printed texts are said not to constitute acting versions but rather doctored ones for reading. Some facsimile versions have been printed, including two Ōkura texts—*Kohon Nō Kyōgen Toraakirabon* (seventeenth c.) and *Torahirobon* (eighteenth c.). There is also a Tenri University Library project to reprint Izumi texts (seventeenth c.).

The plays given below derive from *Kyōgenki*, *Zoku Kyōgenki*, and *Shūi Kyōgenki*, each in five parts of ten plays each. The numbers here run from 1 to 50 for each source. It will be observed that a few titles are shared with nō, although of course the action and tone differ.

Kyōgenki 狂言記

PART 1

 1. *Eboshiori*　烏帽子折り
 2. *Himenori*　ひめ糊
 3. *Ginjimuko*　吟聟
 4. *Nukegara*　抜殻
 5. *Mukomorai*　聟貰
 6. *Shūron*　宗論
 7. *Hagi Daimyō*　萩大名
 8. *Su Hajikami*　酢薑
 9. *Shichiki Ochi*　七騎落
10. *Shikagari*　鹿狩

PART 2

11. *Fuku Watari*　福渡
12. *Konkai*　こんくわい
13. *Tsuto Yamabushi*　苞山伏
14. *Obazake*　伯母酒
15. *Nisengoku*　二千石
16. *Akubō*　悪坊
17. *Uchi Sata*　内沙汰
18. *Munetsuki*　胸つき
19. *Chatsubo*　茶壺
20. *Ikedori Suzuki*　生捕鈴木

PART 3

21. *Sue Hirogari*　末ひろがり

22. *Kakusui*　かくすい
23. *Dokonsō*　鈍根草
24. *Hōshi Monogurui*　法師物狂
25. *Kaki Yamabushi*　柿山伏
26. *Satsuma no Kami*　薩摩守
27. *Tachiubai*　太刀奪
28. *Dobu Katsuchiri*　どぶかつちり
29. *Hakku Renga*　八句連歌
30. *Busshi*　仏師

PART 4

31. *Aiaibakama*　相合袴
32. *Awataguchi*　粟田口
33. *Nasu no Yoichi*　那須の与一
34. *Tsurionna*　釣り女
35. *Kasa no Shita*　笠の下
36. *Akagari*　あかがり
37. *Fumiyamadachi*　文山立
38. *Funefuna*　舟ふな
39. *Kakiuri*　柿売
40. *Ninin Daimyō*　二人大名

PART 5

41. *Kakko Hōroku*　羯鼓炮碌
42. *Imonji*　伊文字
43. *Fumigura*　文蔵
44. *Buaku*　武悪
45. *Fujimatsu*　富士松

PART 4

31. *Mochizake* 餅酒
32. *Hanatori Sumō* 鼻取相撲
33. *Rakuami* 楽阿弥
34. *Inu Yamabushi* 犬山伏
35. *Ryōri Muko* 料理聟
36. *Cha Sanhai* 茶盞拝
37. *Jimba* 人馬
38. *Shidō Hōkaku* 止動方覚
39. *Shujō* しゆでう
40. *Esashi Jūō* ゑさし十王

PART 5

41. *Tsushima Matsuri* 対馬祭
42. *Tako* 鮹
43. *Kane no Ne* 鐘の音
44. *Koshi Inori* 腰いのり
45. *Sado no Kitsune* 佐度狐
46. *Yao Jizō* 八尾地蔵
47. *Fuse Nai* 布施ない
48. *Yoneichi* 米市
49. *Yoroi* 鎧
50. *Sugoroko Sō* 双六僧

Mibu Kyōgen 壬生狂言

The repetoire of Mibu kyōgen consists of thirty pieces. A number share stories with *nō* and yet others feature a rich man, daijin 大尽; this character has some of the qualities of the daimyo who appears so often in *kyōgen*.

1. *Atago Mairi* 愛宕詣リ
2. *Adachigahara* 安達が原
3. *Ōeyama* 大江山
4. *Oharame* 大原女
5. *Oketori* 桶取
6. *Gakizumō* 餓鬼角力
7. *Kanidon* 蟹殿
8. *Kumasaka* 熊坂
9. *Sai no Kawara* 賽の河原
10. *Sakagura Kanegura* 酒蔵金蔵
11. *Setsubun* 節分
12. *Daibutusu Kuyō* 大仏供養
13. *Daikokugari* 大黒狩
14. *Tamamo no Mae* 玉藻前
15. *Tsuchigumo* 土蜘蛛
16. *Dōjōji* 道成寺
17. *Nue* ぬえ
18. *Hashi Benkei* 橋弁慶
19. *Hanaori* 花折
20. *Hana Nusubito* 花盗人
21. *Funa Benkei* 舟弁慶
22. *Hōraku Wari* 炮烙割リ
23. *Horikawa Gosho* 堀川御所
24. *Honnōji* 本能寺
25. *Bōfuri* 棒振
26. *Momijigari* 紅葉狩
27. *Yamabana Tororo* 山端とろろ
28. *Yutate* 湯立
29. *Youchii Soga* 夜討曽我
30. *Rashōmon* 羅生門

I. JŌRURI AND KABUKI

Given the very large numbers of plays, often of the same title, on the same subject, and by different playwrights, it is not feasible to compile a list of titles. For what we can supply, see Part Five D and E. See also section M, below.

J. KYŌKA

Kyōka—"mad *waka*"—were composed from fairly early times, as early as the Kamakura period (see the first entry). But at that period waka was so highly esteemed that "mad waka" was a contradiction in terms, an oxymoron. That fact explains why kyōka really developed in Muromachi, and chiefly in Edo, times. Given the cultivation necessary to effect difference, and the desire to write poems that made the difference, it will be clear that the practice was chiefly that of the warrior aristocracy and of learned townspeople. Dates are given for the two poets not entered in Part Three.

Sake Hyakushu, Gyōgetsubō (1265–1328)
Yūchōrō Ei Hyakushu Kyōka, *Hosokawa Yūsai, etc., 1589
Seisuishō, *Anrakuan Sakuden, 1623
Sakuden Oshō Sōtō Hikae, ibid., pub. after 1643
Bokuyō Kyōkashū, *Nakarai Bokuyō, ca. 1680
Kokin Ikyokushū, *Seihakudō Gyōfū, 1666
Gosen Ikyokushū, ibid., 1672
Gin'yō Kyōkashū, ibid., 1678
Kyōka Iezuto, *Nagata Teiryū, 1729
Zoku Iezuto, ibid., 1731
Manzai Kyōkashū, *Ōta Nampo and Akera Kankō (1740–1800), 1783
Kyōka Wakaba Shū, *Karagoromo Kisshū, 1783
Kyōgen Ōashū, Akera Kankō, 1785

K. SENRYŪ, MAEKUZUKE, AND TSUKEKU

Senryū designates a kind of poetry practiced and collected by an Edo writer whose pen name was *Karai Senryū (1718–1790), whose first large collection (see below) selected about 80,000 stanzas from 2,300,000 he collected in a series of annual senryū drives. Senryū originated as a late Edo *mushin* version of *haikai*, representing one of a group termed zatsuhaikai, miscellaneous or low haikai. It is related to another of that kind, *maekuzuke*, and its offshoot, *tsukeku*. The latter was a single stanza in the form of a *hokku* or *kami no ku*, whereas maekuzuke usually consisted of a small run of stanzas beginning with a first tsukeku as just described (following a *shimo no ku* set by some master). In fact, senryū began as a linked poetry, like *renga* and haikai before it. Yet from the outset it showed a tendency to shorten, and in time it ended in the standard hokku length, although with no need to specify a season, as is the case with a hokku in haikai. Most of the senryū poets also wrote haikai (at the beginning of this satiric art); others wrote *kyōka*, *kokkeibon*, or *sharebon*, and similar kinds of comic literature (as time went on). Senryū therefore offers but one representative, in verse, of a widespread Edo tendency to the comic and what was deemed low (*zoku*). There is ample evidence to show that thousands of people were writing such poems—about their neighbors, no doubt—and the enumeration that follows includes only some important collections.

Maekuzuke
  Saku ya Kono Hana, 1692

Tsukeku
  Kawarigoma, 1701

Senryū
  Senryū Hyō Manku Awase, comp. *Karai Senryū, coll. 1757–1797
  Mutamagawa, comp. *Kei Kiitsu, 1750; pr. 1774
  Haifū Yanagidaru, 1765; with this collection senryū takes on the hokku form
    by which it is later known, see *manku awase* in Part Three.

Kawazoi Yanagi, Akera Kankō (1740–1800); pr. 1780–1783
Yanaibako, 1784
Hako Yanagi, 1786
Suetsumuhana, 1776–1801
Haifū Yanagidaru Shūi, 1776–97

L. WORKS IN CHINESE BY JAPANESE

Although a narrow definition of classical Japanese literature is taken here, Japanese have composed in Chinese as a so-to-speak classical language from the beginnings of literacy. Unlike fallen Rome, of course, China did not stand still, and successive styles of Chinese writing came to Japanese attention. For convenience, we can distinguish writings by Japanese into two serious kinds: verse (*kanshi*) 漢詩 and prose (*kambun*) 漢文; and one comic, verse (*kyōshi*) 狂詩. Although the emphasis falls on collections, there are some works more like treatises, and some of the works also have Japanese writing.

It will be observed that comic writing in Chinese began very late, whereas even in so cursory an enumeration as follows, every century has its monuments of serious work in Chinese. Among the omissions that may be noted by way of example, there is no collection listed in connection with *Yosa Buson, whose Chinese verse has received increasing attention. The three most important poets with names attached to titles are thought by some to be—though agreement does not exist—*Kūkai, *Sugawara Michizane, and *Kan Chazan.

From such titles an obvious "shi" has been omitted in the usual way: that is, *Ryōunshū* rather than *Ryōunshishū*.

Title entries are followed by author/compiler, date, and characters for the title (these often being difficult to judge for works given here) even if they are redundantly given in Part Three.

Verse and Prose

Kaifūsō, ca. 751   懐風藻
Ryōunshū, 814   凌雲集
Bunka Shūreishū, 818   文華秀麗集
Bunkyō Hifuron, *Kūkai, 819
　文鏡秘府論
Bumpitsu Genjinshō, ibid., ca. 820
　文筆眼心抄
Keikokushū, 827   経国集
Seireishū, *Kūkai, 835   性霊集
Toshi Bunshū, Miyako Yoshika, 880
　都氏文集
Denshi Kashū, Shimada Tadaomi, 892
　田氏家集
Kanke Bunsō, *Sugawara Michizane, 900
　菅家文草
Kanke Kōshū, ibid., before 903   菅家後集
Fusōshū, Ki [sic] Tadana (Tokina) 995–
　999   扶桑集

Honchō Reizō, Takashina Moriyoshi, pub.
　1010   本朝麗藻
Wakan Rōeishū, *Fujiwara Kintō, ca. 1013
　和漢朗詠集
Honchō Monzui, *Fujiwara Akihira, 1058–
　1064   本朝文粋
Gōdanshō, *Ōe no Masafusa, 1104–1108?
　江談抄
Sakumon Daitai, Fujiwara Munetada, ca.
　1108   作文大体
Shinsen Rōeishū, *Fujiwara Mototoshi,
　1106–1123   新選朗詠集
Honchō Zoku Monzui, after 1140
　本朝続文粋
Honchō Mudaishi, ca. 1164   本朝無題詩
Saihokushū, *Kokan Shiren, after 1314
　済北集

Mingashū, Sesson Yūbai, 1346　岷峨集
Tōkai Ichiōshū, Chūgan Engetsu, before 1375　東海一漚集
Kūgeshū, Gidō Shūshin, before 1388　空華集
Tōin Gyoshōshū, Keian Genju, before 1495　島隠漁唱集
Kyōunshū, *Ikkyū, before 1481　狂雲集
Nampo Bunshū, Bunshi Genshō, 1625　南浦文集
Seika Sensei Bunshū, *Fujiwara Seika, 1626　惺窩先生文集
Kyōinshū, Hori Kyōan, before 1642　杏陰集
Razan Shishū, *Hayashi Razan, 1662　羅山詩集
Razan Bunshū, ibid., 1662　羅山文集
Kassho Ikō, Nawa Kassho, 1666　活所遺稿
Shōjutsu Sensei Shibunshū, Itō Tōgai, 1736　紹述先生詩文集

Zeigan Shū, Yanada Zeigan, 1746　蛻巌集
Sankaku Shū, Okuda Sankaku, 1756　三角集
Kōyō Sekiyō Sonsha Shi, *Kan Chazan, ca. 1800?　黄葉夕陽村舎詩
San'yō Shishō, *Rai San'yo, 1818　山陽詩鈔

Comic Writings

Taihei Gafu, *Dōmyaku Sensei, i.e., Hata-naka Kanzai, 1769　太平楽府
Neboke Sensei Bunshū, i.e., *Ōta Nampo, 1777　寝惚先生文集
Kokkakō, Ikenaga Hatayoshi, 1787　黒珂稿
Taihei Shinkyoku, Anketsu Sensei, i.e., Nakajima Sōin, 1819　太平新曲
Hanka Sanjin Shishō, i.e. Ueki Gyokusō, 1834　半可山人詩鈔

There are also collections of verses and poems by Chinese poets that greatly influenced Japanese ideas about poetry as an art and about the art of individual Chinese poets. Although this subject is in general beyond the scope of this companion, something will be said to characterize the kinds of Chinese poetry popular at different times. By the time of the *Kokinshū*, the witty poetry of the Six Dynasties was greatly popular. The *Shinkokinshū* reflects a shift in taste to T'ang poets and a graver aesthetic. The Zen priests and especially that part of their literature termed *gosan bungaku* introduced Sung poetry and Sung aesthetics. In the Edo period matters grew more complicated. That would be so in any event, because a longer Chinese tradition had been gained, because more people were reading Chinese, and because varieties of Neoconfucianism were part of the official philosophy of the shogunate. The Gosan priests had made popular a collection, *Santaishi* (三体詩 *San-t'i Shih*) that mostly represents poets after the great T'ang poets, Tu Fu and Li Po. This was the so-to-speak official anthology to Neoconfucianists such as *Hayashi Razan. Its prominence was severely challenged by *Ogyū Sorai, who criticized it (after an earlier enthusiam) for being an inferior collection. In its stead, he propounded the *Tōshisen* (唐詩選 *T'ang-shih Hsüan*), whose collection was falsely attributed to Ri Han-ryō (李攀竜 *Li Pan-lung*). It was, in fact, a kind of pirated edition of another collection, *Tōshi Kunkai* (唐詩訓解 *T'ang-shih Hsün-chieh*). Both the Ming original and the pirated version were highly popular in China and subsequently in Japan. Both feature, as their titles suggest, generous samples of the poems by Tu Fu and Li Po, no doubt approaching then-modern tastes more closely. To relate this at last to Japanese poetry, the preference expressed by *Matsuo Bashō for Tu Fu (To Ho in Japanese) reflects such changing tastes in his time.

M. CRITICISM

Japanese criticism often varies in nature from Western. That being so, no genuine understanding of Japanese literature is possible without attention to the ways Japanese have approached their literature—often in what was assumed rather than said. Among things assumed was practice or technique, the basis of accomplishment: keiko 稽古, etc. Because this was fundamental, exemplary collections (*shūka*[shū] 秀歌[集], *shūku*[shū] 秀句[集], etc.) played a major role. Various styles (*tei* or tai and yō 体, 様) were often distinguished. And because of this technical, stylistic emphasis, a correspondingly heavy emphasis was put on natural expression of feeling as a basis of systematic poetics (see Part One A). Some of the most important criticism is found in prefaces to collections (e.g. the *Kokinshū*), in judgments at poetry matches (e.g. *Ropphakuban Utaawase*), in zuihitsu (e.g. *Sei Shōnagon's Makura no Sōshi*), or in literary creations themselves (e.g. *Murasaki Shikibu's Genji Monogatari*, "Hotaru"). Other sources include more or less secret writing (e.g. *Gotoba's Gotoba no In Gokuden*) and reporting of discussions by famous writers (e.g. *Mukai Kyorai's Kyorai Shō* and *Hozumi Ikan's Naniwa Miyage*). There are also a number of spurious or doubtful writings: for example, forgeries long ascribed as originals by *Fujiwara Teika.

What follows is some attempt to represent these various kinds (excluding the spurious). But it should not be thought that the ensuing list is comprehensive.

An asterisk before a title or author's name indicates that it is included in Part Three. Words, other than titles, underlined will be found in Part Four. Most works are noticed in Part Three.

1. *Waka* (*karon* 歌論)

Kakyō Hyōshiki, *Fujiwara Hamanari, ca. 772

Ki Shishō Gokusui no En Waka, preface by *Ōshikōchi Mitsune, 901

Kokinshū, Japanese preface, *Ki no Tsurayuki, ca. 905–920

Tadamine Juttei, *Mibu no Tadamine, 945

Shinsen Zuinō, *Fujiwara Kintō, ca. 1040

Waka Kuhon, ibid.

Nan Goshūi, *Minamoto Tsunenobu, 1097

Shunrai (or *Toshiyori*) *Zuinō*, *Minamoto Shunrai, ?1115

Fukurozōshi, *Fujiwara Kiyosuke, ca. 1156

Bokuteki Ki, ibid., after 1156

Ōgishō, ibid., 1124–1144

Waka Ichiji Shō, ibid., 1150–1156

Waka Shogakushō, ibid., 1169

Man'yōshū Jidai Nanji, *Kenshō, ca. 1183

Kokin Hichūshō, ibid.

Kokinshū Chū, ibid., 1185—and other titles

Yakumo Mishō, *Juntoku, ca. 1242?

Ropphakuban Utaawase, judgments by *Fujiwara Shunzei, 1193

Man'yōshū Jidaikō, *Fujiwara Shunzei, 1198

Waji (or *Shōji*) *Sōjō*, ibid.; and see the entries in A (Waka), above

Gotoba no In Gokuden, *Gotoba, after 1221?

Mumyōshō, *Kamo no Chōmei, 1209–1210; see also D (Monogatari, etc.), above

Teika Jittei (*Jittai*), *Fujiwara Teika, 1202–1213

Shūka Daitai, ibid.; see also A (Waka), above

Shin Sanjūrokunin Kasen. *Fujiwara Mototoshi, 1260.

Eiga Ittei (*Ittai*), *Fujiwara Tameie, ca. 1274

Tamekane Kyō Wakashō, *Kyōgoku
  Tamekane, ca. 1287
*Fūgashū, prefs. by *Hanazono, 1346
Gumon Kenchū, *Nijō Yoshimoto, 1363

Kinrai Fūteishō, ibid., 1387
Hana ni Yosuru Jukkai Waka no Jo, *Shō-
  tetsu, 1440
Shōtetsu Monogatari, ibid., 1448

With the exception of Shōtetsu, there is little distinguished waka criticism after about 1400, although scholarly study by *kokugakusha* is an important feature of Edo intellectual life. See *Kitamura Kigin, *Keichū, *Kamo no Mabuchi, and *Motoori Norinaga, in Part Three.

2. Monogatari and Other Prose

The most valuable criticism for such works, as for all literature, is that implied by major works. There is not much else for prose literature before the Edo *kokugakusha*. See the preceding paragraph. The discussion of *monogatari* in "Hotaru" in *Murasaki Shikibu's *Genji Monogatari* has been mentioned at the head of section 1, just preceding. But there are numerous other comments on art in the work. *Sugawara Takasue no Musume has a famous account of mono- gatari in her *Sarashina Nikki*. See also *Fūyōshū*.

The *renga* masters are known to have lectured on the *Genji Monogatari*, but little survives apart from *Shōhaku's *Rōkashō*, 1476.

These masters also proved themselves by lecturing on the *Ise Monogatari*, and three important versions of such discussions survive: *Shōhaku's *Shōmonshō*, 1478; *Sōchō's *Sōkan Monjo* (*Kikigaki*) 1478; and *Satomura Jōha's *Ise Monogatari Jōha Shō*, 1580.

For diary literature, there are some comments, as in *Ki no Tsurayuki's *Tosa Nikki*, 935; and *Matsuo Bashō's *Oi no Kobumi*, printed 1709.

3. Renga and Haikai

Because the rules and canons of linked poetry were so complex, a number of guides and rulebooks appeared. In addition to what follows, see section F, above. Because a number of writers wrote both about *renga* and *haikai*, both kinds of criticism are included here, with those after ca. 1650 being devoted chiefly to haikai.

Renri Hishō, *Nijō Yoshimoto, 1349
Tsukuba Mondō, ibid., 1357–1372
Renga Shinshiki, ibid., 1372
Kyūshū Mondō, ibid., 1376
Renga Jūyō, ibid., 1379
Jūmon Saihishō, ibid., 1383
Chōtanshō, *Bontō(an), 1390
Bontōan Shū Hentōsho, ibid., 1417
Shoshin Kyūeishū, *Takayama Sōzei, 1428
Shinshiki Kon'an, ibid., 1452
Hitorigoto, *Shinkei, 1468
Tokorodokoro Hentō, ibid., 1470
Shiyōshō, ibid., 1471

Chōrokubumi, *Sōgi, 1466
Azuma Mondō, ibid., 1467, 1470
Oi no Susami, ibid., 1479
Shitakusa, ibid., 1493
Rōkashō, *Shōhaku, 1479
Nagabumi, *Sōchō, 1490
Sōgi Shūenki, ibid., 1502
Renga Hikyōshū, ibid., 1509
Amayo no Ki, ibid., 1519
Haikai Renga Shō, *Yamazaki Sōkan,
  1532–1546
Renga Shihōshō (or Hon'i Shō), *Satomura
  Jōha, 1585

Renga Kyōkun, ibid., 1587
Shikimoku Hishō, ibid., 1587
Shōzaishū, ibid., 1597
Ubuginu, Konkū, dates unknown, renga treatise
Gosan, *Matsunaga Teitoku, 1651
Zōdanshū, *Enomoto Kikaku, 1692
Bashō Ō Shūenki, ibid., 1694

Sō Kikaku Sensei Sho, *Mukai Kyorai, 1697
Kyorai Shō, ibid., 1702–1704
Sanzōshi, Hattori Tohō, ca. 1702 (the three books are designated White, Red, and Black)
Ten'inron, *Yosa Buson, pr. 1786 (ed. *Takai Kitō)

4. *Nō*

Two seminal critics dominate criticism of *nō*—*Zeami and his son-in-law *Komparu Zenchiku. Although Zeami has been known traditionally as the author of sixteen treatises (jūrokubushū), such has been the industry, and good fortune, of Japanese scholars that he is now known to have written (or supplied the information for) twenty-one. In the order of their composition, and with their usual if not invariable titles, this is his critical canon as known today. Since characters for most of the titles are not given elsewhere, they are included here.

1. *Fūshikaden*　風姿花伝
2. *Kashū*　花習
3. *Ongyoku Kowadashi Kuden* 音曲声出口伝
4. *Shikadō*　至花道
5. *Hitokata (no Zu)*　人形（図）
6. *Nōsakusho*　能作書
7. *Kakyō*　花鏡
8. *Fushizuke Shidai*　曲付次第
9. *Fūgyokushū*　風曲集
10. *Yūgaku Shūdō Fūken*　遊楽習道風見
11. *Goi*　五位
12. *Kyūi*　九位
13. *Rikugi*　六義
14. *Shūgyoku Tokka*　拾玉得花
15. *Goon*　五音
16. *Goongyoku*　五音曲
17. *Shudōsho*　習道書
18. *(Zeshi Rokujū Igo) Sarugaku Dangi* （世子六十以後）申楽談儀
19. *Museki Isshi*　夢跡一紙
20. *Kyakuraika*　却来花
21. *Kintōsho*　金島書

Zenchiku has been somewhat in Zeami's shadow, but his treatises have recently received closer attention. Although they go under various names, the following are those of the standard edition.

1. *Goon no Shidai*　五音之次第
2. *Kabu Zuinōki*　歌舞髄脳記
3. *Goon Jittei*　五音十体
4. *Goon Sankyokushū*　五音三曲集
5. *Rokurin Ichiro no Ki*　六輪一露之記
6. *Rokurin Ichiro no Ki Chū* 六輪一露之記注
7. *Nika Ichirin*　二花一輪
8. *Rokurin Ichiro Taii*　六輪一露大意
9. *Rokurin Kyokumi*　六輪曲味
10. *Rokurin Ichiro Gaishō*　六輪一露概抄
11. *Rokurin Kanchō Hiki*　六輪灌頂秘記
12. *Rokurin Ichiro Hichū* 六輪一露秘注
(version from the Kanshō era, 1460–1466)
13. *Rokurin Ichiro Hichū* (same; version from the Bunshō era, 1466–1467)
14. *Yūgen Sanrin*　幽玄三輪
15. *Shidō Yōshō*　至道要抄
16. *Meishukushū*　明宿集
17. *Emaiza Keizu*　円満井座系図
18. *Sarugaku Engi*　猿楽縁起
19. *Emaiza Hekisho*　円満井座壁書
20. *Bunshō Gannen Waka*　文正元年和歌
21. *Inariyama Sanrō*　稲荷山参籠
22. *Jōdokyō Hihan*　浄土教批判
23. *Sakuzen Nikki*　作善日記

5. Kyōgen

As noticed in Part Five, the very texts of *kyōgen* are only now being recovered in accurate theatrical and readable versions. Criticism is equally difficult to come by, and in fact amounts to one work by *Ōkura Toraakira, *Warambegusa*, in eighty-nine parts, ca. 1660. This is rather miscellaneous although well written. It presents anecdotes about actors and related matters, but it also touches on the nature of comedy and of humor. It gives some instruction in the avoidance of bad performance and in the means to success.

6. Jōruri and Kabuki

Given the relatively low status of these two kinds of theatre in Edo times, it is not surprising, although certainly regrettable, that so little criticism can be mentioned. The opening of *Hozumi Ikan's *Naniwa Miyage* offers remarks by *Chikamatsu Monzaemon that are of great theoretical import. See Part One A. The rest of writing on the theater is mostly anecdotal and so belongs with the next entry. *Jōruri* was best served in terms of historical matters by the approach of *Nishizawa Ippū, whose *Ima Mukashi Ayatsuri Nendaiki* is briefly noticed in Part Three.

7. Theatrical Anecdotes, Comments

Although except for *nō* and Chikamatsu's remarks on *jōruri* there is little formal dramatic criticism, there is a wealth of theatrical records, anecdotes, gossip, and other materials that a theatrical historian may use, and from which a wise critic could no doubt draw important inferences. The *Kojiki* and *Nihongi* refer to wazaoki—entertainers or performers of some kind or kinds, apparently conquered peoples forced to entertain their Yamato conquerors, who received the songs and entertainments as well as the submission of those they defeated. In the Heian period we find sustained accounts. Around 1058 to 1065, *Fujiwara Akihira set down an account of *sarugaku* and its social setting in an account titled *Shinsarugakuki*. Does the title suggest some previous account? Shortly thereafter, in 1096, *Ōe no Masafusa completed a book, *Rakuyō Dengakuki*, on another precursor of nō. He wrote two other, related books by 1111: *Kairaishiki*, dealing with puppeteers, and *Yūjoki*, an account of pleasure girls, as the title says. These early works are observations from above, as it were. By the Edo period (or before, for nō) we hear from the theaters themselves.

When the Edo *bakufu* recognized "four companies and one style" (shiza ichiryū: see Part Five A), the Kita school of nō was not included. Whether for that reason or some other, the criticism of the four established houses seemed to descend on the head of Kita Shichidayū, and although the criticism is very negative, this typifies one kind of anecdotal material that gives the critic as well as the historian insight into what was commonly thought reprehensible, as also, by some degree of implicit contrast, what was esteemed. Each of the companies also created a store of founder's legends. The piety of such material probably tells us less than harsh criticism about actual practice, but it does express some sense of the ideals fostered by the founders or, more likely, assumed by their inheritors.

For examples of such varied writings, one may consult standard works by theater historians. Although now an old compilation, *Nōgaku Kokonki*, edited by Nonomura Kaizō (Shun'yōdō, 1943) generously reprints from a variety of such sources. For nō there is also *Shiza Yakusha Mokuroku*, 四座役者目録 (seventeenth c., compiler uncertain). As its title shows, it concerns the four recognized companies, omitting the Kita. Contrary to the last part of its title, however, it is not a bibliography but a collection of anecdotes and theatrical episodes based on fact, however plain or colored. It concerns such things as quarrels between actors, famous performances, and the incomes of performers.

For *kyōgen*, the *Warambegusa* of *Ōkura Toraakira, mentioned in section 5 above, is the best source of theatrical lore as well as of more general insights.

For kabuki and jōruri, there is *Yakushabanashi* 役者論語 (also read more easily "Yakusha Rongo"). This has some details about jōruri, but as the title implies, it is chiefly about actors and therefore about *kabuki*. It was brought out by Hachimonjiya in Kyoto in 1776, and the fact that was published by a book shop noted for its prose fiction suggests that the appeal of the work may have been not unlike that of many accounts of actors and courtesans in fictionalized or other popular versions. The work is worth mentioning in part because its seven parts are mainly a compilation of earlier materials. The *Ayamegusa* of the *onnagata* Yoshizawa Ayame is one of the earlier works used. The most interesting section is that devoted to the Genroku actor Sakata Tōjūrō. His fame has been kept alive by a story written by the modern novelist and prose fiction writer, Kikuchi Kan. In *Tōjūrō no Koi* he relates how Tōjūrō hired a townswoman to study her life and emotions in order to portray the experience enacted in *sewamono* more faithfully. This catches the spirit of Tōjūrō's account, which of course brought the woman great embarrassment when published. The literary point involves the actor's seeking to define for acting purposes the nature of ordinary life and of female experience in particular. In this respect, we discover a *kamigata* desire to represent faithfully in sewamono what the life of townspeople is truly like. Anyone who goes to kabuki for realism, as that is understood in certain kinds of prose fiction, will not be embarrassed by the abundance of evidence. But it is clear, by contrast with the *aragoto* acting of *Ichikawa Danjūrō so popular in Edo, that Tōjūrō sought for something more nearly akin to realism in the sense known in Western theater.

From *Ihara Saikaku onward, actors feature in Edo prose fiction, and from it one learns a good deal that gives us contemporary understanding of actors, plays, and theaters.

N. Buddhist Sects

Buddhism entered Japan as a major feature of what may be termed the New Learning, in the sixth century: in 538 images of the Buddha were taken to Japan from Korea, and in 588 Hōkōji—the first Buddhist temple—was built. This and the next section treat of such matters, and at the end of this will be found notice of some important omissions.

As the sects of Buddhism proliferated, they were grouped in ever-increasing numerical arrangements; one finds frequent references to, say, the "Six Nara Sects" or the "Thirteen Sects." Generally they were viewed not as competing institutions, each which its sole claim to the truth, but as various ways to enlightenment that the Buddha adapted to the specific needs of individuals. The *Lotus Sūtra* taught that the Buddha ultimately provided a single vehicle (ichijō 一乗; ekayāna) whereby all sentient beings would be brought to enlightenment. But this subsumed every kind of expedient device (provisional teaching, accommodation, hōben 方便) that he freely employed to accommodate the devotee's level of comprehension. Thus, any one sect recognized the others not as wrong, but as more or less appropriate to the needs of the individual and the age. This theoretical basis for Buddhist tolerance is also argued in the *Shōmangyō* and the *Kegonkyō*.

Titles with asterisks will be found in this section O; names with asterisks in Part Three.

The Six Sects of the Southern Capital (Nanto rokushū), that is of Heijō, Nara, is the earliest such classification. They included:

1. Kushashū 倶舎宗. This sect, which derives its name from the *Kusharon* 倶舎論, (*The Treasury of Analyses of the Law* [Abhidharmakośa]), written by the famous Indian philosopher Vasubandhu (Seshin 世親, ca. 350) while he adhered to the (Hīnayāna) Sarvāstivādin school. The *Kusharon* argues that all phenomena arise through the aggregation of ultimate, real, psychophysical entities called dharmas (hō 法). This doctrine is an important moment in the dialectic of Buddhist thought, and was later taught under the auspices of the Hossō sect. The Kusha sect was introduced to Japan in 658 but it did not survive long as an independent institution.

2. Jōjitsushū 成実宗. Introduced to Japan in 625, the Jōjitsu sect likewise never became an independent school, but was recognized as a branch of the Sanron teaching. It takes its name from the *Jōjitsuron* 成実論 (*The Treatise on the Completion of Truth*), by the fourth-century Indian philosopher, Harivarman (Karibatsuma 訶梨跋摩). Like the Kusha, it propounds a dharma theory; but it differs from that sect mainly in denying that these ultimate entities are real. It thus approaches the twofold egolessness of self and dharma as maintained by the Sanron school.

3. Sanronshū 三論宗. The "Three Treatise Sect," introduced to Japan in 625, is based on three works of the Indian Mādhyamika school via China. Two are by the preeminent Mahāyāna philosopher, Nāgārjuna (Ryūju 龍樹, ca. 150–ca. 250): the *Chūron* 中論 (*Treatise on the Middle Path* [*Mādhyamika-śāstra*]) and the *Jūnimonron* 十二門論 (*The Twelve Gates* [*Dvādaśamukhaśāstra*]). The third work is the *Hyakuron* 百論 (*The One-Hundred Verse Treatise*), by Nāgārjuna's leading disciple, Āryadeva (Daiba 提婆, ca. 200). The sect is a Mahāyāna school of dialectical criticism that seeks to refute every dogmatic position because the Real transcends every conceptual formulation. The Sanron sect, like the Kusha and Jōjitsu, did not flourish in Japan as an independent institution. But Nāgārjuna is revered as a major patriarch by all schools of Japanese Mahāyāna Buddhism.

4. Hossōshū 法相宗. The Dharma-Characteristics sect, also known as Yui-

shiki 唯識 (Consciousness Only), is the philosophically important school of Buddhist idealism developed first in India as the Yogācāra school of Asanga (Mujaku 無着, ca. 350) and his brother Vasubandhu (see Kusha, above) after his conversion to the Mahāyāna. (At the Hossō sect's headquarters, the Kōfukuji in Nara, are two remarkable, lifelike statues of Asaṅga and Vasubandhu carved in 1208 by *Unkei.) The Indian tradition was continued in the sixth and seventh centuries by the Vijñānavāda of Dignāga (Jinna 陳那) and Dharmakīrti (Hōshō 法称). The Chinese sect was systematized by the great traveler ~~and~~ translator, Hsüan-tsang (Genjō, 600–664) and his disciple, K'uei-chi (Kiki, 632–682); and it was introduced to Japan in 653 by Hsüan-tsang's disciple, Dōshō 道昭 (629–700). The Kōfukuji and the adjacent Kasuga Shrine were supported by the powerful Fujiwara clan, but Hossō never developed a popular following. Idealism, however, which explains all phenomena as modifications of consciousness, has been a major philosophical current throughout the Mahāyāna, just as it has been in Western thought from Berkeley through Hume, Kant, Hegel, and beyond.

   5. Ritsushū 律宗. The Disciplinary sect, founded by the Chinese monk Chien-chen 鑑真 (Ganjin, 688–763), emphasized the observance of the Buddhist precepts as formulated in the *Shibunritsu* 四分律 (*Vinaya in Four Parts*). Ganjin was influential in establishing regulations for the behavior of the clergy by establishing three official ordination platforms (kaidan). The sect, whose headquarters is the Tōshōdaiji in Nara, never had a popular following, although in later centuries there was considerable concern and dispute over the proper observance of the regulations. In the Kamakura period, Eizon 叡尊 (1201–1290) initiated the Esoteric-Disciplinary sect (Shingon Risshū) at Nara's Saidaiji, a movement continued by *Jiun and others.

   6. Kegonshū 華厳宗. The Hua-yen (Kegon) school was systematized by Fa-tsang 法蔵 (Hōzō, 643–712) and took the *Garland Sūtra* (*Kegonkyō*) as its basic scripture. It is a school of idealism that understands the phenomenal world as the "interdependent arising of the realm of elements" (hokkai engi 法界縁起). Introduced to Japan in the first half of the eighth century, Kegon had its headquarters at the great Tōdaiji in Nara. The Tōdaiji, at which Ganjin (see above, 5) had established a major ordination platform, was the major center of Buddhist studies and ritual during the Nara period and enjoyed royal patronage. Although the sublimity of its speculations was generally admired, Kegon was unable to generate widespread enthusiasm, and its influence was soon superseded by the new sects of the Heian period. Early in the Kamakura period *Myōe attempted, without success, to rejuvenate the Kegon sect at Kyoto's Kōzanji.

   The Eight Sects (hasshū), or Eight Houses (hakke), include the Six Nara sects, with the addition of the two major sects that dominated the Heian period: Tendai and Shingon.

   7. Tendaishū 天台宗. Chih-i 智顗 (538–597) systematized Chinese T'ien T'ai with a philosophy based on the *Lotus Sūtra* (*Myōhōrengekyō*). His Fa-hua Hsüan-i 法華玄義 (*Hokke Gengi, Profound Meaning of the Lotus*); Fa-

hua Wen-chü 法華文句 (*Hokke Mongu, Textual Commentary on the Lotus*); and the *Mo-ho Chih-kuan* 摩訶止観 (**Maka Shikan, Great Cessation and Insight*) make up the Three Great Books (sandaibu) of the Tendai Sect.

The Tendai sect established by *Saichō on his return from China in 805 took Chih-i's T'ien T'ai as its starting point, and over the centuries developed a unique synthesis of disparate ideas and practices. *Ennin introduced esotericism; *Genshin promoted devotion to Amida; and an accommodation with native Shinto beliefs resulted in the doctrine of Sannō Ichijitsu Shintō (Mountain-god One-truth Shintō). The Enryakuji, which Saichō built in 788 on Mount Hiei northeast of Kyoto, was the origin of a great monastic center that was to exert a powerful influence on the religious and civil life of the nation until the temple's destruction in 1571 by Oda Nobunaga. Disputes among the followers of Ennin and Enchin 814–891) split Tendai into two branches: the Sammon (Mountain School) centered at the Enryakuji, and the Jimon (Temple School) with headquarters at the Onjōji (Miidera). Other distinguished members of the Tendai sect are *Henjō, *Jien, and Tenkai (1536–1643).

The *Lotus Sūtra*'s revelation of the Buddha's use of expedient devices (hōben) to speak to different levels of human understanding provided the basis for Chih-i's Five Periods (goji) and the corresponding fivefold classification of the scriptures:

The Garland Period (Kegonji). Immediately after his Enlightenment, Gautama preached the unaccommodated Truth as taught in the *Garland Sūtra* (**Kegonkyō*). But since only the bodhisattvas in the audience were spiritually advanced enough to comprehend his message, the Buddha moved to the Deer Park outside Benares to promulgate the first of a series of accommodations to human understanding.

The Deer Park Period (Rokuonji). Here Gautama expounded the doctrines of Hīnayāna as represented by the *Sūtras of the Tradition* (*Āgamas*, *Agongyō)

The Vaipulya Period (Hōdōji). At this time the Buddha revealed the Mahāyāna sutras that stressed the superiority of the Mahāyāna over Hīnayāna ideals, but that predated the doctrine of Emptiness (śūnyatā; kū 空). Representative works of this period are the *Yuimakyō (*Vimalakīrti Sūtra*), the *Ryōgakyō (*Lankāvatāra Sūtra*), *Ryōgonkyō (*Śūrangama Sūtra*) and the *Konkōmyōkyō (*Suvarnaprabhāsa Sūtra*).

The Perfection of Wisdom Period (Hannyaji). The Buddha then explained the doctrine of Emptiness (śūnyatā) by means of the prajñāpāramitā class of sutras. These include the **Daihannyaharamittakyō*, the *Hannyashingyō (*Prajñāpāramitā-hrdaya-sūtra*), the *Kongōkyō (*Vajracchedika–sūtra*), and the *Ninnōkyō (*Kārunikārājā*).

The Lotus-Nirvana Period (Hokke-nehanji). Finally the fullness of the Buddha's teaching is made manifest through the *Lotus Sūtra* (**Hokkekyō*) and the *Nirvāṇa Sūtra* (**Daihatsunehangyō*). The literary, imaginative character of the *Lotus Sūtra* accounts for no small measure of its appeal to the Japanese. But all of the scriptures are seen to reveal at least a partial truth of the Buddha's teaching, in spite of apparent contradictions. As a famous passage in the "Hotaru" part of *Murasaki Shikibu's *Genji Monogatari* reveals, even the sutras of the second period were thought useful in glossing the superior later ones, and it was thought that in the end all would become one truth—such also being the relation of *monogatari* to nonfictional writing about truth.

Meditation has always been the focus of Buddhist practice, and the philosophical speculations of the religion are for the most part attempts to conceptualize experience from this perspective. Chih-i employed several systems of meditation known as chih kuan 止観 (*shikan*, "cessation and insight"). The "perfect and sudden" (endon 円頓) method described in his *Maka Shikan* is preceded by one of four preliminary practices: (1) constantly sitting (jōza zammai 常坐三昧), (2) constantly walking (jōgyō zammai 常行三昧), (3) half-walking half-seated (hangyō hanza zammai 半行半坐三昧), and (4) neither walking nor sitting (higyō hiza zammai 非行非坐三昧). One result of such meditation is the realization of the Three Truths (santai 三諦), not conceptually but experientially. The multiplicity of the world viewed as arising interdependently (engi 縁起) is empty (*kū* 空) of any self or substance; this reality is ultimately beyond the grasp of concepts. This same world viewed empirically, however, also has a provisional existence (ke 假). To these Two Truths traditionally recognized by the Mahāyāna, Chih-i adds a third: this same world viewed simultaneously as empty and provisional is the truth of the Middle (chū 中).

The goal of religious practice is understood by Buddhism as transcending all concepts, a notion reflected in the Kamakura poetic ideal of using "few words." In his *Korai Futeishō* (*Poetic Styles Past and Present*), Shunzei comments significantly on the Tendai meditation practices, which were frequently employed by the poets of his time who viewed their occupation not merely as a courtly diversion, but as a way—*michi*—to religious understanding.

8. Shingonshū 真言宗. The "True Word," that is, Mantra sect introduced to Japan by *Kūkai emphasizes the use of nonconceptual means to spiritual awareness: maṇḍalas (*mandara*; pictorial representations), mudras (hand gestures and body postures), and mantras (mystic phrases). Its basic scriptures are the *Dainichikyō* and the *Kongōchōgyō*, which respectively describe the assemblies of the Matrix (taizōkai 胎蔵界) and the Diamond (kongōkai 金剛界) mandalas. Whereas some sects, notably Tendai, see esotericism (mikkyō 密教, the "secret teaching") as a complementary practice, for the Shingon sect it is central. Shingon's tōmitsu 東密, to be distinguished from Tendai's taimitsu 台密 (see *Ennin), takes its name from the sect's main temple in Kyoto, the Tōji (Eastern Temple); the sect headquarters is at the Kongōbuji on Mount Kōya.

Kūkai's Shingon teaches that we can "attain Buddhahood in this very body" (sokushin jōbutsu 即身成仏), since all sentient beings have an inherent Buddhanature (bodaishin 菩提心). This state is attained by integrating the Three Actions (sangō 三業: body, voice, and mind) of sentient beings with the corresponding Three Mysteries (sammitsu 三密) of the Great Sun Buddha (Dainichi Nyorai 大日如来, Mahāvairocana). Strictly speaking, of course, nothing is "attained": there is no fundamental difference between man and Buddha, only lack of awareness of their identity.

After Kūkai, Shingon produced few exceptional leaders. Kakuban (1095–1143) split with the orthodox tradition to found the branch known as Shingi ("New Doctrine") Shingon. And priests of other sects frequently sought to graft esoteric practices to their particular doctrinal emphases: *Myōe to Kegon (gonmitsu 厳密), Eizon to the Disciplinary sect (shingon risshū), and a number of Rinzai Zen monks, including *Eisai, *Enni, and *Musō to the meditation techniques introduced in the Kamakura period. In the Tokugawa, *Jiun revived Sanskrit studies in Japan. Because of its emphasis on the nonconceptual, visual aspects of experience, Shingon had a strong influence on the arts.

The grouping of Eight Houses with Nine Sects (hakke kushū) includes the preceding eight sects with the addition of:

9. Zenshū 禅宗. Although meditation has always been an important part of Buddhist teaching, for the Zen sects it is central: hence the name, Zen (Ch'an, dhyāna, "meditation"). The Zen tradition is often characterized by four statements:

A special transmission outside the scriptures;
   (教外別傳 kyōge betsuden)
No dependence upon words and letters;
   (不立文字 furyū monji)
Direct pointing at the heart of man;
   (直指人心 jikishi ninshin)
Seeing into one's nature and the attainment of Buddhahood.
   (見性成佛 kenshō jōbutsu)

Although he died before Gautama (ca. 563 B.C.–483 B.C.), Śāriputra was the leader of the early Buddhist order of monks. Zen, however, traditionally claims a special transmission through Mahākāśyapa when he "smiled faintly [while the Buddha] held out a flower" ("nenge mishō" 拈華微笑) as a nonverbal expression of his teaching. "Transmission from mind to mind" ("ishin denshin" 以心伝心) also refers to the intuitive recognition of that religious truth which, in mainstream Buddhism as well as in Zen, is seen to transcend all conceptualization.

Although Zen argues against dependence upon words and letters, it does not deny their provisional usefulness. Among the scriptures of special importance to this sect are the *Hannyashingyō, *Kongōkyō, *Ryōgakyō, and *Kegonkyō.

The twenty-eighth Indian patriarch, Bodhidharma ([Bodai] Daruma, [菩提] 達磨, d. ca. 528) brought Zen to China to become the first patriarch of Chinese Ch'an. The sixth patriarch of the Chinese line, Hui-neng (Enō 慧能, 638–713), who emphasized the "abrupt" character of the enlightenment experience as opposed to the relative gradualism of the Northern school, is revered by all Japanese Zen sects (except *Saichō's short-lived Gozu school) as the virtual founder of Chinese Ch'an. His *Liu-tsu T'an-ching* (*Rokuso Dangyō* 六祖壇経), *Platform Sūtra of the Sixth Patriarch*, is a major classic of the sect.

Japanese Zen, introduced for the most part during the early Kamakura period, is divided into three principal sects, discussed in separate entries below: the Rinzai sect of *Eisai, *Enni, *Ikkyū, *Kokan, *Musō, *Hakuin, and the Five Mountains (*gosan*) movement; the Sōtō sect of *Dōgen; and the Ōbaku sect of Ingen. The maverick Fuke 普化宗 sect of shakuhachi-playing komusō 虚無僧 monks, said to have been founded by Kakushin 覚心 (Hattō Enmyō Kokushi, 1207–1298), is also classified as an offshoot of Zen.

When the divisions of Japanese Buddhism are referred to as the Ten Sects (jusshū), this indicates the preceding nine with the addition of:

10. Jōdoshū 浄土宗. *Hōnen's founding of the Pure Land sect in 1175 was a landmark in the Amida Pietism movement that had its origins in India and a long prior history in both China and Japan. Amida, earlier known as Amitābha ("Infinite Light") and Amitāyus ("Infinite Life"), may have entered the pantheon from Indian solar myths, or from Persian religion as Buddhism began its long trek across the deserts of Central Asia to China. Amitāyus (Muryōju 無量壽) is depicted in the western direction in both the Diamond and Matrix mandalas employed by esotericism, and devotion to Amida was emphasized as an aid to meditation by Tendai.

For Hōnen, faith in Amida was the "sole-practice" (senju 專修) appropriate to the Latter Days of the Law rather than being a mere adjunct to meditation. (Hōnen himself appears to have been accommodating to the variety of sectarian practices, but the Pure Land movement tended to greater exclusiveness with *Shinran and Rennyo, 1414–1499.) The devotee was to rely solely upon the Other Power (tariki 他力) of Amida rather than on the ego-centered Self-Power (jiriki 自力) of the non-*nembutsu* sects, the traditional schools of the Holy Path (shōdōmon 聖道門). Birth (ōjō 往生) in Amida's Pure Land was possible by virtue of his forty-eight vows in an earlier existence as the bodhisattva Dharmākara (Hōzō 法蔵), which are described in the *Amitāyus Sūtra* (*Muryōjukyō). This work, together with the *Amidakyō* and the *Kammuryōjukyō*, comprise the *Three Pure Land Sūtras* (*Jōdo Sambukyō*).

The Pure Land movement initiated by Hōnen had enormous popular appeal. Its hopeful message that all might enter the Buddha's Western Paradise by the intent invocation of Amida's name brought hope to a nation devastated by the wars between the Taira and the Minamoto. Hōnen's influence also extended to the Jōdo Shinshū and the Jishū (see below).

The Twelve Sects of Buddhism (jūnishū) include the preceding ten with the addition of the following two.

11. (Jōdo) Shinshū (浄土) 真宗 Its closeness to Jōdoshū is testified to by the fact that its founder, *Shinran, studied with Hōnen. It is the first sect formed without direct contact with China or major dependence on Tendai tutelage. Hōnen emphasized invocation of the Buddha. Shinran invested the act with the universal possibility to reach paradise when one did so devotedly, even if one were of the lowliest social status, and even if one were of evil deeds. Besides this emphasis, Shinran was at variance from previous teachers by his willingness to eat meat and his marrying—living in this world. The great hope he offered and his relaxing of clerical rules could only have had wide human appeal.

12. Nichirenshū 日蓮宗. The founder, *Nichiren, did study in the Tendaishū for a time, but his teaching differs in its all but exclusive emphasis on the *Myōhōrengekyō (Lotus Sūtra—see the next section); the sect's founding dates from Nichiren's advocacy of its title (daimoku) in 1253. Another difference sets the Nichirenshū apart from all others of this thirteen: its emphasis on patriotic matters, or at least insistence on Nichiren's teaching as crucial to the country's success.

The Thirteen Sects (jūsanshū) is the most recent classification, not being in common use until about 1940. The grouping reflects the sects' current social prominence more than their basic philosophical differences, or their importance in the history of Buddhist thought. Thus, from among the Six Nara Sects, Kusha, Jōjitsu and Sanron are omitted; Zen is subdivided into Rinzai, Sōtō, and Ōbaku; and to the Pure Land movements are added the Yūzūnembutsu and the Ji sects. The Thirteen Sects, then, include: (1) Hossō, (2) Ritsu, (3) Kegon, (4) Tendai, (5) Shingon, (6) Rinzai, (7) Sōtō, (8) Ōbaku, (9) Jōdo, (10) Jōdo Shinshū, (11) Yūzūnembutsu, (12) Jishū, and (13) Nichiren. The sects not already discussed above are as follows:

(6) Rinzaishū 臨済宗. This first branch of Japanese Zen Buddhism was introduced in 1191 by Myōan *Eisai (1141–1215) who had studied in China, principally at Tendai (T'ien-t'ai) monasteries, who popularized tea in Japan, and who was author of Kissa Yōjōki. This and the next sect therefore had unusually large numbers of monks who were well schooled in Chinese and influenced by Sung aesthetics (see *Gosan Bungaku). Like other Zen sects, it introduced new monastic regulations. Although sometimes depicted as a religion for warrior aristocrats, which is not wholly wrong, this and the other two Zen sects also had great and beneficial popular influence by setting up temple schools (dōjō, later terakoya), thereby spreading literacy in a major way. It has flourished well as an intellectual and aesthetic sect—it has over 6,000 temples, including some of the wealthiest, in all parts of Japan.

(7) Sōtōshū 曹洞宗. With Rinzaishū, this is one of the two principal of the three Zen sects. It was begun in Japan by *Dōgen upon his return from Sung China in 1227. Although not as well known outside Japan, it is very widespread—it has well over 14,000 temples, more than double those of the Rinzaishū.

(8) Ōbakushū 黄檗宗. This last and least important of the three Zen sects can be regarded as an offshoot from the Rinzaishū. It is the sole sect to be founded in the Edo period—by the Chinese priest, Yin-yüan (Ingen, 1592–1673), who began teaching in Nagasaki in 1654. He won a favorable response from the shogunate as well as popular listeners, but the sect remained small.

(11) Yūzūnembutsushū 融通念仏宗. The permeating (yūzū) nembutsu movement introduced by Ryōnin (1071–1132) within Tendai in 1117 was later recognized as an independent sect. Its emphasis influenced the later sects of *Hōnen, *Shinran, and Ippen (see next item).

(12) Jishū 時宗. This is another, lesser offshoot of the Jōdoshū, dating from 1276, when the founder, Ippen (1239–1289), began his teaching. It took its name from a passage in the *Amidakyō (see Section O below), and has affiliations with

esotericism and Zen. It is also termed Yugyōshū from the fact that Ippen and his followers became itinerant preachers of the *nembutsu*. It is further distinguished by its close affiliations with Shinto.

Two very important matters are omitted from this section and the next. The first has been touched on superficially: the accommodation of Buddhism to Shinto and Confucian thought. Shinto emphasis on purity, pollution, lustration, fertility, and generation—along with its close veneration of natural elements and shamanism—has deeply affected Japanese literature, but these are very difficult to specify in terms of Buddhist sects and works. The main thing to be said is that Shinto divinities have often been taken to be bodhisattvas or other figures in the Buddhist pantheon. The phenomenon of ryōbu Shinto 両部神道 was already firmly established by the Kamakura period. This involved not only adapting Shinto divinities to Buddhist figures but also the taking over by certain shrines of tantric practices.

The second omission is easily specified, but its substantive implications are far from clear. The culture of the Buddhist convents is of obvious importance and yet remains obscure, in spite of some initial study. For example, it is known that a nun (ama 尼) is a woman who undertakes spiritual life, renouncing the world like a monk. This usually means taking the tonsure and entering a nunnery. Convents have been conspicuous within the Japanese religious establishment since the early decades after the inception of Buddhism in that country. The *Nihon Shoki* relates that in 584 Soga no Umako (d. 626) installed an image of the Buddha Maitreya (Miroku) in a temple erected next to his dwelling, and that three nuns were assigned to attend it. By 622, the year of Prince *Shōtoku's death, there were more than five hundred nuns throughout Japan, and their numbers continued to grow. Some nuns, however, take vows but not the tonsure, and there are some women who, in old age, reside at home although having taken the tonsure. There are also women—*Gofukakusa in Nijō and *Ukō being conspicuous examples of many—who, like men, took vows not solely for religious reasons but also to be able to move freely in the world, among high and low. There seems to be a wealth of literature and other artistic culture by such women remaining to be explored.

O. A SELECTION OF SUTRAS

Japanese share with other Asian peoples an immense body of Buddhist writings, particularly of the Mahāyāna (Daijō 大乗, Greater Vehicle) kind. Some of these appear to have reached Japan early in the seventh century in their Chinese translations. Although sacred writings, the Buddhist scriptures must be understood differently from the sacred books of Jews, Christians, and Muslims. One difference lies in the extraordinary textual problems of so large a body of writings in so many translations. Another difference lies in the division between major groups of Buddhists—especially between the Mahāyāna and the Hīnayāna—with either different sutras or different emphases and responses to indigenous cultures such as the Chinese (with its strong elements of Confucianism and Taoism). Yet another difference lies in the fact that a given sutra may be a single unit, a part of another, or a collection of yet other units. As far as Japan is concerned, there is also the matter of its receiving, over a period of time, a given sutra in different translations in Chinese of varying completeness, elegance, and accuracy. In view of all this, the ordinary priest learns doctrines and rites from teachers, memorizing parts of sutras.

The list of sutras given here implies certain theological `and ecclesiastical matters. But the main purpose is to present the student of literature with what is excessively difficult to come by, a simple list with elementary remarks on sutras and commentaries that have influenced Japanese writers. (To use this historically, attention will need to be paid to the preceding section in this part, N, Buddhist Sects.) Some of the influences of this writing are immediate, as with the quotation given in the entry for the *Hannyashingyō. Others are far more subtle and comprehensive: for example, from parables such as those in the *Myōhōrengekyō, Chinese and Japanese learned of fiction in explicit ways. The view of the world and expression in esoteric verbal signs and body movements helped define not merely spirituality of one kind but similar approaches in the arts. Buddhist causality, metaphysics, immense temporal and spatial vistas, and large numbers of people in a scene (as in so many sutras) would not by themselves lead to prose narrative, but they help account for the early emergence of great prose narrative in Japan as well as China. The weight of karma might lead to pessimism or a tragic outlook. A sense of evanescence might lead to pensive reflection or to aesthetic definition of what matters because it is so fleeting. Emphasis on the Buddha nature of all sentient things, or on the efficacy of reciting the Amida Buddha's name, would bring hope. Tantrism and meditation define ways of approaching art unknown to an Aristotle or Horace.

The early Buddhist canon of southern Buddhism (Hīnayāna, Shōjō 小乗, Lesser Vehicle) was generally recognized as consisting of "Three Baskets" (tripiṭaka, sanzō 三蔵). The sutras (kyō 経) presented the sermons and life of the historical Buddha, Gautama (ca. 563–483 B.C.). (Predictably, there are differences of opinion about the dating, one prominent medieval Japanese view being that Gautama, or Śākyamuni, died in the year that would correspond to 949 B.C. in the Gregorian calendar; see mappō.) The vinaya (ritsu 律) describe the rules of conduct for monks and nuns, and the abhidharma (ron 論) are various kinds of philosophical writings, including commentaries on the sūtras.

The Mahāyāna generally ignored this early canon, more or less incorporating it into the Sūtras of the Tradition (Āgamas, *Agongyō). A vast array of new scriptures began to appear around the beginning of the Christian era, and these now became the focus of religion and literature. They included such influential writings as the Lotus Sūtra, the Heart of Wisdom Sūtra, and the Three Pure Land Sūtras The word sutra (kyō) was retained, inasmuch as these later works were also seen as having been revealed by the Buddha, in a transfigured state if not in his earthly manifestation; and the term tripiṭaka (sanzō) now generally referred to the entire corpus of the scriptures (issaikyō 一切経). Various classifications were proposed to organize these materials and to reconcile their contradictions, the prominent Tendai view being that the Buddha revealed his teaching during Five Periods (goji) in order to accommodate to human frailty, and that the various scriptures represent one or another, sometimes partial, version of the Truth.

Some sutras are also grouped in triads for sectarian or doctrinal reasons. Perhaps the most prominent is the set of *Three Pure Land Sūtras*, *Jōdo (no) Sambukyō* 浄土(の)三部(経), defined by *Hōnen in his *Senjaku Shū*: *Muryō-jukyō*, *Kammuryōjukyō*, and *Amidakyō*. The *Three Sūtras for the Protection of the Country*, *Chingo Kokka (no) Sambukyō* 鎮護国家(の)三部(経) —*Lotus*, *Ninnōkyō*, and *Konkōmyōkyō*—were conspicuous in early Japanese Buddhism. And Tendai viewed the *Muryōgikyō* and the *Fugengyō*, respectively, as "opening" and "closing" sutras to accompany the *Lotus*; hence, the three are known as the *Hokke (no) Sambukyō* 法華(の)三部(経).

Such conceptions tell something of the ways in which Japanese Buddhists have made sense of, or have applied, many of their sacred texts. In what follows, thirty or so of the more important sutras are discussed briefly. When one is of little importance except for perhaps formal purposes (for example, as just indicated, to make up a sambu or set), little is said of it. For the most important, more detail is given. The ordering is alphabetical according to the common Japanese title, and the entries are cross-referenced to an introductory listing of alternate names, for easy reference. When divisions are mentioned, "fascicle" translates kan 巻, and "part" hon 品.

Modern scholars have devised several numbering systems in an attempt to organize the profusion of Buddhist writings, many of which have several distinct translations into Chinese. The earliest was Nanjō Bunyū 南条文雄 (1849–1927; often romanized as Nanjiō Bunyiu), who published *A Catalogue of the Chinese Translation of the Buddhist Tripitaka* (Oxford, 1883). Books and articles written around the turn of the century may refer to a sutra by its Nanjiō (Nj.) number (much as Mozart's prodigious output is organized by the Köchel listing). This system was superseded with the publication of the one hundred-volume *Taishō Shinshū Daizōkyō* [*Newly Revised Tripitaka of the Taishō Era*] (Tokyo, 1924–1932; 1962 reprint). Each work in the collection was assigned a number that has become the standard means of identifying a specific item in the Buddhist canon; the numbering through volume 55 is also conveniently available in *Hōbōgirin: Fascicule Annexe* (Tokyo: Maison Franco-Japonaise, 1931). The *Daizōkyō* also provides easy access to an (unannotated) text for those who may wish to isolate a particular phrase, and some scholars will cite the volume and page number in their headnotes. The following entries have been identified with their T. (*Taishō Shinshū Daizōkyō*) number.

Finding List

Āgama, see *Agongyō*.
Amitābha Sūtra, see *Amidakyō*.
Amitāyur-dhyāna-sūtra, see *Kam-muryōjukyō*.
Aparimitāyus Sūtra, see *Muryōjukyō*.

Avataṃsaka Sūtra, see *Kegonkyō*.
Bhaiṣajya-guru-sūtra, see *Yakushikyō*.
Brahmajāla Sūtra, see *Bommōkyō*.
Daijōbutsukyō, see *Mirokukyō*.
Gaṇḍavyūha Sūtra, see *Kegonkyō*.

Garland Sūtra, see Kegonkyō.
Geshōkyō, see Mirokukyō.
Heart Sūtra, see Hannyashingyō.
Hokkugyō, see Agongyō.
Ichijōkyō, see Myōhōrengekyō.
Ingakyō, see Kakogenzai Ingakyō.
Jizobosatsugōhōkyō, see Senzatsukyō.
Jōshōkyō, see Mirokukyō.
Kārunikā-rāja-sūtra, see Ninnokyō.
Laṅkāvatāra-sūtra, see Nyūryōgakyō.
Lotus Sūtra, see Myōhōrengekyō.
Mahāparinirvāna-sūtra, see Daihatsune-hangyō.
Mahāprajñāpāramitā-sūtra, see Daihan-nyaharamittakyō.
Mahāvairocana-sūtra, see Dainichikyō.
Maitreya Sūtras, see Mirokukyō.
Perfect Wisdom, Large Sūtra of, see Daihannyaharamittakyō.
Prajñāpāramitā-hrdaya-sūtra, see Hannya-shingyō.
Pratyutpanna-samādhi-sūtra, see Hanju-sammaikyō.
Ryōgakyō, see Nyūryōgakyō.
Ryōgonkyō, see Shuryōgonkyō.
Saddharmapuṇḍarīka-sūtra, see Myōhō-rengekyō.
Saishōōkyō, see Konkōmyōkyō.
Samantabhadra-bodhisattva-sūtra, see Kan-fugenbosatsugyōhōkyō.
Shichibutsuyakushikyō, see Yakushikyō.
Sukhāvatī-vyūha-sūtra, see Amidakyō; Muryōjukyō.
Śūrangama-sūtra, see Shuryōgonkyō.
Susiddhikara-sūtra, see Soshitsujikyō.
Suvarnaprabhāsottama-sūtra, see Konkō-myōkyō.
Tattvasaṃgraha, see Kongōchōgyō.
Ullambana-sūtra, see Urabongyō.
Vajracchedikā-sūtra, see Kongōkyō.
Vajraśekkhara-sūtra, see Kongōchōgyō.
Vimalakīrti-nirdeśa-sūtra, see Yuimakit-sugyō.
Zuiōkyō, see Kakogenzai Ingakyō.

Descriptive List of Sutras (in alphabetical order by Japanese title)

Agongyō 阿含経 (*Āgama, Sūtras of the Tradition*). The teachings of early Buddhism are contained in the Pali Tipiṭaka (Three Baskets; Skt., Tripiṭaka): the *Vinayapiṭaka* (Basket of Discipline), *Suttapiṭaka* (Basket of Discourses), and the *Abhidhammapiṭaka* (Basket of Scholasticism). Most of this southern Buddhist canon has already been extensively translated and published by the Pali Text Society and others.

The second of the "Baskets" consists of five "Nikāyas" ("Discourses"), which more or less correspond to the four Sanskrit *Āgamas* of the Sarvāstivāda (*Setsuissaiu Bu*) canon translated into Chinese. These early scriptures were viewed by most later adherents of Mahāyāna as merely preliminary accommodations (*hōben*) to human weakness of the Buddha's complete teaching, which was only gradually revealed in subsequent scriptures (the Prajñāpāramitā group, etc.) until its most adequate conceptualization was made manifest (according to the Tendai sect, for example) in the *Lotus Sūtra*. (It should be noted, however, that the final Truth of Buddhism was viewed as experiential and beyond all conceptual formulations, even the best.) The four *Āgamas* are:

1. *Jōagongyō* 長阿含経 (*Sūtra of Long Records*, T. 1). *Dīrghāgama-sūtra*, in twenty-two fascicles. Gautama's life, teachings, refutations, cosmology. Cf. the Pali *Dīgha-nikāya* (*Book of Long Discourses*).

2. *Chūagongyō* 中阿含経 (*Sūtra of Middle Length Sayings*, T. 26). *Mādhya-māgama*, in sixty fascicles. Lives of the Buddha and disciples, the Four Noble Truths. Cf. the Pali *Majjhima-nikāya* (*The Middle Length Sayings*).

3. *Zōagongyō* 雜阿含経 (*Sūtra of Miscellaneous Records*, T. 99). *Saṃ-yuktāgama*, in fifty fascicles. Cf. the Pali *Saṃyutta-nikāya* (*Collection of Connected Discourses*).

4. *Zōichiagongyō* 増一阿含経 (*Sūtra of Grouped Records*, T. 125). *Ekot-taragama* in fifty-one fascicles. Cf. the Pali *Aṅguttara-nikāya* (*The Book of Kindred Sayings*).

The fifth of the Pali *nikāyas*, *Khuddaka-nikāya* (*The Book of Little Texts*), is a collection of later items, including the famous Dhammapada (The Path of the Teaching; cf. **Hokkugyō* 法句経, etc., T. 210–13) and the Jātaka tales, accounts of Gautama's former lives (cf. *Honjōmanron* 本生鬘論, T. 160 and others).

Although Japanese Buddhists were familiar with some of the Jātaka tales and were aware of the existence of these early scriptures, they did not study them much. References can be found in a few writers who, like **Myōe, advocated a return to the practices of original Buddhism. In the Five Periods classification of scriptures taught by the Tendai sect, the *Āgamas* belong to the second, the Deer Park Period (rokuonji).

Amidakyō 阿弥陀経 (*Amitābha Sūtra*, T. 366). This is Kumārajīva's translation (ca. 402) of the "smaller" *Sukhāvatī-vyūha* (*Pure Land*) *Sūtra*, in contrast to the larger *Muryōjukyō*. In this scripture, one of the *Three Pure Land Sūtras* (*Jōdo Sambukyō*), the Buddha, Ānanda, and Miroku talk of the Amida Buddha and his Pure Land. For birth in it he prescribes the *nembutsu* 念仏, or invocation, recitation of the Buddha's name in various formulas.

Bommōkyō 梵網経 (*The Net of Brahma*, T. 1484). Kumārajīva's two-fascicle translation of the *Brahmajāla-sūtra* is the major authority of the Mahāyāna disciplinary code, detailing ten major and forty-eight minor rules without distinction between laymen and clergy. **Saichō's support of these Mahāyāna precepts against the Hīnayāna regulations of the Nara clergy was a major issue during his founding of the Tendai sect in Japan.

Daihannyaharamittakyō 大般若波羅密多経 (*Large Sūtra on Perfect Wisdom*, T. 220). Hsüan-tsang's monumental translation of the *Mahāprajñāpāramitā-sūtra* in six hundred fascicles extends for three long volumes (V–VII) in the *Taishō Shinshū Daizōkyō*. Its theme is the wisdom of emptiness (*śūnyatā*, *kū* 空) and thus is representative of the Perfection of Wisdom Period (Hannyaji) in Chih-i's fivefold classification of the Buddha's teaching (see Tendai above). Given the length of the sutra, excerpts were naturally taken from it, or, alternatively, it may be thought of as making up sixteen other sutras. In other words, this consists of sixteen sermons (or sutras) taught by the Buddha at four places (four and sixteen being recurrent Buddhist numbers). These include sermons at Vulture Peak (parts 1–400); in a park (parts 401–57, 591–92); in the highest of one range of heavens (part 578); and at Snowy Heron Pond in Bamboo Park (parts 593–600). This sutra, or collection, is of immense importance for its extended teaching of the doctrine of emptiness. It was also important to early Japan for its rites against national calamities. Although it lost truly central importance after the tenth century, Tendai and Shingon Priests recited and copied it till the beginning of the nineteenth century on crucial occasions—as, for example, a Tendai priest did secretly for Minamoto Yoritomo between 1177 and 1181. Prajñā, wisdom, is here personified as a female, as in Hebrew literature and in Greek.

Daihatsunehangyō 大般涅槃経. The Mahāyāna *Nirvāṇa Sūtra* appears in two similar translations of the *Mahāparinirvāṇa-sūtra*, a "Northern text" (Hokuhon, T. 374) and a "Southern Text" (Nampon, T. 375). Complementing the *Lotus Sūtra*, they distinguish the eternal Law Body of the Buddha from its physical manifestation as Gautama, whose death simply as a historical event is described in the Hīnayāna version (*Daihatsunehangyō*, T. 7). The account of the Buddha's death, or entering nirvāna, has led to many pictures of people weeping about him, as even the animals do, and of the teak trees that surround him scattering their blossoms (nehanzō 涅槃像, or -zu 図).

Daihōshakkyō 大宝積経 (*Great Treasure Store of Sūtras*, T. 310). 120 fascicles. The great treasure of the title of course refers to the Law and to numerous kinds of access to it provided in the sutras of this Mahāyāna collection translated in T'ang China. It represents the Buddha's teaching at forty-nine assemblies.

Dainichikyō 大日経 (*Mahāvairocana-sūtra*, or *Sūtra of the Great Light*, T. 848). Seven fascicles. Probably composed as late as the mid-seventh century, this sutra and the *Kongōchōgyō* are the two basic scriptures of Japanese Shingon as systematized by *Kūkai; the *Three Great Light Sūtras* (*Dainichi*[no] *Sambu*[kyō] 大日[の]三部[経]) additionally includes the *Soshitsujikyō*. The *Dainichikyō* is especially important because it describes the assumbly of the Matrix maṇḍala (taizōkai); see *mandara*.

Hanjusammaikyō 般舟三昧経 (*Visualization* [*of Amida*] *Sūtra*, T. 418). Three fascicles. A translation as early as the second century A.D. of the *Pratyutpanna-samādhi-sūtra*, this describes a meditation practice whose object is to conjure up the Buddha Amitābha before one's eyes. Popular among the early Chinese devotees of the Pure Land movement, the sutra was also an influence on Tendai's Chih-i. But its emphasis on Amida devotion as an adjunct to meditation differs from the total reliance on Amida's Other Power (tariki) advocated by *Hōnen and his successors.

Hannyashingyō 般若心経 (*Heart Sūtra*, T. 251). The 262 characters of Hsüan-tsang's short but famous translation of the *Prajñāpāramitā-hṛdaya-sūtra* is believed to summarize effectively the Mahāyāna doctrine of emptiness (*kū* 空). It represents the Perfection of Wisdom Period (Hannyaji) in Tendai's fivefold classification of the Buddha's teaching, and is highly esteemed by that sect as well as by Shingon and Zen. The quintessential phrase of the *Heart Sūtra* is today a common aphorism: shiki soku ze kū, kū soku ze shiki 色即是空 空即是色: Form is no other than Emptiness, Emptiness is no other than Form. This expresses the basic Mahāyāna position of the Two Truths (nitai 二諦): that the phenomenal world is nothing other than the Absolute viewed through the forms of conceptualization.

Hokkekyō. See *Myōhōrengekyō.*

Jūōgyō 十王経 (*Sūtra of the Ten Kings*). This amalgam of Chinese folk religion with Buddhism is considered to be an apocryphal sutra, gikyō 偽経, originating in China. Yet its account of the judgment of the dead in the underworld and of their tortures for their sins by the ten infernal kings had great influence on popular thought, literature, and art from the late Heian period.

(Kakogenzai) Ingakyō (過去現在) 因果経 (*Sūtra of [Past and Present,] Cause and Effect*, T. 189). A biography of Gautama which shows that his religious achievement resulted from the merit of past actions; hence the indirect title. It includes a paraphrase of the well-known statement ascribed to the Buddha after taking seven steps and raising his right hand: "I alone am most venerable in the heavens and on earth" 天上天下 唯我独尊 "tenjō tenge yuiga dokuson," which is associated with the celebration of the Buddha's birthday on the eighth day of the Fourth Month (Hanamatsuri, the "Flower Festival"). The statement in this precise form appears in the *Zuiōkyō* 瑞應経 (T. 185), of which the *Sūtra of Cause and Effect* is a later and fuller version.

The sutra gained prominence in the Nara period by providing a Buddhist alternative to the Confucian and native theories of kingly legitimation. It is the subject of a famous three-part scroll dating from the Nara period, the *E Ingakyō* 絵因果経.

Kanfugenbosatsugyōhōkyō 観普賢菩薩行法経, or *Fugengyō* 普賢経 (*The Sūtra of Meditation on the Bodhisattva Universal Vow*, T. 277). One fascicle. The only extant version of three translations of the *Samantabhadra-bodhisattva-sūtra*. It carries forward the teaching of the *Lotus Sūtra* and thus has come to be regarded as the "closing sutra" of the *Three-fold Lotus Sūtra* (*Hokke Sambukyō*). It teaches the practice of repentance based on the realization of emptiness and was highly regarded by Tendai's Chih-i.

Kammuryōjukyō 観無量寿経 (*Sūtra of Meditation on Amida Buddha, Amitāyur-dhyāna-sūtra*, T. 365). One fascicle. This sutra tells of Śākyamuni's appearance to the imprisoned Queen Vaidehī, who requested rebirth in a Pure Land without suffering. The Buddha instructs her in thirteen preliminary and three additional forms of meditation, with the promise that even the worst sinner can attain birth in Amida's Pure Land if he recites his name ten times at the moment of death. This sole reliance on Amida as savior differs from the visualization of Amida as an aid to meditation, such as is described in the *Hanjusammaikyō* and advocated by the Tendai sect. The *Kammuryōjukyō* accordingly was selected by *Hōnen as one of the *Three Pure Land Sūtras*.

Kannongyō 観音経 (*Kannon Sūtra*). The twenty-fifth part of the *Lotus Sūtra* (T. 262), treated as an independent sūtra. The "Gateway to Everywhere of the Bodhisattva He Who Observes the Sounds of the World," Kanzeon Bosatsu Fumonbon 観世音菩薩普門品, states that the bodhisattva Avalokiteśvara (Kannon) assumes various forms to save from calamity those who call on his name. The bodhisattva was gradually assumed to be female in popular thought, and was worshiped with particular veneration at Hasedera.

Kegonkyō 華厳経 (*Garland/Flower-Wreath Sūtra*, T. 278, 279, 293). Comprises three translations of the *Avataṃsaka-sūtra* in sixty, eighty, and forty fascicles, respectively. The title Avataṃsaka is applied to all three; but the third version is merely the famous final chapter, "Sudhana's Pilgrimage," of the two earlier versions, and is also referred to as the "Gaṇḍavyūha." Here the youth Sudhana (Zenzai Dōji 善財童子) visits fifty-three "Good Friends" (zenchishiki 善知識, beginning and ending with the bodhisattva Mañjuśrī (Monju 文殊), who guide him on his religious quest to the abode of the bodhisattva Samantabhadra (Fugen 普賢) at the fifty-fourth stage. The *Kegon Sūtra* is the basic scriptural authority for the Kegon Sect, and was also influential in Shingon and Zen, but it tended to be studied by the learned and had little popular appeal. Early in the Kamakura period *Myōe promoted its literary and artistic imagery. Its teachings represent the first phase, the Garland Period (Kegonji), of Tendai's fivefold classification of the Buddha's teaching.

Kongōchōgyō 金剛頂経 (*Diamond Peak Sūtra*, T. 865). The most popular of the three extant Chinese versions of the *Vajraśekkhara-sūtra*, also known as the *Tattvasaṃgraha*. Translated by the tantric master Amoghavajra (Fukū 不空, 704–774) in three fascicles, it is one of the *Three Sūtras of Shingon* (*Shingonshū Sambukyō*), the others being the *Dainichikyō* and the *Soshitsujikyō*. The *Diamond Peak Sūtra* defines the arrangement of the 1,461 deities of the Diamond Maṇḍala (kongōkai 金剛界), whose central ("Karma") assembly represents five Buddhas symbolizing the Five Wisdoms (gochi 五智); the central figure of this assembly, as of the Matrix maṇḍala, is Dainichi Nyorai, the Great Sun Buddha. See *mandara*.

Kongōkyō 金剛経 (*Diamond Sūtra*). Among six Chinese translations of the *Vajracchedikā-sūtra*, the most popular is the version by Kumārajīva (T. 235) ca. 402–412. The *Diamond Sūtra* is one of the best-known representatives of the prajñāpāramitā class of scriptures which emphasize the nature of wisdom (prajñā) and emptiness (śūnyatā, *kū* 空; see the Tendai sect's Perfection of Wisdom Period). The sutra has been especially esteemed by the Zen sect from the time of its sixth Chinese patriarch, Hui-neng (638–713).

Konkōmyōkyō 金光明経 (*Golden Light Sūtra*). Known in three Chinese translations (T. 663–65) of the *Suvarṇaprabhāsottama-sūtra*. The abbreviated first version, in four fascicles from the early fifth century, was of great importance in Japan two centuries later. Because it promises that the Four Deva Kings (Shitennō 四天王) will protect the ruler who follows the teaching of the sutra, it was promoted by Emperor Temmu (r. 672–686) and others of the court. Together with the *Lotus* and *Benevolent Kings Sūtras*, it was considered one of the *Three Sūtras for the Protection of the Country* (*Chingo Kokka no Sambukyō*).

The complete third version in ten fascicles (T. 665), by the famous pilgrim and translator I-ching (Gijō 義浄 635–713), dates from the early eighth century and is known as the *Konkōmyō-Saishōōkyō*, or simply the *Saishōōkyō* 最勝王経, *Sūtra of the Most Victorious Kings*. Besides the materials in the preceding, and somewhat different arrangement, this adds much that is new, including elements left out of the earlier version, particularly the mystic formulas or incantations, dhāraṇī (darani 陀羅尼) so dear to the tantric followers in Tendai and to Shingon practice more generally. *Saichō made one commentary and *Kūkai another. Until the Ōnin War (1467–1477), this sutra was recited as a major annual court event in one of three related festivals begun in Nara. These include the Yuimae (see *Yuimakyō*) of the Hossō sect at Kōfukuji, originally a Fujiwara observance; the Gosaie 御斎会 meeting in the palace; and the Saishōe of the Hossō sect at Yakushiji, originally a Minamoto festival. Both the second and the third of these used this version of the sutra, and the second was one that could be held at a Tendai temple instead of at court. Both the preceding and this went into decline with the royal house.

Mirokukyō 弥勒経 (*Maitreya Sūtras*). Six translations, each in one fascicle (T. 452–57), of writings describing the bodhisattva Maitreya, the future Buddha, who currently resides in the Tuṣita Heaven (Tosotsuten 兜率天) until the time arrives, after billions of years, for him to come to earth after the Law of Śākyamuni has completely disappeared to preach the Dharma again. The so-called *Three Maitreya Sūtras* (*Miroku no Sambukyō*) include the *Geshōkyō* 下生経 (T. 453), the *Daijōbutsukyō* 大成仏経 (T. 456), and the *Jōshōkyō* 上生経 (T. 452).

Muryōgikyō 無量義経 (*Sūtra of Innumerable Meanings*, T. 276). A one-fascicle translation (A.D. 481) of the *Amitārtha-sūtra*. Just as human desires are innumerable, so also are the varieties of the Buddha's teachings, each expressing the One Dharma which, being indeterminate, is not constrained in a single dogmatic conceptual formulation; the merits of belief in this sutra are also innumerable. The sutra has traditionally been treated by the Tendai sect as the "opening" sutra of the *Three-fold Lotus Sūtra* (*Hokke no Sambukyō*).

Muryōjukyō 無量寿経. Literally, the *Amitāyus Sūtra*; but generally known as the (*Larger*) *Sukhāvatī-vyūha* (Pure Land) *Sūtra*; cf. *Amidakyō*, the "smaller." This two-fascicle version (T. 360), one of five extant among twelve known translations into Chinese of the *Aparimitāyus-sūtra*, is traditionally believed to have been rendered by Sanghavarman in A.D. 252. It is the focus of the *Three Pure Land*

Sutras (*Jōdo no Sambukyō*) and has inspired several important commentaries, among them the Jōdoron (T. 1524) of Vasubandhu (Seshin 世親, ca. 350).

The setting for the *Muryōjukyō*, as also for the *Lotus Sūtra*, is Eagle Mountain (Gṛdhrakūta) in Rājagṛha, where Śākyamuni is addressing a large assembly. He describes how the Buddha Amitābha many aeons ago, as the bodhisattva Dharmākara, made forty-eight Original Vows (hongan 本願) which he would fulfill before attaining enlightenment. For Pure Land devotees the most important are vows 18–20, which promise birth (ōjō 往生) in Amida's Pure Land, his Western Paradise, to those who have faith in him and call upon his name (*nembutsu*).

Myōhōrengekyō 妙法蓮華経 (*Scripture of the Lotus Blossom of the Fine Dharma*; or, simply, *Hokkekyō* 法華経, *Lotus Sūtra*). Among several translations of the *Saddharma-puṇḍarīka-sūtra* into Chinese, the version (T. 262) by Kumārajīva in A.D. 406 is the standard. After minor subsequent changes and additions, the current text consists of twenty-eight parts (or chapters) in eight fascicles. The *Lotus Sūtra* has been the preeminent scripture in the Mahāyāna of East Asia, both for its doctrinal position and for providing a rich imagery, largely through the parables, both for literature and for the pictorial arts and architecture. It is the basic revelation for the Tendai and Nichiren sects, and claims many commentaries by, among others, Chih-i, *Shōtoku Taishi, *Saichō, and *Nichiren. It is counted among the *Three Sūtras for the Protection of the Country* (*Chingo Kokka no Sambukyō*); and the popularity of its twenty-fifth chapter has resulted in its being treated as a separate sutra, the *Kannongyō* (q.v.). For the Tendai sect the *Three-fold Lotus Sūtra* (*Hokke no Sambukyō*) consists of the "opening" *Muryōgikyō*, the *Lotus Sūtra* itself, and the "closing" *Fugengyō*.

The message of the *Lotus Sūtra* is that all sentient beings have the Buddha nature (Busshō 佛性; buddhatā) and thus the potential for attaining Buddhahood. Conceptual illusion prevents them from realizing that this is their essential nature, so the Buddha out of compassion uses many devices (hōben 方便), accommodated to their needs, to assist them in seeing through this illusion. Such earlier devices included the teaching that there were Three Vehicles (sanjō 三乗) to enlightenment: that of śrāvaka (shōmon 声聞: hearers, disciples; that is, the Hīnayāna), Pratyekabuddha (engaku 円覚: self-enlightened Buddhas), and Bodhisattva (bosatsu 菩薩: those who seek enlightenment for others as well as themselves). It is now shown that although provisional teachings are not only possible but necessary, there is, in fact, only One Vehicle (ichijō 一乗; ekayāna); and for this reason the *Lotus* is sometimes called the *Ichijōkyō* 一乗経, *Sūtra of the One Vehicle*.

It is important to note that the term does not describe an exclusive dogmatic formulation that is taken to be correct while others are false. The *Lotus Sūtra* may be the fullness of the Buddha's teaching, but other scriptures are seen as expressing at least a partial truth. The *One Vehicle* refers to a single experiential goal to be reached through a variety of conceptual formulations and exercises. This, not political expediency, is the basis of Tendai's proverbial tolerance.

In chapter 16 the Buddha reveals that he is eternal and that the life and death of the historical Gautama had been provided as yet another accommodation. Tendai's Chih-i saw the sutra as falling into two equal parts. The first fourteen chapters are the shakumon 迹門 ("trace gate," applied teaching), in which as a concession to human understanding the eternal life of the Buddha is not yet revealed; the final fourteen are the hommon 本門 ("original gate," basic teaching), which stress the eternal nature of the Buddha. The distinction played a role in the development of the honji-suijaku 本地垂迹 (Original Ground-Manifest Trace) doctrine in Japan, according to which Shintō deities were counted as local manifestations of primary Buddhas and bodhisattvas.

Since the chapter numbering of Kumārajīva's emended version of the *Lotus Sūtra* differs somewhat from a widely available translation from a Sanskrit text of the *Saddharma-puṇḍarīka-sūtra* (Kern, 1909) the following table of contents includes an indication (K) of parallel items. Symbols also show the Four Important Chapters (shiyōbon 四要品) according to Tendai (T)—2, 14, 16, 25—and according to the Nichiren Sect (N)—2, 16, 21, 26. The eight fascicles are indicated by Roman numerals preceding the chapter numbers. The setting, as also for the *Muryōjukyō*, is Eagle Mountain (Gṛdhrakūṭa) in Rājagṛha, where Śākyamuni is addressing a large assembly.

(VI)   17. Fumbetsukudokuhon 分別功徳品. Discrimination of Merits. K16

(VI)   18. Zuikikudokuhon 随喜功徳品. The Merits of Appropriate Joy. K17

(VI)   19. Hosshikudokuhon 法師功徳品. The Merits of the Dharma-Preacher. K18

(VII)   20. Jōfukyō Bosatsuhon 常不軽菩薩品. The Bodhisattva Never Disparaging. K19

(VII)   21. Nyoraijinrikihon 如来神力品. The Supernatural Powers of the Thus Come One. (N), K20

(VII)   22. Zokuruihon 嘱累品. Entrustment. K27

(VII)   23. Yakuōbosatsu Honjihon 薬王菩薩本地品. The Former Affairs of the Bodhisattva Medicine King. K22

(VII)   24. Myōonbosatsuhon 妙音菩薩品. The Bodhisattva Fine Sound.

(VIII) 25. Kanzeonbosatsu Fumonbon 観世音菩薩普門品. The Gateway to Everywhere of the Bodhisattva He Who Observes the Sounds of the World. (T), K24

(VIII) 26. Daranihon 陀羅尼品. Dhāraṇī. (N), K21

(VIII) 27. Myōshōgon'ō Honjihon 妙荘厳王本事品. The Former Affairs of the King Fine Adornment. K25

(VIII) 28. Fugenbosatsu Kambotsuhon 普賢菩薩勧発品. The Encouragement of the Bodhisattva Universally Worthy. K26

The Seven Parables of the *Lotus Sūtra* (Hokke shichiyu 法華七喩) are a major component of the medieval Japanese world of images, just as Noah's Ark, the Walls of Jericho, and the Sermon on the Mount are familiar fixtures in the Western mind, whether of believer or skeptic. Specific doctrinal images were assimilated slowly, and as late as the *Man'yōshū* we find only occasional references to such general religious topics as transmigration and the evanescence of life. In the fourth royal *waka* collection, the *Goshūishū (1086) a special category for Buddhist poems (shakkyōka 釈教歌) appeared for the first time, although isolated examples of such verse had found their way into earlier collections. The powerful influence of the *Lotus Sūtra* on the literature of the time is perhaps reflected in the fact that almost half of these first nineteen shakkyōka make some reference to this scripture, five or six directly to the parables. The influence of the *Lotus* was reinforced by Nichiren's movement from the Kamakura period, but began to wane with the growth of the Zen and Pure Land Sects, which emphasized other scriptures. It is still conspicuous, however, in the *nō* plays of the Ashikaga period. The seven parables are as follows:

1. The Parable of the Burning House (Katakuyu 火宅喩), in part 3. In order to entice his many children from a burning house, a wealthy man promises to give them as playthings a variety of goat-drawn carriages, deer-drawn carriages, and ox-drawn carriages. But once they are safely out of the house he gives to each of them a great carriage yoked to a white ox which exceeds their wildest expec-

tation. So also the Buddha employs the expedient of teaching the Three Vehicles, when in fact there is only One.

2. The Parable of the Prodigal Son (Gūjiyu 窮子喩), in part 4. A son who had run off and forsaken his father for many years returns to his home city, unaware that his father is a man of great wealth. So as not to intimidate his son, the father employs various devices gradually to restore him as his heir. Similarly, the Buddha uses a variety of spiritual devices with the single goal of saving sentient beings.

3. The Parable of the Medicinal Herbs (Yakusōyu 薬草喩), in part 5. Although the Buddha's teaching has the single purpose of saving all sentient beings, each is benefited according to his own needs and capacities. The water of a great rain cloud has a single taste, but it nourishes many kinds of grasses, forests, and medicinal herbs.

4. The Parable of the Magic City (Kejōyu 化城喩), in part 7. The Buddha is likened to a skillful guide leading a band of people over a treacherous road to a cache of precious jewels. In order to give the party a rest and to prevent them from losing heart, the guide conjures up a magic city that fades away after the travelers have been refreshed. So also does the Buddha use religious expedients that are only provisionally true.

5. The Parable of the Hidden Jewel (Eshuyu 衣珠喩), in part 8. A friend sews a precious jewel in the lining of the coat of a man in a drunken stupor, and departs on official business. After the man awakens and leaves he suffers many hardships, not realizing that he has the precious jewel in his possession. So the Buddha in a previous existence taught the Five Hundred Arhants the secret of All-Knowledge (issaichi 一切智), but in their present life they attain nothing more than an understanding of the Lesser Vehicle. Śākyamuni promises their eventual Buddhahood.

6. The Parable of the Topknot Pearl (Keishuyu 髻珠喩), part 14. The *Lotus Sūtra* is likened to a precious pearl that a sage-king wears in his topknot. Although he presents his faithful retainers with lesser rewards (comparable to the scriptures preceding the *Lotus*), he saves this precious jewel for the very last.

7. The Parable of the Physician (Ishiyu 医子喩), part 16. The Buddha is compared to a skillful physician whose many sons have been poisoned in varying degrees, some so ill that in their delirium they refuse the medicine he has prepared. Leaving the medicine behind, the physician goes to another land and sends back a messenger to tell his sons that he has died (just as the historical Śākyamuni is described in the early scriputres as having died). In their sadness and sense of abandonment, the sons are finally impelled to take the medicine, which promptly cures them. The father's deception is seen as an expedient device.

Ninnōkyō 仁王経 (*Benevolent Kings Sūtra*). There are two Chinese translations of the *Kāruṇikā-rājā-sūtra* (?), now lost in Sanskrit. The earlier (T. 245) was done by Kumārajīva in 401; the second (T. 246) by Amoghavajra (see *Kongōchōgyō*) as late as 765. Both are in two fascicles. The *Benevolent Kings Sūtra*, a member of the prajñāpāramitā class of scriptures emphasizing emptiness, explains how benevolent kings protect their countries through the understanding and practice of Buddhism. It is one of the most central to Japanese Buddhism from the seventh to the thirteenth century. Celebration of the Meeting of the Benevolent Kings (Ninnōe 仁王会) was a standard court ritual. The sutra inspired many commentaries by both Chinese and Japanese religious thinkers, including *Saichō (to T. 245) and *Kūkai (to T. 246). Amoghavajra, not surprisingly, added thirty-six dhāraṇīs; so his is the translation used by the Shingon sect. The *Benevolent Kings* is one of the *Three Sūtras for the Protection of the Country* (*Chingo Kokka no Sambukyō*).

(Nyū)Ryōgakyō 入楞伽経 (*Descent to Ceylon*). This takes its name from Mount Laṅkā (Ryōgasen 楞伽山) in Ceylon (?), where the Buddha addresses a great assembly in the form of a dialogue with the bodhisattva Mahāmati. There are three extant Chinese versions of the *Laṅkāvatāra-sūtra*: T. 670 in four fascicles, T. 671 in ten, and T. 672 in seven. The noted translation (1932) and study (1930) by the famous Zen scholar, Suzuki Daisetz (1870–1966) is based largely in a Sanskrit version edited by Nanjō Bunyū (of the numbering system; see above). Tradition says that Bodhidharma, who brought Ch'an (Zen) from India to China, handed down this sutra to his main disciple as expressing the basic thought of the new movement. It propounds a philosophical idealism and was an influence on Hsüan-tsang's *Jōyuishikiron* 成唯識論 translation (T. 1585), the major treatise for the Hossō sect.

Senzatsukyō 占察経; popularly known as *Jizō(bosatsugōhō)kyō* 地蔵 (菩薩業報)経 (*Jizō Sūtra*, T. 839). One fascicle in two parts. Jizō Bosatsu (Kṣitigarbha-bodhisattva) judges good and evil deeds; he is usually shown with a staff in the right hand, and, at least in Japan, is associated with children and fertility. Jizō statues frequently replaced the native phallic deities of the road (dōsojin 道祖神), which may explain the bodhisattva's connection with fertility. Because the sutra seems to be an amalgam of Buddhism and Chinese folk beliefs, it is sometimes thought to be an apocryphal sutra (gikyō) like the *Jūōgyō* (q.v.). But it was considered to be a legitimate sutra during the T'ang, and appears to have been brought to Japan in the late Nara period. It has a particular literary importance because of its influence on *setsuwa*.

(Shu)Ryōgonkyō (首)楞厳経 (*Sūtra of Heroic Deed*). Two different sutras bear this name. The earlier, more properly called *Shuryōgon-zammai-kyō* (*Śūraṅgama-samādhi-sūtra*) is a two-fascicle work (T. 642) translated by Kumārajīva that describes a special kind of mediation from which the title takes its name. The later *Śūraṅgama Sūtra* (T. 945), in ten fascicles and translated in 705, is a discourse on the nature of Mind, with a description of some esoteric practices. Accordingly, it has been of special interest both to the Zen and to the Shingon sects.

Soshitsujikyō 蘇悉地経 (*Sūtra of Excellent Accomplishment*, T. 893). Translated in 726 by the tantric master Śubhākarasiṃha (Zemmui 善無畏), the *Susiddhikara-sūtra* synthesizes the practices of the *Dainichikyō* and the *Kongōchōgyō*. It was introduced to Japan by Tendai's *Ennin and is the third of the *Three Shingon Sūtras* (*Shingon Sambukyō*).

Urabongyō 盂蘭盆経 (*Sūtra for Souls in Suspense*, T. 685; *Ullambana-sūtra*). Of perhaps even greater importance in China than in Japan, this one-fascicle sutra is presented as the Vessel to save those in suspense (that is, souls suspended in hell and waiting to be released by priestly prayers). The Buddha tells Maudgalyāyana that his mother can be released only by the majestic power of the priests of the ten sides. Those wishing to have such rites should offer certain gifts to the priests. The results will be long, happy life for the parents, if still alive, and for the donors. Deceased ancestors back to seven generations will be reborn in heaven, or, by independent rebirth through transformation, enter into the bliss of heavenly light. Some tantric texts and dhāraṇī also became associated with such rites. The efforts on behalf of parents and ancestors naturally led to association with Confucianism and the development in China of a Festival for the Dead. In Japan there developed the Bon Festival (the "bon" of *Urabongyō*) as also the *daimonji* in Kyoto as a mystic fire rite to conclude the festival. This well illustrates kinds of syncretism in the two countries.

Yakushikyō 薬師経 (*Sūtra of the Master of Healing*). Among five Chinese translations of the *Bhaiṣajya-guru-sūtra* the standard is Hsüan-tsang's version of 650 (T. 450). It describes the Medicine Buddha's twelve vows, his Buddha-land, his promise to aid those who hear his name, and the twelve Yakṣa Generals who support him. Worship of Yakushi Nyorai was widespread in the early period of Japanese Buddhism, Nara's Yakushiji being an outstanding architectural and sculptural relic of the time.

   The 707 translation by I-ching is also noteworthy (T. 451), the *Sūtra of the Seven Masters of Healing* (*Shichibutsuyakushikyō* 七仏薬師経), which includes dhāraṇī. This sutra is particularly important for inconographical purposes.

Yuima(kitsu)gyō 維摩 (詰) 経 (*Vimalakīrti Sūtra*). Among several Chinese translations of the *Vimalakīrti-nirdeśa-sūtra*, the most popular is the version by Kumārajīva in 406 (T. 475). It consists of fourteen parts in three fascicles and has been one of the most influential of Mahāyāna sutras, both for literature and the arts. This is a sermon delivered by the Buddha to a host of kings in the Mango Grove presented him by a courtesan. At the time of the sermon, Vimalakīrti—a wise and holy man of great powers though not a monk—assembles tens of thousands of creatures on his right hand to hear the Buddha preach. His names in Japanese include, besides Yuima (kitsu), Jōmyō 浄名, a direct Japanese rendering of Vimalakīrti. The parts are concerned with the following topics:

1. The Buddha-land
2. Expedient Devices
3. The Disciples
4. The Bodhisattvas
5. Mañjuśrī's Visit
6. The Inconceivable Liberation
7. On Living Beings
8. The Way of the Buddha
9. Entering Non-duality
10. Buddha of the Fragrant Land
11. The Life of the Bodhisattva
12. Seeing the Buddha Akṣobhya
13. The Teaching Made Available
14. The Injunction to Promulgate

In the Nara period there arose the practice of Yuima meetings (Yuimae 維摩会). These involved pictures of Vimalakīrti in annual celebrations that continued up to the Nambokuchō (1336–1392) and later, until finally abolished in 1868 (see Part Seven H).

Commentaries, Treatises, Miscellanea

As is wholly natural, Japanese and other peoples learn what they understand about their religions from secondary works as much as from the sacred works themselves. Consideration of such homiletic and other writings opens up an even more complex subject than sutras for students of literature. Buddhist doctrinal literature is enormous, as we can see from the thousands of items catalogued in Ono Gemmyō's *Bussho Kaisetsu Daijiten* (*Dictionary of Buddhist Books with Explanations*), fourteen volumes in the revised edition. From among these we call attention to ten or so of the most important, listed in alphabetical order of their Japanese titles. Others are entered in Part Three, under their authors' names.

(*Abidatsuma*) *Kusharon* (阿毘達磨)倶舍論 (*Treasury of Analyses of the Law*). There are two translations into Chinese (T. 1558, 1559) of Vasubandhu's *Abhidharma-kośa-śāstra*, the major exposition of Hīnayāna doctrine of radical pluralism known to the Mahāyāna. The Japanese Kusha sect, which derived both its name and its philosophical stance from this work, had no great following. But the Kusharon remained important for laying down the initial premises with which the Mahāyāna could define itself by way of contrast.

Daichidoron 大智度論 (*Commentary on the Great Wisdom Sūtra*, T. 1509). Kumārajīva's translation (*Ta-chih-tu-lun*, ca. 402–405) of the 100-fascicle *Mahā-Prajñāpāramitā-Śāstra* attributed to the great Mādhyamika (Chūgan-ha 中觀派) philosopher, Nāgārjuna, three of whose other treatises are the scriptural basis of the Japanese Sanron sect. The encyclopedic commentary emphasizes the doctrine of Emptiness (*kū*) and was a major source for the Japanese knowledge of earlier forms of Buddhism. Its anecdotes also found their way into Japanese literature, especially into *setsuwa*.

Daijō Kishinron 大乘起信論 (*The Awakening of Faith in the Mahāyāna*). Of two translations from a presumed Sanskrit original no longer extant, the version (T. 1666) by Paramārtha (499–569) is the more eminent, having inspired commentaries by the noted Hua-yen (Kegon) philosopher, Fa-tsang (J. Hōzō, 643–712) and an unidentified Nāgārjuna, whose *Explanation of Mahāyāna* (*Shakumakaenron*, T. 1668) was influential in Kūkai's Shingon. *The Awakening of Faith* was traditionally attributed to the famous Aśvaghosha (1st–2nd centuries A.D.), but its Mahāyānist contents make this highly unlikely.

Daitō Saiiki Ki 大唐西域記 (*Record of a Journey from the Great T'ang to the Western Regions*: C. *Ta T'ang Hsi Yü Chi*, T. 2087). Hsüan-tsang (J. Genjō, 600–664), translator and founder of the idealist Fa-hsiang (J. Hossō) school, returned to China after a seventeen-year pilgrimage to India in 645. The account of his travels has for centuries been familiar to Buddhists and to secular audiences, and it inspired the popular Chinese story, *Hsi-yu Chi* (J. *Saiyūki*; *The Journey to the West*; Waley's *Monkey*) by Wu Ch'eng-en (ca. 1506–1582). Both accounts are prominent in the classical Japanese literary imagination.

Hekigan Roku 碧巌録 (*Record of the Green Rock Room*; Ch. *Pi-yen-lu*, T. 2003). This compilation of a hundred *kōan* by Yüan-wu K'o-ch'in (Engo Kokugon, 1063–1135) is the most important of such collections and is still used in all Rinzai monasteries. Each verse is provided with an introduction and several commentaries. The somewhat later *Mumonkan* 無門関 (*The Gateless Barrier*; *Wu-men-kuan*, T. 2005) by Hui-k'ai (Ekai, 1184–1260) collects 48 (sometimes 49) *kōan* with prose and verse commentary.

Honchō Kōsōden 本朝高僧傳 (*Biographies of Eminent Japanese Priests*). This 75-fascicle compilation, published in 1702 by the Rinzai monk Mangen Shiban 卍元師蛮 (1626–1710), includes biographies of more than 1,600 priests of all sects, and remains an important reference tool even today. Shiban's *Empōdentōroku* (*The Empō Era's Record of the Transmission of the Lamp*) of 1678 contained about a thousand biographies of Zen priests; and *Kokan Shiren's early *Genkō Shakusho* fewer than 500 biographies of individuals of various sects.

Jōdoron 淨土論 (*Treatise on the Pure Land*; Skt., *Sukhāvativyūhopadesa*, T. 1524). Attributed to Vasubandhu (J. Seshin), this short treatise on the *Larger Pure Land Sūtra* (*Muryōjukyō*, T. 360) encouraged single-minded faith in Amida. A commentary on this work by T'an-luan (Donran, 476–542), the *Ōjōronchū* (*Commentary on the Treatise on Birth in the Pure Land*, T. 1819) in turn influenced Shan-tao (Zendō, 613–681). All provided the ideological underpinning for the popular Kamakura Pure Land movements initiated by *Hōnen.

Jōyuishikiron 成唯識論 (*The Realization of Consciousness Only*, T. 1585). Hsüan-tsang's 10-fascicle translation of the *Vijnapti-mātratā-siddhi-śāstra* of Dharmapāla (J. Gohō, 530–561) is the basic treatise for the Fa-hsiang (Hossō, Yuishiki) school and a landmark of Mahāyāna thought, for which idealism has been the main philosophical tradition (as in the West from Descartes until the reactions of recent decades). It purports to explicate Vasubandhu's *Trimśikā-vijñapti-mātratā-siddhi* (*Thirty Stanzas on Consciousness Only*; J. *Yuishiki Sanjūju*, T. 1586), also translated by Hsüan-tsang on returning from his pilgrimage to India. Hsüan-tsang's efforts were ably continued by his disciple K'uei-chi (Kiki, 632–682). The first transmission of the Hossō sect to Japan was by Dōshō (629–700), who roomed with K'uei-chi while studying under Hsüan-tsang in China.

Maka Shikan 摩訶止観 (*The Great Cessation and Insight*; C., *Mo-ho Chih-kuan*, T. 1911). The manual of Tendai meditation practice by its noted philosopher, Chih-i (J. Chigi, 538–597), recorded by his disciple Kuan-ting (Kanjō, 561–632) in 594. The "perfect and sudden" (endon) method (see Part Six N, Tendai sect) contrasts with the later Rinzai Zen practice employing the *kōan* (kannazen) and Sōtō Zen's "just sitting" (shikan-taza). The *Maka Shikan*, in 20 fascicles, is one of the Tendai sect's Three Great Books (sandaibu), together with Chih-i's *Hokke Gengi* (*Profound Meaning of the Lotus Sūtra*, T. 1716) and his *Hokke Mongu* (*Textual Commentary on the Lotus Sūtra*, T. 1718). See also *shikan*.

Rokuso Dangyō 六祖壇経 (*Platform Sūtra of the Sixth Patriarch*; C. *Liu-tsu T'an-ching*). Hui-neng (J. Enō, 638–713), sixth Chinese patriarch of Zen after Bodhidharma, founded the Southern School of sudden (as opposed to gradual) enlightenment to which all sects of Japanese Zen (Rinzai, Sōtō, Ōbaku) trace their lineage (except for the short-lived Gozu, Niu-t'ou, school, said to have been introduced by Tendai's *Saichō). The popular version (T. 2008) of *The Platform Sūtra* compiled by Tsung-pao (preface dated 1290) differs somewhat from the recently discovered Tun-huang text (T. 2007), now considered earlier and more authentic, and variously translated into English (Chan, Yampolsky). The popular version contains the well-known line from Hui-neng's gatha: "From the beginning not a thing is."

Note: For convenient modern Japanese translations of some of the sutras and a commentary noted in this section, see *Daijō Butten*, comp. Nakamura Hajime (Chikuma Shobō, 1974). Works translated include *Kegonkyō*, *Myōhōrengekyō*, *Hannyaharamitsukyō*, *Hannyashingyō*, *Yuimakyō*, and *Amidakyō* among sutras; and *Daijō Kishinron* among commentaries.

P. CONFUCIAN AND OTHER PHILOSOPHICAL CLASSICS

The label of this section promises more than is in it. But since, as with Buddhist sects and sutras (sections N and O), information about Confucian classics is hard for the student of Japanese literature to come by, something must be presented here, both by way of narrative and titles.

Japan and China have been alike in being syncretic in philosophical and religious beliefs. Confucianism and Taoism have very ancient origins in China, and some think that both derived from common universalist philosophical points of view. If so, they were seen to acquire different emphases in the course of time. To them Buddhism was of course added. Of these Three Ways, Buddhism was much the most important for Japanese literature, but Confucianism was known from the Nara period, and as early as the *Man'yōshū we observe use made of Taoist stories. Most of this section concerns Confucianism, and that chiefly as important for Japan. This teaching is commonly referred to as *jugaku* 儒学, and is sometimes represented by shorthand for Confucius and Mencius, Kō-Mō 孔孟: short for Kōshi 孔子 for Confucius (K'ung-tzu) and Mōshi 孟子 for Mencius (Meng-tzu).

For the sake of convenience, and also to make certain historical distinctions, the discussion of Confucianism and its classics will be divided into three periods.

1. *Nara and Heian Times*

Confucianism entered Japan with the rest of the New Learning from China. At first it gave Japan Han Dynasty tools of exegesis and a more orderly ethical code taken to be of a practical kind. In the Heian period, however, the court society regarded Confucianism as a definition of its range of interests, particularly as confirmation of its prizing of belles lettres and history. At the Confucian-inspired court school (daigaku), more specialized subjects were taught. Only a small number of works in the Confucian canon were known, and although these mattered to some of the learned, none was of the importance they held in China and Korea. Knowledge was largely confined to the Five Teachings or Classics, Gokyō 五経 (Wu Ching). The *Shiki* (below, Section 3) was something of an exception, in that classically educated boys were expected to memorize parts. In a famous anecdote, *Murasaki Shikibu memorized parts while listening to her brother being taught. It is also mentioned in the "Otome" part of her *Genji Monogatari*, and it seems to have been central to the education received by Yūgiri and other boys in the Heian daigaku.

1. *Shokyō* 書経 *Shu Ching, The Book of Documents*; or, *Shōsho* 尚書 *Shang Shu, Documents of Antiquity*
2. Shikyō 詩経 *Shih Ching, The Book of Songs*; or *Mōshi* 毛詩 *Mao Shih, The Book of Songs with Mao's Commentary*
3. *Ekikyō* 易経 *I Ching, The Book of Changes*; or *Shūeki* 周易 *Chou I, The Duke of Chou's Book of Changes*
4. *Shunjū* 春秋 *Ch'un Ch'iu, The Spring and Autumn Annals*
5. *Raiki* 礼記 *Li Chi, The Book of Rites*

None of these has ever been widely popular in Japan, although the great preface to the second had an important role in defining the systematics of poetry enunciated by *Ki no Tsurayuki in his Japanese preface to the *Kokinshū (see Part One A).

2. *Kamakura and Muromachi Times*

In this period, the Zen monks played an important role in making available to Japan Sung Confucianism, along with so much more in the way of influential Buddhist thought. The most important concepts they introduced were all but untranslatable, designated by the terms ri or kotowari 理 (li) and shō 性 (hsing). The former designates reason, orderly disposition, something for which Confucianism is justly known, although it fared less well in Japanese aesthetic soil, which is far more hospitable to asymmetry, affectivism, and exception. (Its social centrality in the Edo period is an altogether different matter.) The second concept designates nature, so completing one of those polarities much liked by Chinese and rarer in Japan.

Because the Confucian classics introduced by the *Gosan* monks were to achieve currency only in the Edo period, they will not be given here.

3. *Edo Times*

The varieties of Confucian teaching brought in earlier by the Zen monks were spread during this period beyond the confines of the learned, as priests opened temple schools and as other ways of teaching were instituted—giving Japan probably the world's highest rate of literacy for a premodern society. By this time the learned had grown acquainted with two other sets of Confucian writings. The former is the Four Books, *Shisho* 四書 (Ssu Shu):

Daigaku 大学 *Ta Hsüeh, The Great Learning*
Chūyō 中庸 *Chung Yung, The Doctrine of the Mean*
Rongo 論語 *Lun Yü, The Analects of Confucius*
Mōshi 孟子 *Meng-tzu, The Sayings of Mencius*

Although the first is *The Great Learning*, the second offers crucial Chinese thought on the idea of the Mean, and the fourth the teaching of Mencius, they did not achieve very wide currency. The third is different, and will be discussed in brief below.

The latter set is the *Sanshi* 三史 (*San Shih*), which consists of the following:

Shiki 史記 *Shih Chi, Records Compiled by the Historian*, compiled by Ssu-ma Ch'ien (B.C. ?145–86)
Kanjo 漢書 *Han Shu, The History of the Former Han Dynasty*, compiled by Pan Ku (A.D. 32–92)
Gokanjo 後漢書 *Hou Han Shu, The History of the Later Han Dynasty*, compiled by Fan Yeh (398–445)

Once again, the set produced only one work, the first here, that was to become popularly known in Japan.

The two works that became widely known are, then, the *Rongo* (*Lun Yü*) and *Shiki* (*Shih Chi*). The *Rongo*, or *Analects*, consists of twenty short parts, which in turn consist of a series of anecdotes presented as involving twenty-nine people, popularly considered to be disciples of Confucius who pass on his sayings and teachings. The actual historical matter is far more complex, but these sayings were generally accepted in Japan, as in China, with credence as genuine Confucian teaching. The brevity of the entire work and the memorability of so many of the anecdotes give two reasons why this work should have attained currency in Japan, even if often quoted at second or fifth hand.

The *Shiki* (*Shih Chi*) or *Historical Records* is far longer. In Japan, as in China, it was not held in as high formal esteem as the *Analects*, but in Japan it was very popular for accounts of important events to which parallels for present occurrences might be drawn in the time-honored Chinese fashion. The *Historical Records* consists of five different accounts:

Hongi 本紀 *Pen-chi, The Royal Biographies* (12 parts)
Seika 世家 *Shih-chia, Biographies of Noble Houses* (30 parts)
Retsuden 列伝 *Lieh Chuan, Biographies of Commoners* (70 parts)
Hyō 表 *Piao, Historical Compilations* (10 parts)
Sho 書 *Shu, The Treatises* (8 parts)

Altogether these yield 130 parts. The increasing Japanese interest in history, which in any event goes back to ancient times, must have led to the preference for this work. More than just Japanese liking, there must also have been many episodes to cite for historical lessons that did not involve the native royal house. And the first three kinds of history were taken up as models for Japanese writing: see *hongi* in Part Three.

None of these writings of the major canon was as important to the Edo *bakufu* in justifying its policies, however, as was Neoconfucianism. Two main varieties were known in Japan, of which Shushigaku was much the more important. Shuki 朱熹 (Chu Hsi, 1130–1200) was a philosophical dualist (thereby offering a major alternative to the nondualist philosophy of Buddhism). He propounded a distinction between mind and nature, and this gave him a materialist emphasis, which, with his stress on a study of nature, became more and more important as Edo intellectuals grew increasingly scientifically and technologically minded. Shushi also propounded the importance of the *Shisho* (*Ssu Shu*) as the central Confucian canon. Shushigaku was used by bakufu thinkers to give the regime a philosophy at once abstractly rational and very practical. That potent combination helped legitimize Tokugawa polity and justified the theoretically rigid social structure and the ethics of a new age. After a time Shushigaku came to seem rather sterile, and some intellectuals turned to the Neoconfucianism of Yōmeigaku 陽明学. Yōmei or Ōyōmei 陽明, 王陽明 (Yang-ming, Wang Yang-ming, 1472–ca. 1528) opposed Shushi's dualism and materialist emphasis. Shushigaku held its ground as official Neoconfucianism, however, in spite of attempts to introduce Yōmeigaku or other kinds of innovation, which were commonly presented as returns to pristine Confucianism. This so-called Ancient Learning (*kogaku*) was represented by *Yamaga Sokō, *Itō Jinsai, and his son Tōgai (1670–1736). The maverick Confucian, *Ogyū Sorai, posed objections that were among the most interesting, as well as most Japanese, to both the other movements. He was succeeded by a brilliant disciple, Dazai Shundai (1680–1747). Their work is enough of a variant within kogaku to be given a subname, kobunjigaku 古文辞学.

Two of the Taoist classics had some importance in Japan. These are:

Sōshi 荘子 *Chuang-tzu*; attributed to Chuang Chou (B.C. ?369–?286)
Rōshi 老子 *Lao-tzu*; *Dotokukyō* 道徳経 *Tao-te Ching, The Way and Its Power*; 3rd c. B.C.; author unknown.

The usual Japanese names for Taoism are dōkyō 道教 and Rōshi no oshie 老子の教. In each case given above, the work of course bears its author's name, but neither achieved the currency of the *Rongo* or *Shiki*. It would seem that in Edo times the magical arts and legends of Taoism were not wholly agreeable. Yet it is worth mentioning a wider range of these Chinese classics than the two that obtained real currency. A given writer could become interested in one of the lesser-known works and communicate enthusiasm to a circle of acquaintances. By way of example, in the 1680s, *Matsuo Bashō (whose abiding Chinese interests lay much more with the poets Tu Fu and Li Po) was alluding to the *Sōshi* (*Chuang-tzu*), and his followers sometimes do so also, no doubt in some deference to the master's interests. Yet neither of these Taoist classics had anywhere near the widespread influence as had the *Shiki* and *Rongo*, particularly the former.

Note: Chinese writing, including that by Japanese, is not treated as a central matter of this companion. But in Part Three will be found notice of certain works and authors of importance for writing in Chinese. See especially the Chinese collections *Hakushi Monjū* and *Monzen* (to give the Japanese versions of their titles). For Japanese collections, see for example *Kaifūsō*, and such later collections as *Ryōunshū*, *Bunka Shūreishū*, and *Keikokushū*. Among the writers noted in Part Three and earlier in this part for their Chinese compositions there are *Kūkai, *Sugawara Michizane, *Rai San'yō, *Kan Chazan, and *Ōta Nampo. These are but a few examples. The scope of Japanese writing in Chinese is so large that this note constitutes little more than a reminder of the obvious with a few appropriate examples.

Q. DICTIONARIES

According to the *Nihon Shoki*, in 683 Temmu ordered the compilation of what is the earliest known dictionary by Japanese, the *Niina* 新字 (*New Characters*), in forty-four fascicles. The work is no longer extant, and its name was at one time used to reinforce the theory of a native Japanese writing system, *jindai* (or shindai) *moji*. It seems, however, to have been a dictionary of Chinese characters.

This was followed in the 830s by the *Hifuryaku* 秘府略 (*Treasury of Words Defined*), the earliest substantial "classified dictionary" (ruisho); and by *Kūkai's *Tenrei Banshō Myōgi* or *Banshō Meigi* 篆隷万象名義 (*A Myriad Pronunciations and Definitions*).

The first dictionary to provide Japanese readings (*wakun*) for its characters (that is, the first *kan-wa jiten*) was the *Shinsen Jikyō* 新撰字鏡 (*Mirror of Characters Newly Compiled*), compiled ca. 898–901. It was succeeded ca. 934 by the encyclopedic *Wamyō Ruiju Shō* 和名類聚抄 (*Japanese Names for Things Classified and Annotated*) by *Minamoto Shitagō. The student of Japanese frequently finds this work cited in headnotes of standard editions of the classics for early definitions and pronunciations, the Japanified *kun'yomi* being indicated in *man'yōgana*.

Later dictionaries include the *Ruiju Myōgishō* 類聚名義抄 (*Classified Dictionary of Pronunciations and Meanings, Annotated*, 1081), the *Iroha Jiruishō* 色葉字類抄 (*Characters Classified in Iroha Order and Annotated*, ca. 1144–1181), the *Jikyōshū* 字鏡集 (*Mirror of Characters Collection*, 1245), the *Wagyokuhen* 倭玉篇 (*Book of Japanese Jewels*, ca. 1489), the *Kagakushū* 下学集 (*Collection of Mundane Matters*, 1444), the *Setsuyōshū* 節用集 (*Collection of Words for Everyday Use*, 1469–87), and the *Onkochishinsho* 温故知新書 (*Mastery of the Old and Inquiry into the New*, 1484).

The Christian missionaries in the late sixteenth and seventeenth centuries compiled several dictionaries and grammars of special interest because they indicated the *sound* of Japanese pronunciations in a Western alphabet. Printed by the Jesuit Mission at Nagasaki in 1598, the *Rakuyōshū* 落葉集 (*Collection of Fallen Leaves*), in addition to illustrating its characters' *on* and *kun* readings and compounds, was the first dictionary to employ the small raised circle (handa kuten) to indicate the "p" sound.

The *Vocabulario da Lingoa de Iapam* of 1603–1604, commonly known as the *Nippo Jisho* 日葡辞書 (*Japanese-Portuguese Dictionary*), is frequently mentioned in headnotes of annotated texts as an authority for pronunciations and definitions current in the late Ashikaga period. However, the work actually cited is likely to be the *Dictionnaire Japonais-Français* (*Nichifutsu Jisho* 日佛辞書), translated into French by Léon Pagés in 1868 and often reprinted.

João Rodrigues (1561–1633) compiled his *Arte da Lingoa de Iapam* (Japanese translation: *Nippon Daibunten* 日本大文典) sometime between 1604 and 1608; a thoroughly revised edition appeared at Macao in 1620 as the *Arte Breve da Lingoa Iapoa*. The earlier version contains a short treatise on Japanese poetry, the first Western discussion of some facet of Japanese literature.

The *Ars Grammaticae Iaponicae Linguae* (Japanese translation: *Nippon Bunten* 日本文典, 1934), published in Rome in 1632 by the Dominican, Diego Collado (d. 1638), was composed in Latin and had wide circulation in Europe.

The Chinese *K'ang-hsi Dictionary* (*K'ang-hsi Tzu-tien* 康熙字典, familiar to Japanese as *Kōki Jiten*) of 1716 standardized the use of 214 radicals to replace the organization of characters by topic or the *iroha* syllabary. (See *Tsuga Teishō.) This is the system employed by all modern character dictionaries such as Morohashi Tetsuji's thirteen-volume *Dai Kanwa Jiten* 大漢和辞典 (*Great Dictionary of Chinese-Japanese Characters*, 1955–1960), which lists almost 50,000 characters.

In contrast to the *kan-wa* character dictionaries, the familiar "national language dictionaries" (kokugo jiten) organize their entries according to the "fifty-sound arrangement" (gojū onzu) of the forty-seven syllables.

For yet different approaches, see the *Yakubun Sentei* and *Kun'yaku Jimō* of *Ogyū Sorai and the *Tōga* of *Arai Hakuseki.

PART SEVEN Time, Directions, Related Symbolism, and Annual Celebrations

Except for the annual celebrations, the matters treated here are mostly derived from Chinese practice. Aspects of the celebrations are also, but for them indigenous ways of thought and customs make Japanese practice distinct.

A. Zodiac and Element Signs

The basic symbolism in much of what follows involves the twelve signs of the zodiac (jūnishi 十二支) as also, for some matters, the five elements (gogyō 五行). The twelve signs are given with common English renderings. (Actually, the first could be read Mouse as easily as Rat, the second Cow or Bull instead of Ox, etc.) The characters for the animals of the zodiac are distinct from those used for the animals proper.

1. Rat. Ne 子
2. Ox. Ushi 丑
3. Tiger. Tora 寅
4. Rabbit. U 卯
5. Dragon. Tatsu 辰
6. Snake. Mi 巳

7. Horse. Uma 午
8. Ram. Hitsuji 未
9. Monkey. Saru 申
10. Cock. Tori 酉
11. Dog. Inu 戌
12. Boar. I 亥

The five elements have both their Japanese (lower case, below) and Sinified (upper case) readings for various minute calculations.

1. Wood. Ki, MOKU 木
2. Fire. Hi, KA 火
3. Earth. Tsuchi, DO 土
4. Metal. Kane, KIN (or KON) 金
5. Water. Mizu, SUI 水

B. Hours of the Day, Directions

The system of standard reckoning (teijihō 定時法) divided the whole day into twelve long hours of 120 minutes each. At court, these long hours were measured carefully by means of water-clock calculation in order that court ritual, periods of the guards, and so on, could be kept with accuracy. Each of these long hours was named after a zodiac sign. By beginning with the Rat for midnight, going next to the Ox, and so on, the Horse was noon. The twelve long hours can, then, be charted with their times and their durations by Western calculations.

Hour	*Modern Time*	*Modern Duration*
1. Rat	Midnight	11 p.m.–1 a.m.
2. Ox	2 a.m.	1 a.m.–3 a.m.
3. Tiger	4 a.m.	3 a.m.–5 a.m.
4. Rabbit	6 a.m.	5 a.m.–7 a.m.
5. Dragon	8 a.m.	7 a.m.–9 a.m.
6. Snake	10 a.m.	9 a.m.–11 a.m.
7. Horse	Noon	11 a.m.–1 p.m.
8. Ram	2 p.m.	1 p.m.–3 p.m.
9. Monkey	4 p.m.	3 p.m.–5 p.m.
10. Cock	6 p.m.	5 p.m.–7 p.m.
11. Dog	8 p.m.	7 p.m.–9 p.m.
12. Boar	10 p.m.	9 p.m.–11 p.m.

Outside the court, people had to make do with nonstandard reckoning (futeijihō 不定時法). In this system, the day—in the sense of daylight hours—was divided into natural or seasonal durations rather than artificial or measured hours. The hours during darkness were not really calculable. As summer came on, the nonstandard hours steadily expanded in length beyond their presumed 120-minute durations until midsummer, after which their length in minutes gradually decreased. (The presumed hours of night correspondingly shrank and grew.) Nonstandard reckoning was calculated more or less impressionistically by mental division of the sky into six (long-hour) parts determined by what sixth of the sky the sun was deemed to have traversed. Insofar as this reckoning could be accurate, it therefore coincided with standard reckoning only at the vernal and autumnal equinoxes. Apart from a calculation of nonstandard hours by personal impression, there was naturally variance depending on the latitude at which an observer was located in the islands making up Japan.

It has been calculated (on the presumption that one could take a modern clock to classical Japan) that by nonstandard reckoning the hour of the Hare (6 a.m. by modern reckoning) would have fallen as follows in Edo times at the latitude of present Tokyo.

Modern Date	*Present Time*	*Modern Date*	*Present Time*
Spring Equinox		Autumnal Exquinox	
21 March	5:09	23 September	4:54
Summer Solstice		Winter Solstice	
21 June	3:49	22 December	6:11

But of course there were not modern clocks to determine nonstandard any more than standard reckoning (outside the court) in classical Japan, including the Edo period.

As a result of the differences between standard reckoning at court and non-standard elsewhere, care must be taken in translating mention of hours in classical literature. It is one thing if *Sei Shōnagon mentions the hour at court. It is another if the hour is guessed by nonstandard reckoning in the *Heike Monogatari* as Heike and Genji forces engage along the coast of the Inland Sea at some distance from court. It will be observed that *Murasaki Shikibu follows the distinctions carefully in the *Genji Monogatari*, depending on whether action is situated at the court or away from it. Away from it, she may say something vaguely like noon (the Horse) in nonstandard reckoning, "with the sun grown high." Perhaps the best illustration occurs in "Suma," when Genji is going by ship to exile: "With daylight so long at this time [hi nagaki koro nareba], and favored by a good wind astern, he arrived at the bay of his destination while it was still the hour of the Monkey [saru no toki bakari ni]." In other words, what would be 4 p.m. by standard reckoning but which might vary more than three hours by nonstandard. It was presumably about 2 p.m. at Suma.

At court, the long hours could be divided into quarters or smaller divisions (the quarters would be thirty-minute intervals). The time supervisors were called reki hakase, whom we can imagine communicating times to the guards, so that they might go about, twanging their bowstrings to ward off evil and calling out the equivalent of "The Hour of the Boar, and all is well!"

As has been indicated, a given hour (as of the Rat) had both its point (midnight) and its 120-minute duration (11 p.m.–1 a.m.) in standard reckoning, and by modern terms. In the chart that follows, the twelve long hours are specified by number and by sign. With that specification is given the modern point and duration, and also the designation of the period of duration, since that might also need specification to distinguish it from the point designated by the sign. In other words, a sign—again the Rat hour will be the example—specified midnight as a point, and the hours of 11 p.m. to 1 a.m. as the duration. That duration is designated 9th of daybreak. And since the specifications vary so much in the system, and do not coincide either with modern or zodiacal hours in any obvious way, they require setting forth.

Zodiac Hour	Modern Time, Duration	Designation of Period of Duration
1. Rat	Midnight 11 p.m.–1 a.m.	Akatsuki kokonotsu　曉九つ 9th of daybreak
2. Ox	2 a.m. 1–3 a.m.	Akatsuki yatsu　曉八つ 8th of daybreak
3. Tiger	4 a.m. 3–5 a.m.	Akatsuki nanatsu　曉七つ 7th of daybreak
4. Rabbit	6 a.m. 5–7 a.m.	Ake mutsu　明六つ 6th of dawn
5. Dragon	8 a.m. 7–9 a.m.	Asa itsutsu　朝五つ 5th of morning
6. Snake	10 a.m. 9–11 a.m.	Asa yotsu　朝四つ 4th of morning

7. Horse	Noon	Hiru kokonotsu	昼九つ
	11 a.m.–1 p.m.	9th of day	
8. Ram	2 p.m.	Hiru yatsu	昼八つ
	1–3 p.m.	8th of day	
9. Monkey	4 p.m.	Yū nanatsu	夕七つ
	3–5 p.m.	7th of afternoon	
10. Cock	6 p.m.	Kure mutsu	暮六つ
	5–7 p.m.	6th of dusk	
11. Dog	8 p.m.	Yoru itsutsu	夜五つ
	7–9 p.m.	5th of night	
12. Boar	10 p.m.	Yoru yotsu	夜四つ
	9–11 p.m.	4th of night	

Certain of the zodiac signs, as also therefore of the hours, were associated with directions, in particular of the four quarters and of what may be termed the semiquarters between them (northeast, etc.). The semiquarters are indicated by characters read so as to combine the sounds of the two signs they cover. This will be clear from another chart of standard reckoning.

Sign-Hour	Directional Quarter and Character	Directional Semiquarter	Time
Rat 子	North 北		Midnight
Ushitora 艮		Northeast	3 a.m.
Rabbit 卯	East 東		6 a.m.
Tatsumi 巽		Southeast	9 a.m.
Horse 午	South 南		Noon
Hitsujisaru 坤		Southwest	3 p.m.
Cock 酉	West 西		6 p.m.
Inui 乾		Northwest	9 p.m.

These matters can be shown by figures. To serve those with varying degrees of Japanese, Figure 7-1 will combine English with Japanese terms, whereas Figure 7-2 is entirely in Japanese, except for numbers.

C. MONTHS

Months were also designated by zodiac signs but not, as might be expected, beginning with the Rat for the First Month (January, etc., below).

I	January	Tiger	VII	July	Monkey
II	February	Rabbit	VIII	August	Cock
III	March	Dragon	IX	September	Dog
IV	April	Snake	X	October	Boar
V	May	Horse	XI	November	Rat (first sign)
VI	June	Ram	XII	December	Ox

The presently numbered twelve months of the year had a multiplicity of names in the lunar calendar of classical usage, but each month was best known by one.

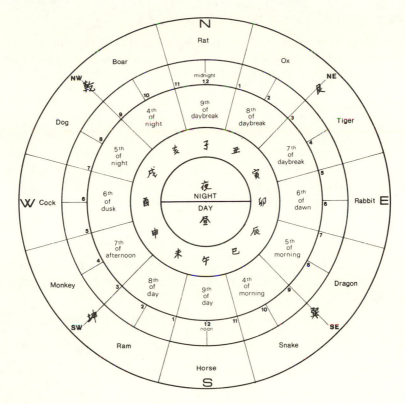

FIGURE 7-1.

Outer Circle: Zodiac Names, Quarters, Semiquarters
Second Circle: Modern Hours
Third Circle: Names of Old Japanese Hours
  (translated)

Fourth Circle: Zodiac signs (Japanese)
Inner Circle: Night and Day Halves

FIGURE 7-2. A Japanese Version
of Figure 7-1

The familiar or standard name is given below, and for a full range—as for the over forty by which the first month was known—see Takayanagi and Takeuchi, ed., *Nihonshi Jiten*, 2nd ed., Kadokawa, 1974 (and reprinted), p. 1,315.

Month	Usual Name			
1	Mutsuki 睦月		7	Fumizuki (Fuzuki) 文月
2	Kisaragi 如月, 衣更着		8	Hazuki 葉月, 八月
3	Yayoi 弥生		9	Nagatsuki (Nagazuki) 長月
4	Uzuki 卯月		10	Kaminazuki (Kannazuki) 神無月
5	Satsuki 五月, 皐月		11	Shimotsuki 霜月
6	Minazuki 水無月, 六月		12	Shiwasu 師走

D. Points, Zodiac Signs, Elements, Colors, and Seasons

The system of correspondences further included relations between the five points (the quarters and center), the zodiac signs, the five elements, colors, and the seasons.

Point Hōi 方位	East 東	West 西	South 南	North 北	Center 中
Zodiac Sign Jūnishi 十二支	Rabbit 卯	Cock 酉	Horse 午	Rat 子	**
Element Gogyō 五行	Wood 木	Metal 金	Fire 火	Water 水	Earth 土
Color Goshiki 五色	Green 青	White 白	Red 赤	Black 黑	Yellow 黃
Season Shiki 四季	Spring 春	Autumn 秋	Summer 夏	Winter 冬	**

As a number of instances will have suggested, the prime quarter in such calculation was East rather than North. East and West came first, and then South and North. This preference can be illustrated by the traditional terms for compound directions. Southwest, as we put it, is termed Westsouth (seinan—Sinified readings of the characters), and Northeast is Eastnorth (tōhoku). The four quarters as a totality are designated east-west, south-north (tōzai namboku). Thus the period of rival northern and southern courts (see Part Two A) is designated Nambokuchō rather than Hokunanchō. Modern weather reports have come to use Westernlike terms, so that a certain wind is now northeastern (hokutō) rather than the designation more familiar in speech, eastnorthern (tōhoku). The northeastern region of Japan and the national university in that area, situated at Sendai, still have their familiar names: Tōhoku (district), Tōhoku Daigaku (University), as is usual in common speech.

E. Seasons, Natural Emblems, Times of the Day, Directions

For poetic purposes, each season of the year was identified with a wealth of words conveying images of flora, fauna, and natural phenomena. These may be found in codified form in various aids to writing modern *haiku*. The most common of these are the various handbooks that give, for each season, the words designating natural phenomena in the sequence of poetic occurrence throughout the season, beginning with spring. These features relate to natural cycles and occurrences, but they are also determined by long poetic tradition in ways often at variance with the natural phenomena. Sometimes the variance involves time of occurrence, sometimes the poetic nature of the phenomenon. The determining factor for poetic nature involves the concept of essential nature (*hon'i* 本意). To take a nonseasonal example, in most of classical literature, love (*koi* 恋) meant unrequited, longing love, not being loved. This was thought the essential nature of love, even if many people who were in love found their love returned. For natural phenomena, haze (kasumi 霞) was thought an essentially spring phenomenon, although in nature it may occur any time of the year. For poetic purposes, the moon (tsuki 月) came to designate autumn unless qualified, as for example the summer moon (natsu no tsuki 夏の月). Spring rains (harusame 春雨) were conceived of poetically as very gentle rains, and the spring wind (harukaze 春風) as a very light breeze, although in nature spring rains often fall very hard and spring winds can blow forcefully. These matters were worked out over a considerable period. Major determinants of such definitions or associations include the *chokusenshū*, whose typical six books on the seasons (including two each for spring and autumn) were arranged according to natural and essentially conceived views of natural phenomena.

*Sei Shōnagon's *Makura no Sōshi* opens with an identification of the times of day especially springlike, summerlike, and so on. She no doubt reflected the poetic views of her time, but her formulation gave explicit sanction to what may have been only implicit earlier. In this respect Japanese ideas are stricter than Chinese ones, which might be invoked, however, when an exception was sought. The decisive stage in such matters was reached when the *renga* masters codified the implications of words for a wide range of natural and human experience in their rule books (*shikimoku* 式目).

It should be added that spring had overtones of love, something implied by the pen name of *Koikawa Harumachi, or by the term shunga (spring pictures), which designates erotic or pornographic pictures.

In the table following, flowers and birds have particular associations. To the

Heian poets, flowers meant those of the plum tree unless qualified by some particular designation of another plant. By about 1500 the implications had shifted decisively to mean flowers of the cherry tree. In other words, for renga a flower stanza (hana no ku 花の句) is uncertain as to whether plum or cherry flowers are meant. And a proper flower stanza was indicated only by the use of the word, "flower" (hana 花), not by designating a specific flower such as kerria or orange flowers (yamabuki 山吹, tachibana 橘). By the time *haikai* came to be practiced, however, the designation of flower had come to mean what was then *the* flower, cherry blossoms (sakura no hana 桜の花).

For similar reasons, the birds that represent summer are conceived by *waka* poets primarily as the hototogisu (時鳥, 子規, etc.) which was poetically thought to delay its singing, while the longing impatience of the poet rose until at last a brief song could be heard—although in nature the bird's mating song could become insistently clamorous.

Season	Natural Emblem	Time of Day	Direction
Spring	Flowers	Dawn	East
Summer	Birds	Night	South
Autumn	Moon	Evening	West
Winter	Snow	First light	North

F. Buddhist Associations, Correspondences

Buddhist analogies enriched the associations already mentioned. The specific kind and set of analogy varied somewhat from one group to another, and from one purpose to another. In general, the older groups in Japan made greater use of correspondences than did the newer. As might be expected, Shingon is one of the richest in its correspondences. Its two basic maṇḍalas (*mandara*), Diamond and Matrix, respectively represent knower and known. As might be expected, both employ a complex symbolism to guide the meditator to that sense of integration of knower and known which *is* Mahāvairocana (Dainichi Nyorai). Shingon's five ritual colors—white, red, yellow, green, and black—can be correlated in various sequences (depending on the scriptural authority) and with various items. For example, I-hsing (Ichigyō, 683—727), in his commentary (T. 1796) on the *Dainichikyō* explains these colors as they apply to the five Buddhas in the central constellation of the Matrix maṇḍala. (The Diamond has its own rules of construction, of course). From this and other sources we can assemble the following chart of correspondences:

Point	Element	Color	Buddha
Center	Water	White	Dainichi Nyorai 大日如来 Skt., Mahāvairocana
East	Fire	Red	Hōtō Nyorai 宝幢如来 Skt., Ratnaketu
South	Earth	Yellow	Kaifukeō Nyorai 開敷華王如来 Skt., Saṃkusumitarāja
West	Space	Green	Muryōju Nyorai 無量寿如来 Skt., Amitāyus (i.e., Amida)
North	Wind	Black	Tenkuraion Nyorai 天皷雷音如来 Skt., Divyadundubhi-megha-nirghoṣa

Some of the reasons, or implications, of these correspondences will be apparent: the green of spring; Amida's Western paradise; the Five Elements comprising the world as *known*, as against the knower represented by the Diamond Maṇḍala, and so on.

G. CALENDAR AND YEARS

The calendar in use throughout the classical period was a lunar one of twelve months of thirty or twenty-nine days. Intercalary units were periodically necessary to prevent the lunar calculations from lagging too far behind the solar.

Years could be indicated by combinations of the senior and junior signs for each of the five elements (a set of ten) and a sequence of the zodiac signs (a set of twelve). Here are the five elements with their senior and junior names.

Element	Senior	Junior
Wood 木	kinoe 甲	kinoto 乙
Fire 火	hinoe 丙	hinoto 丁
Earth 土	tsuchinoe 戊	tsuchinoto 己
Metal 金	kanoe 庚	kanoto 辛
Water 水	mizunoe 壬	mizunoto 癸

By a combinatory process such as will be indicated, a given year in a 240-year period could be designated simply by the sequential use of one of the ten senior-junior element symbols and one of the twelve of the zodiac. The rotation began with the pairing of senior Wood (kinoe) with the Rat; and the second year then was junior Wood (kinoto) with Ox. Every tenth added year (11, 21, 31, 41, 51, etc.) the element set began over; and every twelfth added year (13, 25, 37, 49, 61, etc.) the zodiac set began again. This is not really very complicated, although it is unfamiliar. Since those likely to make use of the system will read Japanese easily, we give in Figure 7-3 the pattern for sixty years of such a cycle in Japanese.

H. ANNUAL OBSERVANCES

With the establishment of a court, numerous indigenous and borrowed rites, customs, and observances gradually became codified. These were specified in codified form as *The Annual Observances* (nenjūgyōji 年中行事). In the course of time, the *bakufu*, beginning with establishment at Kamakura and ending with that at Edo, modified the old system and introduced observances more proper to a society defined by a warrior aristocracy. During the various periods observances were commonly restricted to certain social groups.

In what follows, the year is run through in a way that consolidates the various *Annual Observances*. To distinguish between groups involved, the following symbols will be used:

Pal.   Palace. Observances at court
Mil.   Military. Observances for warriors
Aris.   Aristocracy. Observances for court and shogunate

干　支　表

1 甲子（きのえね）	21 甲申（きのえさる）	41 甲辰（きのえたつ）
2 乙丑（きのとうし）	22 乙酉（きのととり）	42 乙巳（きのとみ）
3 丙寅（ひのえとら）	23 丙戌（ひのえいぬ）	43 丙午（ひのえうま）
4 丁卯（ひのとう）	24 丁亥〈ひのとい〉	44 丁未（ひのとひつじ）
5 戊辰（つちのえたつ）	25 戊子（つちのえね）	45 戊申（つちのえさる）
6 己巳（つちのとみ）	26 己丑（つちのとうし）	46 己酉（つちのととり）
7 庚午（かのえうま）	27 庚寅（かのえとら）	47 庚戌（かのえいぬ）
8 辛未（かのとひつじ）	28 辛卯（かのとう）	48 辛亥（かのとい）
9 壬申〈みづのえさる〉	29 壬辰〈みづのえたつ〉	49 壬子〈みづのえね〉
10 癸酉（みづのととり）	30 癸巳〈みづのとみ〉	50 癸丑〈みづのとうし〉
11 甲戌（きのえいぬ）	31 甲午（きのえうま）	51 甲寅（きのえとら）
12 乙亥〈きのとい〉	32 乙未（きのとひつじ）	52 乙卯（きのとう）
13 丙子（ひのえね）	33 丙申（ひのえさる）	53 丙辰（ひのえたつ）
14 丁丑（ひのとうし）	34 丁酉（ひのととり）	54 丁巳（ひのとみ）
15 戊寅（つちのえとら）	35 戊戌（つちのえいぬ）	55 戊午（つちのえうま）
16 己卯〈つちのとう〉	36 己亥〈つちのとい〉	56 己未（つちのとひつじ）
17 庚辰（かのえたつ）	37 庚子（かのえね）	57 庚申（かのえさる）
18 辛巳（かのとみ）	38 辛丑（かのとうし）	58 辛酉（かのととり）
19 壬午〈みづのえうま〉	39 壬寅〈みづのえとら〉	59 壬戌〈みづのえいぬ〉
20 癸未〈みづのとひつじ〉	40 癸卯〈みづのとう〉	60 癸亥〈みづのとい〉

FIGURE 7-3. Element-Zodiac Rotations for Specifying Years

Pop.　Popular. Observances apart from court, shogunate
Com.　Commoners. Military and popular observances
( )　Other observances, etc.
Moveable.　Celebrations set for certain days rather than dates, so falling on
different days of the month from year to year.

In individual instances, Japanese authorities do not all agree on the distinctions we follow, on the names of the celebrations, or sometimes on details. But we have chosen the main examples, which are least disputed.

Because of the frequent difficulty of the terms, each observance is given in roman and then in Japanese characters.

The importance of the First, Sixth, and Twelfth Months will be obvious, although of course every month had its special features. The doubled dates of the third month (third day), fifth month (day), seventh month (day), and ninth month (day) held special importance.

FIRST MONTH

1st. Ganjitsu, gannichi 元日 Pal. Shihōhai 四方拝
Sovereign's ritual purification of the four quarters
Pal. Kochōhai, kojōhai 小朝拝. Simpler purification, in the morning, by courtiers: also on 2nd

Pal. Ganjitsu no sechie 元日の節会. New Year's festival.

Pal. Toso 屠蘇. Sake-drinking auspice for the year

Mil. Ōban 埦飯. New Year's banqueting; continued to 3rd and repeated on 7th and 15th

Mil. Hatsutōjō 初登城. First greetings of the year to superiors

Pal. Wakamizu 若水. Presentation of fresh water

2nd. Pal. Chōkin no miyuki 朝勤の行幸. Sovereign's visit to father and mother

Pal. Kissho hajime 吉書始め. Sending of New Year's greetings in writing

Mil. Buke Shojihajime 武家諸事始(め). Warriors' version of the preceding

Merchants. Hatsuni 初荷. Exhibition of growing things by merchants; could go to the 3rd

Com. Hime hajime 姫始め. Entreaty of a happy future for couples

(Hatsuyume 初夢. A night for truly predictive dreams; often set for the night of the 1st)

3rd. Com. Matsubayashi 松囃子. Auspicious song and dance

4th. Pal. Matsurigotohajime 政始め. First court work of the year; sometimes from the 9th

Com. Dezome 出初め. Firemen's festival

5th. Pal. Joi 叙位. Lords' court promotions; sometimes on the 6th

Pal. Chōna hajime 手斧始め. Court carpenters begin their work after time off

7th. Pal. Aouma no sechie 白馬節会. Presentation of white (earlier, dark) horses to the sovereign, with banquet for lords

Mil. Yumihajime 弓始め. First day for using bows (on 17th in Muromachi period)

Pop. Nanakusa 七草. Feast of the seven plants; also called Nanoka shōgatsu (New Year's Day of the 7th)

8th. Pal. Gosaie 御斎会. Lecture at court on the *Konkōmyōkyō* (see Part Six O) for preservation of the nation

Pal. Mishio 御修法. Buddhist performances for the nation, individuals; continued for six more days; participants and sites differed from the preceding

Pal. Nyojoi 女叙位. Assignment of ladies to court posts; every other year

Pal. Kosho no sō 古書の奏. Lecture to the sovereign on Chinese classics; sometimes on 2nd and 3rd

11th. Pal. Agatameshi 県召し. Court visitation by, and confirmation of, provincial heads; continued to 13th

Com. Kagamibiraki 鏡開き. Eating of "mirror rice," that is, glutinous rice formed in circular tablets and hardened during the New Year period; originally on the 20th

15th. Pal. Jōgen no shūgi 上元の祝儀. Feast of the middle of the first month (jōgen designates I. 15)

Aris. Mikamagi 御薪. Courtiers' presentation of firewood to the sovereign; in Edo period decoration of the gate of warriors' houses with twelve units of fuel

Pop. Sagichō 左義長. Purification by expelling of evil forces: burning of various New Year's decorations (kadomatsu, etc.)

Pop. Mochigayu no sekku 望粥の節供. Feast of red-bean gruel

16th. Pal. Tōka no sechie 踏歌の節会. Ladies' performance of dance and song; lords performed on the 14th or 15th, and on the 16th there was a banquet for both in the sovereign's presence

Pal., later Pop. Yabuiri 藪入. Day off for servants to return to their homes

17th. Pal. Jarai 射礼. Archery demonstration by princes and lords down to the fifth rank in the sovereign's presence

Pal. Tsuru no hōchō 鶴の庖丁. Lords, wearing ordinary dress, perform the rite of cutting a cooked crane; later held on 18th or 19th

20th. Mil. Renga hajime 連歌始め. First *renga* sitting—*hokku* by Satomura school master; *waki* by shogun

Moveable. Pal. Wakana 若菜. Gathering of young shoots on First Day of the Rat in the New Year

Pal. Uzue or uzuchi 卯杖, 卯槌. Gift to the sovereign of a ritual chastising wand, variously decorated, from the six troops of guards, to ward off evil spirits (other government branches presented similarly appropriate ritual gifts)

Moveable. In first half of month, Risshun 立春, Beginning of Spring

SECOND MONTH

1st. (Nigatsudō shu'nie 二月堂修二会. Drawing of water ceremony at Nigatsudō, Tōdaiji in Nara, a spring observance, from which women were excluded, and otherwise difficult to classify; continued to the 14th)

4th. Pal. Toshigoi (note reversal of characters) no matsuri 祈年祭. Provincial governors' celebration rites for a good harvest of the five grains

8th. Com. Harikuyō 針供養. Appreciation of needles (women)

11th. Pal. Rekken 列見. Inspection of talent; search for lords of outstanding ability below the fifth rank, by ministers of the Great Council of State (an observance made an asset by the astute Fujiwara hegemons)

Moveable. Mil. Sekiten 釈奠. On the first hinoto 丁 in this and the Eighth Month. Rites of sacrifice of animals (living or dead) and of vegetables prepared for divinities; in China a Confucian rite and, some say, also in Japan

THIRD MONTH

3rd. Pal. Kyokusui 曲水. Ostensible purification rite; poems were composed and sake cups floated downstream

Pal. Gotō 御灯. Sovereign's candle service toward northeastern direction

Pal. Tōkei 闘鶏. Cock-fights

Pop. Hinamatsuri 雛祭. Girls' doll festival

(Hanami 花見. Viewing of cherry blossoms)

Moveable. Pal. Jōshi (or minohi) no harae 上巳(巳の日)の祓え. Purification on the First Day of the Snake; later altered into hinamatsuri, above

Pal., later Pop. Hana shizume no matsuri 花鎮祭. Festival at time of cherry blossoms' fall for ease from illness; usually on or near the 30th

FOURTH MONTH

1st. Pal., later Pop. Koromogae 更衣. Change to summer clothes

8th. (Kanbutsue 灌仏会. Feast of the birth of the Buddha)

16th. Pal. Gebana 夏花. Offering of flowers to statues of the Buddha at the beginning of the period of priestly meditation; ended VII. 15

Moveable. Pop. Naka no tori no hi 中酉日. Kamo or Aoi matsuri 賀茂, 葵祭, Hibiscus (mallow) Festival on the Second Day of the Cock

Moveable. In first half of month, Rikka 立夏, Beginning of Summer

FIFTH MONTH

3rd. Pal. Shōbu Kenjō 菖蒲献上. Donation of irises to sovereign

5th. Pal., later Pop. Itsuka no sechie, tango no sekku 五日節会 端午節句. Boys' festival, involving irises (see preceding), later Mil. observance involving armor, etc., and Pop. involving hoisting of paper carp to stream in the air, etc.

17th. Pop. Taishi no Kō 太子講. Carpenters' festival, ostensibly honoring Shōtoku Taishi; also IX and X. 17

25th. Pal. Arinashi no hi 有無の日. Commemoration of Murakami (r. 946–967); a holiday when only essential business was performed

SIXTH MONTH

1st. Pal. Imbi no gohan 忌火の御飯. Celebration of preparing rice with ritual fire for presentation to sovereign; also XI. 1 and XII. 1

Pal. Agamono 贖物. Surrogate purification: dolls used for transfer of human impurities; also XII. 1

Pal. Reishū (shinken) 醴酒(進献). Presentation of sweet sake (brewed the day before) to the sovereign

Pal. Himuro no sechie 氷室の節会. Presentation of ice to the sovereign; later a popular use of ice in hot weather

10th. Pal. (Gotai no) miura no sō (御体)御卜奏. Apostrophe to the sovereign for his good health in adverse weather; also XII. 10

11th. Pal. Tsukinami no matsuri 月次の祭. Prayers for the happiness of the sovereign and nation; also XII. 11

14th. Pop. Gion Matsuri 祇園祭. Gion festival, begun on 14th at Yasaka Shrine

Last day. Pal. Misoka no harae (or Ōharae) 晦日の祓え(大祓え). A very large, old ceremony of purification involving a hundred participants, including princes and ministers; also XII, last day

Pal. Hi shizume no matsuri 火鎮めの祭. Fire prevention festival by fortune tellers, delivering the court of five demons; also XII, last day

Not dated. Pal. Michiae no matsuri 道饗の祭. Festival of the crossroads to prevent demons from entering the capital; also in XII

SEVENTH MONTH

7th. Pop., though at first Pal. Shichiseki or Tanabata 七夕. For Pal., celebration of the star-lovers' annual meeting by decorating bamboo with five-colored strings in a children's celebration for progress in arts (dance, writing, etc.); later, poems were written, songs sung, etc.

13th. Pop. Mukaebi 迎火. Start of fire, opening of the bon season (greeting of the returned souls of the dead)

15th. Pop. Urabone 盂蘭盆会. Sūtra reading for dead parents, ancestors, and others not yet able to enter the Buddha's paradise

Pop. Ikimitama 生き御霊. Begun earlier, this is the proper day when children give living parents gifts: see preceding

Pop. Daimonji no hi and Bon Okuri 大文字の火, 盆送リ. Originally a religious rite, this involves burning a fire on fuel laid out to form the character great, 大; end of bon season

Moveable. In first half of month, Risshū 立秋, Beginning of Autumn

EIGHTH MONTH

1st. Mil. Hassaku 八朔. Harvest festival; for Edo bakufu a celebration of Tokugawa Ieyasu's entering Edo as shogun on this day; retainers celebrated with the shogun, wearing white outer garments; the clothing part of the observance was later taken up by Yoshiwara geisha

Pal. Obanagayu 尾花粥. Taking of gruel flavored with charred pampas grass plumes to ward off contagious disease

11th. Pal. Kōjō 定考. (Note reverse order of the characters); ceremony for promotion of lower-ranking male officials

Pal. Akinojimoku 秋の除目. Promotion, assignment of Kyoto and court officials, not provincial (see I. 11)

(Meigetsu 名月. Harvest moon viewing)

15th. Pop. Iwashimizu (Hachiman) Hōjōe 石清水(八幡)放生会. Freeing of living fish and birds, with prayers for sovereign or shogun; especially common at Hachiman shrines

Moveable. Mil. Sekiten. See II, moveable.

NINTH MONTH

3rd. Pal. Gotō. As on III. 3.

Pal. Fukanden no sō 不堪田奏. Ministers report to sovereign on farming areas deserving tax relief because of drought or floods

8th. Pal. Kise (no) wata (kenjō) 着せ（の）綿（献上）. Chrysanthemum petals were covered with cotton, after which the material with transferred fragrance was used to wipe the face

9th. Pal. Chōyō no sekku 重陽の節供. Presentation of *waka* to the sovereign, in early times involving chrysanthemum-flavored sake (see preceding)
  Com. A counterpart of the preceding that simply involved eating chestnut-flavored rice

11th. Pal. Ise reihei 伊勢例幣. Sovereign sends ritual gifts to Ise shrines

13th. (Nochi no tsuki 後の月. Later full moon [see VIII. 15]; beans and chestnuts eaten; therefore also kurimeigetsu 栗名月)

16th–17th. Pal. Kanname no matsuri 神嘗祭. Sovereign's gifts presented at Ise Outer Shrine on 16th, Inner on 17th

17th. Pop. Taishi no kō, as on V. 17

TENTH MONTH

1st. Pal. Mōtō no shun 孟冬の旬. Recognition of winter
  Pal. later Pop. Koromogae 更衣. Change to winter clothing

5th. Pal. Iba (or yuba) hajime 射場（弓場）始め. Archery celebration

10th. Pop. Yuimae 維摩会. Celebration associated with the *Yuimakyō* (see Part Six M); this Hossō rite is one of the oldest Buddhist celebrations in Japan

15th. Pal. Kagen no shūgi 下元の祝儀. Celebration of Taoism.

17th. Pop. Taishikō, as on V. 17

20th. Merchants. Hatsuka Ebisu 二十日戎. Celebrations by merchants, honoring the divinity Ebisu

21st. Pal. Ōutadokoro Hajime 大歌所始め. Opening of Bureau of Traditional Songs to prepare songs and dances for approaching holidays; closed I. 16

Moveable. Pop. Inokomochi 亥の子餅. Glutinous rice, eaten First Day of the Boar

ELEVENTH MONTH

1st. Pal. Imbi no gohan, as on VI. 1
  Pal. Goryaku no sō 御暦の奏. Presentation to the sovereign by the Court Chronologer (koyomi hakase) of the following year's calendar

Moveable. First Day of the Hare. Pop. Ainame (also aiinbe, ainie) no matsuri 相嘗祭. Twelve days before the next observance below, an offering of new grains to the divinities of seventy-one shrines
  Second Day of the Hare. Pal. Niiname no matsuri (also, shinjōsai) 新嘗祭. Ceremony of presenting the sovereign with the new grains
  Second Day of the Dragon. Pal. Toyo no akari no sechie 豊（の）明節会. Feast provided by the sovereign to court, celebrating the new grain

Pop. Third Day of the Cock. Kamo no rinji matsuri 賀茂の臨時祭. Lesser Kamo festival. See IV.

(Kan no iri no hi 寒の入リの日. Official beginning of cold weather)

In first half of month, Tōji 冬至, Beginning of Winter

TWELFTH MONTH

1st. Pal. Imbi no gohan, Agamono, as on VI. 1

8th. Com. Harikuyō, as on II. 8

10th. Pal. Miura no sō, as on VI. 10

11th. Pal. Tsukinami no matsuri, as on VI. 11

13th. Com. Susuharai 煤払い. A great house-cleaning, celebrating safe conduct through the year (Edo period)

19th. Pop. Obutsumyō 御仏名. At a great throng of priests, the names of 13,000 Buddhas of the past, present, and future were read, with confession of misdeeds and prayers for blessing

30th. Pal. Misoka no harae, Hishizume no matsuri, as on VI. 30

Pal. Tsuina 追儺. Popular versions developed later. One of the official retainers (toneri) dressed like an ogre (oni), wearing only an ogre mask and a loincloth, went about to the four gates of court. Accompanied by twenty younger retainers (shōna), the chief (toneri) of the retainers (taina) put on a golden mask with four eyes and held a halberd and shield in pursuit of the ogre. Courtiers of the fifth grade and up joined, shooting reed arrows from peachwood bows

Moveable. Michiae no matsuri, as above, VI, moveable

2nd auspicious day of month. Pal. Nosaki no tsukai 荷前の使. Donation carried by a messenger on behalf of the sovereign with first ears of new grain to the graves of ten former sovereigns and relatives chosen by the sovereign for his sense of close connection

Pop. Toshi no ichi 年の市. Large market sales for New Year's feasting

Whole month. (Seibo 歳暮. Close of the year)

Later in month. Com. Toshiwasure 年忘れ. Feast to bid the year farewell, with relatives, friends, and servants

PART EIGHT Geography, Maps, Poetic Place Names

A name or title preceded by an asterisk designates an entry in Part Three. Italicized words, other than titles, will be found in Part Four.

Given the nature of this part, we violate convention and supply macrons, even for such familiar place names as Kyōto and Ōsaka.

A. GENERAL DESCRIPTION

From ancient times the country has been known by various names. The present standard names, Nihon or Nippon 日本, are also standard in classical times: cf. *Nihon Shoki*. There have been numerous other names that appear with some frequency in literature. The element Wa 和 is used still, although not the other Wa 倭 (Chinese Wo) used by Chinese and Koreans in early times. Among those most often met with there is Yamato 大和, Ōyashima 大八島 or simply Yashima 八島, along with (Toyo) Ashihara or Ashiwara (no kuni) (豊) 葦原 (の国), and Honchō 本朝. All these names are, of course, far more evocative to Japanese than the non-Japanese "Japan." To them today, the frequent designation in writing is waga kuni 我(わが)国, "my country" or "our country." In modern times, and until the end of World War II, Japan followed the British example and designated itself as the Great(er) Japanese Empire, or Dai Nippon (Nihon) Teikoku 大日本帝国. Because this designation is anachronistic for the entire classical period, we have not used the words "emperor" or "empress" in describing the sovereign and consort.

The origins of the Japanese people are uncertain, and since this companion deals with historical times, it is not the place to represent various hypotheses based on linguistic, archaeological, religious, and other evidence. By the Yamato period, a hegemonous people was settled in the general area of modern Nara, with the capital being shifted from time to time in the area, to the modern Ōsaka area, to beside Lake Biwa, and at last to Kyōto. Indigenous peoples were gradually absorbed or pushed ever farther to the east and north.

Today the nation of Japan occupies an archipelago consisting of four main islands—from the north, Hokkaidō; the main island, Honshū; the smallest of the four, Shikoku; and the largish island to the southwest, Kyūshū (see

Section B). In the late twentieth century, the run of islands formerly known to modern Japanese as the Ryūkyū shotō 琉球諸島 became a prefecture, Okinawa Ken 沖縄県 (see Section I). In ancient times the name was Agonawa 阿児奈波 or Nantō 南島. In the fifteenth century, both Japan and China laid claims to the islands, but by the seventeenth the Kyūshū Shimazu daimate had incorporated it. Much of the north of Japan was only vaguely known for many centuries. The spread of literary and related cultural pursuits during classical times is, then, one primarily of development in the Nara or Yamato area, from there to the Kyōto area, then in Kamakura, thereafter in *kamigata*, and at last with Edo as the center, as its present name of "eastern capital"—Tōkyō—well shows. There were numerous other centers of artistic activity, especially for pottery; and during the Edo period wealthier daimates such as the Maeda centered in modern Kanazawa often became important cultural centers.

The land of these islands is a highly mountainous one, with active volcanoes, earthquakes, and hot springs. The total area of the four main islands, which extend about 2,000 km. (1250 mi.) northeast to southwest, is not large, only about 370,000 sq. km. (ca. 143,000 sq. mi.), but the highly irregular coastline is of great length, ca. 28,800 km. (17,000 mi.). There are numerous small islands lying off the four main ones, of which the most important ones (see Sections B and C) are Sado off the coast of the old province of Echigo or modern Niigata prefecture; Oki, off the coast of old Izumo or modern Shimane; Awaji, lying between Honshū and northeastern Shikoku; and Tsushima, lying north of Kyūshū.

All but innumerable mountains rise to view, and rivers flow down between them to the seas about the islands (see Section J). Given the animistic features of Shintō, various geographical features, particularly mountains and hills, were thought to represent or be the abode of divinities (kami 神). With the advent of Buddhism, temples were associated with mountains or hills. Of many such situations, the most famous are unquestionably Kōya(san) and Hiei(zan), the former situated in the northern part of former Kii province, modern Wakayama, and the latter to the north of Kyōto (again, see Sections B and C). The Yamato homeland is of gentler topography than many other areas, and both in it as well as other districts the natural features of the land were often celebrated in poetry, becoming poetic places (*utamakura*) and famous sites (meisho) for visiting (see Section K).

The highest peak in Japan, as also the most beautiful and famous is Fuji(san), whose conical shape rises some 3775 m. (12,400 feet) among surrounding mountains and volcanic lakes west of Tōkyō. Another particularly handsome mountain is 阿蘇 (山) Aso(san) which is not particularly high—only 1592 m. (5,225 feet) above sea level—but whose top has a lovely and large lake in its crater, extending in length 19.2 km (12 mi.). The largest lake in Japan lies to the east and north of Kyōto: Biwako 琵琶湖, famous for its eight views or scenes, Ōmi hakkei 近江八景. Other sites famous for their beauty include Matsushima 松島, an island or islands lying off the coast of modern Sendai city, which was long thought the most beautiful island of Japan. Another famous island, Itsukushima 厳島, better known today as Miyajima 宮島, lies off the coast of the city of

Hiroshima. Among the most celebrated shorelines there are Amanohashidate 天橋立 in present Kyōto Prefecture (fu) 京都府 and Kisagata 象潟, on the Japan Sea side to the north in old Dewa Province, modern Akita Prefecture.

As in all countries, the nature of the land has determined diet and agriculture. Fish were taken from the seas, lakes, rivers, and ponds. Sea plants and freshwater plants also were staples of diet. The arable land area has always been small, at most about one-sixth of the area of the islands, even as constant efforts were made to increase tillable areas by drainage, irrigation, and other means. The prized grain has been rice, where possible grown in paddies, and in some dry fields. In classical times, however, dry areas were normally used for legumes, millet, and deccan, along with various vegetable plants. Numerous plants, edible or ornamental, were introduced at various times from the continent. These include soya beans, tea, varieties of plum, chrysanthemums, and species of peonies.

Besides such agricultural resources, forests, woods, bamboo groves, reeds, rushes, and clay have furnished Japanese with materials for buildings and many varieties of implements. The country is not devoid of minerals—including copper and tin, iron, gold, silver, and coal. But the country is also not rich in these resources. For most purposes it is fair to say that the people, and therefore the culture they created, have exploited what grew naturally upon the slopes and mountains—trees and plants—or could be cultivated by human effort in lower lands.

The fauna of Japan is numerous and varied, but Japanese attitudes toward it have varied from poetic celebration of the creatures' existence and habits to ambiguous responses to the killing and eating of them, fish being the major exception. The blood associations of killing animals, and contact with death, were sources of pollution to the Shintō view, and required lustration. The great agent of purification was water, with the addition of certain sacred plants such as the sakaki. Buddhism, with its prohibitions of taking the life of living things, strengthened in certain ways Shintō ideas of pollution. Human cremation, slaughter of animals, and tanning were all associated with death, naturally enough, and were activities relegated to outcast groups known by various names over the centuries.

The use of the land and its resources of course came to involve government, social functions or classes, and conceptions of territorial boundaries. These involved, as in other societies, historically altering rules of property and commons. For governmental purposes various social and geographical units were constituted. In what follows only the large units are considered. These are the provinces or kuni 国 of classical Japan (Sections B and C, Figs. 8-1 and 8-2) and the prefectures of contemporary Japan (Section I). The boundaries of these areas were often vague, and sometimes changed to marked extent during classical times. In Figures 8-1 and 8-2, the islands are shown divided into provinces. Figure 8-1 depicts the divisions in early times, although it must be understood that the more remote east and north were then but dimly conceived. Figure 8-2 shows, by contrast, much better defined provinces which, by the Edo period, were carefully delineated. Various barriers or checkpoints were set up to guard the home regions early on and to control movement of people later. Of the many such, the most important for poetry include Shirakawa no Seki 白河の関, made famous by *Nōin and *Matsuo Bashō as a distant point (northeast of Nikkō) beyond which lay remote areas (see Section K). The modern distinction between Kantō 関東, or east of the barriers, and Kansai 関西, or west of the barriers, involves essentially a division among those prefectures lying to the east or west of three ancient barriers such as Suzuka no Seki, which was situated in Ise, what is now Mie Prefecture—although the distinction dates from the Kamakura period and other distinctions exist earlier. The regional divisions given in various contexts for Figures 8-2, 8-3, and elsewhere are selections from a few that have some degree of currency.

The sections following show provinces distinguished in classical times, modern prefectures, and other details. In several instances the maps have numbered provinces (or prefectures) accompanied by two lists keyed to numbers, first in numerical and then in alphabetical order.

B. The Old Provinces in Early Times

Because the geography of Japan was not divisible by scientific measures in classical times, and because more remote parts were but dimly known, no map can adequately represent the conceptions held. In addition, various changes were introduced from time to time as knowledge became more detailed or as political events altered boundaries. This and the next section offer two approximations. In this section, a sketch is offered of the provinces more or less as they were conceived, and named, at about the Nara period. The next section deals with the better-known and delineated provinces in later times.

Following Japanese custom, the listing includes—both in numbering and alphabetically—the islands of Awaji, Iki, Oki, Sado, and Tsushima.

Numbered List of Provinces in Figure 8–1

1. Michinoku (Mutsu) 陸奥
2. Dewa 出羽
3. Shimotsuke 下野
4. Hitachi 常陸
5. Shimōsa 下総
6. Kazusa 上総
7. Awa (1) 安房
8. Musashi 武蔵
9. Kōzuke 上野
10. Sado Isl. 佐渡島
11. Echigo 越後
12. Etchū 越中
13. Hida 飛驒
14. Mino 美濃
15. Shinano 信濃
16. Kai 甲斐
17. Sagami 相模

18. Izu 伊豆
19. Suruga 駿河
20. Tōtōmi 遠江
21. Mikawa 三河
22. Owari 尾張
23. Noto 能登
24. Kaga 加賀
25. Echizen 越前
26. Ōmi 近江
27. Yamashiro 山城
28. Iga 伊賀
29. Ise 伊勢
30. Shima 志摩
31. Yamato 大和
32. Kii 紀伊
33. Wakasa 若狭
34. Tango 丹後

35. Tamba 丹波
36. Settsu 摂津
37. Kawachi 河内
38. Tajima 但馬
39. Harima 播磨
40. Awaji Isl. 淡路島
41. Inaba 因幡
42. Mimasaka 美作
43. Hōki 伯耆
44. Bizen 備前
45. Bitchū 備中
46. Bingo 備後
47. Oki Isl. 隠岐島
48. Izumo 出雲
49. Iwami 石見
50. Aki 安芸
51. Suō 周防

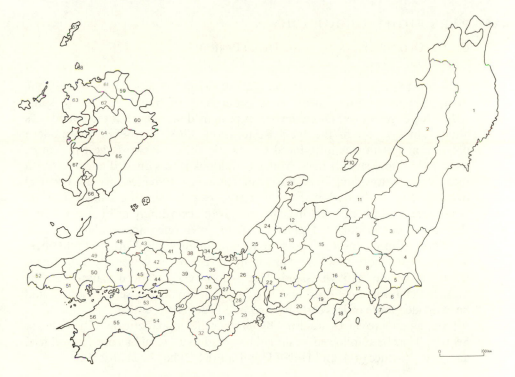

FIGURE 8-1. The Old Provinces in Early Times

52. Nagato　長門	58. Iki Isl.　壱岐	63. Hizen　肥前
53. Sanuki　讃岐	59. Buzen　豊前	64. Higo　肥後
54. Awa (2)　阿波	60. Bungo　豊後	65. Hyūga　日向
55. Tosa　土佐	61. Chikuzen　筑前	66. Ōsumi　大隅
56. Iyo　伊予	62. Chikugo　筑後	67. Satsuma　薩摩
57. Tsushima Isl.　対馬		

Alphabetical List of Provinces in Figure 8-1

Aki 49	Higo 63	Kii 32	Satsuma 66
Awa (1) 7	Hitachi 4	Kōzuke 9	Settsu 36
Awa (2) 53	Hizen 62	Michinoku (Mutsu) 1	Shima 30
Awaji Isl. 40	Hōki 43	Mikawa 21	Shimōsa 5
Bingo 45	Hyūga 65	Mimasaka 42	Shimotsuke 3
Bitchū 44	Iga 28	Mino 14	Shinano 15
Bizen 43	Iki Isl. 58	Musashi 8	Suō 50
Bungo 59	Inaba 41	Mutsu, see Michinoku	Suruga 19
Buzen 58	Ise 29	Nagato 51	Tajima 38
Chikugo 61	Iwami 49	Noto 23	Tamba 35
Chikuzen 60	Iyo 55	Oki 46	Tango 34
Dewa 2	Izu 18	Ōmi 26	Tosa 54
Echigo 11	Izumo 47	Ōsumi 65	Tōtōmi 20
Echizen 25	Kaga 24	Owari 22	Tsushima Isl. 56
Etchū 12	Kai 16	Sado Isl. 10	Wakasa 33
Harima 39	Kawachi 37	Sagami 17	Yamashiro 27
Hida 13	Kazusa 6	Sanuki 52	Yamato 31

C. THE OLD PROVINCES FROM THE HEIAN PERIOD TO THE EDO PERIOD

During the millennium from the ninth through the nineteenth century the many changes in government, society, and sites of population led to some redrawing of provinces. Often the names remained the same but the boundaries altered. In the year of the Meiji Restoration, 1868, but before the modern prefectural system was introduced (see Section D), the two largest provinces were divided into smaller ones. Mutsu (Michinoku) was divided north to south into five provinces, and Dewa into two. These new provinces are not classical ones, strictly speaking, but modern references often use the names. The old boundaries and the new subdivisions are given accordingly in Figure 8-3 after the proper delineation in Figure 8-2. Also, later references include the late subdivisions in parentheses, both to accommodate typical modern references and to locate more precisely what is in Mutsu or in Dewa. By Edo times, Okinawa, or the Ryūkyū Islands (see Section G) had been claimed by the Shimazu clan for some time, and Ezo (modern Hokkaidō, see Section F) had been divided more or less certainly and had been partly settled.

Once again, provinces are listed by number and alphabetically. The order of Section B has been followed. It should be noted that Izumi has been introduced as a new province (41), and Hōki (43 in Figure 8-1) has been absorbed.

Numbered List of Provinces in Figure 8-2

1. Mutsu (Michinoku) 陸奥	24. Kaga 加賀	47. Hōki 伯耆
2. Dewa 出羽	25. Echizen 越前	48. Izumo 出雲
3. Shimotsuke 下野	26. Ōmi 近江	49. Iwami 石見
4. Hitachi 常陸	27. Yamashiro 山城	50. Aki 安芸
5. Shimōsa 下総	28. Iga 伊賀	51. Suō 周防
6. Kazusa 上総	29. Ise 伊勢	52. Nagato 長門
7. Awa (1) 安房	30. Shima 志摩	53. Sanuki 讃岐
8. Musashi 武蔵	31. Yamato 大和	54. Awa (2) 阿波
9. Kōzuke 上野	32. Kii 紀伊	55. Tosa 土佐
10. Sado Isl. 佐渡島	33. Wakasa 若狭	56. Iyo 伊予
11. Echigo 越後	34. Tango 丹後	57. Tsushima Isl. 対馬
12. Etchū 越中	35. Tamba 丹波	58. Iki Isl. 壱岐島
13. Hida 飛驒	36. Settsu 摂津	59. Buzen 豊前
14. Mino 美濃	37. Kawachi 河内	60. Bungo 豊後
15. Shinano 信濃	38. Tajima 但馬	61. Chikuzen 筑前
16. Kai 甲斐	39. Harima 播磨	62. Chikugo 筑後
17. Sagami 相模	40. Awaji Isl. 淡路島	63. Hizen 肥前
18. Izu 伊豆	41. Izumi 和泉	64. Higo 肥後
19. Suruga 駿河	42. Inaba 因幡	65. Hyūga 日向
20. Tōtōmi 遠江	43. Mimasaka 美作	66. Ōsumi 大隅
21. Mikawa 三河	44. Bizen 備前	67. Satsuma 薩摩
22. Owari 尾張	45. Bitchū 備中	68. Oki Isl. 隠岐島
23. Noto 能登	46. Bingo 備後	

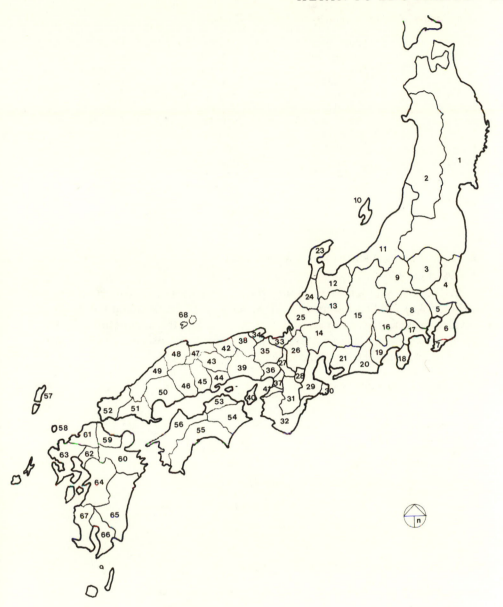

FIGURE 8-2. Provinces, Heian to Edo Times

Alphabetical List of Provinces in Figure 8-2

Aki 50	Bitchū 45	Chikuzen 61	Harima 39
Awa (1) 7	Bizen 44	Dewa 2	Hida 13
Awa (2) 54	Bungo 60	Echigo 11	Higo 64
Awaji Isl. 40	Buzen 59	Echizen 25	Hitachi 4
Bingo 46	Chikugo 62	Etchū 12	Hizen 63

Alphabetical List of Provinces in Figure 8-2 (con't)

Hōki 47	Kawachi 37	Oki Isl. 68	Shinano 15
Hyūga 65	Kazusa 36	Ōmi 26	Suō 51
Iga 28	Kii 32	Ōsumi 66	Suruga 19
Iki Isl. 58	Kōzuke 9	Owari 22	Tajima 38
Inaba 42	Michinoku, see Mutsu	Sado Isl. 10	Tamba 35
Ise 29	Mikawa 21	Sagami 17	Tango 34
Iwami 48	Mimasaka 43	Sanuki 53	Tosa 55
Iyo 56	Mino 14	Satsuma 67	Tōtōmi 20
Izu 18	Musashi 8	Settsu 36	Tsushima Isl. 57
Izumi 41	Mutsu (Michinoku) 1	Shima 30	Wakasa 33
Izumo 48	Nagato 52	Shimōsa 5	Yamashiro 27
Kaga 24	Noto 23	Shimotsuke 3	Yamato 31
Kai 16			

D. EARLY MEIJI SUBDIVISIONS OF MUTSU AND DEWA PROVINCES

In the first year of Meiji, 1868, the large northern provinces of Mutsu (Michinoku) and Dewa were divided. Strictly speaking, the names of the newly divided provinces are not classical. But they predate the designation of prefectures and are often used in writing about classical Japan in order to locate places more exactly than the very large older provinces allowed.

Numbered Listing of Early Divisions of Mutsu and Dewa

Mutsu 陸奥	4. Rikuzen 陸前	Dewa 出羽
1. Mutsu 陸奥	5. Iwaki 磐城	7. Ugo 羽後
2. Rikuchū (1) 陸中	6. Iwashiro 石代	8. Uzen 羽前
3. Rikuchū (2)		

Alphabetical Listing of Early Divisions of Mutsu and Dewa

Iwaki 5	Mutsu 1	Rikuchū (2) 3	Ugo 7
Iwashiro 6	Rikuchū (1) 2	Rikuzen 4	Uzen 8

E. DISTRICT DIVISIONS IN CLASSICAL TIMES

As the map shows, from Heian times the country was commonly thought of as divided into districts, or -dō 道.

District Divisions, with Their Provinces and Major Islands

1. Tōsandō 東山道. Eastern Mountain District
   Mutsu, Dewa, Shimotsuke, Kōzuke, Shinano, Hida, Mino, Ōmi
2. Hokurikudō北陸道. Northern Land District
   Wakasa, Echizen, Kaga, Noto, Etchū, Echigo, Sado Isl.

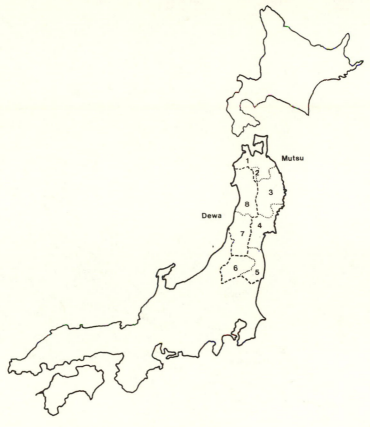

FIGURE 8-3. Early Meiji Divisions of Mutsu and Dewa

3. Tōkaidō　東海道. Eastern Sea District
　　Hitachi, Shimōsa, Kazusa, Awa (1), Musashi, Sagami, Izu, Kai, Suruga,
　　Tōtōmi, Mikawa, Owari, Iga, Ise, Shima
4. Kinai　畿内. Home Provinces; Capital area
　　Yamashiro, Settsu, Kawachi, Yamato, (Izumi)
5. San'indō　山陰道. Transmountain District
　　Tamba, Tango, Tajima, Inaba, (Hōki), Izumo, Iwami, Oki Isl.
6. San'yōdō　山陽道. Cismountain District
　　Harima, Mimasaka, Bizen, Bitchū, Bingo, Aki, Suō, Nagato
7. Nankaidō　南海道. Southern Sea District
　　Kii, Awaji Isl., Sanuki, Awa (2), Tosa, Iyo
8. Saikaidō　西海道. Western Sea District
　　Tsushima Isl., Iki Isl., Chikuzen, Chikugo, Buzen, Bungo, Hizen, Higo,
　　Hyūga, Ōsumi, Satsuma

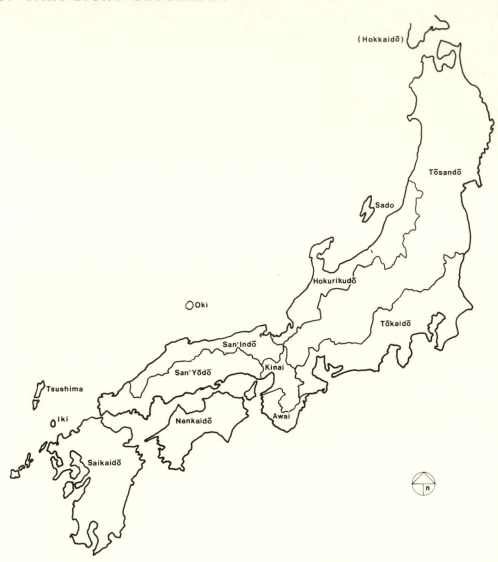

FIGURE 8-4. The Eight Districts

Concepts of such districts have remained into modern times, although often with different boundaries drawn.

It will be observed that all except the Kinai are "roads" 道, reflecting the sense of travel, *tabi*, as something away from the capital at Nara or Kyoto, or between two other points. For the other, modern district or "road," Hokkaidō, and for the southwestern islands off Kyūshū, see the following sections.

F. Hokkaidō

In addition to the divisions noted in the preceding section for the three most populated of the main islands, Japan had in classical times a dimly conceived northernmost island of good size. Its present name, Hokkaidō, was given it early in the modern period (1869). Through most of classical times it was usually referred to as Ezo 蝦夷, much like Barbary, the Barbarian Land. As knowledge grew—and no doubt as Japanese began to develop the island—other, nicer names were employed: Hokushū 北州, Jisshūjima 十州島. The second of these names reflects the fact that the island became divided into ten provinces. Activity involving Hokkaidō really began with exploration during the Muromachi period, and during the Edo period the island, or at least its southwestern reaches, became a Matsumae fief. The fortifications at Hakodate long seemed important, but more to guard the Tsugaru Strait between Hokkaidō and Honshū, more to preserve Honshū, than to protect Hokkaidō itself. Sapporo has come to outrival all other cities in Hokkaidō, perhaps because of its location on the Ishikari Plain, where expansion has been easier than elsewhere on the island.

The Ten Old Provinces of Hokkaidō

1. Kitami 北見   4. Shiribeshi 後志   6. Iburi 胆振   8. Tokachi 十勝
2. Teshio 天塩   5. Ojima 渡島   7. Hidaka 日高   9. Kushiro 釧路
3. Ishikari 石狩   10. Nemuro 根室

Alphabetical Listing

Hidaka 7   Kitami 1   Nemuro 10   Shiribeshi 4
Iburi 6   Kushiro 9   Ojima 5   Teshio 2
Ishikari 3   Tokachi 8

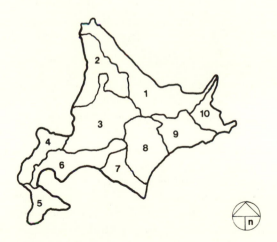

Figure 8-5. Hokkaidō

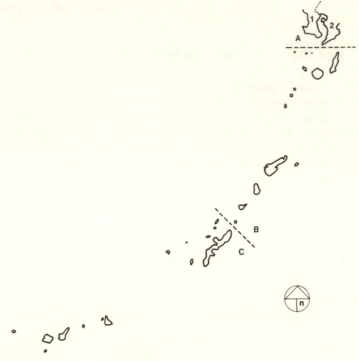

FIGURE 8-6. The Southwestern Islands

G. The Southwestern Islands

To the southwest of Kyūshū, there stretches a chain of islands sometimes referred to as Seinan Shotō 西南諸島, or Nansei Shotō 南西諸島. These include two chains formerly distinguished, Ōsumi—as if part of the province of Ōsumi; and the Ryūkyū chain. These islands now make up Okinawa Prefecture.

A. The southern tip of Kyūshū
 1. Satsuma Province 薩摩
 2. Ōsumi Province 大隅

B. Ōsumi Islands 大隅諸島

C. Ryūkyū Islands 琉球諸島

H. Sinified -Shū Names for Provinces

Many of the provinces were familiarly referred to by names made up of the Sinified pronounciations of their first or, sometimes, their second character, to which shū 州 was added. Since these names are often met with in reading and even in conversation today, they are given here in two lists. The first alphabetizes the Sinified -shū names, followed by the province names. The second gives the names of provinces in alphabetical order followed by the -shū names. Familiar as is Shinshū for old Shinano or modern Nagano prefecture, there are numerous other names for provinces than those given here. They are commonly variants, usually longer for earlier versions and shorter for later. Many of these other names are place names for districts: for example, Kōfu 甲府, for a part of Kai Province and of modern Yamanashi Prefecture. Since whole books exist for Japanese place names, we must be content with specifying the most standard variants for the provincial names. Such specifications are also given for early Meiji subdivisions of Mutsu and Dewa.

Alphabetical List of Sinified -Shū Names for Provinces

Ashū 阿州	Awa (2)	Nōshū (1) 濃州	Mino
Banshū (1) 播州	Harima	Nōshū (2) 能州	Noto
Banshū (2) 磐州	Iwaki	Ōshū 奥州	Michinoku
Bishū 尾州	Owari	Sakushū 作州	Mimasaka
Bōshū (1) 房州	Awa (1)	Sanshū (1) 三州	Mikawa
Bōshū (2) 防州	Suō	Sanshū (2) 讃州	Sanuki
Bushū 武州	Musashi	Sashū 佐州	Sado Isl.
Chōshū 長州	Nagato	Sasshū 薩州	Satsuma
Doshū 土州	Tosa	Seishū 勢州	Ise
Enshū 遠州	Tōtōmi	Sekishū 石州	Iwami
Gashū 賀州	Iga	Senshū 泉州	Izumi
Geishū 芸州	Aki	Sesshū 摂州	Settsu
Gōshū 江州	Ōmi	Shishū 志州	Shima
Hakushū 伯州	Hōki	Shinshū 信州	Shinano
Hishū 飛州	Hida	Sōshū 相州	Sagami
Inshū 因州	Inaba	Taishū 対州	Tsushima
Ishū (1) 伊州	Iga	Tanshū 淡州	Awaji Isl.
Ishū (2) 壱州	Iki Isl.	Unshū 雲州	Izumo
Jōshū 上州	Kōzuke	Ushū 羽州	Dewa
Jakushū 若州	Wakasa	Washū 和州	Yamato
Kashū (1) 加州	Kaga	Yashū 野州	Shimotsuke
Kashū (2) 河州	Kawachi	Yoshū 予州	Iyo
Kishū 紀州	Kii	Zushū 豆州	Izu
Kōshū 甲州	Kai		

Alphabetical List of Provinces with Their Sinified -Shū Names
(When They Exist)

Aki	Geishū	Michinoku	Ōshū
Awa (1)	Bōshū	Mikawa	Sanshū
Awa (2)	Ashū	Mimasaka	Sakushū
Awaji Isl.	Tanshū	Mino	Nōshū
Dewa	Ushū	Musashi	Bushū
Harima	Banshū	Nagato	Chōshū
Hida	Hishū	Noto	Nōshū
Hōki	Hakushū	Ōmi	Gōshū
Iga	Ishū (1), Gashū	Owari	Bishū
Iki Isl.	Ishū (2)	Sado Isl.	Sashū
Inaba	Inshū	Sagami	Sōshū
Ise	Seishū	Sanuki	Sanshū
Iwaki	Banshū	Satsuma	Sasshū
Iwami	Sekishū	Settsu	Sesshū
Iyo	Yoshū	Shima	Shishū
Izu	Zushū	Shimotsuke	Yashū
Izumi	Senshū	Shinano	Shinshū
Izumo	Unshū	Suō	Bōshū
Kaga	Kashū (1)	Tosa	Doshū
Kai	Kōshū	Tōtōmi	Enshū
Kawachi	Kashū (2)	Tsushima	Taishū
Kii	Kishū	Wakasa	Jakushū
Kōzuke	Jōshū	Yamato	Washū

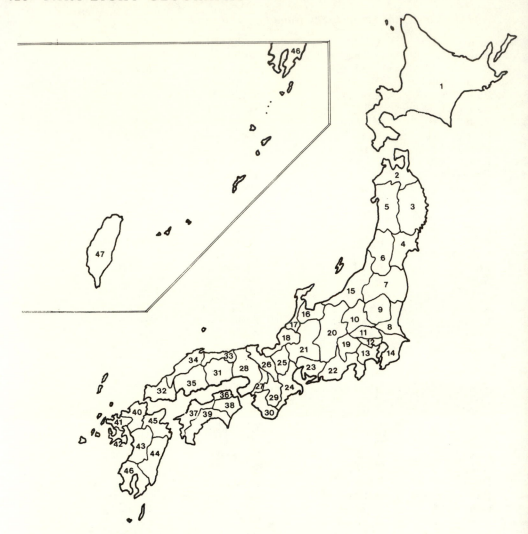

FIGURE 8-7. Modern Prefectures

I. MODERN PREFECTURES

The map and designations are given partly for the sake of completeness, and partly to make possible the locations of classical provinces in works specifying modern names. Modern prefectures are designated ken 県, with three exceptions for metropolitan prefectures. For one of these, Tōkyō, the designation is to 都; for Ōsaka and Kyōto, the designation is fu 府 (cf. Section C, Fig. 8-2).

Prefectures as Numbered on the Map (Ken unless otherwise indicated)

1. Hokkaidō　北海道
Tōhoku Region　東北地方
2. Aomori　青森
3. Iwate　岩手
4. Miyagi　宮城
5. Akita　秋田
6. Yamagata　山形
7. Fukushima　福島
Kantō Region　関東地方
8. Ibaragi　茨城
9. Tochigi　栃木
10. Gumma　群馬
11. Saitama　埼玉
12. Tōkyō To　東京都
13. Kanagawa　神奈川
14. Chiba　千葉
Chūbu Area　中部地方
15. Niigata　新潟
16. Toyama　富山
17. Ishikawa　石川
18. Fukui　福井
19. Yamanashi　山梨
20. Nagano　長野
21. Gifu　岐阜
22. Shizuoka　静岡
23. Aichi　愛知
Kinki Area　返畿地方
24. Mie　三重

25. Shiga　滋賀
26. Kyōto Fu　京都府
27. Ōsaka Fu　大阪府
28. Hyōgo　兵庫
29. Nara　奈良
30. Wakayama　和歌山
Chūgoku Region　中国地方
31. Okayama　岡山
32. Yamaguchi　山口
33. Tottori　鳥取
34. Shimane　島根
35. Hiroshima　広島
Shikoku　四国
36. Kagawa　香川
37. Ehime　愛媛
38. Tokushima　徳島
39. Kōchi　高知
Kyūshū　九州
40. Fukuoka　福岡
41. Saga　佐賀
42. Nagasaki　長崎
43. Kumamoto　熊本
44. Miyazaki　宮崎
45. Ōita　大分
46. Kagoshima　鹿児島
Also
47. Okinawa　沖縄

Prefectures in Alphabetical Listing Keyed by Numbers

Aichi 23	Kagawa 36	Ōsaka Fu 27
Akita 5	Kagoshima 46	Saga 41
Aomori 2	Kanagawa 13	Saitama 11
Chiba 14	Kōchi 39	Shiga 25
Ehime 37	Kumamoto 43	Shimane 34
Fukui 18	Kyōto Fu 26	Shizuoka 22
Fukuoka 40	Mie 24	Tochigi 9
Fukushima 7	Miyagi 4	Tokushima 38
Gifu 21	Miyazaki 44	Tōkyō To 12
Gumma 10	Nagano 20	Tottori 33
Hiroshima 35	Nagasaki 42	Toyama 16
Hokkaidō 1	Nara 29	Wakayama 30
Hyōgo 28	Niigata 15	Yamagata 6
Ibaragi 8	Ōita 45	Yamaguchi 32
Ishikawa 17	Okayama 31	Yamanashi 19
Iwate 3	Okinawa 47	

J. Principal Mountains, Rivers, Bays, Straits

1. Mountains

Three mountains are distinguished as the Three Illustrious Mountains, mei-sanzan 名三山, and, as the alternative characters for the first shows, it is thought essentially peerless.

Fujisan　富士山, 不二山, 不尽山　(and in *Taketori Monogatari* 不死)
　　In Kai and Suruga; west of Edo.
Daisen　大山
　　In Hōki, hence its other name, Hōki Fuji.
Shirayama (Hakuzan)　白山
　　In Mino and Echizen.

Other noteworthy mountains are given alphabetically.

Asamayama　浅間山
　　In Shinano and Shimotsuke.
Asosan　阿蘇山
　　In Buzen and Higo.
Bandaisan　磐梯山
　　In Mutsu (Iwashiro).
Hakoneyama　箱根山
　　Where Sagami, Izu, and Suruga meet.
Hieizan　比叡山
　　Northeast of Kyoto; an area dotted with temples, especially of the Tendai school.
Kōyasan　高野山
　　Northwestern Kii; with the main temples of the Shingon school.
Tateyama　立山
　　In Etchū.
Unzendake　雲仙岳
　　In Hizen.
Yarigatake　槍ケ岳
　　In Shinano and Mino.

For mountains of special importance as poetic names in poetry, see Section K.

2. Islands

From north to southwest, the four main islands are:

Hokkaidō　北海道
Honshū　本州
Shikoku　四国
Kyūshū　九州

As with the four main islands, so with those following: modern versions of names are given, although some have been given in older style in previous maps and their legends.

Amami Ōshima	奄美大島	south of Kagoshima
Awaji Shima	淡路島	west side of Ōsaka Bay
Chishima Rettō	千島列島	the Kurile Islands, north of Hokkaidō
Hachijōjima	八丈島	south of Tōkyō Bay
Iki (no) Shima	壱岐(の)島	between Kyūshū and Korea
Karafuto	樺太	Sakhalin, north of Hokkaidō
Kunashiritō	国後島	off the east coast of Hokkaidō
Ogasawara Shotō	小笠原諸島	the Bonin Islands, southeast of Honshū
Ryūkyū Rettō	琉球列島	the Ryūkyū Islands (Okinawa)
Oki (no) Shima	隠岐(の)島	in the Japan Sea
Ōshima	大島	off Tōkyō Bay
Sado(ga)shima	佐渡(が)島	in the Japan Sea
Shōdojima	小豆島	in the Inland Sea
Tanegashima	種子島	south of Kagoshima
Tsushima	対馬	between Kyūshū and Korea

3. *Bays, Modern Names*

Tōkyō Wan	東京湾	Tōkyō Bay including the Yokohama and Tōkyō harbors
Ōsaka Wan	大阪湾	Ōsaka Bay including the Kōbe and Ōsaka harbors
Ise Wan	伊勢湾	Ise Bay including Nagoya Harbor

4. *Straits, Modern Names*

Naruto Kaikyō	鳴門海峡	the entrance to Ōsaka Bay
Kammon Kaikyō	関門海峡	between Shimonoseki and Moji
Tsushima Kaikyō	対馬海峡	between Iki and Tsushima Island
Tsugaru Kaikyō	津軽海峡	between Honshū and Hokkaidō
Sōya Kaikyō	宗谷海峡	between Hokkaidō and Sakhalin
Mamiya Kaikyō	間宮海峡	between northern Sakhalin and Siberia

5. *Seas, Modern Names*

Setonaikai	瀬戸内海	the Inland Sea, between Honshū and Shikoku
Taiheiyō	太平洋	Pacific Ocean
Nihonkai	日本海	Japan Sea
Higashi Shinakai	東支那海	East China Sea
Minami Shinakai	南支那海	South China Sea
Kōkai	黄海	Yellow Sea

6. *Rivers, Classical Names, but continued in Modern Times*

Kamogawa　賀茂川, 加茂川, 鴨川

Flows south along the eastern side of Kyōto, later turning west to join other streams. See the next two rivers and Yodogawa.

Katsuragawa　桂川

Flows south along the western side of Kyōto, being the downstream name of Hozugawa 保津川 and Ōigawa 大堰川.

Takasegawa　高瀬川

Besides the larger stream of this name in northwestern Shinano, this name designates a part of the Yodogawa system. As a famous story by Mori Ōgai shows, it was the one water route directly from Kyōto to Naniwa (Ōsaka) and the sea.

Ujigawa　宇治川

Above Uji the river is called Setagawa 瀬田川, thereafter the Uji until it reaches Yodo, joining other streams and becoming Yodogawa. See the next and Section K.

Yodogawa　淀川

Issuing into the sea at Naniwa (Ōsaka), this was the principal stream for returning to the capital by water. Small-draft boats might go up the Yodo and finally to Kyōto on the Kamogawa. Larger boats, as recorded in *Ki no Tsurayuki's Tosa Nikki*, had to go up the Yodo, and take the Katsuragawa to the west side of Kyōto; passengers made the rest of the journey by ox-drawn carriage from what is now Arashiyama.

There are four principal rivers that flowed through Edo (Tōkyō):

Edogawa　江戸川

Sumidagawa　隅田川

Tamagawa　多摩川(玉川)

Arakawa　荒川

There are three principal rivers that flow from Fujisan or adjoining slopes:

Fujigawa	富士川	With Mogamigawa and Kumagawa, one of the three fastest currents
Tenryūgawa	天竜川	Flows more westerly, toward Owari (Nagoya)
Ōigawa	大井川	Takes a course like the preceding

Eight other important rivers are often met with in literature:

Sagamigawa　相模川

Of course in Sagami, west of Edo.

Tonegawa　利根川

A long river, originating in Echigo, winding through provinces north and east of Edo, at last entering the Pacific northeast of Edo; of great importance for drinking water, irrigation, and transport.

Kisogawa　木曽川

Of the larger rivers, one of the most famous for beauty; originating in

Shinano, it flowed into Isewan at Owari (Nagoya); from older times it was a principal connection between portions of the Hokurikudō, Tosandō, and western Tōkaidō (Section E).

Nagaragawa　長良川

In southern Mino, near Owari (Nagoya), it is famous for its beauty and cormorant fishing; originating in Echizen, it flows east and south through Hida, southwest through Mino, and empties into Isewan in Ise, west of Owari.

Kitakamigawa　北上川

The principal river in Mutsu, it takes an almost directly southerly course from its origins in Rikuchū to Rikuzen, where it empties into the Pacific northeast of modern Sendai.

Mogamigawa　最上川

The most famous of the rivers emptying into the Japan sea; although it originates in Mutsu (Iwashiro), it is the principal river of Dewa (almost wholly in Uzen); and with Fujigawa and Kumagawa has one of the three fastest currents.

Kumagawa　球磨川

Beginning in eastern Higo, it winds first south, then west, and then north to flow into the sea on the Higo coast; with Fujigawa and Mogamigawa, one of the three fastest currents.

Ishikarigawa　石狩川

The largest river in Hokkaidō, this cuts across the Ishikari plain and flows into the sea at Ishikari Bay.

For information about other rivers and topographical features important to poetry, see the following section.

K. Poetic Place Names

Utamakura 歌枕 include as one category a large number of place names or famous places, meisho 名所, and in particular places celebrated in poetry. Travel pieces, *michiyuki*, in the theater or in prose narrative might also use these words, more for associations and evocative power than for geographical specification. The appeal of specific places is a characteristic of Japanese literature in all periods, including the present, and the effect of skillful handling of such names is more readily felt than explained. Japanese recognized from early times that what could be handled well could also be made routine or mere convenience. For that reason, the stock name is utamakura, poetic pillow (cf. *makurakotoba*).

Because *waka* so often involves places praised for seasonal beauty or used to convey experience of travel or love, or for figurative purposes, almost every place name is a potential utamakura. In the end, it is quite impossible to decide the criteria for distinguishing place names *per se* from utamakura place names, as one example may show. Literature celebrates three little islands in the Ujigawa (see Section J):

Maki no Shima　槙島
Tachibana no Kojima　橘小島
Ume no Shima　梅島

All three identify islands associated with attractive trees. But the last, which has the tree (plum) thought by Heian Japanese to be most attractive of the three, is usually considered simply a place name, whereas the other two are usually accounted utamakura place names.

To codify matters so difficult in distinction, various classical critics attempted to compile lists of utamakura with some discrimination. Among the best are:

*Nōin, *Nōin Utamakura*　能因, 能因歌枕
 Anon., *Godaishū Utamakura*　五代集歌枕
*Juntoku, *Yakumo Mishō*　順徳, 八雲御抄
*Sōgi, *Meisho Hōgakushō*　宗祇, 名所方角鈔

As the second of these shows, some critics thought that proper utamakura place names required the distinction of appearing in one or more of the *chokusenshū*. But many were taken, not always accurately, from the *Man'yōshū*, and others were established in far later times.

In practice, utamakura place names were those that became famous because some poets treated them. The reason for treatment was, in turn, some special feature or features. For example, Tago no Ura 田子の浦, Tago Bay, specified not only the place (Tago) but the feature at the place (the bay). Hitachi 常陸, the name of an entire province, is correspondingly vague, but the utamakura is usually specified further, if still not very narrowly, by an addition, Hitachi no umi 常陸の海 the sea at Hitachi. Katsuragawa (see J6) differs from both of the preceding examples in that the element additionally specified might be the moon, certain flowers or trees, and certain birds. One further complication involves the use of different characters. Seta (in Ōmi province) was usually written 瀬田, but in earlier times was written 勢多 or 勢田. Since it was famous for its strategic bridge southeast of the Kyoto, the usual expression is Seta no hashi or Seta no nagahashi (given below).

The fact that a special feature made the place celebrated was a major reason for compilations of utamakura. Poets and other writers needed guidance to use the expressions properly. That Seta should be distinguished for its bridge is not surprising, in view of its importance to the safety of the capital. Yet literary principles also mattered. The bridge became, as it were, the *hon'i* of Seta. It is no accident that a *renga* poet like Sōgi, for whom hon'i and other directives mattered so much, should have produced one of the major collections of utama-kura. Such hon'i, or at least such specific associations, can be exemplified by three important utamakura place names. To mention Miyagino 宮城野 was to imply hagi, bush clover 萩. Yoshinoyama 吉野山 implied cherry blossoms. Tatsuta(gawa) 竜田(川) implied brightly colored autumnal leaves. There were obviously such colored leaves in autumn not only at Tatsuta, but in nearby Yoshinoyama and in far away Miyagino. But to speak of colored leaves at

Miyagino or cherry blossoms at Tatsuta violated decorum, the hon'i of the place. On the other hand, a given utamakura might be famous for several things. Uji, south of Kyōto, was an utamakura famous for its river, its fish weir, its bridge, and its bridge maiden (or divinity):

Ujigawa　宇治川
Uji no ajiro　宇治の網代
Uji no hashi　宇治の橋
Uji no hashihime　宇治の橋姫

Many of the oldest utamakura place names are those places celebrated in the *Man'yōshū*, the *Kojiki*, and *Nihon Shoki*. One of these is Hatsusegawa(yama) 泊瀬川(山). Syntactically identical attributives are used in expressions like "Makimuku no/Hishiro no miya wa" (*Kojiki*) and in a waka by *Saigyō, beginning "Tsu no kuni no/Naniwa no haru wa" (*Shinkokinshū*). Yet the second examples of place names are usually not considered utamakura (although Naniwae 難波江 is).

Such fine distinctions are often made, even if erroneously. One well-established utamakura place name, Tomaseyama, is nothing other than a very understandable misreading of the characters for Hatsuseyama (given above). Similar misreadings of *man'yōgana* provided the Kakureno and Kakure no yama for what should be Nabarino and Nabari no yama 隠の山.

If such difficulties abound, and they do, they also show that utamakura place names have a special resonance and a degree of canonicity. Few poets who wrote of Miyagino ever saw it. On the other hand, to this day Japanese maintain a differing conception of famous places from that of many other peoples. If one goes to a famous place such as Miyagino, the purpose is not to take it as it is at the moment, or to photograph something unusual, striking. Rather one goes in autumn if possible, and appreciates the hagi, bush clover. One chooses to go to Yoshinoyama in spring to see the cherry blossoms, or to Tatsuta to see autumnal foliage.

Given the special attributes, or hon'i, of a given place name, some skill was required for meaningful use. For a particularly amusing misuse, there is Ōmi no Kimi's poem, with its accompanying letter, in *Murasaki Shikibu's Genji Monogatari*, the "Tokonatsu" part. Ōmi no Kimi has learned without truly understanding the utamakura and other place name tags. Her poem introduces a surprising number of them, and her letter includes the utamakura, Nakoso no seki 勿来の関, which she interprets literally to mean "do not come." It is not surprising that her jumble is answered in similar coinage by an amused, more sophisticated poet. On this general matter, *Kamo no Chōmei wrote in his *Mumyōshō*, "There are well established usages for named places. Throughout the various provinces innumerable poetic places exist, but the place used in a poem should be appropriate to the general outlines (*sugata*)" of the poem. Fitness, not just introducing any old place, was required.

As already mentioned, there are various lists of utamakura place names, which mostly do not wholly agree. What follows presents only a brief sample. Others will be found in the four classical handbooks or sections mentioned, and yet other information will be found in Principal Immediate Sources at the end of this *Companion*.

Akashi　明石
　　In Harima, the shore area next to Suma, whence Hikaru Genji takes exile in the *Genji Monogatari*
Arashiyama　嵐山
　　To the west of Kyōto, a name (Storm Mountain) showing well the association of peaks with winds and storms
Ama no Kaguyama　天香具山
　　In Yamato
Arimayama　有馬山
　　In Settsu
Asajigahara　浅茅が原
　　In Naniwa (Settsu)
Asakayama　浅香山
　　In Mutsu
Asukagawa　飛鳥川
　　In Yamato, a river celebrated for its change of course and for possible play on asu- as "tomorrow"
Fukakusa no Sato　深草の里
　　Sometimes -yama 山. There is a Fukakusa in southeastern Kyōto, but the poetic usage implies a place no longer existing, its old whereabouts indistinct
Futakoyama　二子山
　　A mountain near Hakone (see Section J)
Futami no Ura　二見の浦
　　A sea, or shore, view famous for its beauty; in Ise
Fuwa no Seki(ya)　不波の関(屋)
　　A famous barrier near Ōmi in Mino, which had disappeared by later classical times, in spite of its name (played on by poets), meaning something like "indestructible"
Hakoneyama　箱根山
　　In Sagami
Hakozaki (no Matsu)　箱崎(の松)
　　In northern Kyūshū
Hamana no Hashi　浜名の橋
　　In Tōtōmi, famous as a river crossing and a place in travel accounts
Hatsusegawa (-yama) 初瀬 (or 泊瀬) 川(山)
　　In Yamato (see the preceding discussion)
Hira no Yama　比良山
　　In Ōmi
Hitachi (no Umi)　常陸(の海)
　　The sea view in Hitachi province

Ibukiyama 伊吹山
 In Ōmi
Ikagasaki 如何崎
 In Kawachi-Ōmi provinces; used for a wordplay: ikaga/how
Ikomayama 生駒山
 In Yamato
Ikuno 生野
 In Tamba
Ikuta no Mori 生田森
 In Settsu
Ishiyama 石山
 In Ōmi; famous for Heian visits from the capital to its temple, for as-
 sociations with *Murasaki Shikibu, and for such nearby attractions as
 Hotarugadani
Isuzugawa 五十鈴川
 In Ise
Kagami no Yama 鏡山
 In Ōmi; first appearance in the *Kokinshū*
Kakureno 隠野
 See the preceding discussion
Kakurenoyama 隠山
 See the preceding discussion
Kamakura 鎌倉
 In Sagami; site of the Minamoto *bakufu* and important temples, especially
 of the Rinzai Zen sect
Kaminabiyama 神名備山
 In Yamato
Kamogawa 加茂川
 Flows along the east side of Kyōto
Kasugano 春日野
 In Yamato; a field or plain that was romantic or pastoral to Heian poets
Kasugayama 春日山
 In Yamato; see the preceding
Kasumi no Tani 霞谷
 An imaginary place, thought an utamakura
Katano 交野
 In Kawachi
Katsuragawa 桂川
 See the preceding discussion and Section J
Koromogawa 衣川
 In Mutsu
Kusa no Hara 草の原
 Sometimes treated as an utamakura, it is really a *makurakotoba*, and so
 Kusa no hara
Maki no Shima 槇島

Island in the Uji River

Mika no Hara　甕(瓶)(の)原

In Yamashiro

Mikasayama　三笠山

A hill in Yamato

Mimuroyama　三室山

In Yamato

Miwayama　三輪山

In Yamato

Miyagawa　宮川

A stretch of the Kamo river in Kyōto below Shijō, famous in the Edo period as a cherry-blossom site

Miyagino　宮城野

A plain in Mutsu (Rikuzen) near modern Sendai, famous for its hagi (bush clover)

Moriyama　守山

A posting-station in Ōmi

Nabarino　隠野

Nabari Plain or Moor. See the preceding discussion

Nabariyama　隠山

See the preceding discussion

Nakoso no Seki　勿来関

Nakoso Barrier in Mutsu (Iwaki); used homophonically as a *kakekotoba*: Do not come

Narumigata　鳴海潟

Narumi Inlet in Ise Bay, Owari. Frequent in *kakekotoba*, with naru- as to become or to be, or naru mi, self become something

Natorigawa　名取川

Natori River in Mutsu (Rikuzen), famous as a site for bogwood, but chiefly used by love poets reading the characters to mean one's good name taken or lost as a love affair becomes known

Nigitazu　熟田津

In Iyo

Nio no Umi　鳰海

Another name, or a *makurakotoba*, for Lake Biwa in Ōmi

Obasuteyama　姨捨山

A mountain in Shinano where, according to legend, old women were exposed to die

Odae no Hashi　緒絶の橋

Odae Bridge was thought to be in Mutsu (Rikuzen); an imaginary place based on a misreading of the *Man'yōshū

Ogurayama　小倉山

In Yamashiro

Oiso no Mori　老蘇森

A forest in Ōmi with a well-known shrine

Ōsaka no Seki   逢坂の関

The barrier at Ōtsu in Ōmi, at the south of Lake Biwa and close to the capital. Travelers might be seen off so far or returnees welcomed there. For that reason and because of the *kana* for "ō" (written "afu," modern "au"), it became a favorite utamakura in love poetry or when meeting and parting was a concern

Ōuchiyama   大内山

The courtly mountain, that is, the court itself; also the mountain at Ninnaji in Omuro, where the cloistered sovereign Uda took residence

Sano no Watari   佐野渡

A ford in Yamato

Saoyama   佐保山

In Yamato

Sayo no Nakayama   佐夜中山

A rise in Tōtōmi famous for storms, clouds, and especially the moon, since the characters can be read "little night"

Seta no (Naga) Hashi   瀬田（長）橋

Seta Bridge at Ōtsu in Ōmi was famous for its length and was important as a strategic point east of the capital

Shiga no Ura   志賀浦

Shiga Inlet in Ōmi

Shigitatsusawa   鴫立沢

The Shigitatsu Marsh at Ōiso in Sagami

Shirakawa no Seki   白河関

The barrier at Shirakwa in Mutsu; from a poem by *Nōin it was a famous place in travel poetry, and one who went beyond it to the north was thought of as venturing far away

Sode no Ura   袖浦

This Bay of Sleeves in Dewa (Uzen) was often drawn upon by poets to tell of sleeves wet with tears of love or other grief, and its famous bay wind could be evoked to heighten sadness

Sue no Matsu(yama)   末の松（山）

The pine tree or trees (or the peak on which they stand), perhaps near Matsushima and, in any case, in Mutsu (Rikuzen). Poets used the place name to involve the idea that only some unwelcome or great change could bring waves over the rise or its pines. Love poets adapted the idea for accusations of infidelity, as in the *Kokinshū. *Murasaki Shikibu followed suit on more than one occasion in the *Genji Monogatari*

Suma no Seki   須磨の関

The Suma Barrier in Settsu; not as evocative as the next

Suma no Ura   須磨の浦

Suma Bay in Settsu, famous for the exile there of *Ariwara Yukihira and Genji, as also for its fisher-women (ama) or drawers of seawater for salt kilns

Suminoe   住の江

An older name for the next

Sumiyoshi 住吉

In Settsu, within modern Ōsaka, famous for its divinity, guardian of Japanese poetry, and the pine that is commonly taken to be his manifestation

Suzukayama 鈴鹿山

Mount Suzuka in Ise (there is also a somewhat less famous river there) was famous for its drizzle (shigure) and its remoteness, requiring crossing the mountains (yamagoe). To such sad associations were added the evocation of the name, beautifully joining bell and deer

Tachibana no Kojima 橘の小島

The little island with a kind of orange tree in the Uji; from a poem in the *Kokinshū*; Ukifune there offers Niou the poem that gives her her name in the *Genji Monogatari*

Tago no Ura 田子浦

Tago Bay in Suruga is a lovely inlet with a famous view of Mt. Fuji. Another utamakura, Tago no Ura 多胡浦, in Kōzuke can sometimes be confused with this in *kanabun*, but Tago Bay is famous for its white strand and wisteria

Takasago 高砂

In Harima; famous in art as well as *nō* and other literary versions for the poor but loving and contented old couple located there

Tatsuta(gawa) 竜田(川)

Tatsuta (River) in Yamato, the place most famous for autumn foliage and also known for its divinity

Tomasegawa 泊瀬川

See the preceding discussion

Toribeyama 鳥辺山

In Yamashiro; known for its crematoria

Tsukubasan 筑波山

A mountain in Hitachi, known from poems in the *Man'yōshū; although Tsukuba (no michi) later became synonymous with *renga*

Uchide no Hama 打出浜

Uchide Beach in Ōmi, useful in *kakekotoba*, since the first word means start out

Ujigawa 宇治川

The Uji River in Yamashiro, variously famous, negatively for its noisy waters representing immersion in matters of this world and for the homophonic connection with ushi, misery; and positively by reason of such other things as the next two

Uji no Ajiro 宇治の網代

The (or a) fish weir in the Uji

Uji(no)hashi 宇治(の)橋

The bridge at Uji in Yamashiro. It was the site of the maiden or divinity Uji no hashihime 宇治の橋姫, featured in a *Kokinshū love poem, from which the title for the "Hashihime" chapter in the *Genji Monogatari* is taken

Waka no Ura 和歌の浦

Waka Bay in Kii; useful to poets for the *waka* play

Yamabuki no Hashi   山吹の橋

Some accounts offer this bridge and the Yamabuki Rapids, Yamabuki no Se 山吹の瀬, as an imaginary place introduced late as an utamakura. Since "Yamabuki" designates "mountain blowing," it is treated poetically for its autumn wind. There is also a Yamabuki no Saki, or Yamabuki Point, mentioned in the later chapters of the *Genji Monogatari* and located in Uji; sometimes associated with Ōmi

Yogo no Umi   余吾の湖

A lake near Lake Biwa in Ōmi

Yoshinogawa   吉野川

Yoshino River was known for swiftness, waves over rocks, water falls, wind from the mountains, and a variety of scenery throughout the year

Yoshinoyama   吉野山

Mount Yoshino in Yamato was famous for scenery the whole year, but most for its cherry flowers, the most celebrated of all sites for the mountain (yamazakura) kind

PART NINE Ranks, Offices, and Certain Incumbents

A. RANKS, OFFICES, AND TITLES OF THE COURT

Through nearly the whole of classical times, from 700 onward, the formal or organizational character of the court remained largely the same. This much is clear from the four chief sources, of which a word must be said:

> The Code of the Taihō Era, *Taihō Ritsuryō*, 701
> The Code of the Yōrō Era, *Yōrō Ritsuryō*, 718
> Regulations of the Engi Era, *Engi Shiki*, 927
> Origins of Offices, *Shokugenshō*, 1340

Since there are no major differences for court organization between the Taihō and Yōrō codes, they will be taken as one and referred to as "Code." The term "ritsuryō" combines the two features of this body of ancient regulations. The closest modern equivalents would probably be of laws for ryō and enforcements for ritsu. The Taihō Code has seven parts of ritsu and eleven of ryō. The Yōrō Code has ten of each. The Engi regulations were drawn up at the order of the very active sovereign, Daigo, and it is in fifty parts. The *Origins of Offices* amounts to first historical research into these matters, and it was executed by Kitabatake Chikafusa for Gomurakami. These sources show that the main outlines of the court remained unchanged. Since Japan was of course changing greatly over so long a period, the formal organization corresponded less and less to realities of power and to kinds of office not allowed for in the Code. The first section, A, of this part presents main features of court organization according to the Code, with some attention also to extra-Code matters. The remaining sections (B–F) deal with extra-Code matters and various incumbents of these anomalous offices. For the most part, the description in A can be taken as an idealized or simplified version of the early Heian court, or as a plan of court organization that was laid out in theory for government.

The titular head of the Code organization was of course the sovereign, whose will the Code merely pretended to set forth in rational fashion. Since, however, the sovereigns also gave, by their regnal era names, the basis for calculating years, their names and the characters for them have been given in Part Two. It will be observed that throughout this *Companion*, "sovereign" has been used to render tennō 天皇. It is not altogether satisfactory as an English term, but the frequently heard "emperor" and its variations are quite misleading. Except for a brief period in this century, there has never been a Japanese empire. "King" has the virtue of simplicity, but its Western associations are too many.

Everyone from the sovereign (tennō 天皇) down was effectively appointed to office, since primogeniture was not fully followed by the court. Once appointed and accepted, the sovereign functioned as Shinto shaman, and therefore conductor of rites on behalf of his office and the state; he gave legitimacy to rule. But there were normally a large number of male offspring of the sovereign by various wives and concubines. Depending on the rank of the mother, influence, and so on, the son or daughter of a sovereign might be designated prince (shinnō 親王) or princess (naishinnō 内親王). Otherwise the child might, like Hikaru Genji, be put out to the Minamoto family because of his mother's low rank. It was in such fashion that both the Taira and Minamoto family in their various branches claimed royal ancestry. Princes were designated by the suffixed title, miya 宮. The inheritant or sovereign designate (cf. "crown prince") was known as haru no miya or, commonly, tōgu, the former is more literary; the characters for both are 東宮. Princesses were designated by appellations that indicated their femaleness, their succession as to order or birth, and "miya." For example, Onna sannomiya 女三宮 designated the third princess in order. For both princes and princesses there were grades or ranks (hon). For example, the top or first was ippon no miya 一品宮. These were matters of selection or appointment, and there was no little intrigue, much of which centered on the women who lived with the sovereign.

Marriage customs were extraordinarily complex and varied over the centuries. This discussion more or less presumes a time when the court had real power, what might be termed an idealized version of the system in the Heian period. With such provisos, the sovereign's women aspired to be appointed consort, that is kōgō 皇后 or chūgū 中宮. The consort of an abdicated sovereign was known as kōtaigō or taikōtaigō 皇太后, 太皇太后, depending on position and power behind them (the title was held by some who did not hold the title of consort earlier). Kōtaigō was usually thought of, however, as designating either a dowager consort or the mother of the reigning sovereign. During the Heian period, these women came from certain branches of the Fujiwara family, whose men manipulated the court and held power by becoming fathers-in-law and lineal grandfathers of sovereigns.

The ingenious Fujiwara also invented two extra-Code offices of the utmost power (when held during the heyday of the institution). These were the positions of regent (sesshō) and chancellor (kampaku), which are dealt with in Section B below. Perhaps because of the infusion of so much Fujiwara blood, the sovereigns themselves had the wile to devise a system of abdicated and at least nominally cloistered sovereigns (insei), as described in Section C. By this means, sovereigns who wished to shed the onerous ceremonial duties of their position might relinquish nominal power to exercise some portion of real control of the government. Other motives such as the religious might also be involved. But in all these matters, a combination of circumstances and personalities governed the ways in which matters went. *Murakami managed to reign twenty years or more, and *Daigo his whole reign, without having a regent or chancellor appointed, so exercising power through his office as sovereign and by means of his chosen officials. Some other sovereigns were little more than puppets, even during the heyday of the court.

However, through thick and thin, through moments of power centered here or there, ministers were appointed to offices that meant more or less, according to circumstances. At the peak of officials recognized by the Code were dajōdaijin (modern version daijōdaijin) 太政大臣. In theory this prime among ministers was an exemplary individual. In practice men obtained the office as it became vacant and as they could enter it because of the realities of power. Under this officer were the three principal ministers, the Great Ministers of the Left, of the Right, and of the Center, in decreasing seniority. These lords could count on being appointed to the second rank. (In the heyday of the court, the first rank was usually a fairly rare appointment, commonly being reserved for dajōdaijin or posthumous status.) Although extra-Code and extra-legal matters often proved more important than official appointments, men continued to seek the upper three ranks, because of the high revenues that went with them.

A lord or lady held only one rank at a time. A person (we are really considering men) could hold more than one office, but the salary was that of his rank. Office of course brought status, and with the usual Japanese taste for odd numbers, three offices were thought to sound especially nice. In the nature of the case, it is difficult to estimate other kinds of income, whether from family inheritance (which was chiefly matrilineal in early Japan and seems to have changed gradually during the Heian period) or from practices shading from gifts to downright corruption. The governors of provinces had a bad name for milking the districts they administered. The stewards for the nobility in their manors (shōen 荘園) also were reputed to cheat their masters. Because at some points the highest nobles returned part of their revenues to the sovereign, we must assume that the lucky ones at the top had their hands on the durables. Yet much of what a high nobleman received went, as it were, into circulation by private gifts (roku 禄) to dependents. In her *Genji Monogatari*, *Murasaki Shikibu speaks about this from time to time, and its implications are large. One thing on Genji's mind as he prepares to take orders in "Maboroshi" is the future of those dependent on him, and those who have been his chief officials at court. The part concludes with his ordering such a scale of gifts as shall never recur (have no second, ninō). In pragmatic terms, the system seems to have worked with whatever oppression of the poor.

A government requires more to operate than its ministers. The Code divided the nobility into eight ranks plus initial ranks. In practice, however, the sons of a *Fujiwara Michinaga got off to a very fast start, whereas the non-Fujiwaras or lesser Fujiwaras languished in lower grades.

The eight ranks were further divided. First, second, and third each had two divisions, senior and junior. The other five ranks had four: upper senior and lower senior, upper junior and lower junior.

Since the first rank was bestowed so sparingly, in practice the second and third ranks were the ones sought after, because there was a gulf between the first three and the other five, as also another between the fourth and fifth and those below. These breaking points were recognized by non-Code terms, although they had some exceptions. The terms are:

kugyō　公卿　　　high nobility
tenjōbito　殿上人　attendant nobility
jige　地下　　　　lesser nobility

The kugyō (or kandachibe, kandachime 上達部) group had far greater revenues than the others. Its members were defined partly by rank, partly by office. It included those of the first three ranks and others who sat on the Great Council of State. The chief category of others involved the consultants (sangi 参議) who were of the fourth rank (and extra-Code) and who might number as many as eight. Yet the whole kugyō group seems never to have exceeded thirty in Heian times and often was less as offices went unfilled or were held in multiple fashion. For a subject to enter this group was to reach the pinnacle.

Since they acted in the sovereign's name, the kugyō obviously attended him. The *tenjōbito*, the next lower group, consisted of those nobles of the fourth and fifth ranks whom the sovereign specifically designated as attendants or courtiers. The term takes its name from the courtier's room or hall (that is, tenjō no ma 殿上の間. See Part Ten for its location in the palace). Since one had to be specifically selected, the privilege of attendance was not conferred solely by rank. In some usages, "tenjōbito" includes the nobility of the first three ranks *and* the lesser attendant nobility. There were alternative names as well, such as tōshō 堂上 and unjōbito 雲上人. If we regard the tenjōbito as those separate from the first three ranks, they consisted, it seems, of most nobles of the fourth rank and some from the fifth. Like the kugyō, their numbers would be augmented by one group from a rank below (the sixth). These were the kurōdo 蔵人, the sovereign's secretaries or chamberlains. (Significantly enough, these exceptional persons were also extra-Code.) The number of the tenjōbito varied according to numerous factors (such as the age or power of a sovereign), and is said to have ranged from two or three dozen upwards toward one hundred. It seems safe to say that it would be normal for a mature, alert sovereign to have the company of about one hundred of his nobles, kugyō and tenjōbito. He would be able to know them all.

One other group of people must be included as possible attendants on the sovereign and the consort: the religious. Buddhist priests and nuns, Shinto priests, shrine women, and shamans might be summoned into the presence when a sovereign was ill or a consort was delivering a child. Murasaki Shikibu's diary has a well-known passage describing the tumult in the consort's quarters as she went through an extended labor. Besides the attendant ladies, there were the nobles showing their duty, and the religious in large numbers.

The jige 地下, or lesser nobility, consisted of all those who held ranks from the fourth and lower and who were not tenjōbito. Since these were the people who executed the purposes of government, or were the bureaucracy at the capital and the governors of the provinces, there must have been hundreds of them. The Code allows for one thousand, but there is reason to suppose that there were not always so many and that these were the first offices to go unfilled as the court lost its strength (that is, when there were no revenues to be gained), and when the status of the grand-sounding titles was what held appeal.

Although power and wealth animate individuals in all societies, the court also had a compulsive concern with rank and status. The first page of the *Genji Monogatari* relates the reaction of the court ladies when the sovereign entered into an affair with a woman of low rank. Attendant daughters of ministers felt anger and contempt. Attendant daughters of the lesser nobility were even worse, as feeling the threat closer home. In the *Kagerō Nikki*, *Fujiwara Michitsuna no Haha writhes over the fact that her husband, Kaneie, not only has grown cold toward her but has taken up with a woman greatly her inferior; the diarist later gloats over her inferior's troubles. In *Izumi Shikibu's diary, the prince's consort returns to her home when he installs Izumi Shikibu in his palace. The affront consists not simply of the husband's infidelity but in the low rank of Izumi Shikibu—and no doubt her profligate reputation. Everywhere we find the concern for what people would think and say.

The divisiveness implied by such nervousness and by the system of ranks was eased by the very strength of personal relations that made the society into something other than one relating rank to simple talent. For example, the highest nobility seems to have felt a special obligation to provide for their wet nurses (menoto 乳母). It was also the case that juniors in the nobility attended on seniors, and whatever the distinctions in rank, saw their superiors plain. The happy endings of most *monogatari* also suggest that dreams of becoming a high minister or his wife ran through the heads of the nobility.

For brief discussion of the offices of the early court, see Part Four, *kabane*.

Figures 9-1 and 9-2 offer Japanese versions of offices of court ranks in relation to various offices, beginning with the highest, descending to middle ranks, and then dealing with the lower court ranks. Subsequent tables will present the same information in English with various qualifications dealing with changes over time.

As Table 9-1 shows, the two Code bodies closest to the sovereign were the Jingikan, the Board of Shinto, which reflected the sovereign's religious status, and the Dajōkan, the Grand Council of State. This council included the kugyō, as has been seen. Throughout it should be recalled that Left is senior to Right, which is senior to Center. Under the ministers of the Left and Right were Controlling Boards or Offices (sabenkan, ubenkan). In a line below the minister of the Center were the counsellors. The Dainagon and Chūnagon—Major and Middle Counsellors—sat with him and other ministers on the Great Council. The Shōnagon, or Lesser Counsellors, worked in an office or board (shōnagon no tsubone), lesser than but more or less parallel to the Controllers' offices. The Code envisioned these offices to be the executive of the state. In short, ministers, counsellors, controllers, secretaries, recorders, and their immediate subordinates made up this group.

官 ＼ 位	正一位／従一位	正二位／従二位	正三位	従三位	正四位上	正四位下	従四位上	従四位下	正五位上	正五位下	従五位上	従五位下
神祇官								伯				大副
太政官	太政大臣	左大臣 右大臣 内大臣	大納言	中納言		参議	大弁		中弁	少弁		少納言
中務省					卿				大輔		少輔	侍従 大監物
式部省 治部省 民部省 兵部省 刑部省 大蔵省 宮内省						卿				大輔 大判事		少輔
中宮職 大膳職 京職 修理職 春宮坊				傅			中宮大夫 修理大夫 春宮大夫	大夫				亮 東宮学士
大舎人寮 図書寮 大学寮 雅楽寮 玄蕃寮 諸陵寮 主計寮 主税寮 左右馬寮 木工寮 兵庫寮											頭	文章博士
内蔵寮 縫殿寮 内匠寮 大炊寮 主殿寮 典薬寮 掃部寮 斎宮寮												頭
囚獄司 正親司 内膳司 造酒司 市司												
隼人司 織部司 采女司 主水司 舎人監 主膳監 主蔵監 主工署 主馬署												
弾正台						尹			弼			
近衛府 兵衛府 衛門府				近衛大将				近衛中将 衛門督		近衛少将 兵衛督	衛門佐	兵衛佐
大宰府				帥				大弐				少弐
鎮守府 按察使								按察使			将軍	
斎院司 勘解由使								勘解由長官			斎院長官	勘解由次官
後宮			尚蔵	尚侍	尚膳 尚縫		典侍 典蔵				掌侍	典膳 典縫
大国											守	
上国												守
中国												
下国												

FIGURE 9-1. Upper Court Ranks and Offices

正六位		従六位		正七位		従七位		正八位		従八位		大初位		小初位	
上	下	上	下	上	下	上	下	上	下	上	下	上	下	上	下
少副		大祐	少祐							大史	少史				
大史				大外記	少外史	少外記									
大内記	中判事	中監物·少丞	大蔵大主鈴·少判事	大録	判事大属	大典鈴·典物主	大典鈴	少内記·少監物	少主鈴·少録	少典鑰					
	大丞	少丞·大蔵大主鈴	大蔵少判事·少判事	大録	判事大属	大典鈴	大蔵少鈴	少録	判事少属						
		大進	少進·大京職大進	京職少進·大膳少進	判事大属		大膳大属	大属	少属						
	明経博士·助			大助·明法博士·音博士·算博士·書博士	少音博士·算博士·書博士			大馬医属·医師	少属	少属					
	斎宮助·侍医助	助		陰陽大允·宮大允·天文博士·女医博士·暦博士·医博士	陰陽少允·宮少允·針博士·暦博士·医師·内蔵少主鈴	斎宮属·大属	少属	正親令史·囚獄大令史·少令史	囚獄少令史						
奉正膳						典佑膳									
	正	主水正·主人正·主膳正·主蔵正·首	首		佑			主舎人·主水·主膳·主蔵佑		令史		主水·主人·主膳·主蔵令史	主殿·主工·主馬令史		
大忠	少忠			大疏	巡察		少疏								
	兵衛佐	近衛将監	衛門大尉	衛門将曹	近衛大尉·兵衛大尉	兵衛少尉		衛門大志·兵衛大志	衛門少志·兵衛少志						
	大監	少監	大判事·大典	大工·少典·大典	主神		博士	少算·医師·師工·典師			判事大·令史	判事少·令史			
				軍監				軍曹							
		斎院次官	勘解由判官		斎院判官	勘解由主典				斎院主典					
尚書		尚殿	尚酒	掌蔵·尚兵·尚闈·尚書·尚薬·尚掃·尚水		掌膳·掌鍵·典兵·典闈·典書·典薬·典掃·典水									
	介			大掾	少掾			大目	少目						
		介			掾				目						
	守					掾			目						
		守						掾					目		

FIGURE 9-2. Lower Court Ranks and Offices

TABLE 9–1. DIAGRAM OF THE CENTRAL COURT GOVERNMENT

The figures in square brackets denote the stipulated number of such officials. The order of ranking of the Great Ministers (Daijin) was: 1. Prime Minister, 2. Great Minister of the Left, 3.—of the Right, 4.—of the Center.

Tennō (Sovereign)

Jingikan (Department of Shintō)	Dajōkan (Great Council of State)

Dajōdaijin (Prime Minister) [1]

Sadaijin (Great Minister of the Left) [1]	Udaijin (Great Minister of the Right) [1]

Naidaijin (Great Minister of the Center) [1]

Dainagon (Major Counseller) [4]

Sabenkan (Controlling Board of the Left)	Ubenkan (Controlling Board of the Right)

Chūnagon (Middle Counsellor) [3]

Sadaiben (Major Controller of the Left) [1]	Udaiben (Major Controller of the Right) [1]

Shōnagon (Lesser Counsellor) [3]

Sachūben (Middle Controller of the Left) [1]	Uchūben (Middle Controller of the Right) [1]
Sashōben (Minor Controller of the Left) [1]	Ushōben (Minor Controller of the Right) [1]

Daigeki (Senior Secretary) [2]

Shōgeki (Junior Secretary) [2]

Sadaishi (Senior Recorder of the Left) [2]	Udaishi (Senior Recorder of the Right) [2]
Sashōshi (Junior Recorder of the Left) [2]	Ushōshi (Junior Recorder of the Right) [2]
Sashijō (Scribe of the Left) [10]	Ushijō (Scribe of the Right) [10]
Sakajō (Office Keeper of the Left) [2]	Ukajō (Office Keeper of the Right) [2]

The Four Ministers (Kyō) of the Ministries of Central Affairs (Nakatsukasashō), of Ceremonial (Shikibushō), of Civil Administration (Jibushō), and of Popular Affairs (Mimbushō).	The Four Ministers (Kyō) of the Ministries of War (Hyōbushō), of Justice (Kyōbushō), of the Treasury (Ōkurashō), and of the Royal Household (Kunaishō).

At the bottom of Table 9-1 are named the four ministries associated with the Left and the four with the Right. Table 9-2 sets forth these eight ministries in terms of changes over a period of time. Most originate with the Code, and most continue beyond to the *Engi Shiki* of 927 and the *Shokugenshō* of 1340. The tabular abbreviations for these are "Code," "Engi" and "Offices." Where there is a blank there is a change or an absence. If a line is followed by an entry, there is an addition.

From time to time more in the way of change was introduced in the setting up or disappearance of agencies directly responsible to the Great Council of State, Dajōkan. As Table 9-3 shows, there was far more change in these lesser offices than in the grander ones.

TABLE 9–2. DIAGRAM OF THE EIGHT MINISTRIES

The four ministries (shō) under the Controlling Board of the Left (sabenkan)

	Code	Engi	Offices
1. Nakatsukasahō (Ministry of Central Affairs)	Chūgūshiki (Office of the Consort's Household)	same	same
	Ōtoneriryō (Bureau of Royal Attendants)	same	same
	Zushoryō (Bureau of Books and Drawings)	same	same
	Kuraryō (Bureau of Palace Storehouses)	same	same
	Nuidonoryō (Bureau of the Wardrobe and Court Ladies)	same	same
	On'yōryō (Bureau of Divination)	same	same
	Gakōshi (Painting Office)		
	Naiyakushi (Palace Medical Office)		
	Nairaishi (Palace Etiquette Office)	Takumiryō (Bureau of Skilled Artisans)	same
2. Shikibushō (Ministry of Ceremonial)	Daigakuryō (Bureau of Education)		
	Toneriryō (Bureau of Scattered Ranks)	same	same
3. Jibushō (Ministry of Civil Administration)	Gagakuryō [or Utaryō] (Bureau of Music)	same	same
	Gembaryō (Bureau of Buddhism and Aliens)	same	same
	Shoryōshi (Mausolea Office)	Shoryōryō (Bureau of Mausolea)	
	Sōgishi (Mourning and Burial Office)	same	same
4. Mimbushō (Ministry of Popular Affairs)	Shukeiryō [or Kazueryō] (Bureau of Statistics)	same	same
	Shuzeiryō [or Chikararyō] (Bureau of Taxation)	same	same

The four ministries (shō) under the Controlling Board of the Right (ubenkan)

5. Hyōbushō (Ministry of War)	Heibashi (Military Horses Office)		
	Zōheishi (Weapons-Manufacturing Office)		
	Kusuishi [or Kosuishi] (Drums and Fifes Office)		
	Shusenshi (Ships Office)		
	Shuyōshi (Falcons Office)	Hayato-no-tsukasa (Hayato Office)	same
6. Gyōbushō (Ministry of Justice)	Zōshokushi (Fines, Smuggled Goods, and Lost Articles Office)		
	Shūgokushi (Prisons Office)	same	same

TABLE 9–2. (*continued*)

The four ministries (shō) under the Controlling Board of the Right (sabenkan)

	Code	Engi	Offices
7. Ōkurashō (Ministry of the Treasury)	Imono no tsukasa [or Tenchūshi] (Metal Work Office)		
	Kanimori no tsukasa (Housekeeping Office)		
	Nuribe no tsukasa (Lacquer Office)		
	Nuibe no tsukasa (Wardrobe Office)		
	Oribe no tsukasa (Weaving Office)	same	same
8. Kunaishō (Ministry of the Sovereign's Household)	Dainzenshiki (Office of the Palace Table)	same	same
	Mokuryō (Bureau of Carpentry)	same	same
	Ōiryō (Bureau of the Palace Kitchen)	same	same
	Tonomoryō (Bureau of Palace Equipment and Upkeep)	same	same
	Ten'yakuryō (Bureau of Medicine)	same	same
		Kamonryō (Bureau of Housekeeping)	same
	Ōkimi no Tsukasa (Royal Family Office)	same	same
	Naizenshi (Royal Table Office)	same	same
	Zōshushi [or Sake no tsukasa] (Sake Office)	same	same
	Kaji no Tsukasa (Blacksmiths Office)		
	Kannu no Tsukasa (Government Slaves Office)		
	Enchishi (Gardens and Ponds Office)		
	Dokōshi (Public Works Office)		
	Uneme no Tsukasa (Palace Women Office)	same	same
	Shusuishi (Water Office)	same	same
	Abura no Tsukasa (Oil Office)		
	Uchi no Kanimori no Tsukasa (Inner Housekeeping Office)		
	Hakosuemono no Tsukasa (Vessels Office)		
	Naizenshi (Palace Dyeing Office)		

The appropriate Japanese versions of the relations between ranks and offices have been supplied in Tables 9-1; and in 9-2, variations have been given under versions of the three heads: "*Code, Engi,* and *Offices.*" Comparison of Figures 9-1 and 9-2 with Tables 9-1, 9-2, and 9-3 should make such matters clear apart from a few small differences between the idealized Japanese and the schematic English versions.

Each office had officals divided into four classes, the shitōkan 四等官. These were the Head (kami 長官), the Assistant (suke 次官), the Secretary (jō 判官)

TABLE 9–3. LESSER COURT OFFICES

Code	Engi	Offices
Danjōdai (Board of Censors)	same	same
Kageyushi (Investigators of the Records of Outgoing Officials)		same
Emonfu (Headquarters of the Gate Guards)		same
Konoefu (Headquarters of the Inner Palace Guards)		
1. Sakon'efu (Left Division)		same
2. Ukon'efu (Right Division)		same
Ejifu (Headquarters of the Palace Guards)	Emonfu (Headquarters of the Outer Palace Guards)	same
1. Saejifu (Left Division)	1. Saemonfu (Left Division)	same
2. Uejifu (Right Division)	2. Uemonfu (Right Division)	same
Hyōefu (Headquarters of the Military Guards)	Hyōefu (Headquarters of the Middle Palace Guards)	
1. Sahyōefu (Left Division)	1. Sahyōefu (Left Division)	same
2. Uhyōefu (Right Division)	2. Uhyōefu (Right Division)	same
Hayato no tsukasa (Hayato Office)	[placed under the Hyōbushō (Ministry of war)]	same
Meryō (Bureau of Horses)	same	same
1. Samaryō (Left Division)	same	same
2. Umaryō (Right Division)	same	same
Hyōgoryō (Bureau of Military Storehouses)	same	same
1. Sahyōgoryō (Left Division)	same	
2. Uhyōgoryō (Right Division)	same	
Naihyōgoshi (Palace Military Storehouses Office)		

Code	Engi	Offices
	Kageyushi (Bureau of the High Priestess [of the Great Ise Shrine])	Ise Saigūryō (Bureau of the High Priestess of the Great Ise Shrine)
	Saiinshi (Office of the High Priestess [of the Kamo no Jinja])	Kamo no Saiinshi (Office of the High Priestess of the Kamo no Jinja)

Code	Engi	Offices
		Shurikyūjōshi (Office of Palace Repairs)
		Jusenshi (Mint Office)
		Seyakuinshi (Royal Charity Hospital)
		Junnain [a detached palace that was made into a Buddhist temple]
		Shōgakuin (Private School of the Ariwara Family)
		Gakkanin (Private School of the Tachibana Family)
		Naijudokoro (Royal Pages Office)
		Naikyōbō (Female Dancers and Musicians Office)
		Mizushidokoro (The Sovereign's Dining Room)
		Ōutadokoro (Bureau or Office of Traditional Songs)
		Kirokujo (Records Office)

TABLE 9–3. (*continued*)

Code	Engi	Offices
		Gakusho (Royal Court Music Hall)
		Shurikyūjōshi (Officials in Charge of Repairing the Outer Palace Walls)
		Zōjishi (Officials in Charge of Building Temples)
		Bōkashi (Officials in Charge of Controlling the Kamogawa)

The Tōgūbō (Crown Prince's Quarters)

Code	Engi	Offices
Shajinkan (Division in Charge of Guards)		
Shuzenkan (Division in Charge of Food)	same	same
Shuzōkan (Division in Charge of Valuables)		
Shudensho (Division in Charge of Palace Equipment and Upkeep)	same	same
Shushosho (Division in Charge of Books and Writing Materials)		
Shushōsho (Division in Charge of Gruel and Drinking Water)		
Shukōsho (Division in Charge of Carpentry and Metal Work)		
Shuheisho (Division in Charge of Military and Ceremonial Weapons)		
Shumesho (Division in Charge of Horses and Riding Equipment)		same

The Kōkyū (Women's Quarters of the Imperial Palace)

Code	Engi	Offices
Naishi no Tsukasa (Palace Attendants Office)		
Kura no Tsukasa [or Zōshi] (Treasury Office)		
Fumi no Tsukasa [or Shoshi] (Books and Writing Materials Office)		
Kusuri no Tsukasa [or Yakushi] (Medical Office)		
Tsuwamono no Tsukasa [or Heishi] (Military Equipment Office)		
Kagi no Tsukasa [or Ishi] (Keys Office)		
Tonomo no Tsukasa [or Denshi] (Palace Equipment and Upkeep Office)		

and the Clerk (sakan 主典). For such titles, even with the same pronunciation, Chinese characters may differ from office to office.

For reasons given, there is not always a way of making ranks correspond with offices, but the general outlines can be shown. Table 9-6 sets forth the relation of ranks of the fifth and up to offices in the Great Council of State, the Department of Shinto, the Quarters of the Prince Inheritant, and of one ministry, that for Central Affairs. (Table 9-7 will present the other seven ministries. The tabular abbreviations are Ranks, Council, Shinto, Prince, and Central.)

The next table will set forth the same information, again for the fifth rank and up, for the seven other ministries and for four other kinds of offices: the Board of Censors (danjōdai); the Headquarters of the Inner Palace Guards (konoefu); the Headquarters of the Outer Palace Guards (emonfu) and of the Middle Palace Guards (hyōefu); and the government headquarters in what is now Kyushu (Dazaifu). The tabular abbreviations are Ranks, Minist., Censors, Inner Guards, Out-Mid Guards, and Dazai.

TABLE 9-4. COURT RANKS (*Kurai* 位)

Japanese	English Translation
Ranks of Shinnō 親王	*Ranks of Princes*
1. Ippon 一品	1. First Order
2. Nihon 二品	2. Second Order
3. Sambon 三品	3. Third Order
4. Shihon 四品	4. Fourth Order
Ranks of Ō and Officials 王と令制官	*Ranks of Princes and Officials*
1. Shōichii 正一位	1. Senior First Rank
2. Juichii 従一位	2. Junior First Rank
3. Shōnii 正二位	3. Senior Second Rank
4. Junii 従二位	4. Junior Second Rank
5. Shōsammi 正三位	5. Senior Third Rank
6. Jusammi 従三位	6. Junior Third Rank
7. Shōshiijō 正四位上	7. Senior Fourth Rank, Upper Grade
8. Shōshiige 正四位下	8. Senior Fourth Rank, Lower Grade
9. Jushiijō 従四位上	9. Junior Fourth Rank, Upper Grade
10. Jushiige 従四位下	10. Junior Fourth Rank, Lower Grade
11. Shōgoijō 正五位上	11. Senior Fifth Rank, Upper Grade
12. Shōgoige 正五位下	12. Senior Fifth Rank, Lower Grade
13. Jugoijō 従五位上	13. Junior Fifth Rank, Upper Grade
14. Jugoige 従五位下	14. Junior Fifth Rank, Lower Grade
Ranks of Officials Only	*Ranks of Officials Only*
15. Shōrokuijō 正六位上	15. Senior Sixth Rank, Upper Grade
16. Shōrokuige 正六位下	16. Senior Sixth Rank, Lower Grade
17. Jurokuijō 従六位上	17. Junior Sixth Rank, Upper Grade
18. Jurokuige 従六位下	18. Junior Sixth Rank, Lower Grade
19. Shōshichiijō 正七位上	19. Senior Seventh Rank, Upper Grade
20. Shōshichiige 正七位下	20. Senior Seventh Rank, Lower Grade
21. Jushichiijō 従七位上	21. Junior Seventh Rank, Upper Grade
22. Jushichiige 従七位下	22. Junior Seventh Rank, Lower Grade
23. Shōhachiijō 正八位上	23. Senior Eighth Rank, Upper Grade
24. Shōhachiige 正八位下	24. Senior Eighth Rank, Lower Grade
25. Juhachiijō 従八位上	25. Junior Eighth Rank, Upper Grade
26. Juhachiige 従八位下	26. Junior Eighth Rank, Lower Grade
27. Daishoijō 大初位上	27. Greater Initial Rank, Upper Grade
28. Daishoige 大初位下	28. Greater Initial Rank, Lower Grade
29. Shōshoijō 小初位上	29. Lesser Initial Rank, Upper Grade
30. Shōshoige 小初位下	30. Lesser Initial Rank, Lower Grade

There were some other offices suitable for lords of the fifth rank and above.

It will be observed that a governor of a province and a shogun were rated in the fifth rank. The governor's grade presumably related to the importance of his province. The low grade of the shogun bespeaks a court outlook. Matters were to change when the military took over. But long before that time, the court itself had devised extra-Code offices that are the subjects of Sections B and C below.

TABLE 9–5. THE FOUR CLASSES OF OFFICIALS

Office	Head	Asst.	Sec'y	Clerk
Jingikan (Department of Shintō)	Haku (Head)	Tayū (Senior Assistant Head) Shō (Junior Assistant Head)	Daijō (Senior Secretary) Shōjō (Junior Secretary)	Taishi (Senior Clerk) Shōshi (Junior Clerk)
Dajōkan (Great Council of State)	Dajōdaijin (Prime Minister) Sadaijin (Great Minister of the Left) Udaijin (Great Minister of the Right) [Naidaijin (Great Minister of the Center) worked on the Dajōkan but headed no ministry]	Dainagon (Major Counsellor) Chūnagon (Middle Counsellor)	Shōnagon (Minor Counsellor) Sadaiben (Major Controller of the Left) Udaiben (Major Controller of the Right) Sachūben (Middle Controller of the Left) Uchūben (Middle Controller of the Right) Sashōben (Minor Controller of the Left) Ushōben (Minor Controller of the Right)	Sadaishi (Senior Recorder of the Left) Udaishi (Senior Recorder of the Right) Daigeki (Senior Secretary) Shōgeki (Junior Secretary)
Shō (ministries)	Kyō (Minister)	Tayū (Senior Assistant Minister Shōyū [or Shō] (Junior Assistant Minister)	Daijō (Senior Secretary) Shōjō (Junior Secretary)	Daisakan (Senior Recorder) Shōsakan (Junior Recorder)
Shiki (important offices) and bō (quarters)	Daibu (Master)	Suke (Assistant Master)	Taishin (Senior Secretary) Shōshin (Junior Secretary)	Daisakan (Senior Clerk) Shōsakan (Junior Clerk)

Ryō (bureaus)	Kami (Director)	Suke (Assistant Director)	Daijō (Senior Secretary) Shōjō (Junior secretary)	Daisakan (Senior Clerk) Shōsakan (Junior Clerk)
Shi (lesser offices) and kan or sho (divisions)	Kami (Buzen of the Naizenshi [Sovereign's Table Office]) (Chief)	[none]	Jo (Tenzen of the Naizenshi [Sovereign's Table Office]) (Secretary)	Reishi (Clerk) [Taireishi [Senior Clerk] and Shōreishi [Junior Clerk] of the Ōkimi no tsukasa [Sovereign's Family Office] and the Shūgo-kushi [Prisons Office])
Danjōdai (Board of Censors)	Kami (President)	Daihitsu (Senior Assistant President) Shōhitsu (Junior Assistant President)	Daichū (Senior Secretary) Shōchū (Junior Secretary)	Daisakan (Senior Clerk) Shōsakan (Junior Clerk)
Konoefu (Head-quarters of the Inner Palace Guards)	Taishō (Major Captain)	Chūjō (Middle Captain) Shōshō (Minor Captain)	Shōgen (Lieutenant)	Shōsō (Assistant Lieutenant)
Emonfu (Head-quarters of the Outer Palace Guards) and the Hyōefu (Head-quarters of the Middle Palace Guards)	Kami (Captain)	Suke (Assistant Captain)	Daijō (Senior Lieutenant) Shōjō (Junior Lieutenant)	Daisakan (Senior Assistant Lieutenant) Shōsakan (Junior Assistant Lieutenant)
Chinjufu (Pacifying-Ezo Headquarters)	Shōgun (General)	Fukushōgun (Vice-General)	Gungen (Divisional Commander)	Gunsō (Regimental Commander)

TABLE 9–5. (continued)

Office	Head	Asst.	Sec'y	Clerk
Dazaifu (Government Headquarters in Kyushu)	Sotsu or Sochi (Governor-General)	Daini (Senior Assistant Governor-General) Shōni (Junior Assistant Governor-General)	Taigen (Senior Secretary) Shōgen (Junior Secretary)	Daisakan (Senior Clerk) Shōsakan (Junior Clerk)
Kokushi (Provincial Officials)	Kami (Governor)	Suke (Assistant Governor)	Jō (Secretary) (Daijō [Senior Secretary] and Shōjō [Junior Secretary] in great provinces [taikoku])	Sakan (Clerk) (Daisakan [Senior Clerk] and Shōsakan [Junior Clerk] in great provinces [taikoku])
Gunji (District Officials)	Tairyō (Senior Officer)	Shōryō (Junior Officer)	Shusei (Secretary)	Shuchō (Clerk)

TABLE 9–6. RANKS AND OFFICES (COUNCIL AND OTHER)

Ranks	Council	Shinto	Prince	Central
Shōichii (Senior First Rank) or Juichii (Junior First Rank)	Dajōdaijin (Prime Minister)			
Shōnii (Senior Second Rank) or Junii (Junior Second Rank	Sadaijin (Great Minister of the Left) Udaijin (Great Minister of the Right) Naidaijin (Great Minister of the Center)			
Shōsammi (Senior Third Rank)	Dainagon (Major Counsellor)			
Jusammi (Junior Third Rank)	Chūnagon (Middle Counsellor)			
Shōshiijō (Senior Fourth Rank, Upper Grade)			Fu (Head Tutor)	Kyō (Minister)
Shōshiige (Senior Fourth Rank, Lower Grade)	Sangi (Royal Adviser)			
Jushiijō (Junior Fourth Rank, Upper Grade)	Sadaiben (Major Controller of the Left) Udaiben (Major Controller of the Right)			
Jushiige (Junior Fourth Rank, Lower Grade)		Haku (Head)	Daibu (Master)	

TABLE 9–6. (*continued*)

Ranks	Council	Shinto	Prince	Central
Shōgoijō (Senior Fifth Rank, Upper Grade)	Sachūben (Middle Controller of the Left) Uchūben (Middle Controller of the Right)			Tayū (Senior Assistant Minister)
Shōgoige (Senior Fifth Rank, Lower Grade)	Sashōben (Minor Controller of the Left) Ushōben (Minor Controller of the Right)			
Jugoijō (Junior Fifth Rank, Upper Grade)				Shōyū, or Shō (Junior Assistant Minister)
Jugoige (Junior Fifth Rank, Lower Grade)	Shōnagon (Minor Counsellor)	Tayū (Senior Assistant Head)	Suke (Assistant Master) Gakushi (Teacher of the Classics)	Daikemmotsu (Senior Inspector) Jijū (Chamberlain)

B. REGENTS AND CHANCELLORS

During the Heian period, members of the higher nobility found titles that gave some indication of their actual power or status, while the sovereigns reigned. This gave a certain de jure status, or at least names, to what was the exercise of power even earlier. The two important titles are those of regent (sesshō 摂政) and chancellor (kampaku 関白). The actual power held by men with such titles varied greatly and in general, but not without fluctuations, decreased in time. The first sesshō held the title from 858 to 872; the last in 1867, at the very eve of the modern period. The first kampaku held the title from 880 to 890; the last from 1863 to 1867 (see Table 9-9, pp. 463–467).

In theory at least, the regents tutored, advised, and administered for a given sovereign before he reached an age to rule. In practice the title was devised as a means to control a sovereign and extend family power. A favorite device of Heian times was for a regent to marry a daughter to a young sovereign, thereby creating for himself a position of seniority and status as father-in-law to a sovereign, with hopes of becoming lineal grandfather to the next sovereign, with the greater authority that that relationship held. As time wore on, other appoint-

TABLE 9–7. RANKS AND OFFICES (MINISTRIES, ETC.)

Ranks	Minist.	Censors	Inner Guards	Out-Mid Guards	Dazai
Jusammi (Junior Third Rank)		Kami (President)	Taishō (Major Captain)		Sotsu or Sochi (Governor-General)
Shōshiijō (Senior Fourth Rank, Upper Grade)					
Shōshiige (Senior Fourth Rank, Lower Grade)	Kyō (Minister)				
Jushiijō (Junior Fourth Rank, Upper Grade)					
Jushiige (Junior Fourth Rank, Lower Grade)		Daihitsu (Senior Assistant President)	Chūjō (Middle Captain)	Kami (Captain)	Daini (Senior Assistant Governor-General)
Shōgoijō (Senior Fifth Rank, Upper Grade)					Shōni (Junior Assistant Governor-General)
Shōgoige (Senior Fifth Rank, Lower Grade)	Tayū (Senior Assistant Minister) Daihanji (Major Judge)	Shōhitsu (Junior Assistant President)	Shōshō (Minor Captain)		
Jugoijō (Junior Fifth Rank, Upper Grade)				Suke (Assistant Captain)	
Jugoige (Junior Fifth Rank, Lower Grade)	Shōyū or Shō (Junior Assistant Minister)				

TABLE 9–8. RANKS AND OFFICES (LOWER)

Ranks	Chūgūshiki (Office of the Consort's Household); Daizenshiki (Office of the Palace Table); Kyōshiki (Office of the Capital); Shuri shiki (Office of Palace Repairs)	Kageyushi (Investigators of the Records of Outgoing Offiials); ... Azechifu (Headquarters of the Royal Investigators); ... Chinjufu (Pacifying-Ezo Headquarters)	Provincial Officials (Kokushi) of taikoku (great provinces); ... jōkoku (superior provinces); ... chūkoku (medium provinces); and ... gekoku (inferior provinces)
Jushiige (Junior Fourth Rank, Lower Grade)	Daibu (Master)	Kami (Head Investigator) ... Azechi (Investigator)	
Shōgoijō (Senior Fifth Rank, Upper Grade)	Daibu (Master) [of the Daizenshiki]		
Shōgoige (Senior Fifth Rank, Lower Grade)			
Jugoijō (Junior Fifth Rank, Upper Grade)		... Shōgun (General)	Kami (Governor)
Jugoige (Junior Fifth Rank, Lower Grade)	Suke (Assistant Master)	Suke (Assistant Head Investigator)	... Kami (Governor)

ments (see Sections D and E, below) eroded a regent's power, but the title continued to have considerable status, or men would not have sought it. The title of chancellor was rather similar, except that it was nominally less a relation as tutor to a sovereign than a civil or subject's title of great power, at least during the heyday of chancellors. Like the regents, the chancellors of later times lost power (with ups and downs) as new titles were invested with more of the reality of power. Once again, the title was coveted even when it offered no more than status.

The earlier regents and chancellors bore the name of Fujiwara. With the exceptions of two individuals, later men with these titles were all from branches of the Fujiwara. In Table 9-9, the individuals can be put into three groups, for which the characters for what may be termed surnames are given here rather than repeating them for individuals. The first group is that of men using the surname Fujiwara 藤原. Thereafter the high ministerial branches of that family used five different names and were known as the five regent families (gosekke 五摂家). They are:

Konoe 近衛
Kujō 九条
Nijō 二条
Takatsukasa 鷹司
Ichijō 一条

The third category includes but two individuals, who bore the surname Toyotomi 豊臣 (see Section E).

It will be observed that the titles of regent and of chancellor were regarded as alternate, in the sense that both were not held at the same time, either by the same or different individuals; but also that an individual might hold one title and then another, or hold a title more than once (for example, Fujiwara Tadamichi—see 1121–1158).

Asterisks designate individuals with entries in Part Three. The sovereigns' reigns for the periods of entitlement will be found in Part Two.

TABLE 9-9. REGENTS AND CHANCELLORS

Regent	Chancellor	Dates
Fujiwara Yoshifusa 良房		858–872
Fujiwara Mototsune 基経		872–880
	Fujiwara Mototsune	880–890
Fujiwara Tadahira 忠平		930–941
	Fujiwara Tadahira	941–949
	Fujiwara Saneyori 実頼	967–969
Fujiwara Saneyori		969–970
Fujiwara Koretada 伊尹		970–972
	Fujiwara Kanemichi 兼通	972–977
	Fujiwara Yoritada 頼忠	977–986
Fujiwara Kaneie 兼家		986–990
	Fujiwara Kaneie	990
	Fujiwara Michitaka 道隆	990
Fujiwara Michitaka		990–993
	Fujiwara Michitaka	993–995
	Fujiwara Michikane 道兼	995
*Fujiwara Michinaga 道長		1016–1017
Fujiwara Yorimichi 頼道		1017–1019
	Fujiwara Yorimichi	1019–1067
	Fujiwara Norimichi 教道	1068–1075
	Fujiwara Morozane 師実	1075–1086
Fujiwara Morozane		1086–1090
	Fujiwara Morozane	1090–1094
	Fujiwara Moromichi 師道	1094–1099
	Fujiwara Tadazane 忠実	1105–1107
Fujiwara Tadazane		1107–1113
	Fujiwara Tadazane	1113–1121

TABLE 9–9. (*continued*)

Regent	Chancellor	Dates
	Fujiwara Tadamichi 忠通	1121–1123
Fujiwara Tadamichi		1123–1129
	Fujiwara Tadamichi	1129–1141
Fujiwara Tadamichi		1141–1150
	Fujiwara Tadamichi	1150–1158
	Konoe Motozane 基実	1158–1165
Konoe Motozane		1165–1166
Fujiwara Motofusa 基房		1166–1172
	Fujiwara Motofusa	1172–1179
	Konoe Motomichi 基通	1179–1180
Konoe Motomichi		1180–1183
Fujiwara Moroie 師家		1183–1184
Konoe Motomichi		1184–1186
Kujō Kanezane 兼実		1186–1191
	Kujō Kanezane	1191–1196
	Konoe Motomichi	1196–1198
Konoe Motomichi		1198–1202
Kujō Yoshitsune 良経		1202–1206
	Konoe Iezane 家実	1206–1221
Kujō Michiie 道家		1221
Konoe Iezane		1221–1223
	Konoe Iezane	1223–1228
	Kujō Michiie	1228–1231
	Kujō Norizane 教実	1231–1232
Kujō Norizane		1232–1235
Kujō Michiie		1235–1237
Konoe Kanetsune 兼経		1237–1242
	Konoe Kanetsune	1242
	Nijō Yoshizane 良実	1242–1246
	Ichijō Sanetsune 実経	1246
Ichijō Sanetsune		1246–1247
Konoe Kanetsune		1247–1252
Takatsukasa Kanehira 兼平		1252–1254
	Takatsukasa Kanehira	1254–1261
	Nijō Yoshizane	1261–1265
	Ichijō Sanetsune	1265–1267
	Konoe Motohira 基平	1267–1268
	Takatsukasa Mototada 基忠	1268–1273
	Kujō Tadaie 忠家	1273–1274
Kujō Tadaie		1274
Ichijō Ietsune 家経		1274–1275
Takatsukasa Kanehira		1275–1278
	Takatsukasa Kanehira	1278–1287
	Nijō Morotada 師忠	1287–1289
	Konoe Iemoto 家基	1289–1291
	Kujō Tadanori 忠教	1291–1293
	Konoe Iemoto	1293–1296
	Takatsukasa Kanetada 兼忠	1296–1298
Takatsukasa Kanetada		1298
Nijō Kanemoto 兼基		1298–1300

TABLE 9–9. (*continued*)

Regent	Chancellor	Dates
	Nijō Kanemoto	1300–1305
	Kujō Moronori 師教	1305–1308
Kujō Moronori		1308
Takatsukasa Fuyuhira 冬平		1308–1311
	Takatsukasa Fuyuhira	1311–1313
	Konoe Iehira 家平	1313–1315
	Takatsukasa Fuyuhira	1315–1316
	Nijō Michihira 道平	1316–1318
	Ichijō Uchitsune 内経	1318–1323
	Kujō Fusazane 房実	1323–1324
	Takatsukasa Fuyuhira	1324–1327
	Nijō Michihira	1327–1330
	Takatsukasa Tsunetada 経忠	1330
	Takatsukasa Fuyunori 冬教	1330–1333
	Konoe Tsunetada	1336–1337
	Konoe Mototsugu 基嗣	1337–1338
	Ichijō Tsunemichi 経通	1338–1342
	Kujō Michinori 道教	1342
	Takatsukasa Morohira 師平	1342–1346
	*Nijō Yoshimoto 良基	1346–1358
	Kujō Tsunenori 経教	1358–1361
	Konoe Michitsugu 道嗣	1361–1363
	*Nijō Yoshimoto	1363–1367
	Takatsukasa Fuyumichi 冬通	1367–1369
	Nijō Moroyoshi 師良	1369–1375
	Kujō Tadamoto 忠基	1375–1379
	Nijō Morotsugu 師嗣	1379–1382
*Nijō Yoshimoto		1382–1387
Konoe Kanetsugu 兼嗣		1387–1388
*Nijō Yoshimoto		1388
	Nijō Morotsugu	1388–1394
	Ichijō Tsunetsugu 経嗣	1394–1398
	Nijō Morotsugu	1398–1399
	Ichijō Tsunetsugu	1399–1408
	Konoe Tadatsugu 忠嗣	1408–1409
	Nijō Mitsumoto 満基	1409–1410
	Ichijō Tsunetsugu	1410–1418
	Kujō Mitsunori 満教	1418–1424
	Nijō Mochimoto 持基	1424–1428
Nijō Mochimoto		1428–1432
*Ichijō Kaneyoshi 兼良		1432
Nijō Mochimoto		1432–1433
	Nijō Mochimoto	1433–1445
	Konoe Fusatsugu 房嗣	1445–1447
	*Ichijō Kaneyoshi	1447–1453
	Nijō Mochimichi 持通	1453–1454
	Takatsukasa Fusahira 房平	1454–1455
	Nijō Mochimichi	1455–1458
	Ichijō Norifusa 教房	1458–1463
	Nijō Mochimichi	1463–1467

TABLE 9–9. (*continued*)

Regent	Chancellor	Dates
	* Ichijō Kaneyoshi	1467–1470
	Nijō Masatsugu 政嗣	1470–1476
	Kujō Masamoto 政基	1476–1479
	Konoe Masaie 政家	1479–1483
	Takatsukasa Masahira 政平	1483–1487
	Kujō Masatada 政忠	1487–1488
	Ichijō Fuyuyoshi 冬良	1488–1493
	Konoe Naomichi 尚通	1493–1496
	Ichijō Naomoto 尚基	1497
	Konoe Naomichi	1513–1514
	Takatsukasa Kanesuke 兼輔	1514–1518
	Nijō Tadafusa 忠房	1518–1525
	Konoe Taneie 稙家	1525–1533
	Kujō Tanemichi 稙通	1533–1534
	Nijō Tadafusa 尹房	1534–1536
	Konoe Taneie	1536–1542
	Takatsukasa Tadafuyu 忠冬	1542–1545
	Ichijō Fusamichi 房通	1545–1548
	Nijō Haruyoshi 晴良	1548–1553
	Ichijō Kanefuyu 兼冬	1553–1554
	Konoe Harutsugu 晴嗣	1554–1568
	Nijō Haruyoshi	1568–1578
	Kujō Kanetaka 兼孝	1578–1581
	Ichijō Uchimoto 内基	1581–1584
	Nijō Akizane 昭実	1585
	Toyotomi Hideyoshi 秀吉	1585–1591
	Toyotomi Hidetsugu 秀次	1591–1595
	Kujō Kanetaka	1600–1604
	Konoe Nobutada 信尹	1605–1606
	Takatsukasa Nobufusa 信房	1606–1608
	Kujō Tadasaka 忠栄	1608–1612
	Takatsukasa Nobunao 信尚	1612–1615
	Nijō Akizane	1615–1619
	Kujō Tadasaka	1619–1623
	Konoe Nobuhiro 信尋	1623–1629
	Ichijō Kanetō 兼遐	1629
Ichijō Kanetō		1629–1634
Nijō Yasumichi 康道		1635–1647
Kujō Michifusa 道房		1647
Ichijō Akiyoshi 昭良		1647
	Ichijō Akiyoshi	1647–1651
	Konoe Naotsugu 尚嗣	1651–1653
	Nijō Mitsuhira 光平	1653–1663
Nijō Mitsuhira		1663–1664
Takatsukasa Fusasuke 房輔		1664–1668
	Takatsukasa Fusasuke	1668–1682
	Ichijō Fuyutsune 冬経	1682–1687
Ichijō Fuyutsune		1687–1689
	Ichijō Fuyutsune	1689–1690
	Konoe Motohiro 基熙	1690–1703

TABLE 9–9. (*continued*)

Regent	Chancellor	Dates
	Takatsukasa Kanehiro 兼煕	1703–1707
	Konoe Iehiro 家煕	1707–1709
Konoe Iehiro		1709–1712
Kujō Sukezane 輔実		1712–1716
	Kujō Sukezane	1716–1722
	Nijō Tsunahira 綱平	1722–1726
	Konoe Iehisa 家久	1726–1736
	Nijō Yoshitada 吉忠	1736–1737
	Ichijō Kaneka 兼香	1737–1746
	Ichijō Michika 道香	1746–1747
Ichijō Michika		1747–1755
	Ichijō Michika	1755–1757
	Konoe Uchizaki 内前	1757–1762
Konoe Uchizaki		1762–1772
	Konoe Uchizaki	1772–1778
	Kujō Naozane 尚実	1778–1779
Kujō Naozane		1779–1785
	Kujō Naozane	1785–1787
	Takatsukasa Sukehira 輔平	1787–1791
	Ichijō Teruyoshi 輝良	1791–1795
	Takatsukasa Masahiro 政煕	1795–1814
	Ichijō Tadayoshi 忠良	1814–1823
	Takatsukasa Masamichi 政通	1823–1856
	Kujō Naotada 尚忠	1856–1862
	Konoe Tadahiro 忠煕	1862–1863
	Takatsukasa Sukehiro 輔煕	1863
	Nijō Naritoshi 斉敬	1863–1867
Nijō Naritoshi		1867

C. Cloistered Sovereigns

The onerous ceremonial duties of being sovereign led many individuals to abdicate while still expecting years of life. Abdication might occur so early that there would be more than one ex-sovereign. Other individuals, beginning with Shirakawa, abdicated with the hope that their freedom from ceremony would enable them to take the reigns of power into their hands. So arose the system of cloistered sovereigns (insei 院政): for example, Shirakawa In. Some individuals are less apt to be known, or at least called by, their title as sovereign (tennō 天皇) than by their later cloistered title (in). It is very common to read of *Gotoba In 後鳥羽院 rather than Gotoba Tennō 後鳥羽天皇.

The nomenclature is a bit more complicated than that. Besides the reigning sovereign, there could be one or more abdicated sovereigns properly styled dajō tennō (daijō tennō in modern usage) 太上天皇. In practice, that title is commonly abbreviated to dajōkō (daijōkō) 太上皇 or yet more simply to jōkō 上皇. Sovereigns would often retire to take orders—out of religious purpose, or for some complex of religious and other motives. Such an abdicated sovereign in orders was termed dajō hōō (daijō hōō) written either 太上法皇 or 太上法王. The simplified version of that was hōō: 法皇, or 法王. The system of cloistered (and abdicated) sovereigns is, then, one variation of abdication, and for a time it held genuine political implications. Altogether, there were twenty-six periods when there was a cloistered sovereign, beginning in 1086 and ending in 1840. But the institution had political implications of importance only during the first century or two of use. And later practice is vexed by two matters. Three abdicated sovereigns (Fushimi, Gofushimi, Gouda) held the title of In twice. And the Nambokuchō period, with its rival northern and southern courts, further complicates matters.

Because the page allows room for them, names are given of the then reigning sovereign(s) during a period of a cloistered sovereign, along with the period of cloistered status.

To calculate these matters any more closely, it will be necessary to compare Table 9-10 with the full list of sovereigns in Part Two, where the characters for their regnal names are also given.

Asterisks designate individuals with entries in Part Three, and N designates a sovereign of the Northern line.

TABLE 9-10. CLOISTERED SOVEREIGNS

Cloistered Sovereign	Then Reigning Sovereign(s)	Dates of Cloistering
Shirakawa In	Horikawa, Toba, Sutoku	1086–1129
Toba In	Sutoku, Konoe, Goshirakawa	1129–1156
Goshirakawa In	Nijō, Rokujō, Takakura	1158–1179
Takakura In	Antoku	1180
Goshirakawa In	Antoku, Gotoba	1180–1192
*Gotoba In	Tsuchimikado, Juntoku, Chūkyō	1198–1221
Gotakakura In	Gohorikawa	1221–1223
Gohorikawa In	Shijō	1232–1234
Gosaga In	Gofukakusa, Kameyama	1246–1272
Kameyama In	Gouda	1274–1287
Gofukakusa In	*Fushimi	1287–1298
*Fushimi In	*Gofushimi	1298–1301
Gouda In	Gonijō	1301–1308
*Fushimi In	, *Hanazono	1308–1313
*Gofushimi In	*Hanazono	1313–1318
Gouda In	Gosaga	1318–1321
*Gofushimi In	N Kōgon	1331–1333
N Kōgon In	N Goen'yū	1336–1351
N Gokōgon In	N Goen'yū	1371–1374
N Goen'yū In	N Gokomatsu	1382–1393
Chōkei In	Gokameyama	1385
Gokomatsu In	Shōkō, Gohanazono	1412–1433
Goyōzei In	Gomizunoo	1611–1617
Gomizunoo In	Meishō, Gokōmyō, Reigen	1629–1680
Reigen In	Higashiyama, Nakamikado	1687–1732
Kōkaku In	Ninkō	1817–1840

*Hanazono (r. 1308–1318) is often referred to as "In," but the title seems to have been a courtesy one, perhaps accounting for the strange title of his diary (see Part Three).

The ranks, offices, and titles given in Sections A, B, and C represent court titles, at least in their inception. As such, they relate to the system of rule about a sovereign. To speak of a system is perhaps to use a word that insufficiently accounts for the Japanese genius for exception or anomaly. In any event, in the next sections of this part attention is given to titles and individuals who might or might not work within the system of rule about a sovereign. Of course the line of sovereigns continued as the source of legitimacy for rule, but even as the ranks and titles considered in these three sections continued to be used and enjoyed, new titles reflecting new realities of power also came into use.

D. The Kamakura Bakufu, Shoguns, and Regents

From the twelfth century or so the court began perceptibly to lose some of its power. The sovereign and nobility were not attacked directly but rather through a series of economic and political changes, as also frequently by infiltration. Two warrior families were conspicuous, the Taira or Heike 平, 平家 and the Minamoto or Genji 源, 源氏. Both justly claimed descent from sovereigns, both consisted of many separate groups, much like the Fujiwara, and there was not always agreement among them. The Taira were the first to take on the rule of government, working in effect as a displacement of the Fujiwaras at the court. Taira Kiyomori (1118–1181) rose to a succession of court posts, including that of dajōdaijin (prime minister) in 1167, and five years later had a daughter become consort of Takakura. According to the moral lesson of the *Heike Monogatari*, Kiyomori overreached himself and so was to be humbled from his high station.

The long series of struggles between Taira and Minamoto, the *Gempei* wars, came substantially to its end with the defeat of the red banner of the Taira by the white of the Minamoto at the Battle of Dannoura in 1185. *Fujiwara Teika's famous remark in this diary, *Meigetsuki*, probably typified court attitudes: "The strife between the red and white is no concern of mine." But his kind were involved in the outcome of warrior struggles. In the next few years Minamoto Yoritomo consolidated his power and, in 1192, extracted from the court appointment as shogun in Kamakura. More precisely, his office was seii taishōgun 征夷大将軍, something like "barbarian-quelling generalissimo." He deliberately chose Kamakura as a place distant from Kyoto and what he regarded as the baneful influence of its courtiers. Like Kiyomori, he was ruler of the land— that is, a person than whom no other was more powerful; his rule was obeyed wherever his arms or his authority exercised for the sovereign was acknowledged. He ruled this way from 1192 to 1199, following the time-honored practice of the military houses, by consultation with trusted senior advisors, including in particular his redoubtable wife (Hōjō) Masako (1157–1225). In one sense, the Minamoto triumph went no farther than these few years of Yoritomo. In another, it had lasting effect as a model for later *bakufu*, and more particularly in creating an institution that others might use more immediately.

Yoritomo's eldest son, Yoriie, succeeded as shogun on his father's death. He was, however, so inept and corrupt that Masako worked with her father, Hōjō Tokimasa, to set the Minamoto bakufu in order. This took some years. Before very long, Masako persuaded Yoriie that it would be better if he took the tonsure, and her father saw to it that the ex-shogun was murdered, just to avoid trouble. Then Yoritomo's second son, *Minamoto Sanetomo, was appointed third shogun. A would-be courtier and an alcoholic, he nonetheless had real abilities, not least as a poet. But he was cut down in public by an uncle, who was then done away with. Thereafter the Hōjō family intervened. Acting as regents (shikken 執権), they decided that there was too much trouble involved with Minamoto candidates for shogun, and so decided to import elegant nobodies from Kyoto, first two high-born Fujiwaras and then four princes of the blood. Their idea was to appoint these high ones at as young an age as possible and to get rid of them when they showed any sign of thinking for themselves. They could be persuaded either to take the tonsure or to be packed off to Kyoto, or both. Here, then, are the Minamoto shoguns:

TABLE 9–11. MINAMOTO KAMAKURA SHOGUNS

Shogun	Lifetime	Office
1. Minamoto Yoritomo 源頼朝	1147–1199	1192–1199
2. Minamoto Yoriie 源頼家	1182–1204	1199–1204
3. Minamoto Sanetomo 源実朝	1192–1219	1204–1219
4. Fujiwara (Kujō) 藤原（九条） Yoritsune 頼経	1218–1256	1226–1246
5. Fujiwara 藤原 Yoritsugu 頼嗣	1239–1256	1246–1252
6. Prince Munetaka 宗尊親王	1242–1274	1252–1266
7. Prince Koreyasu 惟康親王	1264–1326	1266–1289
8. Prince Hisaakira 久明親王	1276–1328	1289–1308
9. Prince Morikuni 守邦親王	1301–1333	1308–1333

Considered purely as a shogunate, the Kamakura bakufu set up by Yoritomo went through only three generations, ending in less than thirty years. But from this seeming disaster, the Hōjō regents were able to make a stable government. It is generally agreed that the first half of the Hōjō regency gave Japan a more stable, just, and efficient government than it had long had, and certainly more so than the country would know for a very long time.

Such success was a practical achievement of intelligence snatched from apparent irrationality. The sovereign still reigned, and nobody would dare suggest an alternative to that institution. Around him were the nobility with their grand titles, wealth, and ways—noblemen becoming ministers, regents, and chancellors, positions recognized everywhere as the pinnacles of prestige a subject could reach. Meanwhile, the main actual details of rule had been ceded to the bakufu in Kamakura. There a shogun held the sovereign's appointment to legitimize the exercise of power, but a Hōjō regent actually gave the orders, after consulting trusted advisors among family and allies. The advisors might include women other than Masako, for especially in the first half of the Hōjō regency women might run provinces, defend castles, and fight in the field. Neoconfucianism with its ordering, clarifying, and often suffocating doctrines was not yet public policy. The variety (not to say anomaly) and the undoubted efficiency of this period testifies to something fine and enduring in classical Japanese experience, perhaps also in modern Japanese life.

All told, there were sixteen Hōjō 北条 regents.

TABLE 9-12. HŌJŌ REGENTS

Regent	Lifetime	Office
1. Tokimasa 時政	1138–1216	1203–1205
2. Yoshitoki 義時	1163–1224	1205–1224
3. Yasutoki 泰時	1183–1242	1224–1242
4. Tsunetoki 経時	1214–1246	1242–1246
5. Tokiyori 時頼	1227–1263	1246–1256
6. Nagatoki 長時	1229–1264	1256–1264
7. Masamura 政村	1205–1273	1264–1268
8. Tokimune 時宗	1251–1284	1268–1284
9. Sadatoki 貞時	1272–1311	1284–1301
10. Morotoki 師時	1274–1311	1301–1311
11. Munenobu 宗宣	d. 1312	1311–1312
12. Hirotoki 熙時	1233–1315	1312–1315
13. Mototoki 基時	d. 1332	1315
14. Takatoki 高時	1303–1333	1316–1326
15. Sadaakira 貞顕	d. 1333	1326
16. Moritoki 守時	d. 1333	1326–1333

Apart from the entropy that affects resistant institutions and regimes, the Hōjō regency found sudden trouble from a source it could not have anticipated. Far to the west, at least beyond the Japan Sea, the Mongols were running over country after country in their eastward movement. Kublai Khan, who had completed the Mongol conquest of China, twice attempted to conquer Japan (1274, 1281). Although caught off guard the first time, the Hōjō were saved by luck in the form of a delivering wind, which repelled or sank the invading ships. For the expected second onslaught, the regency impoverished itself, but it succeeded. In saving the country it was left without means to reward those it had called on, and had exhausted most of its power and authority along with its means. As Hōjō power waned, the country gradually slid into the anarchy that would mark it for a considerable period.

E. THE MUROMACHI BAKUFU AND ASHIKAGA SHOGUNS

By 1300, the Kamakura bakufu had become as much a fiction as a reality. The Hōjō family continued to matter, but merely as one of several warrior houses groping for power. So uncertain was the situation that Godaigo (r. 1318–1339) believed that he saw a chance to centralize power once more in Kyoto and about the royal house. Intriguing with various houses disaffected from the Hōjō, he instituted what is often called the Kemmu Restoration, which may more literally be termed the Kemmu Renovation (Kemmu Shinsei 建武新政) in 1334. In the struggles that followed, Godaigo's attempt failed, the Kamakura bakufu was ended, and the Ashikaga house had formed a new bakufu at Muromachi in the capital (1338). In another year, Godaigo was sent into exile.

The successive Ashikaga shoguns from Takauji onward had a taste for glory expressed in their generous support of the arts of drama (nō), painting, architecture, and seemingly everything that bespoke grandeur (see *Zeami, *Nōami). The Medicis in later Italy might have thought them kindred spirits, if, of course, the West had thought much of the glories of the East. The ruder art of power was not one the Ashikagas mastered, however, and although they often had excellent advice, they did not always follow it and, in any event, never extended their rule much beyond the provinces surrounding the capital. The Ashikaga sought to exercise power by appointing certain shugo daimyō (守護大名) to major advisory positions such as administrator general (kanrei 管領) and steward (shitsuji 執事). Among the houses so selected were the Hosokawa, Hatakeyama, and Yamana, the last of which exercised something like rule in ten provinces. The problem with the system was that the supposed subordinates were commonly as ambitious of power, and as ineffectual in achieving or holding to it, as the Ashikagas themselves. The nation was severely fractured into warring factions, so that the Muromachi bakufu was partly a grand illusion and partly a system that somehow continued for lack of a better. Before the reality and its grand fiction exploded completely, there were fifteen Ashikaga 足利 shoguns.

TABLE 9-13. ASHIKAGA OR MUROMACHI SHOGUNS

Name	Lifetime	Office
1. Takauji 尊氏	1305–1358	1338–1358
2. Yoshiakira 義詮	1330–1367	1358–1367
3. Yoshimitsu 義満	1358–1408	1368–1405
4. Yoshimochi 義持	1386–1428	1405–1423
5. Yoshikazu 義量	1407–1425	1423–1425
6. Yoshinori 義教	1394–1441	1429–1441
7. Yoshikatsu 義勝	1434–1443	1442–1443
8. Yoshimasa 義政	1436–1490	1469–1473
9. Yoshihisa 義尚	1465–1489	1473–1489
10. Yoshitane 義稙	1466–1523	1490–1494; 1508–1521
11. Yoshizumi 義澄	1479–1512	1494–1508
12. Yoshiharu 義晴	1511–1550	1521–1546
13. Yoshiteru 義輝	1536–1565	1546–1565
14. Yoshihide 義栄	1546–1568	1568
15. Yoshiaki 義昭	1537–1597	1568–1573

NOTE: Differing dates are given for the periods of office. Those given above are taken from *Chūsei Handbook*, comp. Nagahara Keiji et al. (Tokyo: Kondō Shuppansha, 1973).

The fact that so many Ashigaka shoguns were appointed while still in their nonage amply testifies to the basic powerlessness of many individuals who held the office. One of the more enterprising, Yoshimochi (fourth shogun), affected the title of sovereign in dealing with the Chinese court. Whatever the boast of one shogun or the youth of another, in Japanese fashion the institution could prove stronger than any individual occupant when buttressed by powerful—and loyal—shugo. Such happy circumstances were always a matter of lucky balance, and the Ashikagas can be judged variously as spendthrifts or as brilliant patrons of the arts, as power-seekers or as people who did the best anyone might have done in an increasingly impossible situation.

F. ANARCHY, POTENTATES; FROM THE AZUCHI-MOMOYAMA PERIOD TO THE EDO BAKUFU

Although the Muromachi bakufu continued to have its shoguns till 1573, its last incumbent was really a figurehead. How this came about requires attention to the civil wars that had been ravaging the country. Among these, one was the Ōnin War (1467–1477), which devastated the capital and made it largely un-inhabitable during much of the decade or so of fighting. But the period from 1482 to 1568 was a time of such constant and bloody tumult throughout the land that it (or all of 1467–1568) goes under the name of the Sengoku jidai 戦国 時代, that is, the era of the nation or the provinces at war. Japan was clearly ready either for prostration or for rule by some strong figure capable of government.

The Azuchi-Momoyama period brought strength and government in three stages represented by potentates of quite differing disposition. The first was Oda Nobunaga 織田信長 (1534–1582). From his base of power in Owari and Mikawa (the modern Nagoya region), he gradually moved westward. By 1568, he was acting on behalf of the last Muromachi shogun, Ashikaga Yoshiaki, entering Kyoto nominally to exert *bakufu* authority. Before long, he had made Yoshiaki a puppet and was de facto ruler of much of the country, at least of central Japan. But in 1582 he was murdered.

Nobunaga was succeeded by one of his lieutenants, Toyotomi Hideyoshi 豊臣秀吉 (1536–1598) and his son Hideyori 秀頼 (1593–1615). Hideyoshi was one of the most remarkable figures in Japanese military and political history. As was the case with many in those anarchic times, he was able, in spite of low birth, to rise to very high position. Within three years of Nobunaga's assassination, he had acquired sufficient power to set up government at Momoyama, where he continued the artistic splendors of the Ashikagas. Among other achievements, he opened trade to the continent, waged wars against Korea (even planning one against China). His official appointments are exquisitely revealing of the state of the nation. He was of too low an origin to qualify as shogun. In lieu of holding that office, he managed to get himself appointed chancellor (kampaku) of the court in 1585, and in the next year prime minister (dajō daijin). This settling for mere court ranks tells us how far the court had declined, but the choice of them shows nonetheless that the titles were still far from negligible and might have become the basis for a new system of government, if the Fujiwara and Taira trick could be played again. He took measures to just that end, measures at least of social reorganization and usually termed feudal. He required that commoners relinquish swords and be set in a social hierarchy; he decreed that every person should stay in the occupation of the house into which he or she had been born. In 1594, the symbol of his glory, the Momoyama palace, was built. The effort to found a new dynasty failed at his death, however, because of the weakness of his sons, and even more because of the strength of Nobunaga's other lieutenant, Tokugawa Ieyasu, who had been biding his time patiently.

Ieyasu moved strongly on Hideyoshi's death, and by 1603 was able to make the claim of shogun. He followed Minamoto Yoritomo's example, in choosing a site far from the capital, in Edo. By 1615, with the fall of Osaka Castle and Hideyoshi's descendants, Ieyasu was in greater control of the country than had been anyone since the Hōjō regents. Abandoning Hideyoshi's grand, or grandiose, continental aspirations, Ieyasu concentrated on his own country, using Hideyoshi's centralizing and restrictive measures with a rigor matched by thoroughness. As is detailed in Part One D, this involved a thorough reconstitution of society into social orders that did not include the court. Ieyasu cut the revenues available to the sovereign and the nobility. And if he was not able to do without the sovereign for purposes of legitimacy, he kept a close eye on Kyoto.

The Edo bakufu was designed to be a totalitarian regime. In practice it dispersed degrees of power to various daimyo, allotting rice revenues generously or meagerly depending on a given house's closeness to the Tokugawa, or on past support to its cause. Ieyasu closed the country to foreign entry or native departure, on pain of death. In short, he established a repressive centralized regime whose rule was executed by organs of his household with local supervision by a warrior aristocracy carefully controlled by a system that included triennial visits to Edo, and the leaving of major members of a daimate family as hostages when the daimyo was in his own province. The hard-worked farmers were taxed in an economy determined by units of rice, with artisans and merchants classed still lower. In official theory, at least, society consisted of four major orders—in the descending sequence of samurai, farmers, artisans, and merchants (shi-nō-kō-shō). This was the most systematic and innovative regime the country had known for centuries, perhaps ever. It imported Neoconfucianism as a philosophical justification, if not quite a legitimizing factor or power (see Part Six P). A ravaged, exhausted nation at last found peace, and, as time went on, new energies and new ways to express them in literary activity.

As Table 9-14 shows, the Edo bakufu had at its head a series of fifteen shoguns from the Tokugawa 徳川 family.

Benefiting in different ways from the models and mistakes of the earlier bakufu, Ieyasu designed a system that lasted more than two and a half centuries. His successors added to his plan, but did little to alter its general features. The most important organ of government was the rōjū 老中, the Senior Council, or Council of Elders, as it is variously translated. There, four or five advisors gave

TABLE 9-14. TOKUGAWA OR EDO SHOGUNS

Name	Lifetime	Office
1. Ieyasu 家康	1542–1616	1603–1605
2. Hidetada 秀忠	1570–1623	1605–1623
3. Iemitsu 家光	1604–1651	1623–1651
4. Ietsuna 家綱	1641–1680	1651–1680
5. Tsunayoshi 綱吉	1646–1709	1680–1709
6. Ienobu 家宣	1633–1712	1709–1712
7. Ietsugu 家継	1709–1716	1713–1716
8. Yoshimune 吉宗	1684–1751	1716–1745
9. Ieshige 家重	1711–1761	1745–1760
10. Ieharu 家治	1737–1786	1760–1786
11. Ienari 家斉	1772–1841	1787–1837
12. Ieyoshi 家慶	1793–1853	1837–1853
13. Iesada 家定	1824–1858	1853–1858
14. Iemochi 家茂	1846–1866	1858–1866
15. Yoshinobu 慶喜	1837–1913	1866–1867

their counsel, and if a shogun was too young to rule in his own right, there could always be appointed some sort of regent (hosa, kōken). Because of the lengthy time during which the Edo bakufu lasted, some charting of its government seems desirable. Unfortunately, there is no full, agreed-on list of English versions of offices, as there is for the court. In lieu of that, a briefer chart is offered in Table 9-15.

TABLE 9-15. CHIEF OFFICES OF THE EDO BAKUFU

Shōgun 将軍

The Great Corridor
The Antechamber Regent

—Great Counsellor (1)
  tairō 大老

hosa 輔佐, kōken 後見, etc.

—Senior Counsellors (4–5)
  rōjū 老中
          —Secretaries (about 60)
            yūhitsu 右筆
          —Chamberlains (6–7)
            sobashū 側衆
          —Masters of Official Ceremony (16–26)
            kōke 高家
          —Counsellors for the Three Lords
            karō (Tayasu karō, Hitotsubashi karō,
            Shimizu karō) 家老
          —Keepers of Edo Castle (4–6)
            rusui 留守居
          —Captains of the Great Guards (12)
            ōbangashira 大番頭

TABLE 9–15. (*continued*)

Shōgun 将軍

The Great Corridor
The Antechamber Regent

—Inspectors General (4–5)
ōmetsuke 大目付
—Edo City Magistrates (2)
Edo machi bugyō 江戸町奉行
—Superintendents of Finance (4)
kanjō bugyō 勘定奉行
—Deputies
gundai 郡代 (3); daikan 代官 (40–50)
—Superintendents of the Treasury (4)
kane bugyō 金奉行
—Superintendents of Cereal Stores (2)
kura bugyō 蔵奉行
—Gold Monopoly
kinza 金座
—Silver Monopoly
ginza 銀座
—Copper Monopoly
dōza 銅座
—Cinnabar Monopoly
shuza 朱座
—Comptrollers of Finance (4)
kanjōgimmiyaku 勘定吟味役
—Kantō Deputy (1)
Kantō gundai 関東郡代
—Superintendents of Works (2)
sakuji bugyō 作事奉行
—Superintendents of Public Works (2)
fushin bugyō 普請奉行
—Kyoto City-Magistrates (2)
Kyōto machi bugyō 京都町奉行
—Osaka City-Magistrates (2)
Ōsaka machi bugyō 大阪町奉行
—Magistrates of Nagasaki (3–4), Uraga (1–2), etc.
Nagasaki bugyō, Uraga bugyō 長崎奉行, 浦賀奉行

—Grand Chamberlain (1)
sobayōnin) 側用人
—Junior Councilors (4–5)
wakadoshiyori) 若年寄

—Captains of the Body Guard (6)
shoinbangashira 書院番頭
—Captains of the Inner Guards (6)
koshōgumibangashira 小姓組番頭
—Captains of the New Guards (6)
shimbangashira 新番頭
—Superintendents of Construction and Repair (2)
kobushin bugyō 小普請奉行
—Chiefs of the Pages (6)

TABLE 9–15. (*continued*)

Shōgun 将軍

                                           The Great Corridor
                                       The Antechamber Regent

                    koshō tōdori 小姓頭取
                    —Chiefs of the Attendants (3)
                    ko'nando tōdori 小納戸頭取
                    —Inspectors
                    metsuke 目付
                    —Chiefs of the Castle Accountants (2)
                    nandogashira 納戸頭
                    —Attendant Physicians
                    ishi 医師
                    —Attendant Confucianists
                    jusha 儒者
                    —Superintendents of the Kitchen (3–5)
                    zen bugyō 膳奉行
        —Masters of Shogunal Ceremony (20 or more)
        sōjaban 奏者番
        —Superintendents of Temples and Shrines (4)
        jisha bugyō 寺社奉行
        —Kyoto Deputy (1)
        Kyōto shoshidai 京都所司代
        —Keeper of Osaka Castle (1)
        Ōsaka jōdai 大阪城代

        —Supreme Court of Justice
        hyōjōsho 評定所

Regular duty:
        Superintendents of Temples and Shrines
        Edo City Magistrates
        Superintendents of Finance

Irregular duty:
        A Senior Councilor
        The Grand Chamberlain
        Other Magistrates and Superintendents when residing in Edo

Assisted by:
        Comptrollers of Finance
        Inspectors General and others

The conspicuous feature of the *spirit* of the Edo bakufu is its desire to order everything along lines justified by Neoconfucian rational and moral principles. The conspicuous thing about the *history* of the Edo bakufu is that such philosophy did no more than any other to reduce corruption or prevent change. Change was the one element most resisted by the regime, since its Neoconfucian principles were universal truths. Its system was postulated on a rice-crop fiscal system, on an immobile population, and on total exclusion from the rest of the world. The gap between such theory and reality grew steadily. The fiscal system became monetary, and people began to move about more—socially as well as geographically. Finally, there came pressure from without. Had the bakufu had Hideyoshi's alertness to foreign affairs or the Hōjō regents' practical efficiency, the foreign threat would have meant much less. But if the bakufu had had those things, it would not have been what it was. By the first third of the nineteenth century, matters were increasingly out of hand, opposition was ever stronger. It seems ironic that what neither Gotoba nor Godaigo could do on behalf of the court was finally done by some disgruntled, geographically peripheral houses, when in 1868 the bakufu came to its squeaky end (although not without its loyal adherents, not without a very strong legacy to modern Japan)—restore the tennō to the center of the state.

It will not do to stress only the fixity of the Edo bakufu. At the very top, experiments were tried. The rōjū was a council essential from the beginning. But first in 1636 and intermittently thereafter, there were tairō 大老 appointed. Tanuma Okitsugu 田沼意次, referred to earlier, introduced a liberalized era under Ieharu, getting on famously with corruption, debasement of the currency, profits for the bakufu, and liberal thought, until there were peasant uprisings that gave his enemies an excuse to bring him down.

So there *was* color in the Edo bakufu. And yet if we compare it with previous regimes, one cannot but be struck by the fact that neither these shoguns, nor their chief advisors, are memorable as poets. Once a year the shogun would have to write a *renga* stanza or so after a Satomura master had written the opening stanza. The contrast with Yoritomo and *Sanetomo could hardly be greater. (*Hosokawa Yūsai provides an even better example, however.) In short, it is hard to escape the conclusion that for the first time in their history Japanese continued to create a great literature in spite of their government. It is all the more important, therefore, to point to what imagination there was, Perhaps the fifth shogun, Tsunayoshi, will do. He was so irrationally considerate of dogs that he issued edicts of heinous punishment for people who neglected or mistreated the animals. He became celebrated in plays and known as His Dog Lordship (inu kubō 犬公方). Tokugawa virtue had some more or less redeeming features.

PART TEN Architecture; Clothing, Armor, and Arms; Illustrated Popular Books and Other Genre Representations

The purpose of this part is to present information, by illustration and annotation, that will give readers assistance in visualizing matters referred to in literature. Because the illustrations derive from Japanese sources, both old and modern, the view implied is that of people contemporary either with older writers or with ourselves. We have included some fanciful things, as will be apparent, but we hope that modern imagining by Japanese may assist contemporary foreign readers.

The "architectural" illustrations show first (Section A, Figures 10-1 to 10-14) the disposition of the sovereign's palace in Heian times, very little of which remains in the present gosho, or palace, in Kyoto. Those schematic designs are followed by imagined scenes. The next series, Section B, Figures 10-15 to 10-22, show reconstructed views of what a palace of the high nobility might look like, along with further imagined scenes.

The next series of illustrations, Section C, Figures 10-23 to 10-59, represents clothing worn from ancient to Edo times in terms as accurate as is possible today. There follows a series of illustrations showing armor and arms, Section D, Figures 10-60 to 10-80. No effort has been made to follow the development of warlike gear in any detail, but the terms for the parts of a bow, for example, remain fairly constant.

The last group of illustrations, Section E, Figures 10-80 to 10-93, offers depictions of various kinds of illustrated popular books: *otogizōshi*, *ukiyozōshi*, *kibyōshi*, and *kokkeibon*. There is also one illustrated reading text of a play. It will be found that the emphasis of this group falls on Edo matters (although the series begins with Muromachi pictures), just as the emphasis in the preceding figures falls on earlier times.

We have omitted some of the most familiar examples: the *Genji Monogatari Emaki*, the so-called Toba scroll (we have instead a picture of mice doing human activities), and the portrait of Yoritomo—to name but a few. It is becoming ever clearer that relations between painting and poetry are extraordinarily close in classical Japan, and some token of that connection is therefore given here.

Here, as in the preceding parts, an asterisk designates an entry in Part Three, and an italicized word, other than a title, designates an entry in Part Four.

A. THE HEIAN PALACE

North

平安京大内裏図

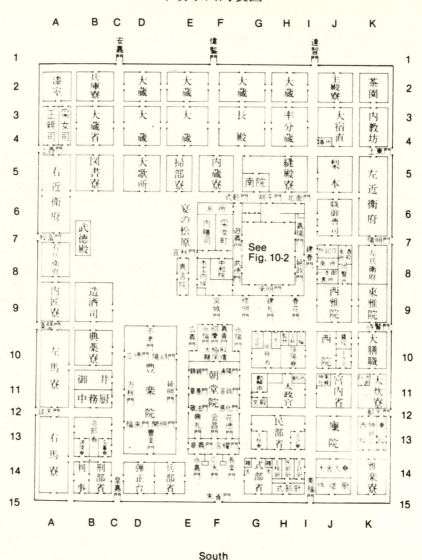

FIGURE 10-1. The Heian Palace, Full View (Heiankyō Daidairi)
By permission of Kadokawa Shoten

Identification of Places in Figure 10-1

R = Right   M = Middle   L = Left   u. = upper   l. = lower

A 1–2	Urushimuro. Lacquer Storehouse
A 3–4	L Ōkimi no Tsukasa. Royal Family Office
	R Uneme no Tsukasa. Palace Women's Office
A 4	Jōsaimon. Jōsai Gate
A 5–6	Ukon'efu. Bodyguards of the Right
A 7	Impumon. Impu Gate
A 8	Uhyōefu. Military Guards of the Right
A 9	Takumiryō. Bureau of Artisans
	l. Sōhekimon. Sōheki Gate
A 10–11	Samaryō. Royal Stables of the Left
A 12	Dantenmon. Danten Gate
A 13–15	Umaryō. Royal Stables of the Right
B 1–2	Hyōgoryō. Bureau of Military Storehouses
B 3–4	Ōkurashō. Treasury Ministry
B 5	Zushoryō. Bureau of Books and Drawings
B 7	Butokuden. Hall of Military Arts
B 9	Miki no Tsukasa. Royal Wine Office
B 10	Ten'yakuryō, Bureau of Medicine
B 11	u. Mii. Palace Well
	l. Nakatsukasa no Kuriya. Central Affairs Kitchen
B 13	Jibushō. Civil Affairs Ministry
	l. L. Shoryōryō. Bureau of Mausoleums
	l. R Genbaryō. Bureau of Buddhism and Aliens.
B 14–15	L Hanji. Judicial Office
	R Gyōbushō. Penal Ministry
C 1	Ankamon. Anka Gate
C 14–15	Kōkamon. Kōka Gate
D 2–4	Ōkura. Government Storehouses
D 10–13	Burakuin. Court of Entertainment
D 10	u. Furōmon. Furō Gate
D 10	l. L Rittokumon. Rittoku Gate
D 10	l. R Yōrokumon. Yōroku Gate
D 11	L Banshūmon. Banshū Gate
D 11	R Emmeimon. Emmei Gate
D 12	L Fukuraimon. Fukurai Gate
D 12	R Kaimeimon. Kaimei Gate
D 14–15	L Danjōdai. Board of Censors
	R Hyōbushō. War Ministry
E 2–4	Ōkura. Government Storehouses
E 5	Kamonryō. Bureau of Housekeeping
E 6–7	En no Matsubara. Pine Grove Banquet Area
	l. Senshūmon. Senshū Gate
E 8	Shingon'in. Shingon Chapel
F 1	Ikammon. Ikan Gate
F 5	Uchi no Kura Ryō. Palace Storehouse Bureau
F 6	Itodokoro. Sewing Office

F 7	L Naizenshi. Royal Table Office
	R Uneme Chō. Palace Women's Office
F 9	Kyūjōmon. Kyūjō Gate
F 10	Daigokuden. Great Hall of State
	u. L outer Kōgimon. Kōgi Gate
	u. L inner Eifukumon. Eifuku Gate
	u. M inner Shōkeimon. Shōkei Gate
	u. R inner Kakimon. Kaki Gate
	u. R outer Eiyōmon. Eiyō Gate
	l. Ryūbidan. Steps to Garden
F 11–13	Chōdōin. Administrative Palace (The Eight Ministries)
F 11	u. L Kenshimmon. Kenshin Gate
	u. R Tsūyōmon. Tsūyō Gate
F 12	l. L Shōzemmon. Shōzen Gate
	l. R Senseimon. Sensei Gate
	l. L Keihōmon. Keihō Gate
	l. R Kankamon. Kanka Gate
F 13	u. L Kōraimon. Kōrai Gate
	u. M Kaishōmon. Kaishō Gate
	u. R Katokumon. Katoku Gate
	l. L Shōgimon. Shōgi Gate
	l. R. Gan'yōmon. Gan'yō Gate
F 14	L Eikamon. Eika Gate
	M. Ōtemmon. Ōten Gate
	R Chōrakumon. Chōraku Gate
F 15	Suzakumon. Suzaku Gate
G 2	Ōkura. Government Storehouse
G 3–4	Nagadono. Treasury Storehouse
G–H 5	Nuidono Ryō. Bureau of Princesses and Wardrobe
	l. L Nan'in. Southern Chapel
G–H 6–8	See Figure 10-2 (Inner Palace Compound)
G–H 9	L Sumeimon. Sumei Gate
	M Kenreimon. Kenrei Gate
	R Shunkamon. Shunka Gate
G 10	Nakatsukasa Shō. Central Affairs Ministry
	u. L Jijū no Tsubone. Chamberlains' Quarters
	u. R Uchitoneri. Palace Retainers' Quarters
G–H 11–12	Dajōkan. Council of State
G–H 13	Mimbushō. Popular Affairs Ministry
	L Shuzeiryō. Bureau of Taxation
	R Shukeiryō. Bureau of Statistics
G 14	Shikibushō. Ministry of Ceremonies
H 14	L Shuzei no Kuriya. Taxation Bureau Kitchen
	M Mimbu no Kuriya. Popular Affairs Ministry Kitchen
	R Shukei no Kuriya. Statistics Bureau Kitchen

	l. Shikibu no Kuriya. Ceremonies Ministry Kitchen	J 11	Kunaishō. Royal Household Ministry
H 2	Ōkura. Government Storehouse		u. L Sonokaranokami Yashiro. Anti-Pestilence Shrine
H 3	Ritsubunzō. Special Goods Store-house	J 13	Rin'in. Tribute Rice Office
H 10	On'yōryō. Bureau of Divination	K 2	Chaen. Tea Plot
I 1	Tatchimon. Tatchi Gate	K 3	Naikyōbō. Female Dancers' and Musicians' Office
I 15	Bifukumon. Bifuku Gate	K 4	Shōtōmon. Shōtō Gate
J 2	Tonomo Ryō. Bureau of Grounds and Repair	K 5–6	Sakon'efu. Bodyguards of the Left
J 3	Ōtonoi. Guards' Quarters	K 7	Yōmeimon. Yōmei Gate
	l. L Bansho. Guards' Office	K 8	Sahyōefu. Military Guards of the Left
J 5	Nashimoto(in). Nashimoto Chapel	K 9	Tōgain. Heir Designate's Eastern Palace
J 6	Shiki no Onzōshi. Apartments of the Consort's Household		l. Taikenmon. Taiken Gate
J 8	Geki no Chō, etc. Secretaries Offices (of the Council of State, etc.)	K 10	Daizenshiki. Palace Table Office
		K 11	Ōiryō. Palace Kitchen Bureau
J 9	Saigain. Heir Designate's Western Palace	K 12	Ikuhōmon. Ikuhō Gate
J 10	L Saiin. Western Shinto Quarters	K 13	M Jingikan. Department of Shinto
	l. L Shōin. Soya Kitchen		L Tōin. Eastern Quarters
	l. R Moitori (Mondo) no Tsukasa. Water Office		R Saiin. Western Quarters
		K 14	Gagakuryō (Uta Ryō). Bureau of Music

Identification of Places in Figure 10-2

NOTE: The empty blocks around the perimeters chiefly designate living areas for lower-ranking servants, along with some offices and guard watches.

R = Right   M = Middle   L = Left   u. = upper   l. = lower

A–G 1–3	Ranrinbō. Female Attendants' Quarters	D 21–22	Shimmotsudokoro. Office of Offerings
A 8–9	Yūgimon. Yūgi Gate	E 14–16	u. Asage no Tsubo. Dining-Room Court
A 10–11	Soto no Shinmotsudokoro. Outside Office of Offerings		l. Daibandokoro no Tsubo. Table-Room Court
A–B 15	Immeimon. Immei Gate	F 5	Kiammon. Kian Gate
A 20	Butokumon. Butoku Gate	F–G 12	Takiguchi no Jin. Guards' Post
A 22–23	Shuri Uchisaburō. Carpenters' Waiting Office	F–G 7–8	Tōkaden. Ladies' Quarters
B 13–14	Uhyōe no Suke no Shuku. Quarters of Assistant Head of the Right Military Guards	F 10–11	Kokiden. Quarters of Junior Consort or Consort
B 16–17	Udaishō Chokuro. Quarters of Head of Right Military Guards	F 12	Chūmon. One of a number of small inner gates or passages
B 22–23	Sōbō. Priests' Office	F–G 12	Takiguchi no Jin. Palace Guards
B–C 21, C–D 22	Tsukumodokoro. Furniture and Other Goods Shop	F 14–16	Seiryōden. Sovereign's Private Residence
C–D 7	Shihōsha (Kannari no Tsubo). Ladies' Quarters	F 16	Ishibaidan. Lime Altar
C–D 8–9	Gyōkasha (Umetsubo). Ladies' Quarters		l. Tenjō (no Ma). Courtiers' Hall
C–E 11	Higyōsha (Fujitsubo). Ladies' Quarters	F 18–20	Kyōshoden. Palace Archives
D 14–16	Kōrōden. Sovereign's Dining Hall	F 20	Gekkamon. Gekka Gate
D 18–20	Kurōdodokoro Machiya. Chamberlains' Quarters	F 21	Ampukuden. Court Physician's Waiting Room
		G 14	Kuretake. "Chinese" Bamboo
		G 16	Kawatake. "River" Bamboo
		G 19	Tachibana. Orange Tree

North

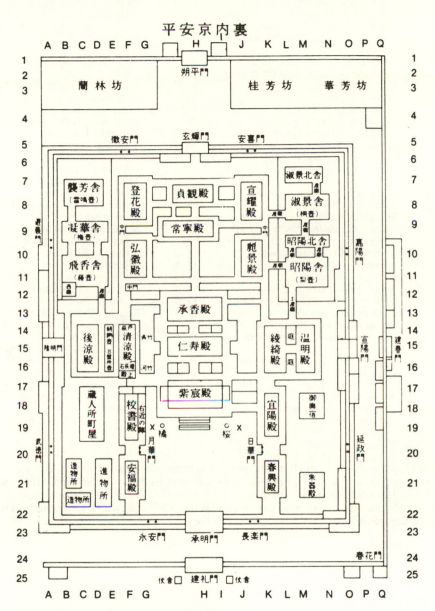

FIGURE 10-2. The Heian Palace, Inner Palace
Inset from Figure 1 (Heiankyō Dairi)
By permission of Kadokawa Shoten

G 20	x Ukon no Jin. Watch of the Right Inner Palace Guards
G 23	Eiammon. Eian Gate
G–H 6	Uhyōe no Suke Shukusho. Post for the Assistant Head of the Right Military Guards
G–H 7	Kawaragaki Katahisashi no Rō. Single-eaved Tiled-Roof Corridor
I–J 7	Same as preceding
H–I 14–16	Rodai. Balcony
H 2	Sakuheimon. Sakuhei gate
H 5	Genkimon. Genki Gate
H 7–8	Jōganden. Wardrobe Office
H 10–12	Kisaimachi no Rō (Kisaki Machi no Rō). Long passage from Shōkyōden to Jōneiden
H 12–14 –16	Watarirō (Watadono). A passage
J 9	Jōneiden. Ladies' Quarters
H 13	Shōkyōden. Ladies' Quarters
H 15	Jijūden. Sovereign's Ordinary Sitting Room
H 18	Shishinden. Ceremonial Court
H 22–23	Shōmeimon. Shōmei Gate
H 25	Kenreimon. Kenrei Gate
I 19	Sakura. Cherry Tree
I 20	x Sakon no Jin. Watch of the Left Inner Palace Guards
I–J 6	Sahyōe no Suke Shukusho. Post for Assistant Head of Left Military Guards
J–Q 2–3	1. Keihōbō. Female Attendants' Quarters r. Kahōbō. The same
J–K 5	Ankimon. Anki Gate
J 7–8	Sen'yōden. Ladies' Quarters
J 10–11	Reikeiden. The same
J–K 20	Nikkamon. Nikka Gate
K 14–16	Ryōkiden. Sovereign's Bathing, Dressing Place
K 18–19	Giyōden. Sovereign's Treasures
K 21	Shunkōden. Military Arms and Stores
L–N 8	Shigeisha (Kiritsubo). Ladies' Quarters
L–N 11	Shōyōsha (Nashitsubo). Ladies' Quarters
L 15, L 16	Niwa. Gardens
M 14–16	Ummeiden. Regalia Court
M–N 18	Mikoshi Yadori. Carriage House
M–N 21	Shukiden. Function not known
N–O 22	Tonomo Uchisaburō. Waiting Place for Bureau of Grounds and Repair
N–O 23	Tori no Zōshi. Falconers' Office
O 10–11	Kayōmon. Kayō Gate
O 11–13	Ijimachi (Ishichō). Small Gate to Inner Palace
O 13–15	Sahyōe no Suke no Shuku. Quarters for Assistant Head of Military Guards of the Left
O 15	Giyōmon. Giyō Gate
O 16–18	Sadaishō Chokuro. Quarters of Head of Left Military Guards
O 20	Enseimon. Ensei Gate
O 21–22	Kamon Uchisaburō. Bureau of Housekeeping's Waiting Office
P 24	Shunkamon. Shunka Gate
P–Q 4–5	Hisumashiden. Resting Room
P–Q 16	Jijūdokoro. Chamberlains' Office
P–Q 17	Edokoro. Office of Arts (chiefly painting)
P–Q 19–20	Goshodokoro. Office of Writing Materials
Q 15	Kenshummon. Kenshun Gate

The Daigokuden, Court of High Ceremony, was where rites of accession (cf. coronation) took place, along with other principal ceremonies, such as the gosaie pictured in these two scenes. This observance ran from the 8th through the 14th of the First Month, and involved sūtra recitations for the nation's well being. See Part Seven H. Later, many of the important ceremonies were performed instead in the Shishinden (see Figures 10-5, 10-6).

FIGURE 10-3.

1. Daigokuden tōmen. Eastern view
2. Tōfukumon. Tōfuku Gate
3. Eiyōmon. Eiyō Gate

FIGURE 10-4.

1. Daigokuden nammen. Southern view

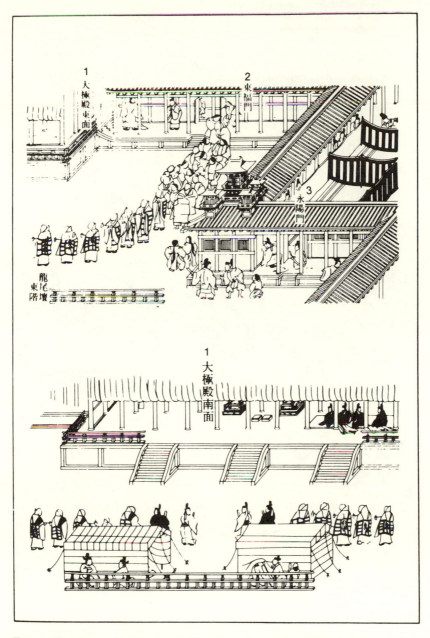

FIGURE 10-3 (top), 10-4 (bottom). The Heian Palace, Imagined Scenes, Daigokuden
By permission of Kadokawa Shoten

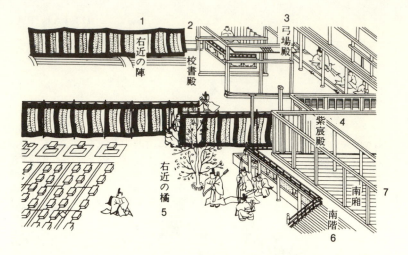

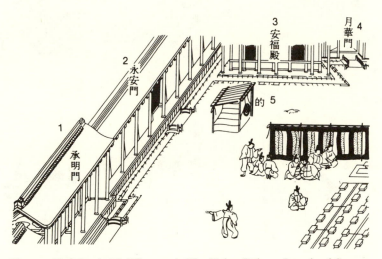

FIGURE 10-5 (top), 10-6 (bottom). The Heian Palace, Imagined Scenes, Shishinden
By permission of Kadokawa Shoten

The Shishinden, Ceremonial Court, is represented here in preparation for the noriyumi no sechi, a guards ceremony something like a royal trooping, held on the 18th of the First Month.

FIGURE 10-5.

1. Ukon no Jin. Watch of the Right Inner Palace Guards
2. Kyōshoden. Palace Archives
3. Yubadono. Archery Grounds
4. Shishinden
5. Ukon no Tachibana. Orange Tree; associated with 1
6. Minami no Kizahashi. Southern Stairs
7. Minami no Hisashi. Southern Eaves

FIGURE 10-6.

1. Shōmeimon. Shōmei Gate
2. Eianmon. Eian Gate
3. Ampukuden. Court Physician's Waiting Room
4. Gekkamon. Gekka Gate
5. Mato. Target

綾綺殿 1 温明殿 2 宣陽門 3

仁寿殿 1 綾綺殿 2

FIGURE 10-7 (top), 10-8 (middle), 10-9 (bottom). The Heian Palace,
Imagined Scenes, Day of the Rat
By permission of Kadokawa Shoten

On the Day of the Rat near the 21st of the First Month, there was an observance
throughout the palace involving various activities, including composing Chinese verse,
drinking, and so on. See Part Seven H. The scenes envision activities in various places.

FIGURE 10-7.

1. Ryōkiden. Sovereign's Bathing and Robing
   Place
2. Ummeiden. Regalia Court
3. Giyōmon. Giyō Gate

FIGURE 10-8.

1. Jijūden. Sovereign's Sitting Quarters (later

these ordinary daytime quarters were shifted
to the Shishinden, to the south)
2. Ryōkiden. See Figure 10-7, 1

FIGURE 10-9. Kenshummon. Kenshun Gate (one
of the twelve outer gates, standing in the middle on the eastern side)

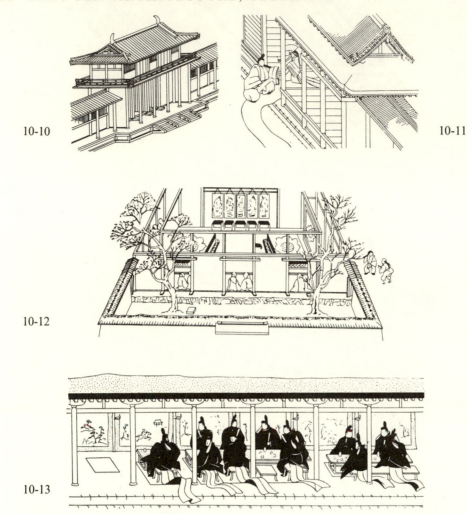

FIGURES 10-10, 10-11, 10-12, 10-13. The Heian Palace, Imagined Scenes
By permission of Kadokawa Shoten

FIGURES 10-10 AND 10-11 show very different gates:

10-10. Ōtemmon. Ōten Gate (one of major entrance and exit)

10-11. Genkimon. Genki Gate (one of twelve inner gates of passage from one part of the palace compound to another).

FIGURE 10-12. Shingon In. Shingon Chapel. The scene envisaged is that of the misuhō observances of tantric rites on the 8th through the 14th of the First Month

FIGURE 10-13. The Hall between Genki Gate and Kian Gate. For the Nigū no Daikyō on the 2nd of the First Month, ministers gathered to pay their respect to the Consort and the Heir Designate

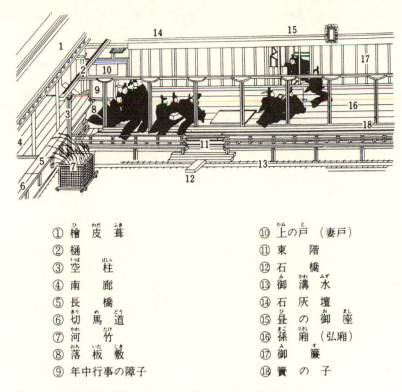

① 檜皮葺
② 樋柱
③ 空柱
④ 南廊
⑤ 長橋
⑥ 切の馬道
⑦ 河竹
⑧ 落板敷
⑨ 年中行事の障子
⑩ 上の戸（妻戸）
⑪ 東階
⑫ 石橋
⑬ 御溝水
⑭ 石灰壇
⑮ 昼の御座
⑯ 孫廂（弘廂）
⑰ 御簾
⑱ 簀の子

FIGURE 10-14. The Seiryōden (see Figure 10-2, E 14–16)
By permission of Kadokawa Shoten

FIGURE 10-14. Seiryōden Tōmen. Eastern view of the Seiryōden, the Sovereign's Residential Palace.

1. Hiwadabuki. Cypress bark roofing
2. Toi (or hi). Rain pipe
3. Utsubobashira. Drainpipe
4. Nanrō. Southern Corridor
5. Nagahashi. Corridor between Seiryōden and Shishinden
6. Kirimedō. Continuation of 5
7. Kawatake. Bamboo
8. Ochiitajiki. Lowered area, wooden-floored
9. Nenjūgyōji no Sōji. Four panels depicting annual observances. See Part Seven H.
10. Kami no To. A hinged (not sliding) door in the corner of the chamber
11. Higashi no Kizahashi. Eastern stairs
12. Ishibashi. Stone paving
13. Mikawamizu. Waterflow for the royal garden
14. Ishibaidan. Lime Altar (an area floored with dirt mixed with lime to purify and harden, where, within the panels of no. 9, the sovereign and female Shinto attendants worshiped each morning, facing the Regalia—Ummeiden, Fig. 10-2, M 15–16—and the Ise Shrine)
15. Hi no Omashi. Sovereign's Sitting Area
16. Magobisashi. The outer of two eaves (this one shingled so the sovereign could hear the rain)
17. Misu. Sovereign's Bamboo Blind of State
18. Sunoko. Weather blinds

B. SHINDENZUKURI. ARCHITECTURE OF THE PALACES OF HEIAN AND KAMAKURA
HIGH NOBILITY

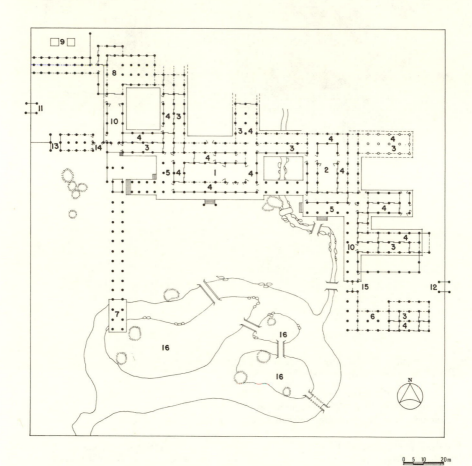

FIGURE 10-15. The Palace of Fujiwara Michinaga's Family (a modern reconstruction)
   Courtesy of the University of California Press

Reconstructed design by Ōta Seiroku, *Higashi Sanjōdono no Kenkyū*. This is as accurate a
depiction as exists of a Fujiwara palace, leaving out the Northern Chamber (kita no tai)
for lack of assured information. See Figure 10-17 for a less accurate but full plan.

FIGURE 10-15.

1. Shinden. Principal Chamber
2. Higashi no Tai. Eastern Chamber
3. Other Chambers
4. Galleries
5. Verandas
6. Carriage House
7. Tsuridono. Pavilion
8. Fudono. Archives

9. Household Shrine
10. Courtyards
11. Seimon. Western Main Gate
12. Tōmon. Eastern Main Gate
13. Minami Chūmon. Southern Inner Gate
14. Nishi Chūmon. Western Inner Gate
15. Higashi Chūmon. Eastern Inner Gate
16. Naka no Shima. Islands in the garden lake

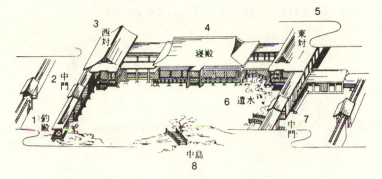

FIGURE 10-16. Shindenzukuri As If Three-Dimensional

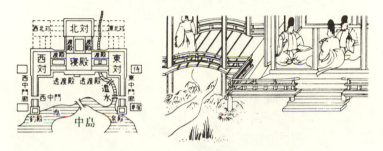

FIGURE 10-17 (left). A Plan of Shindenzukuri (see Figure 10-15)

FIGURE 10-18 (right). Shindenzukuri. Suirō to Higashi no Tai. Gap-Planked Passage and the Eastern Chamber

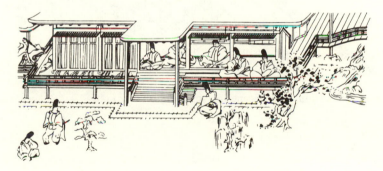

FIGURE 10-19. Shindenzukuri. Shinden Minami Omote. The southern front of the Principal Chamber

FIGURES 10-16 THROUGH 10-22. Shindenzukuri. Imagined Scenes By permission of Kadokawa Shoten

FIGURE 10-16.

1. Tsuridono. Pavilion
2. Chūmon. Inner Gate
3. Nishi no Tai. Western Chamber
4. Shinden. Principal Chamber

5. Higashi no Tai. Eastern Chamber
6. Yarimizu. Garden Stream
7. Chūmon. Inner Gate
8. Naka no Shima. One of the islands in the lake

FIGURES 10-20 (left), 10-21 (right). Izumidono. Western or Water Pavilion, Unwalled

FIGURE 10-22. Chūmon. A Scene Imagined at an Inner Gate

FIGURE 10-22.

1. Chūmon. The Inner Gate
2. Renji mado. Lattice window
3. Yarimizu. Artificial stream in garden

C. CLOTHING

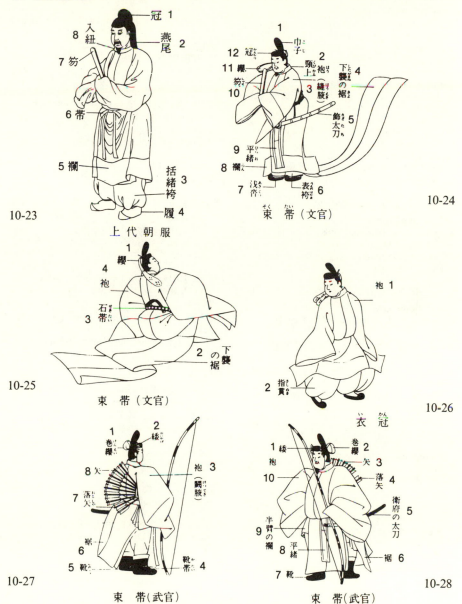

FIGURES 10-23 THROUGH 10-59 by permission of Kadokawa Shoten

FIGURE 10-23. Jōdai Chōfuku. Formal Robe of a
Nara Courtier

1. Kammuri. Crown
2. Embi. Open trail from crown
3. Kukuriobakama. Trousers bound to feet

4. Kutsu. Slipper
5. Ran. Wide cloth attached to train of robe
6. Obi. Sash
7. Shaku. Courtier's wand or scepter
8. Irehimo. Tiestring of robe

FIGURE 10-24. Sokutai (Bunkan). Formal Robe for Sovereign, Civilian Nobles

1. Koji. Projection of the crown
2. Kubikami. High collar
3. Hō(eki). Outer robe (color according to rank)
4. Shitagasane no kyo. Long train; color, crest by rank
5. Kazatachi. Dress sword
6. Ue no hakama. Divided overskirt (like culotte)
7. Asagutsu. Shoes with ties
8. Ran. Wide cloth attached to train of robe
9. Hirao. Skirtfront piece
10. Shaku. Courtier's wand
11. Ei. Part of crown (silk stiffened with bones)
12. Kammuri. Crown

FIGURE 10-25. Sokutai. Rear View

1. Ei. Part of crown
2. Shitagasane no kyo. Long train; color, crest by rank
3. Sekitai. Lacquered belt, gemmed by rank
4. Hō. Outer robe

FIGURE 10-26. Ikan. Formal Robe and Crown

1. Hō. Outer robe
2. Sashinuki. Trousers bound to the feet

FIGURE 10-27. Sokutai (Bukan). Military Formal Dress, Rear View

1. Ken'ei. Inward-rolled ei: see Fig. 10-24, 11; Fig. 10-25, 1
2. Oikake. Decoration of ei at the ear
3. Hō. Outer robe
4. Katai. Upper slipper
5. Kanokutsu. Leather shoes, gilt or silvered toes
6. Kyo. Train
7. Hampi no ran. Train in form of short underjacket
8. Ya. Arrows

FIGURE 10-28. Front View

1. Oikake. Decoration of ei at the ear
2. Ken'ei. Inward-rolled ei: see Fig. 10-24, 11; Fig. 10-25, 1
3. Ya. Arrows
4. Otoshiya. Fanned arrangement of arrows

5. Efu no tachi. Sword of a palace guard
6. Kyo. Train
7. Kanokutsu. Leather shoes with gilt or silvered toes
8. Hirao. Skirtfront piece
9. Hampi no ran. Train in form of short underjacket
10. Hō. Outer robe

FIGURE 10-29. Nōshi (Fuyu). Ordinary Heian Courtier's Robe (Winter)

1. Kubikami. High collar
2. Nōshi. This robe for sovereign and high nobles
3. Sashinuki. Trouser leg bound to foot (greater length than Fig. 10-26, 2)

FIGURE 10-30. Nōshi (Natsu). Summer Court Dress; Ordinary Robe

1. Nōshi. This garment
2. Kariginu. "Hunting robe"—a less formal court robe

FIGURE 10-31. Nōshi Idashiginu (Fuyu). Ordinary Court Winter Robe (showing under layers)

1. Nōshi. Ordinary robe for sovereign and high nobility
2. Sashinuki. Trouser leg bound to foot (see Fig. 10-29, 3)
3. Idashiginu. Under layers visible

FIGURE 10-32. Kariginu. Ordinary Court Robe ("Hunting Robe"—as Fig. 30, 2).

1. Sodekukuri. Sleeve ties
2. Karibakama. A version of sashinuki: Fig. 10-29, 3
3. Kariginu. This garment
4. Kinu. This garment

FIGURE 10-33. Kariginu (Warabe). Young Person's Version of Fig. 10-32

FIGURE 10-34. Kosode Hakama. Heian Common People's Dress with Sleeves Smaller at Wrist, Trousers

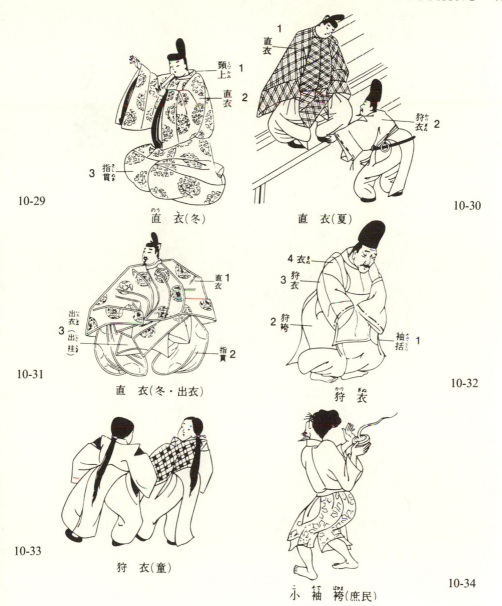

10-29

直 衣(冬)

1 頸上
2 直衣
3 指貫

1 直衣
10-30
直 衣(夏)

2 狩衣

10-31

1 直衣
3 出衣(出桂)
2 指貫

直 衣(冬・出衣)

4 衣
3 狩衣
2 狩袴
1 袖括

10-32

狩 衣

10-33

狩 衣(童)

小 袖 袴(庶民)

10-34

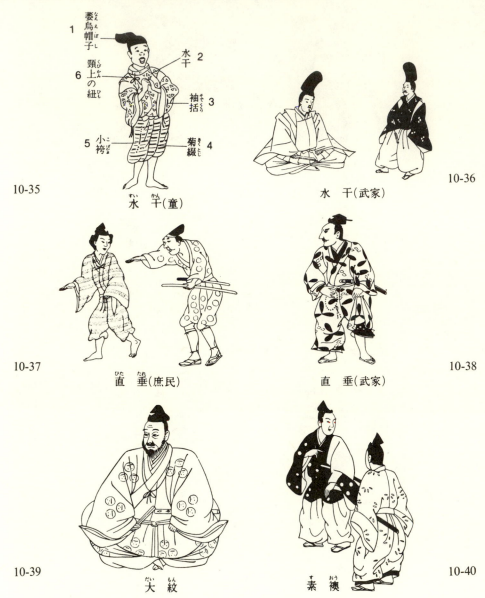

1 萎烏帽子（なええぼし）
6 頭上の紐（くびかみのひも）
2 水干（すいかん）
3 袖括（そでくくり）
5 小袴（こばかま）
4 菊綴（きくとじ）

10-35

水　干（童）（すいかん）

10-36

水　干（武家）

10-37

直　垂（庶民）（ひたたれ）

10-38

直　垂（武家）

10-39

大　紋（だいもん）

10-40

素　襖（すおう）

FIGURE 10-35. Suikan (Warabe). Child's Dress Resembling Kariginu

1. Naeeboshi. Courtiers' softer cap
2. Suikan. With high collar, chrysanthemum design
3. Sodekukuri. Sleeve ties
4. Kikutoji. Chrysanthemum pattern
5. Kobakama. Means the same as sashinuki in Heian times; see Fig. 10-26, 2; Fig. 10-29, 3; Fig. 10-31, 2
6. Kubikami no himo. Tie strings at neck

FIGURE 10-36. Suikan (Buke). Guards' or Soldiers' Version of Suikan

FIGURE 10-37. Hitatare (Shomin). Ordinary Wear, Common People

FIGURE 10-38. Hitatare (Buke). Ordinary Wear, Military

FIGURE 10-39. Daimon. Large Design or Pattern. A Muromachi robe adapted in Edo for daimyō of fifth rank and above.

FIGURE 10-40. Suō. Version of Hitatare; Ordinary Wear for Commoners, Muromachi; Formal Wear for Samurai, Edo.

FIGURE 10-41. Kataginu. Formal Wear before, Ordinary Wear after, Muromachi

1. Kataginu. This garment
2. Hanbakama. Short, narrow hakama; cf. Fig. 10-42, 2
3.

FIGURE 10-42. Nagakamishimo. Samurai Formal Wear, Edo

1. Kataginu, more recently termed kamishimo Overrobe with stiff shoulders
2. Nagabakama. Long hakama or trousers; cf. Fig. 41, 2
3. Noshime. Underrobe

FIGURE 10-43. Hankamishimo. Less Formal Kamishimo

1. Kataginu, kamishimo. Outer robe, stiff shoulders

2. Hanbakama. Trousers bound to the feet: cf. Figs. 10-26, 2; 10-29, 3; 10-32, 2
3. Kosode. Underrobe with sleeves smaller at wrist

FIGURE 10-44. Jōdai Shifuku. Court Women's Informal Wear, Nara Period

1. Suikei tsutsusode uwagi. Over-robe with short sleeves
2. Kagami. Metal mirror
3. Hire. Long, thin white cloth band
4. Obi. Sash
5. Kyo. Train at front of robe

FIGURE 10-45. Karaginumo. Ladies' "Twelve-Layered" Formal Robe, Rear

1. Kasane uchigi. Double overrobe or doublet (cf. 2)
2. Hitoe. A singlet (cf. 1)
3. Uwagi. Overwear, outer robe
4. Hitoe. A singlet
5. Mo. A pleated back skirt
6. Hikigoshi. Two long ties for the mo
7. Hitoe. A singlet
8. Ōgoshi. Wide waistband attached to top of mo
9. Karaginu. More or less the women's counterpart of men's karaginu, Fig. 10-32

FIGURE 10-46. Karaginumo. Ladies' "Twelve-Layered" Formal Robe, Front

1. Karaginu no eri. Collar of karaginu robe
2. Karaginu. Robe; see 10-45, 9; Fig. 10-32
3. Hitoe. A singlet
4. Uwagi. Overwear, outer robe
5. Kasaneuchigi (itsutsuginu). Five- (or more) layered robe
6. Mo. A pleated back skirt
7. Hikigoshi. Long ties for the mo

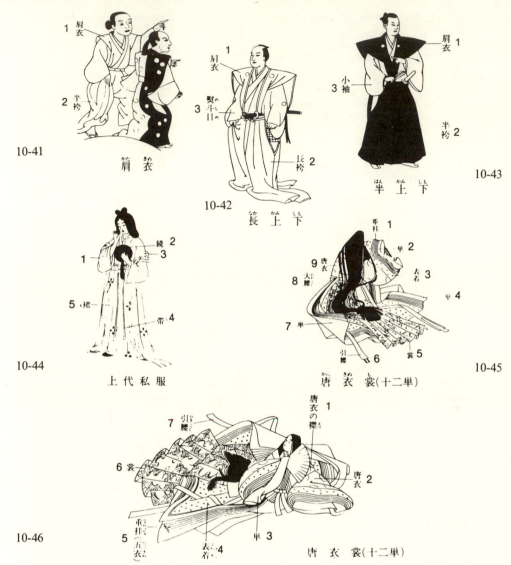

10-41

肩　衣

10-42

長　上　下

10-43

半　上　下

10-44

上　代　私　服

10-45

唐　衣　裳（十二単）

10-46

唐　衣　裳（十二単）

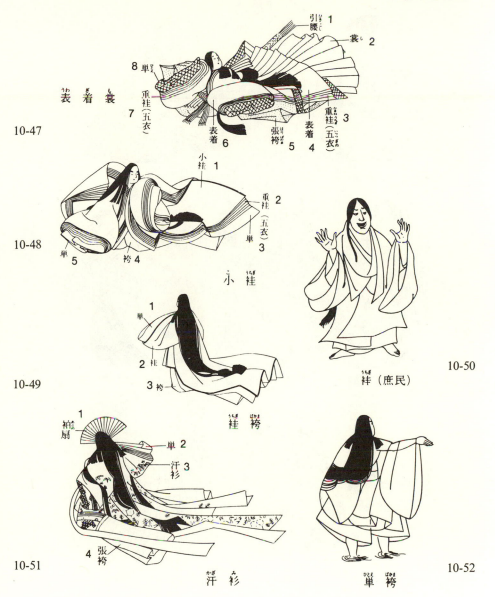

10-47　表着裳

10-48　小袿

10-49　袿袴

10-50　袿（庶民）

10-51　汗衫

10-52　単袴

10-53

小袖袴

腰巻

10-54

10-55

打掛

10-56

小袖（近世）

染女

10-57

10-58

壺装束と被衣

被衣（近世）

10-59

FIGURE 10-47. Uwagimo. Less Elaborate, Less Formal Version of the Preceding

1. Hikigoshi. Two long ties for the mo
2. Mo. A pleated back skirt
3. Kasaneuchigi (Itsutsuginu). Five- (or more) layered robe
4. Uwagi. Overwear, outer robe
5. Haribakama. Divided skirt stiffened with boards
6. Uwagi. Overwear, outer robe
7. Kasaneuchigi (Itsutsuginu). Five- (or more) layered robe
8. Hitoe. A singlet

FIGURE 10-48. Kouchigi. Formal Robe, Embossed Silk Face, Plain Silk Back

1. Kouchigi. Note the absence of karaginu and mo, as in Figs. 10-46, 10-47
2. Kasaneuchigi (Itsutsuginu). Five- (or more) layered robe
3. Hitoe. A singlet
4. Hakama. Divided trouser-skirt with pleats
5. Hitoe. A singlet

FIGURE 10-49. Uchigibakama. Combination of Kouchigi and Hakama, Fig. 10-48, 1 and 4, for Less Formal, More Active Purposes

1. Hitoe. A singlet
2. Uchigi. Overwear, outer robe
3. Hakama. Divided trouser-skirt

FIGURE 10-50. Uchigi (Shomin). An Overrobe for Common People

FIGURE 10-51. Kazami. Heian Ladies' Shorter Robe

1. Akome Ōgi. Cypress fan for formal purposes
2. Hitoe. A singlet
3. Kazami. This robe, showing sleeve
4. Haribakama. Divided skirt stiffened with boards

FIGURE 10-52. Hitoebakama. (Shorter) Divided Trouser Skirt of One Layer of Cloth

FIGURE 10-53. Kosodebakama. Robe with Sleeves Smaller at Wrist and Worn with Divided Trouser-skirt

FIGURE 10-54. Koshimaki. Robe with Sleeves Smaller at Wrist and Worn with Extra Skirt; Dress for Non-nobility

FIGURE 10-55. Uchikake. One of Several Costumes to Bear the Name. This is a kimono over which is worn an outer robe with sleeves smaller at the wrist and a long hang (Edo).

FIGURE 10-56. Kosode. Another (Edo) Version of a Robe with Sleeves Smaller at the Wrist. Women's dress styles (Edo) were generally of foot length, with style changes in matters of dyeing, wrist opening, sashes, and ornaments

FIGURE 10-57. Uneme. A Court Serving-Woman with Her Dress. She would attend the sovereign at meals (pre-Edo)

FIGURE 10-58. Tsuboshōzoku. Women's Walking Clothes in Heian Era

1. Ichimegasa. Hat of lacquered straw, worn from Heian to Edo period as sunshade and for concealing the face
2. Kazuki. Hooded outer garment (Heian). The woman's long hair would be concealed by covering with the ichimegasa and tucking under this outer robe

FIGURE 10-59. Kazuki. Hooded Outer Garment over Robe (Edo)

D. ARMS AND ARMOR

大 鎧 姿

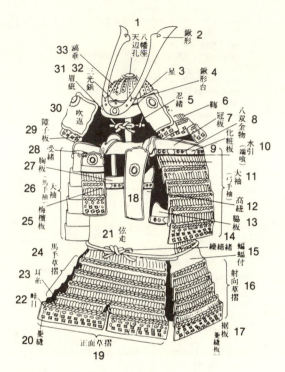

FIGURES 10-60 THROUGH 10-79 by permission of Kadokawa Shoten

FIGURE 10-60. Ōyoroi Sugata. Full Harness. Armor Worn on Horseback by High-ranking Warriors

FIGURE 10-61. Ōyoroi(mae). Full Harness, Front View. 1–6 deal with the helmet (Kabuto 兜).

1. Hachimanza. Top stud of helmet
2. Kuwagata. Metal horn ornament; antlers
3. Hoshi. Rows of studs
4. Kuwagatadai. Base of horn ornament
5. Shinobi no o. Helmet ties
6. Shikoro. Helmet neck-guard
7. Kamuri no ita. Support frame for arm-piece or tasset
8. Hassō kanamono. Metal attachment for frame and tasset
9. Keshō ita. Decorated plate
10. Mizuhiki. Clamp joint
11. Ōsode (yundesode). Tasset (left, bowhand side)
12. Takahimo. Suspender
13. Wakiita. Sideplate

14. Kurishime no o. Waist cord
15. Kōmoritsuke. Flareplate
16. Imuke kusazuri. Left hip-guard or tasset
17. Susoita (hishinuiita). Bottom plate (cross-laced plate)
18. Kyūbi no ita. Stomach ward
19. Shōmen kusazuri. Front hip-tasset
20. Hishinui. Cross-lacing
21. Tsurubashiri. Cuirass
22. Azeme. Holes along the bottom plate
23. Mimiito. Warp cords, joining tassets
24. Mete kusazuri. Right hip-tasset
25. Sendan no ita. Decorated chest plate
26. Ōsode (Metesode). Arm-tasset (right, reins-side)
27. Munaita. Breast-plate
28. Ukeo. Chest cord
29. Sōji no ita. Shoulder harness-plate
30. Fukikaeshi. Head side-guards
31. Mabisashi. Eye-guard
32. Sankōbyō. Helmet-top rivet
33. Shimadare. Protective metal strips

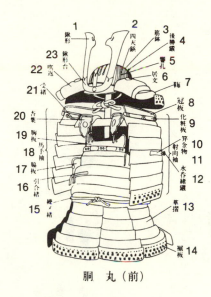

大鎧（前）

胴丸（前）

胴丸姿

FIGURE 10-62. Dōmaru (mae). Helmet and Body Armor (Front)

1. Kuwagata. Horn ornament
2. Shitenbyō. Helmet rivet
3. Sujibachi. Ridged crown
4. Kōsho no kan. Metal ridge
5. Hibikiana. Sound or hearing hole
6. Suemon. Large stud in support frame for tasset
7. Shikoro. Helmet neck-guard
8. Kammuri no ita. Support frame for tasset
9. Keshō ita. Decorated plate
10. Kōgai kanamono. Metal strip for tasset-cord (12) tie to the back
11. Imuke no sode. Left tasset
12. Mizunomi no o no kan. Ring for tasset-cord tie (see 10)

13. Kusazuri. Hip-guard or tasset
14. Susoita. Bottom plate
15. Kurishime no o. Waist-cord
16. Hikiawase no o. Cuirass tie
17. Wakiita. Side plate
18. Mete sode. Right arm-tasset
19. Munaita. Breast-plate
20. Gyōyō. Cuirass suspender guards
21. Ukeo. Chest cord
22. Fukigaeshi. Head side-guards
23. Kuwagatadai. Base of horn ornament

FIGURE 10-63. Dōmaru Sugata. Footsoldier Wearing 62; Heian Period and Later

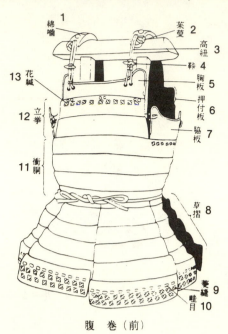

腹 巻（前）

腹 巻 姿

FIGURE 10-64. Haramaki (mae). Foot Soldier's Body Armor (Front); ca. Muromachi Period

1. Watagami. Padded suspender-piece
2. Gumi. Suspender clasp
3. Takahimo. Suspender
4. Kohaze. Suspender holder
5. Munaita. Breast-plate
6. Oshitsuke ita. Back-plate
7. Waki ita. Side-plate
8. Kusazuri. Hip-guard or tasset
9. Hishinui. Cross-lacing
10. Azeme. Holes along the bottom-plate
11. Kabukidō. Lower cuirass
12. Tateage. Upper cuirass
13. Hanaodoshi. Cross-lacing

FIGURE 10-65. Haramaki Sugata. Foot Soldier Wearing 64

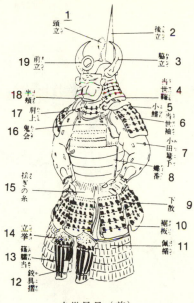

当世具足（前）

当世具足姿

FIGURE 10-66. Tōsei Gusoku (mae). Foot Soldier's Body Armor (Front). Late Muromachi Development of 64–65, More or Less Standard for Sometime Thereafter

1. Zudate. Helmet mid-stand
2. Ushirodate. Helmet back-stand
3. Wakidate. Helmet side-stands: horns
4. Tōsei jigoro. Helmet neck-guard in this style
5. Kobire. Shoulder fins
6. Tōsei sode. Tasset in this style
7. Odagote. Arm-cover
8. Chōtsugai. Cuirass
9. Gesan. Hip-guards

10. Susoita. Bottom plate
11. Haidate. Leg wrap
12. Kakozuri. Metal ankle clamps
13. Shinosuneate. Shin-guards
14. Tateage. Knee-guards
15. Yurugi no ito. Free-hanging cords
16. Onidamari. Joints?
17. Watagami. Padded suspender piece
18. Hambō. Metal face-guard
19. Maedate. Front helmet-stand

FIGURE 10-67. Tōsei Gusoku Sugata. Foot-soldier Wearing 66.

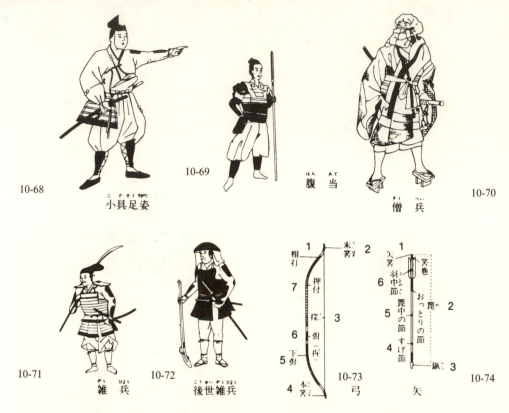

10-68

10-69

腹当
はら あて

10-70

小具足姿
こ ぐ そく すがた

僧兵
そう へい

10-71

10-72

10-73

10-74

雑兵
ぞう ひょう

後世雑兵
こうせい ぞうひょう

弓

矢

FIGURE 10-68. Kogusoku Sugata. Partial Armor (Kamakura)

FIGURE 10-69. Haraate. Partial Armor for Low-ranking Soldiers (Kamakura-Muromachi)

FIGURE 10-70. Sōhei. Warrior Monk (Late Heian and after)

FIGURE 10-71. Zōhyō. Low-ranking Soldier (Post-Muromachi)

FIGURE 10-72. Kōsei Zōhyō. Low-ranking Soldier (Later than 71)

FIGURE 10-73. Yumi. Bow

1. Aiuchi. Stringing grip
2. Urahazu. Upper string-notch
3. Saguri. Bowstring
4. Motohazu. Lower string-notch
5. Shimo Tsuka. Lower shaft
6. Tsuka (Nigiri). Grip
7. Oshitsuke. Draw-shaft

FIGURE 10-74. Ya. Arrow.

1. Yahazu. Notch

2. Me. Shaft
3. Yajiri. Head
4. Sugebushi. Front shaft
5. Menaka no fushi. Mid-shaft
6. Hanaka no fushi. Feathered end of shaft

FIGURE 10-75. Naginata. Long-bladed Halberd; Glaive

1. Wangata. Concave back of blade
2. Itaha. Cutting edge of blade
3. Hoshimenuki. "Star" clasp
4. Nuridome. Lacquered shaft top
5. Chiriharai (Ishizuki). "Dust-sweeper," metal lower tip

FIGURE 10-76. Yari. Pike

1. Mi. Head
2. Shiokubi. Head-joint of shaft (also kerakubi)
3. Tachiuchi. Grip region for use in thrusting, as if a sword
4. Dōgane. Metal holding, fastening ring
5. Chidome. Blood-stopper to keep pike grip from being slippery
6. Tsuka. Main shaft
7. Ishizuki. Metal tip

10-75

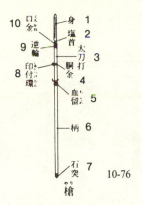

10-76

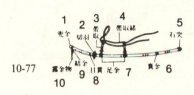

10-77

10-78

10-79

8. Shirushitsuke Kan. Metal attachment like 4, where foreshaft and main shaft join
9. Sakawa. Grip ring to hold head
10. Kuchigane. Metal mouth of head for fixing to shaft

FIGURE 10-77. Katana (Tachi). Sword in Scabbard

1. Kabutogane. Metal end of hilt
2. Seppa. Two metal plates encircling the tang on either side of the guard
3. Obitori. Waist-strap attachments
4. Obitori no o. Cords for joining waist-strap attachments
5. Ishizuki. Metal tip of scabbard
6. Semekane. Metal scabbard constraint
7. Ashikana (Ashikane). Metal fittings for the leather of waist-strap attachments
8. Menuki. Two decorated metal waist-strap attachments
9. Musubigane. Metal to hold the tie for 10
10. Tsuyukanamono. Metal ornament on a tie

FIGURE 10-78. Katana. Sword in Scabbard

1. Menuki. Two decorated metal hilt-ornaments

2. En. Suite
3. Hagigane. Metal scabbard end
4. Sakasazuno. Scabbard
5. Kojiri. Chape, covering the butt
6. Sageo. Suspension string
7. Kurigata. A slotted projection through which 6 passes
8. Koikuchi. "Carp's mouth"; the band surrounding the mouth
9. Tsuba. Guard
10. Mekugi. Peg
11. Tsukagashira. Pommel-cap of hilt

FIGURE 10-79. Katana. Swordblade

1. Shinogi. Ridge
2. Mune. Back of blade; not the cutting edge
3. Munemachi. Notch on back of blade
4. Nakago. Tang
5. Menuki ana. Peg hole
6. Hamachi. Notch on back side
7. Hamon. Blade decoration
8. Yokote(suji). Short transverse ridge
9. Bōshi. Tempered portion of the point

E. ILLUSTRATED POPULAR BOOKS AND OTHER GENRE REPRESENTATIONS

FIGURE 10-80. *Otogizōshi. Issunbōshi.* The Japanese Tom Thumb story, this tale has been loved by children and commoners from Muromachi times. The hero, who will do many feats, is in the utensil in the middle of the room and being presented to the lady. From the special collection in Tōyō Bunko

FIGURE 10-81. *Otogizōshi. Wakakusa Monogatari* (*The Tale of Lady Wakakusa*; Muromachi period). From the special collection in Tōyō Bunko

FIGURE 10-82. *Otogizōshi. Monokusatarō.* The hero of the title is shown setting out on an adventure. (Muromachi period?) From the special collection in Tōyō Bunko

FIGURE 10-83. *Otogizōshi. Kakurezato* (*The Hidden Place*; 1656). The depiction of animals in human roles is a favorite kind of mild satire on the human race. By courtesy of Tōkyō Daigaku, Kokubungaku Kenkyūshitsu

FIGURE 10-84. *Ukiyozōshi.* *Ihara Saikaku, *Kōshoku Ichidai Otoko* (1682). Yonosuke peeps out at prostitutes on Sado Island, comparing them to *kamigata* counterparts (from Part 3). From the special collection in Tōyō Bunko

FIGURE 10-85. The Same. Yonosuke is with rogue *kabuki* actors at Higashiyama in Kyoto (from Part 5). Courtesy of the Kokubungaku Kenkyū Shiryōkan, with gratitude to Professor Oka Masahiko

FIGURE 10-86 (left). The Same. Yonosuke on the roof peeps at maids in a kitchen (from Part 6). By courtesy of the Kokubungaku Kenkyū Shiryōkan, with gratitude to Professor Oka Masahiko

FIGURE 10-87 (right). A *Bikuni*. Some bikuni were proper nuns, some professional entertainers, some prostitutes, with lines hard to draw. In the *ukiyozōshi*, *Kōshoku Ichidai Onna* by *Ihara Saikaku (1686), a woman of this kind features in Part 3. This version is more idealized than many depictions at the time. With gratitude to Professor Toda Yoshio and M O A Museum (Kyūsei Atami Bijitsukan)

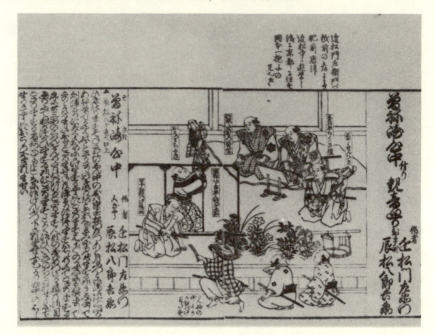

FIGURE 10-88. A Reading Text of *Chikamatsu Monzaemon's *Sonezaki Shinjū* (pub. 1703). By courtesy of Kokuritsu Kokkai Toshokan

FIGURE 10-89. A Wife of a Merchant Household, from *Hyakunin Jorō Shinasadame* (1723). The wronged wife, Osan, in *Chikamatsu Monzaemon's *Shinjū Ten no Amijima* (1720) is so described. By courtesy of Kokuritsu Kokkai Toshokan

FIGURE 10-90. Women of a Teahouse (for Amorous Meetings). From *Hyakunin Jorō Shinasadame*. By courtesy of Kokuritsu Kokkai Toshokan

FIGURE 10-91. *Kibyōshi.* The cover of the first part of *Santō Kyōden's *Edo Umare Uwaki no Kabayaki* (2nd ed., 1793). In the inset we see the feckless hero, Enjirō, of the then famous "peony nose," with the heroine, Ukina. With gratitude to Mr. Hanasaki Kazuo and the Kisho Fukuseikai

FIGURE 10-92. *Kokkeibon.* *Jippensha Ikku, *Dōchū Hizakurige* (1802ff.). The rogue heroes are shown here: A. Yajirōbē and B. Kitahachi (or Yaji and Kita, as usually known). By courtesy of Waseda Daigaku Toshokan

FIGURE 10-93. *Jūhachi Daitsū* (*The Eighteen Great Connoisseurs*) from *Edo no Sachi* (1773). The *daitsū* were men of means, often *haikai* poets under some pen name, and possessors of detailed knowledge of the culture of the demimonde. Contrast Enjirō, as in Fig. 10-91. By courtesy of Kokuritsu Kokkai Toshokan, with gratitude to Professor Nakano Mitsutoshi and Mr. Hanasaki Kazuo

Principal Immediate Sources

Our intent here is to acknowledge our immediate debts to others and our use of previously published material. In doing so, we seek to be as specific as possible without over-much repetition of what has been said in the preface and acknowledgments (which therefore should be considered a part of this section). When, below, a work is referred to more than once, we use abbreviations set in parentheses and small capitals at the head of the first mention. When no place of publication is mentioned, Tokyo is meant. Because this section will be of use only to advanced students, we have not italicized terms appearing in Part Three.

PART ONE. A BRIEF HISTORY

Section A, "The Development of a Systematic Poetics," has been published in other versions in Japanese and English. The English is "Toward a New Conception of Classical Japanese Poetics," *Studies on Japanese Culture*, 2 vols. (Japan P. E. N. Club, 1973), 1, 99–113. Some of the same material was presented in a more theoretical context in "On the Genesis and Development of Literary Systems," *Critical Inquiry*, 5 (1979), 339–53, 553–68.

As stated in the acknowledgments, the scope and temper of the history have been modeled on Konishi Jin'ichi's *Nihon Bungakushi*.

Certain literary histories and jiten have been drawn on. These include Akiyama Ken et al., eds., *Nihon Bungaku Zenshi*, 4 vols. (Gakutōsha, 1978); Takeuchi Rizō et al., eds., *Nihon Rekishi Daijiten*, 10 + 2 vols. (Kawade Shobō, 1968–1969; and Hisamatsu Sen'ichi et al., eds., *Nihon Bungakushi Kaitei Shimpan*, 6 vols. (Kyōbundō, 1966). These works also furnished material for Part Three.

In addition, we have used various other literary and language jiten. These include: (IJICHI) Ijichi Tetsuo et al., eds., *Haikai Daijiten* (Meiji Shoin, 1957); Takagi Ichinosuke et al., eds., *Waka Bungaku Daijiten* (Meiji Shoin, 1962); (TAKAYANAGI) Takayanagi Mitsutoshi et al., *Kadokawa Nihonshi Jiten*, 2nd ed. (Kadokawa Shoten, 1974); (HISAMATSU) Hisamatsu Sen'ichi et al., eds., *Kadokawa Shimpan Kogo Jiten* (Kadokawa Shoten, 1973 and 1982); (KINDAICHI) Kindaichi Haruhiko et al., eds., *Shin Meikai Kogo Jiten* (Sanshōdō, 1972); (SHUZUI) Shuzui Kenji et al., eds., *Ōbunsha Kogo Jiten* (Ōbunsha, 1965); and Ōno

Susumu et al., eds., *Iwanami Kogo Jiten* (Iwanami Shoten, 1974). These were of course useful for many other parts, even when not so noted.

For reference works used for Buddhism, see Part Six, although they have been important for this and other parts. See also the beginning of the next section.

PART TWO. CHRONOLOGIES

The major problem for the brief section A was devising a system of divisions that accorded with Japanese views and yet was sufficiently simple to be useful to our readers. As the preface indicates, we have avoided common Japanese period concepts (kodai, chūko, etc.) on the advice of Japanese friends. But it will be found in Part One and here that we have effected a compromise between those concepts and division by seat of government that are tantamount to some traditional divisions (kodai, etc.).

See also the beginning of Part One B for the common Japanese period concepts.

For the regnal and era names in Section B here, we have adapted the system used in (NELSON) Andrew Nathaniel Nelson, *The Modern Reader's Japanese-English Character Dictionary* (Tuttle, 1962), chiefly by rearrangement and by standardizing era names to those given in (KŌJIEN) Shimmura Izuru et al., eds., *Kōjien*, 2nd ed. (Iwanami Shoten, 1969).

For Section C, the annals of works and events, our model was (ITŌ), Itō Sei, et al., ed., *Shinchō Nihon Bungaku Shōjiten* (Shinchōsha, 1968), from which we have departed by deletion and some addition.

PART THREE. MAJOR AUTHORS AND WORKS

Unfortunately, with one exception, our ability to offer acknowledgments here is at its weakest. The exception, explained in the preface, involves a heavy formal and substantive indebtedness to ITŌ. We have departed by contraction for individual entries, enlargement of others, and by drawing on TAKAYANAGI and other sources, including KŌJIEN. But so much has come from two series familiar to students of classical Japanese literature—the Iwanami *Nihon Koten Bungaku Taikei* and the Shōgakkan *Nihon Koten Bungaku Zenshū*—and various specialized studies that it is difficult to acknowledge our range of indebtedness. Yet we must also mention the Asahi Shimbun Sha *Nihon Koten Zensho*, used by us more in former times than recently, and the *Chikuma Shobō Nihon no Shisō*.

PART FOUR. LITERARY TERMS

Apart from various specialized reference books, we have relied on KINDAICHI and KŌJIEN. The two series of terms (and other matter at the back of the works by KINDAICHI and TAKAYANAGI have been of assistance. We have found suggestive Bruno Lewin, ed., *Japanische Literaturwissenschaft* for its "Fachterminologisches Glossar" (Wiesbaden: Otto Harrasowitz, 1981), for suggesting terms we had missed. We have also drawn on IJICHI and (NAGAHARA) Nagahara Keiji, ed., *Chūsei Handobukku* (Kondō Shuppansha, 1973). We feel we have erred on the side of brevity and fear that readers new to Japanese literature will find this section difficult to use, in spite of our efforts to signal important terms. Yet this part is crucial in the general economy of the *Companion*, as the many italicized words throughout will indicate.

PART FIVE. THEATERS

The most important and least tangible source for this section and counterparts in Part One and Three involves performances we have seen from the 1940s and later (depending on which of us is involved). These include stagings of all the kinds mentioned except kōwakamai, for which our source is James T. Araki, *The Ballad-Drama of Japan* (Berkeley and Los Angeles: University of California Press, 1964).

We had acute difficulty in defining a way to present nō in an idealized but practical model in terms of parts or structure. Miner finally appealed to Konishi Jin'ichi, who wrote what was in effect an essay that Miner translated. Otherwise, we have used a number of works, both for scholarship and illustrative material. Although the two categories overlap, the captions with the figures in Part Five relate to illustrations, and what follows to scholarship and criticism. These include P. G. O'Neill, whose work on early nō is the standard work in English, and whose *Guide to Nō* (Hinoki Shoten, 1953) is handy in its illustration and explanation. Other works on nō of importance to us include: Yokomichi Mario and Omote Akira, eds., *Yōkyokushū*, 2 vols. (Iwanami Shoten, 1960–1963, [TAIKEI] *Nihon Koten Bungaku Taikei*, vols. 40–41), which is important for its approach and detailed stage directions; Koyama Hiroshi et al., eds., *Yōkyokushū*, 2 vols. (*Shōgakkan*, 1973; [ZENSHŪ] *Nihon Koten Bungaku Zenshū*, vols. 33–34); Hayashiya Tatsusaburō, ed., *Kodai Chūsei Geijutsuron* (Iwanami, 1973; *Nihon Shisō Taikei*, vol. 23); and Omote Akira and Katō Shūichi, ed., *Zeami, Zenchiku* (Iwanami, 1974; *Nihon Shisō Taikei*, vol. 24). See also the next section, on Part Six.

For kyōgen: Geinōshi Kenkyūkai, *Kyōgen* (Heibonsha, 1970; *Nihon no Koten Geinō*, vol. 4); Koyama Hiroshi et al., eds., *Kyōgenshū* (Iwanami, 1960, 1961; TAIKEI, vols. 42–43); and Kitagawa Tadahiko et al., eds., *Kyōgenshū* (Shōgakkan, 1972; ZENSHŪ, vol. 35).

For jōruri: Otoba Hiromu and Tsurumi Makoto, eds., *Jōrurishū*, 2 vols. (Iwanami, 1959–1960; TAIKEI, vols. 51–52); Yokoyama Tadashi, *Jōrurishū* (Shōgakkan, 1971; ZENSHŪ, vol. 45); Shigetomo Ki, ed., *Chikamatsu Jōrurishū*, 2 vols. (Iwanami, 1958–1959; TAIKEI, vols. 49–50); and Andō Tsuruo and Charles Dunn, eds. *Bunraku* (Kyoto: Dankō Shinsha, 1965; *Nihon no Dentō*, vol. 3). There is some overlap with kabuki.

For kabuki: Sasahara Nobuo, *Bi to Aku no Dentō* (Ōfūsha, 1969; also on jōruri, etc.); Urayama Masao et al, eds., *Kabuki Kyakuhonshū*, 2 vols. (Iwanami, 1960–1961; TAIKEI, vols. 52–53); Gunji Masakatsu, ed., *Kabuki Jūhachibanshū* (Iwanami, 1965; TAIKEI, vol. 98).

Our information on the annual cycle of kabuki is owed to Barbara Thornbury from conversation, from a talk given at Princeton, and material from a then unpublished study.

PART SIX. COLLECTIONS, ETC.

After Parts One and Three, this is the most difficult part for which to provide adequate designation of sources. Sections A through E are the most indebted to ITŌ. For renga and haikai, IJICHI has been a major source, supplemented by specialized studies and our own work. For nō and kyōgen, we have drawn on the sources mentioned at the head of the sections. For kyōka, senryū, and related kinds we have used many sources, including ITŌ.

For criticism, ITŌ has served us once again as a starting point.

For works in Chinese, we have relied most on advice from Konishi Jin'ichi, as also for Confucian studies, supplemented by ITŌ and specialized studies.

For nō we have relied chiefly on Konishi, *Nōgakuron Kenkyū* (Takama Shobō, 1961); and Omote Akira et al., *Komparu Kodensho Shūsei* (Wan'ya Shoten, 1969), especially in difficult matters of canon and titles for the two critics. Unpublished work as of this writing by J. T. Rimer and Yamazaki Masakazu has assisted us in English titles for Zeami's treatises.

The information on Buddhist sects and sūtras took a disproportionate amount of time. Konishi Jin'ichi offered material assistance to Miner, but in the end Morrell undertook thorough recasting. The major sources follow: Nakamura Hajime, *Bukkyōgo Daijiten*, 3 vols. (Tokyo Shoseki Kabushikigaisha, 1975); Nakamura Hajime, *Shin Bukkyō Jiten* (Seishin Shobō, 1962); Mizuno Kōgen, ed., *Shin Butten Kaidai Jiten* (Shunjūsha, 1966); Leon Hurvitz, *Scripture of the Lotus Blossom of the Fine Dharma* (New York: Columbia University Press, 1976); and Kiyota Minoru, *Shingon Buddhism: Theory and Practice* (Los Angeles and Tokyo, 1978). (DE VISSER) M. W. De Visser, *Ancient Buddhism in Japan*, 2 vols. (Leiden: E. J. Brill, 1935); Iwano Shin'yu [sic], *Japanese-English Dictionary* (Daitō Shuppansha, 1965); and Daigan and Alicia Matsunaga, *Foundations of Japanese Buddhism*, 2 vols. (Los Angeles: Buddhist Books Int'l, 1974–1976) have also been consulted.

PART SEVEN. TIME, DIRECTION, ETC.

Most of our information is taken from KINDAICHI, supplemented by DE VISSER, SHUZUI, and TAKAYANAGI.

PART EIGHT. GEOGRAPHY AND MAPS

Although we have used various sources, the chief are TAKAYANAGI and NELSON. For Section I on utamakura place names, the best listing is that of Katagiri Yōichi, *Heian Utamakura Chimei Sakùin* (Daigakudō Shoten for Himematsu no Kai, 1972). Okumura Tsuneya has an excellent account of the issues and history of these matters in *Utamakura* (Heibonsha, 1977). We have also referred to Sasaki Tadasato, *Utamakura no Sekai* (Ōfūsha, 1979).

PART NINE. RANKS, OFFICES, ETC.

The information on pre-Edo matters derives chiefly from Takayanagi, Nagahara, and two studies in English: (REISCHAUERS) Robert Karl and Jean Reischauer, *Early Japanese History*, 2 vols. (Princeton: Princeton University Press, 1937) and (MCCULLOUGHS) William H. and Helen Craig McCullough, *A Tale of Flowering Fortunes* (a very copiously annotated translation of that great compendium of Heian lore, the *Eiga Monogatari*), 2 vols. (Stanford: Stanford University Press, 1980). The *kinds* of information are modeled on TAKAYANAGI. Our figures and their details are from TAKAYANAGI, supplemented by NAGAHARA, the REISCHAUERS, and the MCCULLOUGHS. Some narrative elements and certain details are also indebted to the MCCULLOUGHS.

For Edo matters, we are indebted again to TAKAYANAGI. Our table of offices is adapted and enlarged (with added Japanese characters) from that in John Whitney Hall, *Tanuma Okitsugu, 1719–88, Forerunner of Modern Japan* (Cambridge: Harvard University Press, 1955).

PART TEN. ARCHITECTURE, ETC.

The tangible nature for our debts in this part makes acknowledgment easier than for other parts. Each figure is accompanied by a statement of provenance, and the "Acknowledgments" states a specific debt. In particular, we wish to express our gratitude to the Kadokawa Shoten.

Glossing the figures, however, proved very difficult in some instances. We drew on the MCCULLOUGHS, the REISCHAUERS, and on such sources as B. W. Robinson, *The Art of the Japanese Sword* (London: Faber & Faber, 1961), and *Arms and Armour of Old Japan* (London: Royal Stationery Office, 1951).

Index

A comprehensive index to Parts One (A Brief Literary History), Three (Major Authors and Works), and Six (Collection, Kinds, Criticism; Buddhism and Confucisnism; Dictionaries), with the topics defined in Part Four (Literary Terms) included to facilitate search. Numbers in bold-face type indicate pages with relatively extensive coverage. The reader is also referred to the table of contents, pp. ix–xi, and the introductions to Parts One, Three, Four, and Six. This index has been prepared by Morrell, with review and tinkering by Miner.

Han Shu (Kanjo), **395**
harai (Shinto ritual purification), **276**
Harima Fudoki, 20, 149
Haritaterai, 359
Haritsu (Ogawa Haritsu), **213**
Harivarman (Karibatsuma), 369
Harumachi (Koikawa Harumachi), 100, **185**, 225
Harumi (Murata Harumi), 93, **207**, 230
Harunobu (Suzuki Harunobu), **242**
Haru no Hi, 255, **349**
Haru no Miyamaji, 143, 345
haru no uta (spring poems topic), 187
Harusame Monogatari, 100, 252
"Harvest, The" (of Edo literature, 1725–1829), **85–108**
Hasedera, 42, 168, 185, 200, 383
Hasedera Reigenki, 347
Hasegawa (school of painting), 160
Hasegawa Tōhaku, **160**
Hashi Benkei, 351, 355, 357, 360
hashikotoba, 276. *See also kotobagaki*, **285**
Hashitomi, 351, 356
Hashitomi Yūgao, 351
hasshū (Eight Sects of Buddhism), 370
Hatanaka Kanzai (Dōmyaku Sensei), **146**
Hatsushigure, 247
Hatsuyuki, 351, 356
Hattō Enmyō Kokushi (Kakushin), 374
Hattori Nankaku, **161**, 214
Hattori Ransetsu, **161**
Hattori Sempo, 350
Hattori Tohō (or Dohō), **160–161**, 345
hayagawari (quick change), **276**
hayashi, 56, **276**
Hayashi Razan, **161**, 363
Hayashi school, 161
hayauta (light songs), 178
head-repeated poem (*sedōka*), 21, 192, 216, 296
Hearing About the West (*Seiyō Kibun*), 142
Heartfelt Worldly Calculations (*Seken Mune San'yō*), 78, 80, 168
Heart (of Wisdom) Sūtra, The (*Hannyashingyō*), 286, 371, 373, 381
Heiankyō (Kyoto), 18, 26, 30
Heian period, literature of the, 17, **26–43**
Heichū Monogatari (*Heichū Nikki*), **161**, 346
Heiji Monogatari (*Heiji Ki*), 49, **161**, 347
Heiji Monogatari Emaki, 162
heike biwa, **276**
heike bushi, **276**
Heike Monogatari, 42, 44, 45, 46, **49–50**, 54, 56, 57, 74, 86, **162–164**, 189, 199, 236, 247, 347
heikyoku, 50, **276**
Heizei (tennō), 221
Hekigan Roku, **392**
Henjō, **163**, 238, 371
Henjō Hakki Seireishū, 190, 362
Henjō Shū, 164

hentaigana (nonstandard syllabary), **277**
hentai kambun, 232, 234
Hibariyama, 351, 355, 356
"Hidden Jewel, Parable of the" ("Eshuyu"), 386, 388
Hideyoshi, *see* Toyotomi Hideyoshi
Hieda no Are, 185
Hiei, Mount, 371
Hifuryaku, 397
Higagoto Kurabe, 70
Higaki, 351, 356
Higaki no Onna, 351
higyō hiza zammai, 372
hijiri (holy man), 210
hikai no uta (*haikaika*), 83, 225, 252, **276**
Hikaru Genji, 35, 41, 79, **204**
hikiage (brought forward), **277**
hikiuta, **277**
Hikobae, 144
Hill of Wakakusa, The (*Wakakusayama*), 169
Himenori, 358
Himuro, 351, 355
Hīnayāna (*shōjō*), 369, 371, 376, 385, 391. *See also Agongyō*, 371, 377, **379**
Hino Chikatsune, 231
Hi no Sake, 359
Hino no Takemuki, **164**
Hiraga Gennai, 100, **101–103**, **164–165**
Hiraga Motoyoshi, **165**
hiragana, 19. *See also kana*, 281
Hiraizumi, 58
hiraku (ordinary stanzas), **277**
Hirata Atsutane, **165**, 243
Hirokata (Yashiro Hirokata), **257**
Hironari (Imbe Hironari), 185
Hirose Tansō, **165**
Hiroshige (Andō Hiroshige), 141
Hisago, 160, 196, 349
Hishikawa Moronobu, **165**, 248
His Majesty's Yakumo Treatise (*Yakumo Mishō*), **173**, 364
Historical Compilations (*Hyō, Piao*), 396
Historical Records (*Shiki*), 394, **395**, 397
histories, mythical and dynastic, 344
History of the Former Han Dynasty, The (*Kanjo*), 395
History of Japan (*Dai Nihonshi*), 247
History of the Later Han Dynasty, The (*Gokanjo*), 395
Hitachi Fudoki, 149
Hitokata (*no Zu*), 366
Hitomaro, *see* Kakinomoto Hitomaro
Hitomaro Kashū (*The Hitomaro Collection, The*), 22, 175
Hitorigoto (Uejima Onitsura), 253
Hitorigoto (Shinkei), 365
Hito to Naru Michi, 172
Hitsujigusa, 251
Hiun, 351, 357
"Hiyubon" (of the *Lotus Sūtra*), 386

This book has been composed by Asco Trade Typesetting Ltd, Hong Kong
Printed by Princeton University Press
Designed by Jan Lilly
Typography: Times Roman
Paper: S.D. Warren's 1854

LIBRARY OF CONGRESS CATALOGING IN PUBLICATION DATA

Miner, Earl Roy.
  The Princeton companion to classical Japanese literature.

  Bibliography: p.
  Includes index.
    1. Japanese literature—To 1868—Handbooks, manuals, etc.   I. Odagiri, Hiroko.
II. Morrell, Robert E.   III. Title.
PL726.1.M495   1984   895.6′09   83-24475
ISBN 0-691-06599-3 (alk. paper)